The Mirage

JAMAL SANAD AL-SUWAIDI

First published in 2015

ISBN 978-9948-23-076-2 Hardback Edition
ISBN 978-9948-23-077-9 Paperback Edition
ISBN 978-9948-23-078-6 Audio Edition
ISBN 978-9948-23-079-3 Electronic Edition

All correspondence should be addressed to:
United Arab Emirates
P.O. Box: 4567
E-mail: jamalalsuwaidi@ecssr.ae

ACKNOWLEDGMENTS

With the publication of this book, it gives me great pleasure to express my thanks and appreciation to all those who strive to maintain the security and stability of my dear homeland, the United Arab Emirates. Through this modest effort, I aim to participate with you in achieving that noble and patriotic objective.

DEDICATION

To those from whom I learned that truth bears
no resemblance to falsehood …

To the souls of my father and mother …

CONTENTS

Part IV: Concluding Remarks

Preface

PREFACE

The mirage is the inspiration for this book. It formed in my mind during the final stages of work on my previous book, *Prospects for the American Age: Sovereignty and Influence in the New World Order.*[1] I developed a conviction that deconstructing the components of the current state of international relations and their repercussions, implications and effects on the Arab and Muslim worlds should go beyond mere understanding of the drivers of these relations and the underlying mechanisms of conflict, competition and cooperation. Indeed, an attempt should also be made to discover the real obstacles preventing serious interaction by many countries of the Arab and Muslim worlds with current global realities. Foremost among these obstacles is the fact that many of these countries and societies have been hooked on the ideology of political religious groups whose ideas have now become – not only in words but in deeds – an obstacle to development, evolution and modernity in these societies.

I have found a striking resemblance between the condition of millions of citizens in some Arab and Muslim countries and that of someone who is exposed to the effects of a unique but common natural phenomenon—namely "the mirage." In a marvelous simile, Almighty God (Allah) mentioned this phenomenon in the Holy Quran: "But the unbelievers—their deeds are like a mirage in sandy deserts, which the man parched with thirst mistakes for water; until when he comes up to it, he finds it to be nothing …"[2]

Through this gracious Holy Quranic verse, Almighty God (Allah) has given a wonderful example reflecting the condition of those who think they are the only ones on the side of truth, when in fact they are not. The term used in the Holy Quran, "Al-Qee'a," is the plural of "Al-Qaa'" which means "low and expansive land"[3] with no plants, where the mirage would usually form. What is meant here is that if a thirsty person sees a mirage, he heads towards it to quench his thirst because, according to his eyes, it is water to be drunk. Yet when he does get there, "he finds it to be nothing." This is the case with those who rely on the rewards of their deeds, but when Almighty God (Allah) holds them to account on the Day of Judgment, they find nothing thereof.[4]

Some literature likens this miscalculation to that of a thirsty person who approaches a mirage thinking that he has found water to drink only to find it is an illusion.[5] It is a painful feeling of disappointment that we hope none of the Arab and Muslim peoples will fall prey to. One can be deceived by the

appearance of a mirage, but the crisis looms when one pursues that mirage, giving up reality for illusion, contenting oneself with the appearance and ignoring the content.[6]

While I stress here that I am not in a position to associate political religious groups with either unbelief or belief, or to describe their ideological status, I mean to draw an analogy between the present situation and the concept of the mirage and its implications in the gracious verse. I consider those millions of people in the Arab and Muslim countries who thought well of political religious groups – believing that they had the capacity to set conditions right, achieve their development aspirations and lead their societies to the shore of modernity and development – to be like those deceived by the phenomenon of the mirage, whereby the viewer sees something where there is nothing—indeed, after a short while such a vision vanishes completely without a trace. Ancient Arabs used the term mirage as a euphemism for lying and anything without basis in truth.

> *Those who thought well of political religious groups are like those who are deceived by the phenomenon of the mirage, which the viewer imagines to be something while in fact it is nothing.*

When I started to work on this book I became more convinced regarding the title I had chosen—from the moment I began to observe the resemblance – or similitude, to be precise – between these two cases. As I mentioned earlier, a mirage is the emergence of an imaginary illusion, of an image that does not really exist. That is, it is an essentially deceptive phenomenon. It emerges as a result of certain natural atmospheric conditions that contribute to its formation. Likewise, under certain societal conditions, millions of people formed erroneous and false impressions that political religious groups were a real alternative capable of providing solutions to development problems and the social, economic, political, cultural and educational obstacles suffered by many Arab and Muslim countries.

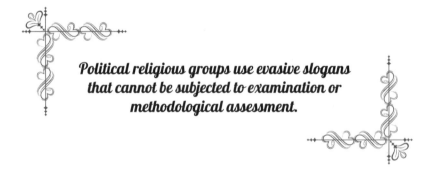

Political religious groups use evasive slogans that cannot be subjected to examination or methodological assessment.

Moreover, there are several common denominators between a mirage in a political context, which I address in this book, and the mirage as a natural phenomenon.[7] However the most notable of these common aspects is the fact that the physical equation of the mirage phenomenon lies in the words of Almighty God (Allah): "… until when he comes up to it, he finds it to be nothing …,"[8] from which interpreters infer that the closer we get to the mirage the farther away it gets from us. This means that the distance between the viewer and the mirage remains constant.[9] That is the case in some Arab and Muslim societies with the mirage of political religious groups that adopt a mercurial discourse and raise evasive slogans and incoherent programs that no objective researcher can subject to examination or methodological assessment. As such, they are like a mirage that remains distant, continuing to recede the closer you get to it.

There are also other shared aspects between the two forms of mirage. In nature, a mirage is an optical illusion that occurs as a result of conditions in the surrounding environment such as high temperature, flat land, and differences in the refractive index, resulting in an intense glow that appears like water on the ground and reflects images of objects as if they were reflected from the surface of a large mirror.[10] In the case of deception by political religious groups, the surrounding environment has played a prominent role in shaping this situation. These groups have exploited living and ideological conditions and the state of chaos and political vacuum resulting from the recent transformations that toppled several regimes in the Arab and Muslim worlds. Similarly, they have exploited, on the one hand, the gap between some of the peoples and their ruling regimes, and on the other the state of instinctive religiosity of the Arab and Muslim peoples, their inclination towards religion in times of crisis and their consequent tendency

to resort to those who speak in its name at times of historical trouble. During crises, the dynamics of reviving religious roots to find remedies for vital problems that the state is powerless to solve become more active.[11] In addition, the social conditions have contributed to the spread of militant ideas and provided a nurturing societal framework. Therefore the necessary conditions for the emergence of this phenomenon ensure its evocation and realization. Consequently, this necessitates a consideration of these conditions and efforts to avoid them, because addressing the root causes will guarantee the avoidance of such outcomes.

There is no better evidence or proof of the failure of political religious groups than the obvious and unmistakable decline – indeed collapse – of their popularity in the last few years. According to the most optimistic estimates in 2010, support for political religious groups ranged from 25 percent to 30 percent, while present estimates indicate that support does not exceed 10 percent in any case.

Recently conducted opinion polls indicate that the overwhelming majority of respondents in different countries in the Arab and Muslim worlds say that they are religious but prefer religion be kept away from both politics and political religious groups. Surprisingly, this response appeared in two countries where political religious groups gained authority, namely the Arab Republic of Egypt and the Republic of Tunisia.[12] Between 2006 and 2013, it was observed that there was a decline in attempts to exploit or use the Islamic religion

in politics. The experience of the Islamists' rule in both countries has made people less enthusiastic to involve religion in politics. Prior to the events of 2011 in the Republic of Tunisia, 20 percent of Tunisians wanted Islam to play a role in political life. However, the subsequent assassinations and polarization resulted in a decline in that percentage.[13]

Paradoxically, political religious groups claim to be defending Islam, although the practices of some of their leaders and members have nothing whatsoever to do with Islam. In fact, they are a crude application of militant ideas and views featured in the books of Sayyid Qutb, the theorist of the Muslim Brotherhood, and Abu Al-A'la Al-Mawdoodi. Qutb's book *Ma'alim fi Al-Tareeq* (Signposts on the Road) is one of the most important intellectual repositories of extremism and terrorism. It was, and still is, a source of inspiration for militant political religious groups, and was the cause of the growth and spread of a culture of violence and extremism in the Arab and Muslim worlds. On the other hand, Abu Al-A'la Al-Mawdoodi was the reference upon which Sayyid Qutb drew in relation to the concept of *hakimiyya* (meaning divine sovereignty; i.e., only *Sharia* principles and rules should be applied, not man-made laws),[14] which classifies Arab and Muslim societies as misguided and heretical, with no hope of rectifying and returning them to the correct path except by applying this concept and adopting the *Sharia* interpretations made by the theorists of political religious groups, who are regarded as agents of God (Allah) on Earth and display an inclination to designate societies as infidel and misguided.

Political religious groups adopt a narrow interpretation of Sharia, based on the concept of hakimiyya, considering themselves the agents of God (Allah) on Earth.

From the standpoint that extremism is a prelude and a precursor to killing,[15] this narrow religious vision is what has ultimately led to the spread of this astonishing level of violence and bloodshed at the hands of members of these groups in various regions of the Arab and Muslim worlds, where no respect exists for the sanctity of blood or human honor. It is inconceivable that the honorable Islamic *Sharia*, one of the main purposes of which is preserving the soul, would be a reference to justify killing, bloodshed and rape when it warns even against frightening a Muslim—albeit in jest. The most gracious Messenger, Muhammad, peace be upon him (pbuh), warned his armies and their leaders against committing such wrongs during war.[16] Despite that, we find people who commit continuous slaughter, killing, looting and destruction in several countries in the name of Islam, using as a reference the sayings of Abu Al-A'la Al-Mawdoodi and Sayyid Qutb instead of the sayings (Hadith) of the Prophet (pbuh), who used to say when he dispatched his armies: "Go out in the name of Allah, fight for Allah's cause those who disbelieve in Allah. Do not transgress, do not commit excesses, do not mutilate and do not kill children or the people at monasteries."[17] The Prophet (pbuh) also said: "By the One in Whose Hand is my soul, killing a believer is more grievous before Allah than the extinction of the whole world." Actually, this second saying (Hadith) by the Prophet (pbuh) is enough to show the greatness of the sanctity of Muslims' blood.[18] This is something that has been emphasized by Almighty God (Allah): "Nor take life – which Allah has made sacred – except for just cause ...,"[19] rendering the crime of killing the innocent among the greatest and most atrocious of sins.

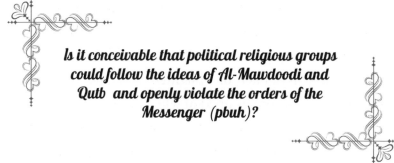

Is it conceivable that political religious groups could follow the ideas of Al-Mawdoodi and Qutb and openly violate the orders of the Messenger (pbuh)?

One wonders how those who claim to be adherents of Islam ignore the directions of the Prophet (pbuh) and persist in their misguided rallying behind the ecstatic utterances of Abu Al-A'la Al-Mawdoodi and Sayyid Qutb and other theorists of extremism and violence! How is it conceivable that some people believe in what these militants proclaim in their defense of Islam and their call for its application when they openly violate the orders of the Messenger (pbuh)?

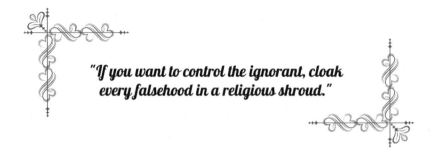

*"If you want to control the ignorant, cloak
every falsehood in a religious shroud."*

Besides, would not the case of political religious groups and
their followers and sympathizers be the best translation of the
saying by the Arab and Muslim philosopher Abu Al-Waleed
Muhammad Ibn Ahmad Ibn Rushd (Averroes): "If you want to
control the ignorant, cloak every falsehood in a religious shroud."[20]
It is a saying whose meaning and significance everybody has
ignored, and hence we ended up in this situation of trade in
religion and the explicit employment thereof.[21] That is what Ibn
Rushd, the philosopher of enlightenment and intellectual
rationality and wisdom, warned of when he said: "The trade in
religions thrives in societies in which ignorance is widespread."[22]
There may not actually have been a time in which ignorance has
dominated, logic has died down and reliance on tradition has
superseded reasoning in the Arab and Muslim countries more
than in the present age, in which conflict between moderation
and extremism seems to be at its peak.[23]

In fact, the misconception regarding the effectiveness of
the solutions and alternatives offered by political religious
groups has not been confined only to millions of people in the
Arab and Muslim countries; that delusion was also deeply

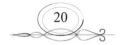

rooted in these groups themselves—which is a bizarre thing in its own right. These groups felt for a relatively long time that they had devised development projects capable of bridging the gap between religion and modernity. This false "mirage-like" feeling was only the result of an inherent, self-imposed intellectual isolation that separated them from the dynamics of the evolution and modernization occurring in the world around them. The result was that they bumped into the hard rock of reality in several political tests, some of which saw them gain the confidence of wide segments of voters only to find themselves facing the economic and development requirements and the complications of reality. These requirements could not wait until these groups returned to reason after they themselves, as well as the people, discovered that they had been selling an illusion, using slogans to gain support at the ballot box. They themselves also soon proved to be nothing more than a mirage for both parties in this equation: political religious groups and the voters. Millions of unemployed youth were not provided with solutions that would create job opportunities, and millions of poor and needy people did not find in those groups any means to secure their subsistence and meet their needs.

Finally, it is paradoxical that talk about the mirage phenomenon necessarily evokes a reference to one of the leading Muslim scholars, namely Al-Hassan Ibn Al-Haitham Al-Basri, the founder of optics, who was considered by some historians the greatest physicist of the Middle Ages. He was the author of the *Kitab Al-Manazir* (Book of Optics) in the 5th century AH (11th century AD)[24] which is considered an encyclopedia of physics and one of the most important scientific works in the field of optics. The paradox here lies in the fact that the scientific monitoring of this phenomenon by Ibn Al-Haitham, who was the first to provide a scientific explanation for it,[25] symbolizes the peak of scientific advancement achieved by the Arabs and Muslims in a previous age, whereas the political mirage we are dealing with today is the complete opposite in terms of its linguistic description and realistic analysis. It reflects a cultural backwardness and decline.

Perhaps one of the reasons for this reality lies in the abandonment of *ijtihad* (independent reasoning) by upholding the value of sticking to the text and limiting the function of the mind.[26] This contradicts the wisdom of God (Allah) who endowed man with a mind to think, create, endeavor and reason in various aspects of life.[27] Perhaps there is no more decisive evidence of the value of *ijtihad* (independent reasoning) and thought in the development of life and the importance of this in Islam than the fact that the number of Holy Quranic verses referring to thinking and *ijtihad* (independent reasoning) and the related aspects of rationalization, learning, contemplation and remembrance is about 300.[28] The Prophet Muhammad (pbuh) also said: "Contemplation for an hour is better than staying up for a whole night of optional prayer."[29]

Hence, this book tolls a warning bell and rings a wake-up call, not just to awaken those who have been tempted by the "mirage" or deceived by its appearance, but also for all of us to

strive together to restore the role of reason, *ijtihad* (independent reasoning), thinking, meditation and contemplation. We must also note that the experience of political religious groups is not devoid of lessons for all the Arab and Muslim societies. Foremost among these lessons is that the appearance avails nothing of the content and exterior avails nothing of the interior, or as the ancient Arab poet Antara Al-Absi said:[30] "Snakes, though silky their skins may feel, it is but a (swift) flip when their fangs deliver death."

Part I

Theoretical and Methodological Framework

Introduction:
The Problem of
the Study

INTRODUCTION:
THE PROBLEM OF THE STUDY

The understanding of Islam in our age is no longer subject to the instinctive and centrist pattern that the majority of Muslims have known and lived with for decades, indeed centuries. The pure Islamic approach is essentially based on centrism[1] and balance in the various aspects of life, in accordance with an explicit divine text in the Holy Quran; as God (Allah) says: "But seek, with the (wealth) which Allah has bestowed on thee, the Home of the Hereafter, nor forget thy portion in this world: but do thou good, as Allah has been good to thee, and seek not (occasions for) mischief in the land: for Allah loves not those who do mischief."[2] Holding to centrism is not optional in Islam; on the contrary, avoiding centrism might be destructive and suicidal, as demonstrated today in some Arab and Muslim states and societies which have lost this balance.[3] Islam is based on moderation and rejects both excess and neglect.[4] This is because centrism is a key feature of pure Islam,[5] which abounds with texts of conclusive significance on the adoption of centrism and moderation, encouraging them, advocating them and warning against surpassing or violating them. Whenever the Messenger, Muhammad (pbuh), had to make a choice between two options he always chose the easiest, unless it was a sin, and he warned against excess and exaggeration when he said: "Beware! The exaggerators perished," meaning exaggerators and transgressors in both word and deed.[6] To underline the option of centrism that Islam has introduced and founded, Almighty God (Allah) says: "Thus, have We made of you a moderate (centrist) nation (*umma*), that ye might be witnesses over the nations, and the Messenger a witness over yourselves…."[7] Ibn Abbas (may God (Allah) be pleased with him) reported that the Prophet (pbuh), said: "beware of exaggeration in religious matters for those who came before you were doomed because of exaggeration in religious matters."[8] However, this moderate (centrist) approach has often been upset by acts of exaggeration, militancy and extremism in both dialogue and application.[9] Such upsetting acts have reached extremes by the issuance of *fatwas* (legal opinions) of *takfir* (branding others as *kuffar*/infidels) and incitement, not only against those who are ideologically different, but also against the followers of the same religion who hold different ideas; not to mention other practices that have now become a danger to religion itself. I would indeed not be exaggerating if I said that the danger to which religion is exposed at the hands of political religious groups within the Arab and Muslim worlds is more serious than the danger stemming from its external enemies and detractors.

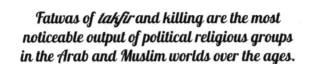

Fatwas of takfir and killing are the most noticeable output of political religious groups in the Arab and Muslim worlds over the ages.

For years, the majority of Arab and Muslim countries have experienced perplexity and confusion that has historically recurred in periods of cultural decline, intellectual weakness and scientific stagnation. Yet this problem now seems much deeper and more impacting. Past decades have witnessed various attempts to mix "religious" matters with "political" matters in a formula of co-existence, whether by establishing political parties with religious frames of reference or by allowing clerics to practice politics. Those experiences have clearly proven that such attempts are doomed to failure. Many scholars and intellectuals have warned about the danger of the approach of political religious groups and their practice of injecting religion into politics. One of those warnings was voiced by Shaikh Muhammad Mutwalli Al-Sha'rawi, when he rejected the idea of linking religious belonging with joining a political religious group or party. Al-Sha'rawi said:

> Belonging to a religious party is not one of the pillars of Islam, and it does not harm my religion if I do not belong to or support this party. I was a Muslim before I

knew the Muslim Brotherhood group or others. I was a Muslim before they became a party and will remain a Muslim after their party fades out and perishes. My Islam will not disappear without them because we are all Muslims, and they are not the only ones who are Muslims. I refuse to join a party begging my support based on my religious conviction and motive before addressing my mind. It is a political party and has nothing to do with religion. It only represents the political thought of its members and does not represent Muslims. I refuse to reduce my religion to a vote in a ballot box because my religion is the link between me and my Creator the Almighty. I hope that religion would reach the people of politics and that people of religion would not reach politics, because if you are people of religion, then there is no merit to you in politics, and if you are people of politics, then it is my right not to choose you and there is no blame or religious fault in that.[10]

Al-Sha'rawi refused to join a party based on "religious conviction and motive" rather than reason. He stated that religion has nothing to do with parties which represent the political thoughts of their members only, rather than that of all Muslims.

In light of the above, the problem lies in the fact that the cost of the failure of political religious groups in managing the affairs of their respective countries and societies is often high and burdensome. This failure has always been associated with turning away from prizing the value of the mind, promoting the knowledge and real understanding of pure religion and the Holy Quran. Indeed, the Holy Quran has preserved the status of knowledge and called for the active use of the mind, reason and contemplation, as in the following verse: "(Here is) a Book which We have sent down unto thee, full of blessings, that they may meditate on its Signs, and that men of understanding may receive admonition";[11] "Do they not then earnestly seek to understand the Holy Quran, or are their hearts locked up by them?"[12]

The disconnect between religion and reality – reinforced by the thoughts and practices of political religious groups – is partly due to the relationship between religion and modernity, which is a subject of historical philosophical debate that has consumed the time of many thinkers and philosophers. Political religious groups in the present time see every attempt at development and keeping up with science as surrender to modernity and westernization, and a rejection of religious, cultural and moral heritage and value. These groups do not for a moment even consider the fact that any building requires a strong foundation, which in this case is cultural and religious heritage. This heritage can neither be denied nor built upon without comprehending its vocabulary and grasping its various aspects in order to reach the stage of modernity grounded on a strong foundation.

On the flipside, this age-long debate is in fact between Islam and modernity, and between fundamentalists and innovative reformists. This chronic debate necessarily evokes an intuitive question: does it mean there is a problem in pairing between religion and the causes of modernity? The answer is emphatically no, because objective theorists and thinkers acknowledge that Islam was a source of inspiration for European and Muslim thinkers in the Middle Ages and the Ages of Enlightenment later on.[13] However, the problem remains visible in the viewpoints of political religious groups and their discussions about religion, modernity and the revival issue; specifically the relationship between religion and modernity, which is dubious and confused, and at best seems loose and sometimes surrounded by distrust; and even stained by deception, equivocation and hidden intentions.

In certain cases, the political practice has proven that political religious groups may ostensibly accept the idea of equality among citizens as a secular constitutional foundation, but they still shy away from the concept of accountability and the idea of equality between men and women, at least in terms of political, economic and social rights. Also, their acceptance of some principles of modernity, such as pluralism, seems highly questionable. For example, the program of the Muslim Brotherhood group mentions its commitment to partisan and political pluralism and respect for the democratic system,[14] but the reality seems quite different. In his answer to a question about the possibility of the Muslim Brotherhood group

accepting the existence of a communist or Christian party, the former General Guide of the group, Mamoon Hassan Al-Hudaibi (2002–2004), said it is impossible to legalize a party that seeks to eradicate religion (in reference to communism). As for the Egyptian Copts, Al-Hudaibi argued that they are not in need of a political party or organization, because the Church plays this role, in his opinion.[15]

Moreover, the experience of the Muslim Brotherhood in government in the Arab Republic of Egypt (June 30, 2012– July 3, 2013), has exposed its narrow-minded view towards others, even if those others are Muslims who just hold different opinions and political orientations.[16] In fact, they did not hesitate to wage fierce campaigns of criticism against religious parties and personalities who hailed from the same ideological background – based on the exploitation of the *fatwa* (legal opinion) for political interest, *takfir* (branding others as *kuffar*/infidels) and killing – with seemingly small intellectual differences. Media campaigns waged by the Muslim Brotherhood group against the Salafi Al-Noor Party during the rule of former Egyptian president Dr. Muhammad Mursi Al-Ayyat in the Arab Republic of Egypt were an example of such differences that cut across ideological frames of reference in pursuit of political self-interest.

Perhaps the fundamental problem in the conduct and discourse of political religious groups lies in their practice of absolute dictatorship. Their political behavior takes an overpowering totalitarian form that does not accept others, no

matter who they are. An analysis of the literature of political religious groups shows the ambiguity of their intellectual and political discourse and its swing between two problematic issues: the first is related to the source of legitimacy—is it the text itself or the *umma* (nation) which is entrusted with the text? The idea of sovereignty – as viewed by Sayyid Qutb – nullifies the dependence of legitimacy on the masses of the *umma* as its source and is confined to divine *hakimiyya* (divine sovereignty), while another different trend maintains that the *umma* is the source of legitimacy within the referential framework of the text. The second issue is related to the definition of the scope of sovereignty (supremacy) of the *umma*; does it refer to *Dar Al-Islam*[17] (Land of Islam) which no longer exists in the modern political structure, or is it the nation-state in its modern political sense rather than religious one?[18]

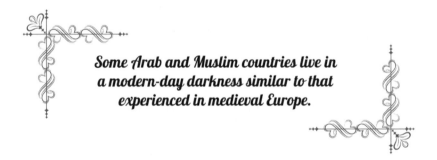

Some Arab and Muslim countries live in a modern-day darkness similar to that experienced in medieval Europe.

This debate seems to represent a darkness engulfing some regions in the Arab and Muslim worlds in this 15th century AH. This situation is similar to the backwardness experienced by the European continent in the Middle Ages, specifically during the 15th century AD. The similarities between the two situations are

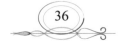

clear and revealing. Also, the similarity between the 15th century AD and the 15th century AH in terms of intellectual and cultural misery is striking and raises questions, given that the time span between the two cases exceeds five centuries. I am afraid that this may be the time span separating some of the Arab and Muslim countries from current Western development and progress.

> *The similarity of the intellectual anguish of the 15th century AD and the 15th century AH raises fears about the existence of a huge time span between the Arab and Muslim worlds from modernity.*

Some researchers argue that the painful experience of European backwardness had a serious negative impact on religion, as it did not lead to punishment of the Church-based religious authority at that time for its misuse of religion by employing it in politics and corrupt financial matters. Instead, it ended up penalizing religion itself. It did not differentiate between religion and its abusers. Therefore, religion became a victim of that struggle, and was totally withdrawn from life. Later, the French Revolution (1789) came to separate religion from the state completely and to become a model for modern political entities in Europe. The issue of separating religion from state was no longer disputable, but became deeply rooted and well-established in the collective Western conscience and consciousness in general.[19]

Linguistically speaking, darkness means the absence of light,[20] which in turn stimulates attempts to escape from it. It requires serious research to provide an intellectual lifeboat for generations of youth who suffer confusion and a lack of prospects as a result of practices that evoke the past without any regard to the factors and dictates of time or developments and changes in the present situation. The deteriorating cultural situation throws some Arab and Muslim countries into a multifaceted unrest that obstructs any attempt at development in those countries. The religious case is part of this unrest, and is perhaps the common denominator between all its elements and dimensions. Talk about religion has changed from being a point of harmony that brings about societal security (in all its components and pillars, particularly moral values and frameworks) and saves societies from decay and disintegration to a factor of division and a subject of contention, as witnessed in various Arab countries, especially in the last ten years, and the bloody conflicts they have endured as a result of sectarian differences.

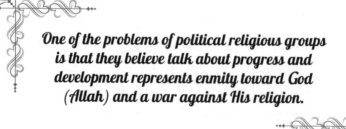

One of the problems of political religious groups is that they believe talk about progress and development represents enmity toward God (Allah) and a war against His religion.

While the disharmonious discourse of political religious groups is split between "Brotherhood," "Salafi," "Sufi," "jihadi" and other types, most of it is characterized by *taqleed* (imitation; reliance on tradition) and lack of *ijtihad* (independent reasoning), without any serious effort to find a formula for coexistence between religion and politics. Many have created an aura of artificial unity and an association between them and religion, where they present themselves as the exclusive agents of the religion of God (Allah), as is the case with political religious groups and their leaders and figures who in many cases have equated the talk about progress and development to enmity against God (Allah) and a war against His pure religion.

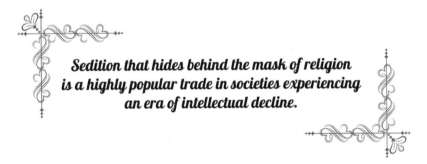

Sedition that hides behind the mask of religion is a highly popular trade in societies experiencing an era of intellectual decline.

The "trade in religion" has become one of the most salient features of this current era of history. The goal of this "trade" is to employ religion in order to achieve political or personal objectives pursued by political religious groups, making religion into a "Trojan Horse"[21] or a disguise to attain their political and personal ends and objectives. In this respect, the writer Bahaa Tahir pointed out that Ibn Khaldoon noted centuries ago the danger of the religious state, the problems of which our Muslim world has suffered and continues to suffer. In his famous *Muqaddima* (Introduction), Ibn Khaldoon argues that sedition that hides behind the mask of religion is a very popular trade. Tahir added to that argument, saying that this trade prospers specifically in eras marked by the intellectual decline of societies, pointing out that Ibn Khaldoon addressed the essence of the matter when he said that false devotees raise religious slogans and seek leadership – the appeal of which fills their souls – but are unable to reach it through conventional means and mechanisms, and hence imagine that exploitation of religion is one of the ways to achieve their desires.[22] Any analysis of the literature of political religious groups will show this fact, in addition to their practices on the ground from which it may easily be concluded that they do not have any clear political, economic, social or cultural program.

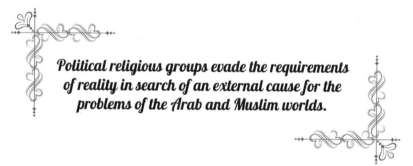

Political religious groups evade the requirements of reality in search of an external cause for the problems of the Arab and Muslim worlds.

The Problem of the Study

This book raises a number of vitally important questions that require investigation and clear, direct answers – without the caution usually taken when discussing such topics for fear of being killed by political religious groups, which was a common

response – given the dark phase through which the Arab and Muslim worlds are passing in the course of their long history, which has seen much brighter and more glorious stages—for example in some periods of the Abbasid dynasty (132–656 AH; 750–1258 AD) when science, arts and literature flourished.

> *One of the goals of The Mirage is to enrich the research debate and sharpen the thought process in order to produce knowledge and necessary solutions.*

In this context, I see no choice but to pose these questions unequivocally, believing in the perfection of the religion of God (Allah, Glorified be He) free of the exploitation of *fatwa* (legal opinion) for political or personal interests or for *takfir* (branding others as *kuffar*/infidels) and killing. I believe in putting religion in its proper high place that keeps it from impurities that might surround it as a result of incorrect and backward practices stained by ignorance, conceit and opportunism among political religious groups which do not look to the past in a critical realistic way that allows them to accept others and see in their progress some lessons to be learned. These groups usually ask themselves the wrong question: "who did this to us?" in an effort to find external causes for our problems. They do not ask themselves the questions needed for achieving progress and catching up with the contemporary world. Such questions were discussed by a researcher in the book *What Went Wrong?* And include: What did we do wrong?" and "What are other people doing right?," in preparation for the answer to the most important question: "How do we catch up with them?"[23]

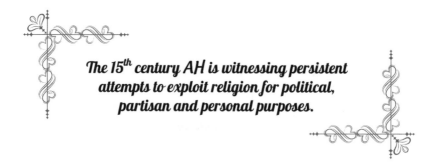

The 15ᵗʰ century AH is witnessing persistent attempts to exploit religion for political, partisan and personal purposes.

In light of this, the book raises the following set of questions, which together constitute the core problem discussed: why was the West successful in separating religion from state at the end of the 15ᵗʰ century AD, while in the Arab and Muslim countries in the 15ᵗʰ century AH we see persistent attempts by political religious groups to exploit religion – by mixing it with politics – in order to achieve partisan and personal interests? Why do these groups monopolize the interpretation of religion and promote unrealistic concepts such as the Caliphate and *bai'a* (oath of allegiance)? And why do many of those groups declare those who disagree with them to be unbelievers and seek to kill them, in violation of key fundamentals entrenched by pure Islam, which seeks to instill the principles of balance, moderation and tolerance? The approach of those groups is in explicit

contrast with the Holy Quranic verses: "Say, 'The truth is from your Lord:' let him who wills believe, and let him who wills, reject (it) …,[24] "Invite (all) to the Way of thy Lord with wisdom and beautiful preaching; and argue with them in ways that are best and most gracious …,"[25] and "Say: O ye that reject Faith! I worship not that which ye worship, nor will ye worship that which I worship, and I will not worship that which ye have been wont to worship, nor will ye worship that which I worship; to you be your Way, and to me mine."[26] These verses reflect an inherent tolerance in our pure religion. Furthermore, why did those groups fail to build a national consensus in their respective countries and to provide an answer to the question of revival or modernization, quickly collapsing after failing to understand the drivers of the collective consciousness of the people who elected them, not because they trusted their religiosity but in order to break out of the development dilemma and find solutions to existing problems?

It is important here to emphasize that this book focuses on the study of political religious groups and their thought within the limits of Sunni Islam, with the aim of refuting their behavior, and dissecting their practices and intellectual and political visions, based on my full awareness of the fact that those groups do not reflect Islam or its pure image. Any yielding to their allegations in this respect is a major offense to this pure religion. Thus, by examining political religious groups and all currents of political Islam, with the exception of Sufism, this book seeks to shed light on the political exploitation of

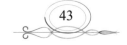

religion, its mechanisms, types, manifestations, consequences and outcomes in order to better understand what is going on in the Arab and Muslim worlds today and to unravel many of the various entanglements and problems that hamper development and progress and fuel the gap separating many Arab and Muslim countries from the progress and development achieved in Western countries.

> *Political religious groups were oblivious to the fact that people did not elect them purely for ideological considerations, so they quickly fell apart.*

To achieve this end, this book provides an insight into, and an in-depth research vision of political religious groups in their various manifestations and practices. It tracks their historical evolution and studies some cases from their inception until the failure of the Muslim Brotherhood group's experience in government in a number of Arab and Muslim countries. It identifies the causes of this failure, which has crushed a long historical legacy of pretentious slogans that had for nearly 80 years been the source of much appreciation and admiration among political religious groups and their sympathizers, and especially the Muslim Brotherhood group itself. As mentioned above, there is a great deal of similarity between the stage of backwardness in the European continent in the Middle Ages and the thought and practices of political religious groups in the Arab and Muslim worlds in the modern era, particularly in terms of intellectual and political structures, the relationship between religion and politics, and the role of clerics in both eras.

The attempt to navigate between these two historical stages will no doubt generate a number of spontaneous questions: why is modernity viewed as the antithesis of religiosity and a rejection of religion and its teachings? Why do some groups think that talk about religion ends where talk about progress and development begins? Why have referential concepts disappeared and given way to destructive ideas like those espoused by political religious groups? What are the circumstances that have paved the way for the growth in the influence of political religious groups in many Arab and Muslim countries? In what ways did some of these groups prove their failure and the emptiness of their political and religious thought when they reached authority in some of those countries?

The "mirage" represents the vast gap between theory and practice in terms of the performance of political religious groups.

This spectrum of questions is the focal point of investigation and scholarly discussion in this book, in which I attempt to pursue a robust scholarly approach to detect what I call the "mirage." This mirage represents the gap revealed between theory and practice in the performance of political religious groups, as well as the now obvious fact that – as experience has shown – alternatives are limited for the many people who have considered political participation as a way out of crises. These people have found that the difficult economic development realities forcibly drive them into the clutches of political religious groups which have then drained much of their efforts and aspirations to achieve a genuine renaissance.

> *One of the problems of political religious groups is that they appoint themselves as agents of religion and monopolize the right to speak in its name like a company that enjoys an exclusive monopoly over a commodity or service.*

The Importance of the Topic

Predicting the future necessitates the study of the topics, issues, developments and events that affect it both directly and indirectly, and an examination of the present to the extent that it affects the future. Such a study should be undertaken according to clear research frameworks and a scholarly methodology that begins with questions and preparatory steps, and proceeds to reach the desired results. Perhaps this book may become a groundbreaking work that will enrich the research debate and sharpen the thought process to expand our knowledge and develop appropriate solutions.

In addressing the topic of this book, I have been keen to strictly observe scholarly and research objectivity, leaving no room for personal opinion, regardless of how far this method contradicts or supports my personal viewpoint or opinion concerning any of the issues I have addressed or their details. In general, the idea of this book emanates from a scholarly belief that it is time to describe political religious groups in a serious scholarly manner for several reasons, including the fact that these groups – at an Arab and Muslim world level – have become a focus of debate and discussion, and in many countries have abandoned their putative role of finding societal solutions to problems and have come to represent obstacles to solving these issues.

Parallel to this are motivations and indicators to consider that should not be underestimated or trivialized, nor can they be analyzed in light of previous historical experiences. Among the most prominent of these are the actions taken by the Muslim Brotherhood group in many countries, both today and in the past, to influence domestic stability. It is quite obvious that the group is attempting to reproduce its failed experiences in government, not to mention its pursuit of political provocation against the ruling authorities in some countries, the escalation

of violence in its ideological discourse, and attempts to incite social and popular unrest to pressure the ruling authorities in order to achieve the demands included in the group's organizational agenda of activity.

If most Arab and Muslim societies today suffer the symptoms of cultural backwardness compared to previous eras, escaping this deteriorating situation will only be possible by undertaking an objective analysis of the causes and factors that have led to it—by understanding identity and the self as a means for change at the societal and individual levels. Such knowledge should allow an intellectual breakthrough and reveal the core of the collective cultural and social consciousness from which social behavior originates.[27] In other words, self-criticism should be exercised in order to build a collective consciousness and subsequent analysis of the causes of backwardness, and to develop alternatives and suggestions for viable ways to overcome this long-standing situation. Needless to say, a critical awareness of the problem is required, because reality can only be changed by unveiling its truths.[28] What is meant here is that the effective treatment of the current problems in the Arab and Muslim worlds starts with a diagnosis of the reality of the ailment, before defining the right remedy, setting the necessary intellectual and cultural foundations necessary for overcoming the current backwardness, and embracing development, progress and salvation from this harsh reality—particularly by taking more interest in education and scholarly research.

Since I started writing this book, I have been undoubtedly aware that attempting any research effort that focuses on the issue of political religious groups is like walking in a minefield, not only because of the complicated, sensitive and controversial nature of the topic, but also because the hidden side of the agendas of these groups is much more than that declared, and what goes on behind the scenes is much more than that which appears in public. Also, what these groups declare is contrary to what they hide. Furthermore, what makes this task more difficult is that these groups are determined to mix various issues in their practices and – as I mentioned earlier – intend to confuse researchers and observers, as well as the ruling authorities. Also, many of these groups are linked to foreign powers and parties that can easily be identified, but it is difficult to track the details of those connections and their real dimensions. As such, the most difficult task I faced was how to remain strictly objective and search for information amidst an almost impenetrable web of secrecy and closely-held information; how to find the truth amidst such a rubble of vagueness; and how to use the appropriate scholarly methods to deal with the large volume of inconsistent and often conflicting information, making the job of a truth-seeker no less dispiriting than chasing a mirage.

Other research difficulties related to the fact that many of the existing books about political religious groups were written in local and regional environments that saw conflicts resulting from the attempts of some countries to regulate those groups and to understand their real intentions, goals and interests. But this book comes into being in a completely different

49

environment—in fact, an environment incompatible with a political landscape, and one that for the most part belongs to the past. In this different environment, the variables of the struggle have changed and resulted in the control of some of those political religious groups over the political scene in some countries of the region. Some of those groups have even reached the helm of government – such as the Muslim Brotherhood group in the Arab Republic of Egypt and the Republic of Tunisia. However, the former failed to retain its position due to its reliance on slogans without having any serious development vision or political, economic, social and cultural programs to turn those slogans into viable action plans and programs—such programs being essential to the people in those countries that once thought these groups really did offer solutions to extricate them from their crises. The Tunisian Ennahdha Party was forced to make political concessions to its competitors, absorbing the important lessons of the Egyptian people's revolution against the rule of the Muslim Brotherhood group on June 30, 2013.

However, these concessions failed to restore the declining popularity of the Ennahdha Party, which resulted in the Nidaa Tounes Party winning the parliamentary elections held on 26 October 2014 as well as the presidency.[29] The above meant that political religious groups, albeit for a short while, moved from the opposition ranks in some Arab and Muslim countries to the position of authority and government. They entered an historic political test that exposed their true intellectual, political, organizational, ideological, economic and cultural weaknesses. These events may help in answering many questions which have

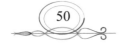

long preoccupied researchers about such groups and their ability to manage government and state affairs while remaining devoted to slogans and the presentation of alternatives from the archives of history without the slightest interest in keeping up with the developments of modern life and the tools needed to achieve real development for millions of people—such as modern age technologies that have become an essential vehicle for development and modernity.

Monopoly of Religion

One of the problems affecting many Arab and Muslim societies is the practice among political religious groups of seeking to entrench the idea of an "agency of religion" through which to attribute lies to God (Allah); i.e. those groups claim to act as agents of God (Allah) on Earth. On this narrow vision they base their monopolistic practice of speaking in the name of religion and determining the fate of Islam and Muslims.

This deficient vision among political religious groups is taken for granted by some, but it is a result of authoritarianism that is practiced without any criticism from other Muslims, for fear of slipping into a sacred–profane controversy. The alleged exclusive agency of religion by political religious groups is specifically not permissible in Islam. In this respect, Islam is intrinsically different from other revealed religions. In Islam, the relationship between a person and his God (Allah) is direct and needs no mediator. There is no *kahanoot* (sacerdotalism, wherein only a special group of men may provide access to God (Allah)), in light of a relationship that

God (Allah) has defined by saying: "When My servants ask thee concerning Me, I am indeed close (to them): I listen to the prayer of every suppliant when he calleth on Me: let them also, with a will, listen to My call, and believe in Me: that they may walk in the right way,"[30] and "Say: "O People of the Book! Come to common terms as between us and you: that we worship none but Allah; that we associate no partners with him; that we establish not, from among ourselves, lords and patrons other than Allah." If then they turn back, say ye: "Bear witness that we (at least) are Muslims (bowing to Allah's Will)."[31]

The relationship between a person and his God (Allah) in the two Holy Quranic verses above is crystal clear and direct, involving no mediation. This is an exclusive attribute of Islam. In fact, the Holy Quran criticizes practices similar to those of former ancient nations, saying:

> They take their priests and their anchorites to be their lords in derogation of Allah, and (they take as their Lord) Christ the son of Mary; yet they were commanded to worship but one Allah: there is no God (Allah) but He. Praise and glory to Him: (far is He) from having the partners they associate (with Him).[32]

It also criticizes those who exaggerate their obedience to other persons, whether within groups, organizations or any form of everyday dealings that may make a person obey another person in a manner almost similar to obedience to Almighty God (Allah). In this regard, God (Allah) says:

> Yet there are men who take (for worship) others besides Allah as equal (with Allah): they love them as they should

love Allah. But those of faith are overflowing in their love for Allah. If only the unrighteous could see, behold, they would see the penalty: that to Allah belongs all power, and Allah will strongly enforce the penalty.[33]

According to the above, in Islam there is no mediation between the Creator and the created, and no such concepts and roles that appear with titles like cleric or guide, or other concepts of this sort that have caused a great deal of confusion and prevented accurate understanding. Many people deal with these concepts as religious truths although they quickly crumble in front of any conscious, insightful jurisprudential reading of the principles of religion. It is possible to find someone who talks about an exclusive right in terms of "commercial agency" or buying and selling, but it would be surprising if someone were to present themselves as the exclusive agent of religion or the sole stakeholder who decides what is legal and what is not, closing the door of *ijtihad* (independent reasoning) and interpretation and rejecting everyone who holds dissenting opinions, without providing the argument and evidence to support that opinion and dispel those of others.[34] The most peculiar problem in this regard is that some members of political religious groups, described as preachers, have become "stars" in recent decades and years, competing with cinema and TV stars in their fame in a manner that is perhaps not in keeping with the status and prestige of a cleric.

The spread of political religious groups geographically and intellectually in the Arab and Muslim worlds is one of the salient features of this phenomenon. Figure (0-1) shows the geographical spread of the groups referred to in the chapters of this book.

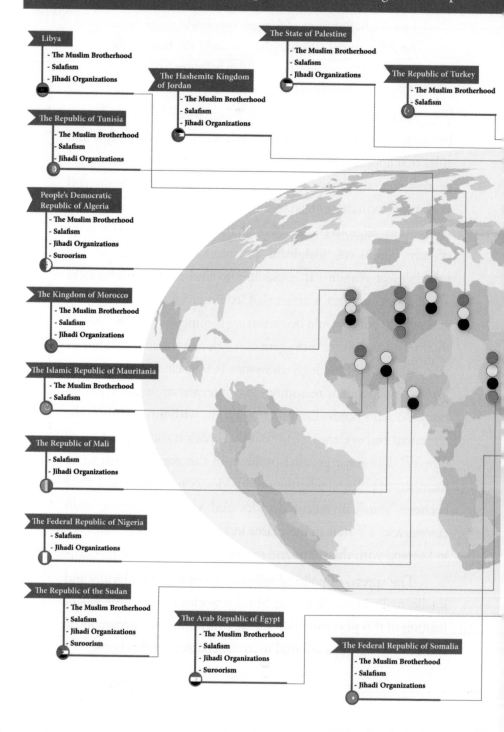

Geographic Distribution of Important Political Religious Groups in

Libya
- The Muslim Brotherhood
- Salafism
- Jihadi Organizations

The State of Palestine
- The Muslim Brotherhood
- Salafism
- Jihadi Organizations

The Republic of Turkey
- The Muslim Brotherhood
- Salafism

The Hashemite Kingdom of Jordan
- The Muslim Brotherhood
- Salafism
- Jihadi Organizations

The Republic of Tunisia
- The Muslim Brotherhood
- Salafism
- Jihadi Organizations

People's Democratic Republic of Algeria
- The Muslim Brotherhood
- Salafism
- Jihadi Organizations
- Suroorism

The Kingdom of Morocco
- The Muslim Brotherhood
- Salafism
- Jihadi Organizations

The Islamic Republic of Mauritania
- The Muslim Brotherhood
- Salafism

The Republic of Mali
- Salafism
- Jihadi Organizations

The Federal Republic of Nigeria
- Salafism
- Jihadi Organizations

The Republic of the Sudan
- The Muslim Brotherhood
- Salafism
- Jihadi Organizations
- Suroorism

The Arab Republic of Egypt
- The Muslim Brotherhood
- Salafism
- Jihadi Organizations
- Suroorism

The Federal Republic of Somalia
- The Muslim Brotherhood
- Salafism
- Jihadi Organizations

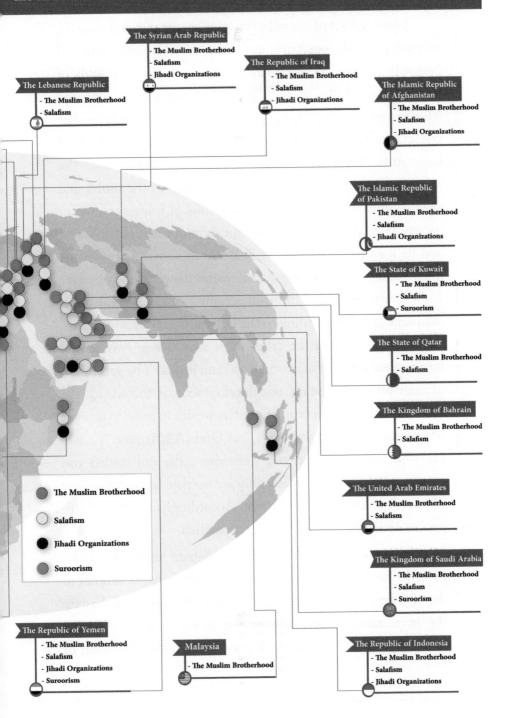

The Syrian Arab Republic
- The Muslim Brotherhood
- Salafism
- Jihadi Organizations

The Republic of Iraq
- The Muslim Brotherhood
- Salafism
- Jihadi Organizations

The Islamic Republic of Afghanistan
- The Muslim Brotherhood
- Salafism
- Jihadi Organizations

The Lebanese Republic
- The Muslim Brotherhood
- Salafism

The Islamic Republic of Pakistan
- The Muslim Brotherhood
- Salafism
- Jihadi Organizations

The State of Kuwait
- The Muslim Brotherhood
- Salafism
- Suroorism

The State of Qatar
- The Muslim Brotherhood
- Salafism

The Kingdom of Bahrain
- The Muslim Brotherhood
- Salafism

The United Arab Emirates
- The Muslim Brotherhood
- Salafism

The Kingdom of Saudi Arabia
- The Muslim Brotherhood
- Salafism
- Suroorism

The Muslim Brotherhood

Salafism

Jihadi Organizations

Suroorism

The Republic of Yemen
- The Muslim Brotherhood
- Salafism
- Jihadi Organizations
- Suroorism

Malaysia
- The Muslim Brotherhood

The Republic of Indonesia
- The Muslim Brotherhood
- Salafism
- Jihadi Organizations

Islam is a set of overall principles meant to guard the self, property, mind, posterity and religion. The attributes of believers are not confined to the marks on the foreheads of worshippers (i.e. the 'prayer marks' which many in the Arab and Muslim worlds develop), but instead shine brightly in the research of scholars, the expertise of producers and efforts of innovators. Religion is the origin of civilization, and the suitability of religion stems from its reform of the moral and value system, where it becomes a means of improvement for society. So, Islam is linked with the development of the Earth and its maintenance; and the link is well known between the maintenance of the mosque, the maintenance of the universe and the attainment of the true meaning of the succession of man on Earth.[35] According to the holistic overall view of Islam, the main purpose of the creation of man lies in two central terms: succession (of man on Earth) and justice. The succession of man on Earth means the development of the world, the extraction, development and use of its wealth in order to achieve happiness and establish justice,[36] as God (Allah) says: "… it is He who hath produced you from the earth and settled you therein…"[37] i.e. the ultimate legitimate purpose is the attainment of benefit and avoidance of harm. Accordingly, the five above-mentioned general purposes were specified.

It is specifically here that the debate arises about the precedence of mind (reason) in deciding the benefits in order to derive rulings and validate them.[38] The Holy Quran emphasizes the importance of the role of the mind (reason) in many verses,[39] such as: "… none will grasp the Message but men of

understanding,"[40] and "… We have made plain to you the signs, if ye have wisdom."[41] Based on the above, one may conclude that there are many factors that help explain the state of disconnect between the Arab and Muslim worlds and development, and understand the reasons why the Arab and Muslim worlds have shunned the reformist calls they have witnessed throughout modern and contemporary history, such as those championed by Qassim Ameen and the Imams Jamal Al-Deen Al-Afghani, Muhammad Abdu, and Rifa'a Raf'i Al-Tahtawi, and why the ideas of militant, text-reliant clerics have triumphed over trends of free and rational thinking.

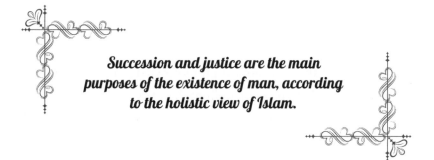

Succession and justice are the main purposes of the existence of man, according to the holistic view of Islam.

There are many viewpoints and conceptions regarding the reasons behind this. Some people consider the Arab–Islamic civilization itself to be one of the obstacles preventing the Arab and Muslim worlds from being influenced by the ages of enlightenment, religious reform and the ripples of the French Revolution (1789–1799). However, such explanations do not deliver the whole truth.[42] As a matter of fact, there is an obvious spread of the term "conspiracy" in the Arab and Muslim worlds.

It is this term that some ruling regimes and political religious groups have used to escape the consequences of suffocating economic crises and weak development, which they blame on external factors. "Westernization" has appeared as a new justification, and refers to attempts by the West to impose the values of globalization and Western culture on the Arabs and Muslims. This accusation is skillfully used by political religious groups that raise charges of heresy, cooperation with the West and being an agent of the West against enlightened and educated Arabs and Muslims who support positive interaction with the West. In fact, these groups used the same accusations when they reached authority in some Arab and Muslim countries, accusing the opponents of their style of governance of conspiracy and being agents of the West.[43]

As stated above, Islam calls for knowledge and encourages it in many noble verses, including: "… Say: are those equal, those who know and those who do not know? It is those who are endowed with understanding that receive admonition?"[44] and: "… Allah will raise up, to (suitable) ranks (and degrees), those of you who believe and who have been granted (mystic) knowledge. And Allah is well-acquainted with all ye do."[45] The same calls also feature in many honorable sayings (Hadith) of the Prophet (pbuh), including: "whoever follows a path to seek knowledge therein, Allah will make easy for him a path to Paradise."[46] However, the consequences of the rigid thought of political religious groups and their failure to accumulate sufficient knowledge capital to improve reality cannot be

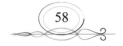

blamed on religion itself, because it is logically impossible to develop the present by returning to a knowledge capital that dates back to several centuries ago, even to the era following the Rightly Guided Caliphate, without renovating it based on the scholarly knowledge accumulated by humanity, West and East, over the course of 14 centuries. These kinds of knowledge are necessary for progress, development and the elimination of all manifestations of backwardness and cultural decline, using modern social sciences to analyze reality and its problems.[47] The lack of such modern knowledge explains the failure of most political religious groups in government, collapsing unexpectedly like meteors that no sooner had sparkled in the skies of some Arab and Muslim countries than burned to ashes.[48] These groups shone and burned to ashes after some of them rose to authority without sufficient experience; societies and countries found themselves facing difficult and tough challenges while these groups led them and their societies through a maze of adventures into the unknown.[49]

Political religious groups appoint themselves as referee, watchman and judge on all forms of thought and adopt the working philosophy of the European Inquisition.

Political Religious Groups and the European Dark Ages

Some researchers may argue that political religious groups mix religion and politics.[50] However, reality confirms that they use the former to serve the latter, and this is one of the reasons for their extremism and hostility towards those who disagree with their opinions. These groups have made themselves referee, watchman and judge on any different form of thought. This is the same logic as that of the European Inquisition, which emerged during the Dark Ages and became active in the 15th and 16th centuries.[51] The Inquisition was the brainchild of ecclesiastics in the first place, and their function was to implement the text of the Bible according to their narrow interpretations and to prosecute anyone who disagreed with them. In this context, they committed many crimes, even against religion itself, in its pure aspect of faith. This is exactly what has been and still is done by political religious groups, which seek to limit history to one version, thought to one school, and culture and art to one outlet.[52] There is a large number of creative citizens and thinkers in the countries of the Arab and Muslim worlds who are subjected to what their European counterparts experienced – like Galileo Galilei and Nicolaus Copernicus – during the Dark Ages at the hand of the courts of the Inquisition, but in a new fashion. The Inquisition courts extended from ancient Rome, Europe, Andalusia, Tehran, Bukhara and Baghdad to reach the Arab and Muslim worlds through different ways; but in the end, they aimed to annihilate creativity and fight everyone who came with anything

contrary to the contents of the old books, even if those contents represented the worst of collectibles.[53]

Perhaps one example of this similarity between the darkness of the Middle Ages in Europe and the present reality in the Arab and Muslim worlds is what political religious groups do in terms of issuing takfiri fatwas (legal opinions branding others as *kuffar*/infidels) or prohibiting literary and artistic works on the basis that they run against the pure principles and foundations of religion. Such practices could be considered as similar to those of the Church during the Middle Ages when it burned about 15,000 scientists and scholars on the charge of heresy and straying from the views of the Church (indeed, the actual numbers were much higher than these estimates).[54] The Inquisition courts forced a scientist like Galileo Galilei to step back from stating a scientific fact – the revolution of the Earth – whose veracity and accuracy have been proven and held true to this day.[55] In that period, the Church was also associated with the burning of books and manuscripts in a public ceremony attended by the masses and supreme religious authorities, as happened in the southern cities of Andalusia, such as Toledo, which became an arena of ignorance and an incinerator of philosophers and their books on charges of heresy, having once been a center of religious tolerance and scientific activity. About 100,000 books and manuscripts were burned and the Muslims of Granada were forced in 1500 AD to hand in millions of books, almost all of which were burned. The few that remained were translated and benefited from in the

West; they constituted the basic building blocks of the knowledge society, which arose on the ruins of the dark Middle Ages.[56]

Historical literature indicates that the ideas of Galileo and Copernicus overturned the concept advanced by the Church regarding the centrality of the Earth (around which everything revolved) and proved that it was the Earth that revolved around the Sun in an infinite solar system.[57] This scientific achievement was a reason for their persecution by the Church. For example, when Galileo struggled to prove the revolution of the Earth and confronted clergymen with their erroneous explanation of this matter, he was persecuted on the charge of breaching an established belief. He would have been burned alive had he not stepped back from voicing those ideas in public.[58]

While European societies and countries managed to extricate themselves from the swamp of darkness that engulfed them for several centuries in the Middle Ages by separating religion and state, many Arab and Muslim thinkers in the modern era reject the idea of secularism. They consider it part of a Western cultural construct that means the separation of Church from state; they do not believe Islam, like the Church, should be separated from the state. One of the proponents of this argument is Muhammad Aabid Al-Jabiri, who advanced the slogan of modernism and rationalism as an alternative that is compatible with Islam and does not exclude it.[59] This proposition ostensibly aims to develop an Islamic-based formula to serve as a mechanism for political practice, but it seems fluid

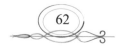

and imprecise, particularly in terms of creating a framework for the relationship between religion and politics. It also fails to clarify whether it intends to find a formula for coexistence between the two or to separate them, as happened in the West but based on a perspective that takes into account the particularities of Islam.

It is important to point out that the development of experimental sciences was primarily based on the development of free critical thinking within the context of relative objectivity provided by free environments where ideas, knowledge and science could be exchanged. Certainly, the development and success of experimental sciences in the West put an end to the allegations of priests and clergymen and their selfish interests. Muhammad Iqbal Al-Lahori (1877–1938) noted this important issue in his writings: "when knowledge is confined in one single source and that source is in the hands of the clerics, this would set the stage for religious despotism. But when there are diverse sources of knowledge, the case is different."[60]

Perhaps the most serious outcome of the experience of political religious groups in the Arab and Muslim worlds during recent years is their attempts to use religion in service of their personal and political ambitions and goals, even if they claim otherwise and proclaim that they separate their preaching–social activities on the one hand and their political activities on the other.[61] There is plenty of evidence that shows such groups exploit religion and the instinctively religious nature of the Arab and Muslim peoples in order to achieve political and personal gains. For example, the Muslim Brotherhood group still clings to its slogan "Islam is the solution" despite the fact that it was not translated into realistic and applicable programs and work plans. Furthermore, their political discourse still tries to impose its "religious" guardianship of society[62] and is still characterized by evasiveness and double standards. This has been demonstrated several times, including by former Egyptian president Muhammad Mursi in relation to the loan offered to Egypt by the International Monetary Fund; he was completely opposed to such loans under previous presidents, but when he became president, he approved the loan and announced that it was compatible with the Islamic principles.[63]

Moreover, political religious groups – particularly the Muslim Brotherhood group – not only politicize religion but also speak in its name and seek to impose their view of religion—sometimes through invitation and at other times through intimidation. They do not tolerate any opinion or word contrary to their understanding of what religious values and behavioral standards should be instilled in society. This is implicitly dangerous, as attempts to impose certain practices by cloaking them in religion will most likely lead to societal violence, in addition to other effects on the relationship between the constituents of societies, and negative impacts on the country's relationship with the outside world. Such practices do not bring anything of value to Arab and Muslim societies, many of which face difficult development problems. The Arab region has one of the highest unemployment rates in the world,

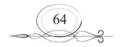

amounting to double the international average, at about 26 percent; i.e. there are an estimated 20 million unemployed in the Arab countries.[64] Some international reports showed noticeably high rates of unemployment in 2013 among youth in Arab countries – such as the Arab Republic of Egypt, where youth unemployment hit 54.1 percent, and the Occupied Palestinian Territories at 49.6 percent[65] – not to mention poverty, corruption and economic weakness.

By carefully examining the political experiences of Islamic political groups in the Arab and Muslim worlds, it seems as though that of the Muslim Brotherhood group in the Arab Republic of Egypt is the most revealing of their *modi operandi* in the political arena and their exploitation of religion in this context. One such example is their abrupt changes of positions towards political partners or rivals, despite belonging to the same religious frames of reference. The Muslim Brotherhood group walked away from political partnerships or entered into tactical alliances based on the self-interest of the group and its leaders, as happened in the Kingdom of Morocco. The vision of the Muslim Brotherhood group – which tries to monopolize speaking in the name of Islam, insists on the foundational frame of reference and claims historical impeccability – remains one of its inherent problems since its establishment in 1928. This vision speaks to an atmosphere of fanaticism, violence and exclusion that grips the group.[66] This is why it rejects alternative intellectual and political trends.

One of the points that should be noted when dealing with the thought of the Muslim Brotherhood group in the Arab Republic of Egypt is that before the events of 2011 the group acknowledged that the Egyptian state relies on Islam in its legislative principles and takes its provisions and rules as pillars of its constitution and laws. This point was conceded by former president Dr. Muhammad Mursi in an article published on August 5, 2007 when he was a member of the Guidance Office of the Muslim Brotherhood group:

> One should note the present differences between the Egyptian state in which the Muslim Brotherhood group lives, with its constitution which stipulates that Islam is the official religion of the state and the principles of *Sharia* are the main source of legislation. This confirms the Islamic nature of the Egyptian state, and no government or authority can change it or even try to, because it represents the identity of the nation both in its history and at present, and its various intellectual and cultural constituents. One should note the differences between this and the ruling Turkish Justice and Development party. After the fall of the Islamic Caliphate and the rise of nationalism and Ataturkism, the Turkish state still recognizes the secularity of the state with its constitution, law and leaning towards Europe, and aims to become part of it despite the obvious difference between the Muslim Turkish people and the secular European people in thought and behavior.[67]

If the Muslim Brotherhood group acknowledged and recognized the superiority of the Egyptian state over the

political system prevailing in the Turkish Republic in terms of its Islamic religious frame of reference, and implicitly condemned the comparison between the orientations of the Turkish Justice and Development party and the goals of the group and its orientations, considering such comparison "erroneous and unfair" given the differences in the fundamentals, foundations, goals, purposes, means and mechanisms.[68] If this were the case, then the course of the relationship between the Muslim Brotherhood group after they reached authority in the Arab Republic of Egypt and the leaders of the Turkish Justice and Development party reflected an abandonment of the ideological position taken by the Muslim Brotherhood group. Consequently, this raises legitimate questions about the belief of the group in what Dr. Muhammad Mursi stated in his article regarding the Islamic frame of reference of the Egyptian state, because the group's explicit acknowledgement of this frame of reference confirms beyond any shadow of doubt that action towards overthrowing the Mubarak regime was only driven by the group's lust for authority and government.

One of the contradictions in the discourse of political religious groups is their promotion of false slogans which accuse Arab and Muslim countries of leniency in confronting the Israeli influence and claim that once such political religious groups reach the position of authority in any Arab or Muslim country they will immediately confront that influence. However, the facts refute this propaganda, and show that in promoting those slogans, political religious groups were using religion to reach a position of authority, and that national interests were

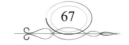

not among the priorities of those groups when they actually reached positions of authority, as the ruling experiences of the Muslim Brotherhood in the Arab Republic of Egypt and the Gaza Strip clearly demonstrate.[69]

Perhaps one of the problems affecting political religious groups is that they deem the religious state the sole alternative to the civil state, and keep pursuing their interests and implementing their plans even if this could lead them to violate the fundamentals and principles of the religious formula for the state they promote. In recent years, the positions of the Muslim Brotherhood group in the various Arab and Muslim countries towards other political currents have fluctuated in ways worthy of monitoring and following up. In this regard, the group has occasionally employed the slogan "participation, not domination," but then felt no shame in practically turning its back on it and trying to exercise an absolute monopoly of authority in a clear expression of dictatorship and authoritarianism.[70]

One may also notice the tendency of political religious groups and their leaders to reproduce the practices of previous ruling regimes in their respective countries through different tools and mechanisms—for example, their tendency towards dictatorship and authoritarianism in a way that ostensibly seems democratic, as was the case with the attempt of the Muslim Brotherhood group to dominate the composition of the Constituent Assembly entrusted with the drafting of the Egyptian constitution in 2012.[71] In that particular case, the group used measures and procedures that were superficially

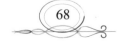

democratic but in essence implied nothing but a clear deception against partners from all political currents. Anyone who observes a line chart of the group's performance throughout the period following the fall of the regime of former president Muhammad Husni Mubarak in the Arab Republic of Egypt in February 2011 will easily discover the extent of political deception it employed against its political opponents and allies alike, in addition to a considerable number of political promises, the fulfillment of even a meager number of which proved later to be an elusive dream.

Perhaps the false promises involved in the so-called "renaissance" program that was promoted by the Muslim Brotherhood group in the Arab Republic of Egypt and the "100-day" program, which was at the forefront of the election campaign of former president Dr. Muhammad Mursi, prove this political deception. It was from here that the moral veil of the Muslim Brotherhood group was removed, as a result of broken promises and agreements and betrayed allies. In April 2013, the slogan "Brotherhood liars" started to appear.[72] Then the one-year rule of former president Muhammad Mursi, who was one of the most prominent leaders of the group, removed what was left of the moral veil in which the Muslim Brotherhood group has covered itself since its birth in 1928, i.e. for more than 80 years.

Egyptian society witnessed a different system of conducts and practices totally unrelated to the political purity that the Muslim Brotherhood group used to claim. Against that

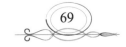

backdrop, the June 30, 2013 revolution broke out and huge numbers of people took to the streets in protest at deteriorating services and anger with the deception represented by the unreal slogans of the Muslim Brotherhood group.[73] The political practices of the Egyptian Muslim Brotherhood group, as a ruling regime, revealed the fallacy of the development programs and projects such political religious groups espoused. Then came the repercussions of the ousting of former president Dr. Muhammad Mursi and the subsequent sit-ins, speeches, acts of violence and militancy, and statements that did not reflect any moral framework but rather a deep-rooted mentality of opportunism that allowed the use of any means to serve the goal of securing authority, government and political influence.[74]

Political Religious Groups and the Question of Modernity

Some researchers suggest that the Muslim world in general has suffered a political, economic and cultural setback since the official abolition of the Ottoman Caliphate by Mustafa Kemal (Ataturk), the founder of the modern Turkish republic, on March 3, 1924, and the subsequent feeling of alienation throughout the entire Muslim world.[75] Those researchers acknowledge that the Ottoman Empire suffered a lack of awareness of the teachings of pure Islam.[76] They consider this to be among the top causes of its political disintegration and inability to influence the international decision-making process, at a time when Europe saw a revolution against the traditional restrictions imposed by the Church and consequently entered

the stage of scholarly research, technology and geographic exploration that opened the way for it to control the world, old and new. Europe benefited from the legacy of previous civilizations, including the Islamic civilization, to expand;[77] Europe opened itself towards the Muslim world and benefited from its civilization and science in the fields of medicine, engineering, astronomy, and other sciences that have contributed to its modern renaissance.[78]

The growing role of the religious factor is a political phenomenon that has nothing to do with religion other than in name, nor is it related to any aspect of renewal of the faith and revival of religious thought. It is only related to literal reading and interpretation of the divine texts.

Now, the question is: why have the Arab and Muslim worlds regressed from being civilizations characterized by religious and ethnic diversity, and failed to adapt to other civilizations and cultures such as those of Persia, India and China, and to interact with other religions such as Judaism and Christianity? Why was the wide religious reform movement initiated by numerous Muslim jurisprudents and thinkers – such as Shaikh Hassan Al-Attar,[79] Qassim Ameen and the Imams Muhammad Abdu, Jamal Al-Deen Al-Afghani, Abdulrahman Al-Kawakibi,

Rifa'a Rafi' Al-Tahtawi and other pioneers of renaissance in the Arab and Muslim worlds since the French Revolution and Napoleon Bonaparte's invasion of Egypt in 1798[80] – aborted? And why was it aborted again by the wave of militancy that coincided with the outbreak of the Cold War—specifically during the 1970s?[81]

Some researchers argue that the call to religion – whether in the West or the East, or in relation to the evocation of religious values – is a strong sign of the employment of religion, not its revival. It is a desire to legitimize political conduct and behaviors. However, the growing role of the religious factor in the West, for example, is not a reaction to the excesses to which secularity supposedly has led the world, but is rather a political phenomenon not related to religion other than in name; neither is it related to any aspect of renewal of the faith or revival of religious thought – it is merely due to widespread literal reading and interpretation of the divine books.[82] An example of this is the *Zahiri* school of thought, which firmly sticks to the literal (or apparent, *zahir*) meaning of texts in the Holy Quran and the Prophet's Noble Sunnah, where there is no personal opinion or use of mind and reason in any provision of *Sharia* law. The *Zahiri* school of thought does not accept analogical reasoning (*Qiyas*) as a source of Islamic law.[83] There are other views suggesting that the glorification of old religious interpretations among political religious groups in the Arab and Muslim worlds is one of the causes of their decline. The bulk of this literature blames the Ottoman era. Advocates of this opinion argue

that the 9th century AD was the golden era of the Islamic civilization,[84] before schools dedicated to interpreting the Holy Quran flourished under the Abbasid state starting from the mid-fourth century AH – i.e. after the tenth century AD – which saw a decline in the use of the mind, the end of independent reasoning (*ijtihad*), and complete reliance on imitation and earlier writings.[85]

Some researchers divide the history of Islamic civilization since its beginnings into four main stages: the first stage starts with the emergence of Islam and includes the next four centuries, in which Islam expanded and established a comprehensive civilization where urbanization grew and sciences developed. Then a second stage, in which the Islamic civilization seemed to be completed and the focus was on safeguarding its gains and resources in the various regions in which its principles spread. Then a third stage in which that balanced image began to shake, and manifestations of decline were seen, and their effects continued until the 19th century. The fourth stage is the revival stage, which began in the 19th century.[86]

Historians and researchers often refer to a period that started at the beginning of the 19th century and continued through the 20th century, sometimes calling it the era of Arab revival and sometimes the era of Islamic revival,[87] depending on the geographic scope in question and according to their intellectual purposes and theoretical orientations. These calls for Islamic revival continued from the early 19th century through the 20th century.[88]

The term "revival" can only apply to a reality which existed in the past, i.e. it does not apply to a nation that wants to create a civilization it has never before possessed, but to a nation wanting to resurrect a civilization that it once had, after a period of decline and decay.[89] That means a return to the root sources and basics and dismantling of all the barriers that this has built between them and the realm of thought.[90] With respect to the Islamic civilization, this means a return to its era of prosperity which started to see a decline in scientific and cultural creativity from the beginning of the 12th century in which Ibn Rushd appeared and had a significant influence on Western thought despite what faced him in the Muslim world.[91] The appearance of Abdul Rahman Ibn Muhammad Ibn Khaldoon during that period, particularly in the 14th century AD was enlightening, but after that the Islamic civilization entered into a stage of stagnancy. It was no longer able to produce anything other than a traditional uncreative education, and hence no longer had the influence it previously enjoyed. The beginning of the decline of the Islamic civilization marked in itself the beginning of the European Renaissance era.[92] The Muslim world emerged as an influential power on the international stage in the 7th century AD and it retained its strength over 10 continuous centuries. It also maintained a civilization which raised the banner of tolerance and was mainly based on the promotion of knowledge and spreading of culture; unlike what exists today in the Arab and Muslim worlds.[93]

> *The thought of enlightenment in the Arab and Muslim worlds never saw an eclipse more serious and damaging than the reality which the forces of darkness tried to entrench at this stage.*

Reformist thought in the Arab and Muslim worlds has been associated with the issue of decline and the search for its causes and manifestations, and hence the formulation of ideas that could help in overcoming the state of backwardness and returning to prosperity and glory.[94] While this decline reached its peak in the 19th century – where the Arab and Muslim worlds witnessed a retreat from the political, social and economic principles that were no longer viable – Europe continued to progress, or, as some researchers suggest, a gap separated a "Muslim world gradually regressing and a European world gradually progressing."[95]

All of the above logically gives rise to questions about whether the Arab and Muslim worlds currently suffer a crisis of thought. In response to that, some researchers believe that this is the worst of the tribulations witnessed by the Arab and Muslim region since the advent of religion. These researchers even argue that thought has never - in any era - seen an eclipse more dangerous and disastrous for humanity than the one currently affecting the Arab and Muslim worlds as a result of raging vain desires and the spread of forces of darkness. This detrimental phenomenon has led to an alienation of contemporary people from religion[96] because of resentment resulting from the practices of political religious groups.

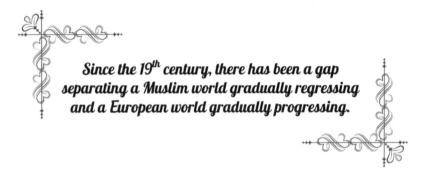

Since the 19th century, there has been a gap separating a Muslim world gradually regressing and a European world gradually progressing.

The above arguments consequently raise an intuitive question: do the Arab and Muslim worlds suffer a religious or a religiosity crisis? It is most probably a religiosity crisis; because the current crisis is not in any way linked to the essence, values and pillars of religion and its prescribed laws, acts of worship and transaction rules. In fact, it is linked to the lack of knowledge and mind (reason), and the inability of Muslims to keep up with the times and to derive from the Islamic religion the appropriate laws to fit modern circumstances.[97] In this context, the problem is that the consequences of this crisis fuel a material, cultural and epistemological decline in the Arab and Muslim worlds, because any crisis that has a link with religion will likely engender a parallel decline in self-confidence and adversely affect accumulated spiritual potency, which is supposed to be compatible with the temporal strength in human life. Hence, it is safe to say that the

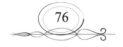

decline of civilization is one of the outcomes of the thought crisis, not the cause of it.

> **Islamic history has witnessed controversy between the mind (reason) and text for centuries.**

Islamic historical literature shows that there is a centuries-old controversy between mind (reason) and text; some researchers suggest that Islam combines both religion and *Sharia*. As for religion, God (Allah) completed and perfected it in the Holy Quran and there was never any role for the minds of people in its creation; while in the case of *Sharia* He provided the overall pillars and left its details and secondary principles for independent reasoning and discretionary judgment.[98] In his *Muqaddima*, Ibn Khaldoon was quoted as saying that early Muslims saw no way other than the divine revelation (Holy Quran) to decide on beliefs; with mind isolated from the text. They saw that the debate and controversy over faith and belief could only lead to alienation from religion.[99] Research and debate about the issues of belief did not exist during the time of the Prophet Muhammad (pbuh) or the days of the Rightly-Guided Caliphs, but when *bid'a* (innovation without basis in Islam) and sedition in religious matters later appeared, Muslims had to ward them off; like the Kharijites,[100] who were extremely audacious in the *takfir* (excommunication) and the shedding of the blood of others, seeing no sanctity in their blood, property and progeny.[101] Then other schools of thought[102] and *Ilm Al-Kalam* (science of discourse/dialectic) appeared gradually as an objective necessity.[103] Methodologically, *Ilm Al-Kalam* means:

> The application of inference on rational certainties, such as perceived and experimented facts. Its aim is the production of knowledge and the objective understanding of it, so that man can move forward and uplift himself from the nadir of tradition and imitation to the zenith of certainty through reasoning, thinking, argument and evidence. It is meant to reconcile the text and mind in order to infer and ascertain the veracity of transmitted (by tradition and imitation) principles of faith concerning the existence of God (Allah) in His essence, attributes and acts.[104]

The use of the mind appeared in religious legal matters initially because the mind supports religion and proves the veracity of its message—whilst also acknowledging the virtue of the mind itself. This in turn opened the way for another parallel effort to prosper, which was the use of the mind in the other aspects of life, or *ijtihad* (independent reasoning) in Islamic laws and practices. On this basis, schools of jurisprudence and the science of the "principles of jurisprudence" emerged. It is known among those concerned with jurisprudence that Imam Muhammad Ibn Idrees Al-Shafi'i (150–204 AH; 767–820 AD) was the first to examine the "principles of jurisprudence" and to write of them independently in his book *Al-Risala* (The Letter).[105]

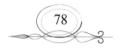

Insightful readers of history will realize that the problem of independent reasoning started when the door was opened for examination of jurisprudential laws and what is known as *Qiyas* (analogy) and personal opinion,[106] where the use of the mind expanded and started to examine matters pertaining to religious doctrine. This eventuality angered the clerics, because rational reasoning led to unfamiliar or unusual outcomes and collided with the opposite thought of tradition and text.[107] It was customary for religious scholars to stick to what they were used to—clinging to the old because it is old and hating the new because it is new. Indeed, this has been a human instinct since ancient times, and could be a logical explanation if other factors are taken into account along with it such as limited thinking, narrow-mindedness and religious intolerance. All these attitudes are absolutely incompatible with freedom of mind and thought and the acknowledgment of the importance of research and *Qiyas* (analogy) in accordance with principles, rules and standards.[108] In this regard, interpreters cite the words of God (Allah) in the Holy Quran: "Therefore do thou give admonition, for thou art one to admonish. Thou art not one to manage (men's) affairs."[109]

The Dynamics of Political Islam

In a previous study, I addressed the role of religion throughout history,[110] and the fact that it has always played a major role in the economic, social, political, cultural and spiritual life of individuals. Religion is a system of beliefs based on the idea that

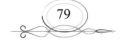

God (Allah) created the world, controls it and gives people life after death. There is a specific system of belief and worship associated with each religion. Spiritually, religion offers a continuity of existence after death and "enables individuals to transcend their earthy existence and attain spiritual satisfaction."[111]

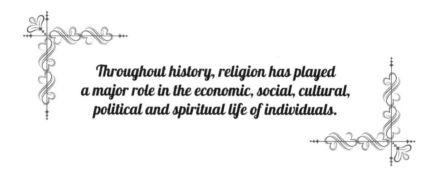

Throughout history, religion has played a major role in the economic, social, cultural, political and spiritual life of individuals.

Socially, religion can be considered a code of conduct, as it defines acceptable moral behavior among its adherents. Furthermore, religion issues moral and religious penalties for those who violate this code of conduct. Politically, religion provides a sense of identity, community, and shared interest. These religious and political values can be used as an ideology of opposition (for example, the role of Islam in the Arab and Muslim worlds during colonialism).

Islam exemplifies these spiritual, political and social functions of religion. It involves submitting oneself to the will of God (Allah).[112] The term Islam can be defined in interrelated dimensions,[113] including the fact that Islam as a religion is based on the belief that the Prophet Muhammad (pbuh) was the last of the messengers and prophets, and the Holy Quran is the final and complete revealed text. These beliefs, as a whole, constitute the essential intellectual structure of devotional observance associated with the practice of Islam as a universal religion.[114] Due to the historical experience of the Islamic community, a culture has thereby been produced. As Alan R. Taylor explains:

> These dimensions of the Islamic heritage differ not only in character but also in durability. Whereas Islam as a religious practice has remained virtually the same since its inception, Islamdom as a political order (*umma*) was unstable and transitory, and the Islamicate [Islamic world] as a cultural tradition changed in emphasis from one era to the next without losing a certain continuity of the whole.[115]

In many Arab and Muslim societies, Islam is considered a foundation that can strengthen and unify the Arab and Muslim worlds. Islam is a very important cultural force and plays a vital role in the socialization process and in social and political identity in all of the Arab and Muslim countries and societies. Mosques can be seen in every city, town and village in the Arab and Muslim countries, and the arts of Islamic architecture and mosque construction seem to be a subject of interest among all Muslims, reflecting their attachment to Islam and their commitment to its teachings, irrespective of living conditions and development indices. Islam encourages the construction of mosques and their maintenance, as stated in the authenticated Prophet's sayings (Hadith); Abu Tharr Al-Ghifari (may God (Allah) be pleased with him) reported that the Prophet (pbuh)

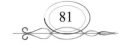

said: "Whoever builds a mosque, the size of a sparrow's nest or even smaller, for the sake of Allah, Allah will build for him a house in Paradise."[116] For example, Hassan Hanafi describes this scene by saying:

> The construction of mosques is taking place in every corner and in every small street. These new, beautiful, and well-ornamented mosques stand side by side with the huts of the poor.[117]

Islam is the most important form of identity and cultural cohesion in the Arab and Muslims worlds.[118] An example of this is the frequency with which followers are called upon to express their attachment to Islam. Some researchers argue that:

> The call of the *muezzin* (ones who recite the call to prayer) to the faithful five times each day; the ritual of prayer throughout the city, village or country; the gathering at the mosque on Fridays; the observance of Islamic ordinances such as the fasting of Ramadan; all of these serve to reinforce the religious foundation of identity for the Muslim.[119]

Islamic traditions and values are widely observed and practiced. Families start to teach children the Islamic values and principles at the early age of three years or so. Parents often teach their children Islamic moralities: what is allowed and what is prohibited, how to pray, and tell them about paradise and hell. In fact, the image of the ideal Muslim person is the backbone of socialization in Arab and Muslim societies. This is the difference between Islam as a tolerant doctrine on one hand and the thoughts of political religious groups on the other.

Those groups exploit the religious upbringing in the Arab and Muslim worlds in order to gain authority and achieve their political and personal interests by turning religion into an ideology that foments political conflict.

Schools also play a key role in teaching Islamic values. Islam is taught in every grade from kindergarten through high school in the form of a mandatory course entitled "The Islamic Religion," and religious education constitutes an essential part of public education.[120] There are secondary schools for religious education in the Arab and Muslim countries, as well as university-level institutions for religious education such as Al-Azhar University in the Arab Republic of Egypt and the Imam Muhammad ibn Saud Islamic University in the Kingdom of Saudi Arabia. Religion is also required in the university curriculum. Religious education is influenced by the prevailing factors and variables, and Arab and Muslim governments often use it as an intellectual barrier to radical and alien ideas or extremist ideology.

The mosque has transformed from a place of worship to a center for recruitment and polarization by political religious groups.

83

For example, Islamic institutions, Islamic banks, and organizations with an Islamic framework play an important role in the Arab and Muslim countries. As James Bill argues, "over the next forty years, populist Islam is going to be the most important ideological force in the world."[121] Had this prospect been taken seriously, the current rise of extremism, militancy and terrorism in several parts of the Arab and Muslim worlds may have been avoided.

The problem is that the traditional function of the mosque as a place of worship has been transformed with the passage of time; religion is increasingly being used in the service of politics, and mosques are used now as forums for political, social and economic debates, and centers for recruiting Muslims by political religious groups. These groups have managed to increase their membership substantially in recent years, and their activities, goals and ideology are "patterned after the Egyptian Muslim Brotherhood, with which they have close ties."[122]

There is a general understanding that Islam has not been perceived or treated as a private personal religion that should be kept separate from public life and confined to private spaces such as places of worship. Separating religious institutions from politics in Arab and Muslim societies is a task which requires efforts be made to resist the inevitable criticisms of political religious groups, because Islam is considered an integral part of the prevailing culture in most Arab and Muslim societies.[123]

Before discussing the nature of the relationship between religion and politics, as explained in Chapter 2, it is important to note that there is a great deal of diversity in Islam:

> Diversity has been discussed and analyzed by sect, school of law, degree of orthodoxy, or tendency toward reform; by whether particular groups tend to be militant, bourgeois, reactionary, socialist; and within particular cultural contexts through which a believer experiences and practices the religion.[124]

One approach to understanding the relationship between Islam and politics is the conservative approach, which stresses a return to what it considers "pure Islam," as perceived by proponents of this approach. They consider this to be the solution to the social, political and economic problems of Arab and Muslim societies. Supporters of this approach argue that Muslim political elites have ignored Islam as well as the welfare, and the rights of their people; therefore, people must be educated to understand that their salvation lies in the return to "pure Islam. They allege that "liberation from … despotism lies in the attribution of all authority to God (Allah),"[125] or the principle of *hakimiyya*.

The fundamentalist approach is based on the necessary unity between religion and state, because "politics needs, above all, to be spiritualized."[126] This argument can be easily refuted in light of the natural contradiction between politics and its practices on the one hand, and religion with its noble spiritual values on the other. The events which have taken place since

2011 have shown that mixing religion with politics distorts the image of religion, weakens politics and is damaging to the public interest. Many political religious groups – particularly the Muslim Brotherhood group – have produced militant thought as a result of a deficient, narrow-minded interpretation of Islam, constituting a real challenge to Arab and Muslim countries and societies.

At the individual and state levels, Islamic values dominate social, political, economic and cultural relations in all Arab and Muslim countries. Even if some people do not apply *Sharia* laws and values to their personal behavior, they still believe that these values are ideal and should theoretically be respected and observed. The fundamental question to be answered is: what are the implications and impacts of these social attitudes and this social system on political reality in the Arab and Muslim worlds? Some countries have always observed religious values in order to legitimize their policies and regimes. Researchers have tended to confuse the opinions of political elites on Islamic values – which are meant to serve the purpose of conferring legitimacy – with the opinion of political religious groups on political practices in Islam.

An examination of the recent history of Arab and Muslim countries reveals the crucial role played by Islam in providing support for existing regimes; and this is natural in light of the referential fundamentals of Arab and Muslim societies. Some Arab and Muslim leaders introduced socialism as a state ideology without challenging Islam. Even when members of the

Muslim Brotherhood group were prosecuted in 1965, former Egyptian president Jamal Abdul Nasser did not blame Islam for the group's activities. Similarly, in 2014 the current president Abdul Fattah Saeed Al-Sisi has been keen to distinguish between Islam and the practices of political religious groups in order to refute their claims and allegations that the Egyptian state was targeting Islam.

The use of religion to enhance the popularity of existing regimes is not limited to a certain country or particular period. In the Arab Republic of Egypt, for example, former president Muhammad Anwar Al-Sadat sought to use religion in order to boost his image among the public, and insisted on being described as the ideal religious family man. He was always keen to appear in the mosque during prayers. In this regard, one researcher observes:

> President Al-Sadat has been given the title "the believing president" and was always called by his first name, Muhammad. In the media, his picture is shown in his white *jallabiyya* [traditional full-length garment], entering the mosque or coming out of it ... with a prayer mark on his forehead.[127]

As a part of the peace treaty signed by former president Muhammad Anwar Al-Sadat with Israel in Washington in 1979, Al-Azhar religious scholars issued a *fatwa* (legal opinion) supporting the treaty. The former Grand Mufti of Egypt, who later became the Sheikh of Al-Azhar, Shaikh Jad Al-Haq Ali Jad Al-Haq, issued a *fatwa* on November 26,

1979 on numerous grounds, including that the inclination of
the enemy towards peace during war must be accepted –
citing the Holy Quranic verse: "But if the enemy inclines
towards peace, do thou (also) incline towards peace, and trust
in Allah: for He is one that heareth and knoweth (all
things)"[128] – that the initiation of peace by Muslims is
permissible as long as it is to bring benefits or avoid harm,
that Muslims' acceptance of some injustice is permissible as
long as that staves off greater damage, and that the articles of
the peace treaty and its annexes did not deny any right or
recognized occupation. He said that those few religious scholars
should not have drifted away or been led from judgments
based on what God (Allah) has revealed, and should not have
descended to insults without referring to the laws of God
(Allah), or *Sharia*, adding that peace with Israel opens the
way to a sense of optimism that may help us regain the land
and protect our honor and bring back Jerusalem, in a dignified
manner, to the realm of Islam.[129]

Former Egyptian president Muhammad Husni Mubarak
began his presidency by giving political religious groups some
freedoms.[130] Hence recent Egyptian history presents a good
example of the continued interaction between religion and
politics.

Islam represents an effective force in maintaining the
status quo, thanks to its centrist, moderate interpretation. This
mainstream Islam alienates militant groups and political
religious groups by classifying them as *Kharijites* (i.e. they do

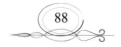

not represent the teachings of pure Islam).[131] This centrist understanding of Islam is what makes states successful in confronting these groups. The question arising here is: why have political religious groups not been effective in the past? This is partly due to efforts which are being made to promote the centrist interpretation of Islam, which rejects extremism and violence, encourages tolerance, and discourages mixing religion with public governance. As such, popular support for political religious groups in the past was not as clear as it appeared following the transformations which began in 2011, because their hierarchical and political structure was, and is still, very traditional and above all, they do not have viable programs, plans, projects or political or developmental visions to challenge those of ruling regimes.

The ruling experience of the Muslim Brotherhood group in the Arab Republic of Egypt in 2012 presents conclusive evidence of the immaturity of political religious groups and their limited abilities to convince people that they are capable of managing state or government affairs, protecting their interests, maintaining their unity and stability and addressing their enormous development challenges. Still, the mere fact that a political religious group reached a position of authority, and the top of the political pyramid, raises serious questions about the continuity of the once-prevalent social traditions of separating religion from politics. This highlights the way these groups manipulate concepts and opinions in order to reach a position of authority.

A report issued by the Carnegie Endowment for International Peace on July 1, 2014 mentioned that the Muslim Brotherhood group in Egypt failed to address the challenge it faced after reaching authority, and this led to the rapid fall of former president Dr. Muhammad Mursi's rule. The report showed a series of consecutive failures of the group; it failed to live up to reality, and only succeeded in maintaining the unity of the group itself. The report also suggested that the participation of the Muslim Brotherhood group in state authority in the Arab Republic of Egypt ruined all previous hopes that this participation would lead to democracy and moderation.[132]

The prevailing centrist interpretation of Islam is relevant to understanding the political history of the Arab and Muslim worlds. The colonial era was the only period in which Arabs and Muslims were united to fight an alien culture due to their Islamic identity. Throughout history, religion had always supported the ruling regimes in the Arab and Muslim worlds as long as these regimes did not adopt radical positions against religion itself; but whenever they did adopt such anti-religious attitudes, that would boost the positions of militant political religious groups.

For example, consider the experience of the Republic of Tunisia in the 1960s, where the Tunisian leadership soon realized the mistake they made when they challenged Islam. Whenever an existing regime challenges Islam, political religious groups become more powerful in response. This happens not only in the Arab and Muslim worlds, but also in

countries with a large Muslim community, as was the case in the Swiss Confederation, the French Republic and the Scandinavian countries. Although the decision to ban the *hijab* (headscarf), *niqab* (veil), *adhan* (call to prayer) and the Islamic (*halal*) animal slaughter was made according to the prevailing laws in those countries, which everyone living on their soil is supposed to accept, political religious groups used such decisions as a pretext to attack the policies of those countries and accuse them of being hostile to Islam.[133]

Islamic Revival

Before discussing the current situations in the Arab and Muslim worlds, it is important to explain some misconceptions and misunderstandings regarding Islam and the relationship between religion and politics. Generally, there are two types of misconceptions about Islam; the first includes misconceptions among Muslims themselves, and the second comprises misconceptions among Western scholars who study Islam.

Throughout history, there has been a general tendency to misinterpret Islamic teachings or to mix them with local customs and traditions. For example, tribal norms, traditions and customs play a key role in interpreting or misinterpreting *Sharia* laws in Arab and Muslim societies. In some Arab and Muslim conservative societies, there are those who believe that women should receive only limited education, be segregated from men and in general be prepared only to become wives and mothers; all of this is contrary to Islamic teachings, which equally honor men and women, as God (Allah) says: "... Never will I suffer to lose the work of any of you, be he male or female: Ye are members, one of another...,"[134] and: "O mankind! We created you from a single (pair) of a male and a female, and made you into nations and tribes, that ye may know each other (not that ye may despise (each other). Verily the most honored of you in the sight of Allah is (he who is) the most righteous of you..."[135] Similarly, the populations in some rural areas have their own codes of conduct regarding social issues, and they claim that these codes are Islamic, as happens in customary reconciliation meetings. Therefore, any in-depth study of the social and political roles of Islam in Arab and Muslim societies should take into account the culture of the society, i.e. its local customs, traditions and values.

Another misconception about Islam among Muslims themselves is related to the role of religious scholars in defining what conforms with Islam and what does not. So the explanation of the relationship between religion and politics in Islam is inseparable from the role played by religious scholars in defining the general framework of centrist moderate Islam.

> *The term "fundamentalism" is misleading and alien to Islamic culture and traditions, while the term "revival" is more accurate.*

The term "fundamentalism" seems misleading and alien to the Islamic culture and traditions.[136] It is generally defined as the "return to orthodoxy in matters of faith and the application of religious rules in a strict literal manner."[137] So, what does fundamentalism mean in the context of Islam? If it means that Muslims believe that the Holy Quran and the Noble Sunnah (prophetic tradition) should both be interpreted literally, then only a few Muslims would be considered fundamentalists since all Muslim schools of thought and jurisprudence recognize the need for *ijtihad* (independent reasoning), and Islam itself appreciates the diversity of views.

In this regard, Imam Abu Abdullah Malik Ibn Anas, the Imam of the Maliki school of jurisprudence, took a commendable position after he compiled his book *Al-Muwatta* on the instructions of the Abbasid Caliph Abu Ja'afar Al-Mansoor (136–158 AH; 754–775 AD) who wanted to force people through the state authority to abide by the rules and laws the book contained.[138] In other words, Abu Ja'afar Al-Mansoor wanted to make it as a general law in the Caliphate state, where all people should abide by it, and for all other views and independent interpretations to be nullified. The story says that when Abu Ja'afar Al-Mansoor undertook pilgrimage, he told Malik: "I decided to order this book of yours to be reproduced, and then send a copy to every Muslim region and order that people abide by it and nobody act contrary to it." Malik replied: "O ye Ameer Al-Mu'mineen (Commander/leader of the Faithful), do not do that. Utterances already went forth to

people, and people heard sayings and told stories; and all people accepted what came forth to them and what they drew from variation of people; so leave people and what the citizens of each region already chose for themselves."[139]

This story reflects the keenness of Imams in Islam to take into consideration *ijtihad* (independent reasoning) and the difference of opinions, not to deny them.

On the other hand, if fundamentalism means strict commitment to the acts of worship, then any practicing Muslim would be considered fundamentalist. Almost all Muslims believe that Islam is a comprehensive system of beliefs and values. They also believe that Islam is an *umma* with its own social, economic, legal and political systems. As the Arab thinker, Saad Al-Deen Ibraheem suggested: "Islamic revival is a phenomenon worthy of study with due care, away from exaggerations and confusing and metaphysical ideas."[140]

Based on the definition of fundamentalism mentioned above, the practice of Islam in several parts of the Arab and Muslim worlds could be called fundamentalist. However, the most important feature of the current revivalist movement is that it advocates an extremely politicized version of Islam.

The term revival is more accurate than terms such as "fundamentalism" or "renewal" because it indicates a direction and a clear historical perspective. Religious revival in the early 21st century is one of the most lasting and complex phenomena facing sociologists and political scientists. It is a universal phenomenon that includes Muslims, Jews, Christians, etc. So,

Islamic revival, as part of this universal phenomenon, can be defined as a cyclical, continuous process of rise and decline, strength and weakness in the activities of political religious groups, political leaders and growing Islamic awareness among the masses. It takes the form of socio-political activism by leaders or opposition political religious groups aiming to maintain or challenge the existing socio-political reality. It is a vital concept to understanding the political dynamics of Islam. It refers to the interaction between religion and social, cultural, economic, political and historical circumstances.

However, a number of problems have emerged in studying Islamic revival:

First, there are few empirical studies that examine the role of religion in the conduct of individuals, organizations and institutions. Second, the meaning of Islamic revival is regularly confused with certain events such as the Iranian revolution and other isolated incidents. Researchers tend to view the political transformations in the Islamic Republic of Iran, the Arab Republic of Egypt and other countries as a new chapter in Islamic history. However, this interpretation of Islamic revival as a recent conservative movement with a fundamentalist approach to social and political issues ignores the historical dimension of the Islamic revival. As Alan R. Taylor explains:

> The origins and import of contemporary Islamic [revival] are best understood from a historical perspective. This phenomenon is actually a manifestation of complex patterns of relations to the decline of Islamic society and institutions in the Middle East, stemming partly from

and then accelerated by economic, political, and cultural intrusion of the West. Therefore, the historical perspective is crucial to studying Islamic revival, especially the ebb and flow movement of the revivalist thought throughout history.[141]

Second, Western literature on Islamic revival is often misleading and frequently lacks an understanding of Islamic culture.[142] The Western world's preoccupation with Islam became evident after the outbreak of the revolution in the Islamic Republic of Iran in February 1979, the attack on the Grand Mosque in Mecca (by Juhayman Al-Utaybi in 1979), the Soviet invasion of the Islamic Republic of Afghanistan (1979), the assassination of former Egyptian president Muhammad Anwar Al-Sadat (1981), the violent events in the Lebanese Republic, the turmoil in the Syrian Arab Republic, the rule of the Muslim Brotherhood group in the Arab Republic of Egypt and the Republic of Tunisia in 2012, the currently unstable situations in the Republic of Yemen, the Republic of Iraq and the Syrian Arab Republic, and the consequent rise of the role of political religious groups in the Arab and Muslim worlds. All these examples show the real presence of Islam in the political agenda in the Arab and Muslim worlds, and the continuous misunderstanding of Islam in the Western world. Books, articles and reports written by Westerners at best reflect a misunderstanding of Islam and its theories; they often contain major errors about the history of Islam and present a confusing picture of the historical and political events that have influenced Islam.[143]

Moreover, Western writings on Islam are characterized by generalizations, sensationalism, distortions and a lack of robust research planning. Talk about this subject often overlaps in a way that reflects a lack of understanding of religious terminologies and concepts in Islam. However, for the sake of objectivity, it must be said that political religious groups and jihadi organizations contribute significantly to this confusion by using Islamic terms and concepts to achieve criminal goals. Al-Qa'ida and other jihadi organizations such as the Islamic State in Iraq and the Levant (ISIL), Jabhat Al-Nusra and others have linked religion with terrorism, causing great damage to Islam.[144] The most dangerous in this respect is that there is an unknown percentage of Muslims in many Arab and Muslim countries, as well as in Western countries, who support the thought of ISIL. There are signs of that, including the arrests made in some countries of elements suspected of supporting ISIL and its thought and carrying its banners and marching with them in the streets.[145] In addition, there are suspicions about growing support and sympathy for this militant thought inside some Arab and Muslim countries.[146]

Third, most definitions of the Islamic revival lack precise criteria for its emergence. The conceptualization of revival should be "clear and well-formulated, devoid of ambiguity and multiplicity of different meanings which cause perplexity and confusion."[147]

 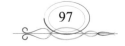

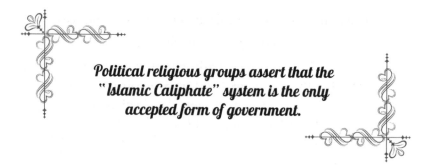

Political religious groups assert that the "Islamic Caliphate" system is the only accepted form of government.

Political religious groups share several characteristics. First, they are committed to a Salafi ideology, collectivism and universalism. Second, they emphasize the application of Islamic *Sharia* as an essential element of the Islamic social system. Third, they assert that the Caliphate system is the main accepted form of government in Islam. Early Islamic society still provides inspiration and an agenda for action among current political religious groups without any independent jurisprudential reasoning that takes into account the developments of the centuries following that era in order to enable Muslim society to interact with the present time and absorb its developments and variables. Most of these groups use religion as an ideology for opposition; they present the Caliphate system as a form of government. So, religion becomes a means or a tool of their rule or political opposition.

Islamic history might be seen as being an ebb and flow movement of revival and religious decline, especially in regard to the vision of the ideal Muslim society based on the Prophet's practices. In this regard, Barbara Regina Freyer Stowasser says:

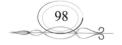

The Islamic past is studded with periods of resurgence, sparked by religious thinkers and religio-political avant-garde groups who called the believers "to return from the abyss" by demanding that they seriously reexamine their heritage as an alternative mode of action, or who translated such visions into political reform.[148]

In order to systematically investigate the role of Islam in the social, political and economic development of the Arab and Muslim worlds, the cyclical pattern or the ebb and flow of political religious groups' activities should be examined. In the last two centuries, the Arab and Muslim worlds have experienced both internal and external crises such as the collapse of the Ottoman Empire, the European penetration, and the struggle against colonialism. There have been three major Islamic responses to these crises: the modernist revivalism of Jamal Al-Deen Al-Afghani and Muhammad Abdu, Arab nationalism, and the religious political response of the Muslim Brotherhood group and others.

There are three main characteristics of the current Islamic revival. The first characteristic is pervasiveness. Political religious groups spread in most of the Arab and Muslim societies, regardless of the size, or political, economic, and social circumstances of thsoe societies (see Figure 0.1, p. 54). Furthermore, the Islamic revival is not limited to a particular socio-economic class. Empirical research has proven that the Islamic revival is spreading from lower and lower-middle classes to upper and upper-middle classes. The second characteristic is polycentrism. Political religious groups "possess no single

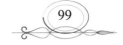

revolutionary leadership or organizational epicenter to bring together their various currents and movements."[149] The return to Islamic values starts at a grass roots level as a reaction to certain social, economic, and political problems in society. The third characteristic of the current Islamic revival is the perseverance of religious revivalist groups and the cyclical nature of their strengths and weaknesses.[150]

Historically, the Islamic revival can be viewed as a reaction to social, economic, moral, political and cultural realities in the Arab and Muslim worlds, i.e. a reaction against poverty, unemployment, corruption, colonialism, Western cultural penetration, and the lack of effective development. As James Bill explains:

> The populist Islamic movements are partly a reaction against corruption and repression which, in the minds of many citizens, have reached intolerable levels in their societies.[151]

The general framework of any study dealing with the relationship between Islam and socio-political change as well as Islamic revival should include a discussion of the relationship between modernity and tradition in Arab and Muslim societies. There is a conflict between those holding traditional Islamic views and those holding modern views which have resulted from education and the adoption of new cultural values. For example, tribal customs and traditions are closely followed by many among the Arab and Muslim peoples. One of the main causes of the Islamic revival is the search for identity and

familiar values that enable individuals to deal with their changing environment. For instance, the discovery of oil, and its resultant wealth, brought many opportunities and experiences to the peoples of the Arab Gulf states. However, social customs and traditions have always been slow to change. Islam is used as a means to deal with the rapid development and change in lifestyle occurring in the Arab and Muslim worlds. Religion becomes the only way for people to adapt themselves to the modern social and political system.

Islam plays an important role, and economic problems influence the religious attitudes of peoples. Islam has become a source of hope in dealing with social, economic and political frustrations, and political realities have made Islam a powerful tool. The most interesting observation in regard to the current situation in the Arab and Muslim worlds is the fact that Islam is equally powerful in countries enjoying economic prosperity and those suffering economic problems.

There is a number of explanations for the current situations in the Arab and Muslim worlds. The first has to do with the impact of development and modernization. Paget Henry argues that religion is a powerful protective shield against Western invasion and the waves of modernization coming from outside.[152] The experience with modernization indicates traditional concepts and modernity can co-exist in developing countries and that modernization processes do not necessarily entail the destruction of religious values or practices. The current changes in the Arab and Muslim worlds can be

101

attributed to socio-economic factors. The gap between tradition and modernity creates psychological tension that drives people to attach themselves to more familiar cultural environments in order to accommodate changes brought about by modernization.

In the development process, religion plays a significant role in dealing with social and psychological problems accompanying rapid social, economic and political developments. G. H. Jansen describes the religious revival by saying:

> The Muslim people turned more than ever to Islam and Islam became more militant ... But while defiant militancy was the public reaction, the elites turning toward Islam was done to find something enduring that would give strength.[153]

Modernization theorists have always argued that developing countries which are in the process of modernization experience a decline in religious influence on the life of society in general. Social scientists and others who apply modernization theories to the Middle East have repeatedly ignored Islam as a social and political force.[154] They consider Islam to be incompatible with science and technology. Hence, when modern values spread and become an essential part of the social structure, they feel that religious values will gradually disappear. One of the major assumptions in the political development literature has been that politics in societies undergoing modernization tend to break away from religion and move towards secularism.[155]

> *The concept of tawheed (the unity/oneness of God [Allah]) is essential to understanding Islam, in which there is no separation between religion and state, or between the spiritual and the temporal.*

The privatization of religion as practiced in the Western world means that religion is an individual concern, whereas politics is a public concern. However, the separation of religion and state as practiced in the West is not necessarily the case in the rest of the world. One needs to remember that some cultures, such as the Arab and Muslim cultures, do not privatize religion. Islam as a comprehensive system of beliefs, concepts and human behavior provides alternative political, ideological, and economic frameworks. The concept of *tawheed* (the unity/oneness of God (Allah)) is essential to understanding Islam, which is an integral part of a Muslim's life. The problem lies in the exploitation of this concept by political religious groups.

Islam is a viable ideology that enables individuals to deal with the gap between new values and the realities of their current lives. Consequently, individuals have become more religious in their private and social lives.

After the attacks of September 11, 2001 and the American invasion of Iraq in March 2003, the Arab and Muslim worlds have witnessed a surge in the religious current, reinforcing the conflict between Islam and the West and fueling extremism.

While some researchers argue that the influence of religion declines during the process of modernization due to factors such as economic development, migration, increased employment opportunities, education and the adoption of new values conflicting with religious teachings, others are of the opinion that religion is not an obstacle to modernization; those who misinterpret its teachings create this obstacle.[156] It appears that rapid political, social and economic changes create an imbalance between individuals and their environment rather than leading to a decline in religion and its influence. In the 1990s, the Arab and Muslim countries – despite their different economic circumstances – witnessed a surge in the religious current at the individual level as well as the state institutional level. This religious surge occurred again after the attacks of September 11, 2001 and the American invasion of Iraq in March 2003, reinforcing the idea of the clash between Islam and the West, which is considered the driving force of propaganda and an engine of mobilization for political religious groups.

The Islamic Revival and Contemporary Realities

The Islamic revival is a reaction to a number of processes and realities, including the social, economic, political and cultural conditions in the Arab and Muslim worlds. Religion becomes a sweeping political force when social, political and economic uncertainty dominates the lives of people and when governments fail to provide acceptable solutions to political, social and economic problems, including the crises of political development such as the search for identity, the just distribution of wealth, the fighting of corruption and the creation of job opportunities. All this is coupled with the inability of political elites to deal with such crises and changes. As in other developing societies, the leadership in many countries of the Arab and Muslim worlds has rarely succeeded in achieving social, economic, or political development. Richard Hrair Dekmejian describes the problems of political elites in these countries as follows:

> Due to their weak legitimacy, the new elites of the [Arab and Muslim] countries have lacked the requisite initial 'political capital' to generate effective policies that could constitute the building blocks of a legitimate public order.[157]

It is important to note that the inclination towards change in the Arab and Muslim worlds has strongly manifested itself in countries where Western cultural, political, economic, and social values are dominant. What has been happening in recent

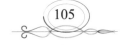

years is a reaction to economic, political and cultural problems including record high unemployment rates, poverty, corruption and political stalemate. In this respect, political religious groups think that the Egyptian state under globalization has become a replica of Western states in terms of values and behavior, and hence these groups claim to be searching for an Arab–Islamic alternative to confront Western cultural and economic hegemony.

This is what the Muslim Brotherhood group sought to exploit in the Arab Republic of Egypt, in addition to its traditional role of filling the vacuum caused by the inability of the Egyptian government to meet the needs of a wide segment of its population in terms of providing livelihoods, healthcare and education (such as the provision of food and free medical care, among others). The group ended up winning a parliamentary majority in 2011 and taking the helm of the country in 2012. The Egyptian economy in the fiscal year 2011–2012 suffered a slowdown in growth, which was only 2.2 percent, and a widening domestic resource gap reaching -8.4 percent of GDP.[158] Also, in 2012 the unemployment rate hit 12.7 percent and the illiteracy rate reached 24.9 percent.[159] Furthermore, the Egyptian economy witnessed increased public subsidies which amounted to 33.5 percent of total government expenditure in the fiscal year 2012–2013, and high public debt reaching 87.1 percent of GDP in the same fiscal year.[160]

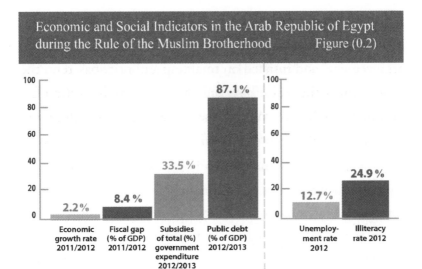

Economic and Social Indicators in the Arab Republic of Egypt during the Rule of the Muslim Brotherhood   Figure (0.2)

The second explanation for what has been happening in the Arab and Muslim worlds since the 1990s has to do with their political realities, such as the failure of some ruling political regimes to address development problems and carry out political and economic reforms that could provide alternative solutions for millions of young people among the new generations who are seeking competitive education and suitable employment opportunities and want to become active members of their societies. As a result, these regimes lack what is called the "legitimacy of achievement." It seems that the future of any ruling regime hinges only on its success in achieving the aspirations and hopes of its people, even if such a regime comes to authority through the legitimacy of the ballot box, which in itself no longer guarantees continuing authority unless there is genuine real fulfillment of promises and pledges. A typical case

at hand is that of former Egyptian president Dr. Muhammad Mursi who failed to move forward to the stage of "legitimacy of achievement" and insisted on retaining authority based on the legitimacy of the ballot box, only to find himself ousted after only one year in government due to his abject failure in every aspect, especially the economic field.[161]

In addition to the above, Islam and public acceptance represent the two pillars of legitimacy in many Arab and Muslim countries. As in most countries in the Arab and Muslim worlds, Islam is the official religion of the state. Arab and Muslim countries generally derive their legitimacy from the distribution of wealth (rent) or national income, rather than from political representation. In this respect, countries of the Cooperation Council for the Arab States of the Gulf (GCC) have developed one of the best and most efficient systems of welfare state in the world. These governments see the welfare state as a way of redistributing wealth. On the other hand, some Arab countries have overcome their huge economic problems through foreign assistance and borrowing (see Figure 0.2, p. 107).

Weakness and decline in many Arab and Muslim countries have deepened their vulnerability and exposure to criticism from political religious groups. In particular, some regimes in the Arab and Muslim countries have been exposed to criticism from these groups for long years past because of their failure to stop the expansion of Israeli influence, their inability to protect Jerusalem against policies pursued by Israel to obliterate identity, and their failure to confront the frequent

Israeli attacks on the Palestinians.[162] These issues in particular exposed, and still expose, some Arab ruling elites to harsh criticism from political religious groups which link such weakness to the loss of religious faith. Political religious groups present themselves as an alternative to these regimes, claiming that they have the ability to take more assertive and committed positions against Israel in defense of Arab and Muslim causes. For example, the 1967 war between the Arabs and Israel placed enormous pressure on Arab governments, as well as on Arab peoples, to find a solution from within. After that war, the problem was to discover "what kind of potential ability there is within the educated community of the Arab society today to address the most humiliating crisis in their entire history."[163] The Muslim Brotherhood group attributed the 1967 defeat to an abandonment of Islamic values and teachings, while the victory of 1973 was considered proof of the miracles of faith. In other words, the decline in the role of religious values and teachings brought defeat to Arabs and Muslims in June 1967, while the return to God (Allah) and seeking His help brought victory in the war of October 6, 1973. The proponents and supporters of this argument say the cry of the soldiers crossing the Suez Canal in the war of victory was "Allah Akbar" (God is Great).[164]

It is obvious that political religious groups find hope and promise in religion during any crisis, and try to exploit crises for their own political purposes. During the 1970s, 1980s and 1990s, there was an unprecedented media presence by these

groups, their leaders and symbols traveling around the world's countries and continents to spread their ideas via various tools of propaganda, media and mobilization.

The domestic contexts of the Arab and Muslim countries have also contributed to the Islamic revival. Western models of development have proven to be ineffective. These models include state capitalism – or "socialism," as it used to be called – and also liberal policies. All these models have failed to distribute goods and services. Moreover, Arab and religious models have failed to achieve political development.

> *Experience indicates that political religious groups are immature and lack the political experience that could enable them to lead their peoples and achieve their development aspirations.*

Due to the failure of some Arab and Muslim states to respond to the aspirations of their people and meet their increasing demands, political religious groups have found convenient room for political activity. They have exploited development problems and the vacuum caused by the absence of a real role of the state to attract the youth and recruit them to their ranks. However, it should be noted that political religious groups are immature and lack the political experience that could enable them to lead their people and achieve their goals.

The third explanation for the current Islamic revival in the Arab and Muslim worlds has to do with the failure of modernization ideologies such as liberalism, Western capitalism, socialism and Marxism, along with their local manifestations such as Arab nationalism, Baathism and Nasserism. These ideologies have failed to attract the people or to compete with Islamic ideology. Political religious groups derive their strength and appeal from the fact that no one would reject a call to Islam. The people have been objects of experimentation for all ideologies. However, the problem in this context lies in that political religious groups believe they are the exclusive, sole representatives of Islam. This creates an atmosphere which is not only unprepared for, but also perhaps opposed to any serious scholarly discussions about the relationship between Islam and modernization ideologies, or even about the relationship between these groups and Islam and how they represent it—whether in a diversified context or an exclusive way.

If the governance model of political religious groups has failed miserably in its latest experience in the Arab Republic of Egypt, and to some extent in the Republic of Tunisia, for reasons related to their lack of any real development programs or projects that could meet the people's demands,[165] as mentioned before, then the question is: why have other ideologies failed miserably to appeal to peoples in the Arab and Muslim worlds? Irrespective of the Nasserist experience which received wide appreciation and popular Arab support,

111

there are many reasons for the failure of other secular ideologies. The first reason is that Arab and Muslim peoples view secular ideologies as foreign systems imported from the West that do not provide the necessary answers to the social, economic and political problems of the Arab and Muslim worlds; political religious groups even accuse them of enmity to Islam. The second reason is the nature of the socialization process in the Arab and Muslim worlds. Socialization into religion takes place early on, in the home and at school, as mentioned above. At this early stage of childhood, civil society organizations and political elites do not make any effort to secure a societal foothold by instilling in these children enlightened political ideas that would help them to effectively participate in opening their societies to modernity and development. As a result, young people become easy prey for political religious groups, who are able to recruit them to their ranks.

Islam has been increasingly used as a political ideology by political religious groups opposing existing regimes because it is compatible with the ideas and ideologies of opposition, and because it is able to mobilize large numbers of people. As Michael Hudson explains:

> "Islam is much more than the historical 'religious institution' in terms of its political significance. It is a salient political ideology. As such, it performs an integrative function in the state political systems of the Middle East."[166]

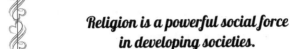

Religion is a powerful social force in developing societies.

The Relationship between Religion and Politics

The study of the role of religion in socio-political life is of great interest to sociologists, historians, political scientists, philosophers and theologians. The role religion plays in socio-political life is of particular interest because it often represents a political ideology, a belief system or a strong socio-political current in modern societies.

Religion and politics have been interrelated since the beginning of human civilization, but scholars have ignored this relationship because they have thought that religious influence on politics is only a fleeting phenomenon. However, during recent decades developing societies have not experienced secularization to the same degree as that experienced by Western societies. Due to the social and cultural realities in developing countries, it has become more common than before to study religion as a socio-political force. There have been different interpretations of the relationship between the level of religiosity and the socio-economic structure of society in the literature on this subject. Researchers have tried to explain high levels of religiosity and religious activism in terms of economic inequalities, lack of political freedom, and social injustice.

The study of the relationship between religion and socio-political life has taken different directions in the last two centuries. The main concern of researchers is to establish a relationship between religion and other social, economic, and political variables. Furthermore, sociologists have taken on the task of analyzing the similarities and differences between modern and traditional societies in dealing with religious traditions.[167] Emile Durkheim recognized the importance of religious studies in understanding social phenomena when he said that "it was through religion that man first became able to think about society."[168]

In Western history, establishing a proper relationship between religion and politics posed a difficult dilemma. Although the relationship between religion and politics is a universal phenomenon, it has been a subject of discussion and debate primarily in Western civilization since the 14th century AD. The evolution in Western societies toward more secular religion (i.e. a secular version of Christianity) did not begin in the 19th century. In fact, the evolution toward secularism is a process that dates back to the Middle Ages. Western societies have experienced what is called horizontal differentiation, i.e. separation and classification of social activities into different and distinct spheres: political, economic, family-related, religious, etc.

An example of differentiation is the separation of education from religion. The relationship between religion and politics reflects a monism/dualism dilemma that has influenced

Western political and intellectual history significantly. The dualism between religion and politics stems from the idea that religion is concerned with the divine and the sacred, whereas politics is concerned with the worldly and the temporal. However, in non-Western cultures and civilizations such as Buddhism, Hinduism and Islam, this duality between religion and politics has no meaning. In other words, the dualistic relationship between religion and politics is culturally specific to Western societies. On the other hand, monism is culturally specific to non-Western Muslim societies. The veracity of the dualistic assumption has been questioned by Emile Durkheim and Max Weber:

> What since the enlightenment had been heralded as rationality and reason had in fact issued in large part from religions; moral and religious ethical foundations [and was thus not truly the antithesis of religion].[169]

Durkheim and Weber have understood the dilemma of the liberal theorists who sought to "disentangle civil society from religious quarrels. But they nevertheless assumed that civil society needed morality and that publicly effective morality rested on religion."[170]

Durkheim and Weber have emphasized the importance of religion in modern industrial societies. For example, Durkheim argued that the French Revolution had succeeded because it was based on moral and religious values that reflected the social reality of that time.[171]

Despite the influence of religion on Western political thought, some researchers argue that religion regulates the relationship between individuals and their Creator. Whereas religion deals with the supernatural, the eternal and the sacred, politics, on the other hand, regulates the relationship between individuals and their society. In Western intellectual traditions, one finds that:

> Politics is the sum total of principles, symbols, means, and actions whereby man endeavors to attain the common good of the population. Religion, on the other hand, is the sum total of principles, symbols, means, and actions whereby man expects to reach the 'highest good' of life.[172]

Based on Western experience, and particularly that of the United States of America, maintaining the distinction between religion and politics has become an art in itself. The dualistic thesis has been fully developed in the United States of America. Thus, it becomes easier for Western researchers "to slip into the thought that religion is what concerns the individual in his own pursuit of integrity and happiness while politics essentially covers the public affairs domain."[173]

Western political thought has identified with and borrowed from two major sources: Christian doctrine and secular Roman law. According to Gilles Kepel:

> These two principles have been articulated throughout all the centuries of Christianity; there has been a relation between them, but never an identification.[174]

Moreover, Western culture has borrowed liberally from ancient Greek culture; Athens came to be seen as a political and cultural model. The myth of Athenian democracy has provided a source of legitimization for the political elites that have governed Western societies throughout history. Similarly, throughout history, the ideal Muslim society in Medina has motivated both the ruling elites and the Muslim opposition in the Arab and Muslim worlds. Early Muslim society provided both a spiritual and a temporal leadership for its members. The early Muslims never made a distinction between the two forms of leadership; they believed that only a righteous, pious man could provide good government for Muslim society. The main function of the Islamic government was to ensure obedience to the law of God (Allah), as explained in the Holy Quran and the Noble Sunnah (Prophet's traditions and practices), and the implementation of *Sharia* laws drawn from its sources: the Holy Quran, Noble Sunnah, *Ijma'* (consensus), and *Qiyas* (Analogy). However, the circumstances today seem different, and taking historical facts for granted without any conscious critical view is a risk.

While there has been a significant influence of secular Roman law on Christian doctrines, Islam has not seen such influence. In Islam, there is harmony and coordination between religion and state, with no mixing between what is religious and what is political. Islam is a religion of *ibadat* (acts of worship) that involves an individual's relationship with God (Allah) and a religion of *muamalat* (everyday human undertakings) that

involves individuals' relationship to other individuals in matters of everyday life without neglecting the fact that these undertakings are also subject to *Sharia* jurisprudence and generally accepted interests.

Religion and Political Development

Theories of modernization or modernity have dominated the field of comparative development in recent decades. Modernization theorists argue that the essential difference between modern and traditional societies lies in the greater control which modern man has over his natural and social environment. This control is based on the expansion of scientific and technological knowledge. According to Weber, rational and bureaucratic organizations have given modern man the tools for effective control over nature and society and have emancipated him from anxiety, magical forces and religious traditions.[175] In modern societies:

> [there are no] mysterious incalculable forces that come into play ... One need no longer have recourse to magical means in order to master or implore the spirits, as did the savage, for whom such mysterious power existed.[176]

The dichotomy between traditional and modern societies has led researchers to analyze the major differences between Western and non-Western societies and people. Just as modern man and traditional man contrast, so do modern societies and traditional societies. It has been argued that traditional man is passive and expects continuity in nature and in society.

118

Moreover, he does not believe that man is able to change or to control either nature or society. Modern man, on the other hand, believes that change is imminent and desirable; he has confidence in his ability to control change in order to accomplish his goals.[177]

Although the traditional–modern dichotomy was popular in the 1960s and 1970s, it has been heavily criticized in recent years. Dichotomous approaches, which were developed by social evolutionists late in the 19th century, have evaluated the progress of nations by their proximity to the institutions and values of Western societies.[178]

> *Classification of societies into "modern" and "traditional" is rigid. It does not take into account the differences between societies and ignores the similarities and links between them.*

These theories speak of modernity as being Western and traditionalism as being non-Western. The distinctions between modern and traditional societies are important parts of modernization theory. Samuel Huntington points out that "Modernity and tradition are essentially asymmetrical concepts. The modern ideal is set forth and then everything which is not modern is labeled traditional."[179]

Hence, the concept of a traditional society is formulated not on the basis of observation but rather as a hypothetical antithesis to modern society. This fact is reflected in a number of conclusions, such as the conventional stereotype that traditional societies are essentially static and non-dynamic.[180]

It has been argued that modern societies are characterized by focusing on achievement, and having functionally specific norms and structures. On the other hand, traditional societies are characterized by particularistic, arbitrary and functionally diffuse norms and structures. The terms "modern" and "traditional" societies are idealized and they do not take into account the differences among traditional societies nor the existence of certain degrees of similarities between traditional and modern societies. These conceptual problems have led to vague definitions of modernization. Modernization is generally defined as a process "through which a traditional or pre-technological society passes as it is transformed into a society characterized by machine technology, rational attitudes and a highly differentiated social structure"[181] The main problem with this definition is the unclear meaning of the descriptive words: What kind of achievements does a society need in order to become modern? What do the terms "traditional" and "modern" mean?

Modernization is also defined as "a multifaceted process involving changes in all areas of human thought and activity."[182] In particular, modernization involves a number of social and economic transformations: from a primitive, underdeveloped economy to a technological, industrialized economy; from

closed, arbitrary systems to open, achievement-oriented systems; and from extended to nuclear families.

The term modernization (transition to modernity) is used to include the overall processes of social, economic, intellectual, political and cultural change that are associated with the movement of societies from relatively poor, rural, agrarian conditions to relatively affluent, urban, technological, industrialized conditions.[183] Most definitions of modernization are generalized rather than discriminating and specific. Since the definition of modernization includes all these processes, it is difficult to formulate a theory of modernization. The concept of modernization is not only vague but also too comprehensive. Modernization theorists have attempted to define the concept of modernization in terms of political participation, education, industrialization, urbanization, secularization, and increased communications.

Organization of the Book

Given the nature of this book's subject and goal, it is logical to rely more on a "descriptive analytical approach." The treatment of the subject is organized in a preface, and four parts divided into an introduction, seven chapters and a conclusion.

The Preface presents a prelude to the topic and briefly explains what the author seeks to discuss through this book.

The Introduction presents a review of the theme of the book, which primarily seeks to shed light on the political exploitation of religion, its mechanisms, patterns, manifestations,

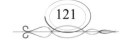

consequences and outcomes. The aim is to provide an in-depth understanding of what is going on in the Arab and Muslim worlds, and to try to deconstruct and unravel many of the entanglements and problems that obstruct development and progress and increase the gap separating many Arab and Muslim countries from progress and development.

Chapter 1, "Political Islam: Between Reality and Myth," presents a conceptual theoretical examination of the frameworks and concepts on which political religious groups and their various intellectual views are based.

Chapter 2 focuses on several issues, and aims to acquaint the reader with the problem of mixing religion and politics, which is the point of focus for the political Islamic trend, with all its various groups, organizations and parties. The chapter provides background on this issue based on the development of societies as a criterion for their existence, absence or administration in the Arab and Muslim worlds. The chapter goes on to discuss the separation of religion and state in the Western, Christian world, and how the objective conditions – internally in the Church and externally in the state – combined to end the era of the Church's control over the state. The second part of this chapter analyzes the causes of this mixture between religion and state in the Arab and Muslim worlds, and the plan of political Islam to perpetuate this situation. At the same time, the chapter presents some Islamic examples of success in separating religion and state. The third part of the chapter analyzes how mixing religious and political matters can cause conflict and division within the same doctrine as well as in

wider society. This refutes, to the extent possible, the idea that the first Islamic state established at the time of the revelation of the Islamic message was free from conflict and dispute because it injected religion into politics.

Chapters 3 to 6 provide a detailed review of political religious groups, with Chapter 3 focusing on the Muslim Brotherhood group, Chapter 4 on the Salafi current, and Chapter 5 on the Suroori current and its intellectual and cultural influence. Chapter 6 focuses on the thought of jihadi Salafism, represented by jihadi groups and organizations, and particularly Al-Qa'ida and ISIL, and discusses the thought of these two organizations and their *modus operandi* while explaining the differences, similarities and common ideological denominators between them.

Chapter 7 discusses an opinion poll of a sample of the Arab–Muslim population in the United Arab Emirates (nationals and other different Arab and Muslim nationalities) to gauge trends in public opinion toward the aims and practices of political religious groups and the extent of their responsibility for the turmoil taking place in several Arab and Muslim countries. It also seeks to determine the views of the public regarding the future role of these groups.

The Conclusion sums up the findings of all the chapters and presents a future vision of political religious groups. It directly discusses the reasons behind the failure of these groups in government and their inability to develop a political theory that could be built upon in order to establish the political

system of government they call for. It also discusses their failure to formulate development programs to keep pace with the modern era and to provide solutions and alternatives to the development problems that exist in many Arab and Muslim countries. They remained content with the raising of slogans and religious and political mobilization—which all soon evaporated when the most powerful and historically deep-rooted of these groups arrived to authority in the most populous Arab country. The Muslim Brotherhood group failed to retain its state authority for more than one year (lasting specifically from June 30, 2012 to July 3, 2013), and was subjected to public exposure unprecedented in its history, which stretches back to 1928. In its experience in government, the Muslim Brotherhood group proved its detachment from reality and its inability to utilize the social and religious momentum of the time. It retained a political religious discourse, which prevented it from overcoming its historical and cultural backwardness in order to move forward along the path to a comprehensive revival that could surpass such historical dreams.[184]

The Muslim Brotherhood group is passing through an unprecedented crisis in its history after having proven its detachment from reality and its inability to lead the social and religious momentum in the Arab and Muslims worlds.

Finally, the Conclusion states that with respect to many Arab and Muslim countries, the alternative to governance by political religious groups might be just as inflexible and its representatives just as inexperienced when it comes to extricating those countries from economic and social problems that have accumulated over decades. It also predicts that the Arab and Muslim worlds in the future may suffer under a continuous duality of the two components of the "mirage": political religious groups and movements seeking authority which they cannot manage efficiently, and dreaming supporters who see in political religious groups a means to overcome the problems of daily life. Of course – as the Conclusion states – this does not change the fact that political religious movements and groups in the Arab and Muslim worlds are witnessing the lowest point of their popularity, and many signs indicate an unprecedented decline in this popularity, especially after the poor experience in government of the Muslim Brotherhood group in the Arab Republic of Egypt.

1

Political Islam: Between Reality and Myth

CHAPTER 1

Political Islam:
Between Reality and Myth

P olitical Islam, with its religious ideology, political
agenda and organizations, emerged in Arab and Muslim
environments and societies at the beginning of the 20th
century. It has generally been a direct reaction against the
deteriorating political, economic, social and cultural conditions
in Arab and Muslim nations following periods of colonization –
which have varied in form and length depending on the colonial
power in question[1] – and after the abolition of the Ottoman
Caliphate by Mustafa Kemal (Ataturk) in 1924.[2] The continued
colonization of regional states and the emergence of a strict
secular state in Turkey angered some circles among religious
Muslims. This led to the gradual appearance of religious groups
which aimed to preserve educational, cultural, intellectual and
religious identity. With time, these groups became organizations
and developed new ideas, including the idea that religion offers

a comprehensive system which deals with all aspects of life, including politics. One of the means used by those organizations to establish an Islamic state in accordance with the theory of *hakimiyya* (divine sovereignty) was *jihad*, both against the outside world and within the Muslim world.[3] This continued for many years, and has most recently led to the emergence of ISIL (the Islamic State of Iraq and the Levant) at the end of June 2014. ISIL announced the establishment of what it called an "Islamic State" with Abu Bakr Al-Baghdadi as the "Caliph" of all Muslims across the world, and asked those Muslims to pledge loyalty to him.[4] Since the start of the popular protests and the subsequent changes in the ruling regimes of some Arab nations in early 2011, the ensuing decline of the state's traditional influence and sovereignty, as well as the deterioration of the security situations in countries such as the Arab Republic of Egypt, the Republic of Tunisia, the Republic of Yemen, the State of Libya, the Republic of Iraq, the Syrian Arab Republic and other countries with Muslim populations like Nigeria and Mali, political religious groups have found ample room to expand, mobilize and act in public, and have managed to exploit prevailing circumstances to assume authority in some of these countries.

This chapter attempts to examine the ideology and *modus operandi* of political religious groups as a broad phenomenon that employs religion to achieve political gains and interests because, by the very nature of their activity, such groups have always sought government or authority. Part one of the chapter focuses on defining the phenomenon and its characteristics.

Part two analyzes the reasons behind the expansion and survival of political religious groups benefiting from the ideological and societal combination of religion and state in the Arab and Muslim countries. The Christian West succeeded in eliminating this centuries ago by separating religious and political matters, and through the formation of distinct political, economic and social classes. Part three discusses patterns of political Islamic thought, their practical manifestations and the agendas of its various factions. Part four reviews the range of criticisms that are leveled against political religious groups, their ways of thinking and their performance in the countries where they assumed authority. The Chapter concludes with a synopsis exploring the short and long term future of these groups.

What is Political Islam?

To define political Islam, it may be useful to distinguish between two Islamic models: first is the traditional model embraced by the majority of Muslims throughout the world, which involves the observance of the pillars of Islam and the obligatory acts of worship such as the attestation that there is no god but Allah and that the Prophet Muhammad (pbuh) is His Messenger, prayer, fasting (in Ramadan), *zakat* (alms) and pilgrimage, commitment to virtuous values of life and religious tolerance, and other general qualities of an ordinary Muslim's life. The second is a model pursued by certain political religious groups and organizations that seek to change the political status quo, as well as economic, social and cultural conditions, using their ability to influence political practices, ideologies and developments in Muslim societies.[5]

131

This latter may generally be described as political Islam, which is practically manifested in political religious groups of all denominations and different ideological and political approaches. The head of a Muslim household who wakes up early to go to the mosque for prayers and strives for a living differs to one who is only interested in changing what he considers contradictory to declared religious laws and principles – which he interprets according to his own views, and political and organizational self-interests – which he dismisses as deviation from the teachings of pure religion and its true path, not serving the life of Muslims in this world and the hereafter, and not reflecting the primary purpose of the revealed Islamic religion— all based on narrow-minded interpretations of some Holy Quranic verses. An example of the Holy Quranic verses taken out of context and used by political religious groups as an excuse for violence and murder is: "And fight them on until there is no more tumult or oppression, and there prevail justice and faith in Allah …"[6] An example of the verses they use in their call for the implementation of the rule of God (Allah) on Earth (the principle of *hakimiyya*), appointing themselves as the guardians of Muslim societies in regards to the application of *Sharia*, is: "… If any do fail to judge by (the light of) what Allah hath revealed, they are (no better than) Unbelievers."[7] The interpretation of these verses requires profound jurisprudential knowledge. Established religious scholars advocate various interpretations of these verses and the definition of not judging "by what God (Allah) hath revealed." These include the view that those who

believe that God (Allah) has revealed the truth but do not judge accordingly as a result of some worldly purpose or personal reason are not committing an act of unbelief that should drive them from the fold of Islam; while those who do so because they consider alternatives to be permissible or preferable to the judgment of God (Allah) are committing an act of unbelief that will result in them being cast out of the faith. Those who deride the judgments of God (Allah) or who deny the judgment He has revealed to His Messengers, and who substitute these judgments with alternatives which they claim are from God (Allah) and proceed to judge by them instead would be committing an act of unbelief that would drive them from the fold Islam. In this regard, militant Islamists cite the example of the Jews, who changed the punishment set by God (Allah) for the adulterer (stoning).[8] Moreover, a Muslim coerced to not judge by what God (Allah) has revealed cannot be considered an unbeliever, because God (Allah) refers to: "… anyone who, after accepting faith in Allah, utters unbelief, except under compulsion, his heart remaining firm in Faith …"[9]

Here, a clear, unequivocal distinction should be made between Islam as a pure heavenly religion encouraging tolerance, love, the spread of virtue and the cultivation of land on the one hand, and political religious groups that seek to use this religion to serve their personal and organizational goals and interests on the other.

Scientific studies, official announcements, experts' writings and media personalities, etc., often use "political Islam" to include all organizations and groups working to materialize the main goal of the "politicization" of Islam; i.e. to place it in the service of a particular political project that could eventually enable the proponents of the ideas of these organizations and groups to secure authority. Other terms derived from the broader term, such as traditional, militant, fundamentalist, extremist and revolutionary Islam, are also commonly used. Each of these derivations has specific characteristics, which apply varyingly to one organization or another, but all these organizations share the primary common goal of achieving authority and controlling the state and its institutions in order to establish what they claim to be the "virtuous Islamic state [utopia or the ideal state, according to their view]."[10] This reflects their narrow-mindedness and exclusionary view towards others, even fellow Muslims. Islam is not an exclusive monopoly for these groups, and its application to various aspects of life is the responsibility and goal of all Muslims, not a certain denomination or group.

For a better definition of the term "political Islam," a number of observations should be noted, deduced from the practices of those who belong to the various political religious groups, which range from traditional to militant, and from old to newly established. The opinions of prominent scholars and jurists about these practices also differ. These observations include the following:

First: political Islam is a term used to identify political religious groups and organizations, which believe that Islam is comprehensive and contains sufficient political, economic,

social and cultural principles to govern both public and private life which each Muslim should follow in every activity, whether in private or when practicing political activity.[11] Therefore, political Islam represents a tendency towards holism based on what are considered flawless principles in the public domain because they are derived from sources of pure religion; i.e. the Holy Quran, Noble Sunnah (the Prophet's sayings and traditions) and consensus. One researcher argues that political Islam is indeed a kind of "molding" of Islam by certain individuals and groups in order to provide political responses to modern socio-economic challenges by seeking a future built upon concepts re-envisioned from Islamic heritage.[12] In my view, fundamentalist, militant and traditional Muslims equally believe that Islam contains everything an individual needs in their life, but that they differ on how to use it politically.[13]

Francois Burgat argues that political Islam is the "recourse to the vocabulary of Islam initially by social classes that have not benefited from the positive aspects of modernization."[14] He points out that the frame of reference of political Islam encourages the emergence of views and interpretations that support autocratic and totalitarian behavior, because a large number of the theorists of this current have declared from the beginning that the use of force and bearing arms against the state are legitimate practices.[15]

Gilles Kepel says that political Islamic movements reached their peak in the Muslim world with the victory of the Iranian

Revolution in 1979, and various factors have led to their spread—most importantly social and political disaffection, particularly among youth and students.[16]

Second: institutional manifestations of political Islam take various forms. Some are clandestine and illegal, such as militant jihadi organizations that seek to change societies by means of violence. Others take on a political nature by forming political groups, organizations and parties that seek to achieve authority and retain it at all costs, be it civil war (like Taliban in Afghanistan, for example), military coup (the Republic of the Sudan), peaceful public revolution followed by liquidation of allies who support secular and national currents (the Iranian Revolution of 1979), parliamentary elections (the Republic of Turkey after the 1980s, specifically after 2002, and the Kingdom of Morocco after the victory of the Moroccan Justice and Development Party in the legislative elections held on November 25, 2011 and its subsequent formation of the government) or mobilization, demonstrations and protests that use Islam as a political rallying call in order to pressure ruling regimes with a view to overthrowing them and changing the entire political landscape (as happened in the Arab Republic of Egypt and the Republic of Tunisia after 2011).

Political religious groups in the Arab and Muslim worlds used to have mostly religious and social orientations, but after the wind of change that began in early 2011 they transformed themselves into political parties whose fate hinged on their political performance as well as on the way other Arab and

Muslim nations dealt with them. Hence, the reality of their disarray and weak intellectual, planning and leadership structures were exposed. The Egyptian Muslim Brotherhood group, for example, formed the Freedom and Justice Party after the ouster of the regime of former president Muhammad Husni Mubarak in 2011. The Egyptian Salafi movement formed the Al-Noor Party, the Tunisian Ennahdha Movement formed the Ennahdha Movement Party and the Islamic current in the Kingdom of Morocco formed the Justice and Development Party. Each of these parties has a different *modus operandi*, but they all share the common political goal of ultimately securing authority.[17]

Political religious groups inject religion into politics, politicize religion and regard it as a criterion for political activity.

Third: an inevitable extension of the second point above is that political Islam injects religion into politics, politicizes religion and regards it as a criterion for political activity, according to its own views. This makes political Islam or political religious groups the main beneficiaries of the current political, social and economic situation in the Arab and Muslim worlds in general, and the lack of any separation between religion and state in particular. It is worth mentioning here that the separation between religion and state succeeded in the West between the 17th and 19th centuries – beginning with the treaties of Westphalia in 1648 which followed the 30-years war in Europe,[18] and developing through the triumph of the ideas of the American and French Revolutions in 1776 and 1789 respectively – and was entrenched by the Western industrial revolution in the second half of the 19th century. These political and economic developments promoted the emergence of new social classes that sought to escape the control of the Church and religion over society.[19]

In the Arab and Muslim worlds, however, the notion of a separation of religion and state collides with the fact that Islam, since the first Islamic state in Medina, has combined religious and political practice and leadership in the person of the Prophet Muhammad (pbuh), who established that state. The Rightly-Guided Caliphs who succeeded him also combined both aspects of leadership in their practices.[20] In reality, this situation was exceptional when the Islamic state was still under formation, but changed following the era of the Rightly-Guided Caliphs. Khalid Al-Dakheel summarizes this case in his argument that the slogan "Islam is both Religion and State" raised by the Muslim Brotherhood group since its establishment – and never uttered by anyone before – is indeed an "ideologized political slogan" meant to serve the political purposes of the group.[21] This was evidenced by the Muslim Brotherhood group's acceptance of the prerequisites of political activity in the Arab Republic of Egypt after the resignation of former president

Muhammad Husni Mubarak.[22] Al-Dakheel argues that the group's acceptance of civil state principles, such as peaceful transfer of authority and the separation of authorities, etc., means the abandonment of the slogan and its requirements and an acknowledgement of the rules established by those secular principles, such as the principle of the separation between religion and state, which intrinsically goes against the declared thought of the group.[23]

Although the literature of political religious groups argues that there was no separation between religion and the state in the early periods of Islam, a study of Islamic history shows that jurisprudence and politics have been separated since at least the ordeal of the Imam Ahmad Ibn Hanbal.[24] Moreover, Muslim society during the era of the Rightly-Guided Caliphs was too simple and homogenous to require such a separation between religion and state. But the reality of the Arab and Muslim worlds today is diametrically different in terms of the development of societies and the complexity of their political, religious, cultural and economic structures, which requires a new perspective regarding the relationship between what is religious and what is political. This, in turn, requires an understanding of the extent of recent changes that have taken place in this relationship, which has been substantially affected by the failure of political religious groups in government. I have carefully and accurately monitored and investigated the failure of these groups in a robust survey I have conducted, and presented its findings in Chapter 7 of this book.

Objectively speaking, the main problem in most countries in the Arab and Muslim worlds does not lie in the relationship between religion and politics or the extent of their separation or connection. It lies basically in the use of religion (a constant) to serve politics (a variable) and in the subordination of religion – with all its enormous spiritual power – to the world of politics, with all its maneuvering, bargains and deals. This entails a misuse of religion as well as a confusion of politics by tying it to fixed principles that are difficult to avoid or escape. Politics changes continuously and requires a great deal of flexibility.[25]

Fourth: political Islam has emerged as a reaction against marginalization and alienation in the Arab and Muslim worlds after centuries of colonization of some states by Western countries. This situation also led to the emergence of Arab national liberation movements.[26] In the particular case of political Islam, the abolition of the Ottoman Caliphate in 1924 by Mustafa Kemal (Ataturk) and the creation of the modern Turkish Republic were earth-shaking events. Political religious groups viewed this as the end of what they considered an Islamic Caliphate that represented a political expression of the *umma*, religion and Islamic history.[27]

Moreover, political religious groups saw the societal decline and decadence resulting from foreign colonization and believed that Muslims broke away from religion, arguing that this brought about difficult problems that could only be solved by going back to religion.[28] In this respect, however, political religious groups tend to forget the fact that the Ottoman

Caliphate was in fact not a good example of the Islamic Caliphate they seek.[29] In fact, the Ottoman Caliphate had many negative aspects and practices alien to the pure nature of the Islamic Caliphate during the era of the Rightly-Guided Caliphs, and pure Islam was never the guiding path of government for the Ottoman sultans. In this respect, there are sufficient historical examples to prove this clearly,[30] but I think the scope of the book does not permit a discussion of these details, as it may distract it from its main goal.

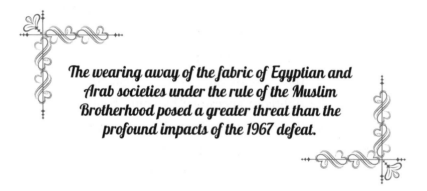

The wearing away of the fabric of Egyptian and Arab societies under the rule of the Muslim Brotherhood posed a greater threat than the profound impacts of the 1967 defeat.

Political religious groups insist on the need to return to the way of the righteous ancestors, represented by the Rightly-Guided Caliphs as a political, social and economic example. They specifically insist on the rebuilding of the Caliphate model as it was seen in the first decades of the Islamic state (i.e., the era of the Rightly-Guided Caliphs).[31] The basis of this idea is that the Islamic state at that time was chronologically closer to pure Islam and its first application, and all authorities were united in the person of one Caliph who drew legitimacy from his companionship of the Prophet Muhammad (pbuh). One researcher argues that political Islam in this aspect combines its criticism against the West as a source of immoral behavior and the inspiration for the modern civil state that alienated religion from daily public life, and also as a source of modernity that substituted hedonistic, materialistic life for the pure religious one.[32]

In its criticism of this, political Islam used and still uses a religious discourse of preaching to inspire people and promote an imaginary idea about how things would be if the political Islamic current were to be allowed to establish what it calls the virtuous state, as mentioned above.[33] The bottom line here is that there are three general principles linking political religious groups in the Arab and Muslim worlds: first, following the example of the righteous ancestors;[34] second, believing in the Islamic *Sharia* as a way of life; and third, believing that the reestablishment of the Caliphate is the path to a good or virtuous life.[35] But what happened in the Arab Republic of Egypt after the Muslim Brotherhood group attained authority in 2012 attested to the failure of political religious groups in translating these convictions into tangible plans and practical realities. In fact, the negative impacts on the fabric of Egyptian and Arab societies resulting from what the Muslim Brotherhood group did during its rule outweigh the profound effects and deep scars inflicted upon the psyches of the Egyptians and Arabs by the 1967 defeat.

Fifth: Political Islam tries to merge its political thought[36] with the values and cultural, social and economic heritage of

Islam. It regards itself as the principal representative of Islam in its comprehensiveness, yet cherry-picks societal and cultural principles of Islam and puts them in the service of its political project. In so doing, it leaves out cultural, social and religious movements and currents that never expressed any interest in politics, preferring to concentrate on their preaching activities.[37] Political Islam strives to blockade political parties and currents that seek to reach authority without mixing religion with politics or exploiting it. In this respect, political Islam resembles the fascist movements[38] that emerged after World War I and manifested themselves in Fascist Italy and Nazi Germany. It also resembles the communist rule in the former Soviet Union, the People's Republic of China or the Democratic People's Republic of Korea (North Korea), etc.

Sixth: political Islam sees that what unites Muslims is their belonging to Islam in its entirety, ignoring the disparate internal conditions of the Muslim countries in which it operates. In other words, political Islam is totalitarian, and believes in the possibility of implementing the principles of the Islamic state, economy and culture in isolation from the objective conditions existing in each individual society.[39]

Political Islam, self-evidently, seeks to "entrench" the religious identity of society, not only in the general principles of government and its practices and in economics and its applications but also in all aspects of public life, from dressing and eating to forums and arts (which will probably be discarded altogether or restricted), etc.[40] It ignores the cultural, ethnic and religious diversity characterizing the Arab and Muslim countries and overlooks the principles of citizenship and its requirement of equal rights and duties among citizens; principles that do not contradict the essence of pure Islam.

The discourse of political religious groups is similar in this regard. Its flag-bearers believe in their ability to apply it equally anywhere; all they need is an opportunity to attain authority, by usual or unusual means. Once they have it, they would embark on applying this totalitarian thought in all its aspects and principles, even if this contradicts the religion they bombastically claim to defend. This appears clearly in various Muslim nations and regions where some movements that believe in the general thought of political Islam have already matured, whether in the Arab world or any other country in the Muslim world. It is also evident where Muslims live in Western countries. Controversies about the *hijab* in the French Republic and Scandinavian countries, the banning of the *adhan* (call to prayer) in Switzerland and of Islamic animal slaughter in some Scandinavian countries are examples of the manipulation of Islam by political religious groups to achieve their goals by exploiting these politically, religiously and legally intermixed issues in order to turn Muslims against the countries in which they live or hold nationality, and to blackmail these countries politically in order to subjugate them to their will and goals.

Seventh: political Islam is a new phenomenon which has emerged as a reaction to contemporary objective circumstances, ranging from political, cultural, economic and social deterioration

to the fall and collapse of the Ottoman Caliphate, Westernization and non-Islamic infiltration in Muslim regions. These circumstances have expanded and Israel's occupation of the Palestine has become one of the pretexts behind the spread of political Islam and its organizations.[41] One researcher estimates that the phenomenon of political Islam dates back 100 years, noting that political Islam originally took the form of revivalist groups aiming to respond to the weakness of the Arab and Muslim worlds by the use of time-honored Islamic symbols.[42] Another researcher considers political Islam as a political ideology rather than a religious system, as two things bundled into one and as a product of modernization as much as a reaction against it.[43]

Political Islam is a religious project which seeks authority by using religion as the ideological grounds for imposing a certain way of life, irrespective of circumstances existing in local contexts.

So, political Islam can be defined as a religious project which seeks political authority in order to be able to rebuild the Islamic Caliphate. To that end, it uses religion as the ideological grounds for its political, economic and social programs and for imposing a certain way of life on all Muslims and non-Muslims, irrespective of objective circumstances existing in local contexts. It attempts to go back to an imagined, blissful past drawn from Islamic history—hence it is fair to describe such political religious groups as attempting to impose not only rigidity, but an escape from reality. This definition is broad and general, but still applies to political religious groups in all Arab and Muslim countries and elsewhere.

Emergence and Intellectual Origins of Political Islam

Since it emerged at the end of the 19th century and the beginning of the 20th century, political Islam has appeared as an attempt to salvage Islam from a state of decline and from Westernization, and to restore the prosperous days of the first decades of Islam. It has emerged in response to the plight of Muslim societies living under the yoke of Western colonization. With the development of secular political theories at the beginning of the 20th century, especially with the rise of nationalism, the attempt to revive religion turned into a political project, which believed that renaissance would only be possible by uniting the *umma*, exerting efforts in the public political arena and using religious text and symbols. The religious project has become an "Islamic nationalism" seeking to unite Muslim peoples and evoke Islamic togetherness and unity. The first appearance of political Islam came with the launch of the Muslim Brotherhood group by Hassan Al-Banna in Egypt in 1928, following the end of World War I in 1918 and the collapse of the Ottoman Caliphate and its abolition in 1924. The Ottoman Empire constituted the

independent political Islamic entity, despite the weakness it suffered for centuries.[44]

The rise and spread of the Muslim Brotherhood group since its inception was striking. Hassan Al-Banna's argument was that Islam as a fully integrated, comprehensive system of belief offered a substitute to Westernization and materialism, which threatened Muslim societies at that time. According to Al-Banna, the only way to forestall social and moral deterioration was to go back to the roots of Islam, precisely the Rightly-Guided Caliphate period in the early decades of Islam.[45] Despite the Muslim Brotherhood group's claim regarding its religious identity at the beginning of its formation, it soon engaged directly in politics the moment it clashed with the Egyptian state, during the British occupation of Egypt (1882–1952).[46] At that time, the group sought to open branches in several Egyptian towns and establish religious, educational and charity organizations, which Egyptian authorities deemed to be an unacceptable expansion and a serious threat to the role of the state as the sole organizer of public life. That threat increased when the group established a secret apparatus in 1938 to pursue its agenda. The group did not respect the existence of Christian citizens, and hence the state authorities considered it a threat to national security and social peace.

After the Muslim Brotherhood group interfered in politics, and the official authorities suspected the activities of its members, a decision was issued to dissolve the group on December 8, 1948. The then Prime Minister of Egypt,

Mahmood Fahmi Al-Nuqrashi, issued a decision to dissolve the group on charges of "incitement and subversive activity against state security."[47] Twenty days later, a member of the group assassinated Al-Nuqrashi on December 28, 1948. This was the first time a decision had been made to ban the group.[48] On February 12, 1949, its founder, Hassan Al-Banna, was assassinated by two unidentified men who shot him and fled. In 1954 (when the relationship between Abdul Nasser's regime and the Muslim Brotherhood group was strong) some Egyptian officials were convicted of plotting to assassinate Al-Banna in revenge for the assassination of Prime Minister Mahmood Fahmi Al-Nuqrashi in 1948.[49] This gave the Muslim Brotherhood group the political cover to increase its influence and activity against the Egyptian state on the pretext of protecting religion.[50]

Hassan Al-Banna's thought was largely influenced by the 19th century Muslim intellectuals who were unhappy with the deteriorating situation of the Muslim *umma* at that time, and who worked within the Arab and Islamic Renaissance Movement, which – most importantly- was concentrated in Egypt, where a stark paradox existed between widespread religious sentiment and religiosity, on the one hand, and an open-minded British occupation on the other. Among those by whom Al-Banna was influenced were Muhib Al-Deen Al-Khateeb and Abu Al-A'la Al-Mawdoodi, who lived in India and wrote about the Islamic state and Caliphate. Those thinkers, in turn, were all influenced by the reformist

Muhammad Abdu who lived at the end of the 19th century and the beginning of the 20th century, but they all, including Hassan Al-Banna, shunned his call for openness towards the West and to derive benefit from it. Instead, they focused on fighting the West and adopted the ideas of the Imam Ahmad ibn Taymiyya.[51]

The absence of religious thought from political life extended until after the Arab and Muslim countries gained national independence in the 1940s and 1950s, where national and secular regimes were established. These regimes were grounded in the armed forces and ideologically influenced by socialism. They faced difficult economic and social situations and prepared a variety of development plans to deal with them. But these regimes – especially in the People's Democratic Republic of Algeria, the Republic of Iraq and the Syrian Arab Republic – excluded religious fundamentalist thought from the political process and created, as an alternative, a centrist religious thought and official religious organizations focused on instilling the values of tolerance, moderation and national belonging. They imposed themselves as the only authorities entitled to define the societal, personal and religious affiliation of the contemporary Arab and Muslim individuals living in the countries they ruled. They also created other political and ideological entities to counter the expansion of political religious groups and their ideas.[52]

The Muslim Brotherhood supported the July 1952 Revolution in Egypt, regarding it as a pathway to achieving their ambition of creating a political religious state free of any dominance of Western colonization and Westernization. They maintained good relationships with some Free Officers such as Jamal Abdul Nasser, Muhammad Anwar Al-Sadat, Muhammad Abdul Hakeem Amir and Kamal Al-Deen Hussain Abdul Rahman, although this relationship was not organizational in the real sense.[53] It did not last long, as political differences between the ruling regime and the group obstructed this cooperation. The regime was suspicious about the intentions and goals of the Muslim Brotherhood group, while the group had sought to seize authority since the 1930s. The January 16, 1953 decision to dissolve political parties did not include the Muslim Brotherhood group, because it was not then classified as a political party.[54] But the clash between the group and the Egyptian government began in 1954 when the government dissolved it and one of its members responded by attempting to assassinate Abdul Nasser at Al-Manshiyya square in Alexandria on October 26, 1954.[55] Moreover, the group considered its decision to cooperate with the government to be misplaced, because the regime was intending to establish a secular national government, while the group sought to realize Hassan Al-Banna's dream of establishing a religious state.[56]

The course of the Muslim Brotherhood group in Egypt was no different from that of the group's branches in other Arab and Muslim countries ruled by nationalist and secular regimes. In those countries, the activities of its members were subjected to scrutiny and examination as they were considered a threat to

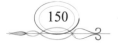

internal security and stability. Over the course of time, the ideological differences turned into an existential battle between secular nationalist thought and political Islamic thought.[57] Political religious groups in the Arab and Muslim countries had one of three options: acquiescence to the notion of citizenship and its requirements and abandonment of their political ambitions, interests and militant religious thinking; continued conflict with the authorities; or exile. While many followers of the group withdrew from the battle against the ruling regimes, others remained in confrontation with them and were imprisoned, and many decided to flee to the Arab Gulf states, both the independent and those under occupation. The strategy of those who fled to the Arab Gulf states was to blend into communities, engage in their institutions and infiltrate minds through their role in establishing educational systems and social institutions in these communities. Among the prominent members of the Muslim Brotherhood group who settled in the Arab Gulf states at that time was Yousuf Abdullah Al-Qaradawi, who settled in Qatar in 1961.[58]

The second half of the 1960s was a critical period in political Islam's shift toward violence, with the appearance of Sayyid Qutb's (1906–1966) writings, especially his book *Ma'alim fi Al-Tareeq* (Signposts on the Road).[59] Sayyid Qutb believed in Abu Al-A'la Al-Mawdoodi's thought and broke away from the ideas of other Islamic thinkers. He pushed towards Islamic agendas that rejected the prevailing realities of the Arab and Muslim societies at that time. He also called for the use of violence in the Arab and Muslim countries, as well as in the West, and the application of the agendas entrenching the Islamic movement (by returning to the primary roots of Islam) in order to establish pure Islamic rule, which is the rule of God (Allah) on Earth—later to become known as *hakimiyya*.[60] Sayyid Qutb maintained that the rule belongs only to God (Allah) and limited to Him by virtue of His divinity, and considered the rule a divine attribute, and whoever disputes God (Allah) over one of His important attributes and claims it is an outright unbeliever and his unbelief becomes a necessarily known matter of religion. Therefore, legislation and enactment of rules and laws become the right of God (Allah) alone; others are not authorized by Him. According to that, Sayyid Qutb argued that anyone who claims the rule to himself, or denies that it belongs to God (Allah) and follows a way other than what has been revealed by God (Allah) is considered an unbeliever and becomes an apostate who is outside Islam.[61]

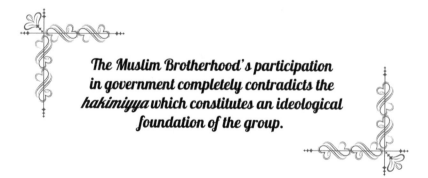

The Muslim Brotherhood's participation in government completely contradicts the hakimiyya which constitutes an ideological foundation of the group.

The concept of divine *hakimiyya* in political Islamic thought is the equivalent of the concept of sovereignty in modern political thought. Debate in Islamic thought revolves around the limits of the overlap between two entities associated with law and its implementation in accordance with modern political thought. There is an entity that is supposed to have the right to make laws (i.e. it exercises "sovereignty") while the other entity has the right to exercise sovereignty and implement laws, even by force, and this is called the "authority"—in this sense, sovereignty is the source of authority, while authority is the exercise of sovereignty.[62] Based on this intellectual framework, it is safe to argue that the Muslim Brotherhood's participation in parliamentary elections in some Arab and Muslim countries, and its engagement within generally recognized political frameworks, represent a clear violation of the concept of *hakimiyya*, and therefore constitutes a violation of *Sharia* (according to the group itself), as main role of legislatures is to draft and enact laws. This reveals a clear contradiction between the theory and practice of the group; while the former focuses on apparent compliance with religion, the latter is guided by the group's political interests.

Sayyid Qutb was one of the first founders of fundamentalism and extremism in political Islam, after being a militant member of the Muslim Brotherhood group. Qutb considered Muslims and non-Muslims as living in *jahiliyya* (ignorance of Islam), and the only way out of cultural and social deterioration and decline was *jihad* against the existing regimes.[63] He believed that the change of societies could be brought about through revolution, violence, application of Islamic law (*Sharia*), rebuilding of the

Islamic Caliphate and the implementation of the rule of God (Allah). In justifying the call for killing, particularly the killing of Muslims by fellow Muslims in the war against *jahiliyya* (ignorance of Islam), Qutb evoked the concept of *takfir* (excommunication) against those whom he considered as violating the teachings of Islam or were not sufficiently Islamic.[64] In his description of the society which he considered as *jahili* (ignorant of Islam), Qutb implicitly condemned many Muslim societies. He described the nature of the *jahili* society as follows:

> Its members do not necessarily deny the existence of God (Allah). A *jahili* (ignorant of Islam) society is the society that allows people to worship in mosques, but forbids them from demanding the arbitration of *Sharia* in matters of their life.[65]

In Sayyid Qutb's view, Islamic society was not a society whose members "proclaim themselves Muslims while the Islamic *Sharia* is not translated into laws applicable by their society and state. Such people will not be forgiven even if they pray, fast and make the pilgrimage."[66] This is in total contradiction with the words of God (Allah) in the Holy Quran: "Therefore do thou give admonition, for thou art one to admonish... Thou art not one to manage (men's) affairs."[67] The addressee in these two Holy Quranic verses is the Prophet Muhammad (pbuh), the greatest and most noble of all creations of God (Allah). According to Ibn Abbas, the interpretation of the Holy Quranic verse "Thou art not one to manage (men's)

affairs" is that you are not required to force things on them, i.e. to create faith in their hearts. Also in this respect, Ibn Zayd said: you are not required to compel them to faith.[68]

Also, on the influence of Sayyid Qutb's thought, Abdulla Azzam[69] said:

> Those who went to Afghanistan knew the profound effect of Sayyid Qutb's thought on the Islamic Jihad and on the entire generation all over the globe. Some of them would not ask you for clothes even if they were naked, food even if they were starving or weapons even if they were unarmed, but they would ask you for Sayyid Qutb's books.[70]

Sayyid Qutb started out from the foundations laid by Abu Al-A'la Al-Mawdoodi and Hassan Al-Banna, but he expanded on the interpretation of jihad.

Sayyid Qutb was a schoolteacher from Upper Egypt. From August 1948 to August 1950, he was sent on a scholarship by Egypt's Ministry of Education to the United States of America to study its educational system.[71] He never thought he would become such a famous figure. During his imprisonment since 1954, he played the role of a "victim," and was portrayed as a victim of torture and defense of truth; and this contributed to the spread of his militant thought.[72] Qutb also made use of his ten years in prison, during which he wrote down his ideas and vision of the Islamic foundations of state and society. Among his most important works were his books *Fi Zilal Al*-Quran (In the Shades of the Quran) and *Ma'alim fi Al-Tareeq* (Signposts on the Road), which was smuggled out of jail by his two sisters.[73] In 1964, Qutb was released from prison only to be arrested again in August 1965 along with thousands of members of political religious groups who were accused of plotting military actions and assassinations against government officials.[74] He was sentenced to death and executed in 1966.[75] In his book *Ma'alim fi Al-Tareeq* (Signposts on the Road), Sayyid Qutb started out from the foundations laid by Abu Al-A'la Al-Mawdoodi and Hassan Al-Banna, but he elaborated on the interpretation of *jihad*, saying: *jihad* is legitimate against the civil current and the enemies of Islam [according to his view, of course] of every kind, and *jihad* in this case is not only a legitimate option but also a holy undertaking to get rid of all forces standing between people and pure Islam. Qutb also rejected any moderate alternative in issues of faith and particularly issues of government.[76]

The defeat of the Arab secular regimes by Israel in the June 1967 war was a turning point in the path of political religious groups. After the failure of these regimes to deliver the political, economic and social development that they had promised their peoples for so many years, the 1967 defeat exposed their true nature: regimes with limited achievement at

the level of government, institutions and policies. I think the failure to confront Israel and restore the rights of the Palestinians, in addition to the loss of more land to Israel caused by the 1967 defeat and the resulting public sense of frustration, defeat and humiliation represented motivating factors for the spread of the thought of political religious groups at that time.[77] In the early 1970s, with the transfer of authority from Abdul Nasser's regime after his death in 1970 to the regime of former president Muhammad Anwar Al-Sadat, space was provided for political religious groups to expand, particularly in universities. These groups started planning for the control of vocational entities and trade unions, and succeeded in their pursuit with the declining influence of Nasserist youth in those entities.[78]

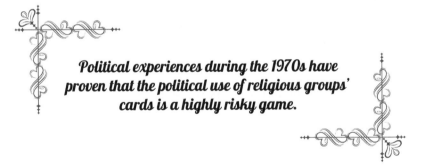

Political experiences during the 1970s have proven that the political use of religious groups' cards is a highly risky game.

The success of the Muslim Brotherhood group in controlling the student unions in Arab universities was a significant tactical achievement towards laying the organizational foundations for the future of trade unions and civil society organizations, after the repression and prosecution to which the group was subjected under the rule of Abdul Nasser.[79] Also, former Egyptian president Muhammad Anwar Al-Sadat considered the Nasserist nationalist current a challenge to his rule and sought to liquidate it;[80] he found that the support for the Islamists in the universities and other areas of public life would help him do that. Even president Al-Sadat's slogan in the mid-1970s – "Knowledge and Faith" – was meant to show his own religiosity and to break away from pre-1970 Egyptian politics – i.e. politics during the rule of Abdul Nasser. Political religious groups found support and were allowed to operate in the early days of President Al-Sadat's rule. In fact, the regime turned a blind eye to their activity in all parts of the country, especially in poor rural areas, where they found that they could provide free social, food and health services for poor segments of the population. In other words, the Egyptian state in the 1970s became implicitly supportive of religious expansion, albeit insisting that this strand of religion should be moderate and should support its policies.[81] However, the Egyptian experience has shown that the political use of the religious groups' card is highly risky.

In addition to the upsurge of religiosity in the public space, sectarian tension mounted without any direct preventive intervention from state institutions. In this context, many attacks were carried out against the Christians in the 1970s, targeting students, clerics and churches, a number of which were burned down between 1977 and 1980.[82] In 1980, president Al-Sadat tried to amend an article in the 1971

Egyptian constitution to stipulate that the Islamic *Sharia* was "the principal source of legislation," subjecting all legislation and laws to the provisions of Islamic jurisprudence and *Sharia*, and getting closer to the Islamic state sought by the Muslim Brotherhood group. Between 1980 and 1981, the official Egyptian discourse regarding the sectarian divide focused on blaming the Copts and Pope Shenouda III, accusing them of receiving weapons from Lebanese Christian militias.[83] Ironically, hardliners in the Egyptian political religious groups assassinated former president Muhammad Anwar Al-Sadat while he was reviewing a military parade in Cairo commemorating the 8th anniversary of the October 1973 war.[84]

In the 1970s a global economic crisis struck. It was caused by a number of factors including: the shift from the "Bretton Woods" system of gold standard to the currency system in 1971, the oil embargo following the October 1973 war and the high rates of inflation in capitalist countries. The crisis greatly harmed the economies of developing countries and forced them to restructure, triggering a host of social and economic problems. Political religious groups took advantage of those problems, touting themselves as the alternative to secular regimes. In addition, the economic policies of the Nasserist regime between the 1950s and 1960s, which were described as unsystematic – from nationalization of industries and banks to the land reform, which the regime did not know how to use in order to increase the national capital, and the high rate of inflation in the public sector and the decline of the private sector – contributed to the further spread of political religious groups. These groups expanded in poor areas to provide assistance as mentioned before, and thus created a growing popular base for themselves.[85]

The expansion of political religious groups in the Arab and Muslim countries was a product of the internal political, economic and social developments in these countries. Followers of these groups focused on filling the vacuum resulting from the crises of the Egyptian ruling regime during the periods of presidents Abdul Nasser and Al-Sadat. However, other external factors converged to add, first, to the problems of the political frame of reference of the Egyptian ruling regime in the 1970s and, second, to give the followers of these groups more room to prove that they were not only active in addressing the problems caused by government failure, but also preoccupied with serving the interests of all Muslims.[86] The Arab openness towards the United States of America in the mid-1970s helped political religious groups in this pursuit. It was not because they admired the Nasserist socialist experience or the former Soviet Union, but because they portrayed the Egyptian–American convergence as a sign of a convergence with, and economic dependence on the Christian West. Nevertheless, it is worth mentioning that many supporters of these groups neither had any problem with American capitalism nor did they see any merit in the resistance of the United States of America against the former Soviet Union.[87]

The reconsideration of Egyptian–Soviet relations affected many local and regional issues. In addition to social change, which he started to achieve domestically in the Arab Republic of Egypt through his open-door policy, president Al-Sadat also played a regional role against the Soviet presence in the region. In addition to getting rid of pro-Soviet elements in Egypt through the "Corrective Movement" launched in May 1971, president Al-Sadat intervened in the Republic of the Sudan the same year to prevent the overthrow of Ja'afar Numairi's regime by the Sudanese Communist Party and military officers sympathetic to it.[88] After that came the cancelation of the friendship and cooperation treaty between the Arab Republic of Egypt and the former Soviet Union, then the October 1973 war and the subsequent Arab oil embargo, placing the Arab Republic of Egypt at the heart of American strategic policy planning towards the Middle East, after strained – and oftentimes severed – relations during the Abdul Nasser era.[89]

However, while former president Muhammad Anwar Al-Sadat was purging his opponents and encouraging the supporters of political religious groups to acquire positions in the Egyptian educational and social institutions, he also went on to change his country's strategic approach. So, after the 1973 war and the disengagement agreements with Israel between 1974 and 1975, the Arab Republic of Egypt, by virtue of its communication with the United States of America, shifted away from its traditional anti-Israeli position. The disengagement treaties required a redeployment of the Egyptian armed forces away from military confrontation lines with Israeli forces.[90] Meanwhile, the Palestinian issue was attracting significant attention across the world, with the international recognition of the Palestine Liberation Organization (PLO) at the United Nations as the sole legitimate representative of the Palestinian people in October 1974.[91] This development forced the Arab Republic of Egypt to play the role of the strongest Arab mediator capable of dealing with the United States of America. But with the rise of the Israeli right to authority in Tel Aviv, represented by Menachem Begin, and the fading hopes for reaching an agreement on Palestinian rights, president Al-Sadat stated in one of his speeches that he was willing to visit Jerusalem to talk with Israeli leaders about peace and the legitimate rights of the Palestinians. Menachem Begin was quick to welcome Al-Sadat's visit, ushering in a new phase in the strategic positioning of the Arab Republic of Egypt; and therefore the position of the political Islam movement within it[92]—particularly the position of political religious groups on former president Muhammad Anwar Al-Sadat's approach towards the United States of America and Israel.

The signing of the Camp David Accords in September 1978 inaugurated a phase of the desired peace between the Arab Republic of Egypt and Israel during President Al-Sadat's era. After that, the peace treaty between the two countries was signed in March 1979, with the mediation of the United States of America, which supported Egypt's move towards peace with funding as well as economic and political openness. The peace

treaty stated the cessation of the state of war between the two countries, the start of diplomatic relations, end of Israeli occupation of the Sinai Peninsula, coordination of security relations and Israel's right of free passage through the Suez Canal and the Strait of Tiran.[93]

It may be safe to argue that the outbreak of the Iranian Islamic revolution in 1979 and the Soviet invasion of Afghanistan in the same year to support the communist regime in Kabul were the most important events in the journey of political religious groups towards more religious militancy during that period in general.[94] In that revolution, which ended in Shiite political Islam seizing authority after the liquidation of allies supporting the Iranian secular current and nationalists who participated in the revolution, Ayatollah Khomeini established *Wilayat Al-Faqeeh* (the Guardianship of the Jurist) and designated clergymen as constitutional guarantors of the state, revolution and regime. This move was considered an unacceptable expansion of the role of Shiite clerics in the government. A large number of Shiite scholars and religious references objected to the principle of *Wilayat Al-Faqeeh* (the Guardianship of the Jurist), including the prominent Shiite religious figure in the Republic of Iraq, Ali Al-Sistani. Contrary to what Khomeini did, Ali Al-Sistani asserts that religious scholars are a mere religious moral force and clerics should not hold any political office.[95] It is clear that Iranian Shiite Islam did not have any significant effect on Sunni political Islam, not only because of the Persian origin of the Iranian revolution but also because of the ideological differences between the Islamic schools of thought themselves, especially given the severe sectarian division, which still characterized the relationship between Sunnis and Shiites.[96]

> *Without Arab and American support, the Arab and Afghan mujahideen could not have defeated a power as sizable as the Soviet Union.*

The second reason – i.e., the Soviet invasion of the Islamic Republic of Afghanistan – had a significant role in the shift of Sunni political Islam towards adopting militant ideas that call for violence and *jihad*. At first, this shift was widely supported by the United States of America and some regional and international powers, because it was directed against the former Soviet Union. In 1983, former American president Ronald Reagan referred to the former Soviet Union as the "evil empire" and decided to support the global Islamic *jihad* instead of fighting the Soviet presence in the Islamic Republic of Afghanistan through political and military means. The jihadi groups managed to recruit thousands of Muslims who were willing to fight the so-called Soviet atheism. They established social institutions, schools and organizations all of which worked to attract ideologically inspired fighters and recruit them.[97]

It is safe to say that without the Arab and American support, Arab and Afghan *mujahideen* could not have defeated a power as sizable as the former Soviet Union.

The support received by these jihadi organizations from western countries – especially the United States of America – and some Arab countries was intensive and advanced. It was driven by strategic considerations aiming primarily to drain the Soviet armed forces and stem the Soviet advance in Central Asia. This helped strengthen these groups and hence made it more difficult for enemies to confront them afterwards.[98] Throughout the 1980s, the United States of America became a frequent destination for the leaders of the Afghan *jihad*, which the American media called "freedom fighters." American intelligence agencies were also active in providing financial and military support for the Afghan *mujahideen*, whether through the Pakistani army and intelligence service or through the advanced military bases they established for training the Afghan *mujahideen* in the Afghan–Pakistani border areas in collaboration with the Pakistani government.[99]

One researcher argues that it is impossible to underestimate the importance of the Afghan *jihad* and its role in the emergence of the jihadi movement and its evolution in general, because doing so would make the evolution of political Islam – as a concept and practice – much more difficult to address for those countries that seek to resist it.[100] The Afghan war factor gave the jihadi organizations new strategic positions and agendas that transformed them into a serious trans-border threat in the field of international relations, not only in the Arab Republic of Egypt but also in the Arab and Muslim worlds, the West and elsewhere.

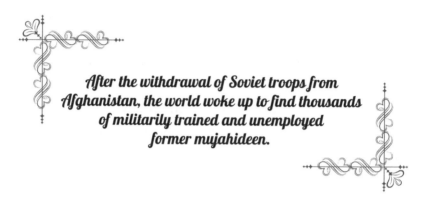

After the withdrawal of Soviet troops from Afghanistan, the world woke up to find thousands of militarily trained and unemployed former mujahideen.

In the 1990s, after the withdrawal of soviet forces from the Islamic Republic of Afghanistan and the disintegration of the former Soviet Union – the Afghan War being one of the causes of its economic and military collapse – the world woke up to find thousands of militarily trained and unemployed former *mujahideen*. Those *mujahideen* came from many Arab and Muslim countries, and among them was the founder of Al-Qa'ida, Usama bin Ladin, who was killed by a team of American Navy SEALs on May 2, 2011.[101]

Dealing with such huge numbers, especially after they embraced militant ideas, was a great dilemma for countries that supported them. The *mujahideen* split into several factions.[102] Some of them engaged in the civil war between Afghan factions and settled in Afghanistan, as was the case with Al-Qa'ida members who allied themselves with the Afghan Taliban

movement. Some left Pakistan and Afghanistan in search of new battlefields – such as Bosnia, Chechnya, Kashmir and Somalia – to complete the march of *jihad*. Some returned to their home countries to engage in acts of political violence there, as happened in the Arab Republic of Egypt, the Republic of Yemen, the People's Democratic Republic of Algeria, the Kingdom of Saudi Arabia and elsewhere, which witnessed a wave of extremism and violence launched by the "Afghan Arabs."

The "Afghan Arabs" were Arab jihadists who returned from Afghanistan and focused on confronting the "near enemy" represented, in their opinion, by the "corrupt" Arab and Muslim ruling regimes. Those returnees formed the nucleus of the various armed groups that later emerged in the Arab and Muslim worlds, such as the Armed Islamic Group in the People's Democratic Republic of Algeria, the Islamic Fighting Group in the State of Libya and other groups sprouting from the Afghan *jihad* experience, in addition to more recent organizations such as the Islamic State (ISIL) and Jabhat Al-Nusra in the Syrian Arab Republic.[103]

During that same period, the Iraqi regime invaded the State of Kuwait on August 2, 1990, prompting the formation of an international coalition consisting of hundreds of thousands of troops from Western, Arab and Muslim countries to liberate the Gulf state. After the end of the Kuwait war, however, the *jihad* against the presence of Western troops in the Arabian

Peninsula was inflamed. That was one of the driving factors for moving the *jihad* to the Arabian Peninsula under the banner of Al-Qa'ida, which included war veterans from the Islamic Republic of Afghanistan who believed that their first new mission was the liberation of "Muslim lands" from invading troops and the expulsion of foreign forces. Throughout the 1990s, therefore, the Arab and Muslim worlds went through all manner of laborious pain, fueled by the civil war in the Islamic Republic of Afghanistan between various factions that participated in the war against the Soviet troops.[104]

The establishment of Al-Qa'ida in 1988 was a critical turning point in the history of jihadi organizations.

The official establishment of Al-Qa'ida in 1988, just one year before the withdrawal of Soviet troops from the Islamic Republic of Afghanistan in 1989, was a critical turning point in the activity of jihadi organizations, especially after its alliance with the Taliban movement. That alliance gave Al-Qa'ida a wider freedom of movement, special areas in which it used to build camps for gathering and training *mujahideen*,[105] and allowed the organization to create a network of relationships with other jihadi groups spreading throughout the Arab and Muslim worlds that provided it with support.

Al-Qa'ida demonstrated its threat to global security by carrying out a series of terrorist operations, such as the bombings of the American embassies in Nairobi (Kenya) and Dar es Salaam (Tanzania) on August 7, 1998, and the bombing of the American Navy ship USS *Cole* in the Gulf of Aden in October 2000 by a suicide operation that killed 17 American soldiers and wounded 38 others. These terrorist activities reached their peak with the attacks of September 11, 2001, which clearly revealed the might of jihadi organizations and the extent of their pervasiveness. With such a combination of mass destruction – made possible by the easy access to modern technologies – the violent nature of the perpetrators of these attacks[106] and the huge number of victims – exceeding 3,000 people, which is more than three times the Americans killed in all terrorist attacks in the preceding 30 years – the attacks of September 11, 2001 represented an historical precedent. It was the first time in history that a militant organization managed to acquire a destructive capability similar to those of sovereign states. This fact has led the international community to launch a global war against this threat to international peace and security.

In the 1990s, the operating theater of militant religious organizations widened out. Countries such as the People's Democratic Republic of Algeria and the Islamic Republic of Afghanistan became hotspots of political, security and social instability. The Al-Qa'ida network, which was established during the Afghan *jihad*, expanded and created branches in a number of Arab and Muslim countries, taking advantage of the shelter, training and financial facilities provided to it by the hard-line Afghan Taliban movement, which took control of the Islamic Republic of Afghanistan in 1995. While it was once a threat to national and regional peace in a large number of Arab and Muslim countries, especially in the Gulf Arab states, Al-Qa'ida became the primary flag-bearer of terrorism after the attacks of September 11, 2001.

Inspired by the thought of Al-Qa'ida, other organizations in Europe and Asia carried out attacks in the Kingdom of Spain, the United Kingdom and the Republic of Indonesia, proving that, first, jihadi Islam has become an indicator for assessing trends in political Islam, and, second, political Islam, represented by political religious groups, has become questionable since the undermining of the credibility of its slogans, political discourse and plans and programs which claim to express Muslim peoples' aspirations for religious-based political agendas that could serve their interests and future lives.[107]

In response to the attacks of September 11, 2001, the United States of America launched what it called the war on terror. Its first major battle was the war in the Islamic Republic of Afghanistan and the elimination of the Taliban regime, which was allied with the Al-Qa'ida organization. In 2003, during the first term of President George W. Bush, the United

States of America also waged a war on the Republic of Iraq based on its supposed support for international terrorism. That war ended with the withdrawal of American troops by the end of 2011. However, after all the wars against militant jihadi organizations, militant *jihad* does not seem to be defeated or even close to being defeated. It is still a dominant feature of the Arab and Muslim landscape and may remain so indefinitely, given the growing danger of the ISIL organization and the US-led international coalition (composed of American allies in Arab, Muslim and Western countries) fighting the threats from this group.

The Various General Currents of Political Islam

When talking about political Islam, it is important to distinguish between its two main Sunni and Shiite[108] branches in order to fully understand it. Although it existed in various forms for decades in the Arab and Muslim worlds, this distinction became important as a local and international political factor after the Iranian Islamic Revolution in 1979, which was the greatest threat felt by the West at that time. In particular, the Iranian Islamic Revolution collided with the greatest international actor, the United States of America,[109] when militant Iranians stormed the American embassy in Tehran on November 4, 1979 and held its staff hostage for 444 days. Because the Shiites are a minority in the Arab and Muslim worlds in general (about 20 percent of total Muslims) and in most countries in which they live, they tend to defend their interests as a "minority" in a broader Sunni environment. Also, because Shiite scholars hold strong and dominant status in Shiite communities, the followers of the sect have remained united. Unlike Sunni communities, they have not witnessed such divisions into different forms of political–religious activity.[110]

In this regard, it is important to recall that all of political Islam is indeed a conservative current, by the very nature of its call for restoring the values of the past and rebuilding the first Islamic state which political religious groups consider as the means to achieve the embodiment of religious traditions that is free from any ideas alien to Islam—especially Westernization and contemporary social globalization. In this context, one researcher argues that political Islam is conservative because its positions "derive their frame of reference and fundaments from the founding past of the Islamic *da'wa* (call to Islam), and because it aspires to improve conditions as a result of its social belonging."[111] Political Islam is indeed a result of the stirring up of socially and morally discontented and frustrated middle classes in society, which try to find some space to work in order to change their reality. It is also a reflection of the failure of the Arab and Muslim liberal right in particular – which is the beneficiary of the existing economic situation – and its inability to provide political, economic and social alternatives to address the prevalent problems in the Arab and Muslim worlds.[112]

Sunni political Islam, on which the West and many researches and studies focus today, appears militant and a threat to Western interests, although political religious groups are not

unified and do not have common principles, visions or intellectual approaches. Also, the West itself does not lump them into one category when dealing with them, as some of these groups – such as the Muslim brotherhood – have remained friends with the West for long periods because they have been thought of as representing a majority of Muslims. This, of course, was the case before recent events in the Arab Republic of Egypt, the failure of the Muslim Brotherhood in authority and their removal in the revolution of June 30, 2013.

Political Islam includes three major currents, and a fourth that has joined national and religious liberation movements. Each current has its own world view and *modus operandi*:[113]

1. **Non-violent Political Islam:** this appears in the form of political religious groups in the Arab and Muslim worlds and in other countries where Muslim communities are allowed to establish political–Islamic entities. Certainly, the goal of political Islam and its groups was and still is to reach authority at the national level. These groups – in spite of their efforts to widen their operating theater, such as the Muslim Brotherhood group, which tried to create organizations fully or partially affiliated to it in the GCC states, for example – claim that they renounce political violence and comply with democratic principles. After the beginning of the waves of Arab change in early 2011, it appeared that these groups intended to completely transform their societies into religious states, as was the case in the Arab Republic of Egypt before mid-2013 and in the

Republic of Tunisia before the collapse of the Ennahdha government in January 2014.[114]

Some researchers and figureheads of political religious groups view the Turkish Justice and Development Party as a model of non-violent political Islam.[115] This party underwent significant change in its orientations after it rid itself of the influence of the first generations that championed the emergence of Turkish political Islam in the 1950s. Before the establishment of this party, there were four Islamic-oriented parties, namely: the National Order Party, the National Salvation Party, the Welfare Party and the Virtue Party, which were all led by Necmettin Erbakan, the conservative Islamist who challenged the Turkish military between the 1960s and 1990s.[116] In 1996, he became Prime Minister but was overthrown by the military in a bloodless coup in 1997. The story of Erbakan and the Turkish military establishment is a long one. However, it is sufficient to say a long historical enmity existed between Erbakan and the Turkish military establishment, which considered itself the guardian and protector of secularism and the country's secular constitution. His first party – the National Order Party – was founded in 1970 but dissolved by the military establishment in 1971; the National Salvation Party was established in 1972 and was also dissolved by the military establishment in 1980; then the "Welfare Party" was formed in 1983 after the approval of the new constitution and the return to parliamentary politics, but was also dissolved in 1997 after Erbakan was deposed. Thereafter Erbakan founded the Virtue Party in 1998, which was banned in 2001. The basis on which all these parties were dissolved was their religious profile and the insistence of Erbakan and his aides and supporters on the idea of transforming Turkish political and social life by changing the history of the modern Turkish state, which was founded by the leader of Turkish secularism Mustafa Kemal (Ataturk) after he abolished the Ottoman empire and Caliphate in 1924.[117]

The Justice and Development Party was founded in 2001 by Recep Tayyip Erdoğan, who was the mayor of Istanbul, and Abdullah Gul, who later became President of Turkey, and others.[118] These two founders were among the youth who worked with Erbakan in the 1990s and made the Islamic current and its ideology a pivot of their political activities. However, it could be argued that Turkish political Islam, since the days of Erbakan, learned to live with a system controlled by the military top brass and subjected to considerable military-backed authoritarian doctrine. The best lesson it learned was to be moderate in its social and political agenda and discourse. While Erbakan started his political life by pushing towards a return to religion and conservative religious life, Erdoğan proposed the idea of conservative democracy instead of the Islamic orientation slogan. Thus, he succeeded in attracting many members of the urban middle class, although it was the Turkish countryside that was a long-time stronghold of any Islamic-oriented party, whatever its name.[119]

Even when Necmettin Erbakan formed a coalition government in 1996 with Tansu Çiller, the leader of the "True Path Party," after the surprise success of his party in the general elections of 1995, winning the largest number of parliamentary seats, he exhibited an attitude of moderation from the first days. Çiller was an advocate of Turkish secularism. She politically grew up among the secularists and maintained wider relations with Europe. She successfully worked together with Erbakan for one year; she served as Prime Minister from 1993 to 1996 before forming a coalition government with Erbakan between June 28, 1996 and June 30 1997.[120] During the coalition government, the Turkish economy achieved reasonable success after the crises that hit it in early 1990s.[121] This indicates that if political religious groups modify their political and religious ideology, they could find political partners who would cooperate with them in achieving national goals. But the problem in the Turkish case also lies in the fanatic adherence of the military establishment to secularism, which Turkish political Islam itself, led by Recep Tayyip Erdoğan, managed to change after more than ten years in authority since 2002.

On the other hand, the success of Turkish political Islam was not a result of its religious background alone, but

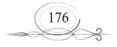

also because it avoided imposing its religious ideology on society at the beginning. Instead, the Justice and Development Party introduced structural and economic reforms in Turkish institutions—especially the military, judicial and security establishments. It focused on trying to join the European Union, a plan initiated by the secularists before it in 1960.

It also opened the doors to Western capitalism and managed to utilize all forms of investment to improve the economic conditions of ordinary Turkish citizens. It helped the industrial bourgeoisie of Anatolia in making the Republic of Turkey an industrial country, by focusing on raising economic performance and efficiency. This is why the Turkish Islamists are viewed as a possible model to be followed by other Arab and Muslim countries, even Erdoğan himself said to those celebrating with him in the parliamentary elections of 2011 that Sarajevo, Beirut, Damascus, the West Bank and Jerusalem also won in the Turkish elections. Nonetheless, what the Party did not succeed in was how to convince the secularists that it did not seek the "Islamization" of society after it weakened secular institutions.[122] In other words, the Turkish Islamists are still facing the difficult task of overcoming their militant history in pursuing what they considered their primary mission behind their involvement in politics, i.e. the achievement of their image of the virtuous Islamic state.

It may also be noted that the Justice and Development Party saw a change in its political practice following its latest electoral success in 2011 when it formed a new government without any alliances with other parties. This allowed it to lead the country in a direction which made it more difficult to convince the secularists that it did not aim to bring more conservatism to the country and its institutions, particularly social conservatism. In 2012–2013, the Party returned to focusing on its Islamic identity and moved away from the pragmatism which enabled it to seize authority in the first place. It introduced laws passed by the parliament regulating dress, curbing alcohol consumption and banning mixed-sex dorms for students.[123] However, criticism recently leveled by the Islamic preacher Fethullah Gülen against the Party and its leader Recep Tayyip Erdoğan, the corruption cases involving the family of Erdoğan himself, the practices of current Turkish President Recep Tayyip Erdoğan when he was Prime Minister and attempted to restrict the public political sphere—all these were indicative of some problems or dilemmas afflicting the rule of Turkish political Islam.[124] The last evidence of Erdoğan's attempts to restrict the public sphere was the banning of the social networking site Twitter in the Republic of Turkey, accusing its users of launching what he called a smear campaign against his government. This measure was criticized by former Turkish President Abdullah Gul, who belongs to the same ruling party, indicating differences within the party over how to deal with issues of public freedoms.[125]

The profound, deep-rooted differences that erupted between the Turkish President Recep Tayyip Erdoğan when he was Prime Minister and the preacher Fethullah Gülen speak to the intent of the political Islamic current to exploit religion to achieve its interests. Gülen always warned of Erdoğan's extremism and his tendency to antagonize the military establishment. Also, Erdoğan's domestic policies and the corruption revealed involving his party and family gave Gülen's religious movement a noticeable local context in Turkey.[126] In foreign policy terms, Gülen represented a challenge to Erdoğan in Central Asia, where his network of schools and newspapers extended. He criticized Erdoğan's policies in the Middle East—from his defiance of Israel and intervention to support the Islamists in the Syrian Arab Republic, to his openness towards the Islamic Republic of Iran and his differences with the Kingdom of Saudi Arabia over the Arab Republic of Egypt and the Republic of Tunisia.

The experience of the Muslim Brotherhood group's rule in the Arab Republic of Egypt proved that the semblance of political moderation was only a means to achieve its political ends.

If "moderation" is a characteristic of political Islam in Turkey, as some researchers argue, the Muslim Brotherhood group in the Arab Republic of Egypt – particularly before the political change that took place in 2011 and its rise to authority after the 2012 elections – was also considered to be among those groups embracing non-violent political Islam. Necmettin Erbakan was influenced by the Muslim Brotherhood group in his youth, when it claimed to work through peaceful means to achieve what it considered to be its goal of helping the Muslim *umma*. However, the events following the rise of the Egyptian Muslim Brotherhood to authority proved it was way far from moderate. The group revealed its exclusionary intentions and used its new political role to present itself as if it were the official mouthpiece of all Muslims. It showed that the attempts to hide behind the veneer of political moderation were nothing but a means to achieve its political goals. In other words, the group, after reaching authority, started to show its militant nature in a way even its most committed ideological enemies did not expect.[127] In the literature of its founder, Hassan Al-Banna, the Muslim Brotherhood group called for a return to the early roots of Islam and for the rebuilding of the unified Islamic *umma* and state, on the pretext of defending Muslim lands against Westernization and Western colonization. The group was not an armed movement. In 1938, however, it developed a military arm and began training its members and forming a special wing – or the so-called 'secret apparatus' – to carry out military operations. That move coincided with the rise of Fascism and Nazism in Europe.[128]

In any case, it is indisputable that political religious groups describing themselves as moderate – or considered so by some researchers[129] – do not object to the use of violence and military action when it serves their political interests.

2. **Religious Preaching Groups:** these groups operate within the framework of preaching and spreading the faith. There are two types of such groups: the faith-spreading (*tabligh*) movement with a hierarchical organization and strong institutional structure, and the unorganized Salafi movement. The latter managed to find for itself a political role in the Arab countries that have recently witnessed change, such as the Arab Republic of Egypt. The Salafi Al-Noor Party in the Arab Republic of Egypt won 121 seats, representing 24 percent of parliamentary seats in the 2012 elections,[130] despite the aversion of the Salafi current to politics in the past when it considered it a distraction from the worship of God (Allah). But authority is ultimately the desire of a broad segment of the Salafi current because they consider it an elevation of the status of Muslims and faith.

The Tablighi Jamaat (the Society for Spreading Faith) group was founded in the third decade of the 20th century by Muhammad Ilyas in India.[131] It then expanded to Arab and Muslim countries and established branches in the Islamic Republic of Pakistan and the People's Republic of Bangladesh, and entered the Syrian Arab Republic, the

Lebanese Republic, the State of Qatar, the Republic of Iraq, the Arab Republic of Egypt, the Republic of the Sudan, the State of Palestine and other countries[132] The goal of the group is the spread of Islam and its teachings to non-Muslims and among Muslims who the group considers has strayed away from the pure religion. The group evokes Islamic history to assert the centrality of the idea of preaching and spreading Islam across the globe. Its method of preaching is based on certain principles: attestation that there is no god but Allah and that the Prophet Muhammad (pbuh) is His last Messenger, and following the way of the Prophet's companions and their moral tradition; performance of prayers with submission and all humility; deep learning of religion to benefit spiritually from it; treatment of fellow Muslims with love and deference and making efforts to guide and teach them; sincerity of intentions and honesty in performing every human action; and going out to preach and spread the faith everywhere. The most important characteristic of this group is its aversion to politics because it distracts Muslims from the worship of God (Allah) and the spreading of His religion, according to its members.[133]

The Salafi current is inherently conservative and passionately adherent to the religious teachings and belief sanctioned by the righteous ancestors—the Rightly-Guided Caliphs, the companions of the Prophet (pbuh) and followers.[134] Salafism is associated with what is known as

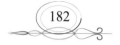

Wahhabism (*Wahhabi da'wa*) which was founded by the Imam Muhammad ibn Abdul Wahhab in the Najd and widely spread after it was adopted by Muhammad ibn Saud as the brand of Islam for the Saudi State in 1745.[135] Salafi preaching is centered on the principle of *tawheed* (the unity/oneness of God (Allah)) and the rejection of unusual Islamic interpretations. It sees that the only pathway to a virtuous life is to follow the Holy Quran and the Noble Sunnah and abstain from personal interpretation of the faith; which essentially means the absence of different ideas and interpretations. According to the Salafi view, any opinion contrary to what is stated by the righteous ancestors is either rejected or at least questionable. At the same time, the Salafis believe that they apply correct religious principles, which are derived from two main sources: the Holy Quran and the Noble Sunnah. According to them, if a person follows their way, he will arrive at the perfect flawless truth.[136]

Several Salafi groups equally rely on principles drawn from the four main sources (the Holy Quran, the Noble Sunnah, Consensus and Analogy) but they differ in their views and stances towards the spread of faith and Islamic thought and the practicing of politics. However, one current of Salafism – jihadi Salafism – adopts a more militant approach, and believes that violence will help change the status quo. This current can include among its enemies other Muslims whom it considers to be deviating from the straight path, from the application of the law (*Sharia*) of God (Allah) and from the consensus of religious jurists and people of the nation.[137] In Chapter 4 of this book, I will discuss the currents of Salafism in more detail to pinpoint the differences between them.

The Egyptian Al-Noor Party represents the Salafi current in the Arab Republic of Egypt. It was formed after the January 25, 2011 protests that toppled former president Muhammad Husni Mubarak. The party – as a political entity – overstepped what were considered the recognized fundamentals of the Salafi discourse, which required abstinence from politics because it distracts the believers from the way of God (Allah). The Egyptian Salafis were previously content with preaching, sermonizing and guiding, and non-interference in politics. They considered opposition to be a disobedience to the Muslim ruler. One researcher states that the Salafis basically did not support change because of this principle, and when they decided to transform themselves into a political party, they were criticized by other Salafi scholars who rejected politicization, [138]and also by mass protestors who did not get their full support. In spite of that, they decided to enter into politics[139] in the 2012 parliamentary elections, the constitutional amendments after the overthrow of former president Dr. Muhammad Mursi and the referendum on the latest constitution in January 2014.

The vice president of the Salafi movement, Yassir Burhami – in his comment about the Egyptian constitution endorsed

in 2014 after the overthrow of the Muslim Brotherhood group in the Arab Republic of Egypt – said the constitution was satisfactory and sufficient because it contains principles that the Salafi movement embraces and defends,[140] such as consensus and legitimacy of its provisions in terms of commitment to religious principles. Burhami used many expressions and explanations that were a far cry from the main, clear and direct demands that the Salafis used to voice before the overthrow of former president Muhammad Husni Mubarak. He also talked about the available and possible options, focusing only on what was legitimately required. This means that the Salafi Al-Noor Party was willing to change its literal interpretation of religion for the sake of entering into politics.[141]

Unlike the Egyptian Salafis, the "Ansar Al-Sharia" (Partisans of Islamic Law) Salafi movement in the Republic of Tunisia chose *jihad* as a means to assert itself politically and socially. It has branches in the State of Libya and eastern parts of the People's Democratic Republic of Algeria. Al-Qa'ida in the Islamic Maghreb (AQIM) appointed Khalid Al-Shaib (aka Abu Luqman) as a leader of the movement.[142] The Ansar Al-Sharia movement itself dates back to the early 1980s, but it suffered major setbacks at the hands of the Tunisian regime during the days of former president Al-Habib Bourguiba. The Tunisian jihadists returned to the scene during the 2011 protests, when they sensed a golden opportunity to assert their political and religious position, but they declared that they were against the Tunisian democracy brought about by the protests and all its subsequent outcomes. The Tunisian "Ansar Al-Sharia" movement once again proved that political Islam, whatever its identity and orientation – be it democratic, peaceful or a promoter and user of violence – strives to establish its own government, although some of its main factions reject political activity.[143] Therefore, it is safe to say that the term Islamic "preaching groups" – except the faith spreading (*tablighi*) movement – has become a vacuous title for what were previously thought to be purely religious groups with no interest attaining authority or controlling the people.

3. **Jihadi Organizations:** these organizations believe in armed struggle on three general fronts: at home, against the regimes they consider not sufficiently Islamic and whose rulers do not apply the law (*Sharia*) of God (Allah); abroad, against those they consider usurpers of Arab and Muslim land and against those they consider "infidels" across the world,[144] and hence may be attacked wherever they are.[145] The most dangerous among these organizations are Al-Qa'ida and its offshoots in North Africa or the Maghreb, the Arabian Peninsula, the Republic of Somalia, the Islamic Republic of Afghanistan, the Islamic Republic of Pakistan and the Chechen Republic, and the Islamic State organization (ISIL) and others. These jihadi organizations can fight specific regimes that they deem "infidel" and "unjust."[146]

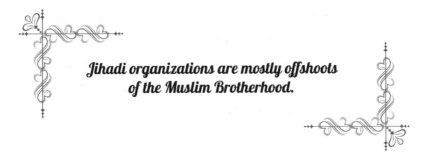

Jihadi organizations are mostly offshoots of the Muslim Brotherhood.

Researchers have tried to investigate the origin of the militancy of jihadi organizations in political Islam, most of which are offshoots of the Muslim Brotherhood, which is considered the parent organization. They investigated the causes of terrorism resulting from militant jihadi thought and jihadi Salafism. They found out that it is possible to group these causes into general categories including: psychological causes, especially mental health problems and deprivation; social causes, especially the economic situation and government and authority affairs; and causes related to the international situation, especially foreign domination and the existence of regional and international powers supportive of these organizations, in addition to failed states, which provide fertile environment for the growth of these organizations.[147]

However, whatever the causes behind the spread of terrorist acts perpetrated by jihadi organizations, the most important goal of these acts is to send a message to Muslims and non-Muslims alike that their perpetrators have an issue that needs be solved, or are trying to exact retribution on those who helped create this issue in the first place, regardless of how just the issue is. Militant jihadis who blow themselves up in attacks on military or civilian targets and kill dozens or even hundreds of Muslims and non-Muslims do not care about the human and material losses they cause; their main goal is to send a specific message, at any cost.[148]

> *Abu Al-A'la Al-Mawdoodi believed the Muslim ummah's decline resulted from practicing a corrupted form of Islam contaminated by non-Islamic ideas and culture.*

Many researchers believe that the source of this evolution of violence are the early theorists of jihadi thought, such as Abu Al-A'la Al-Mawdoodi in the Republic of India, and Hassan Al-Banna and Sayyid Qutb who belonged to the Muslim Brotherhood group in Egypt.[149] Al-Mawdoodi believed that the Muslim *umma*'s decline resulted from practicing a corrupted form of Islam contaminated by non-Islamic ideas and culture.[150] He also believed the acceptance of non-Muslim rule and ideas and non-Islamic regimes was a violation of the law (*Sharia*) of God (Allah), and that the only solution was the establishment of Islamic rule and control of all influences coming from non-Islamic sources. He preached that the only practical way to achieve this was by *jihad* and the use of violence to liberate Muslim societies from Western and Hindu occupations and from *jahili* (un-Islamic) thought, which is alien to Islam.[151]

> *Sayyid Qutb, the theorist of the Muslim Brotherhood, was one of the founders of the violent jihadi current in contemporary political Islam and his writings are a reference for militant extremists and jihadis.*

In regard to Hassan Al-Banna and Sayyid Qutb, through their published works – such as Al-Banna's *jihad* and Qutb's *Fi Zilal Al-Quran* (In the Shades of the Quran) and *Ma'alim fi Al-Tareeq* (Signposts on the Road)[152] – they presented two different models for restoring the dominance of pure Islam against Western hegemony, according to their ideological viewpoint, spreading the pure principles and teachings of Islam among Muslims and achieving their renaissance. In his messages, Al-Banna talked about the gradual implementation of this program, starting by working in schools, mosques, factories and through social entities to provide the social services needed by the poor and destitute.
[153]Al-Banna opted for the gradual implementation of his program, maybe because he lived in a civil state that enjoyed stability and national security under Western/ British occupation. This, at least at the beginning of his movement

until the early 1930s, encouraged him to resort to preaching, guiding and expanding the influence of the Muslim Brotherhood group, instead of embracing militancy in his political and religious discourse.

Sayyid Qutb was one of the proponents of the violent current in contemporary political Islam. He was a former member of the Guidance Office of the Muslim Brotherhood group, and was inspired by the ideas of Abu Al-A'la Al-Mawdoodi and Hassan Al-Banna.[154] His books and writings are considered a reference for most militant extremists and jihadis in justifying their use of violence and their attacks against what they oppose in the near political arena in the Arab and Muslim countries,[155] and the far political arena, i.e. in non-Muslim countries, especially Western countries, as shown by the dozens of attacks and acts of aggression launched by jihadi organizations against civilians in various Muslim and non-Muslim regions and countries. Sayyid Qutb's thought – which aimed to spread the orientations of the Muslim Brotherhood group during the era when secular nationalism dominated the Egyptian landscape under the rule of Jamal Abdul Nasser – led to his long-term imprisonment and ultimate execution in 1966.[156]

To his followers, Sayyid Qutb's thought is characterized by its simplicity and direct nature. It does not contain any jurisprudential ambiguities or complexities. On the practical side, Qutb focused on a top-down strategy of social and political change by removing what he considered *jahili*

(ignorant of Islam) rulers and governments which did not govern their peoples in accordance with the ideal Islamic way and did not fight Western countries and governments which occupied the Muslim land and controlled its resources.[157]

> *In his thought, Sayyid Qutb focused on describing Muslim societies as jahiliyya (ignorant of Islam) and deviant from the correct teachings of Islam.*

In his book *Ma'alim fi Al-Tareeq* (Signposts on the Road), Sayyid Qutb described Muslim societies at that time as *jahiliyya* (ignorant of Islam) and deviant from the correct Islamic teachings and values. According to one researcher, Sayyid Qutb here did not exclude any Muslim sect or denomination from *takfir* or targeting, and did not differentiate between countries and their citizens because they were together the repository of error and deviance from the pure religion. He accused the state of sponsoring this deviance from the law of God (Allah) and acts of worship, and the spread of social and moral corruption through the expanding influence of infidel Western cultures. He believed that the only way to correct Muslim society and bring it back to the way of religion was to apply the principle of *hakimiyya* under which there would be no law or rule but that of God (Allah).[158]

The thoughts of Sayyid Qutb and other theorists of jihadi ideology clearly contradict many modern values and ideas. The jihadis attack freedom, ideas of human rights, modernity and nationalism. They understand them in a completely different way to the general concepts associated with them, and they consider them a reflection of Westerners' domination over Arab and Muslim political and social discourse. To them, freedom means freedom to do "righteous deeds," according to their own narrow-minded understanding of this term, but not freedom to do whatever one wishes as Westerners would understand it. According to them, a deed of righteousness is the work towards the application of the rule of God (Allah) on Earth – or what is known as *hakimiyya* – but not submission to emotions and instincts. As for human rights, they are not a person's rights but a set of obligations and duties ordained upon him in order to follow the path of God (Allah). The concept of secularism, according to them and other currents of political Islam, contradicts Islam, which focuses on religion and state combined. They also believe that nationalism tends to divide Muslims and separate them from each other, and this is wrong, because the Muslim *umma* is one and its goals are the same, and it works to achieve its religious unity in order to serve God (Allah) and His *Sharia*.[159]

One researcher argues that what is called political Islam today is nothing but a militant, fundamentalist and highly politicized Islam. It is used for purposes beyond religious ones, and its objective is to distort the mentality of the *umma* and impose on it a certain opinion instead of allowing it to decide its life and orientation by itself.[160]

In addition to being a jihadi combatant movement fighting on the ground and carrying out attacks against local and international targets, the Al-Qa'ida organization is quite modern in its operation and uses modern technologies in communication, recruitment, training and the execution of operations, as if it is a government that controls institutions and finances their operations. Al-Qa'ida and other jihadi organizations – allied with it or otherwise – have managed to utilize modern technologies for recruitment and to spread their propaganda by building websites and communicating via advanced media in various languages. They have even created their own broadcasting stations, but their locations are unknown. As the French thinker Gilles Kepel says, The "Al-Qa'ida" organization today does not control a specific land that could be occupied or a regime that could be changed, but by its use of technologies, it looks modern and sophisticated. Its former leader and founder, Usama bin Ladin, was not a typical Wahhabi but adapted to modern life and sought to apply his ideas and convictions and translate them into terrorist plots and acts using all available modern means, whether in terms of using advanced weapons and explosives or in recruiting new members and communicating with members of the organization via modern tools.[161]

Abdullah Azzam, Usama bin Ladin and Ayman Al-Zawahiri were among the most prominent students of Qutbism.

The ideology of Al-Qa'ida, which originated in the thoughts of Sayyid Qutb and Abu Al-A'la Al-Mawdoodi, is the perfect expression of the jihadi ideology. Among the students of Qutbism were Abdullah Azzam and Ayman Al-Zawahiri, each of whom helped in attracting Usama bin Ladin to this thought after they met him in the Islamic Republic of Afghanistan during the war against the Soviets. Following the assassination of Azzam in mysterious circumstances in the Islamic Republic of Pakistan in 1989,[162] and the unification of the Services Office – which was run by Usama bin Ladin – with the Egyptian Islamic Jihad group – which was led by Al-Zawahiri – to form the Al-Qa'ida organization, the jihadi ideology made an enormous qualitative leap. The focus now moved to global *jihad*, specifically to fighting the United States of America in order to drain and weaken it through wars across the Arab and Muslim worlds until it would stop supporting Israel and what they considered the "corrupt" Arab regimes. After that, Al-Qa'ida and its allies could attack the United States of America and hit it where it hurts.[163] On the other hand, Usama bin Ladin and Al-Zawahiri may have decided to fight the external enemy as escapism because it was difficult to topple the internal enemy – the Arab and Muslim regimes – or because they believed that their concentration on the external enemy would attract support for Al-Qa'ida from the peoples of the Arab and Muslim worlds.

Before Al-Qa'ida and its affiliates, there were many militant religious parties, such as the Islamic party Hizb-ut-Tahrir (Islamic Party of Liberation) which was founded in Jerusalem in 1953.[164] Hizb-ut-Tahrir is banned in many countries of the world and its leaders are scattered in a number of Arab and Muslim countries.[165] This party believes that there is neither an extreme nor a moderate Islam but only an eternal religious truth that says anyone who does not believe in Islam is a *kafir* (infidel) who should be forced to believe or become a subject of the Islamic state and live as a *thimmi* (non-Muslim citizen). It also believes that there is no option other than fighting the *kuffar* (infidels) through *jihad* and bloodshed, if they refuse to accept Islam. This physical jihadi struggle comes after the intellectual struggle. The party maintains that the current weakness of the Muslim *umma* is nothing but a reflection of the old foreign interventions since the Crusades and the new interventions in the era of colonialism and occupation.

So, the Muslim *umma* does not have any alternative other than fighting for its religious and political liberation through struggle against the infidel West in intellectual and bloody physical wars. Importantly, the party considers so-called moderate Islam to be an unbearable mistake, because there is no moderation in Islam but literal application of the creed and faith as stated in the revealed Holy Quran and the Noble Sunnah.[166]

4. **Islamic National Liberation Movements**: these movements intellectually and ideologically belong to the political Islam current. They operate within their Muslim environment and at the same time constitute a nucleus and key element in the national liberation movements in their respective countries. Geographically, these groups extend from the eastern part of the Arab and Islamic worlds to their western part. Here, I will focus on two movements of this type – one is a Sunni Islamic movement and the other is a Shiite Islamic movement – in order to explore whether the doctrinal differences change their thoughts or their belonging to the main current of political Islam.[167]

The first movement of national liberation, backed by Islamic political thought, is the Islamic Resistance Movement (Hamas) in Palestine, which has been in control of the Gaza Strip since 2007. In short, the Hamas Movement was founded in 1987 at the beginning of the first *intifada* (uprising), after the Islamic jihadi current had already established some movements, such as the Islamic Jihad Movement in 1981 and the Ahmad

Yaseen Group in 1983. It is worth mentioning that that period witnessed various intellectual and operational changes in Palestinian reality and thought. Detractors of the Palestine Liberation Organization (PLO) began to show an intention and will to form a rival faction to the PLO, which, they thought, had become reluctant in its duty to liberate Palestine, and was responsible for the Arab and Muslim worlds losing interest in the just Palestinian cause. The vanguards of Islamic Jihad activity started among students who took upon themselves the task of daily confrontation with the Zionist occupiers of the West Bank and the Gaza Strip. Then armed jihadi operations of the Hamas Movement grew from mere knife attacks against Israeli soldiers to the establishment of a military wing by the end of 1991 called the Izz Al-Deen Al-Qassam Brigades.[168]

Hamas remains connected to political religious groups, and it is a faction affiliated to the Muslim Brotherhood group. This means that non-violent political Islam can include some movements that believe in the use of force.[169] The Hamas Movement, like its parent group in the Arab Republic of Egypt, believes in the religious state, where religion is inseparable from politics.[170] As soon as it secured its control over the Gaza Strip in 2007, Hamas began to impose restrictions on personal and social freedoms, although it did not go as far as imposing the full codes of conduct and dress existing in an Islamic country like the Islamic Republic of Iran. However, the biggest factor affecting the Hamas Movement today, and its evolution and survivability as an Islamic movement is its being a resistance movement to Israel, i.e. it positions itself as part of the Palestinian national liberation movement. It does not recognize any right of the Jews in Palestine, although it accepts a gradual solution and a temporary truce with Israel based on the 1967 borders, pending the advent of the integrated Arab Islamic plan to liberate the entire historical Palestine; from river to sea. The Movement sees the struggle with the Israeli occupation as "a struggle of existence, not a border dispute."[171]

The second movement is the Lebanese Hezbollah Party, which combines a number of concepts, ideologies and practices not wholly confined to the current of political Islam, although considered synonymous with it. Hezbollah is the strongest spearhead of the Islamic Republic of Iran, which adopts a Shiite political religious ideology and governs the state and society according to a creed based on the idea of representing or acting on behalf of the Hidden Imam and preparing for his appearance.[172] In this context, one researcher argues that Hezbollah is an extension of the Shiite parties and groups in the Lebanese Republic and the region, but cannot be studied the same way as other contemporary religious organizations and groups, specifically because it has developed for itself an additional record in the confrontation with Israel.[173]

The Party came into being in response to the Israeli invasion of the Lebanese Republic in 1982. It was formed with strong Iranian support and a key Syrian role due to the Syrian military presence in the Lebanese Republic, where the

Iranian Revolutionary Guard Corps was able to enter the country and provide the necessary training, mobilization and preparation of the surroundings, environment and land. On the political side, which is not devoid of a religious dimension, the formation of the Party was a reflection of militancy that gripped the Shiite sect in the Lebanese Republic following the Israeli invasion and was reinforced by Iranian support and the waning role of the Shiite Amal Movement.[174] Hezbollah was primarily an advocate of overturning the Lebanese political system, or the so-called Lebanese political "Maronism" – where the president of the Republic is required to be a Maronite – and establishing an Islamic state modeled on the Islamic Republic of Iran.[175]

Another researcher says that the Lebanese Hezbollah Party began to define itself in the 1980s as a follower of the principle of *Wilayat Al-Faqeeh* (the Guardianship of the Jurist) in the Islamic Republic of Iran and declared its explicit Shiite identity. Its relationship with the Iranian regime was, and still is, both religious and political.[176] He also says:

> In the literature and practices of the Hezbollah Party at its formation, the Shiite religious tendency was stronger than its Lebanese leaning. However, the problem after the 1980s sprung from the fact that the Party made a strategic decision to enter into politics and try to influence the system of government in a country with a multitude of sects and parties. This made its militant religious discourse quite disturbing and frightened many

people, even among its own non-Shiite allies. To soothe
the situation, the Party and its leaders tried their best to
avoid such a discourse and to focus instead on criticizing
the new world order, which the Party saw as favoring
capitalist and Western countries in general.[177]

The Lebanese Hezbollah Party is Iran's spearhead in the eastern Mediterranean.

In fact, by tracking its recent thoughts and actions, particularly
since the end of the Israeli aggression against the Lebanese
Republic in 2006, the Hezbollah Party appears an odd element
in the Lebanese body politic. This is due to the fact that the
Party is armed like a country and capable of withstanding any
military confrontation. It takes hold of the Shiite street in the
Lebanese Republic, not just by virtue of its presence as a
political representative of Lebanese Shiites (the other representative
being the Amal Movement), but also because it has succeeded
in making the Shiites scared of their wider Sunni Arab
environment, and has succeeded in recruiting thousands of
fighters from among them. Moreover, the Party is the spearhead
of the Iranian regime in the eastern Mediterranean and is
fighting with all its might in the Syrian Arab Republic alongside
the regime of president Bashar Al-Assad. The Hezbollah Party
is accused of playing a visible role in fueling sectarian strife in

the Arab Middle East and the Arabian Gulf region. Meanwhile, it continues in its media and political discourse to defend, first, its Shiite religious identity; second, its role in fighting what it considers a conspiracy against the Islamic "resistance"; and third, political Shiism in the Lebanese Republic, which has become a threat not only to the privileges of other sects but also to the rights of those sects. The Party has even become a real threat to the very survival of the country itself because of its subordination to Iranian policy in the Syrian Arab Republic and the Lebanese Republic.[178]

What connects these various types of political religious groups is that they all take advantage of the development problems afflicting many Arab and Muslim countries and exploit them to expand their role in the Islamic socio-political domain, especially in the Arab and Muslim worlds. In addition, they all criticize financial, administrative and political corruption in the Arab and Muslim countries, claiming that the absence of social justice is a result of politicians' divergence from pure religious teachings and political commitments to serving peoples. Also, before the outbreak of the recent wave of change in the Arab and Muslim worlds, these groups sought to present themselves as suitable and effective alternatives to the ruling regimes. However, after these groups acquired authority in some Arab and Muslim countries, it became clear that they were not as perfect as they claimed, and were just as prone to failure and setback as the political organizations, parties and currents that preceded them.

Evaluation of the Thought of Political Islam

Numerous critiques were directed against the ideological foundation of political Islam and its practices, since its emergence as a movement that uses religion to implement its political project. Critiques can be focused on the following key issues.

1. The goal of rebuilding the Caliphate. The ideological pivot of political Islam, which prioritizes the reestablishment of the Caliphate model, its importance and centrality, is wrong in its belief in the applicability of this concept and in considering it the right answer to the problems facing the Arab and Muslim worlds. The development that human society has seen since the era of the Rightly-Guided Caliphs and the complexity of the structure of society has forced everyone – Muslims and non-Muslims alike – to develop their institutions and structures in order to respond to these changes, and to introduce non-religious criteria into the religious parameters of life.

Also, this issue is not a subject of consensus among political religious groups themselves. According to one researcher, the dream of an Islamic Caliphate is controversial among the Islamists themselves, especially among militant Salafis and traditional currents which agreed to engage in the political process, and the Islamists and secular currents that fear the domination of religious thought on the state, including some groups that may not believe in political Islamic thought or belong to other sects.[179]

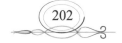

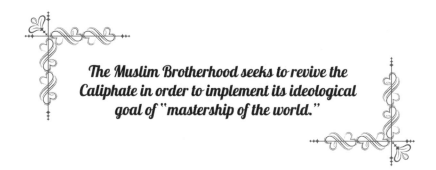

The Muslim Brotherhood seeks to revive the Caliphate in order to implement its ideological goal of "mastership of the world."

Some leaders and figureheads may say that what they mean today by the Caliphate state is not exactly what others understand. They may claim so, although the General Guide of the Muslim Brotherhood group, Muhammed Abdul Majeed Badie, said that the group helped in reviving the Caliphate as a means for Muslims to achieve "mastership of the world."[180] This is the statement that the Muslim Brotherhood tries to reinterpret by saying that what Badie said in early 2011 was just a reminder that the overthrow of the regime of former President Muhammad Husni Mubarak was a step towards achieving the hope of the Arab peoples for an Islamic renaissance project, which would increase the convergence between the Arab and Muslim countries, according to their view. They argue that the Caliphate they mean is not in its old sense, but in a form that emulates modern reality.[181] However, the belief that the revival of the Caliphate contributes to the betterment of the Arab and Muslim worlds ignores many related issues and factors. Moreover, the belief that the early Islamic state was free of political, economic and social problems is contrary to the historical track of that state and what was written about it and its problems.

Every entity or country has its own problems, which vary in their severity and the way they are addressed.

Furthermore, the belief that it is possible to recreate the objective conditions for that Caliphate runs against the laws of nature and human history. Hence – no matter how strong and applicable the call is - it is difficult to convince the majority of Muslims to coexist with a system of government that is historically obsolete and no longer possesses the characteristics of continued positive interaction and engagement with the dynamics of international relations in the modern age, or to convince them to isolate themselves from the international environment in this age of globalization and interdependence among countries and the urgent need for economic, technological, industrial and cultural development. Based on this, I could say that the idea of reviving the Caliphate is controversial and meant to convince Muslims to chase an unobtainable mirage.[182]

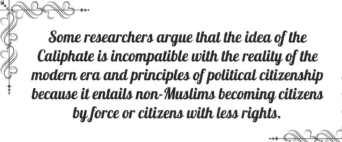

Some researchers argue that the idea of the Caliphate is incompatible with the reality of the modern era and principles of political citizenship because it entails non-Muslims becoming citizens by force or citizens with less rights.

On the other hand, the idea of the Caliphate is incompatible with the reality of the modern era and principles of political and social citizenship. The Islamists see no harm in imposing a head

of state, for example, provided that he is necessarily a Muslim, although sometimes they differ about which religious school of thought he should be from. Each group of Islamists insists that the head of state should be from its school of thought and be male. This means that no non-Muslim citizen or woman has the right to reach the seat of authority.

This debate is associated with what is called the grand guardianship or the supreme Imamate, where some *fatwas* (legal opinions) show that the community of religious scholars has agreed upon specific standards and conditions for the guardianship of Muslim affairs including: responsibility, sound mindedness, and adulthood. Guardianship cannot be handed to a child or someone mentally ill, because they are under the guardianship of others, so they cannot be guardians of Muslims. Also, the guardian should be male, for female guardianship is not acceptable, and guardianship by non-Muslims is not permissible.[183] These two latter requirements in particular have recently become a subject of controversy. Some leading women in several Arab and Muslim countries have asked the Muslim Brotherhood group and the Salafi movements to present a clear explanation of their opinion on the issue of the "grand guardianship" in order to resolve the controversy about women assuming the office of the presidency.[184] The debate has extended to the status of non-Muslims in these countries, where political religious groups, and even some preachers who are not affiliated with these groups, reject handing the grand guardianship to a non-Muslim. This has caused domestic political tensions in many Arab and Muslim countries, as in the case of protests by political religious groups against the appointment in November 2014 of a Christian politician, Tjahaja Purnama, as governor of the Indonesian capital Jakarta for the first time in fifty years, which was seen as an indicator of the strengthening of democratic reforms.[185]

According to some researchers, ignoring the difference between the concept of the Caliphate and contemporary realities would prevent the implementation of real citizenship principles and result in non-Muslims becoming citizens by force or citizens with less rights.[186] Also, there is no mechanism that gives citizens – whoever they are – an idea of how to select the head of state who, once selected, would control them, as he would represent the country at home and abroad.

2. The continued belief in the possibility of fusing religion and politics. The main argument of political religious groups – be they traditional, militant or jihadi – is that Islam is both religion and state, and these two components are inseparable. They consider the civil state incompatible to Islam. The philosophical religious basis of this position relates to the issue of man's relationship with God (Allah). For political religious groups, there is no individual relationship, as the Holy Quran speaks of and deals with the "Muslim community" and thus – according to their view – it is illogical to separate religion from state, because such a separation means the cancellation of nearly 600 Quranic verses, such as those concerning fighting, retribution and others.[187] Moreover, one researcher argues that the slogan

"Islam is both religion and state," though clever and attractive to many people, was invented by the Muslim Brotherhood group in the early 20th century and no one had mentioned it before. Also, that slogan is more an "ideologized" political one than the product of an analysis of the social and political history of Islam.[188]

The insistence on fusing religion and state conceals a failure to answer various questions relating to the thoughts and ideas of political religious groups. If they acknowledge the possibility of separating religion from state, they have to come up with new solutions to many social issues, especially those concerning women and the equality between them and men; private property and human rights which require the abandonment of *hudood* (prescribed punishments) like death, amputation and retribution; freedom of belief and worship for citizens; the position towards non-Muslims; the role of religion in education and its status in systems of knowledge and research; and finally – and most importantly – the role of Islamic *Sharia* in daily life and the rule of the state.[189] Regarding the positions towards these social issues, we find many similarities between political religious groups – Sunni and Shiite alike – and Christian and Jewish right wing fanatics who have tried since the 1960s to introduce amendments to educational systems in the United States of America, such as the imposition of the religious interpretation of natural phenomenon, the Creation and the status of women in society.[190]

Certainly, the separation of religion and state does not mean its separation from society. Religion is deeply rooted and engrained in society, its traditions, customs and history; and the state is neither religion nor society, but a set of institutions, policies and persons whom govern society. Neither is religion society, although it is an important social force. In this context, one researcher has said:

> The slogan "the religion of the state is Islam" is ridiculous, because it portrays the state in the form of a man that goes to the mosque to pray. Indeed, the state does not pray, make pilgrimage, fast or pay *Zakat*. The fear from all of this is that religion may become a tool in the hands of the state to use it whenever it wants. This also undermines the concepts of citizenship, equality and law.[191]

The same researcher argues that the insistence on considering the principles of *Sharia* as the primary or sole source of legislation in the constitution makes the followers of other religions feel like second-class citizens and fuels their sentiments of discontent, non-belonging and exclusion. The problem also lies in making legislation according to *Sharia* principles and considering *Sharia* as the "primary source of legislation," because this negates the importance of law and citizenship.[192]

It would be difficult to achieve a separation between religion and state in the Arab and Muslim worlds in the short term, but this mixture negatively affects religion and makes it

prone to contamination by political impurities such as bargains, deals and the protection of interests. In addition, there is the issue of religious and ethnic minorities in the Islamic state where there is no separation between religion and state. For this reason, some researchers believe that political religious groups stoke racism and sectarianism at the expense of the state and the concept of citizenship, because their discourse automatically classifies non-Muslims as not being afforded the same freedoms and advantages as others; i.e., they are second-class citizens. This status keeps them under a framework of control wrapped in the cloak of Islamic tolerance of other religions.[193]

In fact, these practices are not in keeping with the tolerance of Islam. Muslims and non-Muslims peacefully coexisted in the Islamic state throughout its history and periods of strength and weakness. Non-Muslims were not forced to abandon their beliefs or coerced into Islam. The supreme rule in Islam is "no compulsion in religion".[194] As a result, the *thimmis* (non-Muslims citizens) and others lived under the protection of the Islamic state, with their beliefs and religions left intact. Islam does not persecute non-Muslims, deny their rights, force them to change their beliefs or treat their property, families and relatives unjustly. The history of Islam in this respect is the brightest and cleanest on Earth. It is known among religious scholars that if someone is forced into Islam, his Islam would not be true[195] pursuant to the Quranic verse: "There shall be no compulsion in religion. The right course has become clear from the wrong."[196]

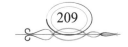

3. The belief that it is possible to establish a single unified Islamic *umma* at the expense of the nation-state. Political religious groups pride themselves on their belief in the idea of a single unified Islamic *umma* instead of the nation-state, which has become the defining feature of political life in a world of diversified cultures, civilizations and religions. Some of these groups call for coordination, not only between Muslim countries but also with non-Muslim countries. Some are militant and call for war against everything non-Islamic and every non-Muslim, and some even call for war within the Arab and Muslim worlds to cleanse the countries of impurities and the creeds that they consider deviant from the principles of pure religion, i.e. Shiism, Sufism and the others.[197] Although some of these groups have succeeded in acquiring authority in some countries – such as the Muslim Brotherhood in the Arab Republic of Egypt, the Republic of Tunisia and the Republic of the Sudan, and the Taliban in the Islamic Republic of Afghanistan, for example – they still call for work to unify the Muslim *umma* instead of dividing Muslims according to their different nationalities, where their Islamic effort is wasted and their identity lost in the views of these groups.

The call to work "for one unified Islamic *umma*" is nothing more than a cover to intervene in the affairs of states on the pretext of changing the current situation of Muslims living within them. For example, the Muslim Brotherhood group gave itself the right to establish branches in the Arab Gulf states – such as the United Arab Emirates – and affiliate religious

associations in other Arab states, and expects loyalty and oath of allegiance to the General Guide of the Muslim Brotherhood in the Arab Republic of Egypt from citizens who are not Egyptians—all this under the cover of the principle of a unified Islamic effort. In this pursuit, it violates the sovereignty of other countries. This can be viewed not only in terms of securing political influence to control the wealth and potential of other countries, but also in terms of the use of religion as a social and political tool acceptable among those who believe in the idea of intervention in the affairs of other nations.[198]

4. A monopoly on political activity and a lack of participation. After the rise of political religious groups to authority in a number of countries in the Arab and Muslim worlds, their political conduct was no different to that of other secular political parties. Political religious groups acquired authority in the Islamic Republic of Iran after the success of the 1979 revolution and the elimination of nationalist, leftist and communist opposition; in the Republic of the Sudan after the Islamist-backed military coup in 1989; in the Islamic Republic of Afghanistan after the arrival of the "Taliban" in Kabul and the end of civil war in 1996; in the Republic of Turkey in 2002; and in the Arab Republic of Egypt and the Republic of Tunisia after the changes that took place in 2011.

In all these cases, these groups pursued their own interests and desires after using religion to reach authority and government, despite the potential pitfalls of such an approach. According to some researchers, political religious groups cannot be credited with initiating the wave of political change in the Republic of Tunisia and the Arab Republic of Egypt, and the political momentum seen in the Arab world would not give these groups any right to claim that they rescued their peoples from the corruption of former ruling regimes. In addition, with their engagement in political activity, political religious groups found themselves face to face with the huge political, cultural and intellectual diversity of their societies, and discovered that they would not be able to transform these societies or change their identity as they would like.[199]

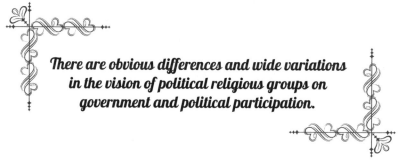

There are obvious differences and wide variations in the vision of political religious groups on government and political participation.

There are many differences among political religious groups – not only at the level of the Arab and Muslim worlds but also within individual countries – in terms of their perception of political participation, and their views on government and various aspects of life; and this reduces their chances to cooperate. For example, there are differences between the Muslim Brotherhood group and the Salafi current. The development of political events in the Arab Republic of Egypt since 2011 revealed these differences, which became a huge obstacle to cooperation between them in achieving their main goal of

establishing the Islamic state.[200] The Muslim Brotherhood group today is considered a pariah and is politically and legally outlawed. Authorities in many Arab countries designate it as a terrorist organization, while the Salafis chose to cooperate with the new public-backed regime and other forces in the country and its institutions. For example, the Al-Noor Party approved the Muslim Brotherhood group's constitution in 2012, but avoided involvement in the issues of removing the former president Dr. Muhammad Mursi in the summer of 2013. However, it supported the army movement, welcomed the new constitution, and voted for it in January 2014.[201]

The Muslim Brotherhood did not consider the opinions of the majority of Egyptian people who rejected the attempt to "Brotherize" the state and its institutions during the rule of former president Dr. Muhammad Mursi. The leaks about suggestions to ban alcohol consumption, impose Islamic dress codes, urge people to pray, and forbid women from going to beaches, in addition to the appointment of Brotherhood members to vital official positions all raised concern among parties, institutions and other forces, because such measures would not only cause unneeded social problems but also adverse economic impacts at a time when the country was suffering mounting economic problems. This situation was not limited to the Arab Republic of Egypt, but had repercussions in the Republic of Tunisia, where the government declared a number of times that it might take measures to reduce aspects of the state's secularism—although it later retracted these statements.[202]

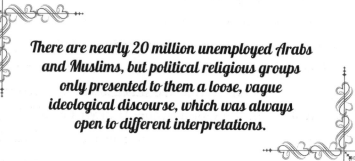

There are nearly 20 million unemployed Arabs and Muslims, but political religious groups only presented to them a loose, vague ideological discourse, which was always open to different interpretations.

5. The lack of a political program. The major problem in the performance of political religious groups – be they traditional or militant – was, and still is, due to the fact that they deal with politics in a reactive manner based on the policies and actions of regimes and governments which they oppose. To them, politics does not depend on specific, calculated political, economic and social programs. Despite differences in their political and national backgrounds and environments, what these political religious groups propose is nothing but arbitrary views, without a theoretical or organizational basis, on well-conceived topics, policies and projects proposed by these governments. Paradoxically, there are high rates of unemployment in the Arab and Muslim countries in which these groups are active – about 20 million people according to 2013 statistics[203] – but they did not present any specific strategic vision to solve this problem other than promoting a loose, vague discourse of propaganda, which is always open to different interpretations. This situation puts the future of Islam at stake, especially given the growing complexity of domestic government matters, the lack of common ground for understanding between political factions about decisive issues, and the confusion in foreign policy as a result of weakness caused by the engagement in political, economic and social globalization.[204]

What complicates the future course of political religious groups is that they do not have the social, political or economic programs like other political groups and parties aspiring to reach authority in order to achieve certain agendas and defend the interests of those who support them. For example, political religious groups did not have any plans or programs to address difficult development problems such as poverty and unemployment, and they left millions of people suffering as a result of these problems during their rule in the Arab Republic of Egypt. They continue to repeat emotional slogans without undertaking any real work on the ground. Thus, these groups lacked the theoretical base of their political proposition, and in place of it they raised non-renewable, non-modifiable Islamic slogans in an environment in which one cannot live and work without adjusting and making interim deals and agreements. With respect to their political programs, political religious groups generally focused on moral, spiritual and social matters. This is not wrong in itself, but it confines the interests of such groups to matters that are not political or economic in nature; and without politics, social life cannot be organized. Furthermore, these groups limit their moral concentration to certain issues, such as women and their status in Islamic society and the protection of Islamic values and morals by controlling means of social contact and preventing gender mixing, and attacking any ideas they consider threatening to Islamic spiritual purity. Some militant political religious groups today even demand the implementation of the *hudood* (prescribed punishments) stated in the *Sharia*.[205]

There is also a general trend among political religious groups to put authority in the hands of a group of people, (the leaders of these groups) whom they describe as benevolent, as the right path to good, effective and pure governance. The Egyptian Muslim Brotherhood group, for example, claims that its General Guide knows what is best for the *umma* above anyone else, and can be relied upon because he is a competent and qualified scholar, planner and politician. With regard to the Shiites, Ayatollah Khomeini, the author of the constitution of the Islamic Republic of Iran, reasoned that giving the authority to clerics by selecting a *wali faqeeh* (jurist guardian) as a temporary stand-in for *Al-Mahdi Al-Muntazar* (the awaited guide) is the right thing in government and the pathway to political, economic and social success. Thus, he replaced a political program with a metaphysical doctrine, pending the formation of a state which would establish its own system of government; i.e. the Islamic Republic of Iran decided, from the outset, to put the cart before the horse, whatever the outcome, in order to serve its political religious project.[206]

Conclusion

Much speculation surrounds the fate of political Islam as a concept – and its groups and parties – since the outbreak of the wave of

political change in the Arab world in 2011 and the rise of some political religious groups to authority, as in the Arab Republic of Egypt, the Republic of Tunisia and the Kingdom of Morocco (in terms of premiership), and the growth of their political and security influence in other countries such as the State of Libya, the Republic of Yemen and the Republic of Iraq. Such speculation has increased since the abject failure of one group in government in the Arab Republic of Egypt, the decline in the role of another in the Republic of Tunisia, and the cessation of religious momentum in other countries, even in the Kingdom of Morocco, where the Prime Minister, Abdullah Bin Kiran, seems unable to use Islamic momentum to achieve the major economic successes required by the country in order to achieve social stability. Moreover, even in non-Arab countries such as the Republic of Turkey there is some reconsideration of the record of the Justice and Development Party and its administration of the government, and whether it is really much different to other Turkish political parties, given the corruption scandals, abuse of authority, restriction of freedoms and other shortcomings.

Political Islam failed to formulate integrated programs and plans other than those drawn from the Holy Quran and the Noble Sunnah. This reduced prospects for its development in light of time-place limitations.

The following summary therefore describes the position of political religious groups and their future prospects, in light of the fact that the Arab Republic of Egypt in December 2013 designated the Muslim Brotherhood group a terrorist organization[207] and subjected its leaders and members to prosecution on a number of criminal cases and others related to compromising the country's national security. It is this group that is considered the pioneer and architect of political Islam and the political religious project in the 20th century. Other currents, groups and movements that have become the main source of concern for all peoples and regimes in the Arab and Muslim worlds and the world at large are offshoots of this group. Here are the summary points:

1- Political religious groups are not different to other political currents and parties—whether traditional or militant. They all seek to seize authority and government in order to achieve the interests of certain elites in society and impose their ideologies on the institutions of the state and society. However, political religious groups differ from other political forces in that seizing authority and government is their absolute priority, irrespective of the method to achieve that. They can reach that goal through elections—as happened in the Republic of Turkey in mid 1990s,[208] the Arab Republic of Egypt and the Republic of Tunisia after the Arab protests in 2011; through popular revolution and mass demonstrations and mobilization, as was the case in the Islamic Republic of Iran in 1979; or a military coup, as happened in the Republic of the Sudan in

1989. Once these groups acquire authority in government, they attempt to change the existing political situation in a way that serves their interests in building a religious state that gradually eliminates all opposition to its various political and intellectual orientations.

2- Political religious groups failed to formulate politically, economically and socially integrated programs, projects and plans. They only produced broad religiously charged slogans and headlines, and what they managed to extract from the Islamic *Sharia* confined them with limitations of time, place and space. Politically, they were forced to define an institutional framework for themselves, which was the Islamic Caliphate. They ideologically confined their discourse to religion and the return to the righteous ancestors as a benchmark for values and goals. Then at a later stage, they found for themselves another institutional framework, which was the Ottoman Caliphate. This way, these groups denied themselves any possibility to develop, because the religious text, being divinely revealed and fixed, has never changed; i.e. these groups could not keep up with development due to their lack of modernity and its absence from their discourse. In terms of place, political religious groups have secluded themselves and refused to be influenced by the positive aspects of non-Muslim societies that have proven their ability to keep up with the modern world and its political, economic and social development through technological, scientific and intellectual progress.

3- The future of political religious groups seems to hinge on addressing two major problems that make it unpredictable and difficult to define. The first intractable problem is the presence of jihadi organizations of all forms – terrorist, militant and those who refuse any kind of compromise, etc. – which have stained every religious-oriented issue with violence, although Islam does not call for war without a *Sharia*-compliant goal, and the overwhelming majority of Muslims are not supportive of the ideology of jihadi groups. This places these organizations in a perpetual confrontation not only with 'the other,' but also with their own societies and states. The second problem lies in the ideology of political Islam itself and its characteristics, because any potential change in its course requires a decision to abandon its ideas and referential determinants. Such a decision is unlikely, given the current facts, especially with regard to political Islam's narrow-minded, rigid interpretations of religious texts extracted from the Holy Quran and the Noble Sunnah. If political Islam abandons the goal of establishing an Islamic Caliphate, or discards the principle of return to the righteous ancestors and their *modus operandi* in an ever-changing globalized world – although these are fundamental principles of its ideology – it will face two difficult problems: first, it will lose the support of many people who were convinced that it would relieve them of their day-to-day problems, because it would no longer be religiously perfect; second, it will be the same as any other political party, with

no religious halo to rely on in order to gain the support or sympathy of ordinary people.

4- In addition to these outcomes, political religious groups are expected to remain on the sidelines of political life in the Arab and Muslim worlds, at least in the short and medium terms, if they still have any remaining legal and political legitimacy or any popularity. These groups exploited the Arab wave of change and did not play any role in initiating it. They attained authority, only to prove their political and economic failings. They have even become a security threat to the stability of their countries, whether in the Arab Republic of Egypt, the Republic of Tunisia, the State of Libya, the Islamic Republic of Pakistan, the Islamic Republic of Afghanistan, the Republic of the Sudan or other countries with Muslim populations like Nigeria and elsewhere.

2 Religion and Politics: Historical Relationship and Continuous Conflict

CHAPTER 2

Religion and Politics: Historical Relationship and Continuous Conflict

The separation of religion and politics is an important dimension of political, social and economic life in the Arab and Muslim worlds, not only because this matter is strongly connected to the history of both, but also because it affects various issues, as well as the range and depth of development plans. This separation is more important today than ever, given the deep political, economic, social and intellectual changes witnessed in the Arab and Muslim worlds, with Islamists reaching positions of authority in some Arab and Muslim countries in 2011. Arab decision-makers need answers to essential questions regarding human development, as they find it difficult to manage the confusion and overlap between religious and worldly matters in an increasingly complex and interconnected world. Furthermore, individuals in all Arab and Muslim countries feel that in their efforts to improve their

political, economic and social conditions, they have to find a way to maintain their religiosity while enjoying worldly advances. At the same time, they are aware that they are in constant competition with others, in both their communities and the world at large, and that they are the only ones who can improve their own living conditions and those of their families and communities.

This chapter introduces the concept of mixing religion and politics, which is practiced by Islamists of various groups and parties. It gives an historical background which relies on the advancement of societies to determine whether such mixing is present, absent or managed in the Arab and Muslim worlds. This is followed by a look at the separation of religion and politics in the Western world, examining how internal factors in the Church together with external factors in the state helped end the Church's control of the state. The second section of this chapter analyses the reasons behind the mixing of religion and politics in the Arab and Muslim worlds, uncovers efforts by the Islamists to maintain this mix, and presents successful Islamic examples of a separation of the two. The third section argues that mixing religion and politics results in discord and conflict between religious schools themselves, and in society as a whole. It refutes, to the extent possible, the idea that the early Islamic state in the revelation period experienced no conflict because it mixed religion and politics. The last section presents a contemporary example of an Islamic state which managed to separate religion and politics, although religion still has presence in institutions and society.

Mixing of Religion and Politics

It is important to begin this chapter by stating in general that the mixing of religious and political aspects is inevitable, due to the objective conditions pertaining to the development of societies, and to human nature itself which seeks to attain spiritual as well as material fulfillment. In its primitive stages, society looked for quick and simple explanations for facts of life, and these were provided by religious institutions over the ages.[1] Religion, as a human system, combines belief in the supernatural and the tangible, has spiritual, economic and social aspects, and reflects man's aspirations for a successful life. The study of the role of religion in socio-political life has been of great interest to sociologists, historians, political scientists, philosophers and theologians because it is a political ideology, a belief system, and a strong socio-political force in society.[2] Some sociologists have tried to disregard the organic relationship between these two elements (religion and politics) of human nature, but their attempts were not successful, at least in recent years, as developing nations, which consider the two elements inseparable, play a bigger role in the system of international social and religious relations.[3]

The following themes should be considered when examining the relationship between religion and politics. First, in order to understand the relationship between religion and politics, one must examine and analyze the relationship between religion and the social, economic and cultural realities of any society. Second, religious phenomena and movements must be examined in the historical context of the society where they are found. Third, scholars should emphasize a methodological approach based on an historical and empirical comparison with a view to obtaining analytical insights into both the implicit and explicit meanings of the religious phenomenon under investigation, especially in relation to the historical context of religion, the development of the religious phenomena, and its flexible and changing nature in both temporal and spatial terms. Each group or movement will have its own interpretation of religion. For example, Islamic liberalism, represented by Muhammad Abdu and others, had different viewpoints from those of conservatives, represented by Muhammad Rasheed Rida and others.[4] In this case, it is possible to combine the two currents (liberalism and conservatism) of Sunni Islam, which represents the majority of Muslims, and understand their similarities and differences in terms of religiosity or the application of religion in one's private and public life.

In their modern history, the Arab and Muslim worlds saw a period of renaissance and enlightenment during the last quarter of the nineteenth century and the first half of the twentieth. Enlightened men tried to change the backward conditions of their countries after long centuries of despotism by the Ottoman Empire, which remained the centre of the Islamic Caliphate for almost five centuries, and material and cultural decline since the Mongol invasion of the old Arabian empire in the mid-thirteenth century AD. These enlightened men included Muhammad Abdu, Abdurrahman Al-Kawakibi,[5]

and a number of Christian Arabs who considered themselves protectors of the Arabic language and culture. This was facilitated by the fact that the region currently comprising Egypt, Lebanon, Syria, Palestine and Iraq benefitted at the time from efforts by the British and French colonizers to develop scientific, cultural and literary fields which were deemed far removed from politics, despite the trouble created by some Arab politicians and enlightened men under the British and French occupations. One scholar describes this period as expressing "a desire to break away from a past characterized by lagging behind other advanced nations,"[6] and a revolt "against sluggishness, backwardness, and degeneration, seeking to achieve vitality, progress and superiority."[7]

What interests us in this era of Arab and Islamic enlightenment is that it saw an attempt by educated people in the Arab and Muslim worlds to get over sectarian and religious divides in order to: 1) improve the status of Arab and Muslim nations following centuries of decline—in this sense, it was a national movement aiming at liberation; and 2) benefit from the experience of the West in separating religion from politics and focusing on science, innovation and social, political, and economic change, thereby entering the age of modernity and world domination. However, following World War I and the abolition of the Ottoman Caliphate, enlightened Arab and Muslim men were faced with the emergence of political religious groups. Influenced by the Fascist ideas of the 1920s, and concerned that secularism might result in depravity in Arab and Muslim societies, these groups started planning to transform a national struggle into an Islamic, mainly Sunni, struggle. It must be pointed out that the secularists paid the price of the victory of the Communist Revolution in Russia in 1917; they were accused of being communists who did not believe in God (Allah) and did not want to apply *Sharia*. As such, they lost popular support for their unionist national project. Instead, Hassan Al-Banna and the Muslim Brotherhood succeeded, and were considered by the West to be a weapon that could be used against the leftists to stop the Arab liberation movement.[8]

As previously indicated, mixing religion and politics in Western Christian history kept Europe in the Dark Ages for several centuries. This period was characterized by the Church's control over the state and all politicians and institutions. It was a typical case of a theocratic state, which is defined as "combining religious and political authority in one hand. Once this happens, the state's authority acquires a sense of infallibility or sanctity, and becomes immune to accountability."[9] From the fourteenth to the sixteenth centuries, Europe was a big religious state ruled by the Pope in Rome by virtue of his undisputable religious authority. Both spiritual and worldly matters were decided by him. He waged wars and mobilized armies for defense and invasion. This period was called the Dark Ages of Europe. The Crusades occurred in the eleventh through the thirteenth centuries AD; Byzantium sought the assistance of Rome's Pope, who offered full indulgence to any Christian participating in the Crusades, alleging that they aimed at liberating Jerusalem. The Crusades started in 1096 AD, and

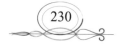

ended with failure in the late thirteenth century AD. The Pope
also supported military campaigns to expand the rule of the
Church in northern Europe, and called for fighting Muslims,
Jews and pagans everywhere.[10] Although divided, the Muslim
world withstood these campaigns under leaders such as Imad
Al-Deen Zengi, his son Nur Al-Deen Zengi, and Salah Al-
Deen Al-Ayyubi (Saladin). In addition, the flood of the Nile
saved Egypt from the campaign of Louis IX.[11]

Simon Newman writes that Europe in the Middle Ages
was dominated by Christianity, particularly the Catholic
Church, the only church in Europe at the time. It built
cathedrals and universities such as Paris, Cambridge and
Oxford universities.[12] The laws of the land and major roles in
the government were all in the hands of Church leaders.[13] From
birth to death, the life of the medieval people was entirely
dominated by the Church, and many religious institutions
gained power and wealth. The control of the Church resulted in
campaigns led by religious leaders against followers of other
religions, who were considered unbelievers. These campaigns
targeted Muslims, Jews, pagans and gypsies. In fact, Jews
suffered the most as they were considered to be the greatest
threat to Christianity, hence the emergence of Anti-Semitism.[14]
To improve its control and maintain its privileges, the Church
relied on businessmen and political leaders.[15] In the fifteenth
century AD, the church was not only a place for worship and
ritual, but a financial institution and a source of wealth. Many
bishops and archbishops became worldly leaders, and the
relation of the Church to politics and economy became more

complicated. For example, Julius II, nicknamed "The Fearsome Pope" sold indulgences, and was involved in favoritism.[16]

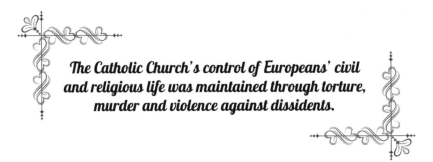

The Catholic Church's control of Europeans' civil and religious life was maintained through torture, murder and violence against dissidents.

The Catholic Church's control of the Europeans' civil and religious life was maintained through torture and violence against dissidents, who were burned, killed, tortured or persecuted until they gave up their beliefs. The Papal inquisition system, instituted by Pope Gregory IX in 1233 AD,[17] and officially sanctioned by Pope Innocent IV in 1252 AD, was one of the most savage and suppressive mechanisms in the history of mankind, and one of the most dangerous weapons used by the Catholic Church against those trying to undermine its authority and influence.[18] Under this system, which lasted until the late eighteenth century, anyone expressing in public ideas against the beliefs of the Church would be burned, his properties confiscated, his house demolished, and two generations of his descendants denied any wealth-generating position, unless they were to report another dissent.[19] It is estimated that this system resulted in the death of hundreds of thousands in the Christian world.[20] This associated religion in the minds of Europeans with backwardness and suppression. Therefore, efforts to change this

situation meant getting rid of all aspects of the religious state and moving towards the civil state, which was the only road to progress and a better future.

At the beginning of the sixteenth century, a number of factors – some attributed to the Church itself, some beyond its control – contributed to weakening its authority. The Church became corrupt, Popes became obsessed with authority and control, and bishops cared more about money and authority than about religion. As a result, the Church was in discord, vulnerable to revolt by domestic opposition.[21] Christians lost their faith in the Church and its ability to take care of their spiritual life and living conditions, especially after it proved helpless in the face of widespread plagues that devastated all of Europe in the fourteenth and fifteenth centuries AD.[22] This gave rise to religious reformation led by Martin Luther and John Calvin, who aimed at liberating Europeans and focused on the individual instead of the Church-controlled group.[23] Most important was the rise of a new class of businessmen and industrialists, helped by new discoveries in America. As such, the Church found itself competing with a new strong capitalist class which relies on science, wealth and urban life.[24] This is the bourgeois class which played a major role in limiting the authority of the Church in the Middle Ages.[25]

Separation of religion and politics is a major, important reason behind the development, progress and modernization of Europe.

The new capitalist class dominated economic and social life in Europe, and was most successful in Britain, where an industrial economy first developed, replacing the feudal class which benefited from its close relations with the Church. Furthermore, the invention of the printing press by Johannes Gutenberg in 1449[26] contributed to spreading the written word to wider audiences and allowed people to learn the truth about the world away from the analyses of the Church and superstitions of the clergy. With the Church and its supporting feudal class weakening, European reformations culminated with the separation of religion and politics, thereby reducing the control of the Pope and clergy over populations.[27]

There is no separation between religion and politics in the Arab and Muslim worlds. I think mixing religion and politics in one system is wrong and results in complex problems; and is even one of the factors behind the current domestic turmoil in several Arab and Muslim countries. The Western (Christian) duality disregards the comprehensive nature of the relationship between religion and politics; this is due primarily to the objective conditions of Western society. In Islam, religious and worldly aspects are strongly connected, and the early Islamic state in Medina succeeded in combining the two, thanks to certain objective circumstances. This success, however, does not justify calls to copy that experience in our present time, especially considering that those trying to implement this tradition reject innovation, modernity and advancement, and present examples which are detrimental to the image of Islam. This, however,

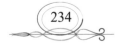

does not negate the fact that early Muslims thought that this combination provided the best formula for governance. In short, "in Islam, what is religious is clearly political, and what is seen as political is also deeply religious."[28]

Table 2.1
Analysis of Religious Systems[29]

		Non-historical	Historical
Analysis of systems	Organic model	Hinduism	Islam
	Church model	Buddhism	Catholicism (Christianity)

Donald E. Smith argues that there are two criteria for classifying religious systems:[30] the religious interpretation of history, and the framework connecting the religious system with the social system. Historical religious systems comprise main world religions: Islam, Christianity and Judaism. Their interpretation of the world is based on the existence of a creator, God (Allah), and the story of the creation of Adam and Eve. On the other hand, history has no specific meaning in Hinduism and Buddhism. For example, Buddhism views history as an endlessly repeated cycle of religious ideas rising and falling.

For Smith, in organic religious systems no distinction can be made between religion and society. Divine law and social order are both inherent in religion.[31] On the other hand,

Church religious systems have a structure built within society, but as a separate institution. Church systems are more tolerant of civil ideas and values, because they stress the development of Church institutions. Organic systems, however, have a limited number of religious institutions and react much less consistently and effectively. According to Smith, ordinary people have to do much to resist secularism, organize political forces, and rewrite social ideology or philosophy.[32]

Although it is difficult to adopt one criterion for measuring the relationship between religion and the state in the Arab and Muslim worlds, due to the differences in political systems (monarchical, republican, military, civil, etc.), religion has a varied but generally strong presence in political and social life in Arab and Muslim countries. It is strong and influential in the Kingdom of Saudi Arabia, and moderate in other GCC nations and republican countries. Therefore, separation between religion and politics can be subject to certain temporary or permanent interpretations, which could result in Arab and Muslim countries losing their identity or internal stability.[33] Many proponents of the political role of religion, particularly political religious groups, view separating religion from the state in terms of true secularism, which is, for them, a form of blasphemy and atheism. The Muslim Brotherhood views supporters of separating religion from the state as unbelievers or untrue Muslims.[34] This strange argument made Khalid Al-Dakheel wonder: if secularism led the West to its current age of progress and scientific advancement, how can it be described as

236

blasphemy? Obviously, he meant to say that this argument
contographs scientific analysis.[35]

> *Hardliners in political religious groups believe that
> violence is the best way to enforce the application of
> Sharia, even if the struggle for that goal results in
> the death of many Muslims.*

Mixing religion and state is one of the most important
principles of political Islam, as represented by various
movements, groups and parties. Other principles stress the
applicability of religion to all aspects of life without leaving any
space for logic and realism. Political Islam calls for a return
to the roots of Islam in the early problem-free era, and a
re-establishment of the first Caliphate state. It views the
political, economic and social problems faced by Muslims today
as the result of authoritarian regimes and colonial powers, and
believes they can be solved only by restoring pure religion and
the application of *Sharia*. For them, *Sharia* provides everything
contemporary people require. Hence, the Muslim Brotherhood's
slogan states that "Islam is the solution." For them, Islam is an
integral system of social and economic ideas. Hardliners in
political religious groups believe that violence is the best way to
enforce *Sharia*, even if the struggle for that goal results in the
death of many Muslims. In this sense, there is no difference

between hardliners, be they Sunni or Shiite, Muslim, Christian or Jewish.[36]

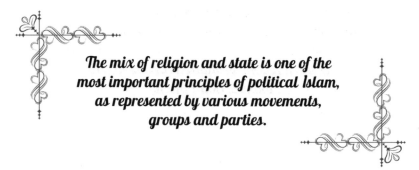

The mix of religion and state is one of the most important principles of political Islam, as represented by various movements, groups and parties.

On the other hand, the separation of religion from politics is an indicator of progress and modernity in the West, not because religion is an element of backwardness, but because modernity requires a change in the human mindset and the adoption of a more scholarly approach. In general, modernization is a difficult process to define, but it comprises a change from poor agricultural village-based communities to industrially, intellectually and socially advanced ones. Against this background, several questions arise: does religion facilitate or hinder this process? The answer depends on the nature and structure of the religion under investigation, and the kind and form of required modernization. Certainly, religion is an important factor in this process, because it offers the means to adapt to new situations. There are also questions about the relationship between secularism and the possibility of a modern state; some scholars believe there is a disproportionate relationship between religion and modernity, meaning that technical and intellectual improvements in societies result in a weaker religion.[37]

*Islam, as a religious system, has no institutions
independent from the state, and Muslims have no
religious obligations toward religious institutions
or clerics; their obligations are basically
toward God (Allah).*

There are other opinions which support the idea that Islam, as
an organic religious system, has no institutions independent
from the state (thereby making the idea of separating religion
from the state more difficult). Therefore, a Muslim does not
feel he has any religious obligations toward any religious
institution or cleric; his obligations are basically toward God
(Allah). The difficulty in establishing a civil state in the Arab
and Muslim worlds stems from the lack of distinction between
religious and secular spheres of activities. Historically, state
expansion in Islam was based on religious values. When a
Western approach is used in trying to understand the
relationship between the religious and the secular in the Arab
and Muslim worlds, enormous analytical difficulties arise,
including the absence of an independent religious institution,
and the fact that the concept of the state, in the sense used in
contemporary political literature, does not occur in the Holy
Quran.[38] In fact, political authority (after the Rightly-Guided
Caliphs) took over religion, and later kings, sultans and caliphs
gave the state – as a group of people and institutions – the

liberty to act without being subject in its actions and duties to religious analysis. An example of this is the concept of *Ahl Al-Hal Wa Al-Akd* (decision makers).[39]

Reasons behind the Mixing of Religion and Politics in the Arab and Muslim Worlds

Some scholars argue that the view that Islam does not distinguish between religion and the state goes back to the days of the early Islamic state established by the Prophet Muhammad (pbuh) in Medina.[40] Muhammad (pbuh) was the Prophet and the political and military leader who led Muslims to a new world they had not experienced in the pre-Islamic era. After the death of Muhammad (pbuh), the Caliphs maintained religious and political leadership. It was their duty to teach religious principles, settle disputes and expand Islamic territory. In this regard, the Caliph's position was unique and absolute in relation to all religious and worldly matters. It is worth mentioning that it was important for the Caliphs that Muslims take the oath of allegiance to them, which reflected an implied recognition of the fact that the *umma* is the real source of authority, to use modern political terms. Despite this indisputable history, developments in the Arab and Muslim worlds contributed to reducing the overlap between religion and politics, as Muslim societies developed and the complexity of their cultural, religious and social structures increased.[41]

The organic relationship between religion and the state can be viewed as serving some political regimes in the Arab and

Muslim worlds.[42] This was true in the case of the Arab Republic of Egypt in the early 1970s, when former Egyptian president Muhammad Anwar Al-Sadat used religion as a tool for political control. Former president Muhammad Husni Mubarak followed the same path. However, he neither gave Islamists an opportunity to influence the state's policies during his rule, nor moved back toward the civil state.[43]

Mixing religion and politics remains a means for various political religious groups to reach positions of authority in an attempt to copy the model of the first Islamic state. Khalid Al-Dakheel argues that the phrase "Islam is a religion and a state" is merely a slogan used to serve the political project of the Muslim Brotherhood.[44] The reason for the spread of this discourse was the belief among the public that it was the solution to the degeneration of the Arab and Muslim worlds following the colonial period and the Western control of local wealth, and the double insult stemming from the fact that the colonizer was the Christian Western world, which, despite its political, economic and social advances, is still home to blasphemy and atheism in the eyes of political religious groups.[45]

The other objective reason for the continued mixing of religion and politics is the absence of an economic factor such as existed in Europe by the end of the Middle Ages, when a new class emerged comprising capitalists and industrialists who benefited from the separation of the Christian Church from the state which they wanted to establish to protect their economic interests. The Arab and Muslim worlds saw no change in terms of their economies and the central role of the state in achieving human and structural development. Furthermore, although there was a wealthy class, it was not independent from the state, and did not have independent capital. The Arab and Islamic capitalist class does not care about the economic circumstances of their countries and peoples; they have transferred their wealth to Western banks to escape state control and avoid the risks of popular protests because of poverty and lack of opportunities.[46]

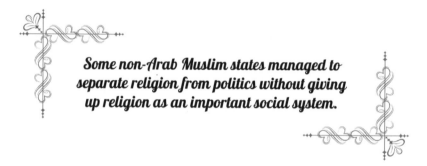

Some non-Arab Muslim states managed to separate religion from politics without giving up religion as an important social system.

On the other hand, certain non-Arab Muslim states, particularly Turkey, Indonesia and Malaysia, have managed to separate religion from politics without giving up religion as a social system compatible with contemporary life. In Turkey, religion was separated from politics after centuries of Ottoman rule over an empire extending at different times from the farthest provinces in North Africa to the Arabian Gulf and Southern Europe. This separation was successful because the Ottoman Empire faced in its last century all manner of economic, political and social problems, especially because it was not capable of embracing modernity and the scientific spirit embraced by Europe following the separation of religion and state.[47]

Ataturk's vision was based on six socially and institutionally important principles: republicanism (although he ruled like a king), secularism, Turkish nationalism (rather than integration with other Muslim nations), populism, building a strong state comprising all interest groups – including clerics – and reformation of all aspects of life in Turkey following centuries of religion-backed despotism.[48] Following World War II and the international polarization between the United States of America and the Soviet Union, this reformist environment in the modern Turkish state helped transform the country from a marginal state (Europeans referred to the Ottoman Empire in its later days as "the sick man of Europe"), to a modern state at the heart of international alliances such as NATO. Today, Turkey is seeking membership of the European Union.[49]

> *Despite development problems, secularism appears to be a settled and non-negotiable issue in Indonesia.*

In Indonesia, following the collapse of the Muhammad Suharto regime in the 1990s and the emergence of an open political environment, state institutions helped open discussions of topics which were previously taboo, such as a female president and limiting the role of *Sharia* in governance. Since its establishment by Ahmad Sukarno, the Indonesian state separated religion from politics, as in Egypt under the rule of former president Jamal Abdul Nasser. The change from Suharto's autocracy to democracy was not an opportunity for Islamists to impose themselves on the state and society; they found themselves unable to answer simple questions about governance, including how to achieve development at various levels and improve the performance of the economy to better serve citizens, and this weakened their position in the political landscape. In addition, Indonesian intellectuals opened public debates about several topics, such as the role of women and *Sharia* in politics, human rights, education and public culture.[50] Although Indonesia, the world's most populated Muslim country, is still suffering economic and social problems associated with the size of its population, the secularism or religiosity of the state does not appear to be a negotiable or disputed issue. Interestingly enough, historical and social circumstances in Indonesia were similar to the ones in the Arab world; it fell under European colonization for centuries and suffered a lot during World War II. Nevertheless, Indonesia successfully separated religion from politics, while Arab countries could not achieve this goal.

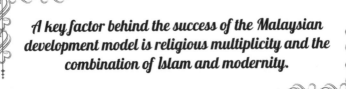

A key factor behind the success of the Malaysian development model is religious multiplicity and the combination of Islam and modernity.

Since independence in 1957, Malaysia has transformed itself from a poor agricultural country which is economically and socially dependent on others to a modern industrial state and a global commercial hub. This is attributed, at least partially, to the separation of religion and state, as well as embracing multi-ethnicity and multi-religiosity. Muslims, who represent 60 percent of the population,[51] do not feel that they have to impose their religion on others or establish a state where non-Muslims are treated as *thimmis*. According to the Turkish journalist Bülent Keneş, Malaysia succeeded as a state because it embraced diversity and because its Muslim leaders hold that Islam is synonymous with moderation, inclusiveness and good governance. Economically, Malaysia is truly an Asian tiger, with the industrial and services sectors contributing 90 percent of national income,[52] average annual per capita income of approximately USD 11,000 in 2014,[53] and an annual growth rate of gross domestic income (economic growth rate) of 5.9 percent in 2014.[54] As such, determined to follow the path of modernization, the Malaysian state faced no problems associated with the separation of religion from politics, but established a peaceful social and political environment which enabled it to achieve prosperity, security and stability in its domestic affairs and international relations.

By contrast, the experience of the Sudan following the coup in June 1989 shows that mixing religion and politics is undesirable, and could result in negative consequences in terms of stability and development. The military *coup d'état* led by

Omar Hassan Al-Bashir, with the encouragement of Hassan Abdullah Al-Turabi, leader of the Islamic movement in Sudan,[55] ended with self-division because the leaders of the Islamic project were politicians seeking authority regardless of the economic, political, social and security problems that their project might cause.[56]

The application of Islamic *Sharia* in a multi-religious multi-ethnic society was the main cause of the civil war which started in the 1980s and ended with the secession of the south and the establishment of the Republic of South Sudan with regional and international guarantees. This would not have occurred without commitment to the vision of establishing an Islamic state.[57] It is worth mentioning that the two main political players in the Sudan, Omar Hassan Al-Bashir and Hassan Abdullah Al-Turabi, were recently forced into a re-union after their political religiously-cloaked adventures weakened and disintegrated the country.

The Islamic Republic of Iran provides another bad example of the consequences of mixing religion and the state on the basis that Islamic *Sharia* offers the state everything required to achieve development and progress. After overthrowing the Shah in 1979 and dissolving all other secular forces which participated in the revolution within two years, leaders of the Islamic Revolution proceeded to establish a totalitarian Islamic regime based on the ideas of the leader of the revolution Ayatollah Khomeini. This regime, however, did not care about changing the economic system which caused the Iranian poor to

suffer under the Shah. Instead, the regime introduced more restrictions on women, and added to the burdens of the economy, which suffered international sanctions that negatively affected the lives of citizens.[58]

Separation of religion and state does not mean removing religion from public life or prohibiting Muslims from practicing religious rituals, going to mosques or attaining spiritual fulfillment.

Potential Effects of Mixing Religion and Politics

A brief analysis was made above regarding the combination of religious and worldly aspects in the Arab and Muslim worlds, including a look at some Muslim countries which have succeeded in separating religion and politics and have enjoyed political, economic and social achievements despite their difficult circumstances and the many obstacles they faced. In this section, I will examine some of the damage resulting from mixing religion and politics—outcomes that were avoided by Western civil states and some Muslim states by separating religion and politics a long time ago, but not in the Arab and Muslim worlds which continue to feature religious politics (i.e. state policies with a religious dimension) and politicized religion (i.e. using religion for political purposes).[59] The separation of religion and state does not in any way mean removing religion from public life or preventing Muslims from practicing religious rituals, going to mosques or attaining spiritual fulfillment.[60] Furthermore, separating religion and politics should not be understood as introducing new ideas to Islamic social life, following the Western social model, or abandoning old religious traditions which form the foundations of Arab and Islamic heritage.

The damage caused by mixing religion and politics in the Arab and Muslim worlds can be summarized as follows:

1. Mixing religion and politics links religion with all the negative practices associated with politics, such as political deals, temporary alliances, shared interests, and short-term plans. This undermines the sanctity of religion and moves it away from the ultimate divine truth. Ridwan Al-Sayyid argues that there are four factors which make the rise of political Islam a threat to religion: 1) the call for the application of *Sharia* is motivated by ideology rather than religion, and is the result of identity conflicts in the Arab and Muslim worlds; 2) the claim that religion is a comprehensive system which provides everything required to conduct politics and run the economy; 3) assigning religious duties, such as the application of *Sharia*, to the state undermines the mandate of the state in supporting equality of citizenship; and 4) involving religion in political conflicts creates problems for everybody.[61]

2. Mixing religion and politics gives some clerics and members of political religious groups the right to determine the destiny of the nation, which detracts from the role of experts

in governance, politics and the economy. Furthermore, allowing politics to be subject to religious interpretation deprives it of dynamism and flexibility, which are two important features of contemporary political work— constant movement and change ensure the renewability of society and the state. For example, the discourse of political religious groups about the Caliphate system is one pillar of the political project of these groups, and they admit that they do not believe in any modern or contemporary form of governance. The same applies to giving the leaders and members of these groups prominent roles in government; the Islamic Republic of Iran assigned the leading positions in the state to mullahs (clerics) who are assumed to be infallible and incorruptible, which is not true.[62]

3. Mixing religion and politics increases the chances of discord and division among Muslims of various sects and schools, and between Muslims and non-Muslims. In the early Islamic state, sedition resulted from the conflict concerning the right to succeed the Prophet (pbuh). This conflict continues today; Muslims are divided into various, often conflicting sects and groups.[63] At present, militant attitudes in various religious schools widen the gaps between them, which adversely affect the unity of Muslims in the Arab and Muslim worlds. In this respect, Ridwan Al-Sayyid states that in addition to the Arab–Iranian conflict, there is conflict between Sunni jihadi political Islam, which is committed to fighting Shiites and the West simultaneously,

and organized partisan political Islam, represented by the
Muslim Brotherhood, which is committed to fighting Arab
regimes. This results in crises in the Arab national
consciousness, especially with the youth who are struggling
with inconsistent religious standards.[64]

4. Mixing religion and politics gives an authoritarian state
using religion in its ideology the right to impose a certain
lifestyle which could limit the ability of Muslims to be
creative and successful in their lives, improve their living
conditions and develop their countries. In this respect, some
scholars argue that regimes which historically mandated the
mixing of religion and politics in their societies imposed a
certain way of living, suppressed individual and social
freedoms, and prevented change, citing its negative effects
on society, while in fact they were simply trying to retain
their positions of authority.[65]

5. Mixing religion and politics opens the door for wars,
violence and crises. The religious model of governance
makes it easy to find "legitimate justifications" for wars in
accordance with the wishes of the regime and regardless of
the state's national security considerations and calculations,
because a religious state, by its nature, prohibits any
discussion of religion, *jihad* and the authorities of the
"Caliph."

Whilst mixing religion and politics has negative effects on
individuals, society, the state and religion itself, their separation
has several advantages, including the following:

1. When religion has a clear role and status in the state, and when the state has a clear secular agenda and ideology, the individual living in such a state is expected to take his rights and duties towards the state more seriously. Promoting a civil state implies the recognition of the importance of co-existence and cooperation among various components of society despite their differences in certain respects. It also means participation in building an open political system which facilitates social stability, citizenship, and the rule of law. This would represent the application of the principles of the Imam Muhammad Abdu, the social and religious reformist who argued that social cooperation was the only way towards social development and stability.[66]

2. The separation of religion and state helps expand the cultural space of society and guarantees contributions by all individuals towards intellectual and artistic enrichment, particularly in multiple societies like those in the Lebanese Republic, the Syrian Arab Republic, the Republic of Iraq, the Arab Republic of Egypt, Northern African states and the GCC states. Once the civil state is established, the population will feel they have equal citizenship, rights and duties, and have the opportunity to occupy any position in public life. This applies in particular to non-Muslims living in countries with Islamic majority populations; they would be able to contribute to the intellectual and cultural evolution of their countries without concern for their future.[67] The

Arab and Islamic renaissance in the nineteenth and twentieth centuries could be taken as a model for equal participation by all in restoring the Arab and Islamic past and enhancing human development.

3. Outside the Arab and Muslim worlds, the separation of religion and state will likely help Muslims integrate in the societies of host countries because they will have been used to living in an open multi-cultural society in their home countries. Once integrated, they may participate in determining their own destiny and the destiny of their families in the future. They will be at the heart of a human experiment where different religions, cultures and ethnicities mix, each providing all they can to enrich their environment and expand the horizons of their knowledge. Furthermore, Muslims familiar with the Western way of thinking could serve their religion by being open to others and forming alliances aimed at serving Muslim communities in Western countries.[68]

4. By separating religion and politics and allowing all segments of society to contribute to social development, any state would earn a positive image abroad and reduce external and international pressure to respect human rights and protect religious freedoms. These rights have become very important internationally, and any state violating them will be held accountable and subject to consequences.

The Secular Alternative to Mixing Religion and State in the Arab and Muslim Countries

Leaving aside the case of Arab and Muslim countries which have not yet been able to clearly separate religion and the state, there are a few alternative models which may be followed by Arab and Muslim countries. The French model is persistent in its commitment to secularism, totally eliminating religion from public life and even preventing Muslim women living in France from wearing the veil in public places.[69] Until recently, Islamic dress was also prohibited in public places in Turkey. This was a literal application of the secular principles upon which Ataturk established the modern Turkish state. The ban ended in early October 2013, when a law allowing the Islamic veil to be worn in government institutions in Turkey was published in the Turkish official gazette.[70]

Another model for the separation of religion and state is the US model. It is a moderate model which does not allow the state to interfere in the lives of individuals as the French state does today or as the Turkish state did in the past. American secularism, which has its ideological foundation in English history and the European religious reform movement of the fifteenth and sixteenth centuries, is based on the freedom of the individual to decide all matters related to his or her private life with little or no interference by the government. In fact, the separation of religion and state in the United States of America is the ultimate product of the idea that the Catholic Church should be denied absolute authority over the state, thereby making the Church merely a source of spiritual authority. All in all, the American model has two sides: on the one hand, churches are not allowed to interfere in politics; and on the other, political institutions do not interfere in religious matters.

This started in the United States of America with the writing of the American Constitution following the declaration of independence and the 1776–1787 war. The Constitution was published in 1787, and the Bill of Rights, comprising 10 Amendments, was published in 1791. The First Amendment provided that the Congress "shall make no law respecting an establishment of religion, or prohibiting the free exercise thereof."[71] However, the Constitution and the Amendments made no reference to the separation of religion and state. Furthermore, the First Amendment did not aim to eliminate religion from public life, rather it declared that the state would fund no plans to either spread or prohibit religion. The Amendment aimed at preventing religion from interfering in the state, and stressed that the state respects all religions and would not put its institutions in the service of one specific religion. In fact, the founders of the new state in the United States of America wanted to avoid repeating the persecution they suffered in Europe, because there had been one state religion which considered adherence to other religions as alien to social and spiritual life.[72]

The separation of religion and the American state was stressed in a promise made by the second American president,

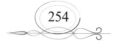

Thomas Jefferson, in the 1800s to a group of Baptists who were concerned that the state would favor one religion. Jefferson said that the First Amendment was a "wall of separation" between religion and the state.[73] The phrase spread and became central to American politics. The United States of America, as a nation and a society, remains religious today. At present, there are several cases before American courts, some demanding more religious aspects in public life, and some arguing for the elimination of religion from public life.[74]

The separation of religion and the state in the United States of America does not mean that religion is prohibited in state institutions. It is not odd to see the American president participating, for example, in prayers at the church or putting his hand on the Bible while making the oath when inaugurated. What is prohibited in the United States of America is to make religion and religiosity a precondition for participation in political life. In fact, what is referred to as "civil religion" governs the relationship between religion and state.[75] The United States of America is a multi-religious country, although Christians of different denominations are the majority. According to a survey by Gallup in 2012, as shown in Figure 2.1, Christians account for 77.3 percent of the population (51.9 percent Protestants, 23.3 percent Catholics, 2.1 percent Mormons), Jews 1.6 percent and Muslims 0.6 percent, with almost 15 percent having no religious identity. 2.6 percent belong to other non-Christian religions, and 2.2 percent did not answer the question about religion.[76]

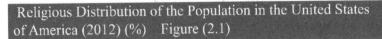

Religious Distribution of the Population in the United States of America (2012) (%)   Figure (2.1)

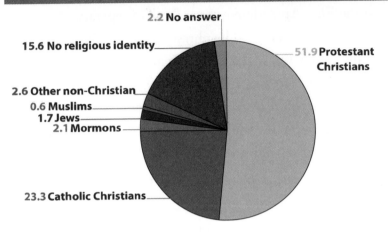

However, constitutional provisions and laws which prohibit the state from having one religion or punish those who do not observe the separation of religion and state in the United States of America have not always succeeded in preventing discrimination, persecution and violence on religious grounds, even by the authorities. The religious history of the United States of America is full of shameful incidents against those considered by the majority to be "unbelievers" or "aliens," including Protestants, Catholics, Jews, Muslims and Native Americans, who were not Christian but had their own faith and deities when the first settlers arrived in America.[77]

The problem faced by Muslims in New York in the 2000s when attempting to build a mosque near Ground Zero (formerly the site of the World Trade Centre twin towers) reflects an unusual attitude by Americans, who are

proud of their openness to all religions, toward what they do not understand.[78]

The good thing about the American model of separating religion and the state is the right to defend personal rights in the press, media and courts, despite the fact that some cases fail in court or in public due to weak argument or ignorance of the public. Even in the case of building a mosque near the site of the 9/11 attacks, social work and cooperation between religions had a big impact. Many Jews, Christians and the civil state – even President Barack Obama himself – supported the cause of the mosque and considered it a symbol of religious openness which could help establish domestic social stability. After much cooperation and communication among activists, politicians, and defenders of personal and religious freedoms, the mosque was eventually opened near the site of the attacks.[79]

Besides the French and American models, there are several other models which can be adopted by any society or state in the Arab and Muslim worlds to achieve the separation of religion and state in a way which enables religion to keep its spiritual holy status and maintain its positive role in promoting virtue and serving humanity, and at the same time gives the state the freedom and flexibility to achieve comprehensive development, prosperity, stability and happiness for all its citizens. Achieving this goal is certainly the only way for Arab and Muslim states to restore the glorious past of the Islamic nation and lead the world. Such a restoration cannot be achieved by hollow resonant slogans which play on the religious and spiritual aspects of people' lives without having a real vision for progress and development.

> *Removing religion from public life is not an option due to the associated social and political risks, as religion plays an important role in controlling the social behavior of individuals, thereby ensuring stability.*

As previously indicated, the call to separate religion and the state does not in any way mean a call to put an end to the role of religion, Westernize Arab and Muslim societies or undermine their culture, heritage and religious identity. Aside from the associated risks, any attempt to remove the role of religion in any society is doomed to fail, as the European experiment itself shows. Despite the lapse of more than two centuries, predictions by prominent Western modernists about the inevitable end of religion in the modern world have been unfounded. On the contrary, there is an increasing tendency towards religiosity in Western societies at both the individual and public levels. French sociologist Frédéric Lenoir cited interesting statistics in this respect: 93 percent of Americans and 67 percent of Europeans believe in God (Allah). He concluded that recent years had seen a change in European psychology, with a tendency towards religion and spirituality.[80]

Nobody is talking about abandoning religion, due to the associated social, cultural and political risks, especially in societies which have not seen stable and natural intellectual development. This is because religion plays an important role in controlling the social behavior of individuals, thereby ensuring stability and security. That is why there have been Western reviews of the status of religion, with post-modernism rejecting talk about the inevitable end of religion[81] and some even stressing the importance of religion, not only in the private lives of individuals but also in public life. This may be attributed to the spiritual values of religion which contribute to achieving psychological and social stability, as one researcher put it:

> Victorious global capitalism is facing little genuine opposition today. That is why religion, with its spiritual values, still has an important role to play. It protects individuals in modern civil societies from being overwhelmed by the requirements of their careers and worldly success. As such, religious values (love, solidarity and piety) can stand in the face of the values of competition, gain, manipulation and control, thereby encouraging human beings to deal with each other as being ends in themselves and not merely means.[82]

Conclusion

The separation of religion and politics is an essential requirement for the political, economic and social development of the Arab and Muslim countries which share a number of similarities in terms of religion, language, heritage, customs and traditions. Just as this separation paved the way for Europe towards scientific progress and human development, it could lead the Arab and Muslim worlds to a similar outcome. Despite poverty in some Arab and Muslim countries, there are huge capabilities which modern Arab and Muslim states could put in the service of a multi-dimensional revival project. At a time when the Arab and Muslim worlds are going through a transformation, the separation of religion and state should be considered as a means to move towards a new revival rather than distancing Muslims from God (Allah). Modernity is not atheism, and a civil state can solve many of the social problems associated with what some researchers call the "identity tensions" experienced by Muslims.[83]

While religious and social reformists of the Arab and Islamic renaissance in the nineteenth and twentieth centuries failed in achieving a true revival of the Arab and Muslim worlds due to internal and external circumstances, political despotism, and the actions of political Islamists serving their own interests, there are currently sufficient intellectual and human capabilities to renew that effort.

Part II

Case Studies

3 Political Religious Groups: The Muslim Brotherhood

CHAPTER 3

Political Religious Groups: The Muslim Brotherhood

One of the most prominent manifestations of the political transformations that have taken place in the Arab world since 2011 is that political religious groups affiliated with the Muslim Brotherhood group have assumed authority in several Arab and Muslim countries. Nearly 86 years since its inception the group was finally able to expand politically and pursue the strategic goal its leadership has maintained since its inception in 1928—the revival of the Caliphate to include all Muslim countries, following what is described in one of the Brotherhood's documents as the "Empowerment Phase."[1] In January 2012, the General Guide of the Muslim Brotherhood group, Dr. Muhammad Badie announced that the group's ultimate goal was to establish the "Rightly Guided Caliphate for the education of the world."[2] Islam, according to the group's founder and first General Guide Hassan Al-Banna, does not

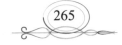

recognize geographical boundaries, and considers the Muslim world to be one nation, regardless of borders or the distances between its countries, and the Muslim Brotherhood considers this unity to be holy, declaring every inch of land inhabited by a Muslim who says "There is no god but Allah and Muhammad is His Messenger" as their fatherland.[3] This entails the abolition of the nation-state and the concept of sovereignty, which has featured in political literature and practice for centuries.

This chapter, through its various topics, examines the history of the Muslim Brotherhood group in terms of its origin, establishment and spread; it also tackles the aims of the group and its means to achieve them, and sheds light on the Muslim Brotherhood's thought, approach and its views regarding the governance system in general, as well as its stance toward parties, *shura* and democracy. It also addresses the Muslim Brotherhood's participation in politics and its engagement in political institutions such as parliaments, legislatures and executive offices in order to identify the implications of this participation and the general layout governing the group in this regard.

The chapter also examines the political experience of the Muslim Brotherhood group in several Arab and Muslim countries, and raises an important question: did the Muslim Brotherhood fail in government?

The Foundation of the Muslim Brotherhood Group

The Arab and Muslim worlds entered the 20th century in a state of unprecedented decline, while Europe was enjoying the fifth

century of its renaissance and was preparing to distribute the inheritance of the Ottoman Empire between its countries. The second decade of that century witnessed events that represented significant milestones in the Arab and Muslim worlds. The Ottoman Caliphate disintegrated after the Ottomans were defeated in World War I. The Arabs contributed to this defeat through the Great Revolt launched by Sharif Hussein bin Ali, the Emir of Mecca on June 10, 1916,[4] in response to the injustice, tyranny and underdevelopment they suffered under the rule of the Turks. Thereafter the Ottoman State was divided between the major colonial powers and the Ottoman Caliphate was abolished, as previously indicated, leaving the Muslims without a Caliph for the first time in history. They entered a phase of unprecedented underdevelopment in most fields of life due to the Caliphate's neglect of science and development, especially in its last two centuries, during which it adopted destructive policies based on directing all the capabilities of Arab and Muslim peoples under its control toward wars that eventually exhausted it and doomed its people.[5]

> *The Ottoman Caliphate neglected the Arab and Muslim worlds and considered them merely a source for recruiting soldiers and collecting taxes.*

The Ottoman Caliphate completely neglected areas that were under its control, especially Arab ones, considering them merely as sources for military recruitment and taxes, and paid no attention to their development and modernization. Thus, during the era of the Ottoman Caliphate, the Arab and Muslim worlds – the Levant included – existed under hard political, social and economic conditions, while the West had come a long way towards progress, and was already leading the movement of history in the world after decades of underdevelopment, backwardness and darkness. This, in fact, was a fulfillment of the law of God (Allah)—i.e., alternating nations experiencing varying fortunes. However, the problem is that the Arab and Muslim worlds, while entering an era of unprecedented decline since the fifteenth century AD, were not aware of the evolution taking place in the world around them at the beginning of that century. In light of this fact, which was a shock to many in the Arab and Muslim worlds, the revival of the Caliphate state was considered the only solution to restore the glories of the past and rise again, perhaps without realizing the fact that the circumstances have changed and that current reality probably requires new a perspective and approach regarding the nature and shape of systems of governance and the nature of the relationship which should link the countries and peoples of the Arab and Muslim worlds. In fact, the fall of the Islamic Caliphate shook the consciousness of many people who had high hopes for the Islamic Caliphate as a protector of Muslims.[6] Writings have emerged – from even decades before the fall of the Caliphate –

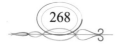

calling for reformation and renewal, such as those of the Imams Jamal Al-Deen Al-Afghani, Muhammad Abdu, Abdurrahman Al-Kawakibi and others.[7]

> *Promoting the idea of reviving the Caliphate state lacks awareness of current facts and circumstances which require a new perspective and approach.*

At that time, Cairo was one of the major Islamic metropolises and was filled with scholars, which resulted in the establishment of religious associations of a social nature that sought to raise a new generation according to Islamic teachings. The most prominent associations included the Principal Sharia Society for Cooperation between Quran and Sunnah Scholars, which was founded in 1912, and today has about 5,000 branches, comprising 5,000 mosques across the Arab Republic of Egypt and more than 50 institutes for the preparation of preachers and Holy Quran readers.[8] There is also the first Salafi association, the Ansar Al-Sunnah Society, which appeared in 1926, two years before the Muslim Brotherhood was established.[9] In addition to the Young Men's Muslim Association (YMMA) which was established in 1927.[10] However, other voices emerged beyond those demanding reform, calling for a revival of what had been lost. One who took advantage of the existing conditions, and later became a pivotal figure in Arab and Muslim history, was a young Egyptian man named Hassan Al-Banna.[11] Al-Banna was associated with the Young Men's Muslim Association, which was founded by a group of Egyptian preachers in 1927 to counter missionary campaigns. However, Al-Banna sensed a need to establish a more comprehensive association, so he established a group called the Muslim Brotherhood on March 22, 1928,[12] the first organized religious group of its kind,[13] and one of the most important political religious groups in the history of contemporary Islam.[14]

At the time of the group's establishment, Al-Banna was accompanied by other people, although it is very rare to find any reference to them or their role; however it is important to mention them here to show the environment from which the group emerged and the nature and orientations of those who contributed to its establishment. These are namely, Hafez Abdul Hameed (a carpenter), Ahmed Al-Husary (a barber), Fouad Ibraheem (a laundryman), Abdul Rahman Hasaballah (a driver), Ismail Ezz (a farmer), and Zaki Al-Mughrabi (a bicycle shop owner).[15] They all had received only a limited education, and represented those who were influenced by Al-Banna's lectures in mosques and public places. This indicates that the group in its infancy did not exhibit deep intellectual or jurisprudential expertise. It is also difficult to accept that this band was aware of the movement of history at that time or understood the dimensions of the international struggle to a

sufficient degree to establish a group to revive the role of the Islamic religion.

The name of the Muslim Brotherhood has been suspicious and questionable since its inception in the late 1920s.

The name of the group, which is still surrounded by questions today, especially as all Muslims are brothers, surfaced during a discussion between the seven founders about a name that would brings them together, and whether their proposed entity would be an organization, a club, or an association. Hassan Al-Banna put an end to the discussion when he told them, "we are brothers in the service of Islam, hence we are (the Muslim Brotherhood)."[16] In line with the existing conditions at that time, the group had three goals: first, to fight against colonialism and to expel the foreign presence;[17] second, to revive the Islamic Caliphate; and third, to achieve the re-Islamization of society.[18] Despite the magnitude of these goals – at least in relation to the size of the newly established group – as well as the narrow-mindedness of its founders, they have remained at the core of the Muslim Brotherhood's thought and ideology since its inception and until its dramatic political fall in the middle of 2013. In order to achieve these goals, the group has employed parallel approaches in its work[19]—while being engaged in the community reform movement, it also appeared as an anti-colonial movement which opposed foreign influence.

Proliferation at Home and Abroad

Hassan Al-Banna adopted a gradual strategy to spread the thought of the Muslim Brotherhood group by focusing initially on the religious and preaching aspects in order to ensure the prevalence of the group's ideals among different segments of society. His aim was fulfilled, and within a few years the Muslim Brotherhood group had spread across Egypt and beyond. It had a presence in most major Egyptian cities and in some other Arab and Muslim countries. In the first decade of its lifetime, the group had 215 branches in Egypt, and by the late 1940s, it had around 3,000 units in Egyptian cities and villages.[20] Hassan Al-Banna roamed across the various regions of the country, he is even said to have visited thousands of them, and delivered speeches, lectures and sermons even in cafes and bars. He also exploited the political, economic and social conditions of the time, which helped him attract a large number of followers, especially among workers and farmers, the most disadvantaged classes in this period.

Moreover, the group managed to present itself as an alternative to the secular currents which sought to adopt a Western lifestyle. The group promoted itself as being able, through religion, to provide solutions to ideological, economic, social, political and other issues, and took advantage of people's innate religiosity to penetrate all different segments of society.

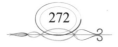

There is no doubt that the group's utilization of the media in Egypt had greatly helped its substantial horizontal spread. Besides direct interaction via lectures and otherwise, the group issued a Muslim Brotherhood newspaper in 1933, and *Al-Natheer* magazine in 1938, which focused in particular on issues in the Arab and Muslim worlds. Moreover, several local newspapers and magazines opened their doors to Al-Banna's writings, such as the *Al-Manar* and *Al-Taaruf* journals, as well as the newspapers *Al-Fateh* and *Al-Amana*.[21]

Following its rapid spread through Egypt, the Muslim Brotherhood group began to disseminate its thought abroad, where its call was well received due to the political, economic and social conditions the Arab and Muslim peoples were experiencing in the wake of the colonial era. Hassan Al-Banna sought to establish relations with Islamic groups and organizations in many Arab and Muslim countries, thus confirming that the Brotherhood was undertaking global outreach based on the calls to restore the Islamic Caliphate. This was evident in the first Muslim Brotherhood by-law which emphasized the universality of the Muslim Brotherhood's call.[22] The group established branches in many of these countries, and others which were organizationally loyal to the Muslim Brotherhood group emerged and promoted it in many Arab and Muslim countries. This was not surprising, especially as the group raised the slogan: "[serving] God (Allah) is our purpose; the Holy Quran is our Constitution; the Prophet is our leader; *jihad* is our way; death for the cause of God (Allah) is our supreme objective."[23]

Such principles are appealing to every Muslim, and they are undisputable as they are drawn directly from Islamic doctrine. However, these principles were turned into slogans, and exploited by the group to achieve group-specific ends and even narrow personal interests.[24]

The Syrian Arab Republic is considered one of the first Arab countries where the Muslim Brotherhood's thought took hold; some sources argue that the group's emergence there dates back to 1935, through a group of Syrian university students.[25] In 1936 it spread in the Sudan; then it entered the Hashemite Kingdom of Jordan in 1945 through Abdullatif Abu Qoura,[26] who was introduced to the group's thought via its magazine *Muslim Brotherhood* which was concerned with the Palestinian cause. The group's headquarters was officially opened in Amman in 1945, under the patronage of King Abdullah Ibn Al Hussein, who expressed his admiration for the call, hoping it would be blissful for the Muslim *umma*.[27] In Kuwait, a division of the Muslim Brotherhood was established in 1947 by Abdulazeez Al-Ali Al-Mutawa and Abdullah Al-Ali Al-Mutawa, from the prominent Kuwaiti Al-Qenaei family, after Abdulazeez Al-Mutawa met Al-Banna in Cairo, where he was studying.[28]

The Kuwaitis feared the prospect of religious control of their lives, especially having witnessed what the Islamists were doing in neighboring countries, besides the negative connotations of the Muslim Brotherhood's name, which brought back memories of attacks by "Brothers" *(Ikhwan)* from tribes in the Arabian Peninsula on Kuwait on January 28, 1928.[29] Nevertheless,

274

the Muslim Brotherhood's call resulted in the Islamic Guidance Society being officially declared as a social front for the group in Kuwait in 1952.[30] This coincided with an influx of a number of Muslim Brotherhood's members from Egypt and other Muslim countries to work in the State of Kuwait. It is noteworthy that membership of the Muslim Brotherhood's division in Kuwait was open even to non-Kuwaitis, so the group exploited this point and instructed its members, who came to Kuwait to work as teachers, to enroll with the division.[31] In 1991, the Islamic Constitutional Movement (ICM) was established to be a political front for the Muslim Brotherhood in Kuwait, and since then the group has had an active and influential presence in the country.[32]

In Tunisia, the emergence of the Brotherhood dates back to the late 1960s under the name Islamic Action, and its early secret meetings were revealed in 1972.[33] Meanwhile, the emergence of the group in Pakistan dates back to 1947, when there was communication between Al-Banna and Muhammad Ali Jinnah, President of Pakistan which had just achieved independence from India.[34]

In the United Arab Emirates, the emergence of the Muslim Brotherhood group was not much different in terms of its incorporation or thought from the parent group in Egypt. The development of the group's activity in the United Arab Emirates took several forms, the first of which was an activist organization promoting conservative religious ideas, which later became a more proactive initiative to influence the state and society in order to benefit its ideological and doctrinal convictions and tendencies, eventually ending in confrontation with the state and its institutions.[35] In the beginning, there was expansion and the spread of influence, and some researchers say that Qatar was the staging point of the Muslim Brotherhood group toward the United Arab Emirates, and particularly to Dubai.[36] The Muslim Brotherhood's branch in the United Arab Emirates began its activity from the headquarters of the Qatari educational mission in Dubai, founded by Abdulbadie Saqr who used to supervise it during his many trips to the United Arab Emirates. Saqr appointed Syrian and Palestinian supervisors from the Muslim Brotherhood at the mission. Moreover, Dr. Yousuf Al-Qaradawi helped Saqr in managing the Muslim Brotherhood's branch when it was founded in Dubai in 1974[37] under the name of the Reform and Social Guidance Association (Al-Islah). Al-Islah had close connections with the Muslim Brotherhood's leaders in the Arab Republic of Egypt, and was able to infiltrate UAE society and take advantage of its strong influence in the educational process. The group employed activities such as preaching, education, religious sermons and lectures, but these methods were a disguise for its real intentions—to recruit new members who believed in the Muslim Brotherhood's ideology, especially among young people.[38] This was a short-term tactic in order to achieve the group's long-term strategic objectives.

Mansour Al-Nogaidan quoted Muhammad Abdullah Al-Rokn, one of the first members of the Muslim Brotherhood group in the United Arab Emirates, saying that some Emirati

students studying in the State of Kuwait at that time wished to establish educational associations and institutions in the UAE similar to those in Kuwait. So in 1974 they founded the Reform and Social Guidance Association (Al-Islah) in Dubai.[39] These students also succeeded in mobilizing support for their call from some dignitaries, businessmen and religious scholars.[40]

After the Reform and Social Guidance Association was founded, the Muslim Brotherhood's cadres became active across the education sector, becoming involved in developing the curriculum and controlling student activities. In this regard, Mansour Al-Nogaidan says that the Association has worked since its inception to attract students and youths, and has targeted education institutions, allowing its members to control student scouting activities and summer centers. By the early 1980s, the Muslim Brotherhood had dominated the public education sector, including curriculum design and management in the Ministry of Education and government universities, and in 1988 it became an influential party in the UAE's educational institutions.[41]

When the wave of regional protests and turmoil began in 2011, culminating in the Muslim Brotherhood winning the 2012 presidential elections in the Arab Republic of Egypt, the group's elements in the UAE, like many other Brotherhood followers and leaders around the world, became inspired by the delusional notion that the establishment of the Caliphate might be possible. Hence, they showed their true colors and engaged in a conspiracy aimed at destabilizing the security of the UAE.

However, the UAE authorities discovered the plot in 2012, countering the Muslim Brotherhood's propaganda and exposing the true goals of the group's elements in the UAE, which were closely linked to the parent organization in the Arab Republic of Egypt and associated with the International Organization of the Muslim Brotherhood. These elements abandoned their national loyalty by pledging their allegiance to the General Guide of the group and seeking to achieve its objectives and serve its interests, ignoring national principles and the requirements of citizenship.

This is consistent with the content of a document issued in July 1982 by the International Organization of the Muslim Brotherhood.[42] This document does not recognize the principle of national loyalty, but rather establishes loyalty to the group or the international organization (and ultimately to the General Guide, the head of the organization). One of the organization's by-laws states that:

> The Muslim Brothers everywhere are one group, brought together by the by-laws, and its objectives are to liberate all parts of the Muslim homeland of any non-Islamic authority and to establish the Islamic state.[43]

The by-laws also suggest that every national organization is part of the International Organization of the Muslim Brotherhood, and that each organization's supervisor owes allegiance to the Supreme Guide in the Arab Republic of Egypt.[44]

The relationship between the Muslim Brotherhood group and the other Gulf Arab states dates back to the 1930s, as there was a connection between Al-Banna and some Saudi officials, which later led to the opening of the Kingdom's doors for Muslim Brotherhood members to live and work there, especially in the field of education. After the confrontation with the regime of former Egyptian President Jamal Abdul Nasser in the mid-1950s, members of the group flocked to the Kingdom, and then gradually to the other Gulf and Arab states, where the call spread unevenly. Although it did not take the shape of a formal regional organization in the Gulf, it was clearly present, and expanded using charitable and societal facades. In Bahrain, in particular, and despite the lack of information about the beginning of the Muslim Brotherhood's call there, the first association bearing the Muslim Brotherhood's thought was founded in 1941 and was called the Students Club.[45] In Yemen, and in spite of the early contacts between the Muslim Brotherhood's leaders in Egypt and some Yemeni religious figures, the organized Islamic action appeared in 1959 at the hands of a group of students, most notably Abdul Majeed Al-Zindani.[46]

Since its inception in 1928, the Muslim Brotherhood has also expressed a great interest in developing a foothold in the Kingdom of Saudi Arabia, due to the Kingdom's spiritual and geographical significance. Since the late 1920s, the group's founder Hassan Al-Banna used to perform Hajj, and successfully exploited his visits to strengthen his ties with the Hijaz dignitaries who have emphasized their support to him.[47]

During the rule of the former Egyptian President, Jamal Abdul Nasser, and particularly since the mid-1950s, a large number of the Muslim Brotherhood's elements have headed to the Kingdom of Saudi Arabia to escape prosecution. They succeeded in penetrating Saudi society, taking advantage of the support provided to them by the Kingdom at that time. These circumstances gave rise to new Muslim Brotherhood leaders in the Kingdom of Saudi Arabia, particularly in charities, universities and other educational institutions.[48]

Over the years, the Muslim Brotherhood in the Kingdom of Saudi Arabia was able to establish an influential presence and later tried to exploit the regional events that began in 2011 to demand the enhancement of popular participation, public freedoms, transparency and accountability, rule of law, and the establishment of a civil state that believes in the principles and values of democracy, thereby ignoring the Kingdom's religious particularity. This was the reason for the increased tension with the authorities, and the deterioration in the status of the Muslim Brotherhood's elements within the country, and in March 2014 the group was designated a terrorist organization along with a number of other organizations inside and outside the country.[49]

For the first time since 1928, the Muslim Brotherhood group and its international organization face widespread popular and official rejection in the Arab and Muslim worlds. The group is renounced socially and legally banned in several countries such the Arab Republic of Egypt, the United Arab

Emirates and the Kingdom of Saudi Arabia, and public opposition to its activities is evident in countries such as the Hashemite Kingdom of Jordan, the State of Kuwait and the Democratic People's Republic of Algeria.

> *After gaining a foothold in the Arab and Muslim worlds, the Muslim Brotherhood expanded globally, and has now spread to about 72 countries.*

The Muslim Brotherhood tried during its early years to establish branches in the Maghreb, so in 1937 it founded two divisions in Morocco, one in Fez led by Muhammad bin Allal Al-Fassi, and the other in Tangier led by Ahmed bin Al-Siddiq, but the French occupiers arrested its prominent leaders such as Al-Fassi, which resulted in the group's decline and halted its expansion.[50] Later, the group became active again in the 1960s under Dr. Abdulkareem Al-Khatib, head of the Moroccan parliament in 1965, who provided political cover to the group through the establishment of the Popular Democratic Constitutional Movement in 1967, which changed its name in 1998 to the Justice and Development Party after some members of the Reform and Renewal Movement joined.[51]

After spreading in many countries in the Arab and Muslim worlds, the Muslim Brotherhood's call began to spread to the West, taking advantage of the free environment in Europe and the United States of America. It also spread in Asian countries, and now the group exists in around 72 countries across the world (see Figure 0.1, p. 54).[52]

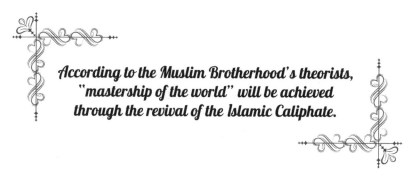

According to the Muslim Brotherhood's theorists, "mastership of the world" will be achieved through the revival of the Islamic Caliphate.

The group's tendency toward foreign expansion was inseparable from the primary goal of its establishment; rather it is an essential stage in the context of its ultimate goal to establish an Islamic Caliphate.[53] The Caliphate, according to Al-Banna, is a religious rite and a symbol of the unity of the Arab and Muslim worlds, but what is more important to the Brotherhood is to achieve what Al-Banna called "mastership of the world."[54] So, Islamic unity, in its framework represented in the Caliphate, is considered one of the essential intellectual assets of the Muslim Brotherhood group, but unlike some groups – such as the Liberation Party, for example, which believes that the change should be from the top down to the base; i.e., changing the ruler to reform the ruled – the group believes that the process should be gradual, and from the bottom up to the top. Therefore, the Muslim Brotherhood's goals were short-term in character but stretched out over a period determined by existing internal

circumstances and the prevailing international environment—this is perhaps one of its most dangerous aspects, and one which enhances its ability to infiltrate the collective consciousness of populations through mechanisms of social and educational indoctrination.

Goals and Means

Any group, party, organization or entity is established in order to achieve specific goals—some interim, others strategic. In this context, identifying the Muslim Brotherhood's goals is particularly important in order to determine the effectiveness of the group and the extent of its success in achieving these goals, which can be listed as stated in the group's by-laws and regulations:[55]

1. Implement Islamic law (*Sharia*) in the various political, economic, social and educational fields.

2. Convey Islam to people in accordance with the Muslim Brotherhood's approach (based, both in its preaching and regulatory aspects, on the vision of the group's founder Hassan Al-Banna, which appeared in *The Collected Epistles of the Martyred Imam Hassan Al-Banna*, a book the group idolizes and confers with spiritual stature comparable to that of the Prophet's sayings (Hadith) and Noble Sunnah, besides the intellectual frameworks stated by the group's former theorist Sayyid Qutb in his book *Ma'alim fi Al-Tareeq* (Signposts on the Road).

3. Exert efforts to raise the standard of living and develop the *umma*.

4. Revive the spirit of *jihad*, pursue the liberation of usurped Muslim lands, and help Muslim minorities.

5. Pursue the unity of the Muslim *umma*.

It is noted that, in their entirety, these goals are sublime and touch the feelings of all Muslims, and are perhaps indisputable. It is also noted that any political religious movement probably has the same goals. However, the truth is only evident in practice, and the secrecy surrounding the group's real objectives indicates that not all of these stated goals are key to the group's approach, vision and understanding; here, specifically, the journey of exaggeration, disagreement and exclusion begins.

In order to achieve its objectives, the group has, since its early years, used a variety of different means, methods and techniques, including individual education, physical and ideological training, propaganda and media (in the form of newspapers and magazines, as well as through general writings, publications and mosques). Insistence on discipline and obedience is a major principle of the group's internal work, and since its first clash with the monarchical regime in Egypt before 1952 it has adopted covert action as a fundamental approach which has become one of the most important characteristics of its work, and perhaps the main reason for the ambiguity of its activities and the evolution of its goals;[56] hence the official resentment and periodic battles with the group.

This was one of the main reasons for the failure of its rule in the Arab Republic of Egypt in 2012–2013, when it acted as an insular group, separate from and not within a political system having its rules and governance institutions. Moreover, the group failed to abandon its rigid ideology and begin acting in the interests of the nation, and refused to treat rival groups and parties in the political arena with equity.[57]

> The book *Ma'alim fi Al-Tareeg* (*Signposts on the Road*) not only rejects governance systems in the Arab and Muslim worlds, but also calls upon political religious groups to challenge the legitimacy of those systems.

The Muslim Brotherhood's Thought and Approach

The Muslim Brotherhood group believes that Islam is a comprehensive religion that should encompass the various social, economic and political aspects of human life,[58] as its founder Hassan Al-Banna writes in one of his letters: "Islam is faith and worship, a state and nationality … a culture and law. A Muslim is required to be familiar with all the affairs of the *umma*."[59]

Thus, the Muslim Brotherhood does not consider itself just a religious preaching group, but also a "political body"; because according to what Al-Banna writes in his letters, it demands governance reform from within; he even went further, stating that: "A Muslim's religion is not perfect unless he is politically active ..."[60]

The group's political participation was originally aimed at reforming society and implementing the teachings and provisions of Islam.[61] The Muslim Brotherhood's interference in politics was based on the idea that Islam advised on all the affairs of life, and tackled all matters of the world, and that Islam without politics is only worship. Moreover, the Muslim Brotherhood considered those who believed in the separation of religion and politics to be adversaries, ignorant of Islam.[62] So the Muslim Brotherhood assumed stances on state-related issues such as governance, democracy, minorities and other aspects of the governance and management of state and society.

Politically, the Muslim Brotherhood supported the *Salafiyya* principle—returning to the ideal society designed by the Prophet Muhammad (pbuh) in the seventh century AD. The political dimension of Islam was crucial to the Muslim Brotherhood's thought. As Al-Banna explains:

> Islam is a comprehensive system, dealing with all spheres of life; it is a state and a homeland, or government and an umma; it is a morality and power, or mercy and justice; it is a culture and law, or knowledge and jurisprudence; it is material and wealth, or gain and prosperity; it is *jihad* and a call or army and an idea, and it is a truthful belief and honest worship.[63]

> *Sayyid Qutb's Ma'alim fi Al-Tareeq (Signposts on the Road) is one of the most prominent intellectual products of the Muslim Brotherhood.*

Sayyid Qutb's *Ma'alim fi Al-Tareeq* (Signposts on the Road) is one of the most important books about the Muslim Brotherhood's philosophy, thought and principles. The Al-Azhar Board of Scholars, however, has repeatedly condemned the book. They considered Qutb to be Kharijite because of his use of the concept of *hakimiyya* that opposed any earthly sovereignty.[64] The book is considered to be a manifesto for militant religious groups in the Arab and Muslim worlds.[65] It is one of the few books that examine the politics of modern societies and compare it with the Islamic political model. Qutb's *Signposts* not only rejects modern regimes in the Arab and Muslim worlds, but also presents the ideology that Islamic groups should challenge the legitimacy of contemporary regimes. The concept of *jahiliyya*:

> is the cornerstone on which the theoretical construction of *Signposts* rests. If it is true that contemporary society can be reduced to pre-Islamic *jahiliyya*, of which it is no more than a sophisticated copy, then Muslims must view it just as the Prophet (pbuh) and his companions viewed their society.[66]

Sayyid Qutb defines *jahiliyya* as:

Any society that is not Muslim ... any society in which
something other than God (Allah) alone is worshipped
... Thus, we must include in this category all societies
that now exist on Earth.[67]

Having defined *jahiliyya* in contrast to Muslim society,
Qutb explained the ways through which *jahiliyya* can be
transformed into an Islamic society. First, in order to change
the conditions of *jahiliyya*, Muslims must return to their
original sources, i.e. the Holy Quran and the Prophet's Noble
Sunnah. Second, *jihad* is emphasized as a legitimate way to
resist the forces of *jahiliyya*.

The Muslim Brotherhood considers Muslim states that
are ruled by secular laws to be living in a state of *jahiliyya*.
Consequently, the Muslim Brotherhood emphasized the
political role of Islam:

This religion did not come only to remain confined in
the corners of places of worship ... it may govern life
and administer it and mold society according to its total
image of life, not by preaching or guidance alone but
also by setting laws and regulations.[68]

For the Muslim Brotherhood, the contract between
Muslims and their governments is conditioned upon the
implementation of *Sharia*. If rulers fail to implement *Sharia*,
then the contract is considered invalid and *jihad* is considered a
legitimate Islamic method to remove the rulers.

The Muslim Brotherhood provided an alternative ideology
during periods of backwardness and turmoil. The group became

active and effective in a period of confrontation between traditional established values and modern values. Talcott Parsons explains that the reaction of religious groups has been prominent in those areas of society where traditional elements have formed the points of reference for guidance and orientation.[69]

Although the Imams Muhammad Abdu and Jamal Al-Deen Al-Afghani's teachings were different from the organized and more political approach of Al-Banna, the Muslim Brothers believed their movement to be a continuation of previous Islamic groups and currents such as Wahhabism. The comprehensive nature of the Muslim Brotherhood influenced its vision of Islam. The Brotherhood rejected secular policies and considered the separation between religion and state to be anti-Islamic because Islam calls for *deen wa dawlah* (a religion and a state.) Muhammad Al-Ghazali, an ideologist from the Muslim Brotherhood said:

> We will not sell our religion for the whole Orient and Occident. This religion of ours, for which we are prepared to sacrifice everything we love, has a theology, an economic doctrine and a world policy all its own. It is a sinister thing to exhort us to discard all of these for nationalism, communism, democracy or any other "ism"; for it is nothing less than asking us to become heathen. The "Islamism" in which we believe and for which we work will automatically take care of our homeland and enable every citizen to live a righteous, abundant, egalitarian, and just life, no matter what his denomination or sect may be.[70]

The Muslim Brotherhood believes that Islam is a comprehensive social, economic, and political system that is adaptable to modern societies. However, Hassan Al-Banna did not look to the West in order to achieve his goals. Rather, he used Islam in defining such goals:

> The [Muslim] Brotherhood is a Salafi message, a Sunni way, a Sufi truth, a political organization, a sporting organization, a cultural–educational union, an economic project, and a social idea.[71]

The Muslim Brotherhood's Stance on Systems of Governance

The government system is a set of general rules under which a state is governed. Usually the system of governance applicable in any state reflects the nature of the evolution of its society and its public values and culture. Hence, the modern era has witnessed the emergence of several types of government system that differ in form and substance. Although it is not one of the objectives of this book to delve into the genesis of these systems or the details of their underlying principles, I would like, however, to examine the most prominent modern systems, to determine their compatibility with the realities of the Arab and Muslim worlds, particularly in countries witnessing domestic transformations since 2011 which have opened the door for the Muslim Brotherhood to participate in government or even to rule. On the other hand, these events provided an unprecedented opportunity to observe how realistic the group's approach was, and how capable it was of applying the slogans and principles it had advocated for decades—especially

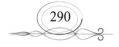

with regard to the government system, its form, nature and practice.

Needless to say, the most important systems prevailing in global political culture today are: the parliamentary system in which the authority is concentrated in the hands of the prime minister whilst the presidency is a ceremonial position, as in the British political system; the presidential system, in which the president enjoys decision-making authority, as in the United States of America; and the mixed system which combines the two, wherein the authorities are divided between the presidency, the government and parliament, as in the French Republic. Regardless of the form of the government system, what matters in the discussion of the Muslim Brotherhood's perspective of the political system and the state – is the system's underlying general rules or principles that allow us to compare between the Muslim Brotherhood's stance on the governance and the extent of its conformity with what the case should be in Islam on the one hand, and the Western liberal thought which produced these systems on the other.

The Muslim Brotherhood, as it claims, seeks to establish an Islamic system of government similar to the Caliphate system. Thus, the nature of the relationship between state and religion was declared, directly and from the very beginning, where the group entirely refuses to separate them, and in this sense Al-Banna says: "Islam is a religion and a state, a government and an *umma*, a Holy Quran and a sword, a rule and an execution, a law and a judiciary, and none can be separated from the other."[72]

Al-Nizam Al-Siyasi fi Al-Islam (The Political System in Islam) by Muhammad Abdulqadir Abu Faris, is one of the most important texts on government and politics for the Muslim Brotherhood.

The Muslim Brotherhood believes that the Islamic government system must be based on a set of rules derived from *Sharia*. Such rules were explained by Muhammad Abdulqadir Abu Faris, a prominent Muslim Brotherhood figure in the Hashemite Kingdom of Jordan, whose book *Al-Nizam Al-Siyasi fi Al-Islam* (The Political System in Islam) is one of the most important texts for the Muslim Brotherhood in this regard.[73] It is a system based on *hakimiyya*, justice and equality, and the Shura Council. Perhaps the most important element of this system is the conclusive text that Islamic *Sharia* is the only source of legislation in the Islamic state, and in this context, it is not possible to separate religion and state. In other words, the Islamic state should derive its laws from Islamic law only (the Holy Quran and the Prophet's Noble Sunnah).

Since its inception, the Muslim Brotherhood group has emphasized an intellectual or ideological reference, which means that the laws governing the Muslim society should be directly derived from a fundamental concept for the Muslim Brotherhood, which is the principle of *hakimiyya*, which stipulates the absolute authority of God (Allah) in the universe, and that God (Allah) alone has the right of legislation and to determine what benefits the people and what harms them, as He is their Creator and their Lord, and He alone, has the right to permit or forbid, and thus no one in this world can come up with different rules. Advocates of this principle also argue that laws and legislation in Islam embody the orders of Almighty God (Allah), and whoever disagrees with this is marked with *jahiliyya*. The Muslim Brotherhood's perspectives regarding Islamic *Sharia* and the interpretation of its texts are based on this principle. Sayyid Qutb[74] played a key role in establishing the concept of *hakimiyya*, which, as mentioned above, has become the most distinguished characteristic of the Muslim Brotherhood's thought, and he had significant influence among the group's youth and others who regarded Qutb's ideas as the exact description of social reality, especially in the 1950s and 1960s, which highlights the need to reform society even if this required the use of violence and force. Therein lies the danger of the Muslim Brotherhood's thought, as the issue is not about discussing doctrinal ideas and accepting them fully or partially, but mainly about how to apply these ideas and the mechanisms of that application which the Muslim Brotherhood group, through the writings of is theorists, has aggressively promoted to the point of violence and bloodshed in order to achieve its ultimate goal of assuming authority.

> *In order to justify violence, Sayyid Qutb relied on what he described as the jahiliyya of Islamic societies and the jahiliyya of the twentieth century.*

In his perspective on the system of governance, Sayyid Qutb relied on the hypothesis of modern society's *jahiliyya*, which he called the "*jahiliyya* of the twentieth century,"[75] arguing that the problems faced by the world were caused by the absence of *hakimiyya* and deviation from the teachings of Islam, to the extent that it became difficult, as Qutb's says, to distinguish between the reality of Muslim society during that period and the reality of the era of *jahiliyya* that preceded the advent of Islam.[76] Qutb suggested that a form of sacrilege against one of the greatest attributes of God (Allah), *hakimiyya*, was occurring not in terms of rejection of God (Allah) by Muslim societies, but rather through the creation of values, perceptions, legislation and rules without regard to, and even conflicting with what God (Allah) has prescribed.[77] The concept is correct, and there is no dispute among Muslims who profess the singularity of authority – which means that God (Allah) alone creates things

and prudently manages the affairs of his creation[78] – and the singularity of divinity, which means that God (Allah) alone should be worshipped through the prayers of his subjects. However, the problem always occurs in relation to the understanding and interpretation of the concept and how it should be put into practice—in particular the tendency to exploit the concept within narrow frameworks to serve certain personal or factional purposes.

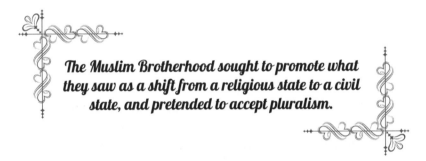

The Muslim Brotherhood sought to promote what they saw as a shift from a religious state to a civil state, and pretended to accept pluralism.

Nevertheless, the Muslim Brotherhood promoted what its ideologues described as an intellectual shift regarding this issue and toward the whole idea of the state and whether it should be secular or religious.[79] A wave of liberalism and democracy began sweeping through many countries around the world, especially after the end of the Cold War. Then, in the context of the Brotherhood's attempts at adjustment to the changes taking place around it – as it realized how unrealistic and even unacceptable its approach was, even to the populace – the group's literature declared a shift in its perception of the state, from a religious state concept, which has been practically exercised within the framework of the Caliphate state,[80] to a civil state based on the principles of democracy such as pluralism and citizenship, but with emphasis on the Islamic reference. However, it transpired that the adoption of this concept was only an attempt to give a secular veneer to its religious discourse directed to the outside world. In truth, there was no intent to apply the principles of a civil state. This was one of the reasons behind the failure of its ruling experience in the Arab Republic of Egypt during the period from June 30, 2012 to July 3, 2013.

> *The Muslim Brotherhood's talk about the civil state was only an attempt to give a different image to its religious discourse directed to the outside, without committing to applying the essence of the civil state and its principles of governance.*

However, the most important shift in the context of the alleged intellectual transformations is the proclaimed acceptance of a mechanism that allows Muslim society to decide on this matter, particularly as there is an assumption that Muslim society, if given sufficient opportunity and freedom, will choose *Sharia*. This might be the basis for making the idea of democracy, as a ruling mechanism, acceptable to the Muslim Brotherhood, and perhaps for many other political religious groups. The Muslim

Brotherhood group, in its recent writings, demonstrated its acceptance of the idea of democracy and that the application of *Sharia* should be left to the people and decided through a referendum;[81] meaning people should be given the choice of whether to implement *Sharia* or not.[82] This approach is contradictory to the concept of *hakimiyya* promoted by Sayyid Qutb, as well as the basis on which the Muslim Brotherhood group was established, i.e., that the application of *Sharia* is not optional because it is from God (Allah), and thus the ruler, assisted by the clerics and society, must apply it. This contradiction reveals political opportunism in the thought of the Muslim Brotherhood and shows that they are willing to take advantage of any social or political condition to serve their own interests, without any consideration of their own religious discourse.

This shift raises many questions: firstly, regarding the extent of the group's commitment to the principles upon which it was established, in terms of there being no contradiction, or at least ambiguity, in the Muslim Brotherhood's thought; and secondly, in the degree of pragmatism (or political deception similar to Shiite political thought, concealing one's true views and motives), in addition to *takfir;* systematic lying;[83] besides other characteristics that have become distinct features of the Brotherhood's interaction with its surrounding ideas, groups, governments or systems.

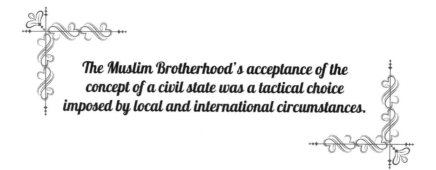

The Muslim Brotherhood's acceptance of the concept of a civil state was a tactical choice imposed by local and international circumstances.

It is claimed that a change has occurred in the Muslim Brotherhood's thought since the mid-1990s, in that it requires an explicit acceptance of democracy along with its associated concepts such as citizenship and the multiparty system. Some observers consider this to be the most significant shift in the Brotherhood's thought regarding the state and the government system, for which it was highly praised by some communities. This, however, made it prone to broad accusations from those of various different views and orientations within Muslim societies, saying that the group has deviated from the pure concept of the Islamic state and what it should be in the present era. Moreover, many accused the Muslim Brotherhood of turning into a self-interest group which did not adhere to its own principles,[84] and even exploited religion to assume authority and achieve narrow personal gains. The Brotherhood realized that its approach was unrealistic and even unacceptable to essential segments of Islamic societies which are wary of religious rule in light of the historical background brought about by the rule of the Church in Central Europe—which had plunged the entire continent into darkness. Thus, the Brotherhood

found itself left with no option but to change its discourse and accept the idea of a civil state. It claims that over the past two decades, the concept of the civil state has become a part of the group's slogan, rhetoric, statements, charters, literature and writings.

The Muslim Brotherhood's stance toward the contemporary state did not necessarily come as a result of firm convictions, it was rather a tactical choice imposed by local, regional and international circumstances. The group has realized that it cannot achieve its goal of establishing an Islamic state in the sense stipulated by Islamic politics without engaging in the existing general political reality which is mostly based on systems and laws derived from Western intellectual, secular and worldly references; this cannot be achieved without adopting the idea of a civil state in its contemporary Western sense. It was not possible to enter the democracy game and then assume authority through elections unless such an idea was adopted. The group has sought to reaffirm its commitments, especially amid doubts raised by many internal and external forces. Thus slogans like civil state and citizenship became an integral part of the Brotherhood's official discourse. The group's prominent figures, leaders and advocates began to vigorously promote such slogans. Perhaps Rashid Al-Ghannooshi, the leader of Ennahdha Movement (Renaissance Party) in Tunisia and one of the Muslim Brotherhood's leaders at the international level, is one of the most prominent figures to introduce the new Muslim Brotherhood's concept of a civil state which is based on democracy and the rights of citizenship similar to that of the

Western example.[85] However the Brotherhood's ideas regarding the nature of this state remained ambiguous, particularly in light of the contrast between some of the group's underlying principles and the underlying principles of the civil state in its modern sense, such as the stance toward minorities, especially regarding the assumption by a non-Muslim of a leadership position (as previously mentioned regarding the appointment of a Christian Indonesian as governor of Jakarta), as well as the issue of the tribute (*jizya*).

The Stance of the Muslim Brotherhood Group toward Parties, Democracy and Shura

The Muslim Brotherhood group was first established as a religious movement, and it was not within its objectives to participate in politics or authority. Article 3 of Part II of the by-laws establishing the Muslim Brotherhood Association in 1930 stated that the group should not interfere in politics or partisan and religious differences,[86] and the preamble of the by-laws also provided for:

> The establishment of a religious association aimed at disseminating *Sharia* laws, urging ethics, seeking to preserve the Book of God (Allah), the Holy Quran, as well as rebuilding ruined houses of worship – mosques ...[87]

Therefore, at that time, issues related to authority or its acquisition, particularly via parties, democracy and elections, were not of any interest to Al-Banna and his group. This period actually saw a good relationship established between the group

and King Farouk, who ruled Egypt from 1936 to 1952. Moreover, the Muslim Brotherhood's stance toward existing political parties and governments was neutral and did not exceed the roles of advising and preaching. Al-Banna wrote in his letters that the most important characteristic of his call was the need for the Muslim Brotherhood to avoid being associated with any party or entity.[88]

However, the group's intellectual position toward political parties was not only different in terms of its commitment to not establishing them or participating in them, but also in terms of their feasibility and legitimacy. Al-Banna discussed political parties in many of his writings, as he said:

> As for our position on political parties, we do not differentiate between them and we are not biased toward any of them, but we believe that they all agree, *inter alia*, that they are not convinced of the necessity of calling for social reform according to the rules and the teachings of Islam[89]

Hence the position of the Muslim Brotherhood toward parties was negative from the beginning and dismissive at a later stage, with Al-Banna demanding that they should be abolished on the grounds that they led to sedition (*fitna*). In 1938, Al-Banna sent a letter to King Farouk calling on him to dissolve the political parties because of their corruption and the division they caused in Egyptian society and the state.[90] In the same context, Al-Banna announced a shift from advocacy to action and struggle, and that the group would consider all parties and leaders as adversaries, whether in government or not, unless they pursued the victory of Islam and the restoration of its rule and glory.[91] This reflected the Brotherhood's early position toward parties that they did not exist in the Islamic religion or its history, that they were imported from, or representative of an alien Western culture that seeks to assume authority, and that they were usually the cause of division and corruption.

The Muslim Brotherhood group gradually realized the need to disguise its ideology in order to achieve its desired political objectives, so it announced a change in its stance on parties, adopting an approach that seemed to be almost the complete opposite. While most of the jurisprudential writings and views were inclined toward rejection and sometimes prohibition, the Muslim Brotherhood began to legitimize the work of parties as regulatory bodies that the group might deal with, participate in or even establish in order to achieve the main objective. So the shift in the Muslim Brotherhood's view of parties was always accompanied by its desire to participate in the elections and assume authority, whether in parliament or at the level of the presidency. The Muslim Brotherhood accepted the multiplicity of political parties,[92] and subsequently established their own, in accordance with the laws they had previously shunned, in many countries including the Hashemite Kingdom of Jordan, the Kingdom of Morocco, the Republic of Tunisia and the Arab Republic of Egypt.

The Muslim Brotherhood's perception and outlook on these parties is inseparable from their outlook on multi-party democracy and accountability. Since its inception, the Muslim

Brotherhood has rejected democracy as a Western concept and was reluctant, to say the least, to engage or work within the framework of democracy or democratic institutions, on an Islamic jurisprudential basis.[93] The Muslim Brotherhood, like other religious groups in this context, was not immune to periodic confusion concerning democracy and basic Islamic concepts like *Shura*, as literature often compared democracy to Islam, although the former is not a religion, and its philosophy is based on the principle of separating religion and politics, or even separating it entirely from the workings of the state.

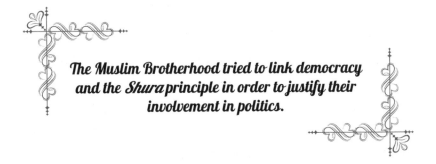

The Muslim Brotherhood tried to link democracy and the Shura principle in order to justify their involvement in politics.

Eventually, using the same logic and pretexts, the Muslim Brotherhood announced its acceptance of democracy as a mechanism to assume, or participate in the exercise of authority to achieve its goals, and began to gradually engage in democracy and to establish parties. As an ideological cover for this, they acted on the hypothesis that there are common denominators between democracy and the principle of *Shura* in Islam, as God (Allah) says in the Holy Quran "and consult them in affairs,"[94] and they view it merely as a tool, rather than in its true spirit. Hence – as many believe – the contrast in perception appears when the issue of choice and compulsion is discussed. Shura is the most important principle underlying the system of government in Islam, as the Muslim Brotherhood and other political religious groups believe, and is perhaps one of the foundations agreed upon by Muslim scholars throughout the ages, but demonstrating democracy as a substitute or equivalent to the concept of *Shura* involves several contradictions. There is extensive disagreement in Islamic jurisprudence as to whether *Shura* is obligatory or not, besides the issue of references to *hakimiyya* and *Sharia*; i.e. religion's role in politics and law.

Al-Banna initially embraced the principle that *Shura* is based on informing, but not obligating, rulers.[95] This, in essence, does not conform to the principle of democracy, where the majority decision is binding in a national framework; hence, it was not possible to engage in politics according to the prevailing rules at that time without embracing this principle, so there was a shift in Al-Banna's thought late in his life when he accepted the principle that *Shura* should be regarded as obligatory rather than merely advisory in nature. In fact the Muslim Brotherhood's position on democracy was a matter of debate within the group itself for many years before deciding in favor the concept on the basis that it best served the long-term interests of the group. At this stage the talk about democracy appeared constantly in Muslim Brotherhood literature and became a platform for them to exploit the situation and then accept the ballot box as a way to assume authority.[96]

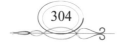

The Muslim Brotherhood's standpoint on the subject of democracy and parties – besides its stance on some jurisprudential issues – has become one of the reasons behind the group's disagreement with other religious currents. It even became a cause for defections that have occurred within the group itself, giving birth to splinter organizations of different ideologies, some of which adopted excommunication-based violence as the basis for their approach and pursuit of change. Disagreement emerged dramatically in the 1990s, when the Islamic Group in the Arab Republic of Egypt resorted to violence and armed confrontation with the Egyptian government.[97] Meanwhile, the Muslim Brotherhood was reconsidering its attitudes to governance and politics, and was working to adapt to contemporary circumstances in light of its desire to participate in government and assume authority. To this end the Brotherhood issued three documents expressing its new viewpoint on the state and governance. These documents are considered the most important – and probably the most dangerous – literature released by the group, to the extent that some consider them to mark the second establishment of the group.[98] The first document, issued in March 1994 and entitled "Women and Shura," emphasized women's rights to work and participate in elections and occupy public and government posts. In the second document, issued in the same month and entitled "Shura and Party Pluralism in Muslim Society," the group announced its acceptance of the constitutional parliamentary rule, the *umma* as the source of all powers, and that people had the right to choose who should rule them. This document also confirmed the Brotherhood's acceptance of the principle of alternating governance by different groups and parties through periodic elections.[99] The third document, entitled "Statement to the People" and issued in April 1995, outlined the general stance on Muslims and non-Muslims and the relationship between religion and politics. It disavowed violence and emphasized the rights of Christians. The highlight of the document was that it pointed out that the legitimacy of rulers should be derived from the consent and choice of the people. Without doubt, these documents represent the Muslim Brotherhood's acceptance of Western political concepts which contradict the principle of *hakimiyya*, without any intellectual or jurisprudential revision reflecting its acceptance of contemporary political realities or relinquishing its intellectual maxims in this regard, which in turn raises questions about the group's commitment to putting these new principles into practice.

> *The Muslim Brotherhood was obliged to embrace democracy, because it realized it to be its only way to assume authority and achieve its goals.*

There are many indications, including in its political practices, that the Muslim Brotherhood has been obliged to embrace democracy and has tried to adapt it to its ideology based on the realization that, under the current circumstances, democracy is its only path to authority. Therefore, the group has once again demonstrated opportunism and clear political deception which has attracted criticism from a variety of Islamic currents – especially Salafi ones – who believed that what the Muslim Brotherhood is doing is in fact contrary to the teachings of Islam as far as rules of governance are concerned. Then these same groups began themselves to exploit democracy to assume authority, including the Salafi Al-Noor Party in Egypt after a review of its approach and jurisprudential options. The issue of democracy – by virtue of the results it was to yield later, such as enabling political religious groups like the Muslim Brotherhood to control politics and government in some Arab and Muslim countries – shows how adaptable such groups are to mechanisms they previously considered man-made and inconsistent with the principle of *hakimiyya*, which once comprised the underlying basis of the Muslim Brotherhood's philosophy regarding its desired system of government. At the same time, it shows a pragmatism that many observers and analysts consider to be a clear demonstration of how all things – including religion – can be exploited in order to assume authority and rule, even if such an act is fundamentally wrong – or unacceptable – in the opinion of widely-recognized religious institutions or scholars.

> *The Muslim Brotherhood's history shows how it exploits and utilizes all mechanisms and means, including religion itself, in order to achieve its goal of assuming authority in various Arab and Muslim countries.*

The Muslim Brotherhood's Participation in Politics (Representative and Parliamentary Councils)

At its inception, the Muslim Brotherhood did not exhibit any interest in political participation or involvement in governance. But as it regarded itself as a comprehensive group concerned with political, social and religious reform, the group emerged as a political group by the late 1930s and early 1940s; it became a major force in some Arab and Muslim countries[100] and began seeking to engage directly in political action.

The Muslim Brotherhood has sought to find a legitimate cover under which to engage with authority in general and to enter parliament in particular, as it believed that entering parliament would provide legal immunity for its organization and protection for its members, as well as a means to spread its call and engage actively in creating legislation in some Arab and Muslim countries.[101]

This began with Hassan Al-Banna himself, who tried to enter the Egyptian parliamentary elections in 1942, but the

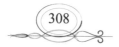

Egyptian Wafdist government headed by Mustafa Muhammad Al-Nahhas (aka. Al-Nahhas Pasha), under pressure from the British occupation, negotiated with Al-Banna to waive his candidacy, in the face of threats to disband the group. Al-Banna agreed but with conditions, including providing guarantees not to prosecute or politically harass the group and allowing it to issue an official gazette in its name.[102] The Muslim Brotherhood then participated in the next elections in 1944 by nominating a number of its leaders, including Al-Banna, but did not win any seats. World War II was then coming to an end, while the Jews were expanding their control and increasing their influence as a prelude to establishing their state in Palestine with the help of the British Mandate. The issue heightened culminating in the 1948 War between Israel and Arab armies.

The Muslim Brotherhood participated in this war with their own forces.[103] Despite this participation, and the fact that the group has boasted of its involvement throughout its literature, it forgets its role and responsibility in this war, and the fact that it blamed the Arab armies for the defeat and accused the Egyptian government in particular of negligence. These accusations escalated with the Muslim Brotherhood's inclination towards a confrontation with the government. As a result, the group's relationship with the regime and the government was strained, and the crisis peaked when the government of Mahmood Fahmi Al-Nuqrashi dissolved the Muslim Brotherhood on December 8, 1948 and confiscated its funds. A member of the group's secret apparatus, named Abdul

Majeed Ahmad Hassan, retaliated by assassinating Prime Minister Al-Nuqrashi Pasha on December 28, 1948.[104]

The group tried to deny its role in this assassination by issuing a statement of condemnation, and Al-Banna himself denounced the murderers with his famous statement that "they are neither brothers nor Muslims."[105] Nonetheless, 24 members of the Muslim Brotherhood were charged. The first defendant was sentenced to death and executed, whilst various other sentences were issued, and some were acquitted. The security apparatus in the Ministry of Interior subsequently retaliated by assassinating Hassan Al-Banna on February 12, 1949.[106] This crisis was the beginning of a new phase of confrontation between the Muslim Brotherhood group and the regime, and henceforth the group's tactics began to shift from working within the framework of the existing political system to working against it to facilitate the desired political change.[107]

The Egyptian army, on the other hand, resented King Farouk's pro-Western policy; hence there was a clear convergence between the Muslim Brotherhood – which was opposed to the British occupation and demanded that the King end it – and the Free Officers organization which was planning to oust the King. As such, a close relationship between the two organizations was established.[108] Perhaps one of the ironies in this context is that Muhammad Anwar Al-Sadat, who later became President of the Arab Republic of Egypt and was ultimately assassinated by extremists, played an essential role in this convergence.[109] The motive behind this convergence was

that the two organizations shared a common goal, to overthrow the regime blamed for the military defeat in Palestine in 1948 as well as the internal problems Egypt was experiencing at that time, so the conditions brought the two organizations together in the same trench against the regime.

The Free Officers, with the help of the Muslim Brotherhood, succeeded in forcing King Farouk to nominally abdicate to his son before being deposed on June 18, 1953, which was followed by the abolition of the monarchy and the proclamation of the Republic.[110] This, in turn, revived the Brotherhood's ambitions to assume authority in the largest Arab country. Then the Muslim Brotherhood stepped up its pressure to participate in government and in all likelihood to share authority with the Free Officers organization. But the latter was aware of the Muslim Brotherhood's motives and goals, so it worked to neutralize the group through its involvement in the government; the group agreed to participate, but tried to exploit the situation to formally impose its conditions on the formation of the cabinet. But in spite of its reservations regarding the number of ministries offered to it – three ministerial portfolios – which it felt would weaken the group whilst strengthening the Revolutionary Command Council – it accepted the offer and nominated three names, all of whom were rejected because they lacked effectiveness or influence. The Free Officers wanted prominent figures from the Muslim Brotherhood to participate, so they offered the Ministry of Awqaf individually to Ahmad Hassan Al-Baqoori, a prominent Muslim Brotherhood leader at that time and a member of the Guidance Office, who accepted the position and consulted the group who in turn did not object, but required him to resign, and he did.[111]

The relationship between the Free Officers and the Muslim Brotherhood did not take long to deteriorate, as the Muslim Brotherhood felt that the new ruling elites did not respond to its demands, especially with regard to its request to form a political party, while the Officers sensed the group's growing negative attitude towards them.[112] The contradictions between the two sides deepened and the indications of a looming clash began to appear. Both sides realized that their objectives were different, and even contradictory,[113] particularly after the Muslim Brotherhood demanded the return of the army to its barracks and the restoration of the country's parliamentary life, so the Revolutionary Command Council decided to dissolve the group and banned it in January 14, 1954, a move that led to the escalation of the confrontation between the two sides. The "Manshiya incident" in Alexandria on October 26, 1954, in which the Brotherhood was accused of attempting to assassinate the President Jamal Abdul Nasser while delivering a speech marking the Evacuation Agreement, ushered in a new confrontational phase in the relationship, with thousands of members of the Muslim Brotherhood being arrested and a special court, called the People's Court, established on November 2, 1954 to try them,[114] which resulted in many of them being sentenced to death.[115]

In the meantime, the struggle for authority between the Free Officers was taking another path, as Major General Muhammed Najeeb Yousuf was deposed from the presidency and put under house arrest, while Jamal Abdul Nasser became Prime Minister and Chairman of the Revolutionary Command Council, and was later elected President of the Republic on June 24, 1956,[116] giving rise to a new phase of the conflict between the Muslim Brotherhood and the regime, characterized by the Muslim Brotherhood's rejection of the authority of the Free Officers, and President Nasser's campaign of arrests and prosecutions of Muslim Brotherhood members. Perhaps the most significant event in the escalation of this conflict was the execution of Sayyid Qutb in 1966 after being convicted on charges of plotting to overthrow the government.

President Nasser was successful in dismantling the Muslim Brotherhood and destroying its organizational structures by the end of 1966; however, the regime was devastated by Israel's victory in the 1967 War. After the decline of Nasser's regime, the Muslim Brotherhood's return to the scene seemed certain. The group perceived the defeat in the 1967 War as a clear indication of the failure of Nasser's secular policies. In short, the consequences of that war generally strengthened the *raison d'être* of political religious groups in the Arab and Muslim worlds.

The defeat resulted, *inter alia*, in the Arabs losing the remaining territory of historic Palestine, and Nasser was held responsible for the defeat. He decided to step down, only to retake office after popular demonstrations called for his reinstatement, but he died suddenly on September 28, 1970, and was succeeded by Muhammad Anwar Al-Sadat as president, and hence began a new phase which differed from its predecessors in terms of the relationship between the Muslim Brotherhood and the regime.

The post-Nasser era saw a clear breakthrough for relations between the regime and the Muslim Brotherhood. President Sadat began his term by introducing a constitutional amendment in 1971 determining the role of religion in politics. That was an indication of Sadat's reconciliatory approach toward the religious mainstream, and was an attempt to establish independent legitimacy based on his own decisions and policies, separating himself from the Nasser era. Sadat released the Muslim Brotherhood's leaders from jail, and even empowered the group to resist opposition forces—particularly the leftists, Nasserists and communists.[117] In turn, the group began returning to the scene and engaging in charitable and social institutions and in the student elections at Egyptian universities.

Although the Muslim Brotherhood refrained from participating in the 1976 elections as a political organization, its members participated individually as independent candidates. One of the Brotherhood's elected candidates was Salah Abu Ismail Muhammad, father of Hazim Salah Abu Ismail, one of the most prominent figures of the Salafi movement today.

The Muslim Brotherhood capitalized on its growing influence to establish an opposition front against President Sadat. Criticism increased and the relationship with the regime descended into confrontation following the Camp David agreement in 1979. The group mounted a fierce campaign denouncing President Sadat's unprecedented, historic visit to Israel on November 19, 1977 as part of his quest to achieve peace. In retaliation, President Sadat launched a campaign of mass arrests, in which many Brotherhood members, including Omar Al-Telmesani, the group's General Guide at that time, were detained.[118] President Sadat's disagreement with the Muslim Brotherhood was neither doctrinal nor ideological, as he wanted to mobilize full support behind the peace negotiations and to ensure their success.[119] The Muslim Brotherhood went on to participate in the 1979 elections, where Salah Abu Ismail was elected again along with Hassan Ahmad Al-Jamal. Muslim Brotherhood sources credit these two members for their efforts in establishing Islamic *Sharia* as the main source of legislation in the constitution of the Arab Republic of Egypt.[120] This is inaccurate, however, as contemporary politicians confirm that credit for the application of *Sharia* should go to none but former President Muhammad Anwar Al-Sadat himself. Sufi Abu Taleb, former Speaker of the Egyptian People's Assembly, points out that Sadat was the real engine behind the project to incorporate *Sharia* in the laws that the Assembly's committees worked on in the late 1970s and completed in the early 1980s:[121]

I can confirm that President Sadat (may God bless his soul) was serious about the application of *Sharia*, and all his deeds and sayings attested to this.[122]

Therefore, the allegations promoted by those sources are clearly inaccurate, and contradict the true events of Sadat's presidency (he was called, among other things, the 'believing' president).[123] Some even propose that President Sadat had sought to Islamize the Egyptian state,[124] although this does not mean that he was a supporter of the Muslim Brotherhood— particularly as he strongly condemned them and leveled several accusations against them, especially after the October 1973 War. He also showed regret for releasing the detained leaders of the Muslim Brotherhood. On September 5, 1981 he stood inside the Egyptian Parliament and denounced the Brotherhood for their conduct and lack of gratitude, saying aloud "I was wrong"[125] and lamenting their release from imprisonment in the early 1970s.[126] Perhaps this position of Sadat towards the Muslim Brotherhood at the beginning of his rule can best be explained in the words of Muhammad Hassanein Haikal, who said that the US strategic vision at that time was based on the need to take the religious current into account.[127]

The tense relationship between President Sadat and the Muslim Brotherhood continued after the Camp David Accords until 1981, when Khalid Shawqi Al-Islambolli, a first lieutenant in the Egyptian army, along with other militants and in coordination with the Islamic Group, assassinated president Muhammad Anwar Al-Sadat on October 6, 1981 during the

commemoration of the October 1973 victory.[128] Sadat's Vice President, Muhammad Husni Mubarak, was appointed as his successor, thus beginning another new phase in the relationship between the Muslim Brotherhood and the Egyptian regime.

At the beginning of the reign of former president Muhammad Husni Mubarak, the relationship witnessed a period of peaceful coexistence. The new president sought to establish his rule through openness to the political forces in Egypt, so he declared his commitment to respecting the rights of people to choose their representatives, and released prisoners the majority of whom were Muslim Brotherhood members. The 1984 elections represented the first test of the President's credibility and commitments. The Muslim Brotherhood took advantage of this new reality to rebuild the organization, and participated in the elections along with other representatives of the Islamic current via the lists of the Al-Wafd Party. It was noteworthy that the regime did not intervene to prevent this alliance, as the Muslim Brotherhood was not yet a political organization, and the election law issued in 1983 did not prohibit inter-party alliances. The total number of winning representatives of the Islamic current under the Al-Wafd Party lists was 10, including six members from the Muslim Brotherhood, while the representatives of Al-Wafd won 48 out of 448 seats.[129]

These were the first elections under the reign of the former President Muhammad Husni Mubarak and a true test of his credibility, thus differentiating his regime from those of his

predecessors. However, the new parliament did not last long, as it was dissolved in 1987 after a court ruled that the law under which the elections were conducted was unconstitutional. The law was amended and new elections were held in 1987, in which the Muslim Brotherhood participated in a coalition with the Labor Party and the Liberal Party under the name "the Islamic Alliance."[130]

It is noteworthy that during these elections, the slogan "Islam is the solution" appeared and was primarily exploited in the electoral campaign. The Muslim Brotherhood participated fully this time, as it wanted to overcome its legal ban – or at least to water down its content in terms of political practice – and demonstrate to the regime and other powers that the Brotherhood was a major force which should not be underestimated or ignored.[131] The economic situation was becoming increasingly difficult, aggravating associated social problems and creating a supportive environment that helped the Brotherhood to achieve a relatively significant result. Of the total 444 seats, the Alliance won 56 seats, 38 of which were held by the Muslim Brotherhood,[132] rendering it the largest opposition bloc in the Egyptian parliament. It was remarkable that a Coptic candidate on the Muslim Brotherhood's list, Jamal Asaad Abdul Malak, won a seat, yet there were no women among the Muslim Brotherhood's members of parliament.[133] The period of coexistence between Mubarak's regime and the Muslim Brotherhood lasted during the 1980s, which can be called the "appeasement" stage.

However, by the late 1980s the situation had changed, as it had with all previous regimes, and a new phase of strained relations began, culminating in hundreds of Muslim Brotherhood members being arrested and referred to military courts, paving the way for a new phase of confrontation. President Mubarak's regime began changing its strategy in dealing with the group, seeking to curtail it politically and socially, especially as its influence was increasing through public services and vocational work. Consequently, the regime amended the Societies Act to limit the Muslim Brotherhood's growing control over charity and union work across the Arab Republic of Egypt. In light of this fact, President Mubarak was not enthusiastic about the participation of the Muslim Brotherhood or any other opposition force in the political process, and the features of confrontation re-emerged. Mubarak did not prevent the Muslim Brotherhood from running in the 1990 elections, but the group decided along with other parties including the Al-Wafd Party, the Liberal Party, and the Labor Party, to boycott the elections due to corruption and the ongoing application of martial law.

The Muslim Brotherhood's support for the Iraqi invasion of Kuwait in 1990 created a rift in the relationship between the group and the Gulf Arab states.

The 1990s witnessed a number of events that affected this relationship between the Muslim Brotherhood and the authorities in the Arab Republic of Egypt, most importantly the Muslim Brotherhood's support for the Iraqi invasion of Kuwait in 1990, which reflected negatively on the relationship between the group and the Arab Gulf states. Later on, the actual confrontation with the Egyptian government was renewed in 1992 in what is known as the "Salsabeel" case, in which the Egyptian government accused the group of attempting to revive its organization.[134] Subsequently, a number of the group's leaders, including Khairat Saad Al-Shatir, were arrested.[135] This coincided with a growing armed confrontation between the state and the Islamic Group, which was conducting terrorist operations in the Arab Republic of Egypt, and in the same context came the attempted assassination of President Muhammad Husni Mubarak in Addis Ababa in Ethiopia, in mid-1995, which Cairo accused Khartoum of plotting in collusion with the Islamic Group.

The confrontation continued, but it took new shape when the first military trial of the Muslim Brotherhood in the era of President Mubarak was conducted in 1995 on charges of creating a secret organization to overthrow the government. The trials continued until 2000, when a number of the group's leaders were convicted and imprisoned, including the current General Guide Muhammad Badie. So the last decade of the last century was characterized by tension and confrontation.[136]

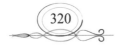

Nonetheless, the trials and the obvious organizational regression did not significantly affect the group's social and union-related activities, as it maintained its presence as part of many trade unions and student associations. It also continued to provide social services through a large number of charities and social associations scattered across various parts of the country.[137] This was accompanied by what some call "grievance" and depiction of the group in the media as a victim, which contributed, with other factors, to increasing the group's proponents and supporters and strengthened its popular base and chances of election.

During the first decade of the third millennium (2000–2010) the relationship, despite its volatility, started taking on the nature of an understanding based on what might be called "mutual deterrence." Such mutual deterrence was based, on one hand, on the fact that the regime recognized the Muslim Brotherhood's strength and influence, especially in trade unions, charities and student movements, and consequently that it would be impossible to shut down the group entirely. On the other hand, this mutual deterrence was also based on the Muslim Brotherhood's sense, in return, that it would not be able to overthrow President Mubarak or change the existing regime. As such, the two sides had a mutual interest in maintaining the status quo; perhaps giving many an impression or even a conviction that the two sides have an implicit alliance that in fact reflects the group's pragmatism in its dealings with existing political regimes with the aim of serving their own interests.[138] Nevertheless, some believe that the Muslim Brotherhood's animosity toward President Mubarak was greater than toward any other after President Nasser, attributing this to the fact that Mubarak dealt shrewdly with the group, and did not face them using the routine methods of employing the police and security forces.[139]

> *The Muslim Brotherhood has exploited the difficult political, economic and social conditions and the deficiencies in existing government policies to increase its popularity and extend its influence.*

The Muslim Brotherhood once again exploited the difficult political, economic and social conditions and the deficiencies in government policies to increase its popularity and extend its influence, which resulted in the group winning 20 percent of the seats in the 2005 parliament—88 out of 454 seats. Although the Muslim Brotherhood's members were running in the elections as independent candidates – given that the group was banned[140] – this was considered an unprecedented victory in its history, and the culmination of the group's relentless quest over the preceding decades to achieve such a victory.[141] There is no doubt that history has served the Muslim Brotherhood. The development failures of President Muhammad Husni Mubarak's

regime and those that preceded it played a key role – and perhaps were the most influential factors – in this relatively major electoral victory.[142]

The internal situation in the Arab Republic of Egypt was worsening in terms of the rates of poverty, unemployment, corruption, social problems, suppression, repression and heavy-handed security control, broadening the base of the popular opposition to the regime. The Muslim Brotherhood was no longer its main organizational front, as a new force had emerged, known as the Kefaya (Enough) Movement which was mainly established following media propagation of the idea of inherited succession of authority in the Arab Republic of Egypt, whereby President Mubarak's son, Jamal, would eventually assume control after his father.[143] While the Muslim Brotherhood participated in the movement, it attempted to exploit it for the benefit of its own aims, building alliances with the leaders of the demonstrations, which had increased dramatically during the three years preceding the protests of January 25, 2011. Meanwhile, however, it maintained its tacit understanding with the regime until the President stepped down.

In the Hashemite Kingdom of Jordan, the Muslim Brotherhood participated early in the state's political and public life, its first direct participation in politics being in 1956, when the group fielded just six electoral candidates, aware of the sweeping popularity of the nationalists and leftists at that time. Four of the group's six candidates were elected,[144] and the

Muslim Brotherhood was offered an opportunity to participate in the government, but it declined the offer because the system was not based on Islam.[145] Political polarization in the Hashemite Kingdom of Jordan intensified between King Hussein bin Talal, who was an ally of the (democratic capitalist) West, and Prime Minister Suleiman Al-Nabulsi, who was seeking to incline towards the (socialist–communist) East. Therefore, and in light of the growing direct threat to stability and order, the King dissolved the House of Representatives, prohibited political parties, and temporarily suspended parliamentary life in 1956. When it was resumed in 1963 the Muslim Brotherhood again participated in the parliament, although they only won two seats, cutting their representation in half.[146]

But the Muslim Brotherhood's activities were not affected by the decision prohibiting political parties or by the decline in its parliamentary representation, as its public and preaching activities continued in mosques and public institutions. This allowed the group to achieve gains within labor, vocational and student unions, controlling most of them until the end of the second millennium. However, perhaps the most important factor was the establishment of Islamic centers in various regions of the Kingdom. Yet, at the beginning of the third millennium, nationalist currents and parties began to emerge and grow increasingly popular at the expense of support for the Muslim Brotherhood.

Once again, as a result of the Arab–Israeli conflict, parliamentary life in the Hashemite Kingdom of Jordan was suspended until 1989, when the "April Uprising" erupted as the masses in the south – known for its traditional allegiance to the Royal Jordanian regime – launched violent demonstrations in protest against the economic conditions and because the Jordanian dinar had plummeted, losing half of its value. The Muslim Brotherhood was not instrumental in these demonstrations, as its influence is diminished in tribal areas.[147] The demands of the demonstrators focused on: first, the dismissal of the Zaid Samir Al-Rifai government on the basis of corruption and its responsibility for the deterioration of the economic situation and the collapse of the currency—this demand was immediately fulfilled. Second, the protesters demanded a resumption of parliamentary life after 22 years of suspension, and King Hussein responded by announcing elections for the 1989 House of Representatives. The Muslim Brotherhood participated separately in these elections and won 22 out of 80 seats, with other Islamists accounting for exactly one third of the House of Representatives. Five Muslim Brotherhood members of parliament were also appointed as ministers in the government of Mudar Badran in 1991.[148]

However, despite its significant support for the government of Mudar Badran, the Muslim Brotherhood did not engage in the four governments that followed while it was represented in parliament up to 1997. During this period, significant shifts occurred within the group, as the wave of excommunication and extremism which prevailed in the 1980s and early 1990s declined significantly, the group also witnessed organizational and ideological differences which were reflected in public forums and media.

Economic and social conditions in the Hashemite Kingdom of Jordan were deteriorating since foreign aid had been cut in response to its position toward the Iraqi invasion of Kuwait in August 1990.[149] Additionally, in light of the increasing popular discontent with the government because of its failure to solve the problems of unemployment, debt and rising prices, the Muslim Brotherhood's popularity was rising considerably as it expanded its charitable, societal, union and educational activities. There were concerns in the Hashemite Kingdom of Jordan that the Muslim Brotherhood might win an absolute majority in the elections, which would have been unacceptable, particularly as the Kingdom in 1994 was due to sign a peace treaty with Israel that would require parliamentary approval.

One of the most important factors in the Muslim Brotherhood's electoral success was the multi-vote system, in which each Jordanian voter has a number of votes equivalent to the number of seats allocated to each constituency, increasing the Muslim Brotherhood's chances of winning because it would at least secure a number of the remaining votes of elites and tribesmen in excess of its need. As a result, an amendment was made to the electoral law, adopting the "one person one vote" system common in electoral and democratic practice around the

world. Prior to the elections and after the Parties Law was endorsed, the Muslim Brotherhood established a political party in 1993 called the Islamic Action Front Party,[150] and the group participated in elections with a unified list for the first time. However, its representation dropped dramatically, winning only 17 out of the total 110 seats.[151] From the Muslim Brotherhood's viewpoint, this was the result of the single-vote system, while other observers considered it to be both a true reflection of the group's popularity in the Jordanian street, and an indication of the rise of the nationalist tribal current. The group later participated in the 1995 municipal elections through its new party; however, it did not achieve a significant victory, since voting in municipalities was governed by tribal, rather than political or religious considerations.

The Muslim Brotherhood's relations with the palace and the government were placed under further strain as a result of the Wadi Araba Treaty, which was strongly opposed by the group.[152] At the same time, polarization intensified due to protests against the single-vote system, which prevented the group from securing a repeat of its result in 1993. Recognizing this fact, the group decided to boycott the 1997 elections. The new circumstances cast a shadow over the Muslim Brotherhood itself, resulting in a state of polarization and intense competition between three streams: the first was realistic and tended to ally with the state; the second was hard line and refused appeasement; and the third was moderate and represented by the younger generation.[153] On February 7, 1999, King Hussein bin Talal died, and was succeeded by his son King Abdullah II who pursued an open-door policy with the Muslim Brotherhood. Despite the decision of the government led by Abdul Raouf Al-Rawabdeh to close down the offices of the Palestinian movement Hamas – which has ideological and organizational ties with the Muslim Brotherhood and whose leaders were expelled from the Hashemite Kingdom of Jordan – the Muslim Brotherhood participated in the 2003 elections represented by the Islamic Action Front Party and won 17 seats.

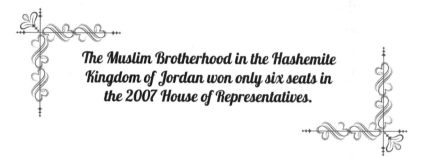

The Muslim Brotherhood in the Hashemite Kingdom of Jordan won only six seats in the 2007 House of Representatives.

The year 2007 represented a real turning point and a test of the Muslim Brotherhood's strength, as it only secured 6 out of 110 seats. This result was a significant political setback. Although the group accused the Jordanian authorities of fraud, many observers and analysts considered the results to be an indication of a genuine erosion of the Muslim Brotherhood's popularity in the Kingdom, and it was highly significant not only at the local level, but also in terms of political Islam across the Arab and Muslim worlds.[154] The group in the Hashemite Kingdom of Jordan was one of the most organized branches of the Muslim Brotherhood, and it had operated legitimately and legally since its inception. Besides, it maintained a good relationship with

the regime, allowing its social and union-related expansion. Therefore its electoral loss had multiple effects, both internally and externally. Perhaps this explains why the group insisted on demanding an amendment to the elections law and to abolish the single-vote system as an excuse to boycott the elections in 2013. Those elections resulted in the unexpected rise of political forces and parties which were represented in the Parliament for the first time, while traditional Islamic forces (the Muslim Brotherhood and the Islamic Action Front) were absent as a result of their decision to boycott the elections—a decision that likely benefited other political forces and currents, particularly the Al-Wasat Islamic Party.[155]

In the Republic of the Sudan, the Muslim Brotherhood established an alliance with the Salafis and the Sufi Tijani followers. They formed a front to run in the 1964 elections after the October Revolution which overthrew the rule of Ibraheem Abbood Shaikh Al-Arab, in which the Islamists, led by Dr. Hassan Abdullah Al-Turabi played a key role. After the 1976 coup attempt by Sudanese organizations and parties whose elements received military training abroad under the support of the State of Libya, the former Sudanese President Ja'afar Muhammad Numairi was concerned regarding parties which had become a threat to his rule, so the following year he took a proactive step to hold what was known as the National Reconciliation in 1977. The parties participated in the reconciliation, and then Al-Turabi, who was a school-friend of President Ja'afar Numairi, dissolved the Muslim Brotherhood because President Numairi did not recognize parties. Al-Turabi played an increasing and visible role in directing affairs in the Republic of the Sudan through his influence on President Ja'afar Numairi himself.[156] As a result of Al-Turabi's role, the Muslim Brotherhood in the Republic of the Sudan was divided into two blocs, one followed Al-Turabi who established the National Islamic Front in 1986, whose primary objective was the Islamization of society, and the second, led by Al-Hibr Yousuf Noor Al-Daiym, was the Muslim Brotherhood, which distanced itself from the Front.[157]

The Muslim Brotherhood participated in the 1986 elections but none of its candidates were successful. On the other hand, the National Islamic Front, led by Al-Turabi, grew more powerful owing to its significant engagement in parliament, the government, the army and even the charities and societal associations, and more importantly the emerging banks, which at the time were the main financier of its activities. The National Islamic Front participated in the 1986 elections and secured 51 seats in the Sudanese parliament.[158] As his ultimate goal was to assume the helm of authority, Al-Turabi, who was known for his shrewdness, engineered the 1989 coup and then personally dissolved the National Islamic Front. In 1991 the (original) Muslim Brotherhood witnessed a split which weakened it, particularly as an Islamic government of mixed orientations had assumed authority in the country following a coup led by Omar Hassan Al-Bashir, who assumed both the premiership and the presidency.

The Islamic Resistance Movement (Hamas) was the first political front for the Muslim Brotherhood in Palestine. Taking into account the nationalist and Islamic dimensions of the Palestinian cause, the Hamas movement was founded in 1987. The intellectual and organizational correlation with the Muslim Brotherhood confirms Hamas as a branch of the group in Palestine.[159] Despite the fact that the purpose of establishing Hamas was primarily to resist the Israeli occupation, it was also undertaking work similar to that of the Muslim Brotherhood in other countries, including activities related to charities, trade unions and students. At the same time, it became politically engaged in municipal and union elections. Social, economic and political conditions were becoming increasingly difficult despite the financial and economic support provided to the Palestinian Authority after the Oslo Accords.

Security conditions had deteriorated under the Palestinian Authority, which mounted an extensive campaign of arrests against prominent Hamas figures and imprisoned many of its leaders and members,[160] which, as a whole, helped to significantly increase Hamas' popularity. It participated in the 2005 municipal elections in the Gaza Strip and won 77 out of 118 seats in the first round, and 30 out of 84 in the second round.[161] The turning point was in 2006, when Hamas participated in the legislative elections and won about 70 percent of the votes (76 out of the 132 seats in the Legislative Council), while Fatah won 43 seats, which enabled Hamas to form the government.[162] It was an unprecedented victory for any group or party representing or

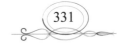

emanating from the Muslim Brotherhood anywhere in the world. However, it was not long before Hamas' popularity began to decline, as it entered into conflict with other Palestinian factions. Hamas' conflict with Fatah eventually led to a military victory which gave Hamas absolute control over the Gaza Strip. This had a significant impact on the Palestinian situation and divisions deepened in an unprecedented way. All this came at a time when Palestinian cause was facing a loss of exposure amid the major events occurring in the region.

On April 23, 2014 Hamas and Fatah signed a reconciliation agreement, and managed to form a national consensus government headed by Rami Al-Hamdallah on June 2, 2014. However this did not solve their differences on some key issues, particularly how to negotiate with Israel in the coming period. The Palestinian issue itself seems to be open to several scenarios, especially after the Israeli war on the Gaza Strip at the end of July 2014, which caused the death of more than two thousand and injured several thousand more Palestinian civilians.

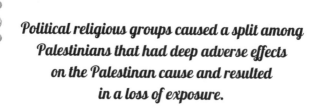

Political religious groups caused a split among Palestinians that had deep adverse effects on the Palestinan cause and resulted in a loss of exposure.

In the Kingdom of Morocco, the political experience of the Muslim Brotherhood is entirely different from most of its other experiences, particularly in the Arab Republic of Egypt, the Hashemite Kingdom of Jordan and Palestine. From the very beginning there was a complete separation between the group's educational activity (represented by the Unification and Reform Movement) and its political activity (represented by the Justice and Development Party).[163] There are not even any common institutions or organizational elements linking the group's educational and political activities. The Justice and Development Party participated in the 1997 legislative elections with 24 candidates, winning 9 out of the 325 seats which constitute the first chamber of the Moroccan Parliament, while the Party was represented by one seat in the second chamber, known as the House of Counselors.[164]

The Kingdom of Morocco's response to regional events was quick and consistent, as it announced important constitutional reforms which maintained stability.

In the 2002 legislative elections, the Party won 42 seats.[165] The terrorist events which took place in the Kingdom of Morocco in 2003 represented a real problem for the Party even though it issued a statement strongly condemning and denouncing the attacks.[166] The Party, however, came under official and popular criticism, not because there were suspicions of its direct involvement in the attacks, but because it was held morally responsible for the attacks as the perpetrators were from the hard-line Salafi current. Some voices within the government demanded the dissolution of the party, but King Muhammad VI intervened to prevent it. Nonetheless, the Party participated in the 2007 elections and won 46 seats, coming in second place for the first time.

Then the events of the so-called "Arab Spring" erupted, and King Muhammad VI's response was both quick and consistent, as he announced important constitutional reforms which paved the way for new elections in 2011.[167] In these elections, the Justice and Development Party managed for the first time to gather more votes than the competing parties and subsequently presided over a coalition government which still exists today—although it faces considerable difficulties, especially as a result of the deterioration of the economic situation and the continuing need for foreign aid. The government has been unable to address the aggravating problems of poverty and unemployment in the country, or achieve the desired development, the promise of which represented the main basis for its election victory.

> *The Muslim Brotherhood does not have a tangible presence or popularity in the Arabian Gulf due to the nature of the society, which is characterized by religiosity, conservatism and the rejection of ideological organizations and parties*

334

In the Arabian Gulf region, the Muslim Brotherhood does not enjoy a noteworthy presence or popularity, not because there is a different outlook that lacks fervent religiosity – on the contrary these societies are overwhelmingly religious and conservative – but rather because the conservative social structure in these societies is predominantly of a stable tribal nature. Arabian Gulf societies do not accept the existence of organizations or groups that may affect their stability or undermine their achievements and the welfare provided to their people. Whilst there are official organizations of the Muslim Brotherhood using social and charitable fronts in some of these countries, politically the Muslim Brotherhood's official presence is limited to the State of Kuwait and the Kingdom of Bahrain.

The Muslim Brotherhood's direct political engagement in the State of Kuwait dates back to the 1960s, as its representatives and other supporters of the religious trend took part in the first elections in the State of Kuwait in 1962. The Muslim Brotherhood aimed to be elected to the constituent assembly to devise a new constitution for the country which had just received its independence from Britain. The results of those elections indicate the weakness of the religious trend in general and the Muslim Brotherhood in particular, as it won only one seat, while the Arab nationalists won 7 seats.[168] In the first Kuwaiti National Assembly elections in 1963 the nationalists won 16 seats, while the Islamic trend secured 7 seats, out of which only two seats were won by the Muslim Brotherhood.[169]

The Brotherhood's organized participation was clearly formed by the early 1990s, when the Islamic Constitutional Movement (Hadas), led by Hamad Hamoud Al-Roomi, was established as a political front for the Kuwaiti Social Reform Association, which in turn is organizationally linked to the Muslim Brotherhood group.[170] Hadas participated in the eight Kuwaiti National Assembly elections that have taken place since 1992. Hadas's average results in the elected councils during this period ranged from 2 to 6 seats, and it claimed only 5 out of 50 seats in the National Assembly elected in 2012. In the same year, the Constitutional Movement competed for the Presidency of the National Assembly against Ahmad Abdulazeez Al-Saadoon, a candidate backed by the leftists and the liberals, but did not succeed. In general, Hadas adopted a policy of appeasement of the regime, as it assumed some ministries and retracted from its previous demands to separate the positions of crown prince and prime minister.[171]

In the Kingdom of Bahrain, the Al-Menbar National Islamic Society was established in 2001[172] to represent the Muslim Brotherhood's orientation and ideology, and as the political arm of the Al-Islah Society which has existed in Bahrain since 1941.[173] Al-Islah did not participate in official political action until the National Action Charter of Bahrain was issued in 2002 to organize the political and parliamentary processes in the country,[174] but before that it used to express its position through statements, seminars or lectures. Al-Islah participated in the 2002 elections, which were boycotted by the

Shiite Al-Wefaq National Islamic Society, and it claimed 7 out of the 40 seats. In the 2006 elections, Al-Islah teamed up with the Al-Asalah Islamic Society which represents the Salafi current in the Kingdom of Bahrain, the aim being to strengthen the Sunni position against other currents which represented a challenge to the state. Once again Al-Islah claimed 7 seats.

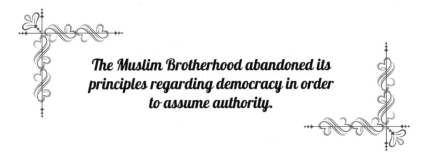

The Muslim Brotherhood abandoned its principles regarding democracy in order to assume authority.

Motives and Implications of Political Participation

Muslim Brotherhood members are spread around the world (see Figure 0.1, p. 54), and there is an uneven presence in terms of their numbers and influence in many Arab and Muslim countries. Proceeding from its primary objective – the pursuit of government and authority under the guise of implementing the *Sharia* and establishing an Islamic state – the Muslim Brotherhood group deemed it necessary, and perhaps inevitable, to participate in existing official institutions, and particularly the legislatures, in order to achieve its goals and objectives.

It had to adapt its principles with regard to democracy, and especially the multiparty system and accountability, because the jurisprudential views of the group on partisanship represented a fundamental obstacle to participation in elections in some of the countries where the Muslim Brotherhood operated.

After the sudden and controversial shift in its position on this issue, the group formed political entities, parties or fronts in order to participate in the elections, which it did in most of the countries where circumstances allowed it to engage in political life. The group took part in the legislative elections in the Arab Republic of Egypt, the Republic of the Sudan, the Hashemite Kingdom of Jordan, the Kingdom of Morocco, the Republic of Tunisia, the Kingdom of Bahrain and the State of Kuwait, and other countries where the Muslim Brotherhood has a presence. Several factors encouraged the group to participate in the elections, including the appeal of its slogan "Islam is the solution" among Arab and Muslim people, and especially those suffering worsening and intractable economic and social problems. Circumstances related to underdevelopment and the suppression of public and individual freedoms worked in the group's favor, making it – by virtue of its efficient organization and infiltration of social and trade unions – the most viable, and sometimes the only alternative to the ruling regimes in certain Arab and Muslim countries.[175]

However, despite its popularity in many of the countries where it participated in political life, the Muslim Brotherhood and the parties emanating from it did not achieve significant results until the victory of Hamas in the 2006 Palestinian legislative elections, the victory of the Freedom and Justice Party in the Arab Republic of Egypt in 2012, the Justice and

Development Party in Morocco, and Ennahdha Movement party in the Republic of Tunisia in 2011. Hamas's victory came as a result of the difficult prevailing conditions at all levels in the occupied territories. The Palestinians were fed up with the Palestine Liberation Organization (PLO), as one faction was controlling it, its policy and direction. Moreover, the authority that emerged from the Oslo Accords failed to achieve the minimum demands of the Palestinian people. As such, there was no choice but change, and the change this time favored Hamas.[176]

On the other hand, the victory of the parties representing the Muslim Brotherhood in the Arab Republic of Egypt, the Kingdom of Morocco and the Republic of Tunisia came after popular protests. There was no other alternative, particularly as the existing regimes had been deposed. The Muslim Brotherhood was the only organized and influential force in society, owing to its social, charitable and trade union activities, so it emerged as the first choice for the majority of people in the countries where these protests occurred.

From its inception in 1928 until 2014, the Muslim Brotherhood's popularity did not exceed 20 percent.

The overall pattern indicates, however, that these groups did not achieve significant electoral success, as their representation in most cases did not exceed 20 percent of the seats in the parliaments and legislatures they entered. However, even more important in this context was that all these groups witnessed a gradual decline and in some cases considerable regression in their popularity, even among their traditional supporters and in areas where they had once received strong backing. Therefore, according to the majority of estimates, from its inception in 1928 until 2014 the Muslim Brotherhood's popularity did not exceed 20 percent. At present the Muslim Brotherhood's popularity in those countries that represented major incubators for the group and its thought is no more than 10 percent.

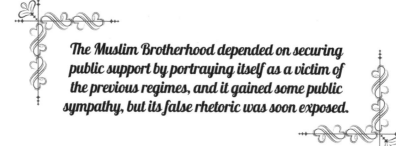

The Muslim Brotherhood depended on securing public support by portraying itself as a victim of the previous regimes, and it gained some public sympathy, but its false rhetoric was soon exposed.

The factors that led to the success of the Muslim Brotherhood in the abovementioned states are as follows. First is the failure of the ruling political elites in most cases to achieve the aspirations of their people or provide them with basic services such as education, health, food, etc.—a situation often accompanied by underdevelopment, corruption, and unemployment. This paved the way for political religious groups to take advantage of these

failings by introducing themselves as an alternative source of aid and services to cities and villages through their associations and institutions, creating a parallel institutional framework to that of the state, which was mostly marginalized and had no tangible role to win people's support.

The Muslim Brotherhood filled the vacuum created by official incompetence, so it established and supervised social and charitable institutions and participated in existing official and non-official organizations, including trade unions which involved the elites of society. Through such institutions, the group provided social services to large segments of society.

The group was often more effective than the government in providing such services, especially in the Arab Republic of Egypt. In addition to exploiting the scarcity of services and the absence of the state in the development process, political religious groups exploited the repressive security conditions to entrench the idea of "injustice" and depict themselves in the media as "victims." This increased the group's popularity, and as a spontaneous response, the voters selected the group in the hope that it would become their savior. However, everyone soon discovered that the Muslim Brotherhood was dependent on gaining public sympathy by portraying itself as the victim of regimes in many Arab and Muslim countries; its false rhetoric was soon exposed, and it was revealed to be an opportunistic organization interested only in assuming authority. This was clearly revealed by the Muslim Brotherhood's time in government in the Arab Republic of Egypt, which came to an end when the people rose up against the group on June 30, 2013 after only one year.

Thus, the Muslim Brotherhood's rule between 2012 and 2013 represents an important turning point in the group's history, as it exposed its true intentions. It also represented a popular and political test that the group failed—perhaps this period brings the curtains down on the group's entire story.

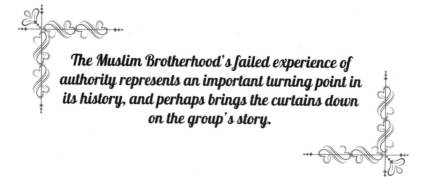

The Muslim Brotherhood's failed experience of authority represents an important turning point in its history, and perhaps brings the curtains down on the group's story.

Second, it is difficult to ignore the role of the religious factor in the electoral choice. Slogans such as "Islam is the solution" and the notion of the implementation of Islamic *Sharia* are appealing to some segments of society—especially young people.[177] Moreover, the West's anti-Islamic policies are exploited by these groups to attract sympathizers and supporters in countries such as France, Switzerland and Norway.[178]

However, the Muslim Brotherhood's overall success is not primarily linked to the implementation of *Sharia* or the goal of establishing an Islamic Caliphate. Indeed, when these parties participated in parliaments they did not play their expected role in this context, as the case was with Hamas in the Gaza Strip in

2006 and the Freedom and Justice Party in the Arab Republic of Egypt in 2011. This reflected their political opportunism rather than their idealism, intellectual standards or doctrinal or dogmatic guidelines.

In this context, Muhammad Hassanein Haikal believes that the Muslim Brotherhood had sold an "idea" which was not the exclusive preserve of the group—this being the religion which belongs to everyone. However, the Muslim Brotherhood was able to associate itself with this idea, and the rise of the group was ultimately down to the rise of the idea itself. This reflects the growing role of religion in society, and was a product of a crisis experienced in most Arab and Muslim societies, where religion, during periods of crisis, plays a vital role in the stability and reassurance of the public. The Muslim Brotherhood benefited considerably from this reality, and group's size and popularity was confused with that of the idea they represented. As such, the group's abilities were overestimated as its promotion of this idea provided it with the substantial political privileges and gains it aspired to.[179]

The Muslim Brotherhood participated in – and in some cases monopolized – authority in three Arab countries, namely: the Republic of the Sudan, the Arab Republic of Egypt and the Republic of Tunisia.

The Muslim Brotherhood in Authority: The Presidency and the Government

The Muslim Brotherhood's declared goal was always to establish an Islamic state or implement the system of a Caliphate. As indicated above, the group adopted a staged approach based on gradual reform and transition from one stage to another according to prevailing conditions. This process mirrored the gradual, staged promotion of individuals in order to identify those most committed to the group's approach and political and religious ideology. It was even possible – although not easy – to promote such a person to the pinnacle of the organization, as their socialization and movement could be adjusted. However, when it comes to authority, this is not possible in light of the numerous inherent difficulties and formidable challenges of governance, in addition to various requirements relating to eligibility, capability, efficiency and credibility that are not always easily satisfied. Moreover, composite or complex internal and external factors overlap in this regard. It is also difficult, if not impossible, to achieve the movement of society as a whole in one direction; in such cases opposition emerges, the idea of resistance develops and in an historic moment it may ignite disorder, widespread rebellion or revolution. The Muslim Brotherhood participated in, and in some cases monopolized authority in three Arab countries, namely the Republic of the Sudan, the Arab Republic of Egypt and the Republic of Tunisia.

This participation and access to authority against the backdrop of radical changes in the countries where the

344

Brotherhood existed, was imposed by difficult economic, social and political circumstances. The experience represented a series of practical tests of the Muslim Brotherhood's political capacities and its ability to govern in light of complex internal, regional and international conditions. Hence there are questions regarding this experience, its course and the results it yielded.

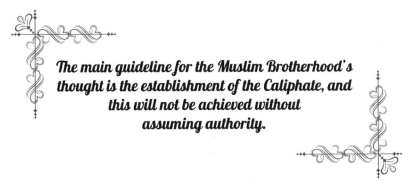

The main guideline for the Muslim Brotherhood's thought is the establishment of the Caliphate, and this will not be achieved without assuming authority.

Discussing both the truth and illusions with regard to the Muslim Brotherhood's primary declared goal – the establishment of a Caliphate – it is clear that achieving such a goal is no easy matter, and cannot be determined by a particular faction, current or group in any Muslim community. The nature, shape and underlying foundations of the government system must be a product of a society's realities, circumstances, potential, ambitions and aspirations in any given period of history. However, talk about a Caliphate remained the focus of the Muslim Brotherhood's thought and narrative, without looking deeply into the requirements of the times and their compatibility with such a narrative. After the fall of the Ottoman Caliphate in 1924, the main guideline of the Muslim Brotherhood's thought and behavior was the establishment of an Islamic state, and the group was well aware that this could not be achieved without entering government and subsequently participating in or monopolizing authority;[180] hence the Muslim Brotherhood's exclusionary political performance in authority. Despite its spread over more than eight decades of its existence, there was no suitable opportunity for the Muslim Brotherhood. Even in light of the unprecedented deterioration of the social, economic and political situations in several Arab and Muslim countries, the Muslim Brotherhood never expected to be in a position to assume authority so quickly. However, the situation changed after the fall of former Tunisian President Zine Al-Abideen bin Ali's regime on January 14, 2011.[181] This was due to several domestic factors, including restrictions on individual freedoms as well as those related to society's identity and culture, and even to the most basic human rights which distinguish Muslims, such as the prohibition of wearing the head scarf (*hijab*) for women at work or praying in the mosque for men. This was accompanied by deteriorating economic and social conditions, and increasing poverty, but the most important factor at this stage was the rising unemployment among young people, who have become an important segment of the population not only in the Republic of Tunisia, but also in other Arab and Muslim societies. Estimates show that those aged 15–24 account for around 19.6 percent of the total population in the Arab countries.[182]

Besides the abovementioned internal environment, the international factor also played a role in the growth of political religious groups and the escalating demands for change in some Arab and Muslim countries, especially after the September 11, 2001 attacks which irrevocably changed the world. Economic conditions were also deteriorating, especially following the global financial crisis that swept across the world after 2007 and which threatened the status and economies of large and small states alike.[183] Furthermore, Israeli aggression against Palestine and other Arab states and US policies toward the Arab and Muslim countries were used by political religious groups as a pretext for their extremist activities—especially US support for Israel's expansionist practices. Thus, all internal and external conditions created a reality that was ready for change, especially in countries with fragile economies; however, what happened was not expected in the foreseeable future.

The events of the so-called "Arab Spring" have in fact triggered surprising unrest, not only in terms of its timing but also the forces behind it. The regimes that were suffering economic and social crises anticipated that they would be opposed in some form, but they focused on the threat from political religious groups without any regard to other social movements produced by the poor living conditions. Regardless of the factors mentioned previously, such as the intentions of those groups who exploit religion to assume authority through political mechanisms or violence, as well as denouncing governors and communities as unholy, etc., the regimes in question were keen to curb or contain such groups – often through their security apparatuses – or even to dismantle and destroy them entirely. However, it seems that it did not occur to many regimes, analysts, observers or local or global intelligence agencies, that such a view was limited and short-sighted. There have been other latent societal forces among which the idea of rebellion has been brewing for years, but they lacked the means, plans and support mechanisms. As soon as these became available to them, these forces rose up against the status quo, and turned it upside down, taking advantage of the regional and international balance of interests and the massive, unprecedented information revolution.

On the other hand, political religious groups – and especially the Muslim Brotherhood – which sought for decades to achieve their interests and bring about the desired transformation and then assume authority, found themselves at the forefront of the change they had always called for. However, although they later participated in it, they did not drive the change. Instead they mistakenly bet on the regimes they had long appeased, and were reluctant even at critical moments to give up on or abandon those regimes, until all indications inevitably signaled their imminent demise.

Several regimes in key Arab countries have fallen; the political and social forces driving this change could have taken over the reins, and perhaps had the chance to offer an alternative to those regimes at these defining moments. But the exact opposite occurred; these transformations gave political

religious groups an opportunity not only to participate in authority – in keeping with their plans and goals – but also to monopolize it.

Varying degrees of participation in parliaments and legislatures were possible for the Muslim Brotherhood in many Arab and Muslim countries, including some of those countries which witnessed unrest. Perhaps participation would also have been acceptable in the context of the political systems that existed; although, it would have been unreasonable or at least unexpected for political religious parties to assume authority in countries whose regimes better understood the true intentions of the Muslim Brotherhood and were the toughest in dealing with the group, such as the Arab Republic of Egypt and the Republic of Tunisia. Events in the Arab Republic of Egypt represent a clear example of what has been achieved by political religious groups, including their dreams and unexpected political gains—although these did not actually last for long.

The January 25, 2011 protests that toppled the Egyptian President Muhammad Husni Mubarak erupted against injustice, marginalization, unemployment, poverty and corruption, and were triggered by youth representing all sections of Egyptian society including Muslims and Christians, conservatives and liberals, nationalists and leftists, workers and farmers, men and women. In this regard they represented the truly collective action of the Egyptian people. It is noted that the Muslim Brotherhood's participation in these protests was late, and even hesitant, as the group officially declared its non-participation on the first day of the protests. The Brotherhood's position in this regard remained unchanged until it became clear from the unprecedented size of the protest movement – previously only the Muslim Brotherhood itself would have had the power to mobilize on this scale – that the protests would not stop. Consequently the group announced its participation on January 28, after 3 days of protests, and called upon its supporters to take to the streets. Nonetheless, the group still entered into negotiations with the regime of former President Muhammad Husni Mubarak in order to end the protests if certain conciliatory demands were met.[184] This was before the group and the regime alike discovered that the popular movement had already moved past these demands, and that there was no option for the head of the regime but to step down, which happened on February 11, 2011, beginning a new and unprecedented phase for the Arab Republic of Egypt and the Muslim Brotherhood.

After the former President Muhammad Husni Mubarak stepped down, authority was transferred to the Supreme Council of the Armed Forces, headed by defense minister Field Marshal Muhammad Hussein Tantawi.[185] Then, talk about the transition period and possible scenarios began, and various forces announced their orientations and positions, whether with regard to the nature of the transition phase or the writing of a new constitution and the associated form of the state and government system, and accordingly the legislative and presidential elections.[186]

The movement began to take shape when various forces established their own political parties. The Muslim Brotherhood officially established its own party, named "Freedom and Justice" on June 6, 2011 to run in the parliamentary elections.[187] The world kept a watchful eye on the developments in the Arab Republic of Egypt, but accurate predictions were not possible; in fact, many observers had not yet recovered from the shock of what had happened. Against this backdrop, the newborn (although from an old parent) Freedom and Justice Party won by a large majority, securing 47 percent of seats in the Egyptian parliament.[188]

Political Islamic parties represented by the Muslim Brotherhood and the Salafis won more than two-thirds of the seats.[189] This result, although expected in light of the balance of political forces in 2011, came as a shock to many. The Egyptian street was clearly inclined toward political religious groups, not necessarily as a result of being attached to their ideologies and ideas and sharing their goals, or in support of their ambitions, but rather in pursuit of restoring security and stability with a desire for change and to fill the vacuum that no other forces were prepared for or capable of.

Just a few months passed before another political surprise occurred—the Egyptian people were shocked by the performance of the new post-Mubarak parliament. Many of the representatives from political religious groups demonstrated incompetence, not only in terms of efficiency but also in understanding the nature and work of parliament, and consequently it was not surprising to see ridiculous manifestations under the dome of the parliament. The fact is that the new parliamentarians were neither up to the occasion nor up to the work of parliament, particularly as the people's hopes as well as the state's future rested with them. Even more dangerous was the fact that a majority of the Egyptian parliament exploited its dominance to impose a particular orientation on a society that is diversified by nature, not only in terms of religion, but also intellectual, cultural and political affiliation. Parliament's inability to meet people's aspirations – regardless of the associated conditions – has had a clear role in the major change that has occurred in Egyptian public opinion. This was clearly reflected in the presidential elections of 2012, in which members of parliament engaged in discussions of secondary and peripheral issues, and raised controversial religious issues instead of tackling the development challenges facing the Egyptian people who had such high expectations of those members.

After the formation of the Egyptian Parliament came the more important presidential elections, as the president enjoys broad authority, while representing the country and its image abroad. Thirteen candidates ran for the Egyptian presidency, including Dr. Muhammad Mursi Al-Ayyat, who was organizationally affiliated with the Muslim Brotherhood, as well as Dr. Abdulmunem Abu Al-Futooh Abdulhadi (who is currently the leader of the Strong Egypt Party, who claimed 20 percent of the votes in the 2012 Egyptian presidential elections but was sacked from the Muslim

Brotherhood for not abiding by the group's decision not to nominate candidates for the presidency—before the group retraced the decision and nominated an official candidate).[190] The elections attracted unprecedented popular participation, and although Dr. Muhammad Mursi assumed first place in the first round, his share of votes did not exceed 25 percent.[191] This indicated a significant decline in the Muslim Brotherhood's popularity, which had been cut in half compared to what they had achieved in the parliamentary elections. This was a lesson worthy of consideration and urgent review; however, the Muslim Brotherhood paid no attention. The run-off election witnessed fierce competition between the Muslim Brotherhood's candidate Dr. Muhammad Mursi and Lieutenant General Ahmad Shafeeq. Even though Shafeeq was considered one of the henchmen of the regime of former President Muhammad Husni Mubarak, being the last prime minister of Mubarak's rule, and Dr. Muhammad Mursi only won by a narrow margin of just 3.4 percent of the vote to claim 51.7 percent, while Shafeeq received 48.3 percent of the vote.[192]

This was also noteworthy, if we take into account the fact that the majority of political forces and many voters opted for Mursi because they feared the return of the regime against which they had rebelled, which simply meant that Dr. Muhammad Mursi would never have received so many votes had it not been for the fear among many of the return of the old regime.

The reign of the former Egyptian President Dr. Muhammad Mursi was characterized by a tendency to monopolize authority and control the state through what is known as Ikhwanization or "Brotherization."

Following the victory of Dr. Muhammad Mursi in the presidential elections on June 30, 2012, and from the first day of his rule, he promised to be a president for all Egyptians, but Mursi had barely completed his first year in office before facing unprecedented popular protests on June 30, 2013 demanding that he step down. This was the result of multiple failures, including those linked to the deteriorating economic situation and those related to the treatment of political partners and opponents alike. Consecutive developments over the Muslim Brotherhood's time in authority and the subsequent state of affairs leading eventually to ending the rule of former President Dr. Muhammad Mursi on July 3, 2013 were in fact a direct result of the Muslim Brotherhood's practices and their quest to monopolize authority and control the state. Although Dr. Muhammad Mursi declared himself to be a president for all Egyptians, reiterating this in his speeches; he gave Islamists the upper hand in many major state institutions, including some key ministries. He also removed several governors and replaced almost half of them with Muslim Brotherhood members, in addition to appointing a former jihadi, Aadel Al-Khayat – who is a member of the Building and Development Party, the political wing of the Islamic Group – as a governor of Luxor, one of the most prominent tourist provinces.[193] This move lacked any political skill, particularly in light of the fact that Islamic Group has been charged with involvement in the Luxor massacre of November 1997[194] which claimed the lives of more than 26 tourists and wounded a further 26 people.[195]

In spite of the justifications provided, such as the fear of a return of the previous regime's symbols or the overwhelming influence of the so-called "deep state," relations with political leaders and with those who had led civil actions appeared to be undermined not only by caution and suspicion, but also with a great deal of distrust of the Muslim Brotherhood and their intentions. Neither the group nor the former President Dr. Muhammad Mursi and his advisers realized that the transitional stages of any state or society cannot be managed based on the mentality of one single faction, particularly when one considers that this faction did not even trigger the mass protests, it simply benefited from them. Major mistakes, hesitance in the decision-making process and the "Brotherization (Ikhwanization) of the State" policy brought about unprecedented popular rejection of the Muslim Brotherhood and their rule, as reflected by frequent marches and demonstrations.

During the year of Muslim Brotherhood rule, the moral disguise was gradually exposed and society saw a different system that contradicted all previously declared slogans and statements, and had nothing to do with any of the Muslim Brotherhood's claimed principles, programs or plans. The June 30, 2013 revolution was born of resentment against the deterioration of services, and rage toward the great moral deception.[196]

At the government level, things were no less intense. Dr. Hisham Qandeel's government came into existence after a long and difficult birth, but it also was not of the correct standard, and was characterized by repeated failures, not least in the economic sphere. Despite much hope and optimism the government came under sharp criticism and suffered a lack of confidence in its ability to meet the requirements of the new reality or even the basic needs of the people.[197] Contrary to expectations, the government included ministers from president Mubarak's era and five ministers from the Muslim Brotherhood but it excluded entire currents, not only from the liberals or other revolutionary forces that assisted the Muslim Brotherhood to assume authority, but also the group's allies like the Salafi Al-Noor Party, which was given only one ministry (the Ministry of the Environment), prompting it to withdraw from participation in the government.[198] Nevertheless, the Egyptian people still had hopes for change. However, without going into details and regardless of the exerted efforts, the result was that the government not only failed to live up to these great aspirations, but also to meet the basic needs for which Egyptian citizens had risen up and made great sacrifices. Eventually,

events accelerated and the Egyptian people demonstrated in massive unprecedented protests on June 30, 2013, leading to the intervention of the army, the deposition of the former President Dr. Mursi, the fall of the Muslim Brotherhood, and the decline of the influence of Islamic and liberal forces, ushering in a new phase in the history of the Egyptian people.[199]

In foreign policy terms, the situation was no less severe or dangerous. Foreign policy played a role in deposing former President Dr. Muhammad Mursi and overthrowing the Muslim Brotherhood's rule. The handling of what the media dubbed the Grand Renaissance Dam crisis – one of the most important Egyptian national security issues – revealed poor management and planning and a lack of strategic vision. This culminated in what was described by the vast majority of observers and politicians as a scandal. The Egyptian presidency at the time aired live proceedings of a presidential meeting on national security with some politicians discussing the dam crisis, and the meeting was broadcast via satellite channels. When the speakers suggested preparing military and intelligence plans to destroy the dam, one of the attendees asked the rest to swear not to leak the proceedings of the meeting to the media, but soon they all discovered that the meeting was being broadcast live on television from the presidential palace.[200] Moreover, Egypt's relations with some Arab countries became strained, as the new government's foreign discourse was not reassuring to the Arab countries—especially the Gulf states and particularly with regard to the security of the Arabian Gulf and its precedence in the new foreign policy of the Arab Republic of Egypt. Most importantly in this context were the Egyptian relations with countries or entities that pose a threat to the security and stability of the Arabian Gulf.

There has been a clear fear of the Muslim Brotherhood's policy with regard to the Islamic Republic of Iran, which represents the biggest challenge to the security and stability of the region in general and to the members of the Cooperation Council for the Arab States of the Gulf (GCC) in particular. The Arab Republic of Egypt, being the largest Arab country and a major regional power, is one of the most important security pillars of the GCC states. Thus, any uncalculated rapprochement or alliance between the Arab Republic of Egypt and the Islamic Republic of Iran could have undermined the Egyptian role in ensuring the security and stability of the Arabian Gulf region. It then would pose a threat to the stability of the GCC states—or at least some of them, as certain GCC members were excluded by virtue of the their relations with the Muslim Brotherhood's government in the Arab Republic of Egypt. As such, there was concern in the Arabian Gulf region regarding Egyptian foreign policy under the rule of the Muslim Brotherhood. Perhaps this is the most important regional factor for the Arab Republic of Egypt, and may have contributed in some way to the removal of the former President Dr. Muhammad Mursi in the name of preserving Egyptian and Arab national security.

> *Rashid Al-Ghannooshi's thought and political approach was affected by his time in Britain, where he became very familiar with the nature of civil states.*

In the Republic of Tunisia, the cradle of the regional uprisings, the Ennahdha Movement, which represents the Muslim Brotherhood, won the legislative elections and formed a government. The Ennahdha Movement was banned in the Republic of Tunisia during the rule of former President Zine Al-Abideen bin Ali, prompting most of the Muslim Brotherhood's leaders – such as Ennahdha's leader Rashid Al-Ghannooshi – to move to Europe.[201] This had many benefits for the thought of the movement and its plans after the fall of bin Ali's regime and the return of Tunisian Muslim Brotherhood leaders to the country in 2011. During his stay in London in early 1990s, Rashid Al-Ghannooshi was able to become closely acquainted with the essence and nature of the civil state on realistic basis. As such, Al-Ghannooshi's thought, and subsequently his writings and political approach, was affected by the new environment in which he enjoyed great freedom that allowed him to communicate with the leaders of the Islamic Movement in Britain.[202] Perhaps this explains, to some extent, the Movement's subsequent more realistic response to political developments compared to its counterpart in the Arab Republic of Egypt. There has been a significant shift in the thought of Al-Ghannooshi and the other leaders of Ennahdha Movement, which reflected clearly on the movement's approach and conduct at home and abroad. Besides, there is also the record of self-criticism expressed by previous leaders who left and joined the movement from time to time, and whose intellectual jurisprudence contributed to the political maturation of the movement and released it from the its limiting ideological and doctrinal fragmentation. What is clearly obvious in this context is the role of Abdul Fattah Moro, one of the leading founders of Tunisia's Ennahdha Movement.[203]

Thus, the circumstances served the Ennahdha Movement, whose leaders benefited from the internal and external political environment in the Arab countries surrounding the Republic of Tunisia to develop a more realistic approach compatible with the actual requirements of the time. This is not to say that Ennahdha has not been repeatedly and harshly criticized, particularly for harboring a strategy to use the political system as a means to achieve the 'Brotherhoodization' (Ikhwanization) of society.

After the regime of the former Tunisian President Zine Al-Abideen bin Ali fell, the scene appeared set for a new transition phase based on fair elections. Indeed, elections were held in late 2011, and Ennahdha claimed victory with 41 percent of the seats in the National Constituent Assembly. The liberal Congress for the Republic came second with 13.4

percent followed by the Popular Petition for Freedom, Justice and Development with 12 percent, and the Democratic Forum for Labor and Liberties with 9.2 percent.[204] Ennahdha formed a coalition government whose premier enjoys authorities similar to those of a prime minister in a parliamentary system.

Indeed, the formation of the troika was a strategic choice even for Ennahdha itself, as it was not alone in government despite its dominance of the Constituent Assembly, and it seems that Ennahdha did not want to be held solely responsible for potential political failures. Despite foreign aid, especially from Arab countries, the European Union and the United States of America,[205] the government could not meet the aspirations of the Tunisian people, as the economy did not improve but instead deteriorated, and high rates of unemployment persisted. Salafi and radical forces emerged and sometimes even played a role in directing Ennahdha party's compass. As this situation worsened, and in the absence of national political consensus, voices began calling for a change of government, and the country entered a state of political instability which was reflected in a security situation in which crime prevailed and militant *jihad* thrived. The Ennahdha Movement party held the biggest share of the burden, as it held the reins of government at the time. However it did not initially make concessions in response to demands for the resignation of the government headed by Ali Laarayedh and the formation of a technocratic replacement. People took to the streets in demonstrations, and it became clear that the country was heading towards the unknown; then the Labor Union proposed an initiative which, after months of dialogue, culminated in the national dialogue document under which the Ennahdha government resigned.

> *After the dispute over the role of Sharia in the constitution, Rashid Al-Ghannooshi said: "Sharia divides the Tunisians and Islam unites them."*

As for the National Constituent Assembly, firstly the issue of writing a constitution emerged, and Ennahdha tried to achieve its vision by introducing an Islamic *Sharia* article, an attempt that was abandoned due to the vast opposition from secular forces. Consequently Al-Ghannooshi said: "*Sharia* divides the Tunisians and Islam unites them."[206] In the end, the constitution was endorsed and an independent government was formed and received great Arab, Islamic and international support.

Despite the many drawbacks and gross errors, the experience of political religious groups in the Republic of Tunisia was significantly different in comparison to its counterpart in the Arab Republic of Egypt. Ennahdha's pragmatism on the one hand, and perhaps the lessons it learned from the fate of its counterpart in the Arab Republic of Egypt (the Muslim Brotherhood) on the other, as well as significant popular pressure, prompted Ennahdha to respond to the requirements of the national dialogue and abandon authority. Ennahdha was hoping to regain its position through the ballot box, but the legislative elections held on October 26, 2014 were disappointing for Ennahdha and the Muslim Brotherhood. As the Nidaa Tounes (Call of Tunisia) list won 85 out of the 217 seats, while the Ennahdha party came second with 69 seats, and the Free Patriotic Union Party came in third place with 16 seats.[207] The result was considered a severe blow to the Muslim Brotherhood's ambitions of returning to authority, and reflects a clear decline in their popularity among Tunisians.

In the Republic of the Sudan the Muslim Brotherhood engaged in politics and government from the very beginning and endeavored to penetrate the institutions of the Sudanese state, especially the army.[208] The Brotherhood's first and most important experience was its participation in the government of the former President Ja'afar Muhammad Numairi in 1977, as previously mentioned. Dr. Hassan Al-Turabi – who was a prominent figure of the Brotherhood before forming a splinter group of his own – played a key role in former President Ja'afar Numairi's adoption of Islamic *Sharia*. Al-Turabi was Numairi's special legal counsel, and then took over the Ministry of Justice and personally oversaw the implementation of September's laws instituting Islamic *Sharia*,[209] which in turn facilitated the spread and empowerment of the Muslim Brotherhood in many government departments – particularly the army itself – and thus paved the way for the group to assume authority. The Muslim Brotherhood, in collaboration with some leaders in the Sudanese army, managed to stage a 1989 coup which overthrew the elected government of Sadiq Al-Mahdi Abdurrahman. However, the hopes resting on the Muslim Brotherhood were as huge as the problems experienced by the Republic of the Sudan, which was in danger of being split into north and a south on ethnic and religious grounds. Moreover, the Sudanese economy was fragile and weak, and famine was spreading despite the country's vast agricultural areas that rightly qualify it to be the bread basket of the Arab region.[210] The country was also suffering from a lack of infrastructure and growing illiteracy, poverty and corruption; albeit magnanimity and Arab dignity prevailed.

After more than two decades under the regime, the situation in the Republic of the Sudan is now worse than ever. The southern part, which has more than 90 percent of the oil, is now separated, the living conditions of the people have worsened and poverty and illiteracy are still widespread. No real development has been achieved even in the simplest areas such as infrastructure to prevent villages being drowned in rainwater, houses falling on the heads of their inhabitants or the population being washed away by floods. Politically, the restrictions on freedoms returned the country to what it was before the October 1964 revolution.[211] In terms of foreign relations, the country now lives under a political

and economic blockade, and not only that, the rest of the old Republic of the Sudan is still threatened by division.

Was Muslim Brotherhood Rule a Failure?

Since its inception in 1928, the Muslim Brotherhood has pursued positions of authority, using its discourse of establishing an Islamic state and implementing *Sharia* to govern various aspects of life as an attractive' political cover. In order to achieve its goal, the group has adopted several methods during the past 86 years, and focused throughout these decades and years on education and media, while heavily depending on the political socialization of its members in accordance with its interests on the one hand, and on engaging in public affairs when circumstances allow on the other. The group's interests have prevailed, despite the fact that they often conflict with the principles it advocates; such conflict has sometimes extended to *Sharia* rules and ideological guidelines. Many analysts and observers consider the Muslim Brotherhood's eagerness to assume authority after the popular protests as the pinnacle of political opportunism led by interests separate to their constants and principles.[212]

Islamists' experience of governance in the Republic of the Sudan ended with the division of the state and worsening economic and living conditions.

365

It is difficult to make generalized judgments on the Muslim Brotherhood group's experiences in authority in various Arab and Muslim countries due to the obvious disparity between the group's political arms in various countries and their existing experiences on the one hand, and the variance in the periods of their rule on the other. However, the overall pattern that can be deduced is that they generally did not achieve their objectives, and in particular they failed to meet the aspirations and expectations of the people. Moreover, the achievements made so far in the countries where the Muslim Brotherhood continued in politics are still well below expectations and are inconsistent with the long history of the group's political and organizational activities in these countries.

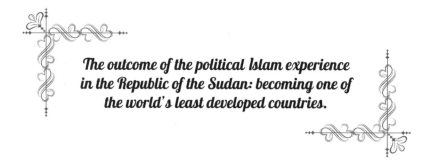

The outcome of the political Islam experience in the Republic of the Sudan: becoming one of the world's least developed countries.

In the Republic of the Sudan, internal and external expectations were largely pinned on the Islamists – who more or less represented the Muslim Brotherhood's thought – to achieve their promises, including ending the war, solving the issue with the South, achieving economic development, eradicating poverty, attaining political openness and promoting democracy.[213] The outcome, after a quarter of a century, is that the circle of internal conflict has expanded to include most of the states in the western and eastern parts of the country. The war in the south ended, but only after the Republic of the Sudan was divided and the territorial integrity of the country was lost. Moreover, the economic crisis has become exacerbated as the government has failed to achieve development—this was one of the most important causes of the insurgency in states like Darfur. Despite the discovery of oil and diversified sources of income, especially after the country opened its doors to foreign investments in agriculture and industry, the Republic of the Sudan is now among the poorest countries in the world. Politically speaking, there are increasing divisions among its various parties and forces, and the ruling party is facing a growing crisis after most other parties became allied against it; it is even experiencing internal defections following the government's suppression of protestors demanding reforms in September 2013. As a result, the Republic of the Sudan ranks as the fifth most fragile country in the world.[214]

In the Arab Republic of Egypt, the Muslim Brotherhood has failed its first true test at the top of the pyramid of authority in the most populous Arab country. Regardless of the limited period of the Muslim Brotherhood's rule – exactly one year – it was obvious during this period that the Muslim Brotherhood does not have the capacity or the real expertise required to manage the affairs of the state. As such, the group's failure to achieve its expected goals during that year in respect of basic services and stimulating the economy, as well as the precursors that have emerged during the period of its rule, showed a lack of strategic vision in dealing with internal and external challenges. It also revealed a lack of experience in administration and governance, especially in relation to a state the size of the Arab Republic of Egypt, as well as a tendency to rely on consultants and administrators who lack practical expertise. This has been associated with a policy of exclusion, not only of national human resources that could be beneficial, but also of the Muslim Brotherhood's partners in the demonstrations and protests. The group monopolized authority and marginalized the very forces that triggered and directed the protests. As such, the Muslim Brotherhood created political discord and attracted animosity from almost everyone, including the main institutions of the state. This was especially true of the judiciary, whose sovereignty was overstepped and whose provisions were rejected at the highest levels of government, which was not acceptable to the public. Furthermore, chaos, thuggery and lawlessness prevailed in several Egyptian governorates. Such pressing circumstances prompted millions of Egyptian people to take to the streets on June 30, 2013 to demand change. The Egyptian army responded to these demands and announced after a few days, on July 3, the deposition of former President Dr. Muhammad Mursi, bringing the curtains down on the reign of the Muslim Brotherhood in the Arab Republic of Egypt and putting an end to the group's aspirations to win the spoils of the most populated Arab state and implement the so-called "Brotherhoodization"[215] policy in order to change the identity of the Egyptian society through subsequent social and cultural transformations.

In the Republic of Tunisia the picture was somewhat different. Ennahdha won a majority of the seats in the Constituent Assembly, qualifying it to dominate the official institutions of the state. However, Ennahdha accurately read the Tunisian situation, which was that the people were not prepared to accept its dominance, even if based on the legitimate ballot through which Ennahdha was elected in October 2011. This prompted Ennahdha to ally itself with other major powers, including the Democratic Forum and the liberals—who themselves probably represent the biggest challenge to the Islamic project adopted by the Muslim Brotherhood. The authority was distributed among these three major groups, and Ennahdha secured the premiership, which provided authority that outweighed those of the president.

Economic reform and countering militant *jihad* were the top priorities of the new government in the Republic of Tunisia. But the transitional government could not achieve the ambitions of the people, and particularly not those of the youth who triggered and conducted the protests at the end of 2010. The economy deteriorated, insecurity increased, and more importantly the influence of Salafi jihadi militants expanded to the extent they had taken control of some areas and begun applying *Sharia* punishments, as perceived by them, for those who consumed alcohol or did not pray.[216] This augmented the strength of jihadi militant groups which carried out unprecedented bombings in Tunisia. Moreover, freedoms were suppressed, journalists were repressed and some opponents were assassinated, and the country was on the brink of slipping into the unknown before being saved by the national dialogue initiative led by the Tunisian General Labor Union.[217]

In spite of the difficulties faced by the national dialogue, the obstacles were defused as all the political parties realized the seriousness of the situation and that clinging to authority could plunge the country into chaos. Ennahdha also realized that this would lead the party itself to an unknown political destiny, or possibly a similar fate to its counterpart in the Arab Republic of Egypt. So Ennahdha had no other option but to make concessions which were the key to the solution that enabled the party to maintain its presence in the political scene and put things back on the road to stability in the Republic of Tunisia. Ultimately, Ennahdha was unable to implement its project or even achieve its interim or permanent goals. However, politically it has nonetheless achieved much more than the parent group in the Arab Republic of Egypt. The latter exited the ring of political competition entirely, and its mere coexistence with the Egyptian people was put in doubt due to its intransigence, despotism, and the narrow-mindedness of its inexperienced political leaders. The lesson which summarizes the Muslim Brotherhood's experiences in various Arab and Muslim countries is the need to recognize the differences between administrating a

state and administrating an institution, a facility or a small entity. Ultimately, whoever practices political activity should be armed with adequate knowledge, expertise and skill to meet the expectations of the role.

Conclusion

This chapter presented a comprehensive analytical review of the Muslim Brotherhood's ruling experiences in several Arab and Muslim countries, and concluded that there are variations in the political performance of the group according to the circumstances of each state and the variables of the internal and external environments. However, the Muslim Brotherhood's experience in authority in the Arab Republic of Egypt was clearly a failure, being the only venture of the group that was brought down permanently after the uprising of the Egyptian people on June 30, 2013 and the subsequent overthrow of former President Dr. Muhammad Mursi. There is no doubt that the Muslim Brotherhood's ruling experience in the Arab Republic of Egypt in particular will cast a long shadow over the group's future, as this experience occurred in the home country of the parent group, the birthplace from which it spread to dozens of countries in the Arab and Muslim worlds. This experience is also unique, as it took place in the most populous Arab country. The Muslim Brotherhood's political experience in the Arab Republic of Egypt clearly revealed the group's incompetence, not only in terms of its leadership, planning and administration of the affairs of state, but also with regard to the lack of any qualified personnel to occupy official positions of authority without endangering the destiny of the nation and the proper management of state affairs. The Muslim Brotherhood's history presented in this chapter indicates substantial conflict and disparity between its principles and practices, as well as between rhetorical idealism and pragmatic opportunism. Throughout its history, the group has never hesitated to exploit the prevailing circumstances to achieve its ends and pursue its objectives, without any prudent examination of the surrounding variables. It has relied on the rhetorical skills of its leaders and speakers to win the hearts of supporters without undertaking any serious work on the ground.

4 Political Religious Groups: The Salafis

CHAPTER 4
Political Religious Groups:
The Salafis

L ike other Islamic currents and groups, Salafism emerged as a result of an historical comparison between the glorious Islamic past (of the eighth through the fifteenth centuries AD) and the current weakness and deterioration in the Arab and Muslim worlds, and among Muslims in general. There was a strong desire to restore the strength of Muslims. To achieve this goal, several approaches were pursued, such as the revival of the Caliphate state – as in the case of the Muslim Brotherhood – refining the Islamic religious practice of *bid'a* (innovation without basis in Islam), going back to pure Islam, as contemplated in Salafi writings,[1] and defending Islam through "*jihad* against the unbelievers," because Muslims were strong when they adopted *jihad* and became weak when they abandoned it,[2] as reflected in the ideology of Al-Qa'ida and other jihadi organizations.

The Arab and Muslim worlds had undergone a period of weakness and degeneration, and largely fell under foreign occupation from the beginning of the nineteenth century. This culminated in the fall of the Caliphate in 1924. Subsequently, Mustafa Kemal (Ataturk) removed all the symbols of Islamic culture and identity in Turkey; he stopped the application of Islamic *Sharia* laws, prohibited women from wearing veils, abolished Islamic endowments, and adopted the Latin alphabet instead of the Arabic script for the Turkish language, etc. Hassan Hanafi explains that:

> Religious reformation was motivated by political factors, such as the weakness of the Ottoman Caliphate, the division and occupation of the nation's territories, falling behind modernized nations, and the existence of a centralized system. These factors encouraged the secession and independence of provinces from the empire, and caught the attention of colonial powers seeking to seize parts of the territory of the "Sick Man," and even led to attempts to take over the empire, as in the case of Muhammad Ali in Egypt and then others following the fall of the Caliphate in 1924.[3]

Following the fall of the Ottoman Caliphate, the Muslim world was burdened with backwardness and corruption, while Europe was heading towards advanced civilization.

One scholar describes this stage as a confrontation between a backward, corrupt and authoritarian Muslim world and a modernized, advanced and industrialized European world which had gone through a political, social, cultural and intellectual revolution.[4] As a result, the Arab and Muslim worlds tried to rise up and resume their role in civilization. Various Islamic currents expressed their desire to effect a change that would enable the nation to rise up and face contemporary challenges.[5]

As such, the backwardness of the situation of Muslims led to a generally strong reaction, and to attempts to identify the causes of this situation and find a solution. According to some scholars, in the face of this new challenge:

> Threatened with marginalization, the Arab and Muslim worlds responded in two ways: a Westernization trend, taking a series of administrative measures aimed at applying the European model, and a reformist trend aimed at reviving and renewing interest in Islam to prevent it from being subordinate to the West.[6]

Obviously, the deterioration of Islam and attempts at its revival are present in all religious currents, although different methods are adopted to effect change. Some have followed the European model, embracing Western culture, as well as its behavioral code and scientific approach. Others advocated violence and a return to pure Islam – according to the interpretation of each group – which gave rise to takfiri ideas and arguments, accusing society and the state of unbelief and using weapons to fight them.[7]

These religious groups and currents involved themselves in politics on the basis that Islam is both religion and state, comprising both theory and practice and encouraging governance in accordance with the rules of *Sharia*. This opened the door for varied interpretations, and resulted in the deviation of certain groups from pure tolerant Islam (which encourages its followers to invite others with wisdom and benign preaching) to accusing others of unbelief and resorting to coercion and violence. As a result, some of these groups have become associated with terrorism.

This chapter sheds light on an intellectually and ideologically influential religious trend: Salafism. According to Salafis, the return to pure Islam, as lived and practiced by the righteous ancestors, is the way forward for the *umma*. It must be stated that various Salafi groups agree with regard to certain matters, but differ in respect of other key issues. Hence, they have developed the varied goals and approaches that are closely examined in this chapter.

The Emergence and Development of Salafism

The term Salafism is derived from the Arabic word *Salaf* which refers to the ancestors.[8] The Arabic word was used in the Holy Quran: "Those who after receiving direction from their Lord, desist, shall be pardoned for the past; their case is for Allah to judge",[9] and "Allah forgives what is past."[10]

Followers of Salafism are referred to as Salafis.[11] *Salaf* (ancestors) used to refer to the Companions of the Prophet (pbuh) and Muslim generations of the first three centuries AH, who were praised by the Prophet (pbuh) in the following saying (Hadith):

> People of my generation are the best, then those who follow them, and then those who follow the latter, then there would be people whose evidence would precede their oath and their oath would precede their evidence.[12]

The reason people of those three centuries were distinguished from others is because they included the direct recipients of the early teachings of Islam, and some of them were even close to the Prophet (pbuh) and learned lessons directly from him. Those teachings and lessons were then passed down to followers, and followers of followers. The more times they were passed down, the more suspicion, sedition and division increased.[13]

Salafis call for a return to the ways of the righteous ancestors. For them, the righteous ancestors applied and lived in accordance with the Islamic teachings as set out in the Holy Quran and the Prophet's Noble Sunnah. Therefore, Salafis call themselves "*Ahl Al-Sunnah Wal Jama'a*" or true representatives of Sunni Islam. They look at the model of the righteous ancestors as being closest to pure Islam as set out in its main sources: the Holy Quran, the Prophet's Noble Sunnah and consensus.[14]

Salafism: Doctrine and Rules, or Groups and Trends?

There are various different opinions regarding Salafism, and whether it is a doctrine with rules to be followed, an organized movement or entity (party, society, current, etc.), or something else.

Proponents of the first opinion argue that Salafism is basically a doctrine derived clearly and indisputably from the Holy Quran and the Prophet's Noble Sunnah. To support their argument, they cite one saying (Hadith) by the Prophet (pbuh) narrated by Abu Huraira: "I have left two matters with you. As long as you hold to them, you will not go the wrong way. They are the Quran and the Sunnah."[15]

According to this argument, the Prophet's saying (Hadith) above is evidence of the validity of the Salafi view that the Holy Quran and the Prophet's Noble Sunnah, together constitute the two main sources of Islam. Accordingly, Salafism, broadly speaking,

> ... respects the sources of *Sharia*, explains them in the light of Arabic linguistics and the understanding of the companions and followers of the Prophet (pbuh), and allows no further interpretations save in exceptional instances."[16]

As such, Salafism is a doctrine which represents a return to the origins of Islam. It is not a group, society, organization or party. According to this opinion, those who think otherwise are simply wrong; Salafism,

… cannot be classified as a movement or group. It is a doctrine which can be adopted by some individuals, a group, or even a state, as in the case of the Kingdom of Saudi Arabia. The history of Salafism started with the companions who followed the ways of the Prophet (pbuh).[17]

So, Salafism follows:

… the ways of the righteous ancestors, including the companions, followers, and followers of followers; they are the best among Muslims, with better knowledge and understanding of the teachings of the Prophet (pbuh). Those who follow this doctrine are Salafis regardless of the name of the group in which they are members.[18]

> *According to Salafis, Salafism is a doctrine. Whoever follows this doctrine is a Salafi regardless of the name of the group of which he is a member.*

According to this view, Salafism involves following in the steps of the righteous ancestors and applying their methods in learning and inference. It stresses the importance of the text of the Holy Quran and the Prophet's Noble Sunnah and follows it to the letter without any attempt at manipulation or reinterpretation.[19] Furthermore, Salafism does not reject *ijtihad* (independent reasoning). It believes that Islam is a comprehensive system which deals with acts of worship, ethics and dealings, and provides for all the spiritual and material needs of Muslims.[20] Hence, Salafism is a doctrine. Whoever follows this doctrine is a Salafi, regardless of the name of the group in which he is a member, and anyone not observing this doctrine is not a Salafi.

It follows, according to the proponents of this opinion, that Salafism has no speaker or representative, and mistakes committed by self-proclaimed Salafis cannot be attributed to Salafism, because words and deeds should be attributed to the individuals or groups adopting them, as in the case of the practices and extremist positions adopted by the "Islamic State" organization (ISIL). According to this argument, the fact that Salafism is a doctrine rather than a group means that Salafis comprise a broad segment in the Arab and Muslim worlds; they represent the majority of Muslims, because a Muslim should follow evidence just like the companions did. As such, according to proponents of this opinion, Salafism is the norm rather than an exception.[21]

Some researchers argue that the general principle of Salafism is adherence rather than innovation. It closely observes the authority of the text and the righteous ancestors (the companions of the Prophet, the followers, and the followers of the followers).[22] This current stems from the Imam Ahmad ibn Hanbal to the Imam Muhammad ibn Abdulwahhab. Fahmi Jad'aan describes it as a religious, moralist, conservative and compliant trend, explaining that all Salafis claim to be following

the path of the *Salaf* (righteous ancestors), but in fact take stances which reflect their own circumstances and ways of thinking.[23]

A second opinion argues that Salafism is a "movement". This means, according to this opinion, that Salafism is a group organized in the form of an association, party, society, etc. It follows the rules of the Salafi doctrine which constitutes an intellectual frame of reference for the group.[24] Scholars defining Salafism as a "current" agree with this opinion:

> Salafism is a reformist educational Islamic current which emerged during a period of backwardness and degeneration in the Arab and Muslim world. It calls for a return to pure Islam, getting rid of all forms of idolatry. Some call it Wahhabism after Sheikh Muhammad ibn Abdulwahhab revived Salafism in modern times.[25]

A third opinion is represented by studies which looked at Salafism as a comprehensive modernizing reformist current which called for a return to fundamentals as well as modernization and independent reasoning, rather than a merely religious current[26] based on a certain religious school. In fact, this opinion views Salafism as an intellectual, cultural and religious reformist movement adopted by figures preoccupied with the deteriorating conditions of Muslims.

According to this opinion, thinkers like Jamal Al-Din Al-Afghani, Muhammad Abdu and others were pioneers of the reformist Salafi current which appeared in the Arab world in the nineteenth century. For example, the Imam Jamal Al-Din

Al-Afghani called for an Islamic awakening in the face of the expansion of European powers in the Arab region. At the same time, he denounced authoritarian regimes in Muslim countries, criticized intolerance and stagnation, promoted a better understanding of Islam, and called for a return to the ways of the "righteous ancestors." That is why his reformist movement was described as a Salafi movement.[27]

Some political religious groups have focused on the concept of "Revival." They emphasize a return to the puritanical practices of early Islam; they are motivated by the development in the West and the deteriorating socio-economic and political conditions in Arab and Muslim societies. In particular, they have attempted to define the role of Islam in the face of great challenges in establishing modern industrial societies.[28]

> *Historically, the relationship between modernization and Islam has gone through several stages, starting with reformists such as Muhammad Abdu and Jamal Al-Din Al-Afghani, and ending with the Muslim Brotherhood and others.*

Historically, the relationship between modernization and Islam has experienced stages characterized by the following:

1. The impact of the West through colonialism and increased personal and social contact with Western culture.

2. The Islamic response through the contribution of Muslim modernists such as Muhammad Abdu and Jamal Al-Din Al-Afghani. Eventually, the Islamic reform movement declined and was replaced by other movements such as the Muslim Brotherhood.

3. In the 1950s and 1960s, the Arab world experienced a decline in Islamic organizations, figures, and values, especially in the political process. There are several reasons for this decline, including the struggle between political religious groups and regimes, as in the case of Egypt, and the popularity of secular ideologies such as Nasserism, Arab socialism, and Baathism.

4. The rise of political religious groups in the 1970s and 1980s was a reaction to the failure of the secular ideologies of the 1960s. The activities of these groups surprised many observers because they contradicted many of the expectations set forth by the theorists of modernization. In the Arab world, modernization did not result in the secularization of state and society.

Forms of Islamic Revival

As mentioned above, modern Islamic political thought is the outcome of an intellectual tradition that began in the nineteenth century with a number of Muslim scholars, researchers, reformists, and politicians.[29] Islamic political thought in the nineteenth and twentieth centuries has been influenced by a number of schools. The first school is Establishment Islam, characterized by attempts to maintain the status quo and resistance to any change in religious interpretation or the introduction of modern institutions. For instance, Al-Azhar scholars have found compromise with different political regimes in Egypt and continued their traditional role as legitimizers.[30] They continue to cooperate with political regimes in defining what is "Islamic" and what is not. Although Al-Azhar, in my opinion, was and remains a stronghold of centrist moderate Islam in the Arab and Muslim worlds, political religious groups have spared no effort in undermining its status and distorting its role. This is because they mix religion and the state, try to use religion in the service of their interests and present themselves as its only representative.[31] They believed, it seems, that any decline in popular support for Al-Azhar would automatically translate into increased popular support for their own organizations, because all Arab and Muslim societies are in need of a religious frame of reference.

The second tradition is Islamic modernism. Muslim modernists such as Jamal Al-Din Al-Afghani and Muhammad Abdu represented a liberal progressive movement which accepted Western technology, institutions, and values and emphasized reason and rationality in interpreting Islam.[32] Independent reasoning was an essential method for Islam to cope with modern society. The philosophy of Islamic modernism was the antithesis of the conservative traditional Islam represented by Islamic scholars. Although this movement was short-lived, it presented Muslims with the ideas and the tools of free rational thinking. Modernizing the backward Muslim societies of the nineteenth century was the ultimate goal of this movement. The Islamic modernism of the nineteenth century was a pure social and religious reformist movement. It emphasized educational and religious reforms and heavily denounced a blind and ignorant interpretation of Islam. One of the major criticisms of Islamic modernism has been that it lacked political programs to establish an Islamic state. However, Muslim modernists perceived social reform to take priority over all other reform. They believed it was impossible to develop a modern polity while the majority of the population was illiterate.[33]

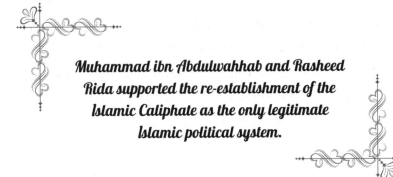

Muhammad ibn Abdulwahhab and Rasheed Rida supported the re-establishment of the Islamic Caliphate as the only legitimate Islamic political system.

The third tradition is conservative reformist Islam. This tradition supported the modernist school in protecting Islam from ignorant interpretations such as *bid'a* (innovation).[34] Conservative reformists strongly opposed *bid'a* (innovation), considering it to be the cause of a number of misconceptions about Islamic values and teachings, and they rejected Western and secular notions in the writings of Muslim modernists. Conservative reformists such as the Imam Muhammad ibn Abdulwahhab supported the establishment of a state in accordance with the doctrine of the righteous ancestors and based on a return to pure Islamic teachings. This implies opposition to the Ottoman Caliphate. Some historical writings even claim that Muhammad ibn Abdulwahhab opposed this Caliphate.[35] In general, the main principles of conservative reformist thinking can be summarized as follows:

1. The Islamic *Sharia* is the only law of the state. Thus, secular laws or any reinterpretation of the *Sharia* to make it compatible with modern needs is strongly rejected. Although they require the application of *Sharia*, it is not clear what action must be taken if the community is faced with an issue that is not explained in *Sharia*. Besides, *Sharia* does not provide for *hudood* (prescribed punishments) only; it provides for the rights of the individual Muslim vis-à-vis society. Nevertheless, there is variation among conservative reformists. For instance, Muhammad Rasheed Rida was more in favor of independent reasoning and gradual change.

2. Some conservative reformists consider the Caliphate system to be the ideal form of Islamic government. Nonetheless, they are willing to compromise the Caliphate system by applying *Sharia* as the only constitution and code of law

for the Islamic state. Thus, regimes in Arab and Muslim states which do not rule according to *Sharia* lose their legitimacy.[36]

3. Conservative reformists emphasize the role of Islamic scholars as advisors on *Sharia* issues; they reject scholars' role as legitimizers of political forces.

> *Salafi scholars argue that Salafism aims to cleanse societies of bid'a (innovation) and habits that are incompatible with Sharia, while jihadists call for resisting modernization and undermining the national state*

The Difference between Salafism and Fundamentalism

To understand the approaches and dynamics of political religious groups, it is necessary to differentiate between Salafism and Fundamentalism. Salafi scholars argue that Salafism aims to cleanse societies of *bid'a* (innovation) and habits that it considers incompatible with *Sharia*, such as magic, fortune-telling, amulets, and visiting tombs of very pious men and appealing to them. Salafism calls for independent reasoning with reliance on the two sources of Islam: the Holy Quran and the Noble Sunnah.[37] Fundamentalism, on the other hand, grew in a different environment. It appeared in what were advanced secular societies at the time (Arab Oriental countries) under complex circumstances and challenges, such as the fall of the

Ottoman Caliphate, the loss of Palestine (the *Nakba*), and the foreign colonization of Arab and Muslim countries. In response to these conditions, fundamentalists called for resisting modernization and undermining the national state, thereby starting a discourse about the Islamic *umma* and the Islamic state. In this sense, fundamentalism is:

> ... an Islamic ideological discourse which presents a conceptual system departing from the present and heading towards the future, unlike Salafism which examines the present and tries to purify it of the wrong practices of the past using the ways and practices of the righteous ancestors as a model. For Fundamentalism, the early Islamic society has gone and been replaced by modernization, subversion, unbelief and despotism.[38]

The Salafi Doctrine and Types of Salafi Groups

Some scholars argue that Salafism has certain principles, rules and characteristics which distinguish it from other religious currents and doctrines. These principles and rules include the following:[39]

- Acceptable evidence is limited to Holy Quranic verses and the Prophet's sayings (Hadith) from the Noble Sunnah.

- The text (i.e. Holy Quranic verses and the Prophet's sayings (Hadith)) takes precedence.[40] As long as the text is authentic and reliable, no reasoning is allowed. As such, reasoning cannot prevail over the text in Salafism. In fact, in all his books, the Imam Ahmad ibn Taymiyya followed the rule which states that reasoning should be subject to the text.[41] This means relying mainly on the text of the Holy Quran and Noble Sunnah and avoiding reasoning whenever an explicit text is available.[42]

- Respect of religious authority and reverence of learned religious scholars.

In addition, the main characteristics of Salafi thought in general can be summarized as follows:[43]

1. Stressing the concept of oneness in worship. There are three types of oneness: 1) Oneness of God (Allah),[44] meaning that only God (Allah) can be worshipped and all acts of worship, direct or indirect, should be intended as worship of God (Allah)—this is the reason God (Allah) sent the Messengers and revealed the holy books; 2) Oneness of the Creator, meaning that only God (Allah) can create creatures, regulate the universe, and give life and death; and 3) Oneness of names and attributes, meaning that all names and attributes of God (Allah), as set out in the Holy Quran and Noble Sunnah, should be limited to Him without manipulation or misinterpretation. Furthermore, no defect or shortcoming can be attributed to Him.[45]

2. Continuously stressing complete obedience to rulers, as long as they observe the teachings of *Sharia*.

3. Highlighting the merits of the companions of the Prophet (pbuh) as well as religious scholars.

4. Avoiding *bid'a* (innovation), superstition and suspicion.

5. *Jihad* is important and should continue. However, by *jihad*, Salafism means the proper spread and promotion of Islam.

6. Avoidance of involvement in problematic political issues.

7. Authorizing rulers to take care of regulations and administrative arrangements. Obedience to the ruler is a key aspect of traditional Salafi thought, which follows the rule that "God (Allah) regulates through rulers matters which He did not regulate in the Holy Quran." This reflects the centrality of the concept of the ruler.[46]

Furthermore, the key formal features of Salafism are as follows:[47]

1. Following the ways of the righteous ancestors and rejecting the ways of the descendants; i.e. returning to the pure teachings of the Holy Quran and Noble Sunnah, modeling practice on the deeds of the righteous ancestors, and rejecting *bid'a* (innovation) and superstition which have increased with the passage of time and distorted religion. This is the essence of the teachings of the Imam Muhammad ibn Abdulwahhab, according to his followers.[48]

2. Favoring traditional interpretations of the Holy Quran based on reference to Islamic texts: the Holy Quran and the Noble Sunnah.[49]

3. Favoring the religious school of the Imam Ahmad ibn Hanbal in jurisprudence, and adopting the views of the

Imam Ahmad ibn Taymiyya. These are two main references of Salafism.[50]

4. Focusing on religious studies, such as the Holy Quran, the Noble Sunnah, jurisprudence and the Prophet's sayings (Hadith).[51]

5. Spreading the ideas of the Imam Muhammad ibn Abdulwahhab, including fighting *bid'a* (innovation) in religion as well as different forms of idolatry, the promotion of virtue and the prevention of vice, etc.

Furthermore, some researchers argue that common characteristics of Salafis include the following:[52]

1. The oneness issue is very important in Salafi thought. This is manifested not only in the stance towards non-Muslims, but also in the rejection of forms of idolatry practiced by some other Muslim groups such as visiting the tombs of very pious men, believing they are infallible, appealing to the Prophet (pbuh) and pious men, or enacting laws which are inconsistent with Islamic *Sharia*.

2. The ideological aspect is strongly present in various positions taken by the Salafis. Historically speaking, they represent the *Ahl Al-Sunnah Wal Jama'a*, particularly the *Ahl Al-Hadith*, which is an Islamic Sunni school which focused on the Prophet's sayings (Hadith), jurisprudence, and the inference of rules from the texts of the Holy Quran and the Noble Sunnah. This is the essence of Salafism, which emerged in response to other groups and schools such as the Shiites, Kharijites, Mu'tazilah, Ash'arites, and others.[53]

3. Favoring the text over reasoning: Salafis stress the precedence of the text (the Holy Quran and the Noble Sunnah); in the case of any conflict between a "clear text" and "sound reasoning," the text shall prevail. This is the opposite of other currents such as the Mu'tazilah, who favor reasoning over the text, and Abi Al-Waleed Muhammad ibn Ahmad Ibn Rushd.[54]

4. Holding to the concept of "following, not innovating,"[55] which means following the Prophet (pbuh) and adopting the religious practices and interpretations of His companions, without any revision. This is because *bid'a* (innovation) in religion will adversely affect its true framework and proper understanding. Islam is perfect, as stated in the following Holy Quranic verse: "This day have I perfected your religion for you, completed My favor upon you, and have chosen for you Islam as your religion."[56] As such, Salafis believe that when it comes to religion, there is no room for innovation.

In my opinion, one of the problems lies in the definition of concepts and terms. *"bid'a* (innovation) has negative connotations, and this might be very true from a religious point of view. However, the conceptual overlap between *bid'a* (innovation) and *ijtihad* (independent reasoning) results in confusing the two concepts not only at the intellectual and ideological levels, but also in terms of application and practice. After all, independent reasoning might be urgently needed, at least to refute the accusations that religion is inflexible and resistant to development and modernization.

Main Currents of Salafism

As discussed above, Salafism is not one coherent body, but has seen several divisions. Some groups adopted Salafism as a doctrine and set of rules. Others used Salafism to create a current which has been involved in politics. A third type went to extremes, adopting force and violence to effect change— these are described as jihadi Salafis.[57] Despite the many subdivisions of Salafism, we can talk about the following three main currents today.

1. Educational or Religious Salafism

This current follows the road of religious education and preaching, and rejects involvement in politics. It aims to spread the teachings of pure Islam and refute ideas which it perceives as un-Islamic, especially those of other Islamic divisions such as the Kharijites and Shiites.[58] This current is represented in the Kingdom of Saudi Arabia by Sheikh Abdulaziz bin Baz, Sheikh Muhammad ibn Salih Al-Uthaymeen and their students. In the Hashemite Kingdom of Jordan, Nasseruddin Al-Albani is closely associated with this current.[59]

I would like to indicate at this point that scholars and experts differ about the definition of educational Salafism. For some, educational and religious Salafism is one current which has chosen the path of education and religious preaching to promote pure religion, and has rejected any involvement in politics.[60] Others have differentiated between educational Salafism and religious Salafism; the former is concerned with religious education, fighting *bid'a* (innovation), and returning to pure Islam,[61] while the latter seeks the reformation of society through education and collective work, and might even form political parties and participate in elections, as seen in the State of Kuwait, the Kingdom of Bahrain, and the Arab Republic of Egypt.[62] The problem with this last definition is that it mixes religion and politics, and mixes religious work with political work. It is agreed that religious work aims at inviting others to Islam and promoting its pure values and teachings, while political work aims at serving the interests and goals of a certain group or current, such as gaining influence at the cost of other rivals.

2. An Intermediate Current Combining Religious Thinking and Activism

This current combines both religious thought and activism. While it holds to Salafi doctrine and principles, it believes in organized activism, political reformation and change through peaceful means. Groups representing this current have different views and stances regarding the political status quo. Still, they agree on the importance of political work, the legitimacy of opposition, and the rejection of violence and armed activism. Groups representing this current include the Al-Noor Party in the Arab Republic of Egypt, the Al-Hikmah Charitable Society and Al-Ihsan Welfare Association in the Republic of Yemen, and Salafi societies in the State of Kuwait and the Kingdom of Bahrain.[63]

3. Jihadi Salafism

Jihadi Salafism requires detailed explanation, because the word "Salafism" in the name of this current suggests that it is part of Salafism, but Salafism – as a doctrine and thought, even as a movement and practice – absolves itself from any relation whatsoever with this jihadi current. Jihadi Salafism believes in violence, armed activism, change by force, and disobedience to rulers. It accuses whole societies of being unbelievers. Some researchers attribute the association between this jihadi current and Salafism to the fact that the intellectual legacy of the Imam Muhammad ibn Abdulwahhab has become a main reference for jihadi Salafism and was added to other sources of its jihadi knowledge created during the *jihad* in Afghanistan.[64]

Some argue that Salafi jihadism combines the new Hanbali concept of oneness, as established by the Imam Ahmad ibn Taymiyya and elaborated as a Salafi principle by the Imam Muhammad ibn Abdulwahhab, and the concept of sovereignty *(hakimiyya)* as established by Sayyid Qutb and Abu Al-A'la Al-Mawdoodi, which means that the application of *Sharia* principles and rules, as perceived by political religious groups, should form the cornerstone of Muslim societies. This means in modern political terms that God (Allah), rather than the people or *umma*, is the source of authority. Furthermore, jihadi Salafism combines the concept of *jihad* against the distant enemy, as in the case of the *jihad* in Afghanistan, and the concept of *jihad* against the near enemy.[65]

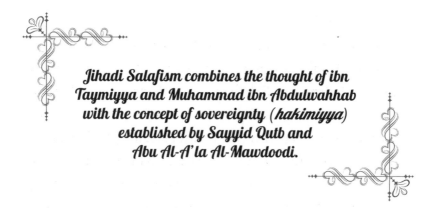

Jihadi Salafism combines the thought of ibn Taymiyya and Muhammad ibn Abdulwahhab with the concept of sovereignty (hakimiyya) established by Sayyid Qutb and Abu Al-A'la Al-Mawdoodi.

On the other hand, some argue that the theoretical link between Salafism and jihadi organizations can be attributed to several factors including the following:[66]

- Many members of the global jihadi current came from the Arabian Peninsula, especially the Kingdom of Saudi Arabia and the Republic of Yemen. This is because some Arab and Muslim countries backed *jihad* in the Islamic Republic of Afghanistan, providing financial support, media coverage, and even religious justification. Many religious scholars popular in jihadi and media circles, such as Muhammad bin Abdulrahman Al-Arifi, Salman bin Fahd Al-Odah and others, have adopted the jihadi cause and promoted it in countries and crises other than Afghanistan, such as Syria and Iraq.[67]

- Jihadi Salafis look at Salafism as a theoretical and practical guide, and consider the Imam Muhammad ibn Abdulwahhab's book *Tawheed* (Oneness) to be one of the main references of jihadi organizations.[68]

- Wahhabi Salafism is divided into two currents: traditional and jihadi. This has allowed for the use of the term jihadi Salafism to differentiate between the two.[69]

> *Followers of Muhammad ibn Abdulwahhab reject the term "Wahhabism." For them, their doctrine calls for a return to pure Islam and fighting against bid'a (innovation), and there is nothing called "Wahhabism."*

Some add that sympathizers of Al-Qa'ida in the Arab and Muslim worlds prefer the name "jihadi Salafism" because it is less suspicious than Al-Qa'ida, which has been associated with terrorism worldwide, especially after the 9/11 attacks, although in fact those sympathizers maintain the same thought as Al-Qa'ida. They seek to present themselves as following the way of the righteous ancestors as the best model, and focusing at the same time on *jihad*, which, according to them, has been ignored by other Salafis.[70]

For jihadi Salafis, Salafism means holding to the way of the righteous ancestors in terms of,

> ... belief, practice, and *jihad*. Jihadi Salafism is a current which combines the call to the oneness [of God (Allah)] and *jihad* to achieve that goal; it is a current which aims at promoting the oneness [of God (Allah)] by fighting evil... this is the identity of the jihadi Salafi current

which differentiates it from other religious and jihadi groups.[71]

The Relationship between Salafism and Wahhabism

There is a strong relationship between Salafism and Wahhabism (named after the Imam Muhammad ibn Abdulwahhab who promoted Salafism in the Najd).[72] Muhammad Abu Zahra explains that:

> Salafis are people who have described themselves as such. They first appeared in the fourth century AH; they were Hanbalis and claimed that their views originated from the Imam Ahmad ibn Hanbal who revived and defended the doctrine of the righteous ancestors. Salafism reappeared in the seventh century AH, revived by the Sheikh of Islam Ahmad ibn Taymiyya, who aggressively promoted the doctrine and, motivated by the prevailing conditions at the time, added to it. Those views emerged again in the Arabian Peninsula in the twelfth century AH, revived this time by the Imam Muhammad ibn Abdulwahhab. Salafism is still promoted by Wahhabists, and zealously endorsed by some religious scholars.[73]

Some argue that there is no difference between Salafism and Wahhabism; they are two sides of the same coin. This argument is based on the view that both have the same ideas and beliefs. When formulated in the Arabian Peninsula, these ideas and beliefs are called Hanbali Wahhabism, and when exported or discussed outside the Arabian Peninsula, they are called Salafism.[74]

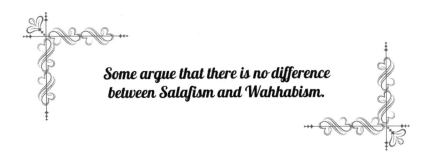

Some argue that there is no difference between Salafism and Wahhabism.

Generally speaking, the term Wahhabism is rejected by the followers of the Imam Muhammad ibn Abdulwahhab.[75] For them, there is nothing called Wahhabism in Islam; it is about returning to pure Islam and fighting *bid'a* (innovation). True, the Imam Muhammad ibn Abdulwahhab is highly respected by his followers, but they do not consider him to have started a new Islamic school called "Wahhabism."[76] They clearly state that their doctrine is based on a return to pure Islam as understood and practiced by the righteous ancestors. The sources of this pure Islam are the Holy Quran, the Noble Sunnah of the Prophet (pbuh), and consensus, in accordance with the school of the Imam Ahmad ibn Hanbal and his followers such as Ahmad ibn Taymiyya. The Imam Muhammad ibn Abdulwahhab only revived this call for a return to pure Islam. As such, he was a follower, rather than an innovator, of Salafism, and the term Wahhabism does not exist in original Salafism.

Regarding the term "Wahhabism," which is attributed to the Imam Muhammad ibn Abdulwahhab, some researchers explain that:

Wahhabism appeared in the Arabian Peninsula as a response to the sanctification of very pious men, visiting their tombs to come nearer to God (Allah), and the spread of *bid'a* (innovation) unheard of in Islam, whether in religious seasons or in daily life. Wahhabism resisted all of these and revived the school of [the Imam] Ahmad ibn Taymiyya.[77]

Hamed Al-Feqqi, founder of the Ansar Al-Sunnah Society in Egypt, agrees with this explanation regarding the origin of Wahhabism. He states that Wahhabists do not claim that the Imam Muhammad ibn Abdulwahhab established a new school or added something which did not exist at the time of the righteous ancestors. He only revived the pure Islam.[78]

That is why Salafis criticize the use of the word Wahhabism to denote their thought. They say this name implies that they are following one person, which is not true. Salafism is about following pure Islam. While critics of Wahhabism allege it is a new school which has introduced views unheard of in Islam, in fact all ideas promoted by the Imam Muhammad ibn Abdulwahhab had their origins in Islam and were previously adopted by Muslim jurists, and his call to fight *bid'a* (innovation) and un-Islamic practices echoes other Islamic schools. Furthermore, the Imam Muhammad ibn Abdulwahhab was a follower of the school of the Imam Ahmad ibn Hanbal.[79]

On the other hand, it must be stated that Wahhabism does not limit itself to preaching, but employs force against those who practice *bid'a* (innovation). This is because innovation is a vice to be combated, in accordance with the

principle of promoting virtue and preventing vice,[80] as set out in the Holy Quranic verse: "You are the best of peoples, evolved for mankind, promoting virtue, preventing vice, and believing in Allah."[81]

Imams of Salafism

The most prominent Imams and authority figures of Salafism are: the Imam Ahmad ibn Hanbal, the Imam Ahmad ibn Taymiyya, and the Imam Muhammad ibn Abdulwahhab. The following section will briefly introduce each of them.

The Imam Ahmad ibn Hanbal (164-241 AH; 780-855 AD)

The Imam Abdullah Ahmad ibn Ahmad ibn Muhammad ibn Hanbal Al-Shaybani (Ahmad ibn Hanbal) was born in Baghdad. He is the founder of the Hanbali religious school, and is highly respected by the Salafis. The Imam Muhammad ibn Abdulwahhab said: "We, thank God (Allah), are followers, not innovators. We follow the school of the Imam Ahmad ibn Hanbal."[82]

The school of the Imam Ahmad ibn Hanbal is one of the most conservative Sunni religious schools. It follows texts to the letter and avoids interpretation. Salafis believe that the doctrine of the Imam Ahmad ibn Hanbal is the same as theirs; it rejects *bid'a* (innovation), relies on the text of the Holy Quran and the Noble Sunnah, promotes virtue and prevents vice. Therefore, Salafis consider Muhammad ibn Hanbal one of the Imams of Salafism.

The Imam Ahmad ibn Hanbal memorized the Holy Quran when he was young. When he was fifteen years old, he started his journey of religious education. He joined lectures on the Prophet's sayings (Hadith) and focused on this discipline, travelling to learn more about the Prophet's sayings, moving between the Levant, the Maghreb, Mecca, Medina, Hijaz, Yemen, Iraq, Persia and Khorasan. Most important among his books is *Al-Musnad*,[83] which is the biggest collection of sayings (Hadith). It contains 40,000 selected by the Imam Ahmad ibn Hanbal out of 750,000 sayings of the Prophet (Hadith).[84]

The Imam Ahmad ibn Hanbal was faced with a difficult test in the form of the controversy over the nature of the Holy Quran which arose during the reign of the Abbasid Caliph Abdullah ibn Haroon Al-Rasheed (also known as Al-Mamoun), who asked religious scholars to endorse the view that the Holy Quran was created. The Imam Ibn Hanbal rejected this view and insisted that the Holy Quran was the Word of God (Allah) revealed to His Prophet Muhammad (pbuh). Despite being tortured, the Imam Ahmad ibn Hanbal resisted and refused to change his position.[85] This is historically known as the plight of Imam Ahmad ibn Hanbal, as previously mentioned.

Salafis look at the rejection by the Imam Ahmad ibn Hanbal of the argument that the Holy Quran was created as a very brave stance. He resisted pressure by three Caliphs (Al-Mamoun, then Al-Mu'tasim, then Al-Wathiq) who adopted the view that the Holy Quran was created. Ibn Hanbal rejected

this view and considered it to be *bid'a* (innovation) with no supporting evidence from the Holy Quran or the Noble Sunnah. Whenever asked to change his mind and endorse the view of the Caliphs, he would demand that they provide evidence from the Holy Quran or the Noble Sunnah to support their view. As they could not provide such evidence, they would find themselves helpless.[86] This explains why Salafism is connected with the Imam Ahmad ibn Hanbal, who is sometimes described as the founder of Salafism.[87]

The Imam Ahmad ibn Taymiyya (661–728 AH, 1263–1328 AD)

Abu Al-Abbas Ahmad ibn Abdulhaleem ibn Taymiyya (the Sheikh of Islam) was born in Harran (in modern day Syria). At the age of seven, he moved with his father to Damascus to escape the Mongol invasion. The Imam Ahmad ibn Taymiyya was raised in a family known for its knowledge, jurisprudence and religiosity. His father, grandfathers, brothers and some other relatives were well known jurists at the time. They include his grandfather Muhammad ibn Al-Khidr, his brother Abdulrahman and other relatives such as Abdulhaleem ibn Muhammad ibn Taymiyya and Abdulghani ibn Muhammad ibn Taymiyya.[88]

The Imam Ahmad ibn Taymiyya started learning from his father and religious scholars of Damascus. He memorized the Holy Quran at an early age,[89] and studied the Prophet's sayings (Hadith), jurisprudence, foundations and interpretation. As a student, he was known for his intelligence, good memory, and hard work. He focused on the study of religious disciplines, and by the time he turned 30, he was widely recognized as a learned, virtuous and scholarly Imam. He was described by his peers, teachers, students and even opponents as knowledgeable, modest and with strong a memory.[90]

According to Abu Abdullah Shamsuddin Al-Dhahabi, the Imam Ahmad ibn Taymiyya was:

> … our Sheikh and the Sheikh of Islam. He was unique in terms of his knowledge, courage, intelligence, enlightenment, generosity, care for the nation, promotion of virtue and prevention of vice. He participated in the *jihad* against the Mongols in 712 AH [1313 AD], and died while incarcerated in the prison of the castle in Damascus in 728 AH [1329 AD].[91]

The Imam Ahmad ibn Taymiyya spent his life trying to restore the purity of Islam by uncovering and removing all traces of Greek philosophy, which, in his opinion, negatively affected Islam.[92] He debated on the *Batiniyya* (esoteric school) and described them as 'innovators' (practicing *bid'a*—innovation) due to the significance they assigned to interpretation. His book, *Al-Siyassa Al-Shar'iya fi Islah Al-Ra'ee wal Ra'iyya* (Sharia Rule on the Reformation of the Ruler and Subjects)[93] is highly influential and has become a reference for all Salafis. It discusses the relationship between the ruler and subjects under Islamic *Sharia*, and emphasizes the literal application of *hudood* (prescribed punishments). However, the book overemphasizes *jihad*, considering it as important as prayer. It even seems that

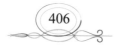

jihad is elevated in importance above the five pillars of Islam (declaration of faith, prayer, fasting, alms and pilgrimage), because the book describes prayer as the body of religion and *jihad* as its head.[94]

In his above mentioned book, the Imam Ahmad ibn Taymiyya states that a Muslim ruler has two main duties. The first is to use all means to serve religion by promoting virtue among the people and applying *hudood* (prescribed punishments), and the second is to carry out *jihad* by fighting warring unbelievers outside Islamic territories. As such, he thought that Islam could achieve the highest success both politically and religiously. The political and religious aspects become inseparable. If political authority does not consider religion, or if religion relinquishes its authority and limits itself to ritual, the result will be the failure of both, according to the Imam Ahmad ibn Taymiyya.[95] This book is different from *Al-Musnad* in terms of its goal, content and approach. As mentioned above, *Al-Musnad* comprises 40,000 sayings (Hadith) by the Prophet (pbuh).

The most important books by ibn Taymiyya are:[96] *Al-Hasaba* (Islamic Police); *Al-Siyassa Al-Shar'iya fi Islah Al-Ra'ee wal Ra'iyya* (Sharia Rules on the Reformation of the Ruler and Subjects); *Al-Furqan bayn Awliya' Al-Rahman wa Awliya' Al-Shaytan* (The Difference between Followers of the Way of God (Allah) and Followers of the Way of the Devil); *Dar' Tanaqud Al-Aql wa Al-Naql* (Averting Conflict between Reason and the Text), 11 volumes; *Al-Istiqamah* (The Straight Path); and *Manahij*

Al-Sunnah *Al-Nabawiyya Al-Shareefa Fi Naqd Kalam Al-Shiah and Al-Qadariyya* (Approaches to Refuting the Allegations of the Shiites and the Proponents of Free Will in the Noble Sunnah). His *fatwas* were collected in 35 volumes.[97]

The Imam Muhammad ibn Abdulwahhab (1115–1206 AH; 1703–1791)

The Imam Muhammad ibn Abdulwahhab ibn Suleiman Al-Tamimi Al-Najdi was born and raised in Al-Uyayna, in the middle of the Najd, currently in the Kingdom of Saudi Arabia. He was taught by his father, who was a judge of Al-Uyayna at the time. The Imam Muhammad ibn Abdulwahhab travelled to Hijaz to perform pilgrimage and pursue his studies. He learned from the Imams of Mecca at the time, then went to Medina and learned from its jurists and scholars such as Abdullah ibn Ibrahim Al-Najdi and Sheikh Muhammad Al-Sindi. After that he went to Basra, where he studied grammar, the Prophet's sayings (Hadith), and jurisprudence, before returning to Najd. On his way back, he visited Al-Ahsa' and learned from Sheikh Abdullah ibn Muhammad ibn Abdullateef Al-Shafe'i Al-Ahsa'i.[98]

The Imam Muhammad ibn Abdulwahhab grew up in a time when the Islamic state was weak, and the Ottoman Caliphate was losing its strength and control. This weakness was aggravated by the spread of *bid'a* (innovation), superstition, and forms of idolatry. Domes, trees and rocks were sanctified, tombs were worshipped, and pious men, both alive and dead, were appealed to.[99] His doctrine focused on purifying the concept of *tawheed* (the unity/oneness of God (Allah)), worshipping Him alone, rejecting idolatry, *bid'a* (innovation) and superstition, promoting virtue and preventing vice, and removing all obstacles on the path to *tawheed* and exclusive worship.[100]

The Imam Muhammad ibn Abdulwahhab considered the concept of *tawheed* to be the basis of Islam. This means that only God (Allah), and nobody else, should be worshipped, and that society should embody the practical application of this concept.[101] He authored several books, including: *Kitab Al-tawheed* (The Book of Oneness); *Kashf Al-Shubuhat* (Uncovering Superstition); *Tafseer Surat Al-Fatiha* (Interpretation of Al-Fatiha Sura); *Usool Al-Eiman* (Fundamentals of Faith); *Ma'na Al-Kalima Al-Tayyiba* (The Meaning of the Goodly Word); *Al-Amr bi Al-Ma'roof wa Al-Nahei an Al-Munkar* (The Promotion of Virtue and the Prevention of Vice); and *Kitab Al-Kabaer* (The Book of the Greater Crimes).[102]

According to his supporters, the Imam Muhammad ibn Abdulwahhab only revived the righteous ancestors' correct understanding and practice of Islam. This explains, in their opinion, the wide influence of Salafism on Muslims; it influenced Islamic reformists in India, Egypt, Iraq, the Levant, and other places, including figures such as Jamal Al-Din Al-Afghani, Jamal Al-Din Al-Qassimi, Khairuddin Al-Tunisi, Seddiq Hassan Khan, and Ameer Ali.[103]

Regarding the influence of the Imam Ahmad ibn Taymiyya on the Imam Muhammad ibn Abdulwahhab, one study states that:

> [The Imam Muhammad] ibn Abdulwahhab was influenced by an important aspect of the thought of [the Imam] ibn Taymiyya; i.e. countering suspicious religious practices and rituals ... This influence came as a response to the needs of the contemporary environment and circumstances as idolatrous forms of worship were prevalent all over the Arabian Peninsula.[104]

Ahmad ibn Hanbal, Ahmad ibn Taymiyya and Muhammad ibn Abdulwahhab share much of their thought. However, there is an increasing aspect of strictness as we move from the former to the latter.

Regarding the convergence of thought between the Imam Ahmad ibn Hanbal, the Imam Ahmad ibn Taymiyya and the Imam Muhammad ibn Abdulwahhab, some argue that an increasing aspect of strictness can be seen as we move from the former to the latter. We begin with relative leniency in the case of the Imam Ahmad ibn Hanbal, move to the radical theoretical criticism of the Imam Ahmad ibn Taymiyya, and end with the

Imam Muhammad ibn Abdulwahhab's sanctioning of violence to purify religion, such as fighting Sufi practices and destroying tombs, to the extent that in the Kingdom of Saudi Arabia, which – under the leadership of Abdulaziz ibn Abdulrahman Al Saud (1902–1953) in the third Al Saud state – adopted the Salafi doctrine and the thought of the Imam Muhammad ibn Abdulwahhab, all tombs of the companions and very pious men were destroyed, and only the tomb of the Prophet (pbuh) remains today.[105]

Some researchers argue that Wahhabi Salafism opened the door for very strict rules, and its focus on the doctrinal concept of *tawheed* resulted in the division of the world into two camps: the camp of idolatrous unbelievers, and the camp of true Muslims as represented by adherents to the concept of *tawheed*. This stance led to an expansion of the concept of *al-Walaa wal-Baraa* (allegiance and enmity) which hard-line takfiri and jihadi currents built on in their writings. This includes the following ten acts which are considered by these currents to result in automatic expulsion from Islam:[106]

1. Whoever practices idolatry, which includes supplicating and invoking the deceased, seeking assistance from them, and sacrificing animals to appease them.[107]

2. Whoever places intermediaries between himself and God (Allah), asking them to intercede on their behalf, and relying on them, has committed an act of disbelief according to the unanimous agreement of scholars.

3. Whoever does not hold the polytheists to be unbelievers, or has doubts about their unbelief or considers their ways and beliefs to be correct, is guilty of unbelief.

4. Whoever believes that some guidance other than that of the Prophet's (pbuh) is more complete than His guidance and that someone else's judgment is superior to His judgment.

5. Whoever hates something that the Prophet (pbuh) said or did.

6. Whoever mocks or ridicules any part of the Prophet's religion.

7. Whoever performs or supports sorcery, which includes magic spells that cause a person to hate or love someone, is guilty of unbelief.

8. Whoever supports and assists the polytheists against the Muslims.

9. Whoever believes that it is permitted for some people to be excused from implementing the *Sharia* of Muhammad (pbuh).

10. Turning away from Islam, not learning it and not implementing it.

Some Salafi scholars reject the name "Wahhabism" as it suggests a new Islamic school, and refuse to associate Salafism with one person—be it the Imam Muhammad ibn Abdulwahhab or the Imam Ahmad ibn Taymiyya. This is because Salafism means returning to pure Islam free of *bid'a* (innovation) or superstition which may have appeared with time. Commenting on the term "Wahhabism," Muhammad Nasseruddin Al-Albani argues that using this term is wrong because Salafism calls for pure

Islam based on the Holy Quran and the Noble Sunnah. He stressed that early Muslims followed this pure Islam, but there was no need to call it Salafi Islam or Salafism.[108] Therefore, according to this view, holding to pure Islam does not necessarily entail using terms like Wahhabi Islam or others. To clarify this, Al-Albani gives the following example:

> People used to speak classical Arabic properly, and there was no need for grammar and linguistic rules, as everyone followed them instinctively. The same applies in the case of Salafism ... It started to emerge after the appearance of other ideas, when foreign cultures started influencing Muslims and distorting pure Islamic practices and rituals.[109]

Some confuse religious Salafism and jihadi currents, considering that the latter developed naturally from the former, meaning that every Salafi group is a potential jihadi project.

Generally speaking, there are several remarks that may be made concerning Salafism:[110]

- Salafi currents share certain characteristics such as the circumstances in which they developed, their spread over a wide geographic area, and their weak organizational structure. The number of Salafis is relatively small, especially when compared with other political religious groups.

- Confusion of religious Salafism and jihadi currents is attributed to the assumption that the jihadi current evolved from Salafi currents. Accordingly, every Salafi group is a potential jihadi project waiting for the appropriate conditions to materialize.

- In its early beginnings, Salafism was not a static or a religious movement limited to preaching and giving lectures in mosques; it was a movement of change and reformation aimed at returning to pure Islam and fighting un-Islamic *bid'a* (innovation) and superstition.

- For some time, it was easy to join Salafi currents. All one has to do was follow the teachings of the Holy Quran and the Noble Sunnah and observe the rules established by them. Apart from certain *Sharia* imperatives, most obligations are between the person and God (Allah). This is how one becomes a Salafi.[111]

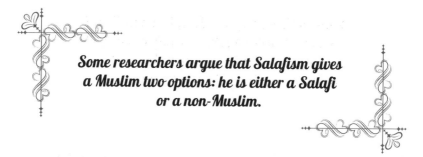

Some researchers argue that Salafism gives a Muslim two options: he is either a Salafi or a non-Muslim.

Criticisms of Salafism

There are several criticisms of Salafism, including ones which accuse it of inflexibility for the following reasons:[112]

1. Salafism used the principle of *tawheed* as a standard to measure the compliance of all acts and statements – even those which are not necessarily religious – with *Sharia*; any act or notion

which is not based on the principle of oneness is a kind of self-worship. According to this opinion, Salafism gives a Muslim two options: he is either a Salafi or a non-Muslim[113]

2. Salafism is very strict compared to contemporary jurisprudence, which does not follow the above tradition (based on a very strict approach and literal observation of the Holy Quran in accordance with the Hanbali school). Salafism rejects the jurisprudence school which calls for current circumstances to be taken into consideration, known as reality-based jurisprudence.[114]

The Salafis' Participation in Politics

At the end of 2010 and the beginning of 2011, the Arab region saw popular protests in several Arab countries, which deeply affected the integrity, security, stability and sovereignty of those countries. An important phenomenon in those protests was the prominent role of political religious groups; i.e. organizations and currents which believe in the importance of linking religion with the state and the inseparability of politics and religion.

The prominence of the Muslim Brotherhood was something expected, given the group's historical legacy and repeated attempts at participation in politics to attain authority.

The prominence of some political religious groups such as the Muslim Brotherhood was something expected, given the group's existence since the 1920s and its repeated attempts at participation in political life with the hope of securing authority. They entered parliament in some Arab countries such the Arab Republic of Egypt, the Hashemite Kingdom of Jordan, the Kingdom of Morocco, the Republic of Tunisia, and others.[115] This means they have a political role and are willing to continue this participation in the future. However, the prominent political role of Salafis in several Arab countries since 2011 and their participation in politics came as a surprise for many experts and observers, especially that they have become active in the political arena in those countries.

The prominent political role of Salafis since 2011 came as a surprise to many experts and observers.

Salafi Involvement in Politics since 2011

The political transformations witnessed in several Arab countries since 2011 constitute an important turning point in the course of Salafi currents, as some decided to participate in political and partisan work and contribute to intellectual and political discussions. This was evident in the cases of Egypt and Tunisia. In Egypt, the Salafi current, represented by the Al-Noor Party, emerged as an

active player in Egyptian politics in 2011. However, Salafis did not play an equal political role in the Republic of Tunisia.

Prior to that, the Salafi current in general, with a few exceptions in the Arab and Muslim worlds, avoided partisan work and political participation for ideological reasons. It focused on religious work, as well as educational work via the establishment of schools run by charitable societies, and rejected any involvement in politics for various reasons and considerations. This new phase came at a cost. Their political gains, public prominence, media coverage, and influence in public life, especially in the countries which have seen domestic turmoil, put the Salafis under the spotlight, which resulted in increasing political opposition to them in the Arab world and led to warnings regarding their social and cultural projects and political goals.

> *Political transformations in the Arab region uncovered differences within the Salafi current regarding democracy and political participation.*

On the other hand, political transformations in these countries uncovered major internal differences among most Salafi groups about the legitimacy of changes within the Salafi current; Arab Salafi circles were not in agreement regarding the acceptance of democracy, political participation, and the main differences between partisan and religious work; some currents resisted this change and continued to reject any involvement in politics altogether, while others insisted on participation in politics despite the fact that they were not ready for such participation.

The Salafis' participation in politics and the creation of political parties began in Egypt and then spread to various other Arab and Muslim countries. In this new phase of their activity, the Salafis had to accept the rules of politics; they had to review their thought and ideology to adapt to their new reality, define their goals and priorities, and decide their position regarding the political work which they had become part of.[116]

The Salafis became new political players, sharing with the Muslim Brotherhood the votes of many segments of society, including religious conservatives, people seeking change, people who trusted political religious groups as an alternative that would end their living and development crises, and those opposed to the previous regimes and fearful of their return. For example, in the Arab Republic of Egypt, the Salafi current entered into confrontation and competition with other political forces. Despite its alliance with the Muslim Brotherhood and its willingness to compete alongside it in the legislative elections held at the end of 2011, the discourse of the Salafi current generally differs from that of the Muslim Brotherhood. Some argue that the Salafis seem to be more committed to the application of *Sharia*, and more opposed to other secular currents.[117] I think these differences are tactical ones and do not reflect strategic differences in vision and objective. They are

basically the result of the Muslim Brotherhood's long history of maneuvering, hiding behind slogans, and political dissimulation to reach their goal and then uncover their true intentions.[118] The Salafis' lack of political experience explains many of their confrontational positions with regard to secular forces, as evidenced by their tendency to change rapidly.[119]

The remarkable success of the Salafis in the Egyptian elections was a surprise even for observers of political religious groups. Others believe the votes won by Islamic currents in the Egyptian parliamentary elections were not surprising; any observer of Egyptian society would have realized in advance that Islamic parties would prevail. Unexpectedly for many people, 40 percent of voters who voted for representatives of political religious groups did not choose the Muslim Brotherhood, which is the biggest and oldest opposition movement in the country. Instead, they supported an alliance of three Salafi parties with no previous experience in politics. The leaders of those parties were not known to most Egyptians before 2011. In addition, with only a few exceptions, Salafis were opposed to the popular protests when they started. They changed their opinions and supported the protests only a few days before former president Muhammad Husni Mubarak stepped down.[120] Nevertheless, the Salafi alliance won 28 percent of votes in the 2011 parliamentary elections,[121] representing 127 seats out of 508. The influence of Salafis was later reaffirmed in the Shura Council elections, when they won 45 seats out of 180.[122]

One observer of Salafism argues that the events of 2011 opened the door for Salafis to enter politics in the Arab Republic of Egypt. They had two options: either holding to their previous positions of non-involvement in politics and rejection of western-style democracy, which would place them on the margins of events in the region, or revising their previous positions by accepting democracy and aligning this with their previous views. The latter option was chosen by many Salafis in the Arab Republic of Egypt, particularly in Alexandria and Cairo.[123]

The Salafis entered politics in 2011 and aligned themselves with the Muslim Brotherhood against secular forces.

The Salafis entered Egyptian politics immediately after former president Muhammad Husni Mubarak stepped down. They mobilized support for the draft constitution in the referendum of March 2011 and aligned themselves with the Muslim Brotherhood in the face of various secular and liberal forces. The draft constitution received popular support. This increased the Salafis' confidence and encouraged them to participate in politics through the establishment of several parties, including the Al-Noor Party, the Al-Asala Party, the Building and Development Party, and others.[124] To justify the change in the

Salafi discourse, focus was placed on the identity of the state. The conflict over the constitution was the pretext used by the Salafis to justify their move from rejecting partisan work and involvement in politics to participation in politics to protect Islamic identity on the one hand and take advantage of democracy to achieve the goal of applying Islamic *Sharia* on the other.[125]

As such, it is safe to state that the change that the Salafis underwent following the events of January 25, 2011 was related to the principle of political participation and the acceptance of political partisan work. Much of their previous activity was focused on religious education and preaching, resisting the temptations of political participation and gain which can be achieved by linking partisan work to religion. Previously, they considered this a complete waste of time and effort. However, this position changed, and they began to focus on active political participation. The importance of this change in the position of the Salafis stems from the fact that it required them to reformulate their position towards political parties and partisan work in general.[126]

Regionally speaking, although the Salafis do not have regional or international organizations like those of the Muslim Brotherhood, they have contacts and lines of communication between their leaders and politically and intellectually similar groups.[127]

After former Egyptian president Muhammad Husni Mubarak stepped down on February 11, 2011, and before the beginning of the race to elect a new president, Salafi leaders made huge efforts to convince the Muslim Brotherhood to nominate Engineer Khairat Al-Shatir, Deputy General Guide of the group, pledging to do all they could to support him. Accordingly, the Muslim Brotherhood nominated Al-Shatir as their candidate for the presidency.[128] However, he was excluded because he had been convicted of a military offence but was not reinstated in accordance with the Egyptian law.[129]

After Khairat Al-Shatir was excluded from the presidential race, there were several candidates from political religious groups. The Salafis announced they would support the presidential candidate Abdulmunem Abu Al-Futooh. Based on this position, the Salafis refused to support the Muslim Brotherhood's candidate, Dr. Muhammad Mursi. One of the reasons cited was that they did not want one party to control the country. This angered the Muslim Brotherhood, whose alternative candidate faced a fierce media attack even before he started his campaign because he was nominated as an alternative after Al-Shatir.[130]

The Muslim Brotherhood insisted on proceeding with their candidate. They made huge efforts and organized a campaign which toured the country. As a result, Dr. Muhammad Mursi came first in the first round, and faced Lieutenant General Ahmad Shafeeq in the second round.

After Dr. Abdulmunem Abu Al-Futooh lost in the first round, the Salafis supported the only other Islamic candidate in the presidential race, Dr. Muhammad Mursi of the Muslim Brotherhood, which helped bridge the gap between the two

groups. The Salafis made huge efforts in support of Dr. Mursi. For them, it was not the battle of the Muslim Brotherhood alone, but the battle of all Islamists and those supporting change against Lieutenant General Ahmad Shafeeq, who was considered the candidate of the former regime.[131] After Dr. Muhammad Mursi beat Shafiq in the elections, the Salafis sought to reap the fruits of their support for the Muslim Brotherhood's candidate in the form of real participation in decision making. They looked forward to the formation of the government and presidential team, but were disappointed as Dr. Mursi did not consult them when forming his presidential team, and in the first cabinet of Hisham Qandeel they were given only the portfolio of the ministry of the environment, which was rejected by the Al-Noor Party.

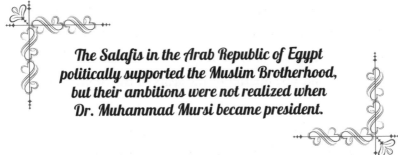

The Salafis in the Arab Republic of Egypt politically supported the Muslim Brotherhood, but their ambitions were not realized when Dr. Muhammad Mursi became president.

The Salafi reaction was swift; the Al-Noor Party denounced the fact that they were not consulted regarding the formation of the presidential team and the government. They had expected the government to be a national coalition government consisting of all parties in the same proportion as their representation in parliament. In an official statement, the Al-Noor Party said its leaders were surprised that consultations, whether with the presidency or with the Freedom and Justice Party, completely stopped after the president's inauguration. Furthermore, they warned that this would have negative effects at a time when they were "looking forward to working together with a new spirit to meet the people's aspirations."[132] The Muslim Brotherhood did not respond to the statement, thereby making it understood by everyone that the Muslim Brotherhood did not want to share authority with anyone.

The Salafi movement in the Arab Republic of Egypt took advantage of the political, economic and social circumstances during and beyond the domestic upheaval of 2011 to achieve very good results in the elections despite its limited experience in political work (such as electioneering and campaigning, manifestos, organizing elections, etc.) compared to the long experience of the Muslim Brotherhood in political work. The Salafi current won one third of the seats in the Egyptian parliament and one quarter of the seats in the Shura Council.

There are several common features of Salafism in various Arab and Muslim countries. For example, the Salafi landscape in the Republic of Yemen is very similar to that in the Arab Republic of Egypt after 2011; there has been a proliferation of Salafi groups and currents, especially in recent years. During the popular protests, the Salafis were divided: some warned of the consequences of disobedience to the ruler and participation in demonstrations, while others, especially the youth, participated in the protests with their leaders who issued *fatwas* allowing

sit-ins and action aimed at toppling the president of Yemen, Ali Abdullah Saleh.[133] During the protests, the Salafis were influenced by the Egyptian experience and started establishing Salafi parties similar to those in Egypt. However, Salafi currents were divided in Yemen as well.[134]

In an article discussing the advantages and disadvantages of the rise of the Egyptian Al-Noor Party, Muhammad bin Musa Al-Aamri, founder of the Sanaa-based Al-Rashad Union Party (a Salafi party established in 2012 in the Republic of Yemen) explained that there were two views.[135] The first comprised the majority of Islamists who viewed the political rise of the Al-Noor Party as a golden opportunity for the Salafis, allowing them to fight corruption and promote reformation as much as possible, which is compatible with *Sharia*,[136] especially if there were coordination with the Freedom and Justice Party (of the Muslim Brotherhood) and other Islamic forces to face liberal and secular currents and their plans in the Arab Republic of Egypt. It also allows them to learn about the problems of the people, and try to attract them to the way of pure Islam. In addition, this offered the Salafis a chance for practical training in political work and optimal utilization of resources, which will open new horizons for Islamic work through popular participation.[137]

The second view is that the participation of the Salafi Al-Noor Party in political work in the Arab Republic of Egypt brings risks which outweigh its advantages, including the following: those involved in politics will inevitably find themselves violating the rules of *Sharia*;[138] political work might distract people from religious education and preaching, and involve them in both conflicts and alliances; the Al-Noor Party has limited experience in politics and will find it difficult to manage the complexities of regional and international politics and deal with secularists, Christians and others; finally, the post-Mubarak Arab Republic of Egypt is struggling with the problems of corruption, poverty, unemployment and underdevelopment, while the Egyptian people can no longer bear their suffering and require immediate change that is difficult for political religious groups to achieve in the foreseeable future given their present capabilities.[139]

As in other Arab countries, the position of the Salafi current towards political work in Tunisia was divided. After the fall of the regime of former president Zine Al-Abideen bin Ali on January 14, 2011, some Salafis adopted the path of political participation while holding to the same religious slogans which were heard in several Arab capitals, such as the inclusion of *Sharia* in the constitution, the Islamization of certain sectors such as labor, production and education, and other well-known Salafi demands. This position was taken by several Salafi parties, including the Jabhat Al-Islah Party, the Al-Rahmah Party, and the Al-Asalah Party. They followed in the footsteps of their counterparts in Egypt and Yemen by giving up their rejection of democracy and elections.[140] The Tunisian Salafi parties have the same intellectual principles as those adopted by the Salafi movement in Egypt, Kuwait and other countries.[141]

In addition, jihadi Salafis emerged among influential forces in the political and security landscape in the Republic of Tunisia. They adopted the same position of jihadi Salafism in other Arab and Muslim countries in terms of rejecting political work and democratic mechanisms. In May 2011, various Tunisian jihadi Salafi groups were united under the umbrella of Ansar Al-Sharia, led by Abu Iyadh Al-Tunisi (Saifullah bin Hussein), who was mentored by Al-Qa'ida members such as Abu Qatada Al-Filistini and Abu Mus'ab Al-Suri, and had met Usama bin Ladin in Kandahar in September 2000. It seems that Ansar Al-Sharia is the same name used by elements carrying the same thought in the State of Libya, the Republic of Yemen, and other countries.[142] In August 2013, Ansar Al-Sharia was officially classified as a terrorist organization in the Republic of Tunisia, and was accused of assassinating political opposition figures, murdering members of the security forces and Tunisian army, and seeking to establish an Islamic emirate.[143]

The Future of Salafism

Some scholars argue that the Salafis benefited from the elections and the attraction of Muslim voters to Islamic parties in light of the increasing domination of conservative Islamic discourse in Egyptian society.[144] Furthermore, many were of the view that those groups deserved to reach a position of authority; as they publicly associated themselves with religion in an instinctively religious society, a certain segment of voters considered them less corrupt than others.

Although Salafism was largely limited to religious scholars and did not attempt to create a political or organizational framework as the Muslim Brotherhood did, it was able to publish, distribute and make available to the public key Salafi works such as *Majmoo' Al-Fatawa wa Maqalat wa Rasael Al-Sheikh ibn Baz* (Complete *fatwas*, Articles and Letters of Sheikh ibn Baz) by Abdulaziz ibn Baz, and *Al-Ahadith Al-Saheeha* (Authentic Prophetic sayings (Hadith)) by Al-Albani.[145] These works were met with increasing interest in the 1970s, especially among students. During this period, Salafism became a larger social and religious phenomenon. All Salafi groups which began participating in political work in the Arab Republic of Egypt in 2011 developed from the social and religious networks which emerged in the 1970s.[146]

One researcher argues that it is still too early to make a final judgment regarding the performance of the Salafis after the recent developments and changes in the Arab and Muslim worlds. All indicators suggest that the Salafi discourse still has a long way to go, and what we see is only the beginning of the transformation.[147] One indicator of the Salafi transformation following the events since 2011 is its position towards democracy, which is a thorny issue for other political currents due to the fact that democracy originates in Western political thought. When the Salafis adopted the concept of democracy within the limits of *Sharia*, they had come a long way from their previous discourse prior to 2011, when they prohibited democracy as "an un-Islamic system imported from the West."[148] The concept of

democracy within the limits of *Sharia* means that democracy should be practiced only to the extent that it is compatible with *Sharia*, and cannot be used to violate *Sharia* rules, such as allowing women to go out unveiled, or destroy the foundations of society as established by religion, such as family cohesion.

Conclusion

This chapter explored in detail the similarities and differences between various Salafi currents and groups which have recently undergone remarkable transformations, particularly in relation to political participation, their position towards existing regimes, and other issues involving the relationship between religion and state.

While the Muslim Brotherhood has experienced governance and reached the pinnacle of authority (the presidency of the Arab Republic of Egypt), some Salafi currents have had experience of political participation at the level of legislatures. This latter experience might not be enough to judge the development of the political thought of these currents and anticipate their direction in the foreseeable future. The transformation has just begun, and is open to all scenarios. However, these scenarios are largely dependent on the position of Arab and Muslim peoples towards political religious groups in general. This is because there is no clear distinction in the public's collective consciousness between different political religious currents and groups such as the Muslim Brotherhood, the Salafis, and others. The stereotypical image of each current or group is affected, both positively and negatively, by the political performance of other currents and groups. This can be attributed to several factors which make it difficult to understand how each of them is perceived by society independently of others. Furthermore, political religious groups are often ideologically classified – within each country and at the broader regional level – under the umbrella of political Islam, because they are aligned against the secular current in relation to several issues, thereby making any distinction between them limited to minor variations within the framework of the political religious current itself.

5 Political Religious Groups: The Surooris

CHAPTER 5

Political Religious Groups: The Surooris

S uroorism is one of the political religious groups that emerged and spread in the 1980s and 1990s. Sources indicate that it was intellectually born of the Muslim Brotherhood, the largest and probably the oldest religious group in the modern era. Suroorism is named after its apparent founder, the Syrian Muhammad bin Suroor bin Nayef Zine Al-Abideen, and was founded when he moved to the Kingdom of Saudi Arabia to teach mathematics there in the late 1960s. It is perhaps ironic that, unlike a lot of his clerical contemporaries, bin Suroor is the founder and guide of an important religious movement and current but does not possess religious knowledge which qualifies him to issue *fatwas* and juristic rulings on issues such as *takfir, jihad* and war, such as those advocated by his Islamic current.

Despite the speed at which the Suroori current emerged, and the activism of thought that characterized it – in an environment that was not conducive to such activism owing to the dominance of one of the most important traditional Salafi approaches in the Muslim world – and despite the presence of older political religious organizations and groups, Suroorism has spread quickly and remarkably, especially in the Kingdom of Saudi Arabia. It is often accused of ambiguity, and there are many doubts about its existence as a 'corporate' organization like the Muslim Brotherhood. Nevertheless, the importance of the Suroori current does not stem from the speed of its expansion, nor even from its large number of supporters, but from the appeal of its view on *jihad*. Suroorism harmonizes the activist aspect, perhaps by virtue of its founder's early life and those of many of his followers within the Muslim Brotherhood. This duality, with its blurred dividing lines between activist and ideological approaches, has raised many questions about the nature of this current and the nature of its approach, and most importantly its role in spreading the culture of *takfir*, which now characterizes many jihadi organizations. How did this current grow, and what are the factors that led to its propagation? What are its goals, methods and approaches? How does it differ from the Muslim Brotherhood or (traditional) Salafism? What is its role in the emergence of the so-called jihadi Salafism which adopts a strict approach to *takfir*? Has this current declined and receded? and if so what factors are behind this decline? Has this trend achieved its objectives? Or is it just a mirage like other political religious groups?

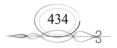

Foundation

The Suroori current, also known as "activist Salafism," was founded by Muhammad bin Suroor, a Syrian cleric born in Horan in 1938. He was an officer in the Syrian army[1] and a member of the Muslim Brotherhood since 1953. At the time of the split in the Syrian Muslim Brotherhood in 1969 between the Aleppo group (that adhered to Hassan al-Banna's ideas) and the Damascus group (that was inspired by the confrontational approach of Sayyid Qutb),[2] Muhammad bin Suroor, highly influenced by Qutb's thought, was drawn to the wing led by Issam Ridha Al-Attar (the former Supreme Guide of the Muslim Brotherhood group in the Syrian Arab Republic and the most influential man in that period, before he broke away from the movement).[3] As a result of the persecution of the Muslim Brotherhood in the 1960s, Muhammad bin Suroor moved to the Kingdom of Saudi Arabia in 1965, where he first stayed in the city of Hail for one year before moving to Buraidah in the Al-Qassim region to work as a teacher in the "Scientific Institute" there.[4] Work was not the motive, however, as Muhammad bin Suroor himself said. He regarded leaving one's country as an "abomination," but was forced to leave because political activity in the Syrian Arab Republic was not possible at the time.[5] Muhammad bin Suroor moved from the Kingdom of Saudi Arabia to Kuwait, where he lived during the period 1973–1990,[6] working as a journalist for the *Al-Mujtamaa* journal, which is considered to be the first publication of the Muslim Brotherhood in the Arab world.[7] He then left Kuwait for Birmingham in the United Kingdom, where he founded the Center for Noble Sunnah Studies[8] and issued the *Al-Sunnah* journal, which was instrumental in spreading his thought and political position. In 2004, he moved to Jordan, where he remains today.[9] Also, he owns a house in the State of Qatar.

Muhammad bin Suroor and many other members of political religious groups – especially members of the Muslim Brotherhood – found a safe haven in the Kingdom of Saudi Arabia, which embraced them during the 1960s and 1970s.[10] Muhammad bin Suroor had been influenced by the Salafi approach prevailing there, and began propagating his call that combined the thought of the Muslim Brotherhood (on which he had been reared for many years) with Salafi ideology, which he believed the Muslim Brotherhood had moved away from. His call spread rapidly through religious platforms and charities, and soon became one of the largest Islamic religious currents in the Kingdom of Saudi Arabia and the rest of the Arabian Gulf region. Despite the lack of accurate statistics on the number of followers of this current, according to various estimates it was considered one of the most prominent religious currents and experienced notable expansion in the 1990s, with supporters in many Islamic countries, and especially the Kingdom of Saudi Arabia.[11] This current became known as Suroorism after its theorist and founder, a description rejected by Muhammad bin Suroor himself and many of his followers who introduce themselves as a Salafi Islamic group without a specific name—although it is always underscored by their opponents, both from

the Muslim Brotherhood or traditional Salafis and other analysts and researchers.[12] Because of its mixture between the two approaches of the Brotherhood and Salafis, which are distinct in thought and practice, Suroorism has become a highly controversial approach that has inspired heated debate; some analysts classify it as a Salafi Islamic current concerned with preaching and scholarship, while others consider it to be a political activist organization with a leadership and institutions based in the Kingdom of Saudi Arabia and many other Arab countries. However, the founder of this current and his supporters deny the existence of any such organization.

Proliferation and Expansion

The Suroori current spread rapidly and concentrated in the Kingdom of Saudi Arabia and the Arab Gulf states, by virtue of its foundation and the predominantly Salafi environment controlled by the Wahhabi–Salafi school and influenced by both its acceptability to society and the political orientation of the rulers of the period. Yet the followers of the Imam Muhammad bin Abdul Wahab's thought differentiate between political affairs – which are the prerogative of the ruler – and religious affairs, which are the prerogative of religious scholars.[13] This is one of the pillars of Salafi ideology, which believes that obedience to the ruler is next to obedience to God (Allah) and His Messenger. It describes the rulers as princes and scholars who must be obeyed, but if one of them commands disobedience to God (Allah) – be he a prince, a king, a scholar, a president of Republic, or otherwise – he must not be obeyed.[14] Muhammad bin Suroor's influence was strongest in the Al-Qassim region, the stronghold of Salafism, where he began his call, and then moved to the eastern and southern regions and the rest of the Kingdom.[15]

The period from the early 1980s through the 1990s was known as the "Islamic Awakening" in the Kingdom of Saudi Arabia. However, despite the departure of the founder of the Suroori current from the country more than two decades ago, Suroori thought – or that of the "awakening" as it is known among scholars in various regions of the Kingdom – has spread. It is believed, however, that the current is centered in a number of universities, schools and government institutions in the Kingdom of Saudi Arabia;[16] there are even reports that it has now penetrated certain levels of leadership, especially in universities.[17]

Besides the adoption of the concept of *jihad* linked to the approach of the righteous ancestors, the financial capabilities of the Suroori current have opened the door for its followers to move outside the Kingdom of Saudi Arabia, and expand geographically and intellectually in a number of Arab and Muslim countries.[18] The Suroori call spread to Kuwait through what was known locally as Scientific Salafism, which was locked in a fierce battle with the Jami current[19] – named after Muhammad Aman Al-Jami – which calls for absolute obedience and loyalty to the ruler and rejects political parties.[20] In 2005, the Surooris tried to form a political party known as the "Umma

Party," and began calling for an elected government, political pluralism and a peaceful transfer of authority. Although this party is banned in Kuwait and the rest of the GCC countries,[21] it participated in the Kuwaiti elections in 2008 with 12 candidates running as independents, none of whom were elected.

The Umma Party in Kuwait and elsewhere – including the United Arab Emirates – adopted the same radical ideas, with separate branches appearing at different times in each country. Their intellectual and organizational convergence is reflected in the convergence of the branches of this party from various Gulf countries at group meetings.[22] These parties have adopted radical stances and opposed the governments of the countries in which they are based, forming an alliance called the "Umma Parties in the Gulf and Arabian Peninsula," which has issued several statements to express its opposition to the policies of GCC governments in relation to both domestic and foreign affairs.[23]

Surooris exist in other Gulf States, like the Kingdom of Bahrain and the State of Qatar, but little information is available in this regard. In the United Arab Emirates, however, although the movement sends a large number of preachers to deliver lessons in the country each year – especially in the Emirate of Sharjah – it no longer has a significant presence.[24] Recently, a group affiliated with the same current established what it called the "UAE Umma Party," but it has not enjoyed any local support or expansion.[25]

Suroorism in Egypt is represented by a current led by Jamal Sultan, the publisher and Editor-in-Chief of the Almesryoon electronic newspaper, who has recently attempted to depart from the traditional Suroori line through intellectual reviews of his earlier writings. Its supporters still exist in the Arab Republic of Egypt,[26] where some people believe it is led by the Salafi preacher, Hazim Salah Abu Ismail. It has gained more exposure since the abdication of former President Muhammad Husni Mubarak, and is similar in its thought and principles to Suroorism. Its leader has sought to create a political bloc or current that blends Salafi ideology and the principles of the Muslim Brotherhood, and imparts a revolutionary character to his intellectual perspective.[27]

In the Republic of the Sudan, the Suroori current found fertile ground and representation in the form of the Legitimate League.[28] The Republic of the Sudan is considered one of the most hospitable environments for Suroorism, and the League's supporters enjoy freedom of expression and speech.

In the People's Democratic Republic of Algeria, Muhammad Ali Belhadj – who is considered to be the vice president of the banned FIS (the Islamic Salvation Front) – is one of the most prominent figures of Suroori thought, which some claim has many followers in Algeria.[29]

In the Republic of Yemen, Activist Salafis are divided into two categories, one follows Muhammad bin Suroor himself, namely the Al-Ihsan Welfare Association,[30] and the other follows Abdurrahman Abdul Khaliq Al-Yousuf, one of the

icons of the Salafi call in the Arab world,[31] who disagreed with Muhammad bin Suroor about political activity, elections, democracy and dealing with ruling authorities.[32]

Suroorism also exists in the West, especially in the United Kingdom, for its founder Muhammad bin Suroor lived in Birmingham after leaving the State of Kuwait in the beginning of the 1990s. He is thought to have left around the time of the Gulf crisis, when the conflict between the Surooris and the Saudi authorities intensified as a result of its opposition to the use of foreign troops in the liberation of Kuwait from Iraqi occupation.[33] Muhammad bin Suroor was known for criticizing the rulers of the Arab Gulf states.[34] The *Al-Sunnah* journal, which was the most important means for the dissemination of his thought,[35] was in great demand during the invasion of Kuwait, especially after it had shown strong opposition to the royal family in the Kingdom of Saudi Arabia with respect to the Gulf War. The journal helped increase the influence of Surooris in the Kingdom of Saudi Arabia and in other parts of the Arab and Muslim worlds.

Surooris Mixed Salafi and Muslim Brotherhood approaches and issued the slogan, "Salafi Approach, Modern Confrontation" to attract support.

Goals

To this day there remains disagreement about the existence of a formal organization behind Suroorism, in the sense that there are no visible institutional structures that operate in accordance with regulations – as in the case of Muslim Brotherhood, for example[36] – and no special publications issued by the Surooris or spokespersons speaking in its name like other political religious groups. Hence, there is no specific literature issued by this movement that clearly indicates its attributes and the nature of its institutional work or its goals and means of achieving them, as is the case for most organized political groups. Despite its large size and broad expansion, especially in the last two decades of the twentieth century, there is little published scholarly literature that tackles this current or studies it in a systematic and scientific way. This may be largely due to the clandestine nature of the current and its theorists – perhaps for security reasons – on the one hand, as well as their narratives, which are seen as contradictory by many specialists, on the other.[37] Despite the existence of websites for some of the associations that adopt the Suroori approach – like the Legitimate League in the Republic of the Sudan[38] which displays the goals that this League seeks to achieve, being derived from the orientations of Muhammad bin Suroor and his writings – there is a need to explore the goals of this current, as well as the means of achieving them cited in the arguments of its proponents, especially in light of the great transformations that have recently occurred in the Arab and Muslim worlds.

442

There may not be much difference in terms of this goal between the Suroori current and the Muslim Brotherhood, which produced Muhammad bin Suroor. However, Suroor tried to develop a way to achieve the goal by spreading new ideas in keeping with the growing role of political and religious groups in the 1980s in a number of Arab and Muslim countries.[39]

> *The Suroori current followed in the footsteps of the Muslim Brotherhood, taking advantage of its experience in order to disseminate its ideas, and focused on spreading rhetoric through teaching and delivering lectures and lessons in mosques.*

The other goal sought by this current is the dissemination of *Sharia* knowledge and the correction of doctrinal concepts. It tries to combine the approaches of Salafis and the Muslim Brotherhood under the slogan: "Salafi approach, modern confrontation." Muhammad bin Suroor believes that the books and literature that dealt with doctrine in ancient Islamic eras are no longer valid in this age and do not help to mobilize or inspire people,[40] and therefore the issue of doctrine should be introduced in a manner suitable to our present time.[41] Therefore, Muhammad bin Suroor wrote his book, *Manhaj Al-Anbiya* (Way of the Prophets),[42] to present activist doctrine and *tawheed*.[43]

Since the issue of government and associated concepts such as *hakimiyya* – the intellectual basis of the writings of Sayyid Qutb – are the main themes in Suroori thought,[44] as is the case with many other religious movements, one of its ultimate objectives is to work toward the establishment of the Islamic State (Caliphate), which rules according to what God (Allah) has revealed. It is rigid in this argument as it denies *hakimiyya* to anyone other than God (Allah), and opposes any source of legislation other than the Holy Quran and the Noble Sunnah. Therefore, the Suroori current attaches particular importance to the issue of *Sharia* in the Islamic *da'wa*, and works primarily to disseminate the understanding of this policy and raise awareness about it within Muslim societies.[45]

In addition to these basic goals, according to its supporters the Suroori current seeks to spread centrism, moderation and tolerance in order to curb excess and neglect, and to revive the promotion of virtue and prevention of vice in accordance with *Sharia* guidelines contained in the Holy Quran and Noble Sunnah, as well as to resist anti-Islamic currents and ideas.[46]

The Suroori current followed the Muslim Brotherhood's approach of political socialization, and relied on so-called "Islamic awareness" groups in schools to attract students.

The Means

The Suroori current employs multiple means of achieving its objectives, but it seems that they do not differ much to those of the Muslim Brotherhood.[47] However, Surooris remain distinct in how they exploit available means, as well as in the substance of the issues or materials which are raised through these means. After leaving the Muslim Brotherhood, Muhammad bin Suroor began to rely on a system of open meetings (*halaqat*) with his disciples and followers,[48] taking advantage of his professional position as a teacher – albeit of mathematics – to provide lessons in mosques and scientific institutes in the Kingdom of Saudi Arabia.

As his following grew, he began to train staff, and especially *Sharia* scholars, enabling them to preach. He therefore paid attention to rhetoric, and his followers took to pulpits and gave lectures and lessons in mosques and Islamic centers. By virtue of their experience in the Muslim Brotherhood, his adherents also realized the potential importance of summer student centers, so they focused their activities on them in schools and universities. The platforms that witnessed the most heated competition with the Muslim Brotherhood were these student camps, where educational, preaching, juristic and activist programs were undertaken. Besides the acceptance by many – especially young people – of this relatively new line of thinking, at least in the Saudi environment, it was also spread by its supporters and followers by establishing and operating charities, which according to some observers served as a source of recruitment and financing.[49]

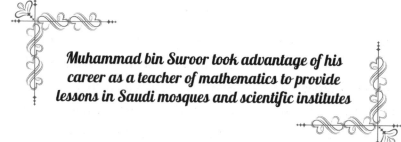

Muhammad bin Suroor took advantage of his career as a teacher of mathematics to provide lessons in Saudi mosques and scientific institutes

A former follower of this current, in an interview with Al-Arabiya website in March 2008,[50] said that it used to depend on the so-called "Islamic Awareness Groups" in schools in order to attract the largest possible number of students. Other important means upon which Muhammad bin Suroor's current depended included meetings and special sessions with students recognized as outstanding in their studies or extra-curricular activities at school or university. These were private sessions (to evade security services), and it was clear that the Surooris believed in the permissibility of secrecy and discretion in the exercise of their activities.[51] The sessions included lessons in commentary on the Holy Quran, as well as debates on intellectual and activist books. There was also a focus on the follow-up of political and preaching events.[52]

One of the most important and efficient means of circulating its message was via audio cassettes.[53] They were used for the dissemination of speeches and lessons by Suroor and other preachers belonging to his current, especially Salman Fahd Al-Odah.[54] This was an important method in the 1990s, before the spread of the Internet and satellite TV channels and

other manifestations of the information revolution in the field of media and communications.

The *Al Sunnah* journal, which Muhammad bin Suroor had established before he left the State of Kuwait for the United Kingdom in the early 1990s against the backdrop of his position towards the Gulf War, was also one of the most important means used to spread his ideas. The journal played a pivotal role in the dissemination of Muhammad bin Suroor's thought and in framing his perspective. He even stated in the journal his explicit political and jurisprudential positions on the existing ruling regimes, which he considered non-Islamic as they did not implement the provisions of the Islamic *Sharia*.[55]

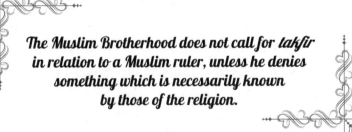

The Muslim Brotherhood does not call for takfir in relation to a Muslim ruler, unless he denies something which is necessarily known by those of the religion.

Thought and Method

Muhammad bin Suroor believed in the permissibility of rebellion against a Muslim ruler if he did not rule according to what God (Allah) has revealed,[56] unlike the Muslim Brotherhood, who do not call for *takfir* in relation to a Muslim ruler, even if he does not rule according to what God (Allah) has revealed, on the basis of a fundamental principle of the *Ahl Al-Sunnah Wal Jama'a* community; i.e. no believer should be excommunicated unless he denies something which is necessarily known by those of the religion.[57]

> *The founder of the Suroori current believes in the permissibility of rebellion against a Muslim ruler if he does not rule according to what God (Allah) has revealed.*

Muhammad bin Suroor found in Britain the environment that would help him to achieve his alternative vision, and he began to be clearly influenced by the Salafi approach prevailing in the Kingdom of Saudi Arabia through the thought of the Imam Muhammad ibn Abdulwahhab.[58] This helped to drastically change Muhammad bin Suroor's thought, and he devised a new approach that combined some ideas of traditional Salafism with the methodology of the Muslim Brotherhood. This new approach combined the Muslim Brotherhood's activist approach – especially the radical aspect – in terms of its view of the nature of society and the ruler, and the violence of Sayyid Qutb, with the Salafi approach, especially in relation to matters of faith, as embodied in the views of the Imam Ahmad ibn Taymiyya.[59] Nevertheless, Muhammad bin Suroor believes that his approach is not different from the approach of the righteous ancestors (*Salaf*); he even considers it to be the way of the prophets. To him, it means only one thing: "abidance by the creed and the way of the righteous ancestors, may God (Allah) bless them, and of those who followed in their footsteps until the day of judgment."[60] Therefore, Muhammad bin Suroor emphasizes frequently in his writings the necessity of adopting the way of *Ahl Al-Sunnah Wal Jama'a* in reform and education, and in the building of people and organizations.[61]

This combination of activism and Salafism is the most distinctive aspect of Suroorism, and perhaps contributed fundamentally to its broad dissemination in the last two decades of the 20th century. The Saudi writer, Ibrahim Al-Sakran Al-Tameemi, a former advocate of this trend,[62] describes Suroorist thought as an "approach that differs from both that of the Muslim Brotherhood and traditional Salafism; it is based on the combination of two Islamic characters, namely the Imam Ahmad ibn Taymiyya and Sayyid Qutb,"[63] from whom, respectively, Muhammad bin Suroor borrows his strict position against dissenters from the Noble Sunnah, especially Shiites (i.e. the dogmatic content) and the principle of *hakimiyya*. Suroor saw in the ideas of Sayyid Qutb – who was executed a year after he left the Syrian Arab Republic for the Kingdom of Saudi Arabia – a true expression of the thought and original approach of the Muslim Brotherhood.[64] Therefore, some people view Sayyid Qutb was the inspiration for Sheikh Muhammad bin Suroor – as he was for many Muslim Brotherhood members and Salafis, and even for other political religious groups including jihadi organizations – and provided analysis of how many Holy Quranic concepts and perceptions could be consistent with the political vision of how Muslim state and society should be in the modern era.[65] It is therefore no wonder that there are Surooris who consider Sayyid Qutb the second guide of the Muslim Brotherhood after Hassan Al-Banna, and some who even consider Muhammad bin Suroor the third guide.[66]

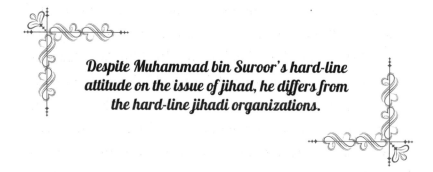

Despite Muhammad bin Suroor's hard-line attitude on the issue of jihad, he differs from the hard-line jihadi organizations.

Despite Muhammad bin Suroor's hard-line attitude toward the issue of *jihad*, he does not agree with jihadi organizations that resort to this weapon, such as the Islamic Jihad in the Arab Republic of Egypt in the 1990s, as well as Al-Qa'ida and ISIL today. Hence, even though he takes a clear position on the necessity of *jihad* to eject the occupiers and liberate the homeland, and permits attacks on groups which refuse to participate in *jihad* against those whom he considers as "infidels," he refuses to use *jihad* randomly and recklessly.[67]

The issue of *al-Walaa wal-Baraa* (allegiance and enmity) has become one of Suroorism's underlying principles with regard to the relationship with non-Muslims, with whom – according to this principle – cooperation is not allowed at all.[68] This was, of course, the baseline of the current in its stand against the 1991 Gulf War, which opposed any assistance from non-Muslims. The principle also stipulates the relationship with the ruling regimes in the Arab and Muslim worlds which Suroor deems "non-Islamic" and therefore not worthy of allegiance or rapprochement; indeed, it is obligatory to rise up against them when conditions allow. Surooris consider Muslim communities as *jahiliyya,* as they suffer from underdevelopment, corruption and decadence in morals and values. Hence the followers of this current believe that their most important duty is to reform governance, guide communities out of darkness and *jahiliyya* and to the light of Islam. The Surooris base their approach on two basic Islamic concepts, namely: "the *da'wa* to God (Allah)" in order to gain supporters and followers, and the "promotion of virtue and prevention of vice" to confront their opponents who disagree with their approach.[69]

These ideas have attracted many grassroots supporters and advocates. However, while Suroor was influential in the Kingdom of Saudi Arabia, he was also influenced by its Salafi environment. He influenced a large segment of the young, even preachers, regarding the issues of organization, *hakimiyya* and politics, which were not among their interests nor those of the Salafi current as a whole at that time, but he was also influenced at the same time by prevailing Salafi ideas.[70] So it was easy for him to emerge from the process of combining activist and Salafi ideas with a new approach which is different in its fundamental principles from those of the Muslim Brotherhood and traditional Salafism. This contributed to the emergence and spread of what is called Activist Salafism on a large scale in many Arab and Muslim countries.

Controls

In addition to the Suroori current's interest in the topic of *Sharia* controls, its supporters usually highlight the issue of the methodical controls employed in their preaching work.[71] One of the most important controls that the Suroori current consider as a determinant of its educational work and the foundation of its activist thought is a view of Islam as a call that includes various aspects of life and may not be fragmented. However, it sets priorities according to the rules of legitimate interests. Moreover, Suroois do not allow excommunication unless the terms of excommunication contained in the Holy Quran and the Noble Sunnah of God's (Allah's) Messenger (pbuh) apply to them. That is, of course, after all the conditions proving their infidelity are substantiated and there are no factors that prevent them from belief.[72]

The allegiance to Muslims who obey God (Allah) and opposition toward those who anger Him, His Messenger, and the Muslim community, are the most important controls that the Suroori current maintains. Related to this is the refusal to

pursue rapprochement with stray sects, like the Rafidites (Shiites), the *Batiniyya* (esoteric schools) and other factions that are considered by the Surooris to be dissenters from religion— by necessity they refuse rapprochement with the Jews and Christians, and all those whom they classify as "those who resist Allah and His Messenger."[73] Their reference in doctrine, worship, transactions, verdicts or ideas is the Book of God (Allah) and the Noble Sunnah of His Messenger (pbuh), and the consensus of the righteous ancestors, without interpretation or modification.[74]

Suroorism and the Muslim Brotherhood

I have previously indicated that Muhammad bin Suroor had been a member of the Muslim Brotherhood, and had been reared intellectually within the group for years, but after splitting from the group in 1969 he sided with the bloc of Issam Al-Attar (Damascus group), which was inclined toward the priority of *jihad*.[75] This was also the opinion of Muhammad bin Suroor, as he believed that the Muslim Brotherhood neglected this religious duty while some Arab and Muslim countries were still under occupation. With his increasing interest in dogma, especially since his time in the Kingdom of Saudi Arabia where Salafi thought prevailed – and the traditional stream in particular[76] – he grew more convinced that the Muslim Brotherhood's approach differed and that it had even abandoned and neglected the dogmatic aspect, and thereby departed from the way of the righteous ancestors in *da'wa* and *tabligh*. Muhammad bin Suroor therefore advocated a third way, which differed from the Muslim Brotherhood on fundamental issues as well as from traditional Salafism. Hence, some points of conflict between Muhammad bin Suroor and the Muslim Brotherhood were a major reason for the emergence of the new approach.[77]

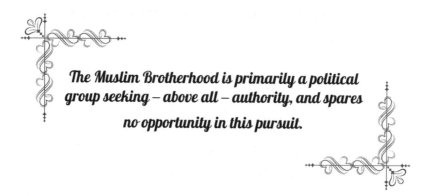

The Muslim Brotherhood is primarily a political group seeking – above all – authority, and spares no opportunity in this pursuit.

Suroorism was originally based on the concept of *takfir* in relation to rulers who do not rule in accordance with what God (Allah) has revealed,[78] though it does not issue verdicts on specific persons. The Muslim Brotherhood does not advocate this approach, but rather deals with these rulers and sometimes engages in their politics and shares their authority.[79] In my opinion, this discrepancy is essentially due to the fact that the Muslim Brotherhood is primarily a political group seeking – above all – authority and does not spare any opportunity in this pursuit. Add to this the Muslim Brotherhood's political duplicity, and tendency to obscure its true attitude towards regimes in order to avoid any repetition of its history of prosecution by judicial and security authorities who have banned the group's activities in the past.

> *The difference between Suroorism and the thought of the Muslim Brotherhood revolves around the perception of an activist concept of hakimiyya and how to apply it on the ground.*

Another major aspect of contrast between Suroorism and the thought of the Muslim Brotherhood is the difference in theoretical references adopted by both groups. While both sides depend, for example, on Sayyid Qutb's commentary *In the Shade of the Quran* for an interpretation that extracts activist, intellectual and political concepts, they differ regarding the authority of the Prophet's biography, especially with regard to activism. Surooris do not feel that the books relied upon by the Muslim Brotherhood in its upbringing and education reflect a true understanding of the Noble Sunnah or its real implications, especially with regard to the concept of activism. Perhaps this is why Muhammad bin Suroor authored his book *Studies in the Biography of the Prophet* from an activist perspective[80] in order to intellectually nurture his followers and supporters. Superficial differences between

Surooris and the Muslim Brotherhood center not only on matters of belief, or the essence of the method of the righteous ancestors, but also revolve around the perspective of the two sides regarding activist concepts associated with the topic of *hakimiyya*, and how to apply it.

The differences between Surooris and the Muslim Brotherhood led to intellectual confrontation described by some observers as a conflict whose battlefields were mosques, student clubs and summer centers,[81] and later municipal elections. The conflict developed into an exchange of accusations and attempts to distort peoples' perception of each other.[82] This had a major impact on the presence of the Muslim Brotherhood in the Kingdom of Saudi Arabia, where the Salafi environment naturally allowed the spread of Suroorism, but often at the expense of the spread of the thought of the Muslim Brotherhood, as it was not possible for the group's members to assume the same presence as Muhammad bin Suroor's supporters.[83]

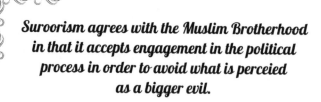

Suroorism agrees with the Muslim Brotherhood in that it accepts engagement in the political process in order to avoid what is perceived as a bigger evil.

Nevertheless, there are intellectual similarities between the two currents: both of them avoid Sufism, and even train their followers to disregard those whom they consider to be people of vain desires, like Jahmis and Mu'tazilah,[84] and instead both currents direct their members and followers to devote themselves to individual, spiritual and organizational education.[85] Suroorism changed its viewpoint about the issue of governance, participation in politics and dealing with existing ruling regimes, although it adopted the principle of *takfir* with regard to regimes that do not rule according to what God (Allah) has revealed.[86] However Suroorism agrees with the Muslim Brotherhood – albeit not at first – on the need to participate in the existing political process in some Arab and Muslim countries, which they both consider to be worthwhile in order to ward off a bigger evil.[87] Therefore, the Suroori current has recently sought to establish political parties to take part in elections, as happened in the State of Kuwait where they participated in the 2008 National Assembly elections (in which they won no seats), and in the Kingdom of Saudi Arabia in the 2011 municipal elections, where it achieved some gains.[88]

Suroorism and the Salafi Call

Given that one of the most important motives in Suroor's decision to split from the Muslim Brotherhood was his accusations that the group was moving away from the path of the righteous ancestors, in addition to its leniency or excessive loyalty to rulers, it is no wonder that Surooris consider themselves only as Salafis, and oppose any other label – including Suroorism or even activist Salafism – arguing that these are invented by their opponents and perpetuated by the media.[89] Thus they see themselves as followers of the righteous ancestors and the way of the prophets in their preaching. There are those who consider Suroori thought to be the product of combining political activism and traditional Salafi ideology, making Suroorism look like a movement of harmonization between the Muslim Brotherhood and Salafism. Nevertheless, some Salafis have abandoned their intellectual constants and turned to political work, as is the case in the Arab Republic of Egypt and elsewhere. Thus the political dimension is no longer a distinctive feature of the Suroori current, especially because the lines that separate political religious groups often fade, not least because the Muslim Brotherhood consider themselves Salafis in thought and orientation—as stated above, Hassan Al-Banna in his epistles describes his call as Salafi.[90]

All of this notwithstanding, there is a clear difference between the Surooris and the Salafi current in general terms. For example, Salafis who follow the Imam Muhammad ibn Abdulwahhab's call consider the Kingdom of Saudi Arabia to be a country of *tawheed* which rules according to what God (Allah) has revealed, and is almost the only country in the world to implement the rules of Islam in many fields of life, as Surooris demand, whereas the Salafis do not recognize that any country today is governed by what God (Allah) has revealed—

this includes the Kingdom of Saudi Arabia,[91] where the movement emerged and was embraced.

On the intellectual side, we find that there is a fundamental difference in understanding the meaning of *tawheed* itself. Salafis believe that the first part of the *Shahada* (the testimony), "there is no god but Allah," means that none is worthy of worship except God (Allah), and that polytheism in any form must be combated. Surooris add another element to this, which is *hakimiyya*[92]—the concept of divine rule and judgment which belong to God (Allah) alone, hence it is not permissible to issue any legislation based on sources other than the Holy Quran and Noble Sunnah. Also related to this is the understanding that Salafis believe obedience to the ruler is obligatory, while Surooris permit revolt against a Muslim ruler who does not rule according to *Sharia*.[93] The subtleties of the understanding and arguments of the Surooris make it difficult to develop an accurate description of their methodology and identify how close or far it is from any corresponding movement such as the Muslim Brotherhood, traditional Salafis or even activist jihadists.

Surooris and Political Participation

I mentioned previously that the Suroori movement emerged amid favorable historical circumstances that provided a fertile environment for Islamic thought and the renewal of its concepts. After the release of Muslim Brotherhood members from prison during the rule of former Egyptian President Muhammad Anwar Al-Sadat, the general opinion among the group – following multiple intellectual, doctrinal and political reviews[94] – was that it should participate in political life and governance. This meant actual involvement in political action and its existing institutions, whilst maintaining allegiance to the ruler – or at least dealing with him – even if he was a corrupt autocrat from the point of view of the Muslim Brotherhood.

In light of the political environment associated with the Palestinian cause and the Arab–Israeli conflict, and in conjunction with the deteriorating economic and social conditions in many Arab and Muslim countries in the second half of the twentieth century, there was general acceptance of the Islamic ideologies promoted by political religious groups. There was even a thirst for change that no political or social forces were capable of delivering – particularly after the 1967 defeat and the subsequent decline in Arab nationalism – other than political religious groups, and mainly the Muslim Brotherhood. In this context, one cannot overlook the role of the Islamic Revolution in Iran, which was seen at the time as a one of the most important events to influence the thought and practice of political and religious groups, and then the emergence of the Islamic tide – or so-called Islamic awakening – and new related concepts in Islamic political thought, such as the concept of political Islam discussed in detail in the first chapter of this book.[95] In a strange paradox, the Islamic Revolution, in spite of its different frame of reference

which conflicted with these groups, inspired the leaders and orientations of political religious groups, including the Muslim Brotherhood.

On the other hand, traditional Salafism, which was influenced by the Imam Muhammad ibn Abdulwahhab's call, recognized the principle of obedience to the ruler.[96] This approach is prevalent in Arab and Muslim countries, including the Kingdom of Saudi Arabia; indeed, traditional Salafism even constitutes one of the most important foundations of the Saudi state. However, the principle of obedience to the ruler in absolute terms,[97] although based on notable jurisprudential foundations, was not acceptable to all Salafis, including Imam Muhammad ibn Abdulwahhab's school itself. With the emergence of the Islamic tide in the 1980s, ideas of change began to spread and the issue of governance received more attention, especially among the younger generation.

When Muhammad bin Suroor moved to the Kingdom of Saudi Arabia in 1965,[98] and regardless of how he initially influenced or was influenced by the surrounding intellectual environment, the situation was favorable to many of the ideas that originally prompted him to leave the Muslim Brotherhood. He found that the Muslim Brotherhood went too far in their loyalty to rulers, showed indulgence or leniency in the application of many *Sharia* rules, and neglected the doctrine of the righteous ancestors. On the other hand, he felt that the traditional Salafis exaggerated the need for obedience to the ruler. There was an appetite for a new and different perspective, which provided the ideal opportunity for bin Suroor to advance his vision, which spread quickly, especially among the students of *Sharia* institutes. Hence we may understand how the Kingdom of Saudi Arabia became a viable incubator for different ideas, such as those of Muhammad bin Suroor.

> *Activist Salafi ideology not only permits rebellion against a ruler who does not rule according to what God (Allah) has revealed, it also obligates the fight against the kafir (infidel) West and accuses it of waging war against Islam.*

The beginning of the third millennium witnessed significant global developments, the most important of which were the September 11, 2001 attacks. Islamic thought in general, and the perspectives of political religious groups and currents of all orientations in particular, became the focus of unprecedented global interest but also of intense criticism. However, the biggest onslaught was focused on Salafi thought in general, and the activist breed in particular.[99] Accusations were made, not only by the West but also by other political religious groups, that Salafism was disseminating ideas which fuelled extremism among young people and inclined them towards terrorism.[100] Some political religious groups permitted – and continue to permit – rebellion against a ruler who does not rule according to what God (Allah) has revealed, and also obligated their members to fight against the West, which they consider to be "infidel" (does not believe in God (Allah)) and waging a war against Islam. Hence, their adherents became the target of direct accusations. It is no wonder that the investigations following the 9/11 attacks identified the hijackers as holding activist Salafi jihadi ideas.[101]

The events even implied the potential danger of a global cultural clash, so it was necessary for some states to adopt policies that encouraged political religious groups – especially Salafi ones – to undertake ideological revisions. The focus on Salafi activists resulted in internal revisions leading to the acceptance of new ideas that might help to dispel the negative perception of Salafism, and so they agreed to participate in elections. Surooris also participated in the municipal elections held in the Kingdom of Saudi Arabia in 2008, and also in the Kuwaiti National Assembly elections in 2005. This direct participation was a clear expression of the nature and orientation of the Suroori current, and confirmed its true interests.[102] Being one of the main reasons for the split from the Muslim Brotherhood, the acceptance of political engagement and participation in elections proved that these interests ran through the Suroori current's thought. The move even prompted criticism from jihadi organizations who regarded Suroorism as one of their intellectual benchmarks. They accused it of loyalty toward rulers and non-acceptance of the jihadi ideology led by

Al-Qa'ida, whether in the Republic of Iraq or in the Islamic Republic of Afghanistan.

Despite the hard-line attitude of this current with respect to the issue of governance, its followers no longer oppose political participation, and call for the establishment of political parties and engagement in ruling regimes even though they are not considered Islamic, in their perspective, the motive being to achieve important interests, the least of which is to ward off or mitigate evil, as they claim. There is no doubt that this excessive pragmatism did not come from a vacuum, but rather a perception that is characteristic of Salafis in particular, that is to maintain their interests at any cost, to the extent that some of their opponents state that they would even accept polytheism if it suited their interests.[103] As with the Muslim Brotherhood, this places them closer to the Shiites in terms of their tendency toward duplicity in the name of pragmatism.[104] Whatever the case may be, a review of the writings and sermons of the founder of the movement, Muhammad bin Suroor, reveal that there is a growing interest in politics, and acceptance of democracy and many of its concepts, including the formation of political parties. Perhaps the greatest practical proof of this is the attempt by some Suroori icons and leaders to establish the Umma Party in the State of Kuwait—although the authorities did not permit it.[105]

A comparison between thought and belief on the one hand, and practice on the other, reveals that Suroorism embraces democracy and a multiparty system, not on the basis of belief in these concepts or acceptance of their compatibility with religious

teachings – especially of a Salafi bent– but as a means that should be exploited in order to ward off the greater evils that may result from the failure to participate.

The Surooris position towards authority does not differ much from their position towards democracy, despite the differences between the two in terms of form and content, yet they were the most influential factors both in turning Muhammad bin Suroor away from the Muslim Brotherhood and in the subsequent major change in his thought, orientation and practice. The most prominent aspect of Suroor's thought had been the issue of *hakimiyya*, which stood his current apart from other political religious groups, including the Muslim Brotherhood.[106] He established his position towards ruling regimes through their position on this principle and the extent of their application of its content: the extent to which they ruled according to the revelations of God (Allah). Those who did not follow this principle were courting disbelief, and this required that people show their opposition to such regimes.

Essentially Suroorism is distinguished from other political religious groups – with the exception of jihadi organizations – by its stance on governance. Surooris are opposed to the Muslim Brotherhood, although it was their original source of reference, and to the Jamis and other groups that are classified as traditional Salafis, and accuse them all of hypocrisy and indulgence of rulers. The Suroori current entered into open intellectual confrontation with these currents in the 1990s.[107] They accused the Muslim Brotherhood of being lenient with regard to many aspects of society that should be regulated according to religious provisions, including partisan and political activity as well as other related concepts such as human rights, women's rights and others. On the other hand, they accuse traditional Salafism, in its different orientations, of marginalizing the consciousness of the nation by promoting unflinching obedience to the ruler, to an extent that even prevents peaceful opposition to his rule.[108]

In light of the above, I would argue that the Muslim Brotherhood does not believe in political action or multiparty participation, and exhibits a tendency toward the monopolization of authority, the exercise of tyranny, and the dismissal of their opponents on ideological grounds. The difference lies only in the political tactic employed, which is in turn linked to the heritage of the Muslim Brotherhood and its attempt to take advantage of its previous experiences, even though its practices in this context appeared to indicate an acceptance of the rules of the political game.[109]

Overview and Evaluation

If one investigates the realities of the Suroori current, one will find that despite its broad dissemination it has neither broken new ground on an intellectual level, nor enjoyed any tangible achievements. Moreover, its founder lacked the intellectual and jurisprudential impact to distinguish it from other interpretations—a criticism often heard from his opponents

among the Muslim Brotherhood and other Salafis themselves.[110] In the eyes of many critics the Suroori current is nothing more than a combination of the Imam Muhammad ibn Abdulwahhab's Salafism and an approach that calls for some reform[111] according to the methods of the righteous ancestors—a call advocated by other political religious currents and groups as well, including the Muslim Brotherhood. Thus Suroorism did not present new concepts that could be built upon to form a new approach, and did not achieve a breakthrough in terms of jurisprudential renewal and modernization, yet it nevertheless achieved widespread influence because of what its supporters considered the appeal of its ideas, especially with regard to *hakimiyya* and *jihad*.

One may also note the apparent contradiction in the thought and practice of the founder and preachers of this current. While they believed in *hakimiyya* and in deposing rulers who did not apply the law of God (Allah), they called for democracy and political participation, and even established parties, which is considered one the drawbacks of their counterparts in the Muslim Brotherhood and a reason for the separation of their founder, Muhammad bin Suroor, from the group.[112] Participating in democracy, albeit merely a mechanism, requires acceptance of its underlying concepts and involvement in state institutions, the responsibility for which is assumed by rulers who, according to Surooris, do not rule in accordance with what God (Allah) has revealed. In addition, the current's founder himself was living in a non-Muslim country at a time when leaving one's country – even if to another Arab or Muslim country – was considered an "abomination," according to an interview featured on the Al-Hiwar channel's Reviews program in London in 2008.[113]

Muhammad bin Suroor is also criticized for his contradictory stance regarding issues other than governance, such as his view of doctrine, which he accused the Muslim Brotherhood of abandoning. While he depends mainly on the writings of the Imam Ahmad ibn Taymiyya, he is a vocal critic of the ancient doctrinal texts, since he deems many of them as belonging to a different age and being in need of urgent review.[114] This has provoked the ire of many Salafi scholars, who consider this to be a departure from their approach. Nasseruddin Al-Albani commented on this view, saying: "Can a Muslim say this?!"[115]

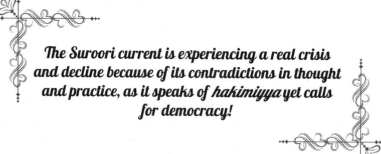

The Suroori current is experiencing a real crisis and decline because of its contradictions in thought and practice, as it speaks of hakimiyya yet calls for democracy!

On the other hand, Surooris are criticized for their contradictory view regarding the call to *jihad*. Some critics believe that Surooris are attached to jihadi organizations by virtue of the intellectual convergence between them and those organizations, as some

Islamists and analysts call them the Jihadi Salafi Movement.[116] Nevertheless, Suroorism does not consider itself to represent the rehabilitation of jihadi Salafism, even though it intersects with it, because it combines activism and Salafism, and it is distinguished from jihadi organizations in that it offers a clear and specific religious vision of many issues, such as human rights, democracy, freedom and the concept of the state, the ruler and the ruled, contrary to jihadi organizations like Al-Qa'ida and others.[117]

The Suroori current lost most of its symbols, like Safar Al-Hawali and Salman Al-Odah, since it became hostile to the GCC countries after they had hosted them in difficult times.

These contradictions were among the most significant factors in the decline in the Suroori current's popularity, and its gradual fade following the period of expansion discussed above. It is true that the Movement still has supporters, even in the Kingdom of Saudi Arabia, and many of its influential leaders remain in institutions in the Kingdom, especially universities and scientific institutes, but Suroorism now faces a real crisis, and is in significant decline.[118] While its supporters, especially the young, numbered in their thousands in the

Kingdom of Saudi Arabia during the 1980s and 1990s, the movement has since lost its young grassroots both in the Kingdom and abroad. While Suroorism used to have popular advocates, such as Safar Abdul Rahman Al-Hawali, Salman bin Fahd bin Abdullah Al-Odah and others, these symbols have since turned their back on the movement, and have even rejected Muhammad bin Suroor's arguments as contradictory, especially after his hostile position toward the GCC countries during the Gulf War,[119] especially the Kingdom of Saudi Arabia and the State of Kuwait, both of which hosted him in difficult circumstances. Many of his former followers saw this as ungrateful and lacking respect for these countries and their rulers who allowed him to move and preach freely and even to engage in important institutions such as the educational establishments.

Conclusion

Muhammad bin Suroor split from the Muslim Brotherhood because of what he regarded as a departure by the group from the way of the righteous ancestors, its growing interest in activism at the expense of doctrine, and its involvement in political action via existing frameworks, which he considered a violation of Islamic *Sharia*. Therefore, Suroor attempted to align activism following the thought of Sayyid Qutb with the doctrine advocated by the Imam Ahmad ibn Taymiyya. The concept of *hakimiyya* and the principle of allegiance were the most important foundations of Suroori thought, as well as the most prominent factors in its expansion and popularity. The Suroori current has spread to many other Arab and Muslim countries, although the Kingdom of Saudi Arabia was its epicenter and incubator, especially at its inception, by virtue of the prevalence of traditional Salafi ideology in the Kingdom. The jihadi ideas of Suroorism were major sources of its attraction, especially among young people, and perhaps contributed to the rise of the activist or jihadi Salafism from which contemporary jihadi organizations have been born or affected. Although Suroorism blended the thought of the Muslim Brotherhood with that of traditional Salafism, it differs from both not only on the subject of *al-Walaa wal-Baraa* (allegiance and enmity) to rulers or non-Muslims, but also in its understanding of the meaning of *tawheed* itself. Surooris are also criticized for their contradictions: the sudden shift in their perception of political engagement based on apparently opportunistic motives deepened the sense of ambiguity among its followers, which probably accounts for the bulk of its loss of support. Suroorism is now experiencing a real crisis, has lost its popular appeal, including among young grassroots adherents, and is now undergoing an unprecedented phase of decline. A movement that is not based on, nor deals with reality, and turns according to the interests and whims of its leaders, will inevitably face this fate.

6 Political Religious Groups: Jihadi Organizations

CHAPTER 6

Political Religious Groups: Jihadi Organizations

The origin of the Al-Qa'ida organization is linked with the jihadi Salafi current which emerged in the mid-1970s.[1] The 1967 war was a turning point in the history of political religious groups. As previously mentioned, they exploited the Arabs' defeat by Israel to promote their argument that the problems in Arab and Muslim countries were due to their neglect of Islamic values. Another factor contributing to the rise of political religious groups, including the militant current within these groups, was the policy adopted by former Egyptian president Muhammad Anwar Al-Sadat between 1970 and 1974, which accommodated and even supported political religious groups. President Sadat gave these groups the opportunity to organize and expand their influence in society in order to minimize the influence of the socialist–leftist trend associated with the era of his predecessor, former president Jamal Abdul Nasser. Another factor was the economic situation in the Arab Republic of Egypt, which contributed to the increased strength and effectiveness of militant jihadi organizations. The Egyptian economy was suffering from serious problems including overpopulation, lack of jobs, lack of planning, an external debt amounting to USD 47.6 billion at the beginning of 1990,[2] and over twenty million people below the poverty line. The militant jihadi organizations took advantage of these difficult conditions to promote their militant ideas and attract members of the poorer classes as well as students who had little hope or future in Egypt, convincing them that it was necessary to resort to violence to achieve their goals and use force to topple governments, eventually resulting in the reformation of society. Many argue that the ideology of Al-Qa'ida is essentially the same as the jihadi ideology which derives its inspiration from the Muslim Brotherhood ideologue Sayyid Qutb, who established the theoretical foundations of the concepts of *hakimiyya* (*Sharia* principles and rules, rather than man-made laws, should be applied) and *jahiliyya* (Muslim societies are reliving the pre-Islamic era because they do not apply the rules of Islam).[3] These two concepts are accepted and adopted by members of Al-Qa'ida and other militant religious organizations.

On the other hand, the Shiite Iranian Islamic Revolution of 1979 and the subsequent establishment of a religious regime provided momentum for jihadi organizations. In addition, the Soviet invasion of the Islamic Republic of Afghanistan in 1979

gave political religious groups an opportunity to launch *jihad* in Afghanistan. This paved the way later for the creation of Al-Qa'ida, which then started growing, developing and expanding.

This chapter examines certain examples of militant jihadi organizations, starting with Al-Qa'ida, which is discussed in several sections. The first section deals with the birth and growth of Al-Qa'ida. The second focuses on differences and defections within the organization. These defections are internal and within the framework of other jihadi organizations rather than breakaways from militant ideology; some defectors even established more extreme organizations. The third section looks at the position of Al-Qa'ida regarding the events which began in 2011; in this regard it is important to understand the way Al-Qa'ida views political participation in general, and how close or far it is from traditional Salafi thought. Finally, the fourth section sheds light on the propaganda and media mechanisms of Al-Qa'ida, which are very important for the organization, whether in terms of promoting ideas, mobilizing and attracting recruits, or in terms of communication, campaigning and raising the spirits of its members through the coverage of its operations.

The second part of this chapter looks at the "Islamic State in Iraq and the Levant" (ISIL) organization, discussing its historical beginnings, intellectual foundations, the differences between it and its parent organization (Al-Qa'ida), the reasons of these differences, and their impact on the organization's working mechanisms and plans.

The Al-Qa'ida Organization

Birth

There are several different opinions explaining how Al-Qa'ida started. This multiplicity of explanations can be attributed to the circumstances in which the organization was born, the variety of ideologies and schools associated with its name, the fact that its leaders moved between several countries (the Islamic Republic of Afghanistan, the Kingdom of Saudi Arabia, the Arab Republic of Egypt, the Republic of Yemen, the Republic of the Sudan, and others), and the reliance by the organization on several intellectual foundations.

According to the first opinion, Al-Qa'ida is a fundamentalist Islamic (multinational) movement which was established to fight the Communists during the Soviet invasion of the Republic of Afghanistan. The United States of America and some Arab and Muslim countries encouraged Muslim youths to join the fight against Soviet forces in the Republic of Afghanistan, because the conflict there was viewed at the time as an act of Soviet expansion and aggression which threatened American and Western interests in the Arabian Gulf and Central Asia. Therefore, the United States of America, in coordination with the Pakistani intelligence services and some Arab countries, provided finance to the Afghan *mujahideen* who fought against the Soviet occupation.[4]

The second opinion is that Al-Qa'ida descended from jihadi Salafism, a term which has been used since the late 1980s

to refer to certain groups in political Islam which adopt *jihad* as a method to achieve change, accuse whole societies of unbelief, and tend to use force. It can be said that jihadi Salafism was the link between various jihadi groups and organizations which later joined Al-Qa'ida. For example, Abu Mus'ab Al-Zarqawi and his organization in Iraq joined Al-Qa'ida, and the Salafi Group for Preaching and Combat in the People's Democratic Republic of Algeria joined Al-Qa'ida (changing its name to Al-Qa'ida in the Islamic Maghreb).[5]

Proponents of the third opinion argue that associating Al-Qa'ida with the jihadi Salafi current is wrong, and that Al-Qa'ida has no doctrine. Some Al-Qa'ida ideologues such as Abdullah Yousuf Azzam have written books, including *Fi Al-Jihad Aadaab wa Ahkam* (The Rules of Jihad) and *Bashaer Al-Nasr* (Signs of Victory).[6] Furthermore, the organization relies on some books drawn from the jihadi Salafi current in relation to certain religious matters which serve its goals. According to this opinion, Al-Qa'ida follows a person rather than a doctrine. Its founder and former leader Usama bin Ladin insisted that the organization should not have a doctrine, because this would give it more freedom to change its goals, alliances and plans. Accordingly, members of the organization followed the orders of bin Ladin himself. The majority of Al-Qa'ida members are Saudis, Yemenis, Pakistanis and Egyptians, and there are links and coordination between the organization and Islamic groups and organizations in many countries.[7]

According to this opinion, Al-Qa'ida shares with jihadi Salafism a number of intellectual foundations including the *fatwas* of the Imam Ahmad ibn Taymiyya, as well as many ideas of the Imam Muhammad ibn Abdulwahhab, Sayyid Qutb and Abu Al-A'la Al-Mawdoodi about *hakimiyya*, and other *fatwas* prohibiting the application of man-made laws and deeming those who apply them in the Arab and Muslim worlds unbelievers.[8]

There are opinions which distinguish between Al-Qa'ida and jihadi Salafism based on the fact that some jihadi Salafi figures have partially or wholly revised their views. One example is Al-Sayyid Imam bin Abdulaziz Al-Shareef (Dr. Fadl), former emir of the Al-Jihad Group (1987–1993), who was arrested in the Republic of Yemen and deported to the Arab Republic of Egypt in 2004, and revised his position several times. He had written two books, *Al-Umdah fi I'dad Al-Uddah* (The Reference Book on Preparing for Jihad), which became a reference for jihadi Salafis, and *Al-Jami' fi Talab Al-Ilm* (A Comprehensive Guide to Religious Learning)[9] (over 1,000 pages), both of which were adopted by Al-Qa'ida as key reference works.[10] In his revision, Imam Al-Shareef accused Al-Qa'ida of summarizing his second book in a way which distorted its message.[11] Although he abandoned jihadi Salafism a long time ago, followers of this current still consider him one of their key ideologues and figures.[12] Dr. Fadl further revised his position in late 2007, when he wrote *Watheeqat Tarsheed Al-Jihad* (The Jihad Rationalization Guide).[13]

Another revision was made by Issam Tahir Al-Barqawi, a Jordanian of Palestinian origin, also known as Abu Muhammad Al-Maqdisi, who was arrested several times by the Jordanian authorities.[14] He is considered a prominent ideologue of jihadi Salafism. He was mentor to Abu Mus'ab Al-Zarqawi when they were together in prison in the Hashemite Kingdom of Jordan. Al-Maqdisi travelled several times to the Islamic Republic of Afghanistan, where he met key figures of the jihadi Salafi current, including Ayman Al-Zawahiri and others.[15] While in the Islamic Republic of Afghanistan, Abu Muhammad Al-Maqdisi wrote *Millat Ibrahim* (The Religion of Abraham), which was his first Salafi Fundamentalist book.[16] He later partially revised his ideas in another book, *Waqafat ma' Thamarat Al-Jihad* (Reflections on the Fruits of Jihad).[17]

Some scholars argue that following those revisions, the influence and presence of Al-Qa'ida jihadi leaders, particularly Usama bin Ladin and Ayman Al-Zawahiri, became the only source of new and continuing direction, even though they were inspired by the jihadi Salafi ideology.[18]

Regarding the impact of those revisions on the relationship between Al-Qa'ida and jihadi Salafism, one researcher explains that:

> These revisions are a reflection of the strong conflict within jihadi Salafism, particularly between Al-Qa'ida, which represents the new leadership of the current, and the old historical leaders who founded jihadi Salafism, particularly in Egypt through the cells of the "Al-Jihad Organization" and then "The Islamic Group."[19]

481

The Islamic Group in the Arab Republic of Egypt was established in the early 1970s by Salah Hashim at Assiut University. It was first called "The Religious Group," and had followers in most Egyptian universities. The list of the group's founders included names which later became prominent in the struggle between the authorities and political religious groups in the Arab Republic of Egypt, such as Abu Al-Ula Madhi, Karam Zuhdi, Abdulmonem Abu Al-Futooh, Aasim Abdulmajid, Usama Hafiz and others. In 1977, many members of the Islamic Group switched to the Muslim Brotherhood, including some members who later became key figures in the Brotherhood, such as Issam Al-Aryan, Abdulmonem Abu Al-Futooh, Helmi Al-Jazzar, and Abu Al-Ula Madhi. The latter left the Muslim Brotherhood to establish the Al-Wasat Party by court order in February 2011.[20] However, he performed a further U-turn and was allied again with the Muslim Brotherhood after former president Dr. Muhammad Mursi reached the presidency, thereby relinquishing all slogans, views and positions adopted by him prior to the events of January 25, 2011.

The Islamic Group focused on trying to change by force what it deemed as 'evil' in university campuses, such as music and singing concerts and other student activities. Politically, it was opposed to hosting the Iranian Shah by former president Muhammad Anwar Al-Sadat. It also rejected the famous visit by Sadat to occupied Jerusalem and his signing of the Camp David Accords with Israel.[21]

The Al-Jihad Organization was founded by Muhammad Abdulsalam Faraj, whose major contribution was a book called *Al-Farida Al-Ghaiba* (The Neglected Duty), which constitutes the ideology of the Organization.[22] There was nothing original in this book; the ideas can be found in Imam Ahmad ibn Taymiyya's book *Al-Siyassa Al-Shar'iya* (Sharia Rule) or in Qutb's writings, in particular *Ma'alim fi Al-Tareeq* (Signposts on the Road). The central theme in *Al-Farida Al-Ghaiba* is the issue of *jihad* and the Islamic justification for the removal of unjust rulers. In June 1981, the Al-Jihad Organization was responsible for a violent sectarian conflict between Muslims and Coptic Christians in the Al-Zawiya Al-Hamra neighborhood of the Arab Republic of Egypt.[23] President Sadat's policies and repression of all opposition groups in 1981 led to his assassination by the Al-Jihad Organization in October 1981. Faraj and the Al-Jihad members who participated in the assassination were executed.[24]

The Inspiration behind the Name Al-Qa'ida

In his book *Mustaqbal Al-Siraa' fi Afghanistan* (The Future of the Conflict in Afghanistan),[25] Al-Sayyid Imam Al-Shareef (Dr. Fadl), who was one of the early participants in the "*jihad* in the Islamic Republic of Afghanistan,"[26] and is referred to as the mentor of Ayman Al-Zawahiri in jihadi ideology,[27] explains the reasons behind choosing the name "Al-Qa'ida." In 1984, Abdullah Azzam arrived at Peshawar (A Pakistani city located near the Khyber Pass, which is a mountain pass connecting the

Afghan capital Kabul to Peshawar in Pakistan) and established the Mujahideen Services Office. As there were increasing facilities to encourage Arab participation in the *jihad*, their numbers grew gradually.[28] Usama bin Ladin used to raise donations for the Services Office. Some Arabs complained to him about what they perceived as violations taking place at the Services Office. Therefore, he decided to work independently from Abdullah Azzam.[29] In 1988, he started a training camp in Jaji, near the border with the Islamic Republic of Pakistan, and called it *Maasadah Al-Ansar Al-Arab* (Lions' Den of Arab Supporters). They decided to attack a nearby fortress occupied by the Communists. However, plans of the attack were leaked and when bin Ladin and his men approached the fortress, they sensed a trap and withdrew. They were ridiculed by other Arabs who said that they fled the first battle. So, the name of the camp was changed from *Maasadah* to *Qa'ida Al-Ansar Al-Arab* (The Base of Arab Supporters), and later shortened to Al-Qa'ida.[30]

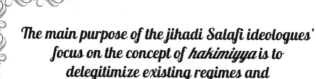

The main purpose of the jihadi Salafi ideologues' focus on the concept of hakimiyya is to delegitimize existing regimes and accuse them of unbelief.

Al-Qa'ida and the Jihadi Salafi Frame of Reference

Jihadi Salafism, which believes in using force and armed violence to effect change, constitutes the main reference for Al-Qa'ida. The following concepts are central to jihadi Salafism:[31]

Hakimiyya versus Contemporary Jahiliyya

Jihadi Salafi ideologues link the concept of *hakimiyya* with the concept of *tawheed* and Islamic faith. As indicated in Chapter 4, the concept of oneness is subdivided into three types: 1) oneness of God (Allah),[32] meaning that only God (Allah) can be worshipped; 2) oneness of the Creator, meaning that only God (Allah) can create creatures, regulate the universe, and give life and death; and 3) oneness of Names and Attributes,[33] meaning that all names and attributes of God (Allah) should be limited to Him.

> *Jihadi Salafi ideologues consider anyone who does not believe that only God (Allah) has the right to set rules to be an unbeliever, and rulers who do not apply Sharia are unbelievers.*

Jihadi Salafi ideologues consider anyone who does not believe that only God (Allah) has the right to set rules to be an unbeliever, while rulers who do not apply *Sharia* are also unbelievers. Furthermore, societies where *Sharia* does not prevail and Islam is not applied in public and private life are un-Islamic.[34] One researcher argues that the main purpose of the jihadi Salafi ideologues' focus on the concept of *hakimiyya* is to delegitimize current regimes and accuse them of unbelief. Sayyid Qutb was a key ideologue who formulated the concepts of *hakimiyya* and *jahiliyya* in the contemporary discourse of political religious groups. His writings have become key intellectual references for jihadi Salafis.[35]

Sayyid Qutb uses the concepts of *hakimiyya* and *jahiliyya* extensively in his writings, stressing them to the extent that he accuses anybody who does not agree with him of unbelief. *Hakimiyya* is the first quality of *tawheed*. According to Qutb, the declaration of faith (I bear witness that there is no god but Allah), means that only God (Allah) can be worshipped, and none of His creatures can share any of His qualities. The first quality of *tawheed* is the right of absolute divine *hakimiyya*, which includes the right to set laws for people to follow, and define principles and values to guide them in their lives.[36]

Jihadi Salafism adopts the same theoretical division adopted by traditional Wahhabi Salafism as mentioned above: *tawheed*, the oneness of the Creator,[37] and the oneness of Names and Attributes. This theoretical aspect is shared by all Salafi schools.[38]

Jihad is the Road to Tawheed

Jihad and *tawheed* are inseparable in the ideology of jihadi Salafism and Al-Qa'ida. Salafism stresses that the aim of *jihad*

is to promote the concept of *tawheed*.[39] Jihadi Salafis differ from other traditional Salafi schools that seek the permission of the ruler when *jihad* is to be declared a duty for all. According to the jihadi Salafis, *jihad* is the duty of every Muslim; it started at the time of the Prophet Musa (Moses), and will continue until Muslims fight against *Al-Maseeh Al-Dajjal* (the false messiah) and his Jewish followers at the end of time.[40]

Furthermore, jihadi Salafism divides states and societies into camps of believers and unbelievers.[41] They use those concepts and project them on the present reality in order to delegitimize many governments and regimes in the Arab and Muslim countries, and then use certain *Sharia* rules to give religious legitimacy to *fatwas* authorizing *jihad* against those governments and political regimes.[42]

Armed Jihad as a Means for Change

After establishing the concepts of *hakimiyya* and un-Islamic contemporary societies (i.e., those deemed so by jihadi Salafism), jihadi Salafism concluded that those regimes must be removed through *jihad*.[43] Therefore, they decided to topple those regimes which did not apply the rules of *Sharia*. According to jihadi Salafis, even though those regimes are headed by Muslim individuals, they are un-Islamic regimes because they rely on secular anti-religious references, and are loyal to the enemies of Islam. Therefore, those regimes should not be tolerated, and *Sharia* rules state that they should be disobeyed and resisted.[44]

The jihadi Salafis completely reject participation in politics and representation in parliaments, because this implies recognition of democracy and of existing regimes. In other words, this would amount to recognizing something other than the rule of God (Allah). For them, *jihad* ranks high among other religious duties. Some of them even argue that *jihad* has become an individual duty since Andalusia fell to the Christians.[45]

> *Al-Walaa, meaning loyalty and support to Muslims, and al-Baraa, meaning denunciation of unbelievers and hostility towards them, are the criterion by which jihadi Salafism distinguishes between believers and unbelievers.*

Al-Walaa wal-Baraa (Allegiance and Enmity)

The concept of allegiance and enmity is central to jihadi Salafism. In general, allegiance means loyalty and support to Muslims, and enmity means repudiation of unbelievers and hostility towards them.[46] Jihadi Salafism considers the concept of allegiance and enmity to be inseparable from Islamic faith; it is even a criterion by which a Muslim's belief in and observation of Islam is measured. Due to the importance and centrality of this concept to the ideology of jihadi Salafism, Al-Maqdisi authored a book titled *Millat Ibrahim* (The Religion of Abraham), referred to above, to discuss allegiance and enmity.[47] Explaining

the concept, Al-Maqdisi considers it essential for the Islamic faith and *tawheed*, and discusses two aspects: denunciation of any god other than God (Allah), and denunciation of unbelievers if they insist on their ways.[48]

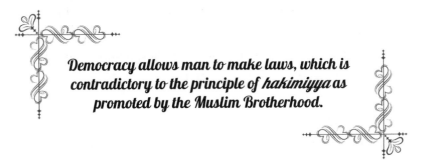

Democracy allows man to make laws, which is contradictory to the principle of hakimiyya as promoted by the Muslim Brotherhood.

Democracy is Un-Islamic

Jihadi Salafi writings consider democracy to be un-Islamic,[49] because it allows man to make laws, which is contradictory to the principle of *hakimiyya*. According to this jihadi Salafi view, *Sharia* is a comprehensive system which covers all aspects of life, and a Muslim should not apply rules other than those of *Sharia*. Further, Abu Muhammad Al-Maqdisi argues that democracy is a word of Greek origin. It means "the rule of the people," which is, according to Wahhabi Salafism, un-Islamic and against the concept of *hakimiyya*, and therefore should be denounced.[50]

The Development of Al-Qa'ida

Some researchers and observers of Al-Qa'ida talk about three main stages which the organization has undergone over the last 20 years.[51]

The Establishment Stage

This stage began in 1993, when the founder of the organization, Usama bin Ladin, began attracting supporters from around the world, and especially from the Arabian Peninsula.[52] At that time, bin Ladin lived in the Republic of the Sudan and invested about USD 200 million in the agriculture and construction sectors.[53] He had a close relationship with the Sudanese regime led by president Omar Hassan Al-Bashir.

Jihadi Militancy

This stage actually began in 1998, when "the World Islamic Front for Jihad against the Jews and the Crusaders"[54] was formed as an alliance of several jihadi organizations, including the Al-Jihad Organization led by Ayman Al-Zawahiri, the Islamic Group led by Rifa'i Ahmad Taha,[55] and an unknown jihadi organization in the People's Republic of Bangladesh.[56] This alliance carried out violent attacks against American interests in different parts of the world, including two attacks at the US Marines barracks in Al-Khobar, eastern Saudi Arabia in 1996,[57] an attack at a Saudi National Guard base in the Saudi capital Riyadh, two attacks at US embassies in Nairobi and Dar es Salaam, the respective capitals of Kenya and Tanzania in 1998, and then the attacks at the World Trade Centre twin towers in New York, on September 11, 2001.

Decentralized Expansion

The decentralized expansion of Al-Qa'ida began with the American invasion and occupation of Iraq in March 2003. This

invasion has arguably saved Al-Qa'ida from a trajectory of decline which started after the 9/11 attacks.[58] This stage is important for several reasons. It gave Al-Qa'ida the chance to directly engage American forces in Iraqi territories. Furthermore, it allowed the organization to expand geographically and establish several branches in the Republic of Yemen, the Islamic Maghreb, Sub-Saharan Africa, the Republic of Somalia, the Syrian Arab Republic, Egypt's Sinai Peninsula, and the Islamic Republic of Afghanistan.[59]

Others recognize several stages in the development of Al-Qa'ida.[60]

1. The camp and the front: this began in late-1987 and was focused on sourcing money and raising donations, as discussed above.[61]

2. Building the organization: this stage started in 1989, with the increasing number of Usama bin Ladin's followers and supporters of various nationalities, but mostly Saudis and Yemenis. Bin Ladin began asking his followers to swear the oath of allegiance to him as their emir and leader. With this, Al-Qa'ida was transformed from a camp and fighting group into an organization.[62]

3. Restructuring: this stage began in 1990. Some of bin Ladin's followers with experience in relief and humanitarian work, originally used as a cover for the organization, noticed that he was changing the goals and plans of the organization from *jihad* in Afghanistan to *jihad* in South Yemen,[63] and preparing the organization to participate in

the Gulf War against the regime of former Iraqi president Saddam Hussein who occupied the State of Kuwait on August 2, 1990 (according to some sources, Usama bin Ladin wanted to form an army of jihadists to fight against the forces of Saddam Hussein and liberate Kuwait, as an alternative to seeking the assistance of foreign forces, which was not acceptable to him. This idea, which was rejected by the Saudi government, reflects bin Ladin's growing sense of power, which began to show in his behavior towards his followers).[64] As a result, there were demands by some followers of Usama bin Ladin that the organization should have a code and guidelines stating its values and objectives on the basis of which the oath of allegiance could be taken. However, Usama bin Ladin refused to accept any rules limiting his freedom to lead the organization in any direction he pleased, and he dismissed from the organization anyone who supported those demands. Thus, he made it clear to the remaining followers that they were expected to blindly obey and follow, or be dismissed from the organization.[65]

4. Global confrontation: in 1993, while in the Republic of the Sudan, Usama bin Ladin announced his intention, as leader of Al-Qa'ida, to fight against international superpowers, particularly the United States of America. As a result of this announcement, some of his followers left the group. When the "World Islamic Front for Jihad against the Jews and the Crusaders" was announced in 1998,[66] there was nothing new

in its contents, save for the announcement itself, preparations were underway, and possible US and European targets around the world had been monitored since 1993. The announcement read as follows:

> Killing Americans and their allies, whether civilian or military, is an individual duty of every Muslim everywhere, and should be done when possible. This way, the Al-Aqsa Mosque and the Holy Mosque in Mecca will be free from them, and their armies will leave the Muslim territory defeated.[67]

This *fatwa* is certainly contradictory with all tolerant teachings of *Sharia* regarding the treatment of non-Muslims. Indeed, Usama bin Ladin was not qualified to issue *fatwas*.

5. Differences and Defections within Al-Qa'ida: following the unprecedented attacks of September 11, 2001 in the United States of America, Al-Qa'ida became the main target of the global war on terrorism. As a result, the organization suffered many remarkable differences and defections which undermined its hierarchal structure and weakened its capabilities. These were greatly aggravated following the death of Usama bin Ladin, the organization's founder and leader, in Pakistan on May 2, 2011. In fact, the situation had deteriorated even before the death of bin Ladin. On September 10, 2010, Nu'man bin Uthman (Abu Muhammad Al-Libi) a Fundamentalist leader of the Shura Council of the Libyan Fighting Group, sent a letter to Usama bin

Ladin on the occasion of the ninth anniversary of the attacks of September 11, 2001, stressing that "Muslims all over the world reject *jihad* as understood and practiced by Al-Qa'ida, and refuse the establishment of an Islamic state which follows the understanding and practice of Al-Qa'ida."[68] Al-Libi invited bin Ladin to revise his strategy of violence which caused much damage to Islam and Muslims.[69] Similar revisions by jihadi leaders in recent years reflect a rejection of the practices of Al-Qa'ida and some of its branches.[70] Those revisions, however, do not necessarily imply a break away from the extremist jihadi ideology, but merely reflect a rejection of the path and plans of Al-Qa'ida. In other words, the differences relate to the tactics, rather than the overall strategy of *jihad*.

These differences emerged in April 2013, as ISIL (then named the "Islamic State of Iraq") gained more strength and influence. Current estimates vary regarding the number of ISIL fighters. (In September 2014, the US Central Intelligence Agency estimated them at 20,000–30,000,[71] while Russia's National Security Council estimated 30,000–50,000 in the same month.[72] These estimates continuously change as the organization's recruitment and mobilization efforts continue). In April 2013, "The Islamic State of Iraq" announced the change of its name to the Islamic State in Iraq and the Levant, and its annexation of Jabhat Al-Nusra, which is estimated to have around 9,000 fighters.[73] However, the annexation was rejected by the leader of

Jabhat Al-Nusra, Muhammad Al-Jawlani, who was supported by Al-Qa'ida leader Ayman Al-Zawahiri.[74]

ISIL's field victories, control of vast territories in Iraq and Syria, and announcement of the Caliphate state in June 2014,[75] resulted in defections from Al-Qa'ida; many groups and thousands of jihadis previously loyal to Al-Qa'ida joined ISIL and shifted their allegiance to it, perhaps explaining the continuous increase in the number of foreign fighters in ISIL. In a report published in June 2014, the Soufan Group, a security intelligence services company based in New York, estimated that at least 12,000 foreign fighters of 81 different nationalities, including around 3,000 Europeans, were fighting in Syria.[76] On the other hand, US President Barack Obama, in his speech before the UN Security Council in September 2014, estimated the number at 15,000 from 80 countries.[77]

One important announcement was the defection to ISIL in September 2014 of several battalions and groups affiliated with Al-Qa'ida in the Islamic Maghreb and its leader Abdulmalik Drudkal, also known as Abu Mus'ab Abdulwadood.[78]

In general, the geographical spread of Al-Qa'ida ideology and the strategic changes and transformations it has experienced is a topic which requires more study and research. At its early stages of *jihad* in the Islamic Republic of Afghanistan in the 1980s, this ideology focused on fighting the faraway enemy, represented by the United States of America and its allies. It was transformed with the passage of time to the current form as adopted by the present jihadi organizations in the Syrian Arab

Republic, the Arab Republic of Egypt (where groups loyal to Al-Qa'ida, such as Ansar Bayt Al-Maqdis, have recently appeared), and the Republic of Iraq, with the increasing influence of the "Islamic State" (ISIL).[79] In its current form, this ideology focuses on fighting the nearby enemy, as represented by the Arab and Muslim regimes, and this resulted in many differences and divisions inside the organization about its vision and doctrine.

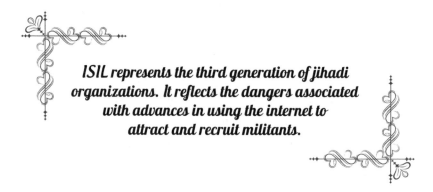

ISIL represents the third generation of jihadi organizations. It reflects the dangers associated with advances in using the internet to attract and recruit militants.

According to some specialists, there are several reasons behind the current defections from Al-Qa'ida. Al-Qa'ida members belong to three generations; the first generation is the generation of old fighters who fought with Usama bin Ladin against the Soviet Union in the 1980s; the second generation joined at the time of the attacks of September 11, 2001 and participated in transferring the battles of the organization abroad; and the third generation is the internet generation which has formed local cells in the Arabian Peninsula, the Maghreb countries, Africa, and some European countries.[80] The generational gaps created differences in terms of thought, planning, means and tactics, which resulted in defections.

Another cause is the large geographical expansion of Al-Qa'ida's operations, which paved the way for such defections away from the parent organization. A further reason is the killing of the organization's founder, Usama bin Ladin, on May 2, 2011, which paved the way for defections and for the rise of other leaders,[81] especially in the light of the apparent weak personality of the organization's new leader, Ayman Al-Zawahiri, compared with that of bin Ladin. All of this resulted in Al-Zawahiri losing control of the organization which has now several, sometimes warring, leaders despite the fact that it appears on the surface that Al-Zawahiri is still in control.

Militant Jihadi Organizations in the Syrian Arab Republic

During the conflict in the Syrian Arab Republic, two militant organizations have appeared among the various factions and groups fighting against the regime of Bashar Al-Assad. These are Jabhat Al-Nusra, which reports directly to Al-Qa'ida's leader Ayman Al-Zawahiri, and the Islamic State organization which defected from Al-Qa'ida and is working independently.[82] This will be discussed in detail in a later section of this Chapter.

Jabhat Al-Nusra Li Ahl Al-Sham

At the beginning of 2012, the conflict in the Syrian Arab Republic saw the emergence of a trend towards armed struggle. There were factors which allowed militant jihadi groups to

penetrate the ranks of protestors against the Syrian regime and use the Syrian conflict to cover and legitimize their activities. These factors included foreign incitement of protestors to take up arms, and the international environment which turned a blind eye to this change in the direction of what was then a political conflict. Some foreign players even provided logistic and military support to these jihadi groups. This coincided with several calls at the beginning of 2012 for the declaration of *jihad* in the Syrian Arab Republic, and jihadi groups exploited those calls to emerge and grow their influence.[83]

There is a varied body of literature expressing the ideology of Jabhat Al-Nusra. However, the writings of Abu Mus'ab Al-Suri (Mustafa bin Abdulqadir Al-Rifa'i) are central. These include: *Da'wat Al-Muqawamah Al-Islamiyya Al-Aalamiyya* (The Doctrine of Global Islamic Resistance),[84] and *Ahl Al-Sunnah fi Al-Sham fi Muwajahat Al-Naseeriyya wa Al-Salibiyya wa Al-Yahood* (The Sunnah in the Levant Against the Alawites, Christians and Jews).[85] The latter book designates the Jews, the Alawites and the Shiites as enemies of the 'jihadi project' in Syria. It seems the name Jabhat Al-Nusra was originally derived from one statement by Abu Mus'ab Al-Suri near the end of his book. It reads as follows:

> *Jihad* started in *Al-Sham* (the Levant/Syria) at the beginning of the 1960s, prospered in Syria in the 1980s, and returns to it now, God (Allah) willing. Let's all, brothers of *jihad*, provide support (Nusra) to our brothers.[86]

In January 2012, Abu Muhammad Al-Jawlani, leader of Jabhat Al-Nusra, announced the establishment of his organization.[87] On April 9, 2013, it became involved in a conflict with another branch of Al-Qa'ida. On that date, Abu Bakr Al-Baghdadi, emir of the so-called Islamic State of Iraq, announced in a recorded statement the merger of The Jabhat Al-Nusra Li Ahl Al-Sham and The Islamic State of Iraq to establish The Islamic State in Iraq and the Levant (ISIL). Al-Baghdadi called upon "all jihadi groups" in Iraq and Syria to give up their names and join ISIL.[88]

In response, Abu Muhammad Al-Jawlani delivered a speech in which he denied all knowledge of the announcement of ISIL, called for a renewed oath of allegiance to Al-Qa'ida (Ayman Al-Zawahiri), referred the issue of the merger to arbitration and talked about the differences between Jabhat Al-Nusra and the Islamic State of Iraq, and their positions regarding Al-Qa'ida, etc. Jabhat Al-Nusra had disapproved several practices by Abu Bakr Al-Baghdadi's group, including its tenancy to accuse others of apostasy on a very wide scale, the killing of anyone who disagreed with them, risking the lives of civilizations in their operations, and their proclivity for offensive operations, etc.[89]

Al-Qa'ida reacted through Ayman Al-Zawahiri in a televised statement broadcasted by Al-Jazeera, rejecting the merger of the two organizations to form ISIL,[90] and stressing that Jabhat Al-Nusra was the branch of Al-Qa'ida in the Syrian Arab Republic. Al-Zawahiri ordered that ISIL be abolished:[91] "The Islamic State in Iraq and the Levant (ISIL) shall be abolished, and the name 'the Islamic State of Iraq' shall continue to be used."[92] He stressed that Jabhat Al-Nusra was an autonomous branch reporting directly to the senior leadership of Al-Qa'ida, and explained[93] that "the Islamic State of Iraq shall have jurisdiction in Iraq, and the Jabhat Al-Nusra shall have jurisdiction in Syria."[94]

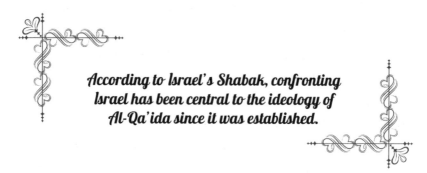

According to Israel's Shabak, confronting Israel has been central to the ideology of Al-Qa'ida since it was established.

Al-Qa'ida and Hostility to Israel

To discuss the position of Israel and the Jews in the ideology of Al-Qa'ida, we may look to a report issued by the Israeli Security Agency (Shabak) in this respect:

> The struggle against the Jews and Israel has always occupied a central position in Al-Qa'ida's doctrine. In February 1998, Usama bin Ladin declared the establishment of the "World Islamic Front for Jihad against the Jews and the Crusaders." The organization's leadership encourages the execution of terror attacks against the Jews around the world and invests effort in promoting terror attacks against Israeli targets. The Jews and Israel in particular became Al-Qa'ida's arch-enemy since, in its view, they settled on land sacred to Muslims and acted against its Palestinian residents.[95]

Despite Al-Qa'ida's pronounced hostility to Israel as acknowledged by Israel itself, it has never targeted Israel or been involved in a struggle against it. In fact, most victims of Al-Qa'ida since its establishment have been Arabs and Muslims. According to some Western reports, during the period 2004–2008, only 15 percent of casualties and injuries of attacks by Al-Qa'ida were of Western nationalities, and the rest were Arabs and Muslims.[96]

The Position of Al-Qa'ida Regarding Events after 2011

Al-Qa'ida never expected the domestic events that occurred in some Arab countries in 2011. This was admitted by Usama bin Ladin in a recording which was broadcast in May 2011 after he was killed. In this tape, he said: "We all were surprised when the sun of the revolution rose from the Maghreb (i.e. west of the Arab world)."[97]

According to one study, the events of the so-called "Arab Spring," triggered intellectual discussions and debates within the circles of jihadi organizations, especially Al-Qa'ida regarding the centralization or decentralization of Al-Qa'ida, as well as the focus on grassroots rather than elitist activism.[98]

Besides failing to anticipate the popular protests and domestic developments which started in the Republic of Tunisia in December 2010, Al-Qa'ida's public reaction was slow; several weeks after the beginning of protests in the Republic of Tunisia, the leadership of Al-Qa'ida published on the internet and social media networks statements clarifying the organization's position regarding those events. In those statements, Al-Qa'ida and other groups affiliated with it welcomed what Ayman Al-Zawahiri described as "blessed uprisings" in the Arab countries.[99]

Before he was killed, Usama bin Ladin wrote one statement regarding the protests in Arab countries. It was published three weeks after he was killed.[100] In this statement, bin Ladin congratulated those who participated in making this change, but at the same time asked them to be cautious regarding any dialogue; they should be careful not to compromise what they have gained. He explained that revolutions offered an opportunity for liberation from despotism,[101] man-made laws, and Western control and development of the nation. He stressed that the goal of the popular protests was to restore dignity and pride, not to get food and clothes, warning that losing this opportunity would be the most severe of mistakes.[102] Ayman Al-Zawahiri's position echoed that of Usama bin Ladin; he pointed out that the journey was not over yet and there was a long way to go. True, the nations had toppled the rulers, but it was important to ensure the establishment of good government, failing which everything would be lost.[103]

Some researchers indicate that Al-Qa'ida was late in responding to the domestic events seen in some Arab countries:

> The media response of the Al-Qa'ida leadership to the Arab Spring was surprisingly slow. After almost one month since the beginning of the Egyptian revolution, Al-Sahab Media Production, which is the main media arm of Al-Qa'ida, published one letter by Ayman Al-Zawahiri.[104]

 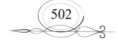

Al-Qa'ida and its affiliated groups tried to take advantage of the fall of these Arab regimes and to ride the tide in the same way that other groups such as the Muslim Brotherhood had. In an effort to link Al-Qa'ida with the political changes occurring in Arab countries,[105] a large section of the Spring 2011 issue of the English online magazine of Al-Qa'ida in the Arabian Peninsula, *Inspire,* was devoted to what the magazine described as the "Tsunami of Change." The magazine stressed that Al-Qa'ida had always cared about issues which are important to average Arab citizens,[106] including the identification of the nearby enemy (ruling regimes in the Arab and Muslim countries) and the far enemy (the West), and better utilization of the natural resources of the region to serve the interests of its citizens. Furthermore, Ayman Al-Zawahiri claimed that the "blessed incursions"[107] (the term used by Al-Qa'ida to refer to the attacks it carries out in various Arab and foreign countries) paved the way for the Arab events and turmoil, which was, in his opinion, a new defeat for the United States of America, which is the main backer of regimes in the region.[108]

Interestingly enough, it seems Al-Qa'ida was waiting for the effects of those events and turmoil to reach the Arabian Gulf countries and topple regimes there too. Anwar Nasser Al-Awlaki (leader of Al-Qa'ida in the Arabian Peninsula, and a US born Yemeni cleric who was killed in a drone raid in the Republic of Yemen on September 30, 2011)[109] likened the turmoil to a collapsing mountain which would open the doors of opportunity for *mujahideen* all over the world. He stated that "thousands of Saudi *mujahideen* in prisons and other places in the Arabian Peninsula were ready to move once regimes in the Gulf start tumbling."[110]

Recent Transformations and the Doctrine of Al-Qa'ida

The doctrine adopted in the recent political transformations and popular protests is completely different from that of Al-Qa'ida. Although Ayman Al-Zawahiri welcomed what he called "the blessed uprisings"[111] in an attempt to exploit their momentum, there was a major debate within Al-Qa'ida and affiliated groups about formulating one position regarding those developments, involving a broad variety of views and opinions. For example, in an online forum in May 2011, Doku Umarov, "Emir of the Caucasus Islamic Emirate,"[112] expressed his aversion of what he called "the game of Democratic Islam" taking place in the Republic of Tunisia and the Arab Republic of Egypt. This feeling was shared by other groups affiliated with Al-Qa'ida. Some groups warned of "democracy becoming the religion of the people and an alternative to *jihad*."[113]

The main argument of Al-Qa'ida was based on the assumption that corruption and Western support of regimes in the Arab and Muslim countries can be changed through *jihad* and attacks which aim at serving the interests of the *umma*,[114] which is similar to the perspective of jihadi Salafism. However, the achievement of political change through popular protest and demonstration, as in the case of the Republic of Tunisia and the Arab Republic of Egypt, without any real contribution by Al-

Qa'ida and without using force and violence, has undermined the validity of Al-Qa'ida's argument.[115] Still, Al-Qa'ida tried to take credit for this achievement itself and claim that it inspired the change.

Besides its failure to anticipate the political change resulting from the events since 2011, Al-Qa'ida has played no significant role after the fall of those regimes. Youth groups in the Republic of Tunisia and the Arab Republic of Egypt did not respond to Al-Qa'ida initiatives. Libyan opposition groups which fought against former president Muammar Al-Qaddafi were not inspired by the concept of *jihad* in the doctrine of Al-Qa'ida. On the contrary, they accepted assistance from the enemies of Al-Qa'ida—NATO.[116]

The truth is that changes in the course of the events in Arab countries, and the political and security chaos which ensued – for example in the State of Libya and the Syrian Arab Republic – brought jihadi organizations, particularly Al-Qa'ida and ISIL, back to the fore. They tried to retake the initiative and restore the appeal of armed *jihad* and other universal intellectual concepts related to extremism.[117.]

One study comments that prior to the political transformations in the region in recent years, Al-Qa'ida was almost dead, with a limited presence in the Islamic Republic of Afghanistan, the Islamic Republic of Pakistan, the Republic of Yemen and the Republic of Somalia. However, according to some researchers, the recent political changes, the fall of several Arab regimes, and the ensuing chaos in some countries, including the Syrian Arab Republic, the State of Libya and the Republic of Iraq offered Al-Qa'ida an opportunity to reimpose itself on the Middle East.[118]

Al-Qa'ida's Media Strategy

The leadership of Al-Qa'ida appreciates the importance of media coverage of the organization by various outlets. Following the attacks of September 11, 2001, this work became central to the organization.[119]

Some researchers familiar with armed fundamentalist groups talk of three generations of Al-Qa'ida, with the current generation being the third[120] as mentioned above. Others point out that the organization was unable to conduct any key operations against the United States of America after September 11, 2001, and that it has instead focused on recruiting new suicide bombers through the internet using social media networks and jihadi websites, especially in countries suffering from security and political chaos under weak central governments.[121]

Electronic media and social media networks have become one of the most dangerous tools used by militant jihadi groups, whether for the purpose of recruitment, propaganda or the promotion of ideology.

There are some studies which have examined the media activities of Al-Qa'ida and talked about the "media ideology of the Al-Qa'ida organization,"[122] referring to a group of ideas which were formulated in the days of *jihad* in Afghanistan. These ideas were re-established, exported theoretically and practically, and expressed through internet, which was the only medium available to Al-Qa'ida. As such, these ideas moved from a limited to an unlimited space in the form of text, sound, images and video, or a combination thereof. The way this ideology is expressed develops alongside the medium used.[123]

There are several stages which may be observed in the media activities of Al-Qa'ida:[124]

The first stage, prior to the attacks of September 11, 2001, was characterized by limited interest in Al-Qa'ida among media outlets, especially those in the West.

In the second stage following September 11, 2001, Al-Qa'ida and its affiliate organizations came under the international media spotlight and consistently made the headlines. The media ideology of Al-Qa'ida was conceived during this stage.

The third stage, in the period 2003–2004, saw Al-Qa'ida's media work become linked to operations on the ground. The organization's media presence preceded field work, as in the case of the attacks on a residential complex inhabited by foreigners in Riyadh in 2003, the US Consulate in Jeddah in 2004, and in Yanbu in 2004 in which six Western nationals were killed.[125]

In the fourth stage (2005–2007), media was not directly linked to ground operations, and became an area of intensive activity in its own right.

Al-Qa'ida leaders understood the key role of the media, and particularly the internet, not only as an important and low-cost means of communication, but also as an effective means of attracting new recruits, thereby allowing the organization to expand horizontally. Al-Qa'ida changed its organizational structure accordingly, and moved towards decentralization, penetrating most countries of the world and creating sleeper cells to grow in the target environment. The role of the central leadership became limited to logistical support and guidance, as seen in the Republic of Iraq, the Republic of Yemen and the Kingdom of Saudi Arabia.[126]

Al-Qa'ida and its affiliated groups and organizations train their members to use the internet professionally and to exploit its potential as a media tool whose users and administrators are difficult to trace, especially with the use of new methods to circumvent controls and avoid identification.[127] The websites of jihadi organizations such as ISIL provide key sources of information about organizations and their activities, as well as their political, military and *Sharia* publications. Examples of such websites include Al-Neda, Al-Jihad, and Azzam.[128]

Some studies indicate that Al-Qa'ida planned to revive[129] the Caliphate state, which is the dream of all political religious groups. This plan continues to comprise three elements, including

a media element which was the most important. These three elements are as follows:

1. The creation of a branch of Al-Qa'ida in the Kingdom of Saudi Arabia in order to wage a long-term war of attrition against Saudi and American forces and drag the United States of America into a war on Saudi territory.[130]

2. Carrying out a major attack against the United States of America on its territory in order to drag it to a war in the Kingdom of Saudi Arabia—this took the form of the September 11, 2001 attacks.[131]

3. Conducting an intensive media campaign through the internet, the only media tool available to promote the ideology of the organization. This would formulate the media ideology of the organization.[132]

The following are the most prominent media outlets used by Al-Qa'ida:[133]

Alneda Website

Alneda (alneda.com) was launched in 1998 by Al-Qa'ida member, Yousuf bin Salih Al-Oyairi. All Al-Qa'ida statements were issued through this website. It was interrupted and restored several times until, following the establishment of Al-Qa'ida in the Arabian Peninsula, it was merged with the official website of the organization Sawt Al-Jihad (Voice of Jihad).[134]

Al-Sahab Media Production

The first release from Al-Sahab was video footage of the attack on the destroyer USS *Cole* in 2000.[135] In recent years, it has released some English language material. Al-Sahab has been the main media arm of Al-Qa'ida, especially for the first generation (Usama bin Ladin and Ayman Al-Zawahiri), and all releases were made through it.

The Media Section of Al-Qa'ida in Mesopotamia

This section was responsible for the media releases of the Al-Qa'ida branch in Iraq. It was shut down recently after the disintegration of "Al-Qa'ida in Mesopotamia" and the emergence of the Islamic State in Iraq organization. The Media Section of Al-Qa'ida in Mesopotamia was replaced by "Al-Furqan" of the Islamic State of Iraq. It developed and later issued "Dabiq," a technologically advanced magazine, to cover the activities of the Islamic State organization.[136] This reflects the interest of militant jihadi organizations and their leaders in media work, drawing the attention of observers to the remarkably advanced use of media by these organizations, particularly the Islamic State organization.[137]

The Media Section of Al-Qa'ida in the Islamic Maghreb

This section works under the name of Al-Andalus Media Production. It prepares and supervises the releases of the Al-Qa'ida in the Islamic Maghreb organization (which covers the People's Democratic Republic of Algeria, the Kingdom of

Morocco, the Republic of Tunisia, the Islamic Republic of Mauritania, and the State of Libya), and posts media and promotional material on websites and social media networks.[138]

Sada Al-Malahim

Sada Al-Malahim (Echoes of Battle) has been responsible for the releases of Al-Qa'ida in the Arabian Peninsula. It is also now responsible for the releases of Al-Qa'ida in the Republic of Yemen, after the two branches of Al-Qa'ida in the Kingdom of Saudi Arabia and the Republic of Yemen were merged.[139]

Al-Fajr Islamic Center

After the Islamic State of Iraq organization was established in 2006, all media efforts were combined into the Al-Fajr Center, which was responsible for distributing all releases of the organization. The purpose of establishing this center was to separate media and field work for security reasons.[140]

According to one study, the war waged by Al-Qa'ida on all fronts is based on attrition, which relies tactically on guerrilla warfare. This form of warfare relies on propaganda to sustain itself. Hence, media work was given priority within the organization. Al-Qa'ida literature explains that guerrilla warfare requires intensive media coverage and propaganda at all levels, as well as media tools which are capable of presenting the organization's viewpoint both domestically and abroad.[141] Ironically, the jihadi organizations' interest in the media and its role in forming trends and changing convictions coincides with a move in some Arab and Muslim countries towards the abolition of the Ministry of Information/ Media at a time when the public in these countries seem to be in a desperate need of an equivalent authority to counter the propaganda and militant ideas promoted by political religious groups through various traditional and electronic media as well as social media.

The Islamic State Organization (ISIL)

Although the Islamic State organization (ISIL) appeared in Syria recently, its roots go back to September 2003, when Abu Mus'ab Al-Zarqawi established and led a group which he called "Jama'at Al-Tawheed wa Al-Jihad" (The Group of Monotheism and Jihad). Between September 2003 and October 2004, the group launched almost 50 car bomb attacks, both driven by suicide bombers and remotely controlled,[142] mostly in Baghdad, the capital of Iraq.[143]

The group developed psychological, political and cyber warfare tactics, and launched an ideological and political campaign against the legitimacy of the government and the state. According to some sources, the United States of America insisted on linking Al-Zarqawi's group to Al-Qa'ida in order to link former Iraqi president Saddam Hussein to Al-Qa'ida, which would form one of its justifications for the invasion of the Republic of Iraq in 2003.[144]

It is well known that Ahmad Fadel Al-Khalaylah, known by the name Abu Mus'ab Al-Zarqawi,[145] who was originally from Jordan, had differences with Al-Qa'ida regarding several intellectual and combat-related issues, although they were all jihadi Salafis. While Al-Zarqawi accused all Arab regimes of infidelity without exception, Usama bin Ladin excluded some countries, especially the Kingdom of Saudi Arabia in the early stages.[146] Furthermore, while Usama bin Ladin took the oath of allegiance to Al-Mulla Muhammad Omar and the Taliban regime, Al-Zarqawi was a hardliner on the issue of allegiance. While Usama bin Ladin and Al-Zawahiri developed their strategy from fighting the near enemy (Arab and Muslim regimes) to fighting the faraway enemy, represented by the Jews and the Christians and led by the United States of America and Israel, Al-Zarqawi held to the objective of fighting the near enemy.[147]

However, things changed after the fall of the Taliban regime in the Islamic Republic of Afghanistan; Al-Qa'ida lost its safe heaven there and decided to attack the Kingdom of Saudi Arabia in order to shake the trust by the United States of America of its Gulf ally and destabilize the relations between the two countries. This began in May 2003 with a series of bomb attacks (including attacks targeting residential complexes inhabited by foreigners in Riyadh). As a result, there was polarization among jihadi Salafis in the Kingdom of Saudi Arabia. Besides, the successes of Saudi security authorities in fighting Al-Qa'ida led to a change in the position of Al-Qa'ida followers; they felt that Al-Zarqawi's strategy in Iraq was preferable and more effective, and that it was useless to continue operations in the Kingdom of Saudi Arabia. A number of Al-Qa'ida leaders began adopting the position of Al-Zarqawi, which paved the way for him to join Al-Qa'ida later on. On October 4, 2004, Al-Zarqawi joined Al-Qa'ida and took the oath of allegiance to Usama bin Ladin. He became the representative of Al-Qa'ida in the region,[148] and changed the name of his group from Al-Tawheed wa Al-Jihad to the Al-Qa'ida Organization in Mesopotamia.[149]

On December 15, 2005, Al-Zarqawi formed the Mujahideen Shura Council from members of Al-Qa'ida in order to coordinate activities against American occupation and to form the kernel of the Islamic state.[150] Al-Zarqawi announced that the Caliphate would soon be established in Iraq, giving a time frame of three months. However, he was killed on June 8, 2006 in a US bombing of Baquba, and the establishment of the state was postponed.[151]

Abu Hamza Al-Muhajir succeeded Al-Zarqawi as leader of Al-Qa'ida in Iraq. On October 15, 2006, a military organization was formed to encompass all fundamentalist organizations in Iraqi territory. It was called the Islamic State of Iraq, and was led by Abu Omar Al-Baghdadi.[152] In April 2010, US forces raided a house where Abu Omar Al-Baghdadi and Abu Hamza Al-Muhajir were hiding. Fierce fighting erupted, and the house was air bombed, killing both of them. Ten days later, the Shura Council of the Islamic State in Iraq met and

chose Abu Bakr Al-Baghdadi to succeed Abu Omar Al-Baghdadi.[153]

Born in 1971 in Samarra, Iraq, Abu Bakr Al-Baghdadi's real name is Ibraheem Awwad Al-Badri. He has several aliases: Ali Al-Badri Al-Samarra'i, Abu Dua'a, Dr. Ibraheem, and Al-Karrar.[154] He is a graduate of the Islamic University in Baghdad, were according to some sources he received his bachelor's, master's and doctoral degrees.[155] Al-Baghdadi started as a religious educator and preacher, but soon became a jihadist. He emerged as a representative of jihadi Salafism in Iraq's Diala and Samarra provinces. He formed small jihadi cells which carried out a number of operations and participated in the street battles witnessed in the Republic of Iraq in the past three years. Then, he established an organization by the name of Jaish Ahl Al-Sunnah wa Al-Jama'a (The Army of the Sunnis) which carried out operations in Baghdad, Samarra and Diala. His organization joined the Mujahideen Shura Council, and he remained a member of the Council until the Islamic State of Iraq was announced.[156] On May 16, 2010, Abu Bakr Al-Baghdadi proclaimed himself emir of the so-called Islamic State of Iraq.[157]

ISIL took a bloodier and more violent course after Abu Bakr Al-Baghdadi assumed its leadership.

The Islamic State of Iraq has a very bloody history. Since Abu Bakr Al-Baghdadi became its leader in May 2010, the organization has carried out a large number of operations and attacks killing thousands of Iraqis (not including attacks by Al-Qa'ida under Al-Zarqawi and his successor). Most notorious was the attack at the Umm Al-Qura Mosque in Baghdad, in which Iraqi member of parliament Khalid Al-Fahdawi was killed.[158] Through the website of Al-Qa'ida in Iraq, the group announced it was responsible for more than 100 suicide attacks conducted in revenge for the murder of Usama bin Ladin, resulting in the death of hundreds of members of the Iraqi army, police and the public. It was also responsible for several high-profile operations in the Republic of Iraq, such as the Central Bank Operation in June 2010.[159]

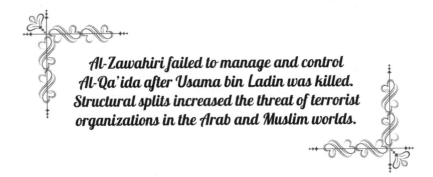

Al-Zawahiri failed to manage and control Al-Qa'ida after Usama bin Ladin was killed. Structural splits increased the threat of terrorist organizations in the Arab and Muslim worlds.

Several writers are of the opinion that following these differences and defections, and Ayman Al-Zawahiri's speech in January 2014 when he appealed to groups in the Syrian Arab Republic to stop fighting each other and elevate themselves above "organizational loyalty and partisan fanaticism,"[160] Al-

Zawahiri is facing a crisis in his ability to control the organization.[161] All this comes in the wake of his decision to abolish the Islamic State in Iraq and the Levant (ISIL), and his insistence in November 2013 that Jabhat Al-Nusra was the only branch of Al-Qa'ida in the Syrian Arab Republic.[162] These internal defections of jihadi Salafi organizations associated with Al-Qa'ida are not without precedent, but they are the most obvious to be seen within these organizations.[163] Differences between ISIL and Jabhat Al-Nusra have increased, leading to assassinations on each side.[164]

The conflict between ISIL and Jabhat Al-Nusra became public after ISIL spokesman Taha Subhi Fallaha, also known as Abu Muhammad Al-Adnani, accused Al-Qa'ida of deviating from the road of *jihad* and dividing the ranks of jihadists.[165] In a recorded statement which appeared on jihadi websites in April 2014, Al-Adnani invited fighters of various jihadi organizations to support his organization during the discord with Al-Qa'ida, which, in his opinion, was no longer the "base of *jihad*."[166] He stressed that the difference between ISIL and Al-Qa'ida:

> … is not about killing someone, or taking the oath of allegiance to someone; it is about deviation from the path of pure religion, adopting pacifism, and following the majority.[167]

There were reports that Usama bin Ladin's letters, which were found by the CIA in his house after he was killed in the Islamic Republic of Pakistan on May 2, 2011, revealed the magnitude of the differences and divisions within Al-Qa'ida.[168]

In light of the above it is safe to say that the Islamic State organization, known in the media as ISIL, developed from the historical ideological and organizational differences between the Al-Qa'ida parent organization and its regional branches. These differences can be traced back to the time when Ahmad Al-Khalaylah (Abu Mus'ab Al-Zarqawi) was leader of "Al-Qa'ida in Mesopotamia," before he was killed in 2006. Although Al-Zarqawi took the oath of allegiance to the founder and previous leader of Al-Qa'ida, Usama bin Ladin, he never observed the *fatwas* of Al-Qa'ida's ideologues in managing his organization's operations in Iraq. He gave priority to fighting the Shiites over fighting the Americans, which reflects the differences between the agenda of the parent organization and that of this branch. Confronting the West in general, and the United States of America in particular, facing foreign hegemony, the application of *Sharia* in domestic affairs, and the establishment of the Caliphate are key pillars of Al-Qa'ida's ideology. On the other hand, the agenda of ISIL gives priority to facing Iranian influence and expansion in the region and fighting what it calls the "Safavid project," especially after the withdrawal of the Americans from the Republic of Iraq. The sectarian Sunni–Shiite division is the key driver of ISIL, and it is the reason why it has become powerful in an environment dominated by sectarian conflict. By contrast, geopolitical interests constitute the key driver of the central leadership of Al-Qa'ida. The establishment of what they describe as the Caliphate state is a shared goal of the two organizations.

Birth and Ideology

Although the Iraqi branch of Al-Qa'ida joined the parent organization and took the oath of allegiance to Usama bin Ladin, as previously mentioned, its founder, Al-Zarqawi, established his own independent network which extended from Jordan to Afghanistan and then to Iraq, before he was killed on June 7, 2006. The Islamic State of Iraq was established on October 15, 2006 under the leadership of Abu Omar Al-Baghdadi, who was killed, together with his military leader Abu Hamza Al-Muhajir, on April 19, 2010. He was succeeded by Abu Bakr Al-Baghdadi on May 16, 2010. This period witnessed a transformation in the organizational structure of the Iraqi branch of Al-Qa'ida, which no longer concerned itself with the opinion of the parent organization or other jihadi organizations. On January 3, 2014, armed conflict erupted between ISIL and other jihadi organizations, including Jabhat Al-Nusra, the Mujahideen Army, the Islamic Front, and the Syria Rebels Front, in addition to parts of the Free Syrian Army and local communities.[169]

While the crisis in Syria uncovered the deep differences between Al-Qa'ida and its regional branches, these differences collectively resulted from a gap which has been widening since US forces withdrew from Iraq in 2011. This coincided with the arrival of popular protests in the Syrian Arab Republic in the middle of March 2011 and in the Republic of Iraq at the end of 2012. These circumstances, according to some analyses, contributed to a rebirth of Al-Qa'ida, a revival of ISIL, and the emergence of a new generation of jihadists who are much more violent and vehement than previous generations. This is when the Iraqi branch of Al-Qa'ida challenged the organization's central leadership, represented by Ayman Al-Zawahiri, through the announcement on April 9, 2013 by Abu Bakr Al-Baghdadi, leader of the Islamic State of Iraq, of a merger with Jabhat Al-Nusra in the Syrian Arab Republic to create the Islamic State in Iraq and the Levant.[170] This confrontation was an inevitable culmination of the historical differences between the branch and the center, which had been contained under Usama bin Ladin.

The situation deteriorated further when the next day, April 10, 2013, the leader of Jabhat Al-Nusra, Abu Muhammad Al-Jawlani, issued a statement in which he refused to join ISIL, announced that his organization reported directly to the parent organization of Al-Qa'ida, and reiterated his oath of allegiance to Al-Zawahiri. Attempting to contain this situation Al-Zawahiri issued a decision on June 9, 2013 in which he abolished the Islamic State in Iraq and the Levant, proclaimed that Jabhat Al-Nusra and the Islamic State of Iraq would remain two separate branches of Al-Qa'ida, and specified the jurisdiction of each group.[171] An online statement attributed to the leadership of Al-Qa'ida read as follows:

> The Al-Qa'ida Organization hereby declares that it has nothing to do with the group "The Islamic State in Iraq and the Levant." Al-Qa'ida has not been notified or consulted regarding the establishment of this group, and

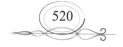

has not approved it. On the contrary, Al-Qa'ida has ordered that this group be dissolved.[172]

In response, the Islamic State in Iraq and the Levant (ISIL) announced that it was not a branch of Al-Qa'ida, indicating that Al-Qa'ida had become something of the past. A statement published on an ISIL's blog Al-I'tissam said that "there is nothing now in Iraq called 'Al-Qa'ida'."[173]

At the end of June 2014 ISIL announced the establishment of "the Caliphate state", with Abu Bakr Al-Baghdadi becoming "the Caliph of Muslims everywhere."[174] The spokesman of the group said that the words "in Iraq and the Levant" have been deleted from the name of the state, which became simply The Islamic State,[175] and invited all Muslims to travel to the state.

The announcement of the "Caliphate" was met with disapproval regionally and internationally. The Association of Muslim Scholars in Iraq stated that "this step does not serve the interests of Iraq and its unity. From the perspective of *Sharia*, this announcement is not binding on any one."[176] Ahmed Al-Raysooni, Vice President of the International Union of Muslim Scholars criticized what he described as "the unreal Caliphate and alleged oath of allegiance which is not binding on any one and concerns nobody other than those who took it."[177]

The announcement of the Islamic Caliphate was opposed and criticized even by prominent figures of the jihadi Salafi current, from which ISIL descended. Issam Al-Barqawi (Abu Muhammad Al-Maqdisi), a prominent ideologue of the Salafi current and its leader in Jordan, issued a *fatwa* delegitimizing the Caliphate state in Iraq and the Levant, and questioning the validity of the oath of allegiance which "did not meet the prescribed conditions."[178] Al-Barqawi's position was echoed by Omar Mahmood Othman (Abu Qatada), one of the leaders of the Salafi current. This criticism of the announcement of the Islamic Caliphate triggered a strong debate in jihadi forums, and revealed an intellectual and organizational gap that could result in an internal split.

This internal crisis turned into a war of statements. Members of jihadi organizations issued a statement signed by "followers of Al-Tawheed wa Al-Jihad in Jordan,"[179] in which they announced their allegiance to the Islamic State and its emir, Al-Baghdadi, called on those fighting under the banner of Jabhat Al-Nusra in Daraa and Ghouta to defect and join ISIL, and strongly criticized the ideologues of those organizations Al-Maqdisi and Abu Qatada for opposing the establishment of the "Caliphate state" and the appointment of Al-Baghdadi as Caliph of all Muslims. On the other hand, the Shura Council of the jihadi Salafi current in Jordan issued a circular asking the Salafis "not to join ISIL or fight in their ranks,"[180] This circular was based on the *fatwa* of Abu Qatada, who called on ISIL fighters to defect and considered anyone fighting with ISIL to be committing a sin.[181]

As a result, followers of the jihadi Salafi current were divided into supporters of the Islamic State organization – who were mostly young people and former supporters of Al-Zarqawi

– and supporters of the Jabhat Al-Nusra, who mostly belonged to the old generation of Al-Maqdisi and Abu Qatada. This suggests that the younger generation is much more radicalized than its predecessor.

For many followers of the jihadi organizations, Al-Baghdadi is carrying on the legacy of Al-Zarqawi. Therefore, members of ISIL are the new, more radicalized generation of jihadi Salafis. This generation tends to ignore old leaders and their *fatwas*, favoring instead field leaders—strength, violence and control is the key criterion for leadership in the organization.

The Islamic State organization is now addressing young people outside the jihadi Salafi environment.[182] It is taking advantage of social and economic conditions to attract poor and unemployed young people by promising better living conditions under the Caliphate, but without presenting any tangible plan.

ISIL: Between Jihadism and Sectarianism

ISIL is the worst mixture of jihadi Salafism and sectarianism. It adopts the concept of *hakimiyya*, accuses others of unbelief, uses violence as a means for radical change, and rejects democracy as an alternative to Islamic rule. Its ideology derives from Sayyid Qutb, the Imam Ahmad ibn Taymiyya and Al-Mawdoodi, and relies on a guided reading of the religious text which looks at individuals, societies and states only from the perspective of pure faith, belief in *tawheed*, and servitude to God (Allah), with the aim of bringing them back to Islam which, according to this perspective, they have abandoned. This reading completely ignores other jurisprudential and *Sharia* sources.

The Holy Quran, the Noble Sunnah, and certain books by the righteous ancestors are almost the only sources used by jihadi Salafism to inform their ideas and organizational experiences. These sources are interpreted literally without considering the context or conditions prevailing at the time. Such literal interpretations underline the problematic relationship between the sacred text and the material world, and the duality of the text and reasoning.

Those organizations use the era of the Prophet (pbuh) and the Rightly Guided Caliphs as a model to be followed. In his ideological vision of society and the state, Sayyid Qutb limits that era to two generations. According to those organizations, the prevailing circumstances of the stage when Islam was in Medina and the following stages were very similar to the prevailing circumstances today. Therefore, violence, or *jihad* as they perceive it, is the means to bring the *umma* back to Islam and re-establish the Islamic state on the same foundations upon which it was established in Medina.[183]

Jihadi Salafism follows the literal interpretation approach, accuses others of unbelief, adopts the concept of *hakimiyya*, and aims to bring society and the state back to Islam through the use of violence. This violence is justified by the fact that, regardless of the religion of the population, it exists in a state of unbelief and does not apply the principle of *hakimiyya*. This has given rise to new concepts and interpretations which allow the

declaration of war not only against one's enemies, but also against Muslim society and anyone opposing such interpretations. These interpretations are backed by historical precedents where *fatwas* were issued to legitimize *jihad* within Islamic territories, such as the *fatwa* of the Imam Ahmad ibn Taymiyya. However, the historical, political and jurisprudential context of such precedents is completely ignored, and those *fatwas* have been used as authoritative texts to justify *jihad* within contemporary Islamic societies. This has paved the way for the rise of a violent and narrow-minded discourse which accuses others of unbelief,[184] and the emergence of cadres who have misused the concept of *jihad*, thereby preparing the political and social landscape for sedition, civil war and sectarian conflict.

Those jihadi organizations still look at regimes in the Arab and Muslim countries as un-Islamic systems which do not apply Islamic rules and principles and exclude religion from their policies, practices and international relations. Furthermore, those organizations reject the concepts of democracy, political parties and participation on the grounds that they constitute "unbelief in God (Allah),"[185] to use the words of Abu Muhammad Al-Tahawai, a leader of the Jordanian jihadi Salafi current.

These organizations view interactions within the framework of the international community based on a certain value system and a certain perspective, which ranks the values of the "other" lower than that of their own. Since the value system of a certain religion is sacred, no movement is possible on this value scale.

Therefore, the jihadi organizations' perspectives of international relations, national interests and political change are based on idealistic perceptions of the nature of Islam, which they consider the only framework to determine political behavior at either the domestic or foreign levels, and a global ideology based on the fact that God (Allah) is the God of the whole world, which goes beyond the political behavior of the *umma*. The failure of these organizations to study the new world order and understand its interactions, and their limited religious value-based view of international relations, result in a failure to understand reality and deal with changes in the new world order, and therefore the loss of any ability to influence that order and direct it to serve the interests of the Arab and Islamic nations.[186]

Political religious groups generally share the goal of establishing an Islamic state, changing the structure and institutions of the political system and effecting a large-scale social change which demands continuous efforts aimed at changing the status quo. However, the vision of jihadi Salafi organizations such as Jabhat Al-Nusra and the Islamic State organization, is completely different from the agenda of other political religious groups in terms of their priorities and tactics. For example, the Muslim Brotherhood is pursuing political tactics to revive the Caliphate, provided certain conditions are met, unlike jihadi Salafism which uses violence as the means to achieve its goal; the Islamic State organization is using violence and murder to expand its control, invade other countries and bring them under the banner of the Caliphate.[187]

ISIL and Changes in Regional Conflicts

Events and developments in the Arab and Muslim worlds since the beginning of the twenty first century which, according to some analyses, have threatened decades-old international and regional power balances,[188] together with the increasing pace of change in the new world order,[189] have created fertile soil for the growth of the Islamic State organization in the territories of the Syrian Arab Republic and the Republic of Iraq. Having promoted sectarianism, adopted violence and accused others of unbelief, the organization is now threatening to expand its so-called Caliphate geographically and politically to neighboring territories. The fictitious map of the "Caliphate" encompasses countries such as the Republic of Iraq, the Syrian Arab Republic, the Hashemite Kingdom of Jordan, the State of Palestine, the Lebanese Republic, and some Gulf states. According to Al-Baghdadi, the mission of ISIL is "to protect Muslims everywhere."[190]

The circumstances of the Syrian crisis have contributed to the rise of the "Islamic State" organization, which has been able to control vast areas of Iraqi territory at a time when the domestic Iraqi scene is dominated by division, sectarianism and insecurity which are driving the country towards further civil war and disintegration. As such, the situation in Iraq is open to all scenarios: either a comprehensive national dialogue aimed at building an all-inclusive consensus-based democracy, thereby containing the influence and threat of ISIL; or a new sectarian setback similar to that witnessed in 2008 when clashes erupted between Sunni and Shiite Islamic groups. The latter scenario would increase the chances of a continuing Iraqi crisis with no political solution, which would strengthen ISIL and extend its control to other areas.

The rise of the Islamic State and the crimes it has committed against civilians in areas under its control have resulted in a US-led international alliance against it. In this context, US Secretary of State John Kerry held several meetings with the ministers of foreign affairs of the Arab countries – with the exception of the Syrian Arab Republic – to discuss aerial bombing of ISIL's sites in the Republic of Iraq and the north of the Syrian Arab Republic. The US began the bombing campaign in August 2014. Although some countries, including the Federal Republic of Germany and the Republic of Turkey, announced they would not participate in this campaign, they stated they were willing to offer help as needed.[191]

The broad regional and international participation in the alliance against ISIL reflects an increasing awareness of the threat of this organization, not only to the security and stability of Arab and Muslim countries, but international security and peace as well. This became evident in UN Security Council Resolution 2170 issued on August 15, 2014,[192] the closing statement of the Arab–American meeting held in Jeddah, Saudi Arabia, on September 11, 2014, as well as the statement issued by the International Conference on Peace and Security in Iraq, held in Paris on September 15, 2014, with the participation of 26 countries. All these statements completely rejected the

terrorist practices of ISIL and other extremist organizations, and stressed the importance of fighting them.

The air strikes conducted by the US-led international alliance of more than 60 countries against ISIL and Jabhat Al-Nusra in the Republic of Iraq and the Syrian Arab Republic reflect a concerted move by the international community to stop terrorist acts carried out by these extremist organizations in the name of religion. Some Arab and Muslim countries, including the United Arab Emirates, play an active and vital role in this international alliance. This role reflects the political conviction of these countries regarding the dangers of the phenomenon of terrorism and its negative effects on regional and international peace and security, besides the fact that it distorts Islam and its tolerant image around the world.

Conclusion

This chapter shows that jihadi organizations represent the most radical and extremist form of political religious groups in the Arab and Muslim worlds. These groups rely on rigid, extremist and closed intellectual frameworks which call for *jihad* and violence as the only means for Muslims to escape their bitter reality. These groups brandish the concept of *hakimiyya*, which is essentially employed to legitimize their existence whilst delegitimizing ruling regimes. These ideas were derived from the ideologues of jihadi thought, notably Sayyid Qutb and Abu Al-A'la Al-Mawdoodi.

Jihadi organizations developed from small local groups to become multinational cross-border organizations, threatening security and stability not only in Arab and Muslim societies, but in communities across the whole world. A number of factors have contributed to the proliferation of these groups, including deteriorating economic conditions and increased rates of poverty and unemployment among the youth.

Al-Qa'ida emerged as an important and far-reaching extremist organization, especially following the 9/11 attacks and the US-led global war on terror targeting Al-Qa'ida and its supporters and financers. The organization developed through three stages: the establishment stage which began in 1993 when Usama bin Ladin was in the Republic of the Sudan; the militant jihadi stage which started in 1998, when the "World Islamic Front for Jihad against the Jews and the Crusaders" was announced; and a stage of decentralized expansion, which began with the American invasion and occupation of the Republic of Iraq in March 2003, and saw Al-Qa'ida establish branches in the Republic of Yemen, the Islamic Maghreb, Sub-Saharan Africa, the Republic of Somalia, the Syrian Arab Republic, the Republic of Iraq and the Islamic Republic of Afghanistan.

Al-Qa'ida suffered serious setbacks during the war on terror, and saw several defections which weakened it—albeit without completely eliminating the organization. Meanwhile, ISIL, another organization with the same jihadi thought, emerged as a greater threat, especially after it assumed control of vast territories in the Syrian Arab Republic and the Republic of Iraq, and

announced the establishment of the "Islamic Caliphate" state at the end of June 2014, suggesting that the territories of the alleged Caliphate extend geographically and politically into neighboring countries. The establishment of ISIL resulted in increasing defections within Al-Qa'ida, with a number of affiliated groups taking the oath of allegiance to the new organization and its emir Abu Bakr Al-Baghdadi, contributing to the deeper intellectual and organizational divisions in the jihadi Salafi current. Just as the mounting regional and international threat of Al-Qa'ida led to the declaration of a global conflict against it, the growing threat of ISIL has result in the formation of a US-led international coalition comprising more than 60 countries. As such, these jihadi organizations have become international actors threatening international peace and security.

Part III

The Survey

7 Public Opinion on Political Religious Groups

A Survey of the UAE Population

CHAPTER 7

Public Opinion on
Political Religious Groups:
A Survey of the UAE Population

Most studies and research depend on polls and surveys as a scientific means to identify public opinion trends regarding topics and issues which are under investigation and relate to social interests or values. Opinion polls are an effective tool for gathering data directly from primary sources. Analyzing this data and linking it to demographic variables offers the information required in formulating and adopting policies in various sectors, and provides a clearer picture and a better understanding of the population's needs and expectations. Furthermore, opinion polls constitute the means for building cognitive and theoretical models of society, testing them, explaining differences in views and values, and understanding behavior.

537

Measuring public opinion has become an important indicator of the advancement of a certain society, and public opinion polls play an important role in rationalizing government decisions and policies, supporting culture and activating mutual feedback mechanisms between the government and citizens.[1]

Therefore, this chapter seeks to determine: how the public in the United Arab Emirates, both UAE nationals and Arab Muslim residents including other GCC citizens, view political religious groups; the extent of their knowledge about these groups and their trust in them; the sources of their information about these groups; their opinion concerning the relationship between religion and politics in terms of political systems, good governance and the drafting of laws; the reasons behind the success of political religious groups in reaching authority; and their evaluation of the ruling experience of these groups and their future prospects.

A key assumption of this study is that the political events and circumstances which have been witnessed in the Arab region since the beginning of 2011, together with their social effects, largely contribute to shaping public opinion in the UAE, including both UAE nationals and Arab Muslim residents, as well as other countries regarding the concepts of religiosity, the relationship between politics and religion, and knowledge about political religious groups. Those events and circumstances contribute also to the view of the public regarding the future of these groups and their role in the political life in the Arab and Muslim worlds.

Methodology

The population of the survey comprises UAE nationals and GCC/Arab Muslim residents of the UAE aged 18 and above.

Data was gathered during the period June 15–26, 2014 using the random sampling method from a multi-stage sample of 1,200 people living in the UAE. The sample was designed in several stages by dividing it into different 'strata,' in accordance with the variables of the study. The population was identified according to place of residence (Emirate), nationality (UAE, Arab Muslims or GCC), gender, age group (20 years or less, 21–30, 31–40, and 40+ years), level of education (secondary or below, diploma or university, and postgraduate), and finally according to level of monthly income (AED 10,000 or less, AED 10,001 – 20,000, AED 20,001 – 30,000, and above AED 30,000).

The sample was designed to fully represent the population of the UAE through proportional representation of all segments of society according to the relative weight of each within the UAE population. An F-test was applied to identify the differences between the response rates of the different groups in the sample. An F-test is a statistical significance test for differences within large samples that are normally distributed. The response rate was 89.1 percent and confidence in the results was 95 percent,[2] with a 2.8 percent[3] margin of error.

Field interviews were conducted with respondents in the period June 15–26, 2014, in which the purpose of the study was explained using a specially prepared questionnaire (see Appendix). The questionnaire was distributed to respondents to complete, expressing their opinions without any influence or interference from those collecting or supervising the collection of data. It was designed to answer the questions and hypotheses raised by the study, and to achieve its goals. A pilot test of the survey was conducted in the field in which the questionnaire was distributed to a small sample of 120 respondents, with a distribution similar to that of the survey sample. Data from this small sample was not included in the results or analysis. The validity of both the content and construct of the questionnaire were tested, as were its reliability and consistency, using Cronbach's alpha. All the tests showed that the questionnaire was suitable for the purposes of the study.[4]

The quality of data collected in the field was verified after being validated and cleansed in SPSS (Statistical Package for the Social Sciences) statistics software to ensure accuracy, completeness, consistency, uniformity and integrity.

The questionnaire covered several topics, and aimed to gather data about the variables of interest. These are: interest in politics and following of the news; the challenges facing the Arab and Muslim worlds; the changes in the Arab region during the last three years; trust in public institutions in the respondents' countries; opinion regarding various political systems, level of religiosity and identity components; the relationship between politics and religion (i.e., religion and the state); knowledge of and trust in political religious groups, as well as sources of information about them; and an evaluation of the ruling experience of some political religious parties.

Demographic Variables

The study sample comprised 1,200 individuals satisfying a number of demographic variables of interest to the study, as previously indicated. These variables are illustrated in Figure 7.1.

Demographic Variables of the Sample (%)   Figure (7.1)

Age Group

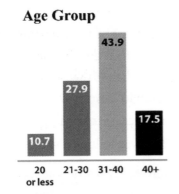

10.7	27.9	43.9	17.5
20 or less	21-30	31-40	40+

Gender

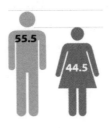

55.5
44.5

Nationality

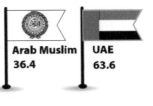

Arab Muslim
36.4

UAE
63.6

Educational Level

Post-graduate degree — 11.2

Diploma or university degree — 61.4

Secondary school and below — 27.4

Area of Residence

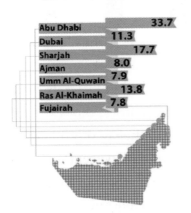

Abu Dhabi	33.7
Dubai	11.3
Sharjah	17.7
Ajman	8.0
Umm Al-Quwain	7.9
Ras Al-Khaimah	13.8
Fujairah	7.8

Monthly Income

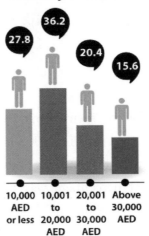

27.8
36.2
20.4
15.6

10,000 AED or less	10,001 to 20,000 AED	20,001 to 30,000 AED	Above 30,000 AED

Results

1. Interest in World Affairs

A reasonable proportion of respondents showed an interest in world news (always or often following news), with 60 percent stating that they followed world news (of which 19.9 percent always followed, and 40.1 percent often followed world news). A significant percentage (28.9 percent) occasionally followed the news, while 11.1 percent stated they never followed world news.

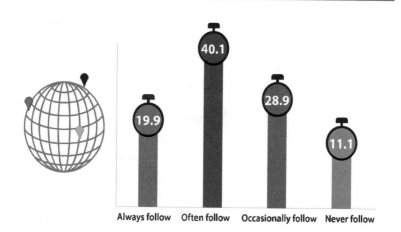

Extent to which Respondents Follow World News (%)   Figure (7.2)

Always follow   Often follow   Occasionally follow   Never follow

It is worth mentioning that the Arab Barometer I[5] survey, conducted in 2006–2007 in 7 Arab countries, showed that 56 percent of respondents followed news (often or very often). The highest percentage was in Palestine (78 percent), followed by the Kingdom of Morocco and the Hashemite Kingdom of Jordan (49 percent), the People's Democratic Republic of

Algeria (45 percent), and finally the State of Kuwait (23 percent only).[6]

The results differed between variables. There was significant variance according to gender, area of residence, age and education, but no variance according to level of income or nationality.

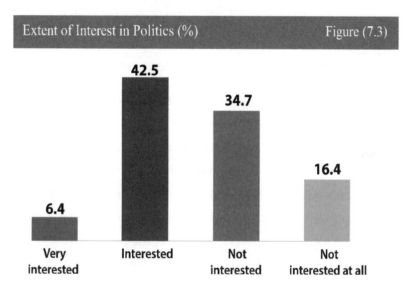

| Extent of Interest in Politics (%) | Figure (7.3) |

A little less than half of respondents (48.9 percent) showed an interest in politics (interested and very interested), with only 6.4 percent stating they were very interested in politics. 34.7 percent of respondents said they were "not interested" in politics, while the remaining percentage (16.4 percent) were "not interested at all."

The Arab Barometer II survey, conducted in 2010–2011 in 11 Arab countries, showed an average interest in politics of

46.4 percent. Among Egyptians, 56 percent said they were interested in politics.[7] In the Hashemite Kingdom of Jordan, 71 percent were interested, compared to 58 percent in the 2006 survey.[8] The percentages fall to 36 percent in the Republic of Tunisia[9] and 32 percent in the Kingdom of Saudi Arabia.[10]

Interest in politics differed between variables. There was significant variance according to gender, area of residence, age and education, but no variance according to level of income or nationality.

2. Challenges Facing the Arab World and Changes in the Region over the Past Three Years

To determine the public's perspective regarding the most important challenges facing the Arab and Muslim worlds, respondents were asked to rank several challenges according to their importance. (In this question, respondents were asked to choose the top three answers; therefore, the percentage total in the results will exceed 100 percent). The top challenge, chosen by 59.5 percent of respondents, was "economic conditions," including poverty, unemployment, corruption and high prices. This was followed by "achieving stability and security" (50 percent), "fighting religious extremism" (40.8 percent), "financial and administrative corruption" (39.8 percent), "solving the Palestinian issue" (35.5 percent), and "stopping foreign interference" (32.0 percent). The challenge of "establishing a democratic system" ranked last (13.6 percent) on the list of challenges facing the Arab and Muslim worlds.

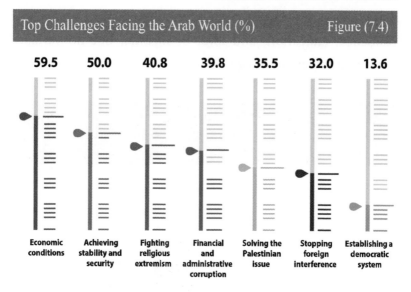

Top Challenges Facing the Arab World (%)   Figure (7.4)

Economic conditions	Achieving stability and security	Fighting religious extremism	Financial and administrative corruption	Solving the Palestinian issue	Stopping foreign interference	Establishing a democratic system
59.5	50.0	40.8	39.8	35.5	32.0	13.6

In the Arab Barometer survey, respondents in all countries stated that economic conditions were the top challenge facing their countries. For Tunisians, economic conditions constituted the top challenge (68 percent) facing their country, followed by financial and administrative corruption, then achieving stability and security.[11] Similarly, economic conditions constituted the top challenge for Egyptians (82 percent), followed by financial and administrative corruption, and then achieving stability and security.[12] Jordanians stated that economic conditions comprised the top challenge facing their country (79 percent in 2010, compared to 66 percent in 2006).[13] Saudis were also of the opinion that economic conditions posed the greatest challenge for the Kingdom of Saudi Arabia.[14]

The respondents' perspectives regarding the top challenges facing the Arab and Muslim worlds differed between variables.

There was significant variance according to nationality, area of residence, education, and level of income, but no variance according to gender or age.

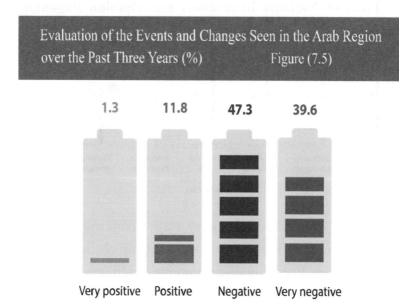

Evaluation of the Events and Changes Seen in the Arab Region over the Past Three Years (%)   Figure (7.5)

1.3   11.8   47.3   39.6

Very positive   Positive   Negative   Very negative

The majority of respondents (86.9 percent) evaluated the events and changes seen in the Arab region over the past three years as negative (both "negative" and "very negative"). Positive evaluation (both "positive" and "very positive") was limited to 13.1 percent, with only 1.3 percent evaluating those changes as "very positive."

The respondents' evaluation of the events and changes seen in the Arab region over the past three years differed between variables. There was significant variance according to

area of residence and education, but no variance according to gender, nationality, age or level of income.

3. Trust in National Institutions and Opinion Regarding Different Political Systems

a) Trust in National Institutions

Respondents were asked about the extent to which they trusted national institutions in their countries. These institutions do not necessarily refer to the United Arab Emirates, because the respondents included, in addition to UAE nationals, Arab Muslim residents and GCC citizens. Results showed that public institutions can be classified into three categories depending on the level of trust in them:

- First category: institutions which enjoy a high level of trust. These include the armed forces (trusted by 89.3 percent), the police (87.1 percent), the cabinet (85.9 percent) and the judiciary (84.5 percent).

- Second category: institutions which enjoy a medium level of trust. These include parliament (74.9 percent) and official religious institutions (68.2 percent).

- Third category: institutions with a lower level of trust. These include the press (59.5 percent), civil society institutions (58.6 percent) and television (56.6 percent).

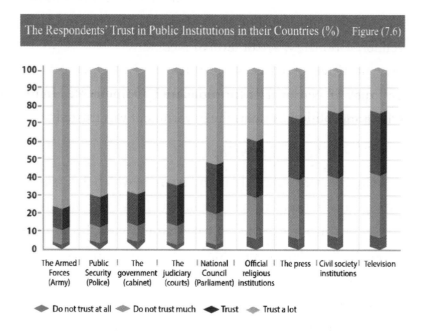

The Respondents' Trust in Public Institutions in their Countries (%)   Figure (7.6)

The Armed Forces (Army) | Public Security (Police) | The government (cabinet) | The judiciary (courts) | National Council (Parliament) | Official religious institutions | The press | Civil society institutions | Television

◆ Do not trust at all ◆ Do not trust much ◆ Trust ◆ Trust a lot

There was no significant variance in the respondents' level of trust in different institutions between independent variables.

Results of the Arab Barometer survey I, conducted in 2006–2007, showed a 50 percent level of trust in both the government (cabinet) and judiciary (courts) in countries covered in the survey.[15] National councils (parliaments) were trusted by 43 percent, and political parties were trusted by only 29 percent.[16] According to the results of the Arab Barometer Survey II (2010–2011), in the Arab Republic of Egypt the armed forces were trusted by 97 percent of the respondents, the judiciary by 88 percent, the government by

81 percent and the police by only 55 percent.[17] In the Republic of Tunisia, the armed forces were trusted by 89 percent of respondents, the government by 62 percent, the police by 58 percent and the judiciary by 51 percent.[18] In the Kingdom of Saudi Arabia, the government was trusted by 82 percent of respondents, the judiciary by 78 percent, the armed forces by 75 percent and the police by 70 percent.[19] In the People's Democratic Republic of Algeria, the government was trusted by only 30 percent of the respondents, the judiciary by 44.5 percent, the police by 47.8 percent and the armed forces by 54.1 percent.[20]

b) *Opinion Regarding Different Political Systems*

The respondents were asked about their opinion of different political systems. The results showed that "a system where senior officials (experts or technocrats) take decisions as they deem best for the country" ranked first, with 80.2 percent having a positive opinion toward it (both "good" and "very good"). Next, "a strong presidential system where the parliament and elections are mere formalities" was positively rated by 75.7 percent of respondents. It was followed by "a military system" (64.6 percent), and "a democratic system where political parties with varied frames of reference compete in elections" (55.8 percent). The system of governance of political religious groups ranked last, with only 32.9 percent of the respondents looking at it positively.

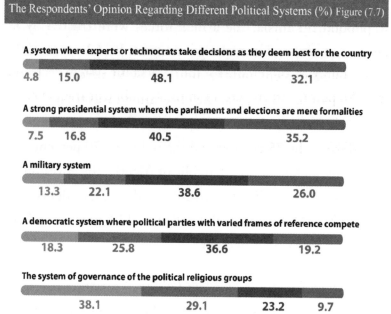

The Respondents' Opinion Regarding Different Political Systems (%) Figure (7.7)

A system where experts or technocrats take decisions as they deem best for the country

4.8   15.0   48.1   32.1

A strong presidential system where the parliament and elections are mere formalities

7.5   16.8   40.5   35.2

A military system

13.3   22.1   38.6   26.0

A democratic system where political parties with varied frames of reference compete

18.3   25.8   36.6   19.2

The system of governance of the political religious groups

38.1   29.1   23.2   9.7

■ Very bad   ■ Bad   ■ Good   ■ Very good

Results showed a slight variance in the respondents' opinion of different political systems according to gender and education only, but no variance according to other variables.

In the Arab Barometer Survey II (2010–2011), the respondents were asked about their preferred political system. The results showed that the democratic system was preferred by 83 percent of respondents in countries covered by the survey. However, this percentage came down to 80 percent in Survey III (2012–2013). The biggest change in the preference of the democratic system between Survey II and Survey III was noticed in countries that had witnessed events and changes in the last three years. In the Arab Republic of Egypt, 79 percent of respondents preferred the democratic system in Survey II, but this percentage increased to 84 percent in Survey III. In other countries, preference for the democratic system decreased from 86 percent to 76 percent in the Republic of Iraq, from 93 percent to 90 percent in the Republic of Tunisia, and from 83 percent to 73 percent in the Republic of Yemen.[21]

4. Extent of Religiosity and Components of Identity

Respondents were asked about the extent to which they were religious and committed to performing certain acts of worship. 78.2 percent of respondents said they were religious (both "very religious" and "religious"), and 21.8 percent said they were not religious (both "not religious" and "not religious at all," with only 1.8 percent in the latter category).

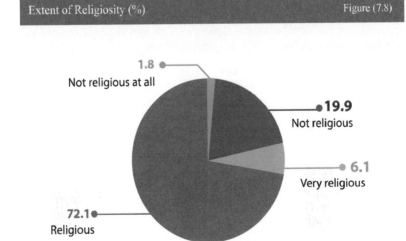

Extent of Religiosity (%)   Figure (7.8)

1.8
Not religious at all

19.9
Not religious

6.1
Very religious

72.1
Religious

In the Arab Barometer Survey II (2010–2011), results showed that 90 percent of Jordanians viewed themselves as religious. In other countries, the percentage was 76 percent in the Republic of Tunisia, 98 percent in the Arab Republic of Egypt, 86 percent in the Kingdom of Saudi Arabia, and 81.1 percent in the People's Democratic Republic of Algeria.[22]

Answering the question about the extent of their commitment to performing certain acts of worship, respondents said they were very committed to performing all acts of worship. This is consistent with the results of the previous question about religiosity. 72.3 percent of the respondents said they were very committed to fasting, and 55.5 percent were very committed to performing prayers and paying alms. The level of commitment to performing acts of worship was a reflection of the level of religiosity. However, the high levels of religiosity and commitment to performing religious duties were not matched by the level of trust in political religious groups, knowledge about those groups, or the mixing of religion and state.

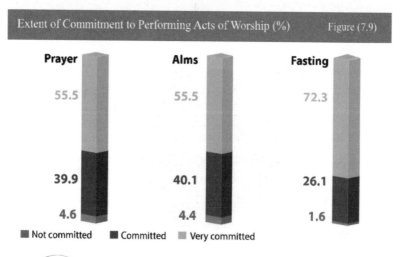

Extent of Commitment to Performing Acts of Worship (%) — Figure (7.9)

Prayer	Alms	Fasting
55.5	55.5	72.3
39.9	40.1	26.1
4.6	4.4	1.6

■ Not committed ■ Committed ▨ Very committed

Respondents were asked several questions relating to the relationship between religion and the state. Their answers were as follows:

The Relationship between Religion and the State (%)	Figure (7.10)

Clerics should not have influence over decisions of the government

4.8	22.6	41.1	31.6

Religion should be separated from politics

10.9	28.0	30.5	30.5

Certain laws should be written in accordance with the wishes of the people, and certain laws should be written in accordance with Sharia

4.1	12.0	41.3	42.6

Laws should be written in accordance with the wishes of the people

5.6	14.9	48.8	30.6

Only Sharia laws should be applied

7.7	39.2	40.2	12.9

■ Strongly disagree ■ disagree ■ agree ■ Strongly agree

72.6 percent of respondents said that clerics should not have influence over the decisions of government and 61.1 percent supported separating religion from politics. A large number (79.4 percent) were of the opinion that laws should be written in accordance with the wishes of the people. 53.1 percent of respondents supported the application of *Sharia* laws only. The majority (83.9 percent) agreed that certain laws should be written in accordance with the wishes of the people, and certain laws should be written in accordance with *Sharia*.

In the Arab Barometer Survey I (2006–2007), 44 percent of respondents said that clerics should not have influence over decisions of the government. This percentage increased to 60 percent in Survey II (2010–2011), and to 64 percent in Survey III (2012–2013).[23] The percentage was 48 percent in the Hashemite Kingdom of Jordan, 42 percent in the People's Democratic Republic of Algeria, 61 percent in the State of Kuwait, 47 percent in the Kingdom of Saudi Arabia, and 63 percent in the Republic of Tunisia.[24]

Regarding the separation of religion from politics, 54 percent of all respondents in the Arab Barometer Survey I supported such a separation. This percentage increased to 67 percent in Survey II, before slightly decreasing to 62 percent in Survey III.[25]

Concerning the drafting of laws, the view that laws should be written in accordance with the Islamic *Sharia* was supported by 91 percent of Saudis, 85 percent of Jordanians, 80 percent of Egyptians, 67.9 percent of Algerians, and 56 percent of Tunisians. On the other hand, 79 percent of Tunisians, 73 percent of Egyptians, 62 percent of Jordanians, 60.3 percent of Algerians, and only 42 percent of Saudis supported the view that laws should be written in accordance with the wishes of the people. The third view which is a compromise of the other two, i.e. certain laws should be written in accordance with the wishes of the people, and certain laws should be written in accordance with *Sharia*, was supported by 78 percent of Egyptians, 77 percent of Jordanians, 76 percent of Tunisians, and 51 percent of Saudis.[26]

Asked about their feelings regarding components of their identities, 58.4 percent of respondents said they were primarily Muslims, 28.4 percent said they were primarily

citizens of their respective countries, while 7.5 percent said Arab, 1.9 percent said GCC citizen, and 3.8 percent identified themselves as global citizens.

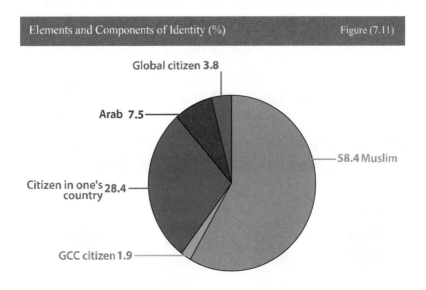

Elements and Components of Identity (%)   Figure (7.11)

Global citizen 3.8

Arab 7.5

58.4 Muslim

Citizen in one's 28.4 country

GCC citizen 1.9

5. Knowledge of, Trust in, and Sources of Information regarding Political Religious Groups

Although the previous question indicated that respondents felt they belonged primarily to Islam, their answers to the question about their knowledge of political religious groups showed that the public does not have good knowledge about these groups in general. This demonstrates that there is no relation between religiosity and belonging to Islam on the one hand and knowledge about political religious groups or trusting

them on the other. 76.8 percent of respondents said they had no knowledge at all about the Surooris, 52.9 percent had no knowledge at all about the jihadis, and 43.7 percent had no knowledge at all about the Salafis. Only 31.9 percent had no knowledge at all about the Muslim Brotherhood. This can be explained by the light shed on this group over the last three years after political religious groups dominated the political landscape in some Arab and Muslim countries.

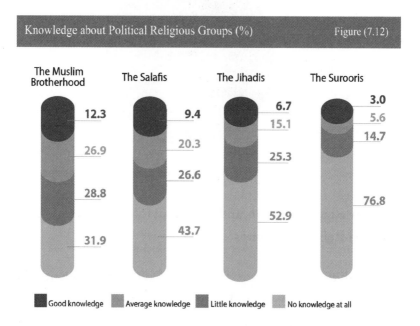

Knowledge about Political Religious Groups (%)   Figure (7.12)

The respondents expressed distrust of political religious groups. Only 6.3 percent of respondents trusted them, while 93.7 percent did not trust them, including 62.3 percent who did not trust them at all. This high level of distrust in these groups could be attributed to the fact that it recently became evident to the public that such groups have used religion to achieve political gains and interests.

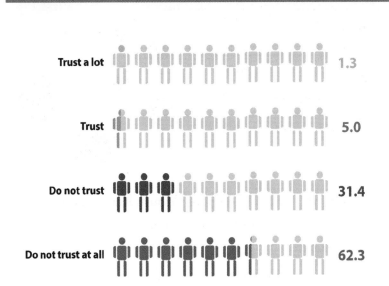

Trust in Political Religious Groups in General (%)   Figure (7.13)

Trust a lot	1.3
Trust	5.0
Do not trust	31.4
Do not trust at all	62.3

The respondents were asked about the sources of their information about political religious groups. Television was the source of information for 60.9 percent of respondents and the Internet was the source for 38.8 percent. Other sources of information included newspapers (31.2 percent), social media networks (29.2 percent), radio (17.3 percent) and books (12.5 percent). 4.1 percent of respondents relied on other sources of information about these groups.

Sources of Information about Political Religious Groups (%)   Figure (7.14)

Television	60.9	
Books	12.5	
Radio	17.3	
Other	4.1	
Internet	38.8	
Social Networks	29.2	
Newspapers	31.2	

6. Reasons for Political Religious Groups Reaching Authority, Evaluation of their Ruling Experience, and View of their Political Future

53.9 percent of respondents believed that the corruption of previous governments was one of the reasons which helped some political religious parties reach positions of authority in some Arab countries, while 47.9 percent of respondents attributed this to the bad economic conditions in those countries. 29.1 percent of respondents said that lack of organized political forces was one of the reasons, and 27.7 percent referred to the power of persuasion of political religious groups as the reason behind their ability to reach a position of authority. The reason was the wide gap between the rich and the poor in the opinion of 24.9 percent of respondents, and authoritative regimes in the opinion of 19.2

percent. 12.6 percent attributed this to the high level of religiosity among the public, and 9.3 percent attributed it to the presence of military regimes in these countries.

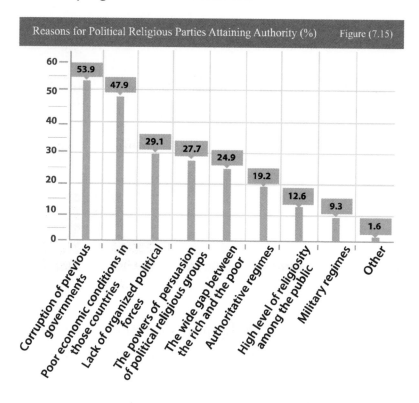

Reasons for Political Religious Parties Attaining Authority (%) Figure (7.15)

After political religious groups reached positions of authority in some Arab countries, such as the Arab Republic of Egypt and the Republic of Tunisia, it was natural to ask respondents to evaluate the performance of those groups. While a very small percentage (5.9 percent) said it was a successful experience, almost two thirds (67.6 percent) said it was unsuccessful. A significant percentage of almost one quarter of the respondents (26.6

percent) were of the opinion that the ruling experience of political religious groups had not yet matured, and therefore it was still too early to judge them.

Evaluating the Ruling Experience of Political Religious Parties (%)	Figure (7.16)

Very successful	Successful	Still too early to judge	Unsuccessful	Very unsuccessful
1.4	4.5	26.6	20.9	46.6

In August 2013, The Egyptian Center for Public Opinion Research, (Baseera,) conducted a survey of opinion regarding Egyptians' assessment of the Muslim Brotherhood. The results revealed that 69 percent of Egyptians do not approve of the Muslim Brotherhood's continued participation in Egyptian politics. Only 6 percent agreed to its continuation, with a further 13 percent agreeing but with certain conditions, such as being limited to religious work with no involvement in politics, abandoning violent means, and revising its positions. 12 percent replied that they could not decide.[27] 78 percent of respondents stated that the Brotherhood's rule was worse than they had

expected, while 3 percent felt it had been better than they expected, 12 percent that it had been as they expected, and 7 percent replied that they could not decide.[28] Regarding the violent events which accompanied and followed the dispersal of the Raba'a and Nahda sit-ins, 57 percent of respondents placed all the blame for those events on the Muslim Brotherhood, while 29 percent replied that the Brotherhood was partially responsible, a small percentage (5 percent) said that the Brotherhood was not responsible for any of the violence that occurred, with the remaining 6 percent replying that they did not know who to assign responsibility to for those events.[29]

A public opinion survey conducted in the Arab Republic of Egypt by the Pew Research Center and published in May 2014 showed a decline in the popularity of the Muslim Brotherhood; the percentage of respondents who viewed the Muslim Brotherhood positively decreased from 63 percent in the 2013 survey to only 38 percent in the most recent one.[30]

Future Outlook for Political Religious Groups in Positions of Authority (%) Figure (7.17)

Yes, religious groups
will have a political future

No, religious groups
will not have a political future

10.5

89.5

Asked about their opinions regarding the future of political religious groups, 89.5 percent of respondents said such groups would have no political future, with the remaining 10.5 percent stating these groups would have political future. A survey carried by the Egyptian Center for Public Opinion Research (Baseera) in October 2013 revealed that 70 percent of Egyptians oppose the Muslim Brotherhood's return to political life. 19 percent of the respondents approved such a return, and 11 percent stated that they were unable to determine their position.[31] Regarding the participation of political religious parties in general in the next parliamentary elections in the Arab Republic of Egypt, 42 percent of the respondents agreed to the participation of these parties, with an equal percentage rejecting participation, and 16 percent unable to determine their position.[32]

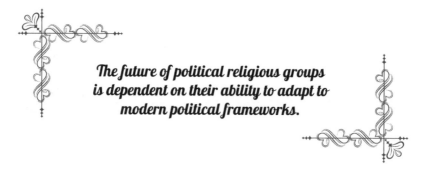

The future of political religious groups is dependent on their ability to adapt to modern political frameworks.

The future of political religious groups will be dependent on their ability to adapt to modern political frameworks, free themselves of their rigid stereotypes, and participate in politics without using religion to serve personal interests and achieve political gains.

Conclusion

The results of the survey in this chapter were interesting: respondents said that the economic conditions in most countries of the Arab and Muslim worlds, including poverty, unemployment, corruption and high prices, were at the top of the list of challenges facing those countries, followed by achieving stability and security, and fighting religious extremism as well as financial and administrative corruption. This is consistent with the results of the Arab Barometer survey which covered 11 Arab countries. The majority of respondents considered the events and changes seen in the Arab region over the past three years to be negative. Results showed that the respondents trusted official institutions highly, but had no trust in political religious groups. Although most respondents considered themselves religious, they said that clerics should not have influence over the decisions of government. They also supported separating religion from politics. The majority believe that certain laws should be written in accordance with the wishes of the people and others in accordance with the Islamic *Sharia*. The system of governance of political religious groups ranked lowest on the list of political systems preferred by the respondents.

Results also showed that the respondents lacked knowledge about political religious groups in general. The group most known was the Muslim Brotherhood, followed by the Salafis, and jihadi organizations.

The results of this survey also show that political religious groups failed to understand the priorities of their societies and the

implications of their natural religiosity. This religiosity does not necessarily mean that people favor a religious model of government. The results were interesting and require further examination. None of those priorities ranked highly on the agendas of the political religious groups which ruled a number of Arab and Muslim countries in recent years; those societal priorities were preceded in those agendas by other issues and interests which had nothing to do with the living conditions and suffering of the people—such as controlling state structures and institutions, monopolizing government positions, social and political expansion, and other autocratic practices. These results are completely consistent with, and confirm, the results of the Arab Barometer survey, especially in relation to the remarkable decline in the popularity of political religious groups following the widespread realization that such groups pursue political interests which bear no relation to the people's goals, interests and development aspirations. The majority of the respondents considered the recent ruling experience of political religious groups in the Arab and Muslim countries to have been unsuccessful, while a very low percentage said it was successful. Most respondents were of the opinion that these groups have no future in political life, especially following their experience in authority in certain Arab countries; the Muslim Brotherhood's experience in the Arab Republic of Egypt ended with failure, and the Ennahdha Movement was unsuccessful in managing the situation in the Republic of Tunisia. This confirms that these groups are completely detached from social and political realities and incapable of comprehending and dealing with current issues. That is why the people of these countries have excluded them from their present and future.

Part IV

Concluding Remarks

Conclusion

Conclusion

CONCLUSION

As you have thumbed through the chapters of this book, I hope it has become clear why it was entitled *The Mirage*. The book has sought to take readers on a journey by examining the experiences of political religious groups and the goals they sought to achieve based on ideas and intentions undermined by fantasy and incompatibility with both modernity and the tolerant principles of religion. The book examined the poor performance of these groups and the ensuing conflict with society which led to their rejection by the people. These groups imagined that they were on the verge of achieving their dream of controlling and dominating the capabilities of societies, assuming that those societies would accept their practices as long as they were disguised by the cloak of religion.

The experience of these political religious groups illustrates that they too labor under a mirage, in a continuous quest to impose on their societies, in the name of religion, ideas that do not fit with reality and modernity. The closer these groups come to achieving their dream, the farther their practices push this dream away toward fading. Likewise, the prospect that these political religious groups could reform political, economic and social conditions was also a mirage, as was their ability to achieve the aspirations of development, progress and prosperity. Some were fascinated by, and supportive of, the ideas and principles of these groups. But when they assume the reins of authority and government, and their principles are put into practice, these groups become like hollow drums producing loud noises but with no factual content, scientific foundation or practical experience to support them. This is particularly the case in a world witnessing increased competition to achieve progress and modernity based on science, research and diligence.

Exploring this book in depth, the reader will see clearly that the inability of religious political groups to efficiently interact and adapt to the requirements of modernity and progress in their societies is a result of a number of factors that can be drawn from their experiences.

The first is the intellectual isolation these groups imposed on themselves by refusing to consider any new ideas or to interact with modernity and scientific progress in other societies whereby their ideas, principles and practices could have been developed in keeping with global progress in science and political, social and economic practices.

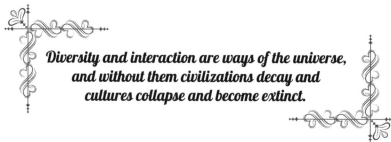

Diversity and interaction are ways of the universe, and without them civilizations decay and cultures collapse and become extinct.

Diversity and interaction with others are the ways of the universe, as the pillars of any society cannot be reinforced without mutually beneficial interaction with other societies and their ideas. This rule, which is based on the need for openness and engagement with others, is actually a part of the natural evolution of life designed by the Almighty Creator. Even at the level of nature, whenever a community secludes itself and does not mingle with others, its evolution will exhibit increasing features of weakness throughout its successive generations, which eventually makes it vulnerable to extinction. As a civilization, we must acknowledge that prosperous Islamic eras were those times that accompanied Islamic conquest and geographical expansion, allowing interaction with different civilizations, resulting in successive leaps forward in science, literature and ideas. It seems that contemporary political religious groups pretend to have forgotten this natural rule, lured toward isolation by their arrogance and sense of exclusivity. Believing they already possess everything they need, and therefore that there is no need to communicate with the rest of the world and benefit from its experiences, they brand such interaction as acts of 'Westernization' that seek to eliminate the (fallacious sense of) distinctiveness and uniqueness these groups have implanted in the minds of their followers and sympathizers.

This reality highlights the importance of ideas from thinkers such as the Imam Muhammad Abdu, who wanted *Sharia* to serve the nation rather than be a restriction to its movement, even if the apparent meanings of texts are in conflict with reality. Abdu's approach in this regard was contrary to that of the traditional

religious currents whose primary concern was to maintain the literal text. He stressed the social function of religion and advocated *Sharia* as the general framework within which Muslims move, whatever the circumstances, and that it was important to widen the scope of reason and open the door of *ijtihad* (independent reasoning). Hence, the Imam Muhammad Abdu has rejected the notion that Muslims should be subject to laws and rules that fit bygone circumstances, and that *Sharia* has one perspective and definite set of rules, arguing that *Sharia* has become rigid and that this rigidity has led people to neglect *Sharia*.[1]

Second, political religious groups lack actual and realistic solutions to the problems facing their societies. They only have pretentious slogans which play on the religiosity of Arab and Muslim societies, such as the Muslim Brotherhood's "Islam is the solution." They also attempt to portray themselves as having projects, plans and strategies to achieve economic development (such as the Muslim Brotherhood's "renaissance project"). However, reality has proven that these groups' slogans are nothing other than empty words, and that these plans and projects are mere general outlines and rhetorical phrases valid only as headlines in newspapers and magazines.

Renaissance projects and plans for modernization promoted by political religious groups are but words and hollow phrases without any basis in thoughtful scientific effort.

So far, in spite of the extensive experience gained by political religious groups and movements in the Arab and Muslim worlds in recent years, no observer or analyst of their activities, publications or speeches can point out a single realistic, detailed economic plan tackling the real-life problems of the public. You will not find any details through which you can judge, in a scientific manner and with practical logic, the plans these groups have to address the problems related to their economies, healthcare or education systems, etc. Their talk about the solutions to these problems is no more than words unsubstantiated by any facts, data or scientific analysis. The development problems suffered by millions of people in the Arab and Muslim worlds confirm that there is an urgent need for someone who plans and devises well-conceived scientific programs to find solutions to the problems of housing, water, unemployment, corruption, late marriage and spinsterhood, and other problems of urgency. These issues outweigh in their importance the attempts of political religious groups to trade in religion and seek only spiritual satisfaction—despite the indisputable significance of this aim.

Political religious groups became entranced by an infinite mirage, thinking that they could easily govern politically by linking their name to religion and thereby justifying their behavior. However, in light of the growing problems in many Arab and Muslim countries, and with the daily suffering experienced by millions of Arabs and Muslims, hollow slogans will not convince people to lend support to any movement or group as long as they do not eventually lead to providing bread for the hungry, cures for the sick, education for the young and the prospects of gainful employment and quality of life.

Third, political religious groups seek to eliminate the realities of development and the modern political and international order, which is represented by the existence of the nation-state; instead these groups advocate a return to a controversial past represented in the concept of the Caliphate.

The international system which was formed after the treaties of Westphalia in 1648 is based on the nation-state concept. It emerged as a result of religious wars that lasted for three decades in Christian Europe, and established a new system in central Europe in accordance with the principles of equality between states, mutual respect for national sovereignty and non-intervention in the internal affairs of other states.[2] However, political religious groups in the Arab and Muslim worlds seem obsessed with the idea of the Caliphate, i.e. the abolition of geographical and sovereign borders between the Arab and Muslim countries, and trying to apply controversial and unrealistic concepts.

Many questions and problems arise in relation to this ambition, which ignores the passage of time and looks to return the Arab and Muslim worlds to a time from their history: what is the "Caliphate" system? How can it be applied? Is it a system like that of the "Rightly Guided Caliphs," each of whom was selected in a different manner? Is it a dynastic governance system as in the Umayyad and Abbasid states, the Ottoman Caliphate, and others? What are the underlying criteria that show a system's superiority compared to another? Was the

progress achieved by Muslims during the Islamic Caliphate, in the era after the Rightly Guided Caliphs, related to religion or merely the everyday policy rules that were effective at the time?

There is no doubt that the unrealistic and ambiguous nature of the Caliphate concept, as currently promoted by political religious groups in the Arab and Muslim worlds – particularly given its rejection of the evolution of international relations – is a source of concern for millions of Arabs and Muslims. Such notions have exposed these groups and promoted awareness that their political visions are unrealistic fantasies, the application of which may have disastrous consequences.

Fourth, political religious groups seek to employ religion politically and attempt to forcibly impose a religious atmosphere on the Arab and Muslim societies to achieve narrow political interests and secure government and authority. They employ the principle of *hakimiyya* and hold this up in the face of any regime that does not adhere to their interpretation of the law of God (Allah).

Some researchers believe that the hakimiyya concept was born as a result of an incorrect interpretation intended to use Holy Quranic verses for purposes other than that for which they were revealed, including to vindicate the fight against others and to justify injustice and evil.

It is generally recognized that divine *hakimiyya* in contemporary political literature is linked to the thought of Abu Al-A'la Al-Mawdoodi who considers it a central idea linked to his interpretation of the concept of *tawheed* itself.[3] Al-Mawdoodi argues that *hakimiyya* embodies human obedience to God (Allah) in its political and legal sense, and that absolute *hakimiyya* in the political sense is represented in God (Allah) who is the obeyed ruler and legislator in the political and legal sense.[4] Al-Mawdoodi considers any president or ruler to be merely a viceroy for God (Allah), executing His orders as stipulated in the Holy Quran and the Noble Sunnah.[5] Hence, Al-Mawdoodi restricts the supreme authority and the right to command, prohibit and legislate to God (Allah), and denies the sovereignty of human beings even if it is legal or democratic, according to contemporary political practices. He justifies this by claiming that God (Allah) has negated the validity of the majority logic in administrating the lives of people based on the verse: "Were thou to follow the common run of those on Earth, they will lead thee away from the way of Allah. They follow nothing but conjecture: they do nothing but lie."[6] Al-Mawdoodi believes that the human mind is incapable of enacting instinctive laws that serve it, because it lacks the full knowledge of the depths of the human psyche and the whims of the people.[7] Al-Mawdoodi, based on this perspective, has denied human being any right to command or legislate – be it an individual, a group or a nation – dubbing societies with secular positivist orientations as *jahiliyya* and infidel, with no middle ground between the two.[8]

> *The Imam Ali ibn Abi Talib thought that the Kharijites' use of the Holy Quranic verse "the command is for none but Allah" as a slogan was "a right word intended for wrong implications," and he stated that "people must have a ruler, be he righteous or vicious."*

Nevertheless, some researchers argue that the concept of *hakimiyya* can be traced to the Kharijites, who broke ranks in the Battle of Siffin, refused arbitration and excommunicated those who accepted, announcing *"la hukma ila lillah"* (the rule is only for God (Allah)) according to what is stated in the Holy Quranic verse: "the command is for none but Allah."[9] Thus, they rejected both the authority of the Imam Ali ibn Abi Talib and Muawiyah ibn Abi Sufyan. Imam Ali realized the danger of using this Holy Quranic verse as a slogan and the magnitude of the confusion and ambiguity that surrounds it, and said in response to their outcry:

> A right word intended for wrong implications. True, command is for none but God (Allah), but those say that the rule is only for God (Allah)… however people must have a ruler be he righteous or vicious.[10]

However, the historical texts indicate that the Kharijites when they used the term *hukm* (rule) actually meant the concept of adjudication in disputes, and did not employ the concept of

hakimiyya at all, since it has appeared only in contemporary
political literature, as I mentioned previously, at the hands of
Abu Al-A'la Al-Mawdoodi. It then moved to Arab countries
through the Muslim Brotherhood's former theorist Sayyid
Qutb, who lent it more radicalism.

Divine *hakimiyya* appears to be the most controversial
demand of political religious groups, and even one of the main
points of conflict in Arab and Muslim political societies, largely
due to the varied perspectives on its meaning and implications
among different political and social groups. For political religious
groups, the application of *Sharia* means that politics and society
should be governed by *Sharia* laws and the requirements of belief
in God (Allah), submission to Him, accepting the rule of the
Holy Quran and the Noble Sunnah of His Messenger in all
matters of life. Meanwhile, others in society see this concept as
an attempt to build a theocratic state that undermines freedoms,
imposes censorship and controls on personal matters, gives the
clergy control over all the affairs of society – although they are
not qualified[11] – and that applies punishments and judgments
that are inconsistent with the spirit of modern times and human
values, such as physical punishments and discrimination between
men and women.[12]

In fact, the controversy over *hakimiyya* does not primarily
stem from the discussion of the benefits of *Sharia* law, but rather
from a sharp contrast in the understanding and application of
these laws.[13]

Counselor Muhammad Saeed Al-Ashmawi argues in his book *Islam and Politics* (2004) that historical events decisively affirm that the verse: "If any do fail to judge by (the light of) what Allah hath revealed, they are (no better than) unbelievers,"[14] was not meant to be an order to forcibly impose the application of the rule of God (Allah), and was wrongly employed to vindicate the fight against others and to justify injustice and evil. Those who employ it in this way base their understanding on a jurisprudential rule which states that meaning lies in the precise wording – rather than the context – of Holy Quranic verses.[15]

Al-Ashmawi states:

> Uthman ibn Affan was killed on the basis of the verse: "If any do fail to judge by (the light of) what Allah hath revealed, they are (no better than) unbelievers," and Ali ibn Abi Talib was killed on the basis of another verse: "The command is for none but Allah," so who killed the former and who killed the latter: the Holy Quranic verses or the evil misinterpretation of them?![16]

Hence, *hakimiyya* seems to be used as a tool or a means of incitement, in the name of which political religious groups aspire to authority, claiming that Islam is based on this concept.[17]

Besides, most scholars agree that this principle, which does not appear in any Holy Quranic verse or in the Prophet's sayings (Hadith), raises many conceptual and jurisprudential problems that can be summarized as follows:

- The verses used by the *hakimiyya* principle's theorists – particularly Sayyid Qutb and before him Abu Al-A'la Al-Mawdoodi – to justify its necessity and denounce its detractors have been truncated and separated from the causes and context of their revelation. They have been interpreted using a narrow perspective in order to allow these theorists to achieve their goals, which are to assume authority by denouncing the ruler and inciting the people against him.[18] One example is the verse referred to above, "If any do fail to judge by (the light of) what Allah hath revealed, they are (no better than) Unbelievers,"[19] which is employed in the context of denouncing rulers and society alike. However, this verse is not – according to scholars – addressed to Muslims, but rather the People of the Book (*Ahl Al Kitab*), and the word "judge" is not meant to have a modern political dimension, but rather refers to the adjudication of disputes.[20]

- The shortsighted unsubstantiated interpretations of some verses of the Holy Quran employed by political religious groups to introduce the *hakimiyya* concept are inconsistent with many other verses in the Holy Quran which call for tolerance and acceptance of the other, even if this other is doctrinally different. These verses include but are not limited to, the following: "To each among you have we prescribed a law and an open way. If Allah had so willed, He would have made you a single people, but (His plan is) to test you in what He hath given you: so strive as in a race

in all virtues. The goal of you all is to Allah; it is He that will show you the truth of the matters in which ye dispute,"²¹ and the verse: "O ye who believe! Enter into Islam whole-heartedly,"²² in addition to other verses that promote tolerance and dialogue, renouncing violence and embracing difference and diversity. As we agree that the book of God (Allah) does not have any contradictions – being from the Lord of the Worlds – then the problem is certainly in these narrow interpretations.

> *Implementing the hakimiyya principle entails restraining the mind and thought, confining it within the circle of texts and re-interpreting and re-producing them, entrenching a state of backwardness and stagnation in the Arab and Muslim worlds.*

- Implementing the *hakimiyya* principle – according to the viewpoint which says that it means no one shall make legislation but God (Allah) – entails restraining the mind and thought and confining it within the context of texts, thus limiting it to re-interpreting and re-producing them, and entrenching a state of backwardness and stagnation in the Arab and Muslim worlds.

- Implementing the *hakimiyya* principle as per the above-mentioned understanding allows for a theocratic despotic (religious) government system that imparts a kind of holiness to the authority of the ruler, who will then claim he applies the laws of God (Allah), from which he derives his authority.[23] This will make it difficult to criticize such a ruler or hold him accountable as a human being who is not infallible. This will reproduce what Europe suffered during the Middle Ages. It is enough in this context to point out some of the inhumane practices carried out by certain jihadi organizations under the guise of applying *Sharia*, in order to envision what might happen if such organizations came to authority in any Arab or Muslim country.

- Those who brandish the concept of *hakimiyya* do not usually have any plans or perceptions regarding how to develop their communities.[24] This was clearly proved by those political religious groups that won authority in countries such as Afghanistan under the rule of Taliban, and the Arab Republic of Egypt under the rule of the Muslim Brotherhood, among other similar experiences. The problem lies not in religion, but in the way it is applied and the interpretation of its provisions by political religious groups whose closed-minded perspectives threaten to plunge societies into the quagmire of underdevelopment, ignorance and violence—as is evident in ISIL's practices in the Republic of Iraq and the Syrian Arab Republic.

It is noteworthy that the rhetoric of political religious groups, whether regarding *hakimiyya* or other concepts, involves employing Holy Quranic verses and the Prophet's sayings (Hadith) to achieve their goals and interests of seizing authority and governance in the Arab and Muslim countries, and to commit crimes and ignite sedition in the name of Islam. Such rhetoric is mostly a fabrication presented in the name of God (Allah), as these groups manipulate the interpretation of the verses and assign to them meanings and interpretations contrary to those for which they were revealed. God (Allah) warned against such acts of forgery in the Holy Quran when He said:

> Say: the things that my Lord hath indeed forbidden are: shameful deeds, whether open or secret; sins and trespasses against truth or reason; assigning of partners to Allah, for which He hath given no authority; and saying things about Allah of which ye have no knowledge.[25]

To lie in the name of God (Allah) is a grave sin that is second only to "assigning partners to God (Allah)."

Holy Quranic commentators consider the gravest sin to be to attribute to God (Allah) things of which you have no knowledge, and in this context they cite the verse:

> And who does more wrong than he who invents a lie against Allah or rejects the Truth when it reaches him? Is there not a home in Hell for those who reject Faith?[26]

This verse equates those who fabricate lies against God (Allah) and invent texts that have no basis in pure religion with

those who deny the truth revealed by God (Allah). In this context some commentators believe that both acts are tantamount to disbelief,[27] as proven in the above verse itself which reads: "Is there not a home in Hell for those who reject Faith?" No one can fail to notice the huge number of *fatwas* issued by the theorists of political religious groups, whether about *hakimiyya* or the *jahiliyya* of societies and other matters which require prudent jurisprudential diligence.[28] As such theorists have become involved and engaged in this issue, resulting in falsifications and allegations which distort the image of Islam and gravely defame it. These *fatwas* are mostly opinions without basis in knowledge, and God (Allah) warned against this in the verse:

> But say not – for any false thing that your tongues may put forth – "This is lawful, and this is forbidden," so as to ascribe false things to Allah. For those who ascribe false things to Allah will never prosper.[29]

These *fatwas* betray even the fundamentals of religion and faith, as they present people with falsehoods.[30] Fabrications in the name of the Almighty Creator, in which these theorists invent words contrary to the words of God (Allah) and to the purposes of *Sharia*, ignore Holy Quranic verses as if they do not exist or deny them in a flagrant misrepresentation that is accurately described in the verse: "ye used to tell lies against Allah, and scornfully to reject of His signs!"[31] and "Say: See ye what things Allah hath sent down to you for sustenance? Yet ye hold forbidden some things thereof and (some things) lawful. Say: Hath Allah indeed permitted you, or do ye invent (things)

to attribute to Allah?"[32] This proliferation of *fatwas* without any basis in knowledge is a very dangerous and serious matter, and some people even consider it to be a great offense, a grave sin and the source of all crime.[33] Altering the texts of the Holy Quran and Noble Sunnah is impermissible, and advice from anyone other than those who have well established knowledge is unreliable.[34]

Most importantly, in my opinion, the warnings against fabricating lies against God (Allah) were mostly regarding matters relating to issues of the daily and political life of Muslims.

Fifth is the tendency of political religious groups to exclude those who differ from them religiously, ideologically, intellectually or politically, in a manner that sometimes amounts to racism or even murder.

> *Political religious groups proceed from the conviction that they possess an absolute right and are the protectors of religion, while their practices are in fact ideologically and politically exclusionary.*

It is clear that these groups who proceed from the conviction that they possess absolute authority, are the protectors of

585

religion, and have a duty to bring societies back to the sound foundations, are actually exclusionary groups. This is clearly manifested in all their practices and dealings with others, starting with their determination to entirely exclude religious minorities from the political process and attempts to exclude advocates of the civil state and modernity, explicitly or implicitly accusing them of heresy, infidelity and atheism. Interestingly, these political religious groups have attempted to exclude even rivals and opponents who belong to the same ideological current, sometimes accusing them of infidelity.[35] The key reason behind this is the insistence on monopolizing religion and its interpretations, and on considering others who do not belong to political religious groups – or even some who do belong to the religious current – unqualified to study and interpret the rules of religion. Furthermore, these groups do not recognize – and sometimes even oppose – historically established religious institutions such as Al-Azhar, defaming its scholars and figures.

The Muslim Brotherhood holds Hassan Al-Banna and Sayyid Qutb in such superior stature that it raises doubts about the extent of the group's commitment to the instructions of Islam, and the need to follow the Noble Sunnah of the Holy Prophet (pbuh).

There is no doubt that the past few years in the Arab and Muslim worlds have witnessed the negative practices of religious political currents that are inconsistent with the foundations of human rights and democracy, and which have sometimes appeared almost comical. No one can ignore the conflict between the Muslim Brotherhood and the Salafi groups. Ironically, exclusion prevails even among jihadi organizations, as seen recently in the struggle between Al-Qa'ida and ISIL, with ISIL accusing Al-Qa'ida leader Ayman Al-Zawahiri of deviating from the correct approach, while the Salafi jihadi Omar Othman (aka, Abu Qatada Al-Filistini) described ISIL as "Kharijites."[36]

Sixth, political religious groups that some people have attempted to portray or classify as "moderate," such as the Muslim Brotherhood, are in fact the source and the parent of all the militant jihadi organizations causing suffering in the Arab and Muslim worlds nowadays.[37]

> *The Muslim Brotherhood has spawned Al-Qa'ida leaders and extremist jihadists like Abdullah Azzam, Usama bin Ladin and Ayman Al-Zawahiri.*

It seems that contemporary advocates of the need for dialogue with those political religious groups which they claim to be

587

"moderate," such as the Muslim Brotherhood, forget that this group was the source of the vast majority of militant jihadi organizations that have plagued the Arab and Muslim worlds over the past decades. The Muslim Brotherhood, which promoted Sayyid Qutb's ideas on the 'excommunication' of society and features the violent "private" or "secret" apparatus, as it is known, spawned Al-Qa'ida leaders and jihadists like Abdullah Azzam, Usama bin Ladin and Ayman Al-Zawahiri. The group also apparently bestows greater stature on its founder Hassan Al-Banna and its theorist Sayyid Qutb than on the Prophet Muhammad (pbuh), as Al-Banna's messages and Qutb's instructions take precedence over the Prophet's sayings (Hadith) and Noble Sunnah in the Muslim Brotherhood's organizational and activist work.

But those who sympathize with the religious political current cannot hide the violent history of political religious groups whom they describe as moderate, particularly as such groups have so obviously resorted to violence in countries that have only recently emerged from corrupt and tyrannical regimes. Moreover, no one can fail to notice the feeble argument of these sympathizers regarding the need to involve political religious groups in public life in the Arab and Muslim countries, claiming that political participation will prevent these groups from resorting to violence. Such arguments make the wise people of these countries feel as if they are hostages to these groups, forced to negotiate for their freedoms in political processes in which they face the constant threat of extremism and violence from these

groups that dominate the political landscape. Besides, political religious groups, and especially the Muslim Brotherhood, focus on exploiting the feelings of Arab and Muslim peoples concerning the Palestinian cause and the Palestinian people, exploiting those feelings to serve the goals and interests of the group in attaining authority. Hamas came to power this way in the Gaza Strip, which led to deteriorating living conditions, splitting Palestinian ranks, and a proliferation of internal conflicts, and achieving no progress in reaching a political or military settlement.

Seventh, the field study reported in Chapter 7 yielded several important results; respondents believed the most important challenges facing the Arab and Muslim worlds were economic conditions, achieving stability and security, fighting religious extremism, and combating financial and administrative corruption. This is consistent with the results of the Arab Barometer II survey, which was conducted in 11 Arab countries.[38] Most of the respondents consider themselves to be religious, and stated that they are highly committed to worship—so the belief is consistent with practice. Although most of the respondents are religious, they said that clerics should not have influence over decisions of the government. They also supported separating religion from politics, in the sense that they do not favor regimes of religious nature. The vast majority of the respondents believe that certain laws should be enacted according to the wishes of the people and other laws according to *Sharia*. Results also showed that a significant percentage of the

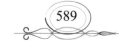

respondents lack good knowledge about political religious groups in general. The most widely-known group was the Muslim Brotherhood, followed by the Salafis and jihadis, particularly Al-Qa'ida and ISIL. A majority of respondents viewed the record of political religious groups in authority in some Arab and Muslim countries to have been unsuccessful, while a very low percentage said it was successful. Most respondents were of the opinion that these groups would have little chance of success in government or in political life in Arab and Muslim countries in the future, especially following their previous experiences of authority in some Arab countries—from the Muslim Brotherhood's time in authority in the Arab Republic of Egypt to the unsuccessful experience of the Ennahdha Movement in the Republic of Tunisia.

These results show that political religious groups were unable to understand the priorities of their societies. They were incapable of comprehending the significance of the innate religiosity that characterizes these societies, or the fact that such religiosity does not necessarily favor the religious model of governance advocated by political religious groups. The results of the survey contained in Chapter 7 reveal some paradoxes, the implications and dimensions of which are noteworthy for researchers and scholars. In the opinion of the respondents, who were UAE nationals and Arab Muslims residing in the United Arab Emirates, the economic situation – including poverty, unemployment, corruption and high prices – topped the most significant challenges facing the Arab and Muslim

worlds. Achieving stability and security ranked second, followed by fighting religious extremism, and then financial and administrative corruption. By contrast, none of these priorities – whether in the same or any other order – ranked high on the agendas of leaders of the political religious groups which attained authority in some Arab and Muslim countries. Such priorities were instead preceded on those agendas by other issues and concerns which had nothing to do with the living conditions and suffering of the people, such as controlling state institutions, monopolizing government positions, and political and social expansion. These results are consistent with, and endorse the findings of the Arab Barometer, particularly with regard to the remarkable decline in popularity of political religious groups, and the finding that the majority of Arab and Muslim people understand the true nature of these groups, their political interests and narrow personal goals, which are completely unrelated to the goals and interests of the people.

The results of the survey also clearly show that recent experiences have left deep scars in the collective Arab and Muslim consciousness, with respondents reporting that they did not trust political religious groups, and that they place such groups at the bottom of their list of viable candidates for office. This was also reflected in the orientations of the respondents with regard to what they considered to be the failed ruling experiences of political religious groups. Hence, it is not surprising that the respondents' outlook for the future of these groups, whether in government or in political life in general,

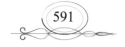

was bleak. These results refute the allegations of the leaders of political religious groups, who insist on adopting the clichéd rhetoric of a "conspiracy," and claim that hidden hands have worked against them, prompting the people to reject them. These groups continue to avoid the facts, as they lack the courage for openness and self-criticism, or to learn from the lessons of previous experiences. These groups prefer to continue to play the role of the "victim" and to claim historical injustice.

Ultimately, an important and pivotal question arises in the context of the ideas and views tackled in this book regarding political religious groups: if the current experience shows clearly that control by political religious groups, acceptance of their rule by societies, and their success in administration and meeting development and modernity ambitions all amount to nothing more than a mirage, then does this recent experience spell the end of these groups and ensure that this failed experience will not be repeated, at least in the near to medium term? The realistic answer is no, unless certain conditions are met.

On the one hand, despite the fact that the threat to religion in the Arab and Muslim worlds at the hands of political religious groups is more severe than that posed by its enemies and opponents abroad, some controversial practices in a number of Western countries give support to the idea of isolation, persecution and self-seclusion advocated by political religious groups. As the experience of the past few years has revealed, some practices, like prohibiting different types of veil –

including the *niqab* and *hijab* – in the French Republic, have led to a negative reaction in the Arab and Muslim worlds. Moreover, decisions like banning the construction of minarets in the Swiss Confederation, the issue of the cartoons defaming the Prophet (pbuh), preventing *halal* slaughter of animals in Scandinavia, have all led to an even more negative reaction in the Arab and Muslim worlds, and resulted in support and sympathy for radical political religious groups that exploit religion for political and opportunistic purposes and to achieve their personal interests, which may conflict with the interests of society and its progress and development.

On the other hand, the American writer Shadi Hamid[39] argues that, from the perspective of political religious groups, "there is a different, deeper failure, one that is likely to plague the Arab and Muslim worlds for decades to come: the fundamental inability of civil state systems to accommodate the participation of political religious groups in politics."[40]

Such logic, which is promoted by some Western writers, can be countered through the historical experience of Europe – and perhaps what some of its countries might witness in the future – in which extremist right-wing currents, such as Nazism and Fascism, enjoyed popular acceptance and democratic authority, but the world now knows well – through harsh cumulative experience – that the acceptance of political models or formulas such as "illiberal democracy,"[41] as described by Shadi Hamid, had very complex consequences, not only for the countries that accepted the existence of such regimes, but for

the whole world. This logic also questions whether it is possible that Western nations would accept a regime or a political system governed by extremist right-wing currents which have the same or similar ideas to those of political religious groups in the Arab and Muslim worlds.

This Western view of political religious groups raises several questions concerning the nature of the relationship between the Muslim Brotherhood and the United States of America,[42] given the latter's leading position at the top of the new world order. One cannot but wonder about the reasons behind the American government's support for the regime of the Muslim Brotherhood in the Arab Republic of Egypt, the guarantees provided by the Muslim Brotherhood to secure such support – including its willingness to recognize the agreements made between former Egyptian governments and Israel – the justification of this relationship from the ideological perspective of the Muslim Brotherhood, and the contradiction between the Muslim Brotherhood's behavior in this respect and the teachings of its founder Hassan Al-Banna.

Regardless of their details, these relations are a vital indicator of the political opportunism that is deeply rooted in the behavior of the Muslim Brotherhood. The United States' support for the Muslim Brotherhood came as no surprise for observers of US foreign policy; historical precedents confirm Washington's readiness to deal with any political religious group which serves US interests and goals in the region. Besides, the relations between the US administration and the

Muslim Brotherhood in particular pre-date this; there have been meetings and coordination between the two sides since the Brotherhood was the main opposition bloc in the Egyptian People's Assembly of 2005, under direct pressure from the administration of former president George W. Bush. Official meetings were held between the Brotherhood's members in the Assembly and official American delegates. There were also unofficial meetings which were not announced for reasons relating to the interests of both sides.[43] This coordination was enhanced after the events of January 25, 2011, as the US administration, in its efforts to deal with the situation after the fall of the regime of former president Muhammad Husni Mubarak, supported the Muslim Brotherhood quest for authority to avoid endangering American interests in the Middle East, as had happened in 1979 when the revolution in the Islamic Republic of Iran created an anti-American regime in the region.

The lack of awareness and education in the Arab and Muslim worlds tempts political religious groups to maintain their practices, bolster their reputations, and entrench a sense of injustice by playing the role of "victim."

But in this context, the commitment of political religious groups to spreading their thought, and to altering democracy to fit their ideas and principles, actually reveals one of the most important characteristics that helps them to endure despite successive failures, namely: mastery of the role of the victim, and the claim that they are indispensable because they cater to popular demand. This means that with time, as the memory of their recent negative experience in government fades, these groups will be capable of returning. This happened in 1976, when the Muslim Brotherhood returned to political participation after the former Egyptian President Muhammad Anwar Al-Sadat assumed the presidency, overturning the hostility toward the group that was a feature of the Nasser era. The Muslim Brotherhood also stepped up to the political arena in an unprecedented manner after their influence and role was curtailed and contained for some time during the rule of former President Muhammad Husni Mubarak, before they ultimately assumed authority in the Arab Republic of Egypt in 2012. What promotes such hypotheses is the existence of societies that are not highly educated or experienced in democratic practice, and which automatically support everything that is linked to religion.

This last point leads us to another which is more important and influential in determining the future of political religious groups, namely, the available political alternatives. It is noted in many Arab and Muslim countries that the alternative to such groups are currents which may not be characterized by flexibility or the effective governance needed to relieve these countries from

economic, social and cultural problems that have accumulated over many decades, which are the most important concerns among electorates. The problems and challenges facing many Arab and Muslim countries are becoming increasingly complicated, and are aggravated by limited resources, the growing aspirations of the peoples of these countries to higher standards of living, and steadily increasing competition from countries all over the world in terms of development and progress in the context of globalization. In light of such circumstances, it is expected that the potential pitfalls of such alternatives may lead some social segments to reconsider religious political movements and groups as the best alternative, regardless of their previous failings.

Moreover, we should not forget that the popularity of political religious groups in the Arab and Muslim worlds is currently very low. Evidence indicates an unprecedented decline in their popularity, especially after the Muslim Brotherhood's experience in authority in the Arab Republic of Egypt, the Republic of Tunisia, and other countries in the Arab and Muslim worlds. Over time people will forget the disadvantages and downsides of this period, and political religious groups may attempt to manipulate the public by yet again portraying themselves as victims. In order to avoid this, strong and effective steps must be taken to fill the current vacuum left by these groups by raising awareness and introducing real economic, social and political reforms in education, media, economy and culture, as well as in religious discourse and socialization. This will gradually lead to comprehensive

597

development and the creating of appropriate job opportunities for young people. This will serve to raise living standards and assist in solving many of the difficult problems facing Arab and Muslim countries. Extremism and fanaticism will not be eliminated from these countries without taking such steps. The current environment seems ideal for achieving a true understanding of the reality of political religious groups and to finally dispel them.

Talk about the future of political religious groups focuses on their view of the world around them and their widely acknowledged organizational ability. These groups have pinned their identity and existence on fighting those who they deem to be "infidels" and enemies, so they target the West, the United States of America and Israel in particular, which in turn raises questions about the legitimacy of their existence in the absence of this existential justification, whether by virtue of the changing policies of the West, or the emergence of new interests.

In light of the above, the Arab and Muslim worlds may continue to suffer the twofold effects of a "mirage": the first is represented by political religious groups and movements seeking authority they are incapable of managing efficiently due to the rigidity of their ideas, their distance from reality and their lack of awareness of the challenges of the times; and the second is represented by supporters who see political religious groups as the key to solving the problems of everyday life and achieving growth and prosperity. Such hopes are based on the promises of

these groups that manipulate the innately religious masses, who will eventually wake up to reality and the need for modernism that these groups lack.

> *Without rectifying the errors, opening up to others and moving towards modernity, scientific development and modern technology, the Arab and Muslim worlds will always suffer the effects of the mirage.*

There is still hope, of course, that the Arab and Muslim peoples will realize that there are no magic solutions for the problems they face, and that they have to be open to others and learn from their experiences. The Arab and Muslim worlds must achieve openness to others, whilst moving toward modernity, scientific progress, invention, creativity and innovation and unleashing the potentials of modernization, research, reform and diligence in religious jurisprudence and Islamic sciences; and if they are to dispel this mirage they must overcome the stagnation and ossification which have dominated the thought of political religious groups seeking to seize government and authority.

Appendix

SURVEY

Public Opinion on Political Religious Groups
A Survey of the UAE Population

1. How often do you follow world news?

    (1) Always   (2) Often   (3) Occasionally

    (4) Never   (5) Other (please specify): ....

2. To what extent are you interested in politics?

    (1) Very interested   (2) Interested   (3) Not interested

    (4) Not interested at all   (5) Other (please specify): ....

3. In your opinion, what are the top three challenges facing the Arab World (please select only three)?

    ☐ Economic conditions (poverty, unemployment, high prices)

    ☐ Financial and administrative corruption

    ☐ Establishing a democratic system

    ☐ Stopping foreign interference

    ☐ Solving the Palestinian issue

    ☐ Achieving stability and security

    ☐ fighting religious extremism

    ☐ Other (please specify) ....

4. How do you view the events and changes seen in the Arab region over the past three years?

    (1) Very positively   (2) Positively   (3) Negatively

    (4) Very negatively   (5) Other (please clarify): ....

5. To what extent do you trust the following institutions in your country?

	Element of Evaluation	Trust a lot	Trust	Do not trust much	Do not trust at all
a	The government (cabinet)	4	3	2	1
b	National Council (Parliament)	4	3	2	1
c	The Armed Forces (Army)	4	3	2	1
d	Public Security (Police)	4	3	2	1
e	The Judiciary (courts)	4	3	2	1
f	The Press	4	3	2	1
g	Television	4	3	2	1
h	Civil society institutions (societies, clubs, youth associations, etc.)	4	3	2	1
i	Official religious institutions	4	3	2	1

6. What is your opinion of the following political systems of governance?

	Element of Evaluation	Very good	good	bad	Very bad
a	A strong presidential system where the parliament and elections are mere formalities	4	3	2	1
b	A system where senior officials (experts or technocrats) take decisions as they deem best for the country	4	3	2	1
c	A military system	4	3	2	1
d	A democratic system where political parties with varied frames of reference compete in elections	4	3	2	1
e	The system of governance of political religious groups	4	3	2	1

7. Some Arab countries have seen changes which have allowed political religious parties to reach positions of authority. In general, how do you rate the ruling experience of these parties?

(1) Very successful (2) Successful (3) Still too early to judge
(4) Unsuccessful (5) Very unsuccessful (6) Other (please specify): ....

8. Please rank the following elements of identity from (1) to (5), where (1) is the most important and (5) is the least important:

Arab	Muslim	Citizen in your country	GCC citizen	Global citizen

9. To what extent are you committed to performing the following acts of worship?

	Acts of worship	Very committed	Committed	Not committed	Not committed at all
a	Prayers	4	3	2	1
b	Paying alms	4	3	2	1
c	Fasting	4	3	2	1

10. To what extent do you think you are religious? Where do you rank yourself on the following scale?

Very religious	religious	not religious	Not religious at all
4	3	2	1

11. To what extent do you agree or disagree with each of the following statements?

Elements of Evaluation		Strongly agree	Agree	Disagree	Strongly disagree
a	Clerics should not have influence over decisions of the government	4	3	2	1
b	Clerics should have influence over decisions of the government	4	3	2	1
c	Religion should be separated from politics	4	3	2	1
d	Religion should not be separated from politics	4	3	2	1

12. What is a good government in your opinion, and how important are the following for a good government?

Elements of Evaluation		Very important	Important	Less important	Not important
a	Laws should be written in accordance with the wishes of the people	4	3	2	1
b	Only Sharia laws should be applied	4	3	2	1
c	Certain laws should be written in accordance with the wishes of the people, and certain laws should be written in accordance with Sharia	4	3	2	1

13. How do you rate your knowledge of the following political Islam groups:

Elements		Good knowledge	Average knowledge	Little knowledge	No knowledge at all
a	The Muslim Brotherhood	4	3	2	1
b	The Salafis	4	3	2	1
c	The jihadis	4	3	2	1
d	The Surooris	4	3	2	1

Other (please specify): ....

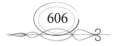

14. To what extent do you generally trust political Islam groups:
    (1) Trust a lot   (2) Trust   (3) Do not trust
    (4) Do not trust at all   (5) Other (please specify): ....

15. What are your sources of information about political Islamic groups?
    ❐ Television   ❐ Internet
    ❐ Radio   ❐ Social Networks
    ❐ Newspapers   ❐ Others (please specify): ....
    ❐ Books

16. What are in your opinion the reasons which helped political Islam groups reach positions of authority in some Arab countries? Please select the top three reasons:

    ❐ Corruption of previous   ❐ The power of persuasion of Political
      governments   Islam groups
    ❐ Lack of organized political forces   ❐ High level of religiosity among the
    ❐ Bad economic conditions in those   public
      countries   ❐ Authoritative regimes
    ❐ The wide gap between the rich   ❐ Military regimes
      and the poor   ❐ Other (please specify): ....

17. In your opinion, do political religious groups have a political future?

    (1) Yes   (2) No

Demographic information

Gender:	(1) Male	(2) Female	
Age:	(1) 20 or less	(2) 21–30	
	(3) 31–40	(4) 40+	
Nationality:	(1) UAE	(2) GCC	(3) Arab
Place of residence	(1) Abu Dhabi	(2) Al Ain	(3) The Western Region
	(4) Dubai	(5) Sharjah	(6) Ajman
	(7) Umm Al Quwain	(8) Ras Al Khaimah	(9) Fujairah
Education:	(1) Below secondary school		(2) Secondary school
	(3) Diploma or university degree		(4) Postgraduate degree
Income:	(1) AED 10,000 or less	(2) AED 10,001 – 20,000	
	(3) AED 20,001 – 30,000	(4) AED 30,001 – 40,000	
	(5) Above AED 40,000		

Notes

NOTES

Preface

1. For more on the book, see: Jamal Sanad Al-Suwaidi, *Prospects for the American Age: Sovereignty and Influence in the New World Order* (Abu Dhabi: The Emirates Center for Strategic Studies and Research, 1st edition, 2014).

2. The Holy Quran (24:39).

3. *Lisan Al-Arab* Dictionary (Beirut: Dar Sadir Publishers, 2003), Part 8, the entry "Qawa'" [in Arabic], p. 304.

4. Hassan Yousuf Shihab Al-Deen, "The Phenomenon of Mirage between Science and the Facts of the Quran," an academic paper presented at the Tenth World Conference on Scientific Miracles in the Qur'an and Sunna [in Arabic], Turkey (March 11-13, 2011); (http://goo.gl/mSIsHR)

5. See: (https://library.islamweb.net/newlibrary/display_book.php?idfrom=2301 &idto=2301&bk_no=61&ID=2326).

6. Talal Abdul Kareem Al-Arab, "I am not the First to be Deceived by the Mirage" [in Arabic], the Kuwaiti daily *Al-Qabas*, March 20, 2014. (http://www.alqabas.com.kw/node/849325).

7. Hassan Yousuf Shihab Al-Deen, op. cit. (http://goo.gl/mSIsHR).

8. The Holy Quran (24:39).

9. Hassan Yousuf Shihab Al-Deen, op. cit. (http://goo.gl/mSIsHR).

10. Ibid. (http://goo.gl/mSIsHR).

11. Muhammad Saeed Al-Fateesi, "The Islamists and the Revolutions of the Arab Spring" [in Arabic]; (n.d.); (http://www.factjo.com/pages/print2.aspx?id=2196).

12. Mark Tessler, "The Civic Orientations of Arab Politics: Selected Findings from the Arab Barometer," Emirates lecture Series no. 115 (Abu Dhabi: The Emirates Center for Strategic Studies and Research, 2014) pp. 1-45. See the video of the lecture at: (http://www.ecssr.ac.ae/ECSSR/appmanager/portal/

ecssr?_nfpb=true&_nfls=false&_pageLabel=ActivitiesPage&eventId=%2FActivities%
2FLectures%2FActivities_4202.xml&_event=viewDetails&lang=ar).

13. Ibid. (http://www.ecssr.ac.ae/ECSSR/appmanager/portal/ecssr?_nfpb=true
&_nfls=false&_pageLabel=ActivitiesPage&eventId=%2FActivities%2FLectures
%2FActivities_4202.xml&_event=viewDetails&lang=ar).

14. The principle of *hakimiyya* means that God (Allah) is the ruler. This concept
was first adopted and announced by Abu Al-A'la Al-Mawdoodi. Later, Sayyid
Qutb provided a realistic dogmatic framework for the transfer of the concept to
its political form. *Hakimiyya* was to become the basis of his thought, as well as
the focus of his books *Signposts on the Road* and *In the Shade of the Quran*. For
more about Sayyid Qutb's view of the concept of *hakimiyya*, see: Hisham
Ahmad Ja'far, Political Dimensions of the hakimiyya Concept: An
Epistemological Perspective [in Arabic]; (Virginia: International Institute of
Islamic Thought, 1995), pp. 221–251. Also see: Muhammad Hafiz Diyab,
Sayyid Qutb: Discourse and Ideologies [in Arabic]; (Cairo: Dar Ru'ya for
Publishing and Distribution, 2010), pp. 197–215.

15. Al-Sadiq al-Mahdi, "Fires of Extremism in the Islamic World" [in Arabic],
Sudaress, electronic newspaper, July 10, 2014. (http://www.sudaress.com/
hurriyat/158115).

16. Jamal Abdul Nasser, "The Muslim is More Sanctified than the Kaaba" [in
Arabic], *Al-Ahram*, July 27, 2013. (http://www.ahram.org.eg/NewsQ/223138.
aspx).

17. The Quran Interpretation of Ibn Katheer [in Arabic]; (http://islamhudaa.
com/e-Quran/images/katheer-p30.htm).

18. Mahir Yaseen El-Fahl, "The Sanctity of the Blood of Muslims" [in Arabic],
Said Al-Fawaid website. (http://www.saaid.net/ahdath/77.htm).

19. The Holy Quran (16:33).

20. Nermine Ishra, "Ibn Rushd Offers a Philosophical Present at the Anniversary
of his Birth" [in Arabic], *Al-Wafd*, April 14, 2014 (http://bit.ly/1wlJdGD).

21. For more on the thought of Ibn Rushd, see: Mahmood Hamdi Zakzook, "The
concept of Enlightenment in the thought of Ibn Rushd" [in Arabic] in Murad

Wehbeh and Mona Abu Sinnah (eds.), *Ibn Rushd and Enlightenment* (Cairo: Dar Al-Thaqafah Al-Jadeeda, Kuwait: Dar Qertas for Publishing and Distribution, 1997), pp. 105–113.

22. Khalid Muntasir, "We have Killed Ibn Rushd to Revive Ibn Taymiyyah" [in Arabic], *Al-Watan* electronic portal, April 14, 2014. (http://www.elwatannews.com/news/details/461576).

23. Ibid. (http://www.elwatannews.com/news/details/461576).

24. Raghib Al-Sirjani, "Ibn Al-Haitham ... the Legendary Scientist" [in Arabic]; (http://goo.gl/JNnd1).

25. Ibraheem Al-Nima, "The Mirage in the Quran: A Scientific Miracle" [in Arabic]; (http://www.beatona.net/CMS/index.php?option=com_content&view=article&id=1341&lang=ar&Itemid=84).

26. Regarding the dialectic of the text and the mind in Islam, see: Muhammad Younis Hashim, *Philosophical Schools: The Dialectic of Text, Mind and Interest* [in Arabic]; (Giza, Egypt: Dar Zohoor Al-Ma'rifa Wa Al-Baraka, 2013), pp. 71–90.

27. Abdullah Ahmad Al-Yousuf, "The Legitimacy of Disagreement: A Methodological basic Study of the Other Opinion in Islamic Thought [in Arabic]. 2nd edition, 2004, p. 87 (http://alyousif.org/?ext=1&act=media&code=books&f=79).

28. Ibid., p. 85.

29. See: (http://www.sahab.net/forums/index.php?showtopic=63204).

30. From the Poetry of Antara Ibn Shadda Al-Absi, the poem "He Who of High Ranks Would not Harbor Hatred" [in Arabic], *The International Encyclopedia of Arabic Poetry* (http://www.adab.com/modules.php?name=Sh3er&doWhat=shqas&qid=10650&r=&rc=5).

Introduction

1. Regarding the concept of centrism in Islam, see: Hassan Hanafi, *The Concept of Centrism in Islam: Centrism in Theory and Practice* [in Arabic]; (Amman: Dar Jareer for Publishing and Distribution, Arabic Thought Forum, 1st Edition, 2005), pp. 57–68.

2. The Holy Quran (28:77).

3. Jad Al-Rab Ameen Abdul Majeed, Speech at a Ramadan evening, Emirates Writers Union, Abu Dhabi, 13 July 2014 (http://www.awqaf.gov.ae/News Item.aspx?SectionID=7&RefID=2343).

4. Regarding the concept of excess in religion, see: Sabir Ta'eema, *Excess and Excessive Groups of Islamists in Light of Ancestors' Doctrine* [in Arabic]; (Cairo: Madbooli Bookshop, 2009), pp. 76–90.

5. Ahmad Abdullah Kassar, "Centrism of Islam in Manners and Behavior" [in Arabic]; (http://www.iasj.net/iasj?func=fulltext&aId=78690).

6. "Pure Islam is Based on Centrism and Moderation" [in Arabic], *Al-Riyadh* newspaper, July 25, 2008 (http://www.alriyadh.com/362159).

7. The Holy Quran (2:143).

8. "Pure Islam is Based on Centrism and Moderation" [in Arabic], op. cit. (http://www.alriyadh.com/362159).

9. Ibn Hajar said in *Fath Al-Bari* (Part 13, p. 278) on Overdoing: "It is exaggeration in something and strictness in it beyond limits" [in Arabic], Sahab Salafi Network (http://www.sahab.net/forums/index.php?showtopic=78515).

10. "Debate: Belonging to a religious party is not one of the pillars of Islam, Imam Muhammad Mutwalli Al-Sha'rawi rejects the linking between belonging to Islam and joining a Brotherhood organization or party" [in Arabic]. Al-Arab newspaper, London, October 23, 2013 (http://alarab.co.uk/?id=6604).

11. The Holy Quran (38:29).

12. The Holy Quran (47:24).

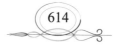

13. Ingmar Karlsson, "Islam and Europe: Confrontation or Coexistence?" Sameer Butani (trans.); (Cairo: Al-Shurooq International Bookshop, 1ˢᵗ edition, 2003), p. 77.

14. The Freedom and Justice Party Program, the Arab Republic of Egypt [in Arabic]; (http://www.fj-p.com/Party_Program.aspx#الحريات_والإصلاح_السياسي).

15. Ingmar Karlsson, op. cit., p. 82.

16. Abdullah Ibn Musa Al-Ta'ir, "Muslim Brotherhood and Demonization of Others" [in Arabic], Al-Riyadh newspaper, July 23, 2013 (http://www.alriyadh.com/854218).

17. Dar Al-Islam is the land of Muslims wherever they are. As Muhammad Abid Al-Jabiri argues, it is a land of peace where warring among its – Muslim - people is impermissible unless it is a war against bandits who disobey the general order and attack people and their properties. The conceptual contrast of that is Dar Al-Harb (the land of war) which is the non-Muslim land engaging in war with Muslims and whose people have no peace treaties with Muslims. See: Muhammad Abid Al-Jabiri, "Islamic Concepts: Dar Al-Islam and Dar Al-Harb" [in Arabic], Al-Ittihad newspaper, UAE, August 18, 2009 (http://www.alittihad.ae/wajhatdetails.php?id=47406).

18. Al-Sayyid Walad Abah, "Political Islam and the Concept of Umma: The National Trap" [in Arabic], Al-Ittihad newspaper, February 17, 2014, p. 30.

19. Sudfa Muhammad Mahmood, Historical Evolution of Religion in International Relations [in Arabic], May 2010, p. 29 (http://www.academia.edu/4097083/_).

20. Al-Waseet Dictionary (Cairo: Al-Shurooq International Bookshop, 4ᵗʰ edition, 2008), p. 598.

21. See: N. S. Gill, "Trojan Horse," About website (http://ancienthistory.about.com/od/troyilium/g/TrojanHorse.htm).

22. Bahaa Tahir, "Secular State and Religious State" [in Arabic], Al-Ahram newspaper, September 11, 2011 (http://www.ahram.org.eg/archive/The-Writers/News/113764.aspx).

23. Bernard Lewis, "What Went Wrong? Western Impact and Middle Eastern Response," *Phoenix*, London, 2002, p. 75.

24. The Holy Quran (18:29).

25. The Holy Quran (16:125).

26. The Holy Quran (109).

27. Hassan Jabir, et al., *Renewal of Religious Thought* [in Arabic]; (Beirut: Institution of Contemporary Religious Thought, 2009), pp. 5–7. See also: Tawfeeq Al-Saif, *Modernity as a Religious Need* [in Arabic]; (Beirut: Arab Scientific Publishers, 2006), pp. 69–80.

28. Muhammad Al-Waqeedi, op. cit., p. 363.

29. "Caid Essebsi is President of Tunisia, and Al-Marzooqi Congratulates him" [in Arabic], Alarabiya.net, 21 December 2014 (http://goo.gl/AVa8GD).

30. The Holy Quran (2:186).

31. The Holy Quran (3:64).

32. The Holy Quran (9:31).

33. The Holy Quran (2:165).

34. Saad Al-Deen Hilali, "Falsehood about Marriage of Minor Girls" [in Arabic], *Al-Watan* newspaper, October 4, 2012 (http://www.elwatannews.com/news/details/57129).

35. Saif Al-Deen Abdul Fattah, *State's Nationalization of Religion: a Look into the Records of Egyptian Citizenship: The Unholy March* [in Arabic] (Cairo: Al-Shurroq international bookshop, 2005), pp. 14–15.

36. Fahmi Jadaan, "Is it Possible to have an Islamic Secularism?" in Sameer Maqdisi et al., *Arab Culture and the Issues of Development and Modernization* [in Arabic]; (Amman: Dar Al-Farsi Publishing and Distribution, 2011), pp. 66–68.

37. The Holy Quran (11:61).

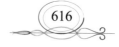

38. Fahmi Jadaan, op. cit., pp. 66–68.

39. Sayyid Muhammad Saeed Al-Tabatabai Al-Hakeem, "The Importance of Mind in the Quran and Sunna" [in Arabic], Dar Sayyida Ruqayya for the Holy Quran website, September 5, 2012 (http://www.ruqayah.net/subject.php?id= 1566).

40. The Holy Quran (2:269).

41. The Holy Quran (3:118).

42. Ingmar Karlsson, op. cit., pp. 82–83.

43. Ibid., pp. 82–83.

44. The Holy Quran (39:9).

45. The Holy Quran (58:11).

46. Saheeh Al-Bukhari, *Book of Knowledge, Chapter on Knowledge before Saying and Action* [in Arabic]; and Saheeh Muslim, *Book of Remembrance of Allah, Chapter on the Merit of an Assembly for the Recitation of the Quran* [in Arabic]; (http://www. alminbar.net/alkhutab/khutbaa.asp?mediaURL=1811#_ftn3).

47. Muhammad Al-Waqeedi & Ahmeeda Al-Naifar, *Why Did the Arab Renaissance Fail?* [in Arabic]; (Beirut: Dar Al-Fikr Al-Muaasir, 2002), pp. 369–370.

48. Ibraheem Gharaiba, "Political Islam … Meteors Sparkled in the Sky of the Arab World and Burned out" [in Arabic], *Al-Majalla* journal, December 31, 2013 (http://www.majalla.com/arb/2013/12/article55249377).

49. Ibid. (http://www.majalla.com/arb/2013/12/article55249377).

50. Regarding the position of political religious groups towards the dialectic of religion and politics, see: Muhammad Helmi Abdulwahhab, *The Religious and the Sacrilegious: Religion and Politics in the Thought of Islamic Movements* [in Arabic]; (Cairo: Dar Al-Ain Publishing, 2009), pp. 15–49.

51. The Galileo Project (http://galileo.rice.edu/chr/inquisition.html).

52. Laila Zaidan, "Palestine and the New Inquisition Colors" [in Arabic], Palestine Website, December 2012 (http://palestine.assafir.com/Article.aspx?Article ID=2413).

53. Ahmad Abdul Malik, "Inquisition Courts Republics" [in Arabic], *Al-Ittihad* newspaper, UAE, August 30, 2012 (http://www.alittihad.ae/wajhatdetails. php?id=67764).

54. There are various estimates of the number of victims of the church in that period. Some sources estimate the number of victims of torture, killing and burning perpetrated by the Inquisition courts during 1570–1630 to be about 50,000 persons. See: Muhammad Ibn Ali Al-Mahmood, "Europe and the Ages of Darkness ... the Struggle of Enlightened Mind" [in Arabic], *Al-Riyadh* newspaper, Saudi Arabia, no. 14332, September 20, 2007 (http://www.alriyadh.com/280951). Other estimates indicate that there were about 32,000 scholars among 300,000 persons brought to the Inquisition courts by the church. See: Hassan Jabir, "The Church in Confrontation with Reason and Science" [in Arabic], Al-Najaf website (http://www.al-najaf.org/resalah/13/04_jaber.htm).

55. Faisal Al-Soofi, "The Salafi Thought and the Church Obscurantism in the Middle Ages" [in Arabic], Al-motamar.net (http://www.almotamar.net/1775. htm).

56. Ibid (http://www.almotamar.net/1775.htm).

57. Ashraf Salih Muhammad, "Our Glorious Civilization during the Middle Ages," *Alwaei Al-Islamic* magazine (Kuwait), no date [in Arabic]; (http://alwaei. gov.kw/site/Pages/ChildDetails.aspx?PageId=168&Vol=581).

58. Muhammad Ibn Ali Al-Mahmood, op. cit. (http://www.alriyadh.com/280 951).

59. Abdul Wahhab Al-Maseeri, *Partial Secularism and Total Secularism* [in Arabic]; (Cairo: Dar Al-Shurooq, 3rd edition, 2008), vol. 1, p. 122.

60. Abdul Kareem Soroush, *Tradition and Secularism: Structures and Pillars, Backgrounds and Facts*, Ahmad Al-Qabanji (trans.); (Beirut: Al-Jamal Publications, 2009), p. 141. For further details on Muhammad Iqbal's thought and opinions about the revival and renewal of religious thought, see: Muhammad Iqbal, *Renewal of Religious Thought in Islam* [in Arabic], Muhammad Yousef Adas (trans.); (Cairo/Beirut: Egyptian and Lebanese Bookshop, 2011), pp. 243–301.

61. Hamada Mahmood Ismaeel, *Hassan Al-Banna and the Muslim Brotherhood group between Religion and Politics 1928–1949* [in Arabic]; (Cairo: Dar Al-Shurooq, 2010), pp. 6–141; Hussam Tammam, *The Transformation of the Muslim Brotherhood: Disintegration of Ideology and the End of the Organization* [in Arabic]; (Cairo: Madbouly Bookshop, 2006), pp. 98–181; and Tawfeeq Al-Wa'ee, *The Muslim Brotherhood – the Largest Islamic Movement: Suspicions and Responses* [in Arabic]; (Cairo: Al-Manar Islamic bookshop, 2001), pp. 141–170.

62. Abdul Raheem Ali, *The Muslim Brotherhood: A Look into the Secret Files* [in Arabic]; (Cairo: the General Egyptian Book Organization, 2011), p. 265.

63. "The IMF Loan Changes the Positions of Political Forces in Egypt" [in Arabic], *Al-Sharq Al-Awsat* (London), 29 August 2012 (http://classic.aawsat.com/details.asp?section=6&issueno=12328&article=692882#.VJ-JHULbE).

64. "ILO: Unemployment in Arab Countries Twice the Global Rate" [in Arabic], Elaph electronic newspaper, February 27, 2014 (http://www.elaph.com/Web/Economics/2014/2/881222.html).

65. United Nations (UN), "The 2013 Human Development Report," the United Nations Development Programme in the Arab States [in Arabic], March 14, 2013 (http://bit.ly/1CGM7cj).

66. Assad Ahmad Mustafa, "The Muslim Brotherhood and the Unanswered Questions," in *The Formation of the Muslim Brotherhood* [in Arabic]; (Dubai: Al-Mesbar Studies and Research Centre, vol. 12, December 2007), pp. 170–171.

67. Muhammad Mursi, "The Muslim Brotherhood and Contemporary Islamic Parties" [in Arabic], August 5, 2007, Ikhawanonline website (http://www.ikhwanonline.com/Article.aspx?ArtID=30200&SecID=390).

68. Ibid. (http://www.ikhwanonline.com/Article.aspx?ArtID=30200&SecID=390).

69. For the position of the Muslim Brotherhood regarding Israel during the rule of former president Muhammad Mursi in the Arab Republic of Egypt, see: "Mursi: Signs of Calming down between Hamas and Israel" [in Arabic], Sky News Arabia, November 18, 2012 (http://goo.gl/RuslB5). See also: "Imad Al-Deen Hussein, "Why did not Mursi Fight Israel?" [in Arabic], Alarabiya.net, 12 July 2014 (http://goo.gl/Si67yK).

70. Ammar Ali Hasan, *Suicide of the Muslim Brotherhood: The Fade of Thought, Fall of Ethics and Collapse of the Organization* [in Arabic]; (Cairo: Dar Nahdat Misr for Publishing, 2013), pp. 152–168.

71. "Growing Fears of Transforming Egypt into a Religious State" [in Arabic], November 28, 2012, Deutsche Welle website (http://bit.ly/1pdZcp5).

72. "'The Free Egyptians' and 'Khanaqtoona' Movement Organize 'Brotherhood Liars' Campaign in Alexandria" [in Arabic], *Al-Shurooq* newspaper, Egypt, April 1, 2013 (http://goo.gl/fflpt1).

73. Nasr Muhammad Arif, "The Fatalist Circle: The End of Modernist Islamism of the Muslim Brotherhood" [in Arabic], *Al-Siyassa Al-Dawliyya* Journal, no. 194, October 2013, pp. 63–64.

74. Ibid., p. 63.

75. Salah Al-Deen Arga Dan, *Political Backwardness in Contemporary Islamic Thought* [in Arabic]; (Beirut: Dar. Al-Nafa'is for Printing, Publishing and Distribution, 2002), p. 17.

76. Ibid., p. 18.

77. Ibid., p. 18.

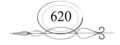

78. Sifat Salama, "An Insight into the Contributions of Islamic Civilization in the Renaissance" [in Arabic], *Al-Sharq Al-Awsat* newspaper, London, July 19, 2011 (http://goo.gl/ekcRej).

79. Imam Sheikh Hassan bin Muhammad bin Al-Attar (1181–1250 AH, 1767–1834 AD) is a Moroccan born in Cairo. He studied religion, geometry, mathematics, and astronomy. He combined both Arab Islamic and Western culture, was fluent in French, and mixed with Arab, French and Turkish contemporary scholars. He called for the study of philosophy, geography, history and literature, and criticized scholars who relied on imitating others. One of his students was Rifa'a Rafi Al-Tahtawi, and Al-Attar played a role in sending Al-Tahtawi to France, and directed him to learn as much as could of the French civilization, hence Al-Tahtawi wrote *Takhlis Al-Ibriz Fi Talkhis Pariz* [The Refinement of Gold: The Abstract of Paris]. Works by Imam Al-Attar include *Hashiyat Al-Attar Ala Al-Jawahir Al-Muntazimat Fi Ukood Al-Makolat* [Al-Attar's Commentary on the Jewels of Writing], a paper on the Ilm Al-Kalam [Science of Discourse], *Manzomat Al-Attar Fi Ilm Al-Nahou* [Al-Attar's Grammar System], and *Rasael Fi Al-Raml Wa Al-Zairja Wa Al-Tib Wa Al-Tashreeh* [Papers on Prescience, Astrology, Medicine and Anatomy]. For more, see: Imam Hasan Al-Attar, "Biographies," at Egyptian Dar Al-Ifta website (http://dar-alifta.org/ViewScientist.aspx?ID=34&LangID=1).

80. Regarding the role of Jamal Al-Deen Al-Afghani, Muhammad Abdu and Rasheed Rida, see: Al-Qutb Muhammad Al-Qutb Tabliyya, *Pioneers of Islamic Thought in Modern Age* [in Arabic]; (Cairo: Dar Al-Fikr Al-Arabi, 1ˢᵗ Edition, 2000), pp. 7–332.

81. Georges Corm, *The Religious Question in the 21st Century*, Khaleel Ahmad Khaleel (trans.); (Beirut: Dar Al-Farabi, 2007), pp. 360–362.

82. Georges Corm, ibid., pp. 71–74.

83. Abdulbaqi Al-Sayyid, *Zahiri School of Thought: Birth, Development, Doctrine and Key Features* [in Arabic], Ahl Al-Zahir website (http://www.zahereyah.com/vb/showthread.php?t=83). See also: Abdulfattah Ahmad Fuad, *Islamic Schools and their Origins of Faith* [in Arabic]; (Alexandria: Dar Al-Wafa for Printing and Publishing, vol. 1, 2003), pp. 467–534.

84. Adam Mitz, *The Islamic Civilization in the Fourth Century AH or the Renaissance* [in Arabic], translated by Muhammad Abdulhadi Abu Zaid (Beirut: Dar Al-Kitab Al-Arabi, vol. 1, no date), pp. 387–388.

85. Ibid., pp. 387–388.

86. Muhammad Al-Waqeedi, op. cit., pp. 166–167.

87. "Project for Revival of Islamic Heritage" [in Arabic], Islam Today website, February 11, 2012 (http://islamtoday.net/nawafeth/artshow-53-163032.htm).

88. Muhammad Al-Waqeedi, op. cit., p. 117.

89. Ibid., 118. 'Revival' could be part of a renaissance movement in the sense of revisiting heritage with the aim of achieving renaissance.

90. The concept of cultural decadence refers to the stagnation of intellectual and cultural life of a civilization or a nation and its backwardness and decline in different aspects of life after a period of development and prosperity. See: Ibraheem Gharaiba, "Book Review: The Islam of the eras of Decadence" [in Arabic], Aljazeera.net, February 12, 2008 (http://aljazeera.net/home/print/92804797-74a7-4675-b919-6682990f8cbe/37a440bd-c4f4-42aa-b715-1b3feb5f436a).

91. Abdul Salam bin Mees, "The Influence of Averroes on Western Political Thought" [in Arabic], *Arab History* journal, no. 15, Summer 2000 (http://www.attarikh-alarabi.ma/Html/adad15partie13.htm).

92. Muhammad Al-Waqeedi, op. cit., p. 121.

93. For further details, see: Imam Muhammad Abdu, *Islam between Science and Civility* [in Arabic], (Damascus, Dar Al-Mada for Culture and Publishing, 2002), pp. 91-99. See also: Mufeed Shihab, "Prospects for Cooperation between Research Centers in the Muslim World" [in Arabic], the Supreme Council for Islamic Affairs, the Arab Republic of Egypt, July 1998 (http://www.elazhar.com/conf_au/10/46.asp).

94. Izz Al-Deen Al-Khattabi, *Modernity Questions and Bets in Society, Politics and Education* [in Arabic]; (Beirut: Arab Scientific Publishers, and Dubai: Muhammad bin Rashid Al Maktoum Foundation, 2009), pp. 44–45.

95. Muhammad Al-Waqeedi, op. cit., p. 165.

96. Maqboola Mas'ood Al-Awami, *Effect of Religious Factor on Emergence of Civilizations* [in Arabic]; (Cairo: Modern Dar Qiba, 2008), pp. 280–281.

97. Ibid., p. 283.

98. Tawfeeq Al-Taweel, *The Story of Conflict between Religion and Philosophy* [in Arabic]; (Cairo: the General Egyptian Book Organization, 2011), p. 136.

99. Ibid., p. 136.

100. Regarding the development and thought of the Kharijites, see: Atallah Najeeb Al-Ma'aita, *Islamic Denominations and the Position of Sunni Muslims Towards Them* [in Arabic]; (Amman: Dar Al-Farooq for Publishing and Distribution), pp. 161–213.

101. "The Kharijites" [in Arabic], Ahl Al-Quran website, January 1, 2012 (http://goo.gl/eU6eBZ).

102. Regarding the development of denominations in Islamic history, see: Abdulfattah Ahmad Fuad, *Islamic Schools and their Origins of Faith* [in Arabic]; (Alexandria: Dar Al-Wafa for Printing and Publishing, vol. 1, 2003), pp. 21–51.

103. Tawfeeq Al-Taweel, op. cit., p. 137.

104. "A Brief Overview on the Emergence of Ilm Al-Kalam" [in Arabic], Ministry of Endowments and Islamic Affairs, Kingdom of Morocco, February 5, 2012 (http://habous.gov.ma/2012-01-26-16-15-16/57-2012-08-28-14-34-54.html).

105. Hussein Al-Ghareeb, "Principles of Islamic Jurisprudence: Origins, Importance and Evolution" [in Arabic], Muslimonline website, August 13, 2009 (http://www.moslimonline.com/?page=artical&id=946).

106. The movement of independent reasoning and interpretation went through several stages in Islamic history. Its origin goes back to the time of the Companions of the Prophet (pbuh), as indicated by some sources, including the following narrative by Maimoon bin Mahran: "When Abu Bakr was presented with a matter to be decided by him, he used to look for an answer in

the Holy Quran. If such an answer was found, he would issue his decision. If not, he would see if the Prophet (pbuh) had decided a similar matter. If he found no similar matter in the Sunnah of the Prophet (pbuh), he would go out and ask Muslims saying: 'I need to decide on this matter. I looked in the Holy Quran and the Sunnah of the Prophet, but found nothing. Are you aware of any similar matter which was decided by the Prophet?' Sometimes the answer would be 'yes,' and people would tell him what the Prophet decided, and he would adopt it." Ja'afar said: "I was told by somebody other than Maimoon that Abu Bakr would then say 'Thank God. Some of us are remembering what the Prophet said and did,' and when he found no answer, he would gather the scholars and consult with them, and if a consensus is reached, he would adopt such a decision." Narrated by Al-Baihaqi (10/114) and deemed as authentic by Al-Hafiz Ibn Hijr in *Al-Fath* (13/342). This was followed by the stage of the four Imams between the 2nd and 4th centuries AH, when jurisprudential terms and schools appeared. This does not mean that the door was wide open for independent reasoning (*ijtihad*) since the time of the Companions; it was within the limits of *qiyas* (analogy) and other similar practices aimed at resolving issues which were not provided for in the Holy Quran or the Prophet's Sunnah. As such, it was not independent reasoning (*ijtihad*) aimed at inferring rules from religious texts, but it became so later with the appearance of the four jurisprudential schools in the 2nd and 3rd centuries AH, when independent reasoning became a source of *Sharia*, besides the Holy Quran, the Prophet's Sunnah, and consensus. Therefore, independent reasoning (*ijtihad*) was used as a source of *Sharia* only if no answer was found in the other three sources, and the early ancestors were conservative about issuing *fatwas*, as indicated by Al-Bara': "I have seen three hundred Companions who participated in the Badr incursion, and they all like that somebody else would issue *fatwas*." See: Ahmad Zooman, "Abu Bakr's Policy when Issuing Judgments" [in Arabic], *Al-Ahram* (Egypt), 18 August 2013 (http://islam.ahram.org.eg/Category/24/40/NewsQ/2231.aspx). See also: Yahya Muhammad, *History and Development of Jurisprudential Reasoning* [in Arabic], Fahm Al-Din website, no date (http://www.fahmaldin.com/index.php?id=98).

107. Abdul Azeez Kaheel, *False Conflict between Text and Reason* [in Arabic], Yaqzat Fikr website, December 16, 2012 (http://feker.net/ar/2012/12/16/ 12933/).

108. Tawfeeq Al-Taweel, op. cit., p. 137.

109. The Holy Quran (88:21–22).

110. Jamal Sanad Al-Suwaidi, "Islam and Socio-Political Change: A Comparative Study of Egyptian, Kuwaiti, and Palestinian Attitudes," unpublished Dissertation Manuscript, University of Wisconsin, 1990.

111. Amira El-Azhary Sonbol, "Egypt," in Shireen T. Hunter (ed.), *The Politics of Islamic Revivalism: Diversity and Unity* (Indianapolis, IN: Indiana University Press, 1988), p. 23. It is worth noting that not all religions believe in God (Allah) and life after death; Buddhism, for example, does not.

112. Religion is a rational, logical and balanced system of beliefs, principles, values and rituals relating to worship of God (Allah) and submission to His will, heavenly orders and teachings, and commitment to His divine message which He reveals to people through messengers and prophets. Abrahamic religions – Islam, Christianity and Judaism – differ from each other in terms of concepts, ideas, beliefs and practices, but the religious feeling is the same. See: Ihsan Muhammad Al-Hassan, *Religious Anthropology: Analytical Study of the Interactive Relationship between Religious Establishment and Society* [in Arabic]; (Amman: Dar Wa'il for publishing, 1st edition, 2005), p. 45. Religion is also defined as the belief in the Creator of the universe and humans and in the teachings and practical functions appropriate for this belief. It is a belief in something that one submits to it and commits himself to it with desire, fear and sanctification, see: Kareem Al-Siraji, *Religious Principles of the Salafi Trends* (Beirut: Dar Al-Salam, 1st edition, 2010), p. 15. In this book, religion is often used to refer to the Islamic religion, which has five pillars as mentioned in the honorable Hadith of the prophet Muhammad (pbuh): "Islam has been built upon five pillars: testifying that there is no God (Allah) but Allah and that Muhammad is the Messenger of Allah, establishing the *salat* (prayer), paying the zakat (obligatory charity), making the *hajj* (pilgrimage) to the House (*Ka'ba*), and fasting in Ramadan." For an explanation of this Hadith, see: "Explanation of the Forty Nawawi Hadeeths," website of Sheikh Muhammad bin Salih Al-Uthaymeen, May 4, 2005 (http://www.ibn othaimeen.com/all/books/article_17764.shtml).

113. These dimensions are based on the explanatory framework presented by Marshall Hodgson. See: Marshall G. S. Hodgson, *The Venture of Islam:*

Conscience and History in a World Civilization, three volumes (Chicago, IL: University of Chicago Press, 1974), vol. 1, pp. 57–60.

114. Ibraheem Khaleel Alyan, "Religious State and Secular State," a working paper presented at the Third Baitul-Maqdis Conference 2012 (http://www.qou.edu/ arabic/researchProgram/researchersPages/ibrahimElaian/r4_ibrahimElaian.pdf).

115. See: Alan R. Taylor, *The Islamic Question in Middle East Politics* (Boulder, CO: Westview Press, 1988), p. 15. See also: Yvonne Y. Haddad, B. Haines and E. Findly, *The Islamic Impact* (New York: Syracuse University Press, 1984), pp. 1–7.

116. Al-Minbar website, a sermon on the merit of mosque construction [in Arabic]; (http://www.alminbar.net/alkhutab/khutbaa.asp?mediaURL=9198).

117. Hassan Hanafi, op. cit., p. 66.

118. Terrance G. Carroll, "Islam and Political Community in the Arab World," *International Journal of Middle East Studies*, no. 18 (1986), 185–204, in particular, p. 189. For more discussion of religion and political identity, see: Crawford Young , *The Politics of Cultural Pluralism* (Madison, WI: University of Wisconsin Press, 1976), Chapter Two. In addition to the above mentioned books, the following two books also discuss this topic: Charles W. Anderson, F. von der Mehden and Crawford Young, *Issues of Political Development* (Englewood Cliffs, NJ: Prentice Hall, Inc., 1967); and Hans Mol (ed.), *Identity and Religion: International, Cross-cultural Approaches* (Thousand Oaks, CA: Sage Publications Inc., 1978).

119. Terrance G. Carroll, op. cit, p. 189.

120. Egyptian teachers and Egyptian curricula have dominated the educational system in many Arab countries for decades. The scores of the student in religious studies may affect his/her academic status.

121. Quoted in: Robin Wright, "'Quiet' Revolution: Islamic Movement's New Phase," *The Christian Science Monitor*, Friday, November 6, 1987.

122. R. Hrair Dekmejian, *Islam in Revolution: Fundamentalism in the Arab World* (Syracuse, NY: Syracuse University Press, 1985), p. 151.

123. To read about the nature of Islam as a religious system, see chapter 2 of this book, pp. 225–260. See also: Donald E. Smith, *Religion, Politics and Social Change in the Third World* (New York, NY: The Free Press, 1971), p. 26.

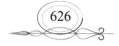

124. Heather Strange, "Traditional Ceremony in an Islamic Milieu: Meleggan Perut Among Malaysian Women," in Freda Hussain (ed.), *Muslim Women* (London: Croom Helm Ltd., 1984), pp. 127–128.

125. Muhammad Qutb, "Shubahat Hawl al-Islam" (Misperceptions of Islam), quoted in James P. Piscatori (ed.), *Islam in the Political Process* (London: Cambridge University Press, 1983), p. 3.

126. Ibid. p. 4

127. Hassan Hanafi, op. cit., p. 63. See also: Fadwa El-Guindi, "Religious Revival and Islamic Survival in Egypt," *International Insight*, vol. 2, no. 1, November and December, 1981, pp. 32–34.

128. The Holy Quran (8:61).

129. "*Fatwas* of Dar Al-Iftaa Al-Massriyya, *fatwa* issued by the former Grand Imam of al-Azhar, Jad Al-Haq Ali Jad Al-Haq concerning the 1979 Peace Treaty" [in Arabic], Al-Maktaba Al-Shamila (http://shamela.ws/browse.php/book-432/page-2571).

130. Hamdi Al-Saeed Salim, "Secret Communications and Connections between Mubarak's Regime and the Muslim Brotherhood before the Revolution" [in Arabic], Middle East Panorama website, March 25, 2013 (http://bit.ly/1qT8Y0q).

131. This group was the first political opposition in Islamic history. For a brief review of the importance of this group, see: James Bill and C. Leiden, *Politics in the Middle East* (Boston, MA: Little, Brown and Company, 1984), pp. 59–60. See also: B.F. Stowasser (ed.), *The Islamic Impulse* (London: Croom Helm, 1987), pp. 303–306.

132. For further details, see: Ashraf El-Sherif, "The Egyptian Muslim Brotherhood's Failures," Carnegie Endowment for International Peace, July 1, 2014 (http://ceip.org/1ueqaNs).

133. The application of Marxism in what was previously known as South Yemen was a unique case. Although Article 9 of the country's constitution stated that: "the State shall direct the society's activity with the aim of achieving the tasks of the national democratic revolution as paving the way for the complete abolition of the exploitation of man by man," Article 47 of the same constitution stipulated that: "Islam is the State Religion." That means South Yemen was different from most communist countries in that it was not secular according to the constitution.

134. The Holy Quran (3:195).

135. The Holy Quran (49:13).

136. Fundamentalism is originally a Protestant term, but has no political connotations for contemporary Protestants, unlike Revivalism, which is a politicized term. Revivalism is a better term to refer to political religious groups, and it is something different from the Islamic traditional current, as argued by several scholars and researchers, including Dr. Ridwan Al-Sayyid. For more on Islam and fundamentalism, see: Bruce B. Lawrence, "Muslim Fundamentalist Movements: Reflections toward a New Approach," in Barbara F. Stowasser (ed.), *The Islamic Impulse*, op. cit., pp. 17–20. People to whom the term fundamentalism applies do not like being called so because they often feel it is "an offensive and derogatory term that suggests narrow-mindedness, bigotry, obscurantism and sectarianism." See: James Barr, *Fundamentalism* (Philadelphia, PA: The Westminster Press, 1978), p. 2. In short, it is important to note the differences between Christian fundamentalism and Islamic fundamentalism (revivalism).

Christian fundamentalism	Islamic fundamentalism
(a) A very strong emphasis on the faultlessness of the Bible; (b) a strong hostility to modern theology and to the methods, results, and implications of modern critical studies of the Bible; (c) an assurance that those who do not share their religious viewpoints are not really true Christians at all.*	a) "A deep and transforming concern with the socio-moral degeneration of Muslim society; (b) a call to go back to original Islam and shed the superstitions inculcated by popular forms of sufism, to overturn the primacy of traditional schools of law, and to attempt to perform *ijtihad*— that is, to rethink for oneself the meaning of the original message; (c) call to remove the crushing burden of a predeterministic outlook produced by popular religion but also materially contribute to the almost ubiquitous influence of Ash'ari theology; and (d) a call to carry out this revivalist reform through armed force (*jihad*) if necessary."**

*   James Barr, p. 1.

**   Fazlur Rahman, "Islam: Challenges and Opportunities," in Alford T. Welch and Pierre Cachia (eds.), *Islam: Past Influence and Present Challenge* (Edinburgh: Edinburgh University Press, 1979), p. 317.

137. Shireen T. Hunter, "Islamic Fundamentalism: What it Really is and Why it Frightens the West," *SAIS Review*, vol. 6, no. 1, Winter, 1986, p. 191.

138. Abdullah Ahmad Al-Yousuf, op. cit., p. 80 (http://alyousif.org/?ext=1&act=media&code=books&f=79).

139. Ibid., p. 80 (http://alyousif.org/?ext=1&act=media&code=books&f=79).

140. Saad Eddin Ibrahim, "Anatomy of Egypt's Militant Islamic Groups: Methodological Notes and Preliminary Findings," *International Journal of Middle East Studies*, vol. 12, no. 4, December, 1980, pp. 423–424.

141. Alan R. Taylor, op. cit., p. 1.

142. For a detailed discussion of the Western misconception of Islam as a religion and culture, see: Bernard Lewis, "The Return to Islam," *Commentary*, January, 1976, pp. 39–41. See also: Mohammad Ayoob, "Introduction: The Myth of the Monolith," in Mohammad Ayoob (ed.), *The Politics of Islamic Reassertion* (London: Croom Helm Ltd., 1981), p. 1, and James Bill and Carol Leiden, op. cit., pp. 134 ff.

143. See: (http://www.alittihad.ae/wajhatdetails.php?id=72658).

144. Sulaiman Jawda, "It is not a State and it is not Islamic" [in Arabic], *Al-Sharq Al-Awsat* newspaper, September 8, 2014 (http://www.aawsat.com/home/article/177041).

145. Riad Mansoor, Jordan: Security Forces Arrest a "Terrorist ISIL" Cell in Central Amman" [in Arabic], *Al-Madeena* newspaper, Saudi Arabia, September 11, 2014 (http://www.al-madina.com/node/556495).

146. "Riyadh Wants to Make Sure of the Percentage of Saudis who Support ISIL" [in Arabic], Erem News Agency, July 23, 2014 (http://www.eremnews.com/?id=52353).

147. Ronald Chilcote, *Theories of Comparative Politics: The Search for a Paradigm* (Boulder, CO: Westview Press, 1981), pp. 16–17.

148. B.F. Stowasser, op. cit., p. 3.

149. These characteristics are based on: Hrair Dekmejian's discussion in *Islam in Revolution: Fundamentalism in the Arab World* (Syracuse, NY: Syracuse University Press, 1985), p. 4.

150. Ridwan Al-Sayyid, *Political Islamic Movements and the Future* [in Arabic], Emirates Lecture Series no. 2 (Abu Dhabi: The Emirates Center for Strategic Studies and Research, 1997), pp. 16–27.

151. James A. Bill, "Resurgent Islam in the Persian Gulf," in *Foreign Affairs*, vol. 63, no. 1, 1984, p. 112.

152. Quoted in: Robin Wright, "Religion and Politics: A Global Phenomenon," *The Christian Science Monitor,* November 4, 1987 (http://www.csmonitor.com/1987/1104/zfun1.html).

153. G.H. Jansen, "Militant Islam: The Historic Whirlwind," *New York Times Magazine,* January 6, 1980, p. 43. Quoted in: John O. Voll, *Islam: Continuity and Changes in the Modern World* (Boulder, CO: Westview Press, 1982), p. 350).

154. Saad Eddin Ibrahim, op. cit., p. 423.

155. For further discussion, see: John Esposito (ed.), *Islam and Development: Religion and Socio-political Change* (Syracuse, NY: Syracuse University Press, 1980), pp. ix–xii. Esposito explains: "while modernization has often meant the curtailment of the traditional power and influence of the religious establishment (clerics) as government advisors and protectors of the law, religion itself has not been weakened appreciably." See also: Bernard Lewis, preface, in Gilles Kepel, *Muslim Extremism in Egypt: The Prophet and Pharaoh* (Berkeley and Los Angeles, CA: University of California Press, 1986), p. 11. Bernard Lewis argues that "the doctrine of the separation of church and state is now accepted in much though not all of the Christian or post-Christian world. In historic Islam, such a doctrine was not only non-existent but would have been meaningless. One can separate two things; one can hardly separate one. For a traditional Muslim, mosque and state are one and the same. They are not separate or separable institutions, and there is no way of cutting through the tangled web of human activities and allocating certain things to religion, others to politics, some to the state and some to a specifically religious authority."

156. Mahathir Mohamad, "Islam is not an Obstacle to Modernization; the Problem Lies in Some Scholars Who Misinterpret Religion" [in Arabic], *Al-Sharq Al-Awsat* (London), 22 February 2002 (http://classic.aawsat.com/details.asp?article=89611&issueno=8487#.VKJ_eULbE).

157. Richard Hrair Dekmejian, "The Islamic Revival in the Middle East and North Africa," *Current History*, April 1980, p. 170.

158. "Main Macroeconomic Indicators Issued by the Central Bank of Egypt," Central Bank of Egypt website (http://cbe.org.eg/CBE_Bulletin/2014/Bulletin_2014_5_May/08_Indicator(Real_Sector)1.pdf).

159. Ibid. (http://cbe.org.eg/CBE_Bulletin/2014/Bulletin_2014_5_May/09_Indicator (Real_Sector)2.pdf).

160. Ibid. (http://cbe.org.eg/CBE_Bulletin/2014/Bulletin_2014_5_May/07_Indicator (Fiscal_Sector).pdf).

161. Abdul Qadir Shuhaib, "Legitimacy of Achievement" [in Arabic], *Veto* newspaper, June 30, 2014 (http://www.vetogate.com/1093012).

162. This issue arose clearly during the Israeli aggression on the Gaza Strip in August 2014 when political religious groups strongly criticized the moderate Arab regimes accusing them of supporting Israel in that conflict. See: Amr Ameenu, "A Disclosure: the Position of Each Arab State towards the War on Gaza" [in Arabic], Al-Taqreer website, August 4, 2014 (http://bit.ly/1tN 11Mc).

163. Sami A. Hanna, "Islam, Socialism, and National Trials," *The Muslim World*, vol. 58, 1968, p. 284.

164. Hassan Hanafi, op. cit., pp. 61–62. For similar views, see: Fouad Ajami, *The Arab Predicament: Arab Political Thought and Practice Since 1967* (Cambridge: Cambridge University Press, 1981), p. 5. In the views of political religious groups, "the Arabs had lost the wars against Israel not because they were worshiping, but because they had lost their faith." Ajami, p. 54.

165. Jamal Sanad Al-Suwaidi and Ahmed Rashad El Safti (eds.), *Political Islamic Movements and Authority in the Arab World: The Rise and Fall* [in Arabic]; (Abu Dhabi: The Emirates Center for Strategic Studies and Research, 2014), pp. 9–10.

166. Michael C. Hudson, "Islam and Political Development," in John L. Esposito (ed.), *Islam and Development, Religion and Socio-political Change* (New York, NY: Syracuse University Press, 1980), p. 15. Hudson's chapter is very informative on the role of Islam as a political ideology.

167. Roland Robertson, *The Sociological Interpretation of Religion* (New York, NY: Schocken Books, 1970), p. 154.

168. Ibid., p. 154. For further details on the history and the various approaches to the study of religion and society, see Robertson, op. cit., Chapter Two, pp. 7–33. Also see one of the most powerful and stimulating analyses about the study of religion by Robert Wuthnow, "Two Traditions in the Study of Religion," *Journal for the Scientific Study of Religion*, 1981, pp. 16–32.

169. Roland Robertson, "The Development and Modern Implications of the Classical Sociological Perspective on Religion and Revolution," in Bruce Lincoln (ed.), *Religion, Rebellion, Revolution: An Interdisciplinary and Cross-Cultural Collection of Essays* (London: The Macmillan Press Ltd., 1985), pp. 242–243.

170. William A. Galston, "Public Morality and Religion in the Liberal State," *Political Studies*, Fall 1986, vol. XIX, no. 4, published by APSA, p. 807. See pp. 801–832 for a thorough discussion of religion and politics in Western societies.

171. Ahmad Anwar, "Theory and Methodology of Sociology" [in Arabic]; (faculty.ksu.edu.sa/75863/Publications/1.doc).

172. Raimundo Panikkar, "Religion or Politics: The Western Dilemma," in Peter H. Merkl and Ninian Smart (ed.), Religion and Politics in the Modern World (New York, NY: New York University Press, 1983), p. 45. The highest good [*Summum bonum*] is defined as the realization of the plentitude of human life.

173. Ninian Smart, "Conclusion," in Peter H. Merkl and Ninian Smart, op. cit., p. 268.

174. Gilles Kepel, *Muslim Extremism in Egypt: The Prophet and Pharaoh* (Berkeley and Los Angeles: University of California Press, 1984), p. 228.

175. Bryan S. Turner, *Weber and Islam: A Critical Study* (London and Boston, MA: Routledge and Kegal Paul, 1974), p. 153.

176. Ibid., p. 153.

177. For a detailed discussion of the modernization approach see: Frank X. Sutton, "Social Theory and Comparative Politics," in Harry Eckstein and David Apter (eds.), *Comparative Politics: A Reader* (New York, NY: Free Press of Glencoe,

1963); Marion Levy, *Modernization and the Structure of Societies* (Princeton, NJ: Princeton University Press, 1966); Cyril E. Black, *The Dynamics of Modernization* (New York, NY: The Free Press, 1966); Cyril E. Black (ed.), *Comparative Modernization: A Reader* (New York, NY: The Free Press, 1976); and Dankwart A. Rustow, *A World of Nations: Problems of Political Modernization* (Washington, DC: Brookings Institution, 1976).

178. Samuel P. Huntington, "The Change to Change: Modernization, Development and Politics," in Cyril E. Black, op. cit., 1976, p. 35.

179. Ibid., p. 35. It may be noted that the vague and imprecise definition of modernization has influenced scholars' distinctions between modern and traditional societies. For instance, Frank Sutton described the main characteristics of modern and traditional societies as follows:

Modern Society	Traditional Society
1- Predominance of universalistic, specific, and achievement norms.	1- Predominance of ascriptive, particularistic, diffuse patterns.
2- High degree of social mobility (in a general, not necessarily in a "vertical" sense).	2- Stable local groups and limited spatial mobility.
3- Well-developed occupational system, insulated from other social structures.	3- Relatively simple and stable "occupational" differentiation.
4- "Egalitarian" class system based on generalized patterns of occupational achievement.	4- A "differential" stratification system of diffuse impact.
5- Prevalence of "associations," i.e., functionally specific, non-ascriptive structures.	

For further details, see: Frank X. Sutton, op. cit., p. 67.

180. Dean C. Tipps, op. cit., p. 75. For a similar critique, see Tom Bottomore, *The New York Review of Books*, October 8, 1970, p. 16. Naomi Caiden and Aaron Wildavsky summarize the critique against modernization theories as follows: "Modernization theories assume transformation from a traditional to a modern state, but it gives little indication how this journey may be achieved; it is static, not dynamic. They assume a dichotomy between traditional and modern without considering the stages in between and patterns of behavior that may even prevent modernization taking place as worthy of discussion in their own right. They equate

modernization with Westernization, and consider current Western society as the ultimate goal for development of other nations ... worst of all modernization theories were culture-bound, seeing economic growth not only as the most important aim, but stipulating that its attainment was irrevocably intertwined with Western organizational forms and values." See: Naomi Caiden and Aaron Wildavsky, *Planning and Budgeting in Poor Countries* (New York: John Wiley, 1974), pp. 27–28. Quoted in: Donald Rothchild and Robert L. Curry, Jr., *Scarcity, Choice, and Public Policy in Middle Africa* (Berkeley, CA: University of California Press, 1978), p. 95.

181. James O'Connell, "The Concept of Modernization," *South Atlantic Quarterly*, LXIV (Autumn, 1965), pp. 549.

182. Samuel Huntington, *Political Order in Changing Societies* (New Haven, CT: Yale University Press, 1968), p. 32.

183. Samuel Huntington and Joan Nelson, *No Easy Choice: Political Participation in Developing Countries* (Cambridge, MA: Harvard University Press, 1977), p. 17.

184. Muhammad Al-Waqeedi, op. cit., p. 365.

Chapter 1

1. The Arab and Muslim worlds, in Asia and Africa alone, in different periods in the 20th century were under the rule of colonial powers including the United Kingdom, the French Republic, the Kingdom of Holland, the Kingdom of Belgium and the Kingdom of Spain; all of which were European Christian nations. For further details, see: Jamal Hamdan, *Colonization and Liberation Strategy* (Cairo: Dar Al-Shurooq, 1983), pp. 64–76, 130–141.

2. The Ottoman Empire, which was a religious and temporal extension of the Caliphate, expanded to the north, east, south and west of the Mediterranean Sea. It was considered the sole legitimate religious authority by most Muslims, even those who were not under its control. For further details on the Ottoman state, see: Andrew Wheatcroft, *The Ottomans: Dissolving Images* [in Arabic]; (Abu Dhabi: The Emirates Center for Strategic Studies and Research, 2014), pp. 31–49. See also: Jamal Hamdan, op. cit. pp. 41–48.

3. Abdulla Muhammad Ali Al-Falahi, "From Misconceptions to Misbeliefs: the Phenomenon of Ideological Extremism and its Practice among some Contemporary (Islamic) Groups" [in Arabic], *Al-Jamhooriyya* newspaper, Yemen, February 7, 2010 (http://www.algomhoriah.net/atach.php?id=27755).

4. "ISIL's Proclamation of an Islamic Caliphate and Reactions to it" [in Arabic], Al-Sharq Al-Arabi Center for Cultural and Strategic Studies, July 2, 2014 (http://bit.ly/1pfcihc).

5. Graham Fuller, "The Future of Political Islam," *Foreign Affairs*, vol. 81, no. 2, March–April 2002 (http://bit.ly/1pYGSfw).

6. The Holy Quran (2:193).

7. The Holy Quran (5:44).

8. Ahmad Sha'ban, "Following the Teachings of Previous Religions" [in Arabic], *Al-Ittihad* (UAE), July 23, 2014 (http://www.alittihad.ae/details.php?id=64586&y=2014&article=full).

9. The Holy Quran (16:106). For more about the interpretation of this verse, see: Rabi bin Hadi Al-Madkhali, "Islamic Sharia is Lenient and God Encourages

Muslims to do What He has Allowed Them" [in Arabic], Sahab Salafi Network, February 13, 2011, (http://www.sahab.net/home/?p=94).

10. Are Knudsen, "Political Islam in the Middle East," Chr. Michelsen Institute (CMI) Reports, Bergen, Norway, 2003 (http://goo.gl/mUIbcn).

11. Charles Hirschkind, "What Is Political Islam?" *Middle East Report*, vol. 27, no. 205, Winter 1997 (http://www.merip.org/mer/mer205/what-political-islam).

12. Mohammed Ayoob, "The future of political Islam: the importance of external variables," *International Affairs* (Royal Institute of International Affairs), vol. 81, no. 5, October 2005 (http://onlinelibrary.wiley.com/Doi/10.1111/j.1468-2346.2005.00496.x/pdf). Also see: Fuller, "The Future…" op. cit.

13. Jamal Sanad Al-Suwaidi, op. cit., pp. 6–70.

14. François Burgat, *Political Islam: the Voice of the South: New Insight into the Islamic Movement in North Africa*, Lauren Fawzi Zikra (trans.); Nasr Hamid Abu Zaid (reviewer); (Cairo: Dar Al-Aalam Al-Thalith, 2001), p. 72.

15. Ibid., p. 128.

16. Gilles Kepel, *Jihad: the Expansion and Decline of Islamism*, Nabeel Saad (trans.), Anwar Mugheeth (reviewer); (Cairo: Dar Al-Aalam Al-Thalith, 1st edition, 2005), p. 84.

17. Usama Salih, "Cautious Approach: Will the Rising Islamic Movements Restructure the Arab State?" [in Arabic], *Al-Siyassan Al-Dawliyya*, no. 188, April 2012 (http://www.siyassa.org.eg/NewsQ/2369.aspx). For information about Morocco's "Justice and Development Party," see (http://www.pjd.ma).

18. The 30 Years War between Protestants and Catholics (1618–1648) was one of the bloodiest and most destructive wars in European history before World Wars I and II in the 20th century. In his book *The Thirty Years War: The European Tragedy*, British historian Peter H. Wilson estimated the number of victims of that war at 1.8 million troops and at least 3.2 million civilians. The German Empire lost more than fifth of its population. For further information see: "The Thirty-Year War: Europe's Tragedy" [in Arabic], *Al-Bayan* (UAE); (http://www.albayan.ae/paths/books/1288543294499-2010-11-13-1.303983).

19. Robert Marks, *The Origins of the Modern World: Fate and Fortune in the Rise of the West* (New York, NY: Rowman & Littlefield Publishers, Inc., 2007).

20. Abduljawad Yaseen, *Authority in Islam: A Critique of Political Theory* [in Arabic]; (Casablanca: Arab Cultural Center, 2009), pp. 91–97.

21. Khalid Al-Dakheel, "Separation of Religion and State in the Islamic History" [in Arabic], *Al Hayat* newspaper, London, February 22, 2014 (http://alhayat.com/Opinion/Khaled-El-Dakheel/729863/), accessed: March 6, 2014.

22. Regarding the Muslim Brotherhood's concept of the civil state, see: Abdulmonem Saeed, *Religion and the State in Egypt: Thought, Politics and the Muslim Brotherhood* [in Arabic]; (Cairo: Nahdat Misr for Printing, Publishing and Distribution, 2008), pp. 232–235.

23. Khalid Al-Dakheel, op. cit. (http://alhayat.com/Opinion/Khaled-El-Dakheel/729863/).

24. During the reign of Al-Mamoun (Abdullah bin Haroon Al-Rasheed, seventh Abbasid Caliph, 170–218 AH), the Mu'tazilah managed to convince him to ask scholars to endorse the argument that the Quran was created and that people must accept it. However, the Imam Ahmad Ibn Hanbal refused to do so, and held to his position despite the fact that most contemporary scholars withdrew. At the orders of Al-Mamoun, Ibn Hanbal was imprisoned and tortured. This continued even after Al-Mamoun died, as his successor, Al-Muatasim, followed in the path of his predecessor. Ibn Hanbal was tortured for over 28 months, then was released, and went back to his studies at the mosque. For more, see: "The Ordeal of Imam Ahmad Ibn Hanbal" [in Arabic], The General Presidency for Scholarly Research and Ifta, Kingdom of Saudi Arabia, no date (http://www.alifta.net/Fatawa/fatawaDetails.aspx?BookID=2&View=Page&PageNo=1&PageID=3591&languagename=). See also: Nimrod Hurvitz, *The Formation of Hanbalism: Piety into Power* [in Arabic], Ghassan Alam Al-Deen (trans.), revised and introduced by Ridwan Al-Sayyid (Beirut: Arab Network for Research and Publication, 2011), pp. 199–257.

25. Abdulhaq Azzouzi, "Islamic Parties and the Political Landscape in the Arab World: A Comparative Study of the Religionization of Politics and the

Politicization of Religion," in Jamal Sanad Al-Suwaidi and Ahmad Rashad El-Safti, op. cit., p. 193.

26. Lutfi Hatim, "The Evolution of the Nation State and the Thought of Political Islam" [in Arabic], Al-Hiwar Al-Mutamaddin website, October 7, 2012 (http://www.ahewar.org/debat/s.asp?aid=327279&t=4).

27. A number of Muslim thinkers, including those affiliated with the Arab reform and modernity current, opined that the continuation of the Ottoman Caliphate was necessary to maintain the unity and strength of Muslims. Jamal Al-Deen Al-Afghani called for Pan-Islamic unity. Muhammad Rasheed Rida, who one of the most conservative and influential figures in Arab and Islamic reform movements between the two world wars, published a series of articles defending the Caliphate and calling for its preservation as an improved institution. The renowned poet Ahmad Shawqi wrote the time-honored poem 'The Fall of the Caliphate" expressing disappointment in Kemal Ataturk's regime and the deep sorrow for the fall of the Caliphate. This poem can be read at (http://goo.gl/1QyJ6s). See also Nesrine Mahran, "The last decade of the Ottoman State was the most turbulent between the Arabs and the Turks" [in Arabic] *Al Ahram* newspaper, February 20, 2012 (http://digital.ahram.org.eg/articles.aspx?Serial=809438&eid=840).

28. Carrie Rosefsky Wickham, *The Muslim Brotherhood: Evolution of an Islamist Movement* (Princeton, NJ: Princeton University Press, 2013), p. 22.

29. Ibraheem Al-Arees, "Islam and the Principle of Government according to Ali Abdul Raziq: A Battle over the Caliphate" [in Arabic], *Al-Hayat* newspaper, London, September 27, 2014 (http://bit.ly/ZuoUML).

30. There is a large body of literature that deals with the manifestations of backwardness and decline of the Ottoman State. See: Carter V. Findley, "The Turks in World History, Book Review" [in Arabic], *Al-Bayan* newspaper, UAE, October 10, 2005 (http://www.albayan.ae/paths/books/1128856924261-2005-10-10-1.983904).

31. Ahmad Al-Baghdadi, *Renewal of Religious Thought: A Call for Reasoning* (Beirut: Dar Al-Intishar Al-Arabi, 2008), p. 139.

32. M.A. Muqtedar Khan, "The Political Philosophy of Islamic Resurgence," *Cultural Dynamics*, vol. 13, no. 2, 2001, pp. 211–229.

33. M.A. Muqtedar Khan, ibid., pp. 211–229.

34. For the meaning of *Salaf* (Righteous Ancestors), see: Muhammad Saeed Ramadhan Al-Booti, *Salafism: A Blessed Stage, not an Islamic School* [in Arabic]; (Beirut: Dar Al-Fikr Al-Mu'asir, 1998), pp. 9–23.

35. Jamal Sanad Al-Suwaidi, op. cit., p. 16.

36. Fuller, op. cit. (http://goo.gl/vB9sL).

37. Fuller, ibid. (http://goo.gl/vB9sL).

38. Khaleel Ali Haidar, "Religious Extremism ... and Fascism" [in Arabic], *Al-Ittihad* newspaper, August 27 2006 (http://www.alittihad.ae/wajhatdetails.php?id=22421).

39. Dale Eickelman and James Piscatori, *Muslim Politics* (Princeton, NJ: Princeton University Press, 1996), p. 4.

40. Muqtedar Khan, op. cit.

41. Jamal Sanad Al-Suwaidi, op. cit., p. 18.

42. Ali Mamouri, "The Roots of Radicalism in Political Islam," Al-Monitor, October 18, 2013 (http://bit.ly/1sk2bLw).

43. Mohammed Ayoob, op. cit.(http://bit.ly/V3MCw5).

44. Wickham, op. cit., pp. 22–26.

45. Beverley Milton-Edwards, *Contemporary Politics in the Middle East* (Cambridge, UK: Polity Press, 2000), p. 129.

46. Hirschkind, op. cit (http://www.merip.org/mer/mer205/what-political-islam).

47. Muhammad Kassab, "Muslim Brotherhood ... Three Decisions of 'Dissolution and Ban' in 85 Years" [in Arabic], Al-Masri Al-Yawm website, September 23, 2013 (http://www.almasryalyoum.com/news/details/321644).

48. Ibid. (http://www.almasryalyoum.com/news/details/321644).

49. "The Assassination of Hassan Al-Banna, Part 2" [in Arabic], Political Crime (Documentary) Aljazeera.net, February 5, 2006, (http://www.aljazeera.net/programs/pages/1af85e43-e9b5-4143-a93a-3eb022f4cd3e).

50. Max Guirguis, "Islamic Resurgence and its Consequences in the Egyptian Experience," *Mediterranean Studies*, vol. 20, no. 2, 2012, p. 193.

51. Richard P. Mitchell, *The Society of the Muslim Brothers* (New York, NY: Oxford University Press, 1969), pp. 320–327.

52. Fouad Ajami, *The Arab Predicament: Arab Political Thought and Practice since 1967* (Cambridge: Cambridge University Press, 1981), pp. 213–232.

53. P.J. Vatikiotis, *The Egyptian Army in Politics: Pattern for New Nations?* (Bloomington, IN: Indiana University Press, 1961), Table, pp. 48–49.

54. Muhammad Najeeb "I was Egypt's President" [in Arabic]; (Cairo: Egypt, Modern Egyptian Office, 1984), pp. 168–169.

55. Ahmad Al-Janabi, "Al-Manshiyya Incident," Aljazeera.net, 7 January 2013 (http://goo.gl/v9lCuF).

56. Ahmad Al-Hubaishi, "Why do the Muslim Brothers Hate Jamal Abdul Nasser? (3)," February 21, 2008 (http://www.metransparent.com/spip.php?page=article&id_article=3389&var_lang=ar&lang=ar)

57. Wickham, op. cit., p. 27–29.

58. For more details about the spread of the Muslim Brotherhood to the Kingdom Saudi Arabia, see: Qassim Qaseer, "Brotherhood and Saudi Arabia: Conflict and Convergence," Islamyun.net, October 5, 2013 (http://www.islamyun.net/index.php?option=com_k2&view=item&id=1711). Also see: Mahmood Mamdani, "Whither Political Islam?" *Foreign Affairs*, January/ February, 2005 (http://www.foreignaffairs.com/articles/60445/ mahmood-mamdani/whither-political-islam).

59. For more about the thought of Sayyid Qutb, see: Sayyid Qutb, *Ma'alim fi Al-Tariq* [*Signposts on the Road*, in Arabic]; (Cairo: Dar Al-Shurooq, 1983), pp. 5–202.

60. Dale C. Eikmeier, "Qutbism: An Ideology of Islamic Fascism," *Parameters*, Strategic Studies Institute, Spring 2007 (http://strategicstudiesinstitute.army.mil/pubs/parameters/articles/07spring/eikmeier.pdf).

61. Abdul Ghani Imad, "God's (Allah) Sovereignty and the Guardianship of the Jurist: The Concept and Discourse" [in Arabic], tourathtripoli.org (http://tourathtripoli.org/phocadownload/dirasset_isslamieh/7akimiet%20ala h%20w%20wilayat%20alfakieh.pdf).

62. Sabri Muhammad Khaleel, "The Concept of hakimiyya [divine sovereignty] in Political Islamic Thought" [in Arabic], September 15, 2010 (http://www. sudanile.com/index.php/2008-05-19-17-39-36/252-2009-09-06-09-34-16/1 8652-2010-09-15-15-34-33).

63. For more about Sayyid Qutb's view of the concept of *hakimiyya*, see: Hisham Ahmad Ja'far, *Political Dimensions of the Hakimiyya Concept: An Epistemological Perspective* [in Arabic]; (Virginia: International Institute of Islamic Thought, 1995), pp. 221–251. Also see: Muhammad Hafiz Diyab, *Sayyid Qutb: Discourse and Ideologies* [in Arabic]; (Cairo: Dar Ru'ya for Publishing and Distribution, 2010), pp. 197–215.

64. Olivier Roy, *The Failure of Political Islam* (London: I.B. Tauris, 1994), p. 41.

65. Abdullah Al-Rasheed, "The Master of Hakimiyya [divine sovereignty] City: Papers of Muhammad Qutb (2)" [in Arabic], *Al-Sharq Al-Awsat* newspaper, London, May 19, 2014 (http://www.aawsat.com/home/article/99311).

66. Ibid (http://www.aawsat.com/home/article/99311).

67. The Holy Quran (88:21–22).

68. Electronic Mus'haf Project, King Saud University [in Arabic]; (http://quran. ksu.edu.sa/tafseer/tabary/sura88-aya22.html).

69. Abdullah Azzam was among the first to be called Afghan Arabs. He played the most important role in the emergence of this phenomenon which later produced Al-Qa'ida. He was a teacher and inspirer of the founder and leader of the organization, Usama bin Ladin. Abdullah Azzam was born in a village near the city of Jenin in Palestine in 1941. He died in November 24, 1989. Abdullah Kamal, "The Black Banners: Abdullah Azzam from Jihad to Assassination (1)" [in Arabic], *Al-Sharq Al-Awsat* newspaper, London, May 1, 2002 (http://classic.aawsat.com/details.asp?issueno=8555&article=100961#.VGRd XzqoWRs).

70.   Yousuf A'la Boona, op. cit. (http://elw3yalarabi.org/modules.php?name=News &file=article&sid=10645.

71.   Salah Abdul Fattah Al-Khalidi, *American War through the Lens of Sayyid Qutb* [in Arabic]; (Amman: Dar Al-Uloom for Publishing and Distribution, 2003), pp. 5–59.

72.   Usama Shahada, "Excommunication and Violence … A Muslim Brotherhood Product!" [in Arabic], Alalukah website, May 22, 2011 (http://majles. alukah.net/t82739/).

73.   John Calvert, *Sayyid Qutb and the Origins of Radical Islamism* (New York, NY: Columbia University Press, 2010), p. 231.

74.   Ahmad Al Hubaishi, op.cit (http://www.metransparent.com/spip.php?page= article&id_article=3389&var_lang=ar&lang=ar).

75.   Ahmad Azb, "On this Day the Execution of the Muslim Brotherhood Member Sayyid Qutb" [in Arabic], Al-Bawwaba News website (http://www.albawabh news.com/759960).

76.   Robin Wright, *Dreams and Shadows: the Future of the Middle East* (New York, NY: Penguin Books, 2008), p. 108. Also see: Muhammad Hafiz Diyab, op. cit., pp. 183–186.

77.   Jamal Sanad Al-Suwaidi, op. cit., p. 24.

78.   Riyadh Al-Saidawi, "On the Rise and Fall of Islamic Movements in the Arab World" [in Arabic], Al-Hiwar Al-Mutamaddin website, June 29, 2007 (http://www.ahewar.org/debat/show.art.asp?aid=101224). For a discussion of the Ideological Underpinnings and Principles of Nasser's Regime, see: Jamal Sanad Al-Suwaidi, op. cit., pp. 33–37.

79.   See, for example: Ahmed Abdalla, *The Student Movement and National Politics in Egypt, 1923–1973* (London: Al-Saqi Books, 1985), p. 35.

80.   For insights on this topic, see: Ali Al-Deen Hilal, *The Evolution of Political System in Egypt 1803–1997* [in Arabic]; (Cairo: Center for political Studies and Research, Cairo University, 1997).

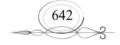

81. Wickham, op. cit., pp. 34–41.

82. Ibid (http://m.ahewar.org/s.asp?aid=419761&r=0&cid=0&u=&i=5396&q=).

83. Guirguis, op. cit., pp. 200–202.

84. "Anwar Al-Sadat: The Reasons and Repercussions of his Assassination, Part 2" [in Arabic], Aljazeera.net website, October 24, 2005 (http://bit.ly/1qUpEzP).

85. For more information about the economy during Nasser's regime, see, for example, Anouar Abdel-Malek, *Egypt: A New Society Built by the Militarists* [in Arabic]; (Berirut: Dar Al-Talee'a, 1964); As'ad Abdul Rahman, *The Nasserism: Bureaucratic Revolution or Revolution Bureaucracy?* [in Arabic]; (Kuwait: Kuwait University Publications, 1977); see also, Alan Richards and John Waterbury, *A Political Economy of the Middle East*, 2nd edition (Boulder, CO: Westview Press, 1996); and Anouar Abdel-Malek, *Egypt: Military Society; the Army Regime, the Left, and Social Change Under Nasser* (New York, NY: Vintage Books, 1986).

86. Fuller, op. cit. (http://search.proquest.com.ezproxy.aub.edu.lb/docview/2142 89242).

87. Michael N. Barnett and Jack S. Levy, "Domestic Sources of Alliances and Alignments: The Case of Egypt, 1962–1973," *International Organization*, vol. 45, no. 3, Summer 1991.

88. Saif Al-Deen Khawaja, "The Role of Egypt … in the Coup of Hashim Al-Ata" [in Arabic], the website of the Sudanese electronic newspaper Al-Rakooba, September 23, 2014 (http://www.alrakoba.net/articles-action-show-id-53725.htm).

89. Ibrahim A. Karawan, "Sadat and the Egyptian-Israeli Peace Revisited," *International Journal of Middle East Studies*, vol. 26, no. 2, July 1994, pp. 253–254.

90. Ibraheem Nuwwar, "Egypt–Israel Relations: The Structure and Outcomes after One Year of Normalization" [in Arabic], *Al-Ahram* newspaper, Egypt, July 1, 1981 (http://digital.ahram.org.eg/articles.aspx?Serial=215095&eid=13).

91. See: "Palestinian Liberation Organization" [in Arabic], Al-Jazeera.net, October 3, 2004 (http://www.aljazeera.net/specialfiles/pages/74244504-9c64-41ff-8887-b2d2dc94858e).

92. For details about this period and the environment surrounding the Egyptian–Israeli Peace Treaty, see: Hussein Al-Sayyid Hussein, "The Egyptian–Israeli Peace Treaty 1979 and its Impact of Egypt's Regional Role" [in Arabic], *Historical Studies* journal, nos. 117–118, January–June 2012, pp. 447–497 (http://www.damascusuniversity.edu.sy/mag/history/images/stories/pdf/14.pdf).

93. Ibid. (http://www.damascusuniversity.edu.sy/mag/history/images/stories/pdf/14.pdf), p. 413.

94. Mamdani, op. cit. (http://www.foreignaffairs.com/articles/60445/mahmood-mamdani/whither-political-islam).

95. Susan Sachs, "Ayatullah Al-Sistani Rejects the Guardianship of the Jurist and Does not Pursue Political Ambitions" [in Arabic], *Al-Sharq Al-Awsat* newspaper, London, January 19, 2004 (http://classic.aawsat.com/details.asp?article=2135 14&issueno=9183).

96. Mamdani, op. cit. (http://www.foreignaffairs.com/articles/60445/mahmood-mamdani/whither-political-islam).

97. Ibid. (http://www.foreignaffairs.com/articles/60445/mahmood-mamdani/whither-political-islam).

98. Muhammad Al-Saeed Jamal Al-deen, *Afghanistan between Domination Tendencies and the Will of Struggle* [in Arabic]; (Abu Dhabi: Zayed Center for Coordination and Follow-Up, March 2003), p. 70.

99. Nash'at Hamid Abdul Majid, "The Afghan Arabs... An Attempt for Definition" [in Arabic], Iman1.net., October 7, 2001 (http://www.imam1.net/archive/showthread.php?t=68208&s=80c0d87bdc281941fe96de92b5b46301).

100. Mamdani, op. cit (http://www.foreignaffairs.com/articles/60445/mahmood-mamdani/whither-political-islam).

101. "Obama: The killing of Usama bin Ladin 'A Good Day for America'" [in Arabic], BBC Arabic, May 3, 2011 (http://www.bbc.co.uk/arabic/worldnews/2011/05/110503_bin_laden_safer_world.shtml).

102. Nash'at Hamid Abdul Majid, op. cit., October 7, 2001 (http://www.Iman1.net/archive/showthread.php?t=68208&s=80c0d87bdc281941fe96de92b5b46301).

103. Kameel Al-Taweel, *Al-Qa'ida and its Sister Organizations: The Story of the Arab Mujahideen* [in Arabic]; (Beirut: Dar Al-Saqi, 2007), p. 50.

104. See the analysis of these issues in Saeed Al-Shihabi, "Two Competing Islamic Enterprises: A Political and a Jihadi" [in Arabic], *Al-Quds Al-Arabi* newspaper, November 12, 2013 (http://www.alquds.co.uk/?p=102771).

105. "Al-Qa'ida and the Internationalization of Suicide Terrorism" [in Arabic], Aljazeera.net, September 21, 2005 (http://www.aljazeera.net/NR/exeres/1D63 6886-D4FD-4736-AB8C-F41D2343FCB8.htm).

106. Joschka Fischer, *The Return of History: The World after September 11 and the Renewal of the West*, Hani Al-Salih (trans.); (Riyadh: Obeikan Publishing, 2009), p. 14.

107. Salim Salimeen Al-Na'eemi, "The Summer of the Fall of Activist Political Islam" [in Arabic], opinion section, *Al-Ittihad* newspaper, UAE, June 25, 2013 (http://www.alittihad.ae/wajhatdetails.php?id=73227).

108. For more on Shiite Islam, see: *Large Encyclopedia of Schools, Sects and Religions: Shiites* [in Arabic]; (Beirut: Middle East Cultural Center for Printing, Publishing, Translation and Distribution, 2008), pp. 5–229.

109. "34 Years after the Hostage Crisis at the American Embassy in Tehran" [in Arabic], *Al-Shaq Al-Awsat*, London, December 12, 2013 (http://classic.aawsat.com/details.asp?section=34&article=753594&issueno=12798#.U_MvI_2oWic).

110. Karim Sadjadpour, "The Supreme Leader," in Robin Wright (ed.), *The Iran Primer: Power, Politics and US Policy* (Washington, DC: United States Institute of Peace Press, 2009).

111. Muhammad Al-Hilali, "Moderate Political Islam: From Mosque to Government, or the Paradoxes of Conservative Social Islam" [in Arabic], Al-Hiwar Al-Mutamaddin website, November 30, 2013 (http://www.ahewar.org/debat/show.art.asp?aid=285435).

112. Ibid. (http://www.ahewar.org/debat/show.art.asp?aid=285435).

113. In my view, it is important to distinguish between the traditional Islam as adopted by the Al-Azhar institution and the unofficial political Islamic groups and currents, such as: Wahhabism, modernist Islamism, the Muslim Brotherhood and militant Islamists. See: Jamal Sanad Al-Suwaidi, op. cit., pp. 180–221.

114. Mohammed Ayoob, op. cit., 2005 (http://bit.ly/V3MCw5).

115. Basheer Abdulfattah, "Beyond Political Islam in Turkey" [in Arabic], Aljazeera.net, April 9, 2014 (http://goo.gl/dEGMBw).

116. Ibid. (http://goo.gl/dEGMBw).

117. Omer Taspinar, "Turkey: The New Model?" Brookings Institution, April 2012 (http://bit.ly/1i2Ttud).

118. Sa'ad Abdul Azeez Muslat, "The Political Project of the Justice and Development Party in Turkey [in Arabic]. *Regional Studies*, no. 12, 2008 (http://www.iasj.net/iasj?func=fulltext&aId=6499).

119. Taspinar, op. cit. (http://bit.ly/1i2Ttud).

120. Carmen Rodriguez, Antonio Avalos, Hakan Yilmaz and Ana I. Planet (eds.), *Turkey's Democratization Process* (London: Routledge Studies in Middle Eastern Politics, 2014), p. 263.

121. "Erbakan and Ciller say coalition government functioning in harmony," Hurriyet, March 25, 1997 (http://goo.gl/C0hk1E).

122. Taspinar, op. cit. (http://bit.ly/1i2Ttud).

123. Wa'il Nuwwar and Feyzi Baban, "The Future of Political Islam: Two Lessons from Turkey and Egypt" [in Arabic] Al Monitor, January 29, 2014 (http://bit.ly/1vewCIs).

124. See, for example, "Opinion Poll: Dispute between Erdogan and the Religious Cleric 'Gulen' Damaged the Reputation of Both" [in Arabic], *Al-Shurooq* newspaper, Egypt, January 30, 2014 (http://www.shorouknews.com/news/view.aspx?cdate=30012014&id=871cf977-a832-4654-98f5-09783a1ed181).

125. "Turkey Enforced Erdogan's Threats by Banning 'Twitter'" [in Arabic], *Al-Ittihad* newspaper, UAE, March 22, 2014 (http://www.alittihad.ae/details.php?id=25435&y=2014).

126. Huda Rizq, "Struggles of Moderate Islam in Turkey" [in Arabic], *Al-Akhbar* newspaper, Lebanon, January 21, 2014 (http://www.al-akhbar.com/node/199034).

127. "Militancy and Violence are Extension of Qutbism in Muslim Brotherhood's Behavior" [in Arabic], *Al-Arab* newspaper, London, April 11, 2014 (http://www.alarabonline.org/pdf/2014/04/11-04/p13.pdf).

128. For a brief look at the Muslim Brotherhood's military apparatus, see Wickham, op. cit., p. 26 (http://www.alarabonline.org/pdf/2014/04/11-04/ p13.pdf).

129. Shihata Awadh, "Enmity to the Muslim Brotherhood is an Obstacle in the Face of Egypt's Regional Role" [in Arabic], Al-Jazeera.net, October 22, 2014 (http://studies.aljazeera.net/reports/2014/10/2014102184431755105.htm).

130. Abdulrahman Abu Al-Ola, *A Reading of the Results of Egyptian Elections* [in Arabic], Aljazeera.net, January 22, 2012 (http://goo.gl/cc4IPA).

131. Haytham Al-Kiswani, "Tablighi Jamaat from India to the World" in *Tablighi Jamaat*, by a group of researchers [in Arabic]; (Abu Dhabi: Al-Misbar Center for Studies and Research, Book 35, November 2009), pp. 31–57.

132. "Tablighi Jamaat" [in Arabic], Said Al-Fawaid website. (http://www.saaid.net/feraq/mthahb/9.htm).

133. "Tablighi Jamaat" [in Arabic], Umm Al-Qura University, Kingdom of Saudi Arabia (https://uqu.edu.sa/page/ar/199450).

134. For more about Salafi thought, see Ammar Ali Hassan, "Salafism: Discourse and Practice" [in Arabic], Emirates Lectures Series no. 162 (Abu Dhabi: The Emirates Center for Strategic Studies and Research, 2013), pp. 43–48; Abduljawad Yaseen, op. cit., pp. 19–87; and Muhammad Salih Al-Marakishi, *Ideology and Modernism in the Thought of Salafi Pioneers* [in Arabic]; (Tunis: Dar Al-Ma'arif for Printing and Publishing, 1995), pp. 10–21.

135. Ibraheem Abu Dah, "Democracy and the Caliphate (2)" [in Arabic], *Al-Ahram* (Egypt), April 9, 2013. (http://digital.ahram.org.eg/articles.aspx?Serial=12479 43&eid=1252). For more on the history of the Kingdom of Saudi Arabia, see: Salah Abu Al-Saud, *Ancient, Modern and Contemporary History of the Kingdom of Saudi Arabia* [in Arabic]; (Giza, Egypt: Al-Nafiza Bookshop, 2014), pp. 67–170.

136. Quintan Wiktorowicz, "Anatomy of the Salafi Movement," *Studies in Conflict and Terrorism*, vol. 29, no. 3, 2006, p. 214.

137. Ibid., pp. 208–208.

138. Usama Salih, op. cit. (http://www.siyassa.org.eg/NewsQ/2369.aspx).

139. Ibid. (http://www.siyassa.org.eg/NewsQ/2369.aspx).

140. Bassam Ramadan, "Burhami: Interpretation of Sharia Principles in the Constitution 'Satisfactory'" [in Arabic], *Al-Masri Al-Yawm*, December 4, 2013 (http://www.almasryalyoum.com/news/details/352377#).

141. Ibid. (http://www.almasryalyoum.com/news/details/352377#).

142. "Al-Qa'ida Appoints Algerian Abu Luqman as a New Leader of 'Ansar Al-Sharia' Movement" [in Arabic], *Al-Ittihad* newspaper, UAE, January 14, 2014 (http://www.alittihad.ae/details.php?id=3880&y=2014).

143. "Jihadi Salafism in Tunisia: Manpower and Sources of Finance" [in Arabic], *Al-Maghrib* newspaper, Tunisia, February 19, 2014 (http://www.lemaghreb.tn/5722).

144. There is what is known as defensive *jihad*, which is defined as the expulsion of an "infidel" enemy, whether an apostate or originally an infidel; and offensive *jihad*, in which the enemy is sought out in his own land and Muslims invade the infidels in their own land. For further details, see: "Islamic Battles between Offensive and

Defensive Jihads" [in Arabic], Islamweb.net, the Da'wa and Religious Guidance Department of the Ministry of Awqaf (Religious Endowments) and Islamic Affairs, Qatar, April 5, 2012. (http://fatwa.islamweb.net/fatwa/index.php?page=showfatwa&Option=fatwaId&Id=177109).

145. Brynjar Lia and Katja H.-W. Skjolberg, "Why Terrorism Occurs: A Survey of Theories and Hypotheses on the Causes of Terrorism," Norwegian Defense Research Establishment (FFI), 2000 (http://www.ffi.no/no/rapporter/00-02769.pdf).

146. Uthman Al-Rawwaf, "The Puzzle of ISIL in Syria and Iraq" [in Arabic], Elaph electronic newspaper, July 13, 2014 (http://www.elaph.com/Web/opinion/2014/7/922955.html?entry=opinion).

147. Brynjar Lia and Katja H.-W Skjolberg, op. cit. (http://www.ffi.no/no/rapporter/00-02769.pdf).

148. Ibid. (http://www.ffi.no/no/rapporter/00-02769.pdf).

149. Abdullah Al-Rasheed, op. cit. (http://www.aawsat.com/home/article/99311).

150. Eikmeier, op. cit. (http://strategicstudiesinstitute.army.mil/pubs/parameters/articles/07 spring/eikmeier.pdf).

151. Ibid.   (http://strategicstudiesinstitute.army.mil/pubs/parameters/articles/07 spring/eikmeier.pdf).

152. Yousuf A'la Boona, "A Look into the Thought of Sayyid Qutb" (http://elw3yalarabi.org/modules.php?name=News&file=article&sid=10645). For more about the thought of Sayyid Qutb, see: Sayyid Qutb: *Ma'alim fi Al-Tareeq* [in Arabic]; (Cairo: Dar Al-Shurooq, 1983), pp. 5–202.

153. Muhammad Falah Al-Zu'bi, "Do the 'Muslim Brothers' Betray their Approach and the Founder of their Group?" [in Arabic], *Fact International* (Jordan), June 16, 2012 (http://www.factjo.com/pages/print2.aspx?id=3858).

154. Muhammad Hafiz Diyab, op. cit., pp. 184–185.

155. Regarding the Muslim Brotherhood's tendency towards violence in the 1950s and 1960s, see: Rifaat Al-Saeed, *The Islamists: Terrorism and Sectarian Sedition*

[in Arabic]; (Damascus, Al-Ahali for Publishing and Distribution, 1994), pp. 59–185.

156. Muhammad Hafiz Diyab, op. cit., pp. 149–156.

157. Eikmeier, op. cit. (http://strategicstudiesinstitute.army.mil/pubs/parameters/articles/07 spring/eikmeier.pdf).

158. Fakhri Kareem, "The Extremism Industry and its Most Inflammatory Elements (9), Incubators of Extremism and their Beginnings: The Muslim Brotherhood" [in Arabic], *Al-Mada* newspaper, Iraq, February 11, 2014 (http://goo.gl/ScQSTO).

159. Khan, op. cit., pp. 216–217.

160. Usama Hasan, "Viewpoint: What do radical Islamists actually believe in?" *BBC News Magazine*, May 24, 2013 (http://www.bbc.com/news/magazine-22640614).

161. Gilles Kepel, *Jihad: The Trail of Political Islam* (London: I.B. Tauris, 2002) cited in Mamdani, op. cit.

162. "The Story of Abdullah Azzam and bin Ladin in Afghanistan" [in Arabic], Donia Al-Watan electronic newspaper (Palestine), 28 July 2005 (http://www.alwatanvoice.com/arabic/news/2005/07/28/25812.html).

163. Bruce Riedel, "Al Qaeda Strikes Back," *Foreign Affairs*, May/June 2007 (http://www.foreignaffairs.com/articles/62608/bruce-riedel/al-qaeda-strikes-back).

164. Regarding the birth and thought of Hizbut-Tahrir, see: Adnan Abdulraheem Al-Soos, *Hizbut-Tahrir and Political Practice* [in Arabic]; (Amman, no publisher, 1st edition, 2007), pp. 7–38.

165. For more about the activities and current thought of Hizbut-Tahrir, see: (http://www.hizb-ut-tahrir.info/info/index.php/contents/entry_65), accessed September 29, 2013,

166. "The Falsehood of Moderate Islam" [in Arabic], a statement issued by Hizbut-Tahrir, November 25, 2002 (http://arabic.hizbuttahrir.org/index.php/culture/politics/195-moderate-islam).

167. The scope of this volume does not permit discussion of all political Islamic groups operating as Islamic liberation movements. However, the aim here is to note that these groups exist and are classified within the current of political Islam, be they Sunni or Shiite.

168. The Charter of the Islamic Resistance Movement (Hamas); [in Arabic], Aljazeera.net website, 16 July 2005 (http://www.aljazeera.net/specialfiles/pages/0b4f24e4-7c14-4f50-a831-ea2b6e73217d).

169. For more details on the birth of Hamas and its relation to the Muslim Brotherhood, see: Khalid Al-Haroob, *Hamas: Thought and Political Practice* [in Arabic]; (Beirut: Palestinian Studies Institution, 1997), pp. 39–46.

170. Ibid., pp. 39–46

171. "The Establishment of Hamas," Alhoria website, December 14, 2012 (http://www.alhoria.net/article.php?id=12904).

172. Regarding the difference between Sunni and Shiite Islam on governance theory, see: Mustafa Al-Jiddawi, *Shiite Theory on Islamic Governance and Comparison with Western Principles of Democracy* [in Arabic], Ph.D. Dissertation (Alexandria, no publisher, 1988), pp. 55–490.

173. Muhammad Harfoosh, "Hizbullah: The Origins and Challenges" [in Arabic], Al-Monitor (Lebanon), July 11, 2013 (http://www.al-monitor.com/pulse/ar/originals/2013/02/hezbollah-beginnings-challenges.html#).

174. The Amal Movement is a Lebanese armed Shiite movement founded by Musa Al-Sadr in Lebanon in 1975 as a military wing to defend the interests of all Lebanese against Israeli aggression, as it describes itself. For further details about the birth and history of the Amal Movement, see: Tawfeeq Al-Madeeni, *Amal and Hizbullah in Local and Regional Confrontations* [in Arabic]; (Damascus, Dar Al-Ahali for Printing, Publishing and Distribution, 1999), pp. 49–88.

175. Muhammad Harfoosh, op. cit. (http://www.al-monitor.com/pulse/ar/originals/2013/02/hezbollah-beginnings-challenges.html#).

176. Jamal Abdul Jawad, "Hizbullah's Political Document: What is New?" [in Arabic], digital Ahram, December 11, 2009 (http://digital.ahram.org.eg/articles.aspx?Serial=18068).

177. Ibid. (http://digital.ahram.org.eg/articles.aspx?Serial=18068).

178. For more on these issues, see: Jonathan Masters and Zachary Laub, "Hezbollah (a.k.a. Hizbollah, Hizbu'llah)," Council on Foreign Relations, Nabeel Zulf (trans.), in Al-Watan newspaper, Kuwait, January 14, 2014 (http://alwatan.kuwait.tt/articledetails.aspx?Id=331527).

179. Usama Salih, op. cit. (http://www.siyassa.org.eg/NewsQ/2369.aspx).

180. "Badie to his 'Clan': Be Prepared to Carry the Banner of the 'Mastership of the World' and Raise it in 'Al-Aqsa'" [in Arabic], Al-Watan (Egypt), May 14, 2013 (http://www.elwatannews.com/news/details/181456).

181. Usama Salih, op. cit. (http://www.siyassa.org.eg/NewsQ/2369.aspx).

182. Haitham Al-Awni, "The Illusion of the Caliphate State" [in Arabic] Al-Arab newspaper website, London, January 6, 2014 (http://alarab.co.uk/pdf/2014/01/06-01/p13.pdf).

183. The Requirements of the (Supreme Imamate); [in Arabic], Islamweb.net, the Da'wa and Religious Guidance Department of the Ministry of Awqaf (Religious Endowments) and Islamic Affairs, Qatar, June 19, 2001 (http://library.islamweb.org/fatwa/index.php?page=showfatwa&Option=fatwaId&Id=8696).

184. Leading Women Ask the "Islamists" for a "Clear Explanation" of the "Supreme Imamate" [in Arabic], Al-Masri Al-Yawm newspaper, December 27, 2011 (http://www.almasryalyoum.com/news/details/137825).

185. "First Christian Governor of Jacarta in 50 years" [in Arabic], Aljazeera.net, November 20, 2014 (http://goo.gl/5D8WVj).

186. Majdi Khaleel, "Citizenship Rights of the Copts between the Ruling Regime's Conduct and the Thought of the Islamists" [in Arabic], Elaph electronic newspaper, May 6, 2007 (http://www.elaph.com/ElaphWeb/ElaphWriter/2007/5/231612.htm).

187. As quoted by Usama Salih from Subhi Salih, the member of the Muslim Brotherhood group and of the Egyptian constitution drafting committee (2011), at a symposium held in Alexandria in April 2011. Usama Salih, op. cit. (http://www.siyassa.org.eg/NewsQ/2369.aspx).

188. Khalid Al-Dakheel, op. cit. (http://alhayat.com/Opinion/Khaled-El-Dakheel/729863/).

189. Muhammad Al-Hilali, op. cit. (http://www.ahewar.org/debat/show.art.asp?aid=285435).

190. Muhammad Al-Sayyid Saeed, "Resistance between Religious Sects" [in Arabic], *Al-Ahram* newspaper (http://www.ahram.org.eg/archive/2002/11/9/REPO4.HTM).

191. Nasr Hamid Abu Zaid, "Fear of Secularism: Separation of Religion and State" [in Arabic], Al-Hiwar Al-Mutamaddin website, May 5, 2010 (http://www.ahewar.org/debat/show.art.asp?aid=215277).

192. Ibid. (http://www.ahewar.org/debat/show.art.asp?aid=215277).

193. Rania Mustafa, "From the 'Constant' of Popular Religiosity to the 'Variable' of Political Islam" [in Arabic], Al-Arab online, February 3, 2014 (http://www.alarabonline.org/?id=14392).

194. "Apostasy and Freedom of Belief: A New Islamic Perspective" [in Arabic], Religion and Politics Center for Studies, August 9, 2011 (http://www.rpcst.com/news.php?action=show&id=3910).

195. "Tolerance of Islam in Treating non-Muslims" [in Arabic], Assakina website, February 11, 2011 (http://www.assakina.com/politics/6565.html).

196. The Holy Quran (2:256)

197. Mohammed Ayoob, op. cit. (http://onlinelibrary.wiley.com/doi/10.1111/j.1468-2346.2005.00496.x/pdf).

198. On "the Muslim Brotherhood" and the United Arab Emirates, see Abdullah Al-Rasheed, "The Muslim Brotherhood in the UAE ... the Complete Story" [in Arabic], *Al-Sharq Al-Awsat* newspaper, London, February 1, 2013 (http://www.aawsat.com/details.asp?article=715512&issueno=12484&section=4#.UzWrtvldWSo).

199. Usama Salih, op. cit. (http://www.siyassa.org.eg/NewsQ/2369.aspx).

200. Mahir Farghali, "The Salifis and Muslim Brotherhood: Disagreement of Ideology and Conflict of Politics" [in Arabic], *Al-Hayat*, February 6, 2012.

201. Bassam Ramadan, December 4, 2013, op. cit. (http://www.almasryalyoum.com/news/details/352377#).

202. Basma Al-Mahdi, "An American Researcher: The Opposition should Worry more about the 'Islamization' than 'Brotherhoodization' of the State" [in Arabic], *Al-Masri Al-Yawm* newspaper, May 15, 2013 (http://www.almasryalyoum.com/news/details/316548).

203. "The ILO: Unemployment Rate in Arab Countries Double the Global Average" [in Arabic], Elaph electronic newspaper, February 27, 2014 (http://www.elaph.com/Web/Economics/2014/2/881222.html).

204. Mohammed Ayoob, op. cit. (http://onlinelibrary.wiley.com/doi/10.1111/j.1468-2346.2005.00496.x/pdf).

205. Katerina Dalacoura, "The Uncertain Future of Political Islam," Global Brief, February 18, 2011 (http://globalbrief.ca/blog/2011/02/18/the-uncertain-future-of-political-islam/). For more on the concepts and thought of political religious groups, see also: Olivier Roy, *The Experience of Political Islam* [in Arabic], Naseer Marwa (trans.); (Beirut: Dar Al-Saqi, 1st Edition, 1994), pp. 41–52.

206. Katerina Dalacoura, op. cit. (http://globalbrief.ca/blog/2011/02/18/the-uncertain-future-of-political-islam/).

207. "The text of the government's statement designating the Muslim Brotherhood as a terrorist group" [in Arabic], *Al-Masri Al-Yawm* newspaper, December 25, 2013 (http://www.almasryalyoum.com/news/details/363925).

208. The Turkish Islamic-based Welfare Party in the mid-1990s became the leading party in the country and, in alliance with a conservative secular party led by Tansu Çiller, managed to form a government in 1996 for the first time in the history of the modern Turkish state. See: Muammar Atawi, "The Islamists of Turkey: from Sufism to Authority" [in Arabic], *Al-Akhbar* newspaper website, January 22, 2010 (http://www.al-akhbar.com/node/59621).

Chapter 2

1. Emile Durkheim, *The Elementary Forms of the Religious Life*, translated by Joseph Ward Swain (London: George Allen and Unwin, Ltd., 1915), Ch. 1.

2. Jamal Sanad Al-Suwaidi, "Islam and Socio-Political Change: A Comparative Study of Egyptian, Kuwaiti, and Palestinian Attitudes," Unpublished Dissertation Manuscript, University of Wisconsin, 1990, p. 58.

3. Ibid. p. 59.

4. Regarding Rasheed Rida's relationship with both Jamal Al-Deen Al-Afghani and Muhammad Abdu, and the influence on him of ibn Taymiyya and others, see: Manooba Burhani, *The Pragmatic Thought of Muhammad Rasheed Rida* [in Arabic]; (Beirut: Dar Ibn Hazm, 2010), pp. 115–145.

5. Zaki Al-Milad, "Reform Thought of Sheikh Abdurrahman Al-Kawakibi," in Zaki Ali Al-Awadi (ed.), *The Reform Movement in the Modern Age* [in Arabic] (various authors), minutes of the forum held at the Royal Cultural Center in Amman during the period 8–10 Sha'ban 1423 AH, corresponding to October 15–17, 2002 (Amman: Dar Al-Razi for Printing and Publishing, 2004), pp. 50–74.

6. Saeed bin Saeed Al-Alawi, "Strategy for a Second Arab Renaissance" [in Arabic], *Al-Sharq Al-Awsat* (London), December 20, 2013 (http://bit.ly/1oFKLcw).

7. Ibid. (http://bit.ly/1oFKLcw).

8. Usama Al-Ghazali Harb, "Political Interest in the Behavior of the Muslim Brotherhood" [in Arabic], lecture presented at The Future of Arab-Islamic Culture Conference, The Emirates Center for Strategic Studies and Research, Abu Dhabi, UAE, 27–28 May 2013, *Al-Arab* (London), May 29, 2013 (http://www.alarab.co.uk/?p=40183).

9. Waheed Abdulmajeed, "The Religious State between Islam and Christianity" [in Arabic], *Al-Ahram*, November 23, 2010 (http://digital.ahram.org.eg/articles.aspx?Serial=339605&eid=891).

10. "How Christianity Rose to Dominate Europe," Worldology, September 8, 2010 (http://www.worldology.com/Christianity/rise_christianity.htm).

11. Muhammad Abdulsattar Al-Badri, "From History: Failure of the Crusades and the Beginning of European Reformation" [in Arabic], *Al-Sharq Al-Awsat* (London), April 29, 2014 (http://www.aawsat.com/home/article/87181).

12. Simon Newman, "Religion in the Middle Ages," The Finer Times, no date (http://bit.ly/1szj1YM).

13. Ibid. (http://bit.ly/1szj1YM).

14. "Western Innovation" [in Arabic], *Al-Ahram* (Egypt), November 2, 2004 (http://www.ahram.org.eg/Archive/2004/11/2/FACE7.HTM).

15. Simon Newman, op. cit. (http://bit.ly/1szj1YM).

16. Ali Sirini, "Conclusions Regarding Political Reforms in Christian Europe in the Middle Ages" [in Arabic], November 29, 2011 (http://www.ahl-alquran.com/arabic/show_article.php?main_id=8978).

17. Tawfeeq Al-Taweel, *The Story of the Conflict between Religion and Philosophy* [in Arabic]; (Cairo: General Egyptian Book Organization, 2011), p. 37.

18. Ibid. p. 37.

19. J. Bury, *A History of Freedom of Thought* [in Arabic], Translated by Muhammad Abdulaziz Ishaq (Cairo: National Translation Center, 2010), pp. 53–54.

20. Hashim Salih, "Christian Fundamentalism in the West: The Inquisition was the Culmination of Fanaticism and Violence" [in Arabic], *Al-Sharq Al-Awsat* (London), October 4, 2000 (http://www.aawsat.com/details.asp?issueno=8059&article=7390).

21. "How Christianity ...," op. cit. (http://www.worldology.com/Christianity/rise_christianity.htm).

22. Ibid. (http://www.worldology.com/Christianity/rise_christianity.htm).

23. Ashraf Mansour, "Modern Philosophy: Development and General Features" [in Arabic], Al-Hiwar Al-Mutamaddin website, December 12, 2010. (http://www.ahewar.org/debat/show.art.asp?aid=238064).

24. Bruce Robinson, "An Overview of the Reformation," BBC History, February 17, 2011 (http://www.bbc.co.uk/history/british/tudors/reformation_overview_01.shtml).

25. Yoachim Rizq Markas, "Lectures on the History of the Western Church" [in Arabic], St. Takla Church (http://goo.gl/YtjZ3i).

26. See: (http://www.ideafinder.com/history/inventors/gutenberg.htm).

27. Jared Rubin, "Printing and Protestants: Reforming the Economics of the Reformation," Munich Personal RePEc Archive (MPRA), June 2011 (http://mpra.ub.uni-muenchen.de/31267/1/MPRA_paper_31267.pdf).

28. Jamal Sanad Al-Suwaidi, op. cit., pp. 66–67.

29. Donald E. Smith (ed.), *Religion and Political Modernization* (New Haven, CT: Yale University Press, 1974), p. 7.

30. Ibid. p. 7.

31. Ibid. p. 6.

32. Ibid. pp. 6–7.

33. Dawood Khairallah, "The Relationship between Religion and the State in the Arab Spring Era" [in Arabic], *Al-Akhbar* (Lebanon), December 11, 2012 (http://www.al-akhbar.com/node/173416).

34. Al-Sayyid Yaseen, "Egypt: the Problematic Relation between Religion and Politics" [in Arabic], *Al-Nahar* (Lebanon), August 15, 2013 (http://newspaper.annahar.com/article/58042).

35. Khalid Al-Dakheel, "Separation of Religion from the State: Same Question Put Differently" [in Arabic], Alarabiya.net, February 16, 2014 (http://goo.gl/86NMhD).

36. Ali Mamouri, "The Roots of Radicalism in Political Islam," Al-Monitor, October 18, 2013 (http://www.al-monitor.com/pulse/originals/2013/10/radicalism-political-islam-roots-sunni-shiite-fundamentalist.html).

37. Jamal Sanad Al-Suwaidi, op. cit., pp. 71–74.

38. Ibid., pp. 98–99.

39. For more about the concept of *Ahl Al-Hal Wa Al-Akd* [decision makers], see: Bilal Safi Al-Deen, *Decision Makers in the Islamic Government System: A Comparative Study* [in Arabic]; (Damascus: Dar Al-Nawadir, 2008), pp. 39–79.

40. Ira M. Lapidus, "The Separation of State and Religion in the Development of Early Islamic Society," *International Journal of Middle Eastern Studies*, vol. 6 (1975), pp. 363–364.

41. Ibid., pp. 363–364.

42. Muhammad Jumaih, "When Religion is a Means" [in Arabic], Ma'reb Press, December 22, 2009 (http://marebpress.net/articles.php?lng=arabic&id=6224).

43. Badr Muhammad Badr, "Religious Politics and Secular States" [in Arabic], a review of a book with the same title by Scott W. Hibbard, Aljazeera.net, January 22, 2014 (http://www.aljazeera.net/home/print/92804797-74a7-4675-b919-6682990f8cbe/2c0e676c-4cc8-454d-9ebb-3b1f4d9eec4).

44. Khalid Al-Dakheel, "Separation of Religion from the State in Islamic History" [in Arabic], *Al-Hayat* (London), February 22, 2014 (http://alhayat.com/Opinion/Khaled-El-Dakheel/729863/).

45. M.A. Muqtedar Khan, "The Political Philosophy of Islamic Resurgence," *Cultural Dynamics*, vol. 13, no. 2, 2001, pp. 211–229.

46. The Union of Arab Banks estimates that Arab countries are losing USD 25 billion every year as a result of money laundered and smuggled outside the Arab world. See: "USD 25 Billion Smuggled from the Arab World Every Year" [in Arabic], Sky News Arabia, October 29, 2013 (http://www.skynewsarabia.com/web/article/462271/).

47. Ergun Ozbudun, "Turkey: Crises, Interruptions, and Reequilibrations," in Larry Diamond, Juan Linz, and Seymour Martin Lipset (eds.), *Politics in Developing Countries: Comparing Experiences with Democracy* (Boulder, CO: 1995), pp. 222–224.

48. Metin Heper, "The Strong State as a Problem for the Consolidation of Democracy: Turkey and Germany Compared," *Comparative Political Studies*, vol. 25, no. 2 (July 1992), p. 175.

49. Nilufer Gole, "Secularism and Islamism in Turkey: The Making of Elites and Counter-Elites," *Middle East Journal*, vol. 51, no. 1 (Winter 1997), p. 49.

50. Luthfi Assyaukanie, *Islam and the Secular State in Indonesia* (Singapore: Institute of Southeast Asian Studies, 2009), pp. 180–184.

51. Bulent Kenes, "Moderation, Modernization and Malaysia," Today's Zaman, January 19, 2012 (http://www.todayszaman.com/columnists/bulent-kenes_269054-moderation-modernization-and-malaysia.html).

52. Ibid. (http://www.todayszaman.com/columnists/bulent-kenes_269054-moderation-modernization-and-malaysia.html).

53. International Monetary Fund (IMF) Database, October 2014 (http://www.imf.org/external/pubs/ft/weo/2014/02/weodata/weorept.aspx?sy=2012&ey=2019&scsm=1&ssd=1&sort=country&ds=.&br=1&pr1.x=33&pr1.y=8&c=548&s=NGDPDPC&grp=0&a=).

54. International Monetary Fund (IMF), "Malaysia and the IMF" (http://www.imf.org/external/country/MYS/index.htm).

55. "The History of Coups d'état in Sudan: 13 Attempts since Independence with 4 Successes; Al-Numairi's and Al-Basheer's Regimes are the Most Lasting" [in Arabic], *Al-Sharq Al-Awsat* (London), September 9, 2014 (http://classic.aawsat.com/details.asp?section=4&article=254457&issueno=9417).

56. Experts point to a lack of a clear vision, the adoption of erroneous policies by the Sudanese regime, and the presence of indicators of macroeconomic mismanagement, such as increasing money supply and low development expenditure compared to total government spending. According to these

experts, the main problem was the lack of political and strategic vision needed to manage the economy, which resulted in an inability to implement proper economic policies taking into consideration the new situation after the secession of South Sudan and the loss of 75 percent of the Sudanese oil revenues. See "Inflation and Political Conflict Threats to the Sudanese Economy" [in Arabic], Aljazeera.net, September 4, 2014 (http://goo.gl/PzWFhE).

57. Ahmad Khamis Kamil, "The Dilemma of Empowerment: The Gap between Discourse and Practice in the Experience of the Islamic Movement in the Sudan" [in Arabic], *Al-Siyassa Al-Dawliyya*, January 29, 2013 (http://goo.gl/3GfhY4).

58. Katerina Dalacoura, "The Uncertain Future of Political Islam," Global Brief, February 18, 2011 (http://globalbrief.ca/blog/2011/02/18/the-uncertain-future-of-political-islam).

59. Alsayyid Wald Abah, "The Islamists: Politicizing Religion or Religionizing Politics?" [in Arabic], *Al-Ittihad* (UAE), February 27, 2012 (http://www.alittihad.ae/wajhatdetails.php?id=64388).

60. Jamal Sanad Al-Suwaidi, op. cit., p. 98.

61. Ridwan Al-Sayyid, "Fears for Religion: from the West, the Elite or Society?" [in Arabic], *Al-Sharq Al-Awsat* (London), October 19, 2012 (http://bit.ly/1sfA8jK). See also: Ridwan Al-Sayyid, *Revival, Reform and Other Options: Protecting Religion amidst Transformational Crises* [in Arabic], Emirates Lectures Series no. 170 (Abu Dhabi: Emirates Center for Strategic Studies and Research, 2013), pp. 13–22.

62. Dalacoura, op. cit. (http://globalbrief.ca/blog/2011/02/18/the-uncertain-future-of-political-islam).

63. Basim Al-Makki, "Power Struggle after the Death of the Prophet: Al-Saqifa Meeting as an Example" [in Arabic], Mominoun Without Borders, November 29, 2013 (http://bit.ly/1q3rUUU).

64. Ridwan Al-Sayyid, "Religious and National Imbalances and Interferences Aimed at Dividing" [in Arabic], *Al-Sharq Al-Awsat* (London), October 4, 2013

(http://classic.aawsat.com/leader.asp?section=3&article=745530&issueno=1272
9#.VFYJVTqoUSs).

65. Mahdi Saad, "Mixing Religion and Politics is a Big Mistake" [in Arabic], Al-
Hiwar Al-Mutamdden, November 20, 2006 (http://www.ahewar.org/debat/
show.art.asp?aid=81288).

66. Ahmad Zayed, "The Islamists ... Fear of Secularism" [in Arabic], Middle East
Online, January 6, 2014 (http://www.middle-east-online.com/?id=168890).

67. Atiyya Massooh, "Secularism and the Arab Reality" [in Arabic], Maaber
(http://www.maaber.org/issue_december08/spotlights2.htm).

68. Ghassan Al-Hammoori, "Challenges Facing Muslims in Western Societies"
[in Arabic], *Al-Waie Magazine*, issues 282–283, July/August 2010
(http://www.al-waie.org/issues/282-283/article.php?id=934_0_72_0_M).

69. "Prohibition of Veils Expands in France ... Most Recently in Universities" [in
Arabic], Alarabiya.net, August 7, 2013 (http://goo.gl/9hTIz9).

70. "Islamic Hijab Allowed in Public Institution in Turkey" [in Arabic], Voice of
Russia Radio, October 8, 2013 (http://arabic.ruvr.ru/2013_10_08/122568
913/).

71. "US Constitution" [in Arabic], Human Rights Library, University of Minnesota,
1996 (http://www1.umn.edu/humanrts/arab/us-con.html).

72. Bill McCarthy, "Separation of Church and State, not Separation of God from
State," Free Republic, n.d. (http://www.freerepublic.com/focus/news/987191/
posts).

73. Rhea Myerscough, "The Relationship between the State and Religion in the
United States of America" [in Arabic], Aljazeera.net, 27 December 2006
(http://www.aljazeera.net/specialfiles/pages/a02d95a9-ebda-4ac3-8dfe-c45c01
302ba3).

74. For the relationship between religion and politics in the United States
of America, see: Americans United for Separation of Church and State
(https://www.au.org).

75. Robert N. Bellah, "Civil Religion in America," *Journal of the American Academy of Arts and Sciences*, vol. 96, no. 1 (Winter 1967), pp. 1–21.

76. Frank Newport, "In US, 77% Identify as Christian," Gallup, December 24, 2012 (http://www.gallup.com/poll/159548/identify-christian.aspx).

77. Kenneth C. Davis, "America's True History of Religious Tolerance," *Smithsonian* magazine, October 2010 (http://www.smithsonianmag.com/ history/americas-true-history-of-religious-tolerance-61312684/?no-ist).

78. Ibid. (http://www.smithsonianmag.com/history/americas-true-history-of-religious-tolerance-61312684/?no-ist).

79. Karen Zraick, "Ground zero mosque opened to public Wednesday," *Christian Science Monitor*, September 22, 2011 (http://www.csmonitor.com/USA/ Latest-News-Wires/2011/0922/Ground-zero-mosque-opened-to-public-Wednesday).

80. Hashim Salih, "Europe Combines Religion and Modernity after Centuries of Separation" [in Arabic], *Al-Sharq Al-Awsat* (London), March 7, 2004.

81. Hani Khamis Ahmad Abdo, "Religion and Political Revolutions: Egypt as an Example" [in Arabic], *Strategic Visions*, The Emirates Center for Strategic Studies and Research, Issue 3, June 2013, p. 40.

82. Thaer Deeb, "From Hegel to Habermas: Religion and Secularism in Western Thought," Al-Hiwar Al-Mutamdden, 13 July 2006 (http://www.ahewar.org/ debat/show.art.asp?aid=69855).

83. Ridwan Al-Sayyid, "Fears for Religion…" op. cit. (http://bit.ly/1sfA8jK).

Chapter 3

1. A document published by the Egyptian weekly Magazine *Al Musawar* on 10 June 1994, pp. 19–22.

2. "Controversy Regarding the Remarks by the General Guide of the Muslim Brotherhood group that the Group is Close to Establishing a Global Islamic Caliphate" [in Arabic], *Al-Sharq Al-Awsat* newspaper, London, January 1, 2012 (http://classic.aawsat.com/details.asp?section=4&issueno=12087&article=656 946&feature=#.U_w_8_mSzYA).

3. Hassan Al-Banna, "The Collected Epistles of Hassan Al-Banna" [in Arabic]; (the fifth general meeting), Daawa (http://www.daawa-info.net/books1. php?id=5126&bn=195&page=6).

4. Muhammad Anagreh, "Sharif Hussein bin Ali ... the Rebel King" [in Arabic], *Addustour* newspaper, 13 June 2012 (http://bit.ly/1y10Af2).

5. Muhammad bin Ali Al-Mahmoud, "We and Colonialism ... Reading through Ideology" [in Arabic], *Al Riyadh* newspaper, May 27, 2010 (http://www.alriyadh.com/529448).

6. Refaat Al-Saeed, *Hassan Al-Banna the Founder of the Muslim Brotherhood, When .. How .. and Why?* [in Arabic]; (Beirut: Dar Al-Talia Publishers, 1988), p. 18.

7. Ahmad Dakeer, "The Reform Movement in the Modern Era: Abdurrahman Ahmad Al-Kawakibi as a Model" [in Arabic], Al-Dhiaa for Contemporary Studies (http://aldhiaa.com/arabic/show_articles.php?articles_id=640&link_ articles=alderasat_almoasereh/harakat_alaslah).

8. "Principal Shari'a Society for Cooperation between Quran and Sunnah Scholars" (http://kfip.org/ar/principal-*Sharia*-society-for-cooperation-between-Quran-and-Sunnah-scholars/)

9. For more information about the Ansar Al-Sunnah Society in the Arab Republic of Egypt, see its website (http://www.ansaralsonna.com/web/page other-659.html).

10. Refaat Al-Saeed, "The Muslim Brotherhood and Hassan Al-Banna: The March of Progressing Downward" [in Arabic], in Al-Mesbar Studies and Research Centre, *The Muslim Brotherhood: The Establishment* (various authors), 1st edition (Dubai: Al-Mesbar Studies and Research Centre, 2007) p. 17.

11. Hassan al-Banna was born in 1906 in the town of Mahmudiyya where he received his elementary and secondary education. He was also taught *Sahria* at the hands of his father the watchmaker Sheikh Abdulrahman Al-Banna and the Sufi order Sheikh Abdulwahhab Al-Hassafi. He joined Dar Al Uloom (the House of Science) in Cairo in 1923, where he came to know Sheikh Muhammad Rasheed Rida and Sheikh Muhibudeen Al-Khatib, and he graduated in 1927 to work as a teacher in Dar Al Uloom. He was assassinated in 1949 by the secret police in retaliation for the assassination of the then Prime Minister Mahmood Pasha Al-Nuqrashi at the hands of elements from the Muslim Brotherhood. See: Qasem Jameel Al-Thubetat, *The Muslim Brotherhood Group in Jordan 1945–1997: A Case Study* [in Arabic]; (Amman: Kunouz Al-Ma'refa Publishers, 2008), pp. 16–17. For further details regarding the Muslim Brotherhood's formation and establishment see: Hamada Mahmood Ismael, *Hassan Al-Banna and the Muslim Brotherhood Group between Religion and Politics 1928–1949* [in Arabic]; (Cairo: Dar Al-Shurooq, 2010), pp. 43–175.

12. Refaat Al-Saeed, *Hassan Al-Banna* ... op. cit., p. 18.

13. Muge Aknur, "The Muslim Brotherhood in Politics in Egypt: From Moderation to Authoritarianism?" *Uluslararasi Hukuk ve Politika*, vol. 9, no. 33 (2013), p. 4.

14. Jamal Sanad Al-Suwaidi, "Islam and Socio-Political Change: A Comparative Study of Egyptian, Kuwaiti and Palestinian Attitudes," unpublished dissertation manuscript, University of Wisconsin, 1990, p. 197.

15. Qasem Jameel Al-Thubetat, op. cit., p. 19.

16. Al-Sayyid Yousuf, *The Muslim Brotherhood: Is it an Islamic Awakening?* part 1 [in Arabic], "Hassan Al-Banna and the Organization" (Cairo: Al Mahrousa Center for Publishing, Press Services and Information, 1994), p. 158; also see

Hassan Al-Banna, *Memoirs of the Call and the Preacher* [in Arabic]; (Kuwait: Afaq Book Store, 2012), p. 72.

17. Laurence Caromba and Hussein Solomon, "Understanding Egypt's Muslim Brotherhood," *African Security Review*, vol. 17, no. 3 (July 2010) p. 119.

18. Aknur and Muge, op. cit., p. 4.

19. Caromba and Solomon, op. cit., p. 119.

20. Saaid Al-Fawaid, "The Muslim Brotherhood" (http://www.saaid.net/feraq/mthahb/10.htm).

21. Hamada Mahmood Ismaeel, *Hassan Al-Banna ...* op. cit., pp. 114–117.

22. Jumna Ameen Abdulaziz, *Leaves from the History of the Muslim Brotherhood* [in Arabic], part 3 (Cairo: Islamic House for Distribution and Publishing, 2003), pp. 253–254.

23. Ibid., pp. 253–263.

24. Taj Al-Sir Othman, "The Cover of Exploiting Religion in Politics is Exposed ... What Does it Mean that Islam is the Solution? A Solution for What?" [in Arabic], *Al-Rakoba* newspaper, Sudan, April 9, 2012 (http://www.alrakoba.net/news-action-show-id-70531.htm).

25. Diana Ahmad, "The Muslim Brotherhood in Syria: A Suspicious Emergence and a Black History" [in Arabic], Modern Discussion website, Issue 4002, February 13, 2013 (http://www.ahewar.org/debat/show.art.asp?aid=345458).

26. Ibrahim Gharaibeh, *The Muslim Brotherhood Group in Jordan 1946–1996* (Amman: Al-Urdun Al-Jadid Research Center and Sindbad Publishing House, 1997), p. 47.

27. Aouni Jaddou Al-Obaidi, *The Muslim Brotherhood group in Jordan and Palestine 1945-1970: Historical Pages* (Amman: 1st edition, 1991), p. 37.

28. Falah Abdullah Al-Mdaires, *The Muslim Brotherhood Group in Kuwait* [in Arabic]; (Kuwait: Qurtas Publishing House, 1999), p. 12.

29. Ibid., p. 13.

30. "The Muslim Brotherhood in Kuwait: A Journey of Understandings and Clashes with the Authorities" [in Arabic], Islamic Movements portal, June 15, 2014 (http://www.islamist-movements.com/2800).

31. Falah Abdullah Al-Mdaires, op. cit., p. 14.

32. Ibid., p. 14.

33. "The Relationship between the Islamic Group and the Salafi Approach" [in Arabic], the Arab Observatory for Extremism and Terrorism, April 25, 2013 (http://arabobservatory.com/?p=6948).

34. "The Muslim Brotherhood in Pakistan: 60 Years of Conflict between the Group and the Generals" [in Arabic], Islamic Movements portal, August 16, 2014 (http://www.islamist-movements.com/3225).

35. Abdullah Al-Rasheed, "The Muslim Brotherhood in UAE: The Roots of the Thought and the Organization" [in Arabic], *Al-Majalla* magazine, London, February 10, 2013 (http://www.majalla.com/arb/2013/02/article55242417).

36. Abdulghaffar Hussain, "The Muslim Brotherhood in UAE" [in Arabic], *Al-Khaleej* newspaper, UAE, August 1, 2012 (http://www.alkhaleej.ae/studiesand opinions/page/f386335f-a354-4fc7-a6c2-dd476e573d3c).

37. Ibid. (http://www.alkhaleej.ae/studiesandopinions/page/f386335f-a354-4fc7-a6c2-dd476e573d3c).

38. Salem Humaid, "The Story of the Brotherhood's Plot in the UAE, from the Infiltration of Thought to the Failure of the Scheme and Prosecuting the Accused Individuals" (Dubai: Al-Mezmaah Studies and Research Centre, Issue 4, 2013), pp. 39–42.

39. Mansour Al-Nogaidan, "The Muslim Brothers in the UAE: Ebb and Tide" [in Arabic], in Al-Mesbar Studies and Research Centre, *The Muslim Brotherhood and the Salafis in the Gulf*, 2010, p. 87.

40. Ibid., p. 87.

41. Al-Mezmaah Studies and Research Centre, "Before Issuing the Verdict" [in Arabic], part 4 (http://almezmaah.com/ar/news-print-1389.html) Also see: Abdullah Al-Rasheed, op. cit. (http://www.majalla.com/arb/2013/02/article 55242417).

42. A Document from "The Unified Global Organization of the Muslim Brotherhood" [in Arabic], *Al-Watan* newspaper, Egypt, September 2, 2013 (http://elwatannews.com/news/details/296054).

43. Ibid. (http://elwatannews.com/news/details/296054).

44. Abdul Raheem Ali, *The Muslim Brotherhood: A Look into the Confidential Files* [in Arabic]; (Cairo: General Egyptian Book Organization, 2011), p. 265.

45. Ghassan Al-Shehabi, "The Bahraini Muslim Brotherhood: The Particularity of Thought and the Future of Activism" [in Arabic], Al-Jazeera Center for Studies, June 10, 2014 (http://studies.aljazeera.net/reports/2014/06/2014 61062637721417.htm).

46. "The Story of the Muslim Brotherhood's Emergence in Yemen (2-3)" [in Arabic], April 29, 2007, Mareb Press (http://marebpress.net/articles.php? print=1647).

47. Hussam Tammam, "The Brotherhood and Saudi: Is it the Time for Divorce?" [in Arabic], *Al-Qahira* newspaper, Egypt, 2003.

48. Abdullah bin Bejad Al-Otaibi, "Saudi Arabia and the Muslim Brotherhood: A Glimpse of History" [in Arabic], *Al-Sharq Al-Awsat* newspaper, London, Issue 12072, December 17, 2011.

49. "First Saudi List of Terrorist Organizations Includes the Brotherhood, Al-Nusra and ISIL" [in Arabic], BBC, March 7, 2014 (http://www.bbc.co.uk/ arabic/middleeast/2014/03/140307_saudi_terror_organizations).

50. "The Muslim Brotherhood Group in Morocco: The Justice and Development Party" [in Arabic], Islamic Movements portal, May 28, 2014 (http://www. islamist-movements.com/2674).

51. Noor Al-Deen Qurbal, "Morocco's Justice and Development Party and Political Participation" [in Arabic], *Hespress* newspaper portal, November 6, 2013 (http://www.hespress.com/writers/93243.html).

52. "Secrets and Mysteries of the Muslim Brotherhood's Wealth: Investments Amounting to 180 Billion Pounds in 72 Countries" [in Arabic], *Al-Ahram Al-Arabi* magazine, Cairo, November 20, 2013.

53. Hussam Tammam, *Transformations of the Muslim Brotherhood: Disintegration of the Ideology and the End of the Organization* [in Arabic]; (Cairo: Madbouly Bookshop, 2006), p. 18.

54. Ibid., p. 18.

55. Ibrahim Gharaibeh, op. cit., pp. 33–34.

56. Aknur and Muge, op. cit., p. 4.

57. Muhammad Mursi, "The Muslim Brotherhood and the Contemporary Islamic Parties" [in Arabic], August 5, 2007, Ikhwan Online portal (http://www.ikhwanonline.com/Article.aspx?ArtID=30200&SecID=390).

58. Jamal Sanad Al-Suwaidi, op. cit., p. 210.

59. Hassan Al-Banna, *The Collected Epistles of the Martyred Imam Hassan Al-Banna* [in Arabic]; (Alexandria: Islamic House for Distribution and Publishing, 1992), p. 119.

60. Ibid., p. 119.

61. Ibid., p. 119.

62. Tawfeeq Al-Wa'ee, *The Muslim Brotherhood: The Largest Islamic Movement: Suspicions and Responses* [in Arabic]; (Cairo: Al-Manar Islamic Bookshop, 2001), pp. 141–170.

63. Hassan Al-Banna, *Risalat al-Mu'tamar al-Khamis* (Beirut, n.d.) in Arabic, p. 10, quoted in Abd al-Monein [sic] Said Aly and Manfred W. Wenner, "Modern Islamic Reform Movements: The Muslim Brotherhood in Contemporary Egypt," *The Middle East Journal*, vol. 36, no. 3, September 1982, p. 340.

64. "A Scholar from Al-Azhar Responds to Sayyid Qutb and his Sedition" [in Arabic], Alukah portal, September 6, 2008 (http://majles.alukah.net/t19695/).

65. Gilles Kepel, *Jihad: The Expansion and Decline of Islamism*, Nabeel Saad (trans.); (Cairo: Dar Al-Aalam Al-Thalith, 1st edition, 2005), p. 40.

66. Gilles Kepel, *Muslim Extremism in Egypt: The Prophet and Pharaoh* (Berkeley and Los Angeles, CA: University of California Press, 1984), p. 46.

67. Sayyid Qutb, *Ma'alim Fi'l-Tariq* [Signposts on the Road, in Arabic]; (Beirut and Cairo: Dar Al-Shurooq, 1980), p. 98, quoted in Gilles Kepel, op. cit., p. 47.

68. Yvonne Y. Haddad, "Sayyid Qutb: Ideologue of Islamic Revival," in John L. Esposito (ed.), *Voices of Resurgent Islam* (New York, NY: Oxford University Press, 1983), p. 70.

69. Talcott Parsons, "Some Sociological Aspects of the Fascist Movements," *Social Forces* vol. 21 (December 1942), p. 140.

70. Said Ramadan, "Rakaiz Dawat Al-Islam," *Al-Musliman*, vol. 1, no. 6, n.d., p. 37.

71. Richard P. Mitchell, *The Society of the Muslim Brothers* (London: Oxford University Press, 1969), pp. 9, 14.

72. Hassan Al-Banna, *The Collected Epistles* (Alexandria: Islamic House for Distribution and Publishing, 1992), p. 102.

73. For more information see: Muhammad Abdulqadir Abu Faris "The Political System in Islam" [in Arabic]; (Amman: Dar Al-Furqan for Publishing and Distribution, 2013).

74. Sayyid Qutb was executed during the reign of the former Egyptian President Jamal Abdul Nasser because of his ideas, which were deemed dangerous, and because he was affiliated with a secret organization which aimed to take over the government. See: Noori Ahmad, "Why Jamal Abdul Nasser executed Sayyid Qutb?" [in Arabic], *Al-Mustashar* newspaper, Iraq, October 3, 2013 (http://almustashar-iq.net/index.php/permalink/33278.html).

75. Tharwat Al-Kharbawi, "Sayyid Qutb from America to Jahiliyya 1-2" [in Arabic], *Al-Dostor* newspaper, Egypt, February 16, 2014 (http://www.dostor. org/81191).

76. "Illusion of the Religious State: between Caliphate, hakimiyya [divine sovereignty] and the Guardianship of the Jurist" [in Arabic], *Al-Arab* newspaper, London, January 8, 2014 (http://alarab.co.uk/m/?id=12317); and Tamer Wajeeh, "Sayyid Qutb: Confrontation between the Group of Believers and the Jahiliyya of the Twentieth Century" [in Arabic], *Al-Masry Al-Youm* newspaper, Egypt, May 8, 2012 (http://www.almasryalyoum.com/news/ details/177399#).

77. Sayyid Qutb, *Ma'alim fi Al-Tareeq*, op. cit., p. 6

78. For more information on the Godliness principle see: Muhammad bin Abdurrahman Abu Yousuf Al-Jehni, "The Meaning, Evidence and Rules of Godliness and the Refutation of Denying it" [in Arabic], pp. 2–10 (http://bit.ly/1pdemKP).

79. Sabri Muhammad Khalil, "The Muslim Brotherhood: A Methodological Examination of its Intellectual Origins" [in Arabic], Sudanile portal, June 5, 2012 (http://bit.ly/1pDHTwc).

80. Ibid. (http://bit.ly/1pDHTwc).

81. Ali Al-Sayyid Al-Waseefi, *The Muslim Brotherhood between Religious Innovation and Political Bankruptcy* [in Arabic]; (Cairo: Dar Sabeel Al-Mumineen for Publishing and Distribution, 2012), p. 33.

82. For more information about the Muslim Brotherhood group's stance on implementing Sharia, see: Salah Al-Sadiq Al-Jehani, "The Muslim Brotherhood's Stance on Implementing Sharia" [in Arabic], Modern Discussion website, July 03, 2014 (http://www.ahewar.org/debat/show. art.asp?aid=422203).

83. Minister of Awqaf: "The Brotherhood Embraced Dissimulation just like the Shiites and We are Purging them from the Ministry" [in Arabic], *Al-Masry Al-Youm* newspaper, Egypt, March 7, 2014 (http://www.almasryalyoum. com/news/details/406187#).

84. Hussam Tammam, "The Democratic Trend in the Brotherhood: Map of Proliferation and Obstacles" [in Arabic], Modern Discussion website, Issue 1082, January 18, 2005 (http://www.ahewar.org/debat/show.art.asp?aid= 30046).

85. Rashid Al-Ghannooshi, *Approaches in Secularism and Civil Society* [in Arabic] (Tunisia: Al-Mujtahid Publishing and Distribution House, 2011), pp. 5–6, 64–91.

86. For further information about the by-laws of the Muslim Brotherhood Society, see: "A Reading in the Intellectual Structure of the Muslim Brotherhood" [in Arabic], February 2010, pp. 12–14 (www.asharqalarabi.org.uk/markaz/dr-19-02-2011.doc).

87. "The Law of the Muslim Brotherhood Society (1930)" [in Arabic], Wikisource (http://bit.ly/1vdRfo6).

88. Hassan Al-Banna, *The Collected Epistles*, op. cit., p. 159.

89. Ibid., pp. 159, 180, 181.

90. Youssef H. Aboul-Enein, "Al-Ikhwan Al-Muslimeen: The Muslim Brotherhood," *Military Review* (July–August 2003), pp. 26–31.

91. Ibid., pp. 26–31.

92. Muhiy Hamed, "Key issues in the Thought of Imam Hassan Al-Banna: The Brotherhood's Stance on Governments, Parties and Issues of Terrorism" [in Arabic], *Al-Mujtama* magazine, Kuwait, issue 2069, March 5, 2014.

93. Haidar Hobballah, "Key Paper on Human Rights in Islam" [in Arabic] (http://www.shahrodi.com/al-menhaj/Almen39/39000015.htm).

94. The Holy Quran (3:159).

95. Helmi Al-Namnam, citing the diaries of Abdulaziz Kamel, former Egyptian Minister of Awqaf and former member of the Muslim Brotherhood and Hassan Al-Banna's contemporary [in Arabic], *Al-Ittihad* newspaper, UAE, February 17, 2007 (http://www.alittihad.ae/details.php?id=98315&y=2007& article=full).

96. Ibid. (http://www.alittihad.ae/details.php?id=98315&y=2007&article=full).

97. Muhammad Abu Zaid, "The Islamic Group in Egypt from Years of Anger to Initiative to Stop Violence" [in Arabic], *Al-Sharq Al-Awsat* newspaper, London, February 13, 2005 (http://classic.aawsat.com/details.asp?article=282 643&issueno=9574).

98. Waleed Nuwaihidh, *The Political Contract: The Islamists, The State and the Issue of Democracy (1984–1996)*, [in Arabic]; (Manama: Dar Al-Wasat for Publishing and Distribution, 2nd edition, 2009); (http://arabsfordemocracy. org/democracy/pages/view/pageId/1025).

99. Ibid. (http://arabsfordemocracy.org/democracy/pages/view/pageId/1025).

100. L. Carl Brown, *Religion and State: The Muslim Approach to Politics* (New York, NY: Columbia University Press, October 2000), p. 144

101. Amr Hashim Rabie, "The Muslim Brotherhood and the Egyptian Parliament," in *The Muslim Brotherhood: The Challenges*, Part 2 [in Arabic]; (Dubai: Al-Mesbar Studies and Research Centre, January 2008), pp. 64–95.

102. Mahmoud Abdul Haleem, *The Muslim Brotherhood: Events that Made History (an inside look)*, Part 1, 1928–1948 [in Arabic]; (Alexandria: Dar Al-Da'wah for Printing, Publishing and Distribution, 1979).

103. For further information regarding the role of the Muslim Brotherhood in the 1948 war, see: Ali Al-Sayyid Al-Wasifi, *The Muslim Brotherhood between Religious Innovation and Political Bankruptcy* [in Arabic]; (Cairo: Dar Sabeel Al-Mumineen for Publishing and Distribution, 2012), pp. 531–548.

104. Amer Shammakh, *The Muslim Brotherhood and Violence: Reading in the Thought and the Reality of the Muslim Brotherhood* [in Arabic]; (Cairo: Al-Saad for Publication and Distribution, 2008), pp. 122–123.

105. Hamada Mahmood Ismaeel, op. cit., p. 434.

106. Amr Al-Shoubaki, "The Challenges of Integrating the Muslim Brotherhood in the Political Process" [in Arabic] in *The Muslim Brotherhood: The Establishment*, various authors (Dubai: Al-Mesbar Studies and Research Centre, January 2007), p. 131.

107. Youssef H. Aboul-Enein, op. cit., p. 28.

108. Ahmad Abu Shousha, "Nasser and the Brotherhood from Reconciliation to Rivalry: The Brotherhood's Support for Sidqi's Authoritarian Government Accelerated the Conflict; The Mansheya Incident Put an End to the Group" [in Arabic], *Sada Al-Balad* newspaper, Egypt, September 29, 2013 (http://www.el-balad.com/631747).

109. Refaat Sayyid Ahmad, "Abdul Nasser and the Brotherhood: The Story of Blood and Fire (1/5) [in Arabic], May 7, 2013, Arab and Muslim Assembly to Support the Choice of Resistance (http://www.khayaralmoukawama.com/DETAILS.ASP?id=2970&param=NEWS).

110. "History of Islamic Civilization," Rulers of Egypt Encyclopedia [in Arabic]; (http://www.islamichistory.net/forum/showthread.php?p=48001).

111. Hala Mustafa, *State and Islamic Opposition Movements between Appeasement and Confrontation in the Reigns of Sadat and Mubarak: The Political Regime and the Islamic Opposition in Egypt* [in Arabic]; (Cairo: Al Mahrousa Center for Publishing, Press Services and Information, 1996), p. 130. For further details regarding the relationship between the Muslim Brotherhood and the Free Officers in Egypt during that period, see: Richard Mitchel, *The Muslim Brotherhood* [in Arabic], Abdulsalam Ridwan (trans.); (Cairo: Madbooli Bookshop, 2nd Edition, 1985), pp. 171–255.

112. Hala Mustafa, op. cit., p. 131.

113. Ibid., p. 131.

114. Richard Mitchel, op. cit., p. 242.

115. Hala Mustafa, op. cit., p. 132.

116. Huda Abdul Nasser, "Biography of President Jamal Abdul Nasser," website of President Jamal Abdul Nasser (http://nasser.bibalex.org/Common/pictures01-%20sira.htm).

117. Waheed Abdulmajeed, *The Muslim Brotherhood between History and the Future: How the Group Was and How it Will Be?* [in Arabic]; (Cairo: Al-Ahram Center for Translation, Publishing and Distribution, 2010), pp. 130–145.

118. "Egypt: A Harsh Blow to the Brotherhood that May Escalate Violence" [in Arabic], Sky News Arabia, August 20, 2013 (http://bit.ly/1q6f6gK).

119. Mustapha Al-Dessouki, "Egypt from One Revolution to Another" [in Arabic], *Al-Majalla* magazine, London, September 28, 2012 (http://www.majalla. com/arb/2012/09/article55238815).

120. "Parliamentary Performance of the Brotherhood Deputies in the Balance" [in Arabic], Swiss Info Portal, October 20, 2005 (www.swissinfo.ch/ara/detail/ content.html?cid=4777302).

121. "Dr. Sufi Abu Taleb: the Project to Incorporate Sharia in the Laws has been Ready since 1983!" [in Arabic], On Islam website, May 22, 2007 (http:// www.onislam.net/arabic/fiqh-a-tazkia/fiqh-papers/8081/95402-2007-05-22% 2013-51-30.html).

122. Ibid. (http://www.onislam.net/arabic/fiqh-a-tazkia/fiqh-papers/8081/95402-2007- 05-22%2013-51-30.html).

123. Samir Atallah, "Sadat's Last Surprise" [in Arabic], *Al-Sharq Al-Awsat* newspaper, London, September 20, 2010 (http://classic.aawsat.com/leader. asp?section=3&article=587449&issueno=11619).

124. "Minister of Culture: Sadat Reconciled with the Muslim Brotherhood and Sought State Islamization" [in Arabic], Al-Youm Al-Sabie electronic newspaper, July 14, 2014 (http://bit.ly/1uGXgoZ).

125. To hear the audio recording of former Egyptian President Anwar Sadat admitting his mistake of releasing imprisoned elements of the Muslim Brotherhood, visit: (http://www.youtube.com/watch?v=TCOXfk519d8).

126. Muhammad Fadhel Ali, "When Sadat Cried I was Wrong Laminating Releasing the Muslim Brotherhood Members from Prison" [in Arabic], Sudanile Electronic Newspaper, August 17, 2013 (http://www.sudanile. com/index.php/2008-05-19-17-39-36/120-2009-02-03-19-32-31/57320- 2013-08-17-11-52-13).

127. "Haikal: 'the Brotherhood is Innocent of Sadat's Assassination and Nasser is the only President who did not Taste the Joy of Ceremonies" [in Arabic], *Al-Watan* newspaper, Egypt, March 28, 2013 (http://www.elwatannews. com/news/details/155259).

128. Muhammad Hassanein Haikal, *Autumn of Fury: The Beginning and End of the Reign of Anwar Al-Sadat* [in Arabic] (Cairo: Al-Ahram Center for Translation and Publication, 1988), pp. 427–436.

129. Amr Hashim Rabie, "The Muslim Brotherhood and the Egyptian Parliament," in *The Muslim Brotherhood: The Challenges* [in Arabic] (Dubai: Al-Mesbar, 2008), p. 68.

130. Kamal Habib, "The New Islamic Alliance in Egypt" [in Arabic], *Al-Youm Al-Sabie* newspaper, Egypt, June 24, 2013 (http://www1.youm7.com/News.asp?NewsID=1131000).

131. "Parliamentary Performance …" op. cit. (http://bit.ly/1oFMxKM).

132. Amr Hashim Rabie, op. cit., p. 70.

133. Ibid., p. 71.

134. Muhammad Al-Baz, "Treason Valley: Final Episode" [in Arabic], *Al-Youm Al-Sabie* newspaper, Egypt, December 28, 2013 (http://www.youm7.com/News.asp?NewsID=1421279).

135. Ibid. (http://www.youm7.com/News.asp?NewsID=1421279).

136. For more details, see: Waheed Abdulmajeed, op. cit., pp. 125ff.

137. Ahmad Zaghlool, "The Islamists and Charity Work in Egypt" [in Arabic], Non Post portal, December 27, 2013 (http://www.noonpost.net/content/1361).

138. Khaleel Al-Anani, "Mubarak and the Brotherhood: A Thirty-Year Experience [in Arabic], Al-Jazeera Center for Studies, October 13, 2011 (http://studies.aljazeera.net/files/2011/08/201187113648385131.htm).

139. Fares Al-Khattab, "The Muslim Brotherhood in Egypt: A Journey of an Obscured Organization Exposed by Light" [in Arabic], *Al-Ittihad* newspaper, UAE, June 8, 2014 (http://www.alittihad.ae/details.php?id=50721&y=2014&article=full).

140. Jeremy M. Sharp, "Egypt: 2005 Presidential and Parliamentary Elections," Congressional Research Service (Washington, DC: GPO for the Library of Congress, 2006), p. 1.

141. Brown, op. cit., p. 12.

142. Ibid., p. 12.

143. Joseph Beshara, "Inheritance, the Muslim Brotherhood and the Crisis of Political Parties in Egypt," Elaph electronic newspaper, June 3, 2006 (http://www.elaph.com/Web/AsdaElaph/2006/6/153224.htm?sectionarchive =AsdaElaph).

144. Ibrahim Gharaibeh, op. cit., p. 12.

145. Aouni Jaddou Al-Obaidi, op. cit., p. 166.

146. Ibrahim Gharaibeh, op. cit., p. 12.

147. For more information about the protests known as the "April Uprising," see: (http://abeash.files.wordpress.com/2013/04/d8a7d984d8a3d8b1d8afd986-d8a7d984d8acd8afd98ad8af.pdf).

148. Ibrahim Gharaibeh, op. cit., p. 14.

149. "Lion of Jordan: Story of a King" [in Arabic] (part 14), *Al-Sharq Al-Awsat* newspaper, London, November 4, 2007 (http://classic.aawsat.com/details. asp?issueno=10568&article=444116#.VBaUbjqoWic).

150. Ibrahim Gharaibeh, op. cit., p. 138.

151. Ibid., p. 133.

152. Khalid Fakhida, "Questions to the Muslim Brotherhood" [in Arabic], *Al-Rai* newspaper, Jordan, March 24, 2012 (http://www.alrai.com/article/500913. html).

153. Qasem Jameel Al-Thubetat, op. cit., pp. 84–85.

154. Muhammad Abu Ramman, "The Muslim Brotherhood in Jordan's 2007 Parliamentary Elections: A Temporary Political Setback or an Erosion of Popularity?" [in Arabic], Judran portal, December 23, 2007 (www.judran. net/?p=48).

155. Muhammad Essam Ayesh, "Jordanian Political Map after the Elections and Constitutional Amendments" [in Arabic], Al-Arabiya Institute for Studies, May 8, 2013 (http://bit.ly/1qXPvxB).

156. Muhammad Al-Demerdash, "Hassan Al-Turabi the Wizard of Sudan, Part 2" [in Arabic], *Al-Masaeya* newspaper, Egypt (http://almsaeya.com/index.php/2014-02-11-17-19-41/item/5502-2).

157. Gabriel R. Warburg, *The Muslim Brotherhood in Sudan: From Reforms to Radicalism* [in Arabic], translated and summarized by Badr Al-Deen Hamid Al-Hashemi, February 19, 2014 (http://www.alrakoba.net/articles-action-show-id-55537.htm). Also see: "The Muslim Brotherhood in Sudan" *Al-Turabi's Ambitions: The Journey of the Rise and Fall* [in Arabic], Islamic Movements portal, June 2, 2014 (http://www.islamist-movements.com/2701).

158. Ali Muhammad Ali, "Islamic Movement's Experience in Sudan: the Gap between Rhetoric and Practice" [in Arabic], Digital Ahram portal, April 1, 2013 (http://digital.ahram.org.eg/articles.aspx?Serial=1383545&eid=592).

159. "Hamas: Inception and Relationship with the Muslim Brotherhood" [in Arabic], *Al-Sharq Al-Awsat* newspaper, London, June 9, 2001 (http://classic.aawsat.com/details.asp?section=28&article=42016&issueno=8229#.U_NNDP 2oWic).

160. Khalaf Khalaf, "Roots and Facts of the Hidden Conflict between Fatah and Hamas" [in Arabic], Elaph electronic newspaper, December 17, 2007 (http://www.elaph.com/ElaphWeb/AkhbarKhasa/2007/12/288608.htm).

161. Bissan Adwan, "Hamas and the Culture of Elections" [in Arabic], Modern Discussion website, April 12, 2006 (http://www.ahewar.org/debat/show.art.asp?aid=82523).

162. "Hamas Wins the Palestinian Legislative Elections" [in Arabic], Al-Quds Center for Political Studies, January 1, 2006 (http://www.alqudscenter.org/arabic/pages.php?local_type=123&local_details=2&id1=86&menu_id=-1).

163. Hussam Tammam, "The Moroccan Experience in Distinguishing between Preaching and Politics" [in Arabic], Islamism Scope portal, July 25, 2007 (http://www.islamismscope.net/index.php?option=com_content&view=article &id=140:2010-02-09-13-43-12&catid=37:articles&Itemid=67).

164. For more details on the political evolution of the Justice and Development Party in the Kingdom of Morocco, see: Amr Hamzawy "Party for Justice and

Development in Morocco: Participation and Its Discontents" [in Arabic] Carnegie Papers, Carnegie Endowment, July 2008 (http://carnegieendowment. org/files/cp93_hamzawy_pjd_arabic.pdf).

165. Muhammad Maleki, "Morocco's Justice and Development Party: Reform in the Context of Stability" [in Arabic], Al-Jazeera Center for Studies, March 20, 2012 (http://studies.aljazeera.net/reports/2012/03/201231913332423267.htm).

166. Saeed Al-Kuhl, "Morocco's Justice and Development Party: Its Positions and Convictions Contradict its Slogans" [in Arabic], Modern Discussion website, April 28, 2012 (http://www.ahewar.org/debat/show.art.asp?aid=36301).

167. Salah Khaleel, "Legislative Elections in Morocco: Division and Challenges" [in Arabic], Digital Ahram portal, January 1, 2012 (http://digital.ahram.org.eg/ articles.aspx?Serial=813871&eid=5239).

168. Falah Abdullah Al-Mdaires, op. cit., p. 26.

169. Ibid., p. 28.

170. "In the Words of its President, the Social Reform Society is in Line with the Thought of the Muslim Brotherhood" [in Arabic], Kuwait Sound electronic newspaper, December 1, 2013 (http://bit.ly/1pdNL0B).

171. Falah Abdullah Al-Mdaires, op. cit., p. 48.

172. Al-Menbar National Islamic Society, a brief introduction (http://www. almenber.bh/about.php).

173. Ghassan Al-Shehabi, "The Bahraini Muslim Brotherhood: The Particularity of Thought and the Future of Activism" [in Arabic], Al-Jazeera Center for Studies, June 10, 2014 (http://studies.aljazeera.net/reports/2014/06/201461 062637721417.htm).

174. Ibid. (http://studies.aljazeera.net/reports/2014/06/201461062637721417.htm).

175. Heather Brown, "Islamist Anomalies: The FIS in 1991, Muslim Brotherhood in 2005 and Hamas in 2006," paper presented at the Annual Meeting of the Northeastern Political Science Association (Omni Parker House, Boston, MA, November 11, 2010), p. 23.

176. "Statistical and Political Examination of the Results of the Second Palestinian Legislative Elections" [in Arabic], January 25, 2006, a report issued by the Middle East Studies Center in the Hashemite Kingdom of Jordan (http://www.mesc.com.jo/OurVision/vision_mesc/vote/vote1.pdf).

177. Amani Zayed, "The Implementation of Sharia: The Brotherhood's Burned Card" [in Arabic], *Al-Wafd* newspaper, Egypt, June 30 2013 (http://bit.ly/1qDDKvi).

178. "The Danger Organizations: 'Al-Qaradawi Union,' 'Cair,' the 'Islamic Organizations' and the 'American Society,' [in Arabic], *Al-Watan* newspaper, Egypt, August 22, 2014 (http://www.elwatannews.com/news/details/543704).

179. "Haikal: Part of Mursi's 'Decisive' Tone in the 'Summit' is Directed to the Brotherhood .. and the 'Group' is Experiencing a 'Shock'," [in Arabic], *Al-Watan* newspaper, Egypt, March 28, 2013 (http://www.elwatannews.com/news/details/155186).

180. Ahmad Othman, "Will the Islamic Caliphate Return in Cairo?" [in Arabic], *Al-Sharq Al-Awsat* newspaper, London, January 2, 2012 (http://classic.aawsat.com/leader.asp?section=3&issueno=12088&article=657119).

181. "The Empowerment Document and the Brotherhood's Intentions" [in Arabic], *Al-Majalla* magazine, London, April 12, 2010 (http://www.majalla.com/arb/2010/04/article5542290).

182. United Nations (UN), "Human Development Report 2014, Sustaining Human Progress: Reducing Vulnerabilities and Building Resilience" [in Arabic]; (http://www.un.org/ar/esa/hdr/pdf/hdr14.pdf).

183. Manoj Singh, "The 2007-08 Financial Crisis in Review," Investopedia (http://www.investopedia.com/articles/economics/09/financial-crisis-review.asp).

184. "The Brotherhood after Meeting Suleiman: Reform Proposals are Inadequate" [in Arabic], BBC, February 6, 2011 (http://www.bbc.co.uk/arabic/middleeast/2011/02/110206_suleiman_meeting_opposition.shtml).

185. *Al-Ittihad* newspaper, UAE, February 11, 2011 (http://www.alittihad.ae/details.php?id=14534&y=2011).

186. Yusri Ahmad Azbawi, "The Future of the New Political Parties after the January Revolution" [in Arabic], Digital Ahram portal, August 1, 2011 (http://digital.ahram.org.eg/articles.aspx?Serial=672651&eid=8011).

187. "A Year Since the Establishment of the Freedom and Justice Party" [in Arabic], *Al-Masry Al-Youm* newspaper, Egypt, June 6, 2012 (http://www.almasryalyoum.com/news/details/184089).

188. "Egypt's Parliament between Consensus and Alliances" [in Arabic], Aljazeera.net, January 23, 2012 (http://bit.ly/1qQqm5X).

189. Khairy Omar, "A Look into the Results of the Egyptian Parliamentary Elections" [in Arabic], *Middle East Studies Journal*, Issue 5, Year 16, Spring 2012.

190. Abdulmunem Abu Al-Futooh –a doctor and former member of the Guidance Office of the Muslim Brotherhood – was dismissed by the group for non-compliance with its decisions when he nominated himself for the presidency. He later established the Strong Egypt Party in 2012. See: "The Parties Affairs Committee Approves the Establishment of the Strong Egypt Party" [in Arabic], *Al-Masry Al-Yaum* (Egypt), November 12, 2012 (http://www.almasryalyoum.com/news/details/240914#).

191. "Results of the First Round of the Presidential Elections" [in Arabic], *Al-Youm Al-Sabie*, May 28, 2012 (http://www.youm7.com/News.asp?NewsID=690592#.U48z5P1kpUY).

192. Official Website of the 2012 Egyptian Presidential Elections (http://presidential2012.elections.eg/index.php/round2-results).

193. "Governor of Luxor a 'Jihadist' who was Arrested after Sadat's Assassination" [in Arabic], CNN Arabic, July 18, 2013 (http://goo.gl/VZr7Ph).

194. "The Islamic Group at a Dangerous Junction" [in Arabic], Al-Quds Center for Political Studies, July 25, 2002 (http://bit.ly/1BMMnGj).

195. Muhammad Fouad, "15 Terrorist Incidents, the Most Infamous is the Luxor Massacre" *Al-Ahram* newspaper, Egypt, February 18, 2014 (http://digital.ahram.org.eg/articles.aspx?Serial=1540976&eid=749).

196. Nasr Muhammad Arif, "The Fatalist Circle: The End of Modernist Islamism of the Muslim Brotherhood" [in Arabic], *Al-Siyassa Al-Dawliyya*, Issue 194, October 2013, pp. 63–64.

197. "Economists: Qandeel's Government is Confused, 'its Decisions are Ill-considered' and it is Operating without a Clear Vision or Goal" [in Arabic], *Al-Youm Al-Sabie* electronic newspaper, Egypt, November 4, 2012 (http://bit.ly/1qYmVuj).

198. "After Getting Only the Ministry of Environment: Al-Noor Party Withdraws from Qandeel's Government" [in Arabic], *Al-Ahram* newspaper, Egypt, August 2, 2012 (http://digital.ahram.org.eg/articles.aspx?Serial=981853&eid=7266).

199. Muhammad Abu Al-Aineen, "Expectations of the Future of Political Islam after the June 30 Revolution" [in Arabic], *Al-Ahram*, September 13, 2013 (http://www.ahram.org.eg/NewsQ/231537.aspx).

200. Sabri Abdulhafeez Hassanein, "An Egyptian Scandal: A Presidential Meeting on National Security Regarding the Renaissance Dam was Broadcasted Live" [in Arabic], *Elaph* newspaper, June 4, 2013 (http://www.elaph.com/Web/news/2013/6/816307.html).

201. Emma Hayward, "Assessing Ennahda, Tunisia's Winning Islamist Party" [in Arabic], the Washington Institute, November 18, 2011 (http://bit.ly/1tg3Wf9).

202. "[Rashid] Al-Ghannooshi does not take a Firm Stand and Quickly Changes his Mind" [in Arabic], *Al-Arab* newspaper, issue 9328, London, September 22, 2013, p. 6.

203. "Interview .. Shaikh Abdul Fattah Moro: Ennahdha's Government has More Cons than Pros" [in Arabic], Islam Online portal, February 17, 2013 (http://bit.ly/1qjtHGl).

204. "The Final Results of the October 23 Elections" [in Arabic], Attounissia electronic newspaper, November 15, 2011 (http://bit.ly/XuBZ7u).

205. Munther Baldhiafi, "Ennahdha Exiting the Government in Tunisia! Factors and Possible Scenarios" [in Arabic], Al-Arabiya.net, January 13, 2014 (http://bit.ly/1pgospX).

206. Mustafa Farhat interviewing Rashid Al-Ghannooshi, Islam Online portal, April 7, 2012 (http://islamonline.net/selected/1665).

207. "Final Results: Nidaa Tounes Wins the Tunisian Elections" [in Arabic], Ahdath Info portal, October 30, 2014 (http://www.ssrcaw.org/ar/news.asp?nid =1844388).

208. Abdulwahid Ibraheem, "The Muslim Brotherhood's Ruling Experience in Sudan" [in Arabic], Civic Egypt, January 28, 2013 (http://civicegypt. org/?p=34060).

209. Hassan Abdullah, "Hollow Political Islam Slogans Thwarted the Implementation of Sharia 3-2" [in Arabic], *Al-Ittihad* newspaper, UAE (http://www.alittihad. ae/investigations_details.php?id=33).

210. "The World's Neglected Food Basket" [in Arabic], *Al-Sharq Al-Awsat* newspaper, London, April 11, 2008 (http://classic.aawsat.com/details.asp? issueno=10626&article=466415).

211. Yasir Mahgoub Al-Hussein, "The Future of the Political System in Sudan" [in Arabic], Al-Sharq Portal, May 31, 2014 (http://www.al-sharq.com/ news/details/242469#.U-MYGf2oWic).

212. As an example for such a shift, see: "Egypt's Brotherhood are Shifting their Policy and Pressing Hamas to Make Compromises with Fatah" [in Arabic], *Al-Sharq Al-Awsat* newspaper, London, March 25, 2012 (http://bit.ly/1teLkej).

213. Musa Hamid, "Sudan's Impossible Democracy" [in Arabic], Ashorooq.net, January 29, 2013 (http://goo.gl/B9EVhU).

214. "Disintegration Threats: The Internal Situations of the Middle East according to the 'Fragile States Index'" [in Arabic], Regional Centre for Strategic Studies in Cairo, website of the Arab Orient Center for Cultural and Strategic Studies, August 3, 2014 (https://gallery.mailchimp.com/7e569236ec7284d7724bc0525/ files/c05d5385-f374-41af-8cf9-a0e244b1904a.pdf).

215. Majdi Helmi, "The Brotherhoodization of State: Plan and Execution" [in Arabic], *Al-Wafd* newspaper, Egypt, September 6, 2012 (http://bit.ly/1y8rt 0M).

216. Salaheddine Jourchi, "Tunisia's Salafism: A Critical Issue in a Fragile Transitional Period" [in Arabic], Swiss Info Portal, September 3, 2012 (http://bit.ly/1sWMmgj).

217. "General Labor Union Proposes a New Initiative to Resolve the Political Crisis in Tunisia" [in Arabic], *Al-Arab* newspaper, London, September 19, 2013 (http://www.alarab.co.uk/?id=4172).

Chapter 4

1. Muhammad Abduwahhab Rafiqi, "Renewal and Revival in Salafi Thought" [in Arabic], Aljazeera.net, March 13, 2014 (http://bit.ly/1BFlEvb).

2. Abdullah Al-Ahdal, "Jihad for Allah: Wasting Jihad Efforts by Acts of Sabotage" [in Arabic], Ahl Al-Hadeeth Forum, August 5, 2014 (http://www.ahlalhdeeth.com/vb/showthread.php?p=2105371).

3. Hassan Hanafi, "Political Islam in Theory and Practice," in *Islamic Movements and their Influence on Political Stability in the Arab World* [in Arabic]; (Abu Dhabi: The Emirates Center for Strategic Studies and Research, 2002), p. 59.

4. Abbas Arheelah, "Reformation Movements in the Muslim World" [in Arabic], *Al-Manhal*, issue 528, year 21, Sha'ban 1416 AH, December 1995; and website of Abbas Arheelah (http://bit.ly/1lvUP7H).

5. Ibid. (http://bit.ly/1lvUP7H).

6. Charles Saint-Prot, *The Future of Tradition between Revolution and Westernization* [in Arabic], translated by Wajeeh Jameel Al-Buaini, Refereed Works Series no. 113 (Riyadh: King Abdulaziz Public Library, 2010), p. 318.

7. Ibid., pp. 318–319.

8. For a linguistic explanation of the Arabic word 'Salaf', see: Ibn Manzoor, *Lisan Al-Arab* vol. 9 (Beirut: Dar Sader, 1994). For the technical meaning of the word, see: Muhammad Saeed Ramadhan Al-Booti, *Salafism: A Blessed Stage, not an Islamic School* [in Arabic]; (Beirut: Dar Al-Fikr Al-Mu'asir, 1998), pp. 9–23. Also see: Abdullah bin Ibrahim bin Ali Al-Tareeqi, "Contemporary Salafi Schools: Diversity and Relationship with the Other" [in Arabic], May 21, 2011 (http://www.alukah.net/web/triqi/0/32046/).

9. The Holy Quran (2:275).

10. The Holy Quran (5:95).

11. Ahmad Zaghlool Shalatah, *Contemporary Salafism in Egypt* [in Arabic]; (Cairo: Madbooli Bookshop, 2011), p. 25.

12. Ibid. p. 26.

13. Encyclopedia of Denominations Belonging to Islam, "Section Nine: the Cause of Difference" [in Arabic], *Al-Dorar Al-Sunniyya*, no date (http://www.dorar. net/enc/firq/670).

14. Ahmad Zaghlool Shalatah, op. cit., pp. 26–29.

15. "Milestones on the Road to One Nation" [in Arabic], Saaid Al-Fawaed website, no date (http://www.saaid.net/aldawah/r/010.htm).

16. Abdullah bin Ibrahim bin Ali Al-Tareeqi, "Contemporary Salafi Schools: Diversity and Relationship with the Other" [in Arabic], Al-Alukah (http://bit.ly/1lA0c2u).

17. Ibid. (http://bit.ly/1lA0c2u).

18. Fahd bin Salih Al-Ajlan, "Salafism: A Doctrine or a Group?" [in Arabic], Al-Minhaj Preaching Blog (Islamic Electronic Magazine), no date (http://bit.ly/1qF33Z3).

19. Ahmad Al-Ghamidi, "Salafism: A Group or a Doctrine? (1)" [in Arabic], *Fi Al-Yaum*, April 5, 2014 (http://www.alyaum.com/article/3130981).

20. Fahd bin Salih Al-Ajlan, op. cit. (http://bit.ly/1qF33Z3).

21. Ibid. (http://bit.ly/1qF33Z3).

22. "Fahmi Jad'an Calls for Liberating Islam of Misconceptions" [in Arabic], *Al-Mirsad*, August 18, 2014 (http://goo.gl/8TF19A).

23. Musa Barhomeh, "Interview: Fahmi Jad'an 'Political Islam' is an Ideological Innovation and a Deviation from the Purpose of Religion" [in Arabic], Mominoun Without Borders, June 16, 2013 (http://goo.gl/2SeQXo).

24. Ahmad Zaghlool Shalatah, op. cit., p. 30.

25. Ridwan Ahmad Shamsan Al-Shaybani, *Fundamental Islamic Movements in the Arab World* [in Arabic]; (Cairo: Madbooli Bookshop, 2005), p. 205.

26. Rafiq Habeeb, "Transformations of Contemporary Salafism between Reformation and Revival" [in Arabic]; (http://www.cha3biahli.net/kbirelhoma/index.php/2009-01-05-08-55-02/670-2009-07-13-12-02-34.html).

27. Charles Saint-Prot, op. cit., pp. 326–327.

28. Jamal Sanad Al-Suwaidi, "Islam and Socio-Political Change: A Comparative Study of Egyptian, Kuwaiti and Palestinian Attitudes," unpublished dissertation manuscript, University of Wisconsin, 1990, p. 150.

29. Salih Hussein Al-Regeb, *Our Contemporary Reality and Intellectual Invasion* [in Arabic]; (Gaza: Islamic University, 7th ed., 2004), pp. 90–95 (http://www.drsregeb.com/index.php?action=vb-k&nid=22).

30. Waleed Abdulrahman, "Al-Azhar in the Gown of the Revolution" [in Arabic], *Al-Sharq Al-Awsat* (London), November 11, 2011 (http://classic.aawsat.com/details.asp?section=45&article=649395&issueno=12036#.U-MrbP2oWic).

31. "Observers Talk about a Conspiracy to Remove the Sheikh of Al-Azhar after his Successful Tours in Saudi Arabia and the UAE while Mursi Failed to Build Bridges with the Gulf" [in Arabic], *Al-Quds Al-Arabi* (London), April 30, 2013 (http://www.alquds.co.uk/?p=39267).

32. Muhammad Abdulfattah Al-Suroori, "Islamic Architecture: Debates on Modernity; Dissertation Review" [in Arabic], *Al-Hayat* (London), March 21, 2014 (http://bit.ly/1vf0pkm).

33. Ibid. (http://bit.ly/1vf0pkm).

34. Yasir Ba Amer, "Conservatives and Reformists in Muslim Saudi Arabia" [in Arabic], book review, Aafaq Center for Research and Studies, January 8, 2012 (http://aafaqcenter.com/index.php/post/969).

35. Yaseen Bin Ali, "Wahhabi Dissent against the Ottoman Caliphate" (Historical Reading and Sharia Discussion) [in Arabic], 2014 (https://da3msyria2.files.wordpress.com/2014/07/khourouj-wahabia.pdf).

36. Fouad Ajami, op. cit., p. 186.

37. Abdulghani Imad, "Jihadi Salafism… or the Survivor Denomination" [in Arabic], On Islam website, 10 March 2010 (http://bit.ly/O828n9).

38. Ibid. (http://bit.ly/O828n9).

39. Ahmad Zaghlool Shalatah, op. cit., pp. 30–35.

40. Imam Muhammad Abu Zahra, *History of Islamic Schools in Politics and Faith and History of Jurisprudential Schools* [in Arabic]; (Cairo: Dar Al-Fikr Al-Arabi, 1987), vol. 1, p. 189.

41. Ibid. p. 189.

42. Ibid. p. 189.

43. Abdullah bin Ibrahim bin Ali Al-Tareeqi, 2011, op. cit. (http://bit.ly/11A0c2u). See also Akram Hijazi, "Substantial Issues in the Thought of Jihadi Salafism" (From Tawheed to Leadership Making) [in Arabic], Jihadi Salafism Studies Series no. 3, October 2007, p. 5.

44. Oneness or unity of the Lord [*tawheed rububiyya*] means that there is only one Lord, with all His names, attributes and acts. Oneness or unity of God (Allah) [*tawheed uluhiyya*] means that all acts of worship, such as prayers and supplications, should be intended for God (Allah) alone. When mentioned separately, both terms have the same meaning. However, when mentioned together, they have different meanings; in this case the 'Lord' means the Creator and the Master ("Say: I seek refuge with the Lord and Cherisher of Mankind * the King of Mankind"), while 'God (Allah)' means ("Say: I seek refuge with the Lord and Cherisher of Mankind, He is the only One to be worshipped, the God (Allah) of Mankind * From the mischief of the Whisperer who withdraws * who whispers into the hearts of Mankind * among Jinns and among men." According to religious scholars, belief in the oneness of the Lord is necessary for belief in the oneness of God (Allah); i.e. acknowledging that God (Allah) alone is the Lord, the Creator, the Master, and the Provider entails acknowledging that He is the only One to be worshipped, and all prayers and supplications should be directed to Him. As such, belief in the oneness of God (Allah) is based on belief in the oneness of the Lord. They are both required for acts of worship to be acceptable; neither is

sufficient on its own; acknowledging the oneness of the Lord is not sufficient on its own as proof of having faith in God (Allah). For more information, see the meaning of the oneness of the Lord and the oneness of God (Allah) in the "Encyclopedia of Islamic Jurisprudence" (http://bit.ly/1qVeT0n).

45. Akram Hijazi, op. cit., p. 5.

46. Hisham bin Ghalib, "Saudi Salafism in the Field of Authority" [in Arabic], Al-Jazeera Studies Center, April 11, 2013 (http://studies.aljazeera.net/reports/2013/04/20134794152127903.htm).

47. Abdullah bin Ibrahim bin Ali Al-Tareeqi, op. cit. (http://bit.ly/1lA0c2u).

48. Ibid. (http://bit.ly/1lA0c2u).

49. Haidar Hoballah, "The Muslims' Tradition-based Interpretation of the Holy Quran: Concept, Roles, History, Works and Issues" [in Arabic] (http://bit.ly/1pxW3A4).

50. Ibid. (http://bit.ly/1pxW3A4).

51. Akram Hijazi, op. cit., p. 5.

52. Muhammad Abu Rumman, "The Salafis and the Arab Spring: the Question of Religion and Democracy in Arab Politics" [in Arabic], *Al-Mustaqbal Al-Arabi* no. 411, May 2013 (Beirut: Center for Arab Unity Studies, 2013), pp. 52–53.

53. Ibid., p. 52.

54. Ibid., p. 52.

55. Muhammad Ratib Al-Nabulsi, "The Concept of Following rather than Innovating" [in Arabic], Lesson 11-70: Following rather than Innovating, January 13, 2009 (http://www.nabulsi.com/blue/ar/art.php?art=2410&id=150&sid=775&ssid=776&sssid=777).

56. The Holy Quran (5:3).

57. Sabri Muhammad Khalil, "Jihadi Salafism: Intellectual Origins and Various Stances Towards it" [in Arabic], *Sudanile*, July 30, 2012. (http://www.sudanile.

com/index.php/2008-05-19-17-39-36/252-2009-09-06-09-34-16/43048-2012-07-30-08-07-56).

58. Hasheem bin Basheer, "Invaluable Statements by Imam ibn Taymiyya regarding the Kharijites" [in Arabic], Majlis Alukah (http://majles.alukah.net/t26910/).

59. Muhammad Abu Rumman, op. cit., p. 50.

60. Ibid. p. 50.

61. Ahmad Fahmi, "Salafi Currents and Future Options," Majlis Al-Alukah, April 10, 2008 (http://majles.alukah.net/t14556).

62. Ibid. (http://majles.alukah.net/t14556).

63. Muhammad Abu Rumman, op. cit., pp. 51–52.

64. Hani Naseera, *Al-Qa'eda and Jihadi Salafism: Intellectual Sources and Limits of Revisions* [in Arabic], Strategic Booklets Series (Cairo: Al-Ahram Center for Political and Strategic Studies, Issue 188, August 2008), p. 8.

65. Ibid. p. 8.

66. Akram Hijazi, "Introduction to Jihadi Salafism and its Jihadi Enterprise: Iraq" [in Arabic], Jihadi Salafism Studies Series no. 4 (Amman: Arab Institute for Research and Strategic Studies, February 2008), pp. 6–7.

67. Ibid., pp. 6–7.

68. Ibid., p. 6.

69. Ibid., p. 6.

70. Ahmad Zaghlool Shalatah, op. cit., pp. 47–48.

71. Akram Hijazi, *Introduction to Jihadi Salafism and its Jihadi Enterprise*, op. cit., p. 7. See also: "A Special Interview with 'Abu Muhammad Al-Maqdisi' (1) On the Doctrine of the Jihadi Salafi Current" [in Arabic], Al-Asr website, July 24, 2005 (http://alasr.ws/articles/view/6872/).

688

72. Imam Muhammad Abu Zahra, op. cit., p. 187.

73. Ibid. p. 187.

74. Ahmad Zaghlool Shalatah, op. cit., p. 32.

75. "Wahhabism is not a New School but a Call to Unite Ahl Al-Sunna Wal Jama'a" [in Arabic], discussion, Al-Alukah website, August 6, 2011 (http://www.alukah.net/web/triqi/0/33757/).

76. Ibid. (http://www.alukah.net/web/triqi/0/33757/).

77. Imam Muhammad Abu Zahra, op. cit., p. 208.

78. Ahmad Zaghlool Shalatah, op. cit., p. 32.

79. "Biographies of Religious Scholars: The Sheikh of Islam Muhammad ibn Abdulwahhab" [in Arabic], Al-Tawheed website (http://bit.ly/1iY07bC).

80. Ibid. (http://bit.ly/1iY07bC).

81. The Holy Quran (3:110).

82. Salah bin Muhammad bin Abdulrahman Al Al-Sheikh, *The Jurisprudential Approach of Salafi Imams in the Najd* [in Arabic]; (Riyadh: Dar Al-Somaie for Publishing and Distribution, 2009), p. 6.

83. "Comprehensive Encyclopedia" [in Arabic]; (http://islamport.com/d/1/mtn/1/89/3501.html).

84. "Imam Ahmad ibn Hanbal" [in Arabic], Islam Story website (http://bit.ly/1njd5T6).

85. Ibid. (http://bit.ly/1njd5T6).

86. Abdulhadi bin Abdullateef Al-Salih Al-Khleif, *Efforts of Salafi Scholars in Najd in Responding to their Opponents (1200–1350 AH)*; [in Arabic]; (http://bit.ly/1ogcKha).

87. "Fahmi Jad'an Calls for Liberating Islam of Misconceptions," op. cit. (http://goo.gl/8TF19A).

88. "The Sheikh of Islam ibn Taymiyya" [in Arabic], Islam Story website (http://bit.ly/1cPxVFf).

89. Ibid. (http://bit.ly/1cPxVFf).

90. Ibid. (http://bit.ly/1cPxVFf).

91. Salah bin Muhammad bin Abdulrahman Al Al-Sheikh, op. cit., pp. 201–207.

92. Abdulmajeed Al-Najjar, "Ibn Taymiyya's Approach in Evaluating Actions Using Sacred Text and Reasoning" in *Ibn Taymiyya: Works and Reformist Approach* [in Arabic]; (a group of authors), papers presented at the symposium held at Mutah University, Karak, Jordan, during the period Muharram 3–4, 1422 AH, corresponding to March 28–29, 2001 (Amman, Dar Ward for Publishing and Distribution), pp. 227–288.

93. Abdulghani Imad, op. cit. (http://bit.ly/O828n9).

94. Ibid. (http://bit.ly/O828n9).

95. Ibid. (http://bit.ly/O828n9).

96. Bassam Atiyya Ismael Faraj, *Ibn Taymiyya's Political Thought* [in Arabic]; (Amman: Dar Al-Yaqoot for Printing, Publishing and Distribution, 2001), p. 40.

97. "Imam Ahmad ibn Hanbal" [in Arabic], Islam Story website (http://bit.ly/1njd5T6).

98. "The School of Sheikh Muhammad ibn Abdulwahhab and its Influence in the Muslim World," op. cit. (http://madrasato-mohammed.com/abd%20elwahab/pg_048_0004.htm).

99. Salih bin Abdulaziz bin Muhammad Al Al-Sheikh, "Research on Sheikh Muhammad ibn Abdulwahhab and his Revivalist Movement" [in Arabic], February 12, 1999 (http://www.saaid.net/muslm/13.htm).

100. "Biographies of Religious Scholars: The Sheikh of Islam Muhammad ibn Abdulwahhab" op. cit. (http://bit.ly/1iY07bC).

101. Abdulghani Imad, op. cit. (http://bit.ly/O828n9).

102. Abu Abdullah Al-Dhahabi, "Biography of Imam Muhammad ibn Abdulwahhab" [in Arabic], Saaid Al-Fawaed website (http://www.saaid.net/monawein/t/4.htm).

103. "Biographies of Religious Scholars: The Sheikh of Islam Muhammad ibn Abdulwahhab" op. cit. (http://bit.ly/1iY07bC).

104. Hasan Konakata, *Ibn Taymiyya's Political Theory* [in Arabic]; (Dammam: Dar Al-Akhella' for Publishing and Distribution, 1994), pp. 231–240.

105. Abdulghani Imad, op. cit. (http://bit.ly/O828n9).

106. Ibid. (http://bit.ly/O828n9).

107. Khalid Al-Waeli, "Appealing to the Dead: A More Serious Form of Idolatry" [in Arabic], Saaid Al-Fawaed website (http://www.saaid.net/feraq/shia/a/52.htm).

108. A Lecture by Sheikh Muhammad Nasseruddin Al-Albani titled "Reality of Salafism" [in Arabic], Islam Web (http://audio.islamweb.net/audio/index.php?page=FullContent&audioid=4842&full=1).

109. Ibid. (http://audio.islamweb.net/audio/index.php?page=FullContent&audioid=4842&full=1).

110. Ahmad Fahmi, op. cit. (http://bit.ly/1gWlfxr).

111. Ibid. (http://bit.ly/1gWlfxr).

112. Abdulhakeem Abu Al-Louz, "Inflexibility of the New Salafi Ideology" [in Arabic], *Idafat Magazine*, Arab Sociological Association, issues 3–4, Summer and Autumn, 2008, p. 98.

113. Ibid., p. 98.

114. Ibid., p. 98.

115. Khalid Mahmood, "Why did the Islamists Win the Elections in Egypt, Tunisia, Libya and Morocco?" [in Arabic], Islam Times (http://islamtimes.org/vdcjyxev8uqe8vz.3ffu.html).

116. Muhammad Abu Rumman, op. cit., p. 7.

117. Ibid. p. 8.

118. "The Empowerment Document and the Intentions of the Muslim Brotherhood" [in Arabic], *Al-Majalla*, April 12, 2010 (http://www.majalla.com/arb/2010/04/article5542290).

119. For example, the Salafi current in the Arab Republic of Egypt has been through several transformations since 2011. See: Ashraf Al-Shareef, "Transformations of the Salafis in Egypt: Politics Takes Ideology Apart" [in Arabic], Al-Qantara (http://ar.qantara.de/content/lslfywn-fy-msr-thwlt-lslfyyn-fy-msr-ltsyys-mfkk-lydywlwjy).

120. "The True Position of Egyptian Salafism toward the January 25 Revolution" [in Arabic], Arab Center for Human Studies (http://www.arab-center.org/index.php?option=com_content&view=article&id=167:25jan-revolution&catid=41:analysis-articles&Itemid=79).

121. Stephane Lacroix, "Sheikhs and Politicians: Inside the New Egyptian Salafism" [in Arabic], Brookings Doha Center, June 2012 (http://bit.ly/1s1WtPK).

122. Ibid. (http://bit.ly/1s1WtPK).

123. Muhammad Abu Rumman, op. cit., p. 20.

124. Ibid., p. 21.

125. Ibid., p. 21.

126. Ibid., p. 22.

127. Ibid., p. 23.

128. Ali Abdulaal, "The Disagreement between the Muslim Brotherhood and the Salafis in Egypt" [in Arabic], *Democracy* (http://bit.ly/1iZmRDQ).

129. "We are Publishing the Reasons why the Supreme Committee Excluded Noor, Suleiman and Al-Shatir from the Presidential Race" [in Arabic], *Al-Yaum Al-Sabi'* (Egypt), April 15, 2012 (http://goo.gl/ypNQbM).

130. Ali Abdulaal, op. cit. (http://bit.ly/1iZmRDQ).

131. "Egypt Presidential Elections and the Theory of Political Poisoning" [in Arabic], The Contemporary Studies Center, June 4, 2012 (http://derasat.ara-star.com/full.php?ID=569).

132. Ali Abdulaal, op. cit. (http://bit.ly/1iZmRDQ).

133. Muhammad Abu Rumman, op. cit., pp. 16–17.

134. Ibid., pp. 16–17.

135. Muhammad bin Musa Al-Aamri, "Egypt's Al-Noor Party: an Opportunity or a Predicament?" [in Arabic], Yemen's Scholars Forum (http://bit.ly/1gLZB9j).

136. Ibid. (http://bit.ly/1gLZB9j).

137. Ibid. (http://bit.ly/1gLZB9j).

138. Ibid. (http://bit.ly/1gLZB9j).

139. Ibid. (http://bit.ly/1gLZB9j).

140. Ahmad Al-Nazeef, "Map of Salafi Groups in Tunisia" [in Arabic], Africa News Gate, January 3, 2014 (http://bit.ly/1nWZcFL).

141. Riyadh Al-Shuaibi, "Tunisian Salafism: Labor of Transformation" [in Arabic], Al-Jazeera Studies Center, November 15, 2012 (http://studies.aljazeera.net/reports/2012/11/20121115111741423396.htm).

142. Ahmad Al-Nazeef, op. cit. (http://bit.ly/1nWZcFL).

143. Ibid. (http://bit.ly/1nWZcFL).

144. Stephane Lacroix, op. cit. (http://bit.ly/1s1WtPK).

145. For more on books by Al-Albani see: (http://www.islamport.com/isp_eBooks/alb/).

146. Stephane Lacroix, op. cit. (http://bit.ly/1s1WtPK).

147. Muhammad Abu Rumman, op. cit., p. 20.

148. Ibid., p. 15.

Chapter 5

1. "The Story of the Founder of Suroorism: From Syria to the Najd" [in Arabic], Middle East Online, November 8, 2013 (http://www.middle-east-online. com/?id=165277).

2. Ibid. (http://www.middle-east-online.com/?id=165277).

3. Muhammad bin Hassan bin Hijazi, "Disassociating the Salafi Call from the Qutbi Suroori Thought" [in Arabic], Sudaress (Sudan Press), June 25, 2010 (http://www.sudaress.com/alsahafa/9001). Also see: Yousuf Al-Deeni, "Suroor Left Buraidah and his Ideas Remained" [in Arabic], in *Suroorism* (Dubai: Al-Mesbar, 2007), p. 44.

4. "The Suroori School, a 'Hybrid' Version of the Muslim Brotherhood and Salafism" [in Arabic], *Al-Arab* newspaper, London, August 19, 2013, issue 9294, p. 13 (http://www.alarab.co.uk/?id=1702).

5. Muhammad Suroor Zine Al-Abideen, 'Murajaat' Talk Show, Al-Hiwar TV Channel (http://www.youtube.com/watch?v=N5RSpkknVG4).

6. Tawfeeq Al-Saif, "Transformations and Future of Political Islam in Saudi Arabia" [in Arabic], Afaq Center for Research and Studies, November 30, 2013 (http://aafaqcenter.com/index.php/post/1970).

7. "The Story of the Founder of Suroorism ...," op. cit. (http://www.middle-east-online.com/?id=165277).

8. Ibid. (http://www.middle-east-online.com/?id=165277).

9. "The Leader of Suroorism 'Sheikh Zine Al-Abideen' leaves Britain and moves to Jordan" [in Arabic], Al-Arabiya website, October 27, 2004 (http://www. alarabiya.net/articles/2004/10/27/7492.html).

10. "Flashback from 13 Years Ago: Prince Nayef Speaking about the Muslim Brotherhood" [in Arabic], Assakina website, March 2014 (http://www. assakina.com/news/news2/40123.html).

11. Abdul Hai Shaheen, "Saudi Suroorism: A Phenomenon or an Intellectual Current?" [in Arabic], Religion and Politics Center for Studies, September 21, 2010 (http://www.rpcst.com/articles.php?action=show&id=195).

12. Nabeel Al-Bakeeri, "Suroorism: A Map of its Spread and Presence" [in Arabic], On Islam website, March 4, 2010 (http://bit.ly/1qXZR0b).

13. Muhammad Abdullah Nab, "Bickering between the Jamis and the Surooris in Saudi Arabia" [in Arabic], Elaph electronic newspaper, May 20, 2005 (http://www.elaph.com/ElaphWeb/Politics/2005/5/63497.htm).

14. "Stating the Rights of Guardians on the Umma" [in Arabic], website of Shaikh Abdulaziz bin Abdullah bin Baz, September 13, 1996 (http://www.binbaz.org.sa/mat/8647).

15. Muhammad Al-Shayookh, "Suroorism: An Affinity between Salafism and the Muslim Brotherhood" [in Arabic], Middle East Online, February 27, 2013 (http://middle-east-online.com/?id=150137).

16. "A Former Revivalist Reveals the Secrets and Mysteries of 'Suroorism' in Saudi Arabia" [in Arabic], Al-Arabiya website, January 15, 2008 (http://www.alarabiya.net/articles/2008/01/15/44239.html).

17. Interview with the writer and academic Dr. Ahmad Faraj, adviser to the Minister of Higher Education in Saudi Arabia, *Al-Hayat* newspaper, London, April 16, 2014 (http://alhayat.com/Articles/1614402).

18. "The Story of the Founder of Suroorism…," op. cit., November 8, 2013 (http://www.middle-east-online.com/?id=165277).

19. Jamism, sometimes called Madkhalism, is a Salafi school critical of all Islamic groups, especially Da'wa and Tabligh, the Muslim Brotherhood and Suroorism in the Gulf region and beyond. The differences between Jamism and these groups are major and are in fundamental rather than the subsidiary principals (http://www.almesbar.net/38). Also see: "Suroorism in the Region: The Muslim Brotherhood Salafi version" [in Arabic], Middle East Online, August 15, 2013 (http://www.middle-east-online.com/?id=160465).

20. Mansour Al-Nogaidan, "Islamist Map in Saudi Arabia and the Story of Excommunication" [in Arabic], *Al-Wasat* newspaper, Bahrain, February 28,

2003 (http://www.alwasatnews.com/175/news/read/198071/1.html). Also see: "Jami Salafism: Loyalty to Rulers, Aversion of Politics, and Attacking the Muslim Brotherhood" [in Arabic], Islamic Movements Portal, December 19, 2014 (http://www.islamist-movements.com/13327).

21. *Al-Sharq Al-Awsat* newspaper, London, Issue 9660, May 10, 2005.

22. "Gulf Umma Parties Gather in Kuwait" [in Arabic], *Al-Watan* newspaper, Kuwait, March 30, 2013 (http://alwatan.kuwait.tt/articledetails.aspx?Id=264204).

23. A statement to this effect was issued on February 8, 2014. It was signed by Hakim Al-Mutairi, General Coordinator of the Umma Conference and President of the Umma Party in Kuwait, Hassan Ahmad Al-Deqqi, Secretary General of the UAE Umma Party, Muhammad bin Saad Al Mefrih, Secretary General of the Islamic Umma Party in the Kingdom of Saudi Arabia, and Saif Al-Hajiri, Secretary General of the Umma Party in Kuwait. For further details, see: "Statement: Umma Parties in the Gulf and Arabian Peninsula Reject Domestic and Foreign Policies Followed by GCC Governments which Pose a Threat to the Future of the Gulf" (http://bit.ly/1tZW3bD).

24. "Suroorism in the Region ...," op. cit. (http://www.middle-east-online.com/?id=160465).

25. "UAE's Umma Party announces incorporation" [in Arabic], National Kuwait Network, August 2, 2012 (http://www.nationalkuwait.com/forum/index.php?threads/239884).

26. "Suroorism in the region ...," op. cit. (http://www.middle-east-online.com/?id=160465).

27. "New Islamic currents in post-revolution Egypt" [in Arabic], Assakina website, September 7, 2012 (http://www.assakina.com/center/files/17922.html).

28. "Suroorism: A Current that Excommunicates Shiites, considers South Sudan as 'crusaders' and accuses Al-Turabi of blasphemy" [in Arabic], Al-Arabiya website, December 10, 2010 (http://www.alarabiya.net/articles/2010/12/10/129058.html).

29. "Suroorism in the region ...," op. cit. (http://www.middle-east-online.com/?id=160465).

30. Abu Ammar Ali Al-Huthaifi, "Reservations concerning the Al-Ihsan Association" [in Arabic]; (http://wahyain.com/forums/showthread.php?t=3355).

31. "The truth about the Salafi call" [in Arabic], Religion and Life Program, Aljazeera.net, March 25, 2001 (http://www.aljazeera.net/programs/pages/409e086e-2203-478e-a9af-ae34f57c5d1b).

32. Nabeel Al-Bakeeri, op. cit. (http://bit.ly/1qXZR0b).

33. Ibid. (http://bit.ly/1qXZR0b).

34. "Salafi Scholars to 'Al-Anba': Muhammad Suroor's thought is a Dangerous Revolutionary *takfiri* (excommunicating) one and is a product of the Muslim Brotherhood's Qutbi approach" [in Arabic], *Al-Anab* newspaper, Kuwait, March 13, 2011 (http://www.alanba.com.kw/ar/kuwait-news/178645/13-03-2011).

35. Ibid. (http://www.alanba.com.kw/ar/kuwait-news/178645/13-03-2011).

36. Khalid Al-Mushawah, "Religious currents in Saudi Arabia: Suroorism (3)" [in Arabic], Jasad Al-Thaqafa website, November 16, 2007 (http://aljsad.com/forum9/thread113550/).

37. Ahmad Saad Al-Kinani, "Salafis of Najd and Al-Ouda … a red line or hidden alliances?" [in Arabic], Middle East Online, August 9, 2012 (http://www.middle-east-online.com/?id=136769).

38. "A former revivalist …" op. cit. (http://www.alarabiya.net/articles/2008/01/15/44239.html)

39. For more information about the Suroori thought and its relation to the Muslim Brotherhood's thought, see: Usama Awadhalla, "The Salafi Suroois: Who are they, who is their God (Allah), who is their Sheikh, who are their leaders and institutions in Sudan? [in Arabic], Al-Rakoba electronic newspaper, Sudan, April 12, 2013 (http://www.alrakoba.net/articles-action-show-id-42587.htm).

40. Muhammad bin Hassan bin Hijazi, op. cit. (http://www.sudaress.com/alsahafa/9001)

41. Muhammad Suroor Zine Al-Abideen, "Refuting the Fabrications of Falsifiers" [in Arabic], website of Shaikh Muhammad Suroor Zine Al-Abideen, June 24, 2012 (http://www.surour.net/index.php?group=view&rid=852).

42. "Who is Muhammad bin Suroor bin Nayef Zine Al-Abideen and the Suroori group?" [in Arabic], Al-Rabanyon Religious Network, November 25, 2011 (http://www.alrbanyon.com/vb/showthread.php?t=8115).

43. Muhammad bin Hassan bin Hijazi, op. cit. (http://www.sudaress.com/ alsahafa/9001).

44. Ibid. (http://www.sudaress.com/alsahafa/9001).

45. "Charter of the Legitimate League of Scholars and Preachers in Sudan" [in Arabic], the Legitimate League website, May 28, 2011 (http://rabetasud. org/index.php/welcome/fullarticle/1).

46. Ibid. (http://rabetasud.org/index.php/welcome/fullarticle/1).

47. To learn about the Surooris advocacy and socialization methods, see: "A former Revivalist ...," op. cit. (http://www.alarabiya.net/articles/2008/01/15/44239. html).

48. Ibid. (http://www.alarabiya.net/articles/2008/01/15/44239.html).

49. Ibid. (http://www.alarabiya.net/articles/2008/01/15/44239.html).

50. Ibid. (http://www.alarabiya.net/articles/2008/01/15/44239.html).

51. Othman Qadri Makansi, "Reticence and Secrecy are Methods of Education in the Quran (21)" [in Arabic], website of Al-Sham League of Writers, September 4, 2010 (http://www.odabasham.net/show.php?sid=38662).

52. "A Former Revivalist ...," op. cit. (http://www.alarabiya.net/articles/2008/01/ 15/44239.html).

53. "Opinions of Scholars about Salman and Safar" [in Arabic], Al-Salafy network, July 6, 2012 (http://alsalafy.com/vb/showthread.php?t=335).

54. Ibid. (http://alsalafy.com/vb/showthread.php?t=335).

55. "A Former Revivalist …," op. cit. (http://www.alarabiya.net/articles/2008/01/15/44239.html).

56. "Who is Muhammad bin Suroor …," op. cit. (http://www.alrbanyon.com/vb/showthread.php?t=8115).

57. Abdulqader Battar, "When Excommunication becomes a Crime According to Islamic Sharia" [in Arabic]; (http://bit.ly/V0uxiJ).

58. Tariq Abdelhaleem, "Suroorism in the Balance" (http://www.tariqabdelhaleem.net/new/Artical-72524).

59. Haytham Sarhan, "Book Review of Awakening Time," by Stephane Lacroix (http://goo.gl/wCDJOx).

60. Muhammad Suroor Zine Al-Abideen, "Refuting the Fabrications of Falsifiers" (http://www.surour.net/index.php?group=view&rid=852).

61. Abu Qatada Al-Filistini, "A New Viewpoint on Discrediting and Accrediting: Muhammad Suroor" [in Arabic], Ana Al-Muslim network for Islamic dialogue (http://www.muslm.org/vb/showthread.php?353829).

62. Abdul Hai Shaheen, op. cit. (http://www.rpcst.com/articles.php?action=show&id=195).

63. Ibid. (http://www.rpcst.com/articles.php?action=show&id=195).

64. Muhammad Suroor Zine Al-Abideen, Studies in the Life of the Prophet [in Arabic]; (Birmingham: Dar Al-Arqam Publishing and Distribution, 2nd Edition, 1988), p. 321.

65. Ibid., p. 321.

66. "Suroorism" [in Arabic], Yemen Sound website, February 26, 2007 (http://www.yemen-sound.com/vb/showthread.php?t=19646).

67. "The Origin of Suroorism: Suroorism and Tawheed" [in Arabic], Jihadi Media Platform, January 6, 2014 (http://alplatformmedia.com/vb/showthread.php?t=34811).

68. Ahmad Al-Hubaishi, "Homeland in the Mirror of Deviant Thought?" [in Arabic], *September* newspaper, Yemen, June 23, 2011 (http://26sep.net/articles. php?lng=arabic&id=4824).

69. Al-Sayed Zayed, "Suroorism: A Preaching Current or an Activist Organization?" [in Arabic], On Islam net, December 31, 2008 (http://goo.gl/ y0lkVF).

70. Abdulwahb Faqi, "The Revolving Door Game: Saudi Arabia and Smuggling Terrorism" [in Arabic], Al-Hejaz.org, no date (http://www.alhejaz.org/ qadaya/038801.htm).

71. "Charter of the Legitimate League ...," op. cit. (http://rabetasud.org/index. php/welcome/fullarticle/1).

72. Ibid. (http://rabetasud.org/index.php/welcome/fullarticle/1).

73. Meaning "those who oppose God (Allah) and His Messenger," King Saud University's E-Quran project (http://quran.ksu.edu.sa/tafseer/tabary/sura58-aya22.html).

74. "Charter of the Legitimate League...," op.cit. (http://rabetasud.org/index.php/ welcome/fullarticle/1).

75. "The Story of the Founder of Suroorism ...," op. cit. (http://www.middle-east-online.com/?id=165277).

76. Ibid. (http://www.middle-east-online.com/?id=165277).

77. Tariq Al-Mughrabi, "Muhammad Abdulkareem, Abdul Hai Yousuf and Suroorism: Al-Qa'ida Sleeper Cells in Sudan" [in Arabic], Kul Al-Salafiyeen website, August 14, 2012 (http://kulalsalafiyeen.com/vb/showthread.php?t=40499).

78. Abdul Hai Shaheen, op. cit. (http://www.rpcst.com/articles.php?action=show &id=195).

79. Ibid. (http://www.rpcst.com/articles.php?action=show&id=195).

80. Ibid. (http://www.rpcst.com/articles.php?action=show&id=195).

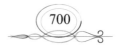

81. Fares bin Hizam, "Islamist–Islamist Race: Dammam Elections Ignite the Suroorism and the Brotherhood" [in Arabic], Al-Arabiya website, February 28, 2005 (http://www.alarabiya.net/articles/2005/02/28/10767.html).

82. Ibid. (http://www.alarabiya.net/articles/2005/02/28/10767.html).

83. Hadi Ahmad Hassan Ateen, *The Muslim Brotherhood Invades the Gulf* [in Arabic]; (Cairo: Dar El-Hekma Printing, Publishing and Distribution) 2013, p. 45.

84. Aljazeera.net, Interview with Shaikh Muhammad Suroor Zine Al-Abideen (talking about democracy), Today Interview Program, June 9, 2013 (http://bit.ly/1u0Ts4L).

85. Usama Awadhalla, op. cit. (http://www.alrakoba.net/articles-action-show-id-42587.htm).

86. Nabeel Al-Bakeeri, op. cit. (http://bit.ly/1qXZR0b).

87. Tariq Abdelhaleem, op. cit. (http://www.tariqabdelhaleem.net/new/Artical-72524).

88. Muhammad Al-Shayookh, op. cit. (http://middle-east-online.com/?id=1501 37).

89. Ibid. (http://middle-east-online.com/?id=150137).

90. Hassan Al-Banna, *The Collected Epistles* (Alexandria: Islamic House for Distribution and Publishing, 1992), pp. 89–90.

91. The Suroori School, a 'Hybrid' Version of the Muslim Brotherhood and Salafism [in Arabic], *Al-Arab* newspaper, London, August 19, 2013 (http://www.alarab.co.uk/?id=1702).

92. Usama Awadhalla, op. cit. (http://www.alrakoba.net/articles-action-show-id-42587.htm).

93. "Suroorism" [in Arabic], Arab Forum website, May 28, 2008 (http://arabcom.mam9.com/t80-topic).

94. Ahmad Al-Henaki, "The Muslim Brotherhood between Abdul Nasser and Al-Sadat" [in Arabic], *Al-Majalla* magazine, London, April 29, 2014 (http://www.majalla.com/arb/2014/04/article55250938).

95. "The Emergence and Development of the Term Political Islam" [in Arabic], Babelmed electronic magazine (http://arabic.babelmed.net/societe/36-generale-culture/552-2012-04-27-19-54-55.html).

96. Sameer Al-Hammadi, "Wahhabism and Jihadi Salafism: Questions about the Relationship" [in Arabic], Modern Discussion website, Issue 4461, May 23, 2014 (http://www.ahewar.org/debat/show.art.asp?aid=416173).

97. Ibid. (http://www.ahewar.org/debat/show.art.asp?aid=416173).

98. "The Story of the Founder of Suroorism …," op. cit. (http://www.middle-east-online.com/?id=165277).

99. Book Review by Jalal Al-Deen Ezz Al-Deen Ali of "Islamists Shifts (From the Flames of September to the Spring of Revolutions)" [in Arabic], Aljazeera.net, November 20, 2012 (http://bit.ly/1qY0Ai6).

100. Ibid. (http://bit.ly/1qY0Ai6).

101. Elizabeth Rubin. "A Story of Reverting from Wahhabism: The Jihadi Who Kept Asking Why" [in Arabic], Al-Hejaz.org (http://www.alhejaz.org/qadaya/031705.htm).

102. Abdullah Al-Rasheed, "How Surooris in the Gulf Think: Democracy and the Dreams of the Caliphate" [in Arabic], *Al-Majalla* magazine, London, March 25, 2013 (http://www.majalla.com/arb/2013/03/article55243687).

103. "The Origin of Suroorism: Suroorism and Tawheed," op. cit. (http://alplatform media.com/vb/showthread.php?t=34811).

104. Ibid. (http://alplatformmedia.com/vb/showthread.php?t=34811).

105. Abdullah Al-Rasheed, op. cit. (http://www.majalla.com/arb/2013/03/article 55243687).

106. Rashid Al-Khayoun, "Suroorism and Ahbash: The *Hakimiyya* Project and the Excommunication Weapon" [in Arabic], *Al-Sharq Al-Awsat* newspaper, London, Issue 10305, February 10, 2007 (http://bit.ly/1pE0Crr).

107. Fuad Abu Al-Ghaith, "The Group 'S' and the Disagreement that Brings One out of *Ahl Al-Sunnah Wal Jama'a*" [in Arabic], March 26, 2012 (http://bit.ly/1pdGDAY).

108. Nabeel Al-Bakeeri, op. cit. (http://bit.ly/1qXZR0b).

109. Eric Trager, "Egypt's Muslim Brotherhood Pursues a Political Monopoly" [in Arabic], April 4, 2012, The Washington Institute (http://www.washington institute.org/ar/policy-analysis/view/egypts-muslim-brotherhood-pursues-a-political-monopoly).

110. Abu Qatada Al-Filistini, op. cit. (http://www.muslm.org/vb/showthread.php?353829).

111. Muhammad Al-Shayookh, op. cit. (http://middle-east-online.com/?id=1501 37).

112. "The Story of the Founder of Suroorism ...," op. cit. (http://www.middle-east-online.com/?id=165277).

113. "'Murajaat' Talk Show, Episode (1)," website of Shaikh Muhammad Suroor Zine Al-Abideen (http://www.surour.net/index.php?group=view&rid=786 &rp=2).

114. Muhammad Suroor Zine Al-Abideen, *Way of the Prophets ...*, op. cit. p. 8.

115. Collection of scholars' opinions about Muhammad Suroor and Suroorism [in Arabic]; (http://www.anti-ikhwan.com/?p=166).

116. Muhammad Al-Shayookh, op. cit. (http://middle-east-online.com/?id=1501 37).

117. Tariq Abdelhaleem, op. cit. (http://www.tariqabdelhaleem.net/new/Artical-72524).

118. Muhammad Al-Shayookh, op. cit. (http://middle-east-online.com/?id=1501 37).

119. "Salafi Scholars to 'Al-Anba' ...," op. cit. (http://www.alanba.com.kw/ar/kuwait-news/178645/13-03-2011).

Chapter 6

1. Nawwaf Al-Qadimi, "The Jihadi Current in Saudi Arabia and Experiences of Dialogue and Reconciliation" [in Arabic], Al-Asr website, May 12, 2009 (http://alasr.ws/articles/view/10859).

2. Abdulhafiz Al-Sawi, "The Story of the Egyptian Economy: From Muhammad Ali to Mubarak," book review [in Arabic], Aljazeera.net, January 4, 2013 (http://bit.ly/1qEjaea).

3. Hani Naseera, *Al-Qa'eda and Jihadi Salafism: Intellectual Sources and Limits of Revisions* [in Arabic], Strategic Booklets Series vol. 18, issue 188 (Cairo: Al-Ahram Center for Political and Strategic Studies, August 2008), p. 32.

4. "The Future of the Struggle in Afghanistan (Episode 1): Dr. Fadl, Founder of 'Al-Jihad,' Writes the Full Story of the Birth of 'Al-Qa'eda' in Afghanistan" [in Arabic], *Al-Sharq Al-Awsat* (London), January 25, 2010 (http://www.aawsat.com/home/declassified/744).

5. Hani Naseera, op. cit., p. 11.

6. "The Future of the Struggle in Afghanistan," op. cit. (http://www.aawsat.com/home/declassified/744).

7. Ibid. (http://www.aawsat.com/home/declassified/744).

8. Hani Naseera, op. cit., p. 11.

9. Muhammad Abu Rumman, "Revisions of Egyptian 'Al-Jihad Group' against the Revisions of 'Jihadis' in Jordan" [in Arabic], Intellectual Revisions website (http://bit.ly/1gVTwr4).

10. Ibid. (http://bit.ly/1gVTwr4).

11. Ibid. (http://bit.ly/1gVTwr4).

12. Ibid. (http://bit.ly/1gVTwr4).

13. Ibid. (http://bit.ly/1gVTwr4).

14. "Abu Muhammad Al-Maqdisi: A Jihadi Ideologue who never Performed Jihad" [in Arabic], Al-Araby Al-Jadeed website, June 17, 2014 (http://www.alaraby.co.uk/politics/09d87ce9-982b-4950-9d9c-736f28b4a690).

15. Alaa Al-Lami, "Al-Barqawi, Al-Zarqawi and the Beginnings of Suicidal Salafism" [in Arabic], *Al-Akhbar* (Lebanon); (http://bit.ly/1eAnV3C).

16. Ibid. (http://bit.ly/1eAnV3C).

17. Hani Naseera, op. cit., p. 12.

18. Ibid. p. 13.

19. Muhammad Abu Rumman, op. cit. (http://bit.ly/1gVTwr4).

20. "The Supreme Administrative Court Approves the Establishment of Al-Wasat Party" [in Arabic], *Al-Ahram* (Egypt), February 19, 2011 (http://gate.ahram.org.eg/News/41458.aspx).

21. "The Islamic Group in Egypt" [in Arabic], Aljazeera.net, March 16, 2011 (http://goo.gl/FGJfj2).

22. "The Beginning of Jihadi Groups in Egypt and the World" [in Arabic], Assakina website, November 29, 2011 (http://www.assakina.com/news/news2/11005.html).

23. "Sectarian Sedition in Egypt: Political Fires Disguised in the Gown of Religion" [in Arabic], Alarabiya.net, January 3, 2011 (http://www.alarabiya.net/articles/2011/01/03/132018.html).

24. "Murderers of Al-Sadat: Executed by Shooting" [in Arabic], *Al-Rai* (Kuwait), September 6, 2009 (http://www.alraimedia.com/Articles.aspx?id=144567).

25. "The Future of the Struggle in Afghanistan," op. cit. (http://www.aawsat.com/home/declassified/744).

26. Ibid. (http://www.aawsat.com/home/declassified/744).

27. For certain published parts of the book, see *Al-Sharq Al-Awsat* January 25–February 2, 2010 (http://classic.aawsat.com/files.asp?fileid=63).

28. "The Future of the Struggle in Afghanistan," op. cit. (http://www.aawsat.com/home/declassified/744).

29. Ibid. (http://www.aawsat.com/home/declassified/744).

30. Ibid. (http://www.aawsat.com/home/declassified/744).

31. Hani Naseera, op. cit., pp. 19–21.

32. Akram Hijazi, "Substantial Issues in the Thought of Jihadi Salafism" (From Tawheed to Leadership Making), [in Arabic], Jihadi Salafism Studies Series 3 (Irbid: No Publisher, September 2007), p. 5.

33. Ibid. p. 5.

34. Ibid. p. 5.

35. Muhammad Abu Rumman and Hasan Abu Haniya, *The Islamic Solution in Jordan: The Islamists, the State and the Bets of Democracy and Security* [in Arabic] (Amman: Friedrich Ebert Institution, Strategic Studies Center, University of Jordan, 2012), p. 330.

36. Ibid. p. 331.

37. *Tawheed* is explained in detail in note no. 42 of Chapter 4.

38. Hani Naseera, op. cit., pp. 32.

39. Ibid. p. 32.

40. Ibid. p. 37.

41. Ibid. p. 37.

42. Muhammad Abu Rumman and Hasan Abu Haniya, op. cit., p. 339.

43. Saud Al-Mawla, *Islamic Groups and Violence: Encyclopedia of Jihad and Jihadis* [in Arabic]; (Dubai: Al-Misbar Center for Studies and Research, 2012), pp. 466–467.

44. Muhammad Abu Rumman and Hasan Abu Haniya, op. cit., p. 339.

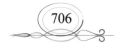

45. Ibid. p. 339.

46. Ibid. p. 383.

47. Ibid. p. 383.

48. Ibid. p. 338. See also: Hani Naseera, op. cit., p. 38.

49. Muhammad Abu Rumman and Hasan Abu Haniya, op. cit., p. 338.

50. Ibid., pp. 332–333.

51. Abdulbari Atwan, *Beyond bin Ladin: The Next Generation of Al-Qa'eda* [in Arabic], translated by Saeed Al-Azm (Beirut: Dar Al-Saqi, 2013), pp. 11–12.

52. Muhammad Abu Rumman and Hasan Abu Haniya, op. cit., p. 332.

53. Ibid. p. 332.

54. Marwan Shehada, *Transformations of the Salafi Discourse: Salafi Movements – A Case Study 1990-2007),* [in Arabic]; (Beirut: Arab Network for Research and Publishing, 2010), p. 271.

55. "New York Trial: The Prosecution Closes by Presenting Documents to Prove the Alliance between Al-Qa'eda, Al-Jihad and The Islamic Group" [in Arabic], *Al-Sharq Al-Awsat* (London), April 6, 2001 (http://classic.aawsat.com/details. asp?section=4&article=33862&issueno=8165).

56. Maha Ali, "Lords of War" [in Arabic], *Al-Ahram* (Egypt), January 1, 2014 (http://digital.ahram.org.eg/Policy.aspx?Serial=1546067).

57. Marwan Shehada, op. cit., pp. 333–334.

58. "Expert on Terrorism: Number of Al-Qae'da Members Reduced to Half, but Funding Unchanged" [in Arabic], *Al-Sharq Al-Awsat* (London), October 13, 2002 (http://classic.aawsat.com/details.asp?section=4&issueno=8720&article=129763&feature=).

59. Fawaz Gerges, *The Rise and Fall of Al-Qa'eda: Debunking the Terrorism Narrative* [in Arabic], translated by Muhammad Shiyya (Beirut: Center for Arab Unity Studies, 2012), pp. 120–121.

60. Ahmad bin Hasan Al-Muwakkali, "Media Ideology of Al-Qa'eda: Challenges to Intellectual Security on the Internet" [in Arabic], paper presented to the First National Conference for Intellectual Security: Concepts and Challenges, 22–25 Jamada Al-Oola 1430 AH (May 16–19, 2009), Prince Nayef bin Abdulaziz Chair for Intellectual Security Studies, King Saud University, pp. 8–9.

61. Ibid. pp. 8–9.

62. Ibid. pp. 8–9.

63. Ibid. p. 9.

64. Jamal Khashoggi, "Prince Turki Al-Faisal: Changes in the Personality of bin Ladin Started in 1990 When he Imagined he could form an Army to Fight Saddam in Kuwait" [in Arabic], *Al-Sharq Al-Awsat* (London), November 7, 2001 (http://classic.aawsat.com/details.asp?section=4&article=65264&issueno=8380#.VBb5YzqoWic).

65. Ahmad bin Hasan Al-Muwakkali, op. cit., pp. 8–9.

66. Sabri Muhammad Khalil, "Al-Qa'eda: Birth, Intellectual Origins and Various Stances Towards it" [in Arabic], *Sudanile*, November 16, 2011 (http://bit.ly/1lBflng).

67. Ibid. (http://bit.ly/1lBflng).

68. "Numan bin Uthman, Comrade in Arms of bin Ladin on the 9th Anniversary of the Attacks: Your Alleged Path to Heaven is Full of Blood and Innocent Victims" [in Arabic], *Al-Sharq Al-Awsat* (London), September 10, 2010 (http://classic.aawsat.com/details.asp?section=4&issueno=11609&article=586097#.VFdGAzqoVaR).

69. Ibid. (http://classic.aawsat.com/details.asp?section=4&issueno=11609&article=586097#.VFdGAzqoVaR).

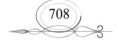

70. "Defections within Al-Qa'eda and Al-Zawahiri Loses Control" [in Arabic], Assakina website, February 4, 2014 (http://www.assakina.com/news/news2/37512.html#ixzz3Exb6rQt0).

71. "CIA: ISIL has about 30,000 Fighters" [in Arabic], BBC Arabic, September 12, 2014.

72. "Russia's National Security Council Estimates ISIL's Fighters at 50,000" [in Arabic], Russia Voice Radio, September 26, 2014.

73. "Warnings from Increasing Number of Foreign Fighters in Syria" [in Arabic], Aljazeera.net, May 29, 2014 (http://bit.ly/1qZAlDg).

74. "Al-Zawahiri Announces the Cancellation of ISIL and Al-Baghdadi Rejects the Decision" [in Arabic], Alarabiya.net, November 9, 2013 (http://bit.ly/1uNr8C9).

75. "ISIL Announces the Establishment of the 'Islamic State' and Takes the Oath of Allegiance to Abu Bakr Al-Baghdadi as Caliphate of Muslims" [in Arabic], France 24 website, June 30, 2014.

76. "ISIL has Fighters from 81 Nationalities around the World" [in Arabic], Al-Sharq Al-Awsat (London), August 31, 2014 (http://www.aawsat.com/home/article/172201).

77. "Obama before the Security Council: Number of Foreign Fighters on their Way to Conflict Zones in the Middle East is above 15,000 from 80 Countries," CNN Arabia, September 24, 2014 (http://arabic.cnn.com/world/2014/09/24/obama-security-council-foreign-fighters).

78. Some battalions affiliated with Al-Qa'eda accused the leaders of the organization of deviating from the right path and announced a shift of their allegiance to ISIL. Those battalions include the so-called Mantiqat Al-Wasat [the Middle Region], Hoda Battalion, and the Mantiqat Al-Sharq [Eastern Region], which together formed what came to be known as "The Caliphate Soldiers in Algeria." See: "Al-Qa'eda's Battalions in the Maghrib Defect and Join ISIL" [in Arabic], Al-Ittihad (UAE), September 15, 2014 (http://www.alittihad.ae/details.php?id=80560&y=2014).

79. "Study: 7 Stages Planned by Al-Qa'eda's Strategic Ideologues to build their State in 2016" [in Arabic], Assakina website, October 5, 2009 (http://www.assakina.com/center/files/4487.html).

80. Jasim Muhammad, "Al-Qa'eda's Generations Cloning" [in Arabic], Al-Roaya News Network, July 28, 2014 (http://bit.ly/1oFLc2e).

81. "Defections and Divisions in the Ranks of Al-Qa'eda because of Conflicting Interests" [in Arabic], Al-Nahar Al-Jadeed (Algeria), April 18, 2014 (http://bit.ly/1p02Imc).

82. "ISIL Criticizes Al-Zawahiri, Denies being a Branch of Al-Qa'ida, and States its Position regarding Al-Sisi and Mursi in Egypt" [in Arabic], CNN Arabia, December 23, 2014 (http://arabic.cnn.com/middleast/2014/05/12/isis-zawahiri-egypt-army-sisi-morsi).

83. Hamza Mustafa Al-Mustafa, "Jabhat Al-Nusra Li Ahl Al-Sham: From Establishment to Division" [in Arabic], Siyasat Arabiyya, no. 5, November 2013 (Doha: Arab Center for Research and Policy Studies), p. 8.

84. Ibid. p. 9.

85. Ibid. p. 9.

86. Ibid. p. 9.

87. Ibid. p. 9.

88. Ibid. p. 9.

89. Ibid. pp. 18–19.

90. Ibid. p. 9.

91. "Al-Zawahiri Cancels the Islamic State in Iraq and the Levant" [in Arabic], Aljazeera.net, November 8, 2013 (http://bit.ly/1nKG8JG).

92. Hamza Mustafa Al-Mustafa, op. cit., p. 9.

93. "Al-Zawahiri Denounces ISIL and Stresses that 'Al-Nusra is our Branch in Syria'," [in Arabic], Al-Watan Al-Arabi website, January 20, 2014 (http://bit.ly/1qHVIJX).

94. Ibid. (http://bit.ly/1qHVIJX).

95. "A Review of Al-Qa'eda and the Diffusion of its Ideas in the Region" [in Arabic], Israeli Security Agency, Terror Portal (http://bit.ly/1pHvZRp).

96. Muhammad Barhomeh, "85% of Al-Qa'eda's Victims are Muslims" [in Arabic], *Al-Ghad* (Jordan), January 17, 2010 (http://bit.ly/1uAmF5A).

97. Abdulbari Atwan, op. cit., p. 78.

98. Hamza Mustafa Al-Mustafa, op. cit., p. 6.

99. Abdulbari Atwan, op. cit., p. 79.

100. "In a Voice Statement Recorded before he was Killed, bin Ladin Praises the Revolutions of Egypt and Tunisia" [in Arabic], Alarabiya.net, May 19, 2011 (http://www.alarabiya.net/articles/2011/05/19/149662.html).

101. Hajer Abu Zaid (trans.), "Al-Qa'eda's Position Regarding the Arab Spring" [in Arabic], Baghdad Center for Studies, Consulting and Media, December 2012 (http://bit.ly/1kzfPuE).

102. Ibid. (http://bit.ly/1kzfPuE).

103. Ibid. (http://bit.ly/1kzfPuE).

104. Ibid. (http://bit.ly/1kzfPuE).

105. Ibid. (http://bit.ly/1kzfPuE).

106. Ibid. (http://bit.ly/1kzfPuE).

107. Abdulbari Atwan, op. cit., pp. 79–80.

108. Ibid., pp. 79–80.

109. "Washington and Sanaa Confirm Anwar Al-Awlaqi was Killed" [in Arabic], BBC Arabic, September 30, 2011 (http://www.bbc.co.uk/arabic/middleeast/2011/09/110930_yemen_alawlaqi.shtml).

110. Abdulbari Atwan, op. cit., p. 80.

111. Hajer Abu Zaid, op. cit. (http://bit.ly/1kzfPuE).

112. Abdulbari Atwan, op. cit., p. 80.

113. Ibid. pp. 78–79.

114. "Al-Qa'eda's Position Regarding the Arab Spring" op. cit. (http://bit.ly/1kzfPuE).

115. Ibid. (http://bit.ly/1kzfPuE).

116. Ibid. (http://bit.ly/1kzfPuE).

117. Hamza Mustafa Al-Mustafa, op. cit., p. 7.

118. "Defections within Al-Qa'eda and Al-Zawahiri Loses Control" op. cit. (http://bit.ly/1eURJWS).

119. "Al-Qa'eda's Position Regarding the Arab Spring" op. cit. (http://bit.ly/1kzfPuE).

120. "Al-Qa'eda's Third Generation and Electronic Jihad," [in Arabic] (http://bit.ly/1vAYGpw).

121. "Al-Qa'eda's Position Regarding the Arab Spring" op. cit. (http://bit.ly/1kzfPuE).

122. Ahmad bin Hasan Al-Muwakkali, op. cit., p. 24.

123. Ibid., p. 24.

124. Ibid., p. 24; and Alaa Al-Lami, "Al-Barqawi, Al-Zarqawi and the Beginnings of Suicidal Salafism," op. cit. (http://bit.ly/1eAnV3C).

125. "Major Terrorist Operations in Saudi Arabia" [in Arabic], Assakina website, February 9, 2013 (http://www.assakina.com/center/parties/21860.html).

126. Ahmad bin Hasan Al-Muwakkali, op. cit., p. 24.

127. "Al-Qa'eda and Technology: From the War of Faxes to Facebook" [in Arabic], Religion and Politics Center for Studies, February 10, 2011 (http://www.rpcst.com/downloads.php?action=show&id=28).

128. Marwan Shehada, op. cit., pp. 259–260.

129. For more on 'revival' and its key figures and movements in the Arab world see: Jamal Sanad Al-Suwaidi, "Islam and Socio-Political Change: A Comparative Study of Egyptian, Kuwaiti and Palestinian Attitudes," unpublished Dissertation Manuscript, University of Wisconsin, 1990, pp. 150–230.

130. Ahmad bin Hasan Al-Muwakkali, op. cit., p. 21.

131. Ibid. p. 21.

132. Ibid. pp. 35–37.

133. Ibid. pp. 35–37.

134. Yassin Musharbash, "Al-Qa'eda in the Arabian Peninsula: Jihad over the Internet" [in Arabic], translated by Khadeejto Al-Hamid, in *Al-Qa'eda in the Arabian Peninsula*, Al-Misbar Monthly Book, no. 10 (Dubai: Al-Misbar Center for Studies and Research, October 2007), p. 95.

135. To view the footage of the attack on the USS Cole, see Al-Sahab Media Production's film, "Status of the Islamic Nation: USS Cole Attack" (https://archive.org/details/state-of-the-ommah).

136. "Dabiq: Media Arm of the 'Caliphate State'," [in Arabic], *Al-Sharq Al-Awsat* (London), July 21, 2014 (http://classic.aawsat.com/details.asp?section=37&article=780177&issueno=13019).

137. Ibid. (http://classic.aawsat.com/details.asp?section=37&article=780177&issueno=13019).

138. For more on the media section of Al-Qa'ida in the Islamic Maghrib, see: (http://andalus-media.blogspot.ae/2013/08/blog-post.html).

139. "Numan bin Uthman to *Al-Sharq Al-Awsat*: 'Sada Al-Malahim' is the Media Arm of 'Al-Qa'eda in Yemen'" [in Arabic], *Al-Sharq Al-Awsat* (London), November 4, 2010 (http://classic.aawsat.com/details.asp?section=4&article=593832&issueno=11664).

140. "Al-Fajr Media Center" [in Arabic], Assakina website, April 6, 2012 (http://www.assakina.com/center/parties/14220.html).

141. Ahmad bin Hasan Al-Muwakkali, op. cit., p. 40.

142. "Al-Qa'eda in Iraq" [in Arabic], Islamist Movements Portal, May 15, 2014 (http://www.islamist-movements.com/2602).

143. Marwan Shehada, op. cit., p. 251.

144. Ibid. p. 253.

145. "Abu Mus'ab Al-Zarqawi" [in Arabic], Aljazeera.net, June 9, 2006 (http://bit.ly/1pDLJFM).

146. "Usama bin Ladin as Peter Bergen Knows him" [in Arabic], Islamist Movements Portal, January 12, 2014 (http://www.islamist-movements.com/2187).

147. Marwan Shehada, op. cit., pp. 254–255.

148. Ibid. pp. 255–256.

149. Ibid. pp. 255–256.

150. "A Statement Announcing the Formation of the Mujahideen Shura Council in Iraq" [in Arabic], Muslim Portal, January 15, 2005 (http://bit.ly/1kYCFg9).

151. Marwan Shehada, op. cit., pp. 264–265.

152. "ISIL: History and Organization" [in Arabic], Noon Post, May 7, 2014 (http://www.noonpost.net/taxonomy/term/3508/all).

153. Marwan Shehada, op. cit., p. 269.

154. "Who is ISIL and what are its Goals?" [in Arabic], Al-Alam website, January 7, 2014 (http://www.alalam.ir/news/1552479).

155. Ibid. (http://www.alalam.ir/news/1552479).

156. Ibid. (http://www.alalam.ir/news/1552479).

157. Ibid. (http://www.alalam.ir/news/1552479).

158. "Suicide Bombing Kills MP Khalid Al-Fahdawi and Injures Chief of Sunni Endowment Court Ahmad Abdulghafoor Al-Samarra'i" [in Arabic], Mawtani,

August 31, 2011 (http://mawtani.al-shorfa.com/ar/articles/iii/features/iraq today/2011/08/31/feature-01).

159. "Who is ISIL? and What are its Goals? ISIL: A Terrorist Organization Fighting Everybody" [in Arabic], *Al-Nahar* (Iraq), no date (http://bit.ly/1p9 JOeG).

160. Arrahmah Islamic Network (http://www.arrahmah.com/arabic/tnzym-qadt-al-jhad-al-qyadt-al-amt-byan-bshan-alaqt-jmat-qadt-al-jhad-bjmat-ad-dwlt-al-islamyt.html).

161. "ISIL Assassinates Emir of 'Al-Nusra' in Idlib" [in Arabic], *Al-Hayat* (London), April 17, 2014 (http://bit.ly/1szR6HW).

162. Ibid. (http://bit.ly/1szR6HW).

163. "Defections within Al-Qa'eda and Al-Zawahiri Loses Control," op. cit. (http://bit.ly/1eURJWS).

164. "ISIL Assassinates Emir of 'Al-Nusra' in Idlib," op. cit. (http://bit.ly/1szR6HW).

165. "ISIL Accuses Al-Qa'eda of 'Deviation from the Path of Jihad'" [in Arabic], *Al-Wasat* (Bahrain), April 19, 2014 (http://www.alwasatnews.com/4242/news/read/877400/1.html).

166. Ibid. (http://www.alwasatnews.com/4242/news/read/877400/1.html).

167. Ibid. (http://www.alwasatnews.com/4242/news/read/877400/1.html).

168. Ibid. (http://www.alwasatnews.com/4242/news/read/877400/1.html).

169. "Is it Al-Maliki's Policies and Miscalculations or it is the Islamic State in Iraq and the Levant?" [in Arabic], Situation Evaluation Paper, Arab Center for Research and Policy Studies, June 15, 2014 (http://bit.ly/1Dkpo78), pp. 4–5.

170. "Al-Zawahiri Dissolves 'ISIL' and Gives 'Al-Nusra' Jurisdiction in Syria …. and Al-Baghdadi Rejects" [in Arabic], *Al-Sharq Al-Awsat* (London), November 9, 2013 (http://classic.aawsat.com/details.asp?section=4&article=74 9530&issueno=12765).

171. "Is it Al-Maliki's Policies and Miscalculations or it is the Islamic State in Iraq and the Levant?" op. cit. (http://bit.ly/1Dkpo78).

172. For Al-Qa'eda's Statement Posted on the Arrahmah Islamic Network, see: (http://bit.ly/1oG6Vfc).

173. "ISIL: Al-Qa'eda in Iraq has become History" [in Arabic], *Al-Quds Al-Arabi* (London), February 23, 2014 (http://www.alquds.co.uk/?p=136497).

174. "ISIL Announces the Establishment of an Islamic Caliphate and Takes the Oath of Allegiance to Al-Baghdadi" [in Arabic], *Al-Hayat* (London), June 29, 2014 (http://bit.ly/1wwb1e7).

175. "ISIL Announces the Establishment of an Islamic Caliphate and Takes the Oath of Allegiance to Al-Baghdadi as Caliph of Muslims" [in Arabic], France 24, June 30, 2014 (http://f24.my/1y8wA0Y).

176. "A Statement Issued by the Association of Muslim Scholars in Iraq," [in Arabic], July 1, 2014, website of the Association of Muslim Scholars in Iraq (http://www.iraq.amsi.com/Portal/news.php?action=view&id=75741&a1bfc6 5ffeb113d564f8878229f9aa54).

177. "A Statement Issued by the International Union for Muslim Scholars" [in Arabic], July 22, 2014, website of the International Union for Muslim Scholars (http://iumsonline.org/ar/Default.asp?ContentID=8198&menuID=7).

178. "Islamic Parties and Organizations Reject the Announcement by ISIL of the Caliphate State" [in Arabic], *Al-Arab Al-Yawm* (Jordan), July 3, 2014, p. 3 (http://alarabalyawm.net/?p=332891).

179. "A Statement by Abu Muhammad Al-Maqdisi" [in Arabic], Tawheed and Jihad Website, September 7, 2014 (http://www.tawhed.ws/r?i=07091401).

180. "Jordan Jihadis Divided: Some Support ISIL and Some Loyal to Al-Qa'eda" [in Arabic], *Al-Arab* (London), July 24, 2014, p. 4 (http://www.alarabonline.org/?id=28746).

181. Ibid. (http://www.alarabonline.org/?id=28746).

182. Hazim Al-Ameen, "Jihadi Salafism in Jordan on its Way to ISIL after Spending Years with Al-Nusra" [in Arabic], *Al-Hayat* (London), July 4, 2014 (http://bit.ly/1qUWbsL).

183. "What is ISIL? Journey since Defection from Al-Qa'eda until Announcing the Caliphate State" [in Arabic], *Al-Hayat* (London), June 11, 2014, p. 9 (http://bit.ly/1p1YFmb).

184. Sayyid Qutb, *Milestones in the Road* [in Arabic], 9th Edition (Cairo: Dar Al-Shurooq, 1982), p. 39.

185. Abdulghani Imad, "Salafism and the Problem of the Other between Negotiation and Preference" [in Arabic], Beirut, *Al-Mustaqbal Al-Arabi*, issue 224, February 2006, pp. 65–69.

186. "Al-Tahawi: Democracy is Un-Islamic" [in Arabic], Ammon News Website, June 1, 2013 (http://www.ammonnews.net/article.aspx?articleno=141318).

187. Naseef Hatti, "The Transformational Course of the New Arab Order" [in Arabic], Beirut, *Palestinian Studies*, Issue 93, Winter 2013, p. 23.

188. Ibid., p. 23.

189. For more on factors affecting the structure of the new world order, see: Jamal Sanad Al-Suwaidi, *Prospects for the American Age: Sovereignty and Influence in the New World Order* [in Arabic]; (Abu Dhabi: ECSSR, 2014), pp. 138–249.

190. "First Statement by 'Caliph' Al-Baghdadi to the Muslim Nation" [in Arabic], *Elaph*, July 1, 2014 (http://www.elaph.com/Web/News/2014/7/919276.html).

191. "Arab Countries and Turkey Support US Plan to 'Protect the World' from the Violence of ISIL" [in Arabic], *Al-Hayat* (London), September 12, 2014 (http://goo.gl/582ZyH).

192. See the text of the decision at: (http://www.mofa.gov.iq/documentfiles/130529094121306074.pdf).

Chapter 7

1. Hisham Basheer, *Theoretical Study on the Nature and Methods of Public Opinion Surveys* [in Arabic]; (Egypt: The Center for the Study of Developing Countries, no date), p. 3.

2. The confidence level tells you how sure you can be of the results using a sample of the population to study a certain phenomenon. It is expressed as a percentage and represents how often the true percentage of the population who would pick an answer lies within the confidence interval. The 95% confidence level means that out of 100 persons, 95 would pick an answer similar to the results of the survey. As such, the results of the survey can be generalized to 95% of the population. Most researchers use the 95% confidence level, especially in social studies. This percentage goes up to 99%, or more, in laboratory studies. For further details, see: (http://www.surveysystem.com/sscalc.htm).

3. Sampling error is the deviation of the selected sample from the true characteristics, traits, behaviors, qualities or figures of the entire population. Sampling process error occurs because researchers draw different subjects from the same population but still the subjects have individual differences. A sample is only a subset of the entire population; therefore, there may be a difference between the sample and the population. Given two identical studies using the same sampling methods on the same population, the study with a larger sample size will have less sampling process error than to the study with a smaller sample size. As the sample size increases, it approaches the size of the entire population, therefore, it also approaches all the characteristics of the population, thus, decreasing sampling process error. There is only one way to eliminate this error. This solution is to eliminate the concept of the sample, and to test the entire population, which is not practical. For further details, see: (https://explorable.com/sampling-error).

4. See: E. G. Carmines and R.A. Zeller, *Reliability and Validity Assessment* (Newbury Park, CA: Sage Publications, 1991).

5. The Arab Barometer was established in 2005 by scholars in the Arab world and the United States. It was headed by Mark Tessler of the University of

Michigan, Amaney Jamal of Princeton University and others from universities and research centers in Jordan, Palestine, Morocco, Algeria and Kuwait. In 2010, a partnership was formed with the Arab Reform Initiative in order to expand the project's scope and range of activities, building on the results of the first regional survey work carried out in 2006–2008. The Arab Barometer was developed in consultation with the Global Barometer, which is a network of regional barometers of Latin America, Sub-Saharan Africa, East Asia, South Asia and elsewhere. The Arab Barometer aims to gather scientifically trustworthy data concerning relevant political positions through surveys and field studies from representative samples of citizens of various countries, and then to publish the results to contribute to political reform and enhance the institutional capabilities of public opinion research (http://www.arabbarometer.org).

6.   See: Amaney Jamal and Mark Tessler, "Attitudes in the Arab World," The Democracy Barometers, *Journal of Democracy*, vol. 19, no. 1, January 2008.

7.   Jamal Abduljawad, et al., *Citizens' Attitudes Concerning the Most Important Political and Social Issues in Egypt* [in Arabic], Arab Barometer Survey (Cairo: Al-Ahram Center for Political and Strategic Studies, June 2011); (http://www.arabbarometer.org/sites/default/files/countyreportyegyptII.pdf).

8.   Muhammad Al-Masri, *Arab Barometer Survey: The Hashemite Kingdom of Jordan* [in Arabic], August 2011, Strategic Studies Center, University of Jordan (http://www.arabbarometer.org/sites/default/files/countyreportjordan2_0.pdf).

9.   Saud Al-Sarhan, *Arab Barometer Survey: The Kingdom of Saudi Arabia* [in Arabic], February 2011 (http://www.arabbarometer.org/sites/default/files/countyreportysaudi2.pdf).

10. Muhammad Al-Masri, *Arab Barometer Survey II, Tunisia* [in Arabic], September 2012 (http://www.arabbarometer.org/sites/default/files/Tunisia%20Country%20Report%20ABII.pdf).

11. Ibid. (http://www.arabbarometer.org/sites/default/files/Tunisia%20Country%20Report%20ABII.pdf).

12. Jamal Abduljawad, et al., op. cit. (http://www.arabbarometer.org/sites/default/files/countyreportyegyptII.pdf).

13. Muhammad Al-Masri, op. cit. (http://www.arabbarometer.org/sites/default/files/countyreportjordan2_0.pdf).

14. Saud Al-Sarhan, op. cit. (http://www.arabbarometer.org/sites/default/files/countyreportysaudi2.pdf).

15. Mark Tessler, et al., *Determinants of Political Participation and Electoral Behavior in the Arab World: Findings and Insights from the Arab Barometer* (http://www.arabbarometer.org/sites/default/files/files/Determinants%20of%20Political.pdf).

16. Ibid. (http://www.arabbarometer.org/sites/default/files/files/Determinants%20of%20Political.pdf).

17. Jamal Abduljawad, et al., op. cit. (http://www.arabbarometer.org/sites/default/files/countyreportyegyptII.pdf).

18. Muhammad Al-Masri, op. cit. (http://www.arabbarometer.org/sites/default/files/Tunisia%20Country%20Report%20ABII.pdf).

19. Saud Al-Sarhan, op. cit. (http://www.arabbarometer.org/sites/default/files/countyreportysaudi2.pdf).

20. Nasser Al-Jabi, *Report on Arab Barometer Survey (2011)* [in Arabic], July 2011 (http://www.arabbarometer.org/sites/default/files/countyreportyAlgeriaII.pdf).

21. Mark Tessler, *The Civic Orientations of Arab Publics: Selected Findings from the Arab Barometer*, June 25, 2014 (http://www.arabbarometer.org/reports-presentation-abwave/arab-barometer-iii).

22. Nasser Al-Jabi, op. cit. (http://www.arabbarometer.org/sites/default/files/countyreportyAlgeriaII.pdf).

23. Mark Tessler, op. cit. (http://www.arabbarometer.org/reports-presentation-abwave/arab-barometer-iii).

24. Mark Tessler, "Accounting for Variance in Popular Attitudes toward the Place of Islam in Political Life: Findings from the Arab Barometer Surveys

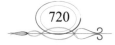

in Algeria, Morocco and Other Arab Countries" (http://www.yale.edu/
macmillan/africadissent/tessler.pdf).

25. Mark Tessler, "Religion, Religiosity and the Place of Islam in Political Life:
    Insights from the Arab Barometer Surveys," *Middle East Law and Governance*,
    vol. 2, 2010 (http://www.researchgate.net/publication/233570622_Religion_
    Religiosity_and_the_Place_of_Islam_in_Political_Life_Insights_from_the_
    Arab_Barometer_Surveys).

26. Saud Al-Sarhan, op. cit. (http://www.arabbarometer.org/sites/default/files/
    countyreportysaudi2.pdf).

27. Majid Uthman, "Results of a Public Opinion Survey on Egyptians' Assessment
    of the Muslim Brotherhood" [in Arabic], The Egyptian Center for Public
    Opinion Research (Baseera); (http://www.baseera.com.eg/pdf_poll_file_
    ar/Towards-the-Muslim-Brotherhood-ar.pdf).

28. Ibid. (http://www.baseera.com.eg/pdf_poll_file_ar/Towards-the-Muslim-
    Brotherhood-ar.pdf).

29. Ibid. (http://www.baseera.com.eg/pdf_poll_file_ar/Towards-the-Muslim-
    Brotherhood-ar.pdf).

30. "US PEW Center: 39% of Egyptians are optimistic about the Future" [in
    Arabic], *Al-Shurooq* (Egypt), May 24, 2014 (http://www.shorouknews.com/
    mobile/news/view.aspx?cdate=24052014&id=27d3b556-0b6c-4213-b4e0-
    77597f43258d).

31. Majid Uthman, "Results of a Public Opinion Survey on the Return of the
    Muslim Brotherhood to Political Life" [in Arabic], The Egyptian Center for
    Public Opinion Research (Baseera) (http://www.baseera.com.eg/pdf_poll_file_
    ar/the%20return%20of%20the%20Muslim%20Brotherhood%20-ar.pdf).

32. Ibid. (http://www.baseera.com.eg/pdf_poll_file_ar/the%20return%20of%20the
    %20Muslim%20Brotherhood%20-ar.pdf).

Conclusion

1. Abdulati Muhammad Ahmad, *Political Thought of the Imam Muhammad Abdu* [in Arabic]; (Cairo: General Egyptian Book Organization, 2012), pp. 144–153.

2. Jamal Sand Al-Suwaidi, *Prospects for the American Age: Sovereignty and Influence in the New World Order* [in Arabic]; (Abu Dhabi: ECSSR, 2014), p. 98.

3. Suhaila Allawa Azeemi, *Revival Methodology according to Abu Al-A'la Al-Mawdoodi* [in Arabic]; (Damascus: Annahdah Publishing House 2008), p. 336.

4. Ibid., p. 340.

5. Ibid., p. 331.

6. The Holy Quran (6:116).

7. Suhaila Allawa Azeemi, op. cit., p. 332.

8. Muhammad Abu al-Qasim Haj Hamad, *Hakimiyya* [in Arabic]; (Beirut: Dar Al-Saqi, 1st edition, 2010), p. 40.

9. The Holy Quran, (12:40).

10. Abdulghani Imad, *God (Allah)'s Hakimiyya and Jurist's Authority: Examining the Discourse of Contemporary Islamic Movements* [in Arabic]; (Beirut: Dar Al-Talia Publishers, June 1997), p. 12.

11. Burhan Ghalioun, *Critiquing Politics: State and Religion* [in Arabic]; (Beirut: Arab Institute for Research and Publishing, 2nd edition, 1993), p. 424.

12. Ibid., p. 424.

13. Ibid., p. 432.

14. The Holy Quran, (5:44).

15. Muhammad Saeed Al-Ashmawi, *Islam and Politics* [in Arabic]; (Beirut: Alintishar Alarabi, 1st edition, 2004), pp. 30–31.

16. Ibid., pp. 36–37.

17. Hisham Ahmad Awadh Jaafar, *Political Dimensions of the Hakimiyya Concept: Epistemological Perspective* [in Arabic]; (Herndon, VA: International Institute of Islamic Thought, Theses Series 14, 1995), p. 24.

18. Abdulghani Imad, *God (Allah)'s Hakimiyya* ... op. cit., pp. 84–85.

19. The Holy Quran, (5:45).

20. Abdulghani Imad, op. cit., pp. 84–85.

21. The Holy Quran, (5:48).

22. The Holy Quran, (2:208).

23. Samer Islamboli, *Divinity and Hakimiyya: A Scientific Study through the Quran* [in Arabic]; (Damascus: Dar Al-Awael Publishing, Distribution and Printing Services, 2000), pp. 216–217.

24. Ibid., p. 217.

25. The Holy Quran (7:33).

26. The Holy Quran (29:68).

27. Mohammed Rateb Nabulsi, "Interpretation of Quran, The Short Version, Surat Al-Ankabut (29)" Lesson 9-9, Verses 68-69 [in Arabic], September 28, 1995 (http://www.nabulsi.com/blue/ar/print.php?art=5791).

28. See: "ISIL's Black Fatwas" [in Arabic], *Addustor* newspaper, Egypt, October 26, 2014 (http://goo.gl/9pblbi). Also see: "In the dictionary of the Islamic State, even the eyes of veiled women are *Awra* [a part of the body that should be covered]" [in Arabic], Middle East Online, July 31, 2014 (http://www.middle-east-online.com/?id=181431!).

29. The Holy Quran, (16:116).

30. Nasser bin Suleiman Al-Omar, "Attributing unto God (Allah) Something of which you have no Knowledge" [in Arabic], Al-Moslim website, August 7, 2011 (http://www.almoslim.net/node/150949).

31. The Holy Quran (6:93).

32. The Holy Quran (10:59).

33. "Issuing a *Fatwa* without having the Required Knowledge is a Crime that Deserves *Tazeer* [a discretionary punishment]," [in Arabic] Assakina website, January 28, 2012 (http://www.assakina.com/news/news1/12446.html).

34. Mohammed bin Abdullah Al-Meshouah, "Preventing God's Mercy" [in Arabic], *Okaz* newspaper, November 12, 2013 (http://www.okaz.com.sa/new/issues/20131112/Con20131112654043.htm).

35. For further details on political conflicts between the Muslim Brotherhood and the Salafis, see: Ammar Ali Hasan, *Suicide of the Muslim Brotherhood: The Fade of Thought, Fall of Ethics and Collapse of the Organization* [in Arabic]; (Cairo: Dar Nahdat Misr for Publishing, 2013), pp. 152–168.

36. "The Salafi Abu Qatada Al-Felistini Describes ISIL as Kharijites and Dogs of the Inhabitants of Hellfire," [in Arabic], Watan News, April 29, 2014 (http://www.elwtanews.net/alarab-news/37239.html).

37. Gilles Kepel, *Jihad: the Expansion and Decline of Islamism*, Nabeel Saad (trans.), Anwar Mugheeth (review); (Cairo: Dar Al-Aalam Al-Thalith, 1st edition, 2005), pp. 42–80.

38. Mark Tessler, "The Civic Orientations of Arab Publics: Selected Findings from the Arab Barometer," *Emirates Lecture Series* No. 115 (Abu Dhabi: The Emirates Center for Strategic Studies and Research, 2014), pp. 1–45. To view the lecture see: (http://www.ecssr.ac.ae/ECSSR/appmanager/portal/ecssr?_nfpb=true&_nfls=false&_pageLabel=ActivitiesPage&eventId=%2FActivities%2FLectures%2FActivities_4202.xml&_event=viewDetails&lang=ar).

39. The American writer Shadi Hamid explains that, "in religiously conservative societies, there is widespread support for more mixing of religion and politics, not less ... If the popular demand is there, someone will need to supply it." Further, "Islamic democracy ... is supposed to rely on a fundamentally different philosophical basis (from the Western concept of democracy) ... If elected Islamic parties have to give up their Islamism, then this runs counter to the essence of democracy – the notion that governments should be responsive to, or at least accommodate, public preferences." Therefore, he calls for the concept of "Illiberal Democracy" in the Arab and Muslim worlds on the basis that it is

the best formula to achieve democracy and incorporate political religious groups. See: Shadi Hamid, "The Brotherhood Will Be Back," *The New York Times*, May 23, 2014 (http://nyti.ms/1im2ijF).

40. Ibid. (http://nyti.ms/1im2ijF).

41. Ibid. (http://nyti.ms/1im2ijF).

42. For further information concerning the Muslim Brotherhood's relations with foreign powers, see: Ali Al-Sayyid Al-Wasifi, *The Muslim Brotherhood between Religious Innovation and Political Bankruptcy* [in Arabic]; (Cairo: Dar Sabeel Al-Mumineen for Publishing and Distribution, 2012), pp. 890–908. Also see: Helmi Al-Namnam, *Hassan Al-Banna as Nobody Knows Him* [in Arabic]; (Cairo: Madbooli Bookshop, 2011), pp. 117–134.

43. Imad Mas'ad Muhammad Al-Saba', "The Future of the Relations between the Muslim Brotherhood and America" [in Arabic], Al-Hiwar Al-Mutamaddin website, August 16, 2011 (http://www.ahewar.org/debat/show.art.asp?aid=27 1596).

Bibliography

Bibliography

BIBLIOGRAPHY

"[Rashid] Al-Ghannooshi does not take a Firm Stand and Quickly Changes his Mind" [in Arabic]. *Al-Arab* newspaper, issue 9328, London, September 22, 2013.

"'Murajaat' Talk Show, Episode (1)," website of Shaikh Muhammad Suroor Zine Al-Abideen (http://www.surour.net/index.php?group=view&rid=786&rp=2).

"'The Free Egyptians' and 'Khanaqtoona' Movement Organize 'Brotherhood Liars' Campaign in Alexandria" [in Arabic]. *Al-Shurooq* newspaper, Egypt, April 1, 2013 (http://goo.gl/fflpt1).

"34 Years after the Hostage Crisis at the American Embassy in Tehran" [in Arabic]. *Al-Sharq Al-Awsat*, London, December 12, 2013 (http://classic. aawsat.com/details.asp?section=34&article=753594&issueno=12798#.U_Mv I_2oWic).

"A Brief Overview on the Emergence of Ilm Al-Kalam" [in Arabic]. Ministry of Endowments and Islamic Affairs, Kingdom of Morocco, February 5, 2012 (http://habous.gov.ma/2012-01-26-16-15-16/57-2012-08-28-14-34-54. html).

"A Former Revivalist Reveals the Secrets and Mysteries of 'Suroorism' in Saudi Arabia" [in Arabic]. Al-Arabiya website, January 15, 2008 (http://www. alarabiya.net/articles/2008/01/15/44239.html).

"A Reading in the Intellectual Structure of the Muslim Brotherhood" [in Arabic]. Al Sharq Al-Arabi, February 2010 (www.asharqalarabi.org.uk/markaz/dr-19-02-2011.doc).

"A Review of Al-Qa'eda and the Diffusion of its Ideas in the Region" [in Arabic]. Israeli Security Agency, Terror Portal (http://bit.ly/1pHvZRp).

"A Scholar from Al-Azhar Responds to Sayyid Qutb and his Sedition" [in Arabic]. Alukah portal, September 6, 2008 (http://majles.alukah.net/t19 695/).

"A Special Interview with 'Abu Muhammad Al-Maqdisi' (1) On the Doctrine of the Jihadi Salafi Current" [in Arabic]. Al-Asr website, July 24, 2005 (http://alasr.ws/articles/view/6872/).

"A Statement Announcing the Formation of the Mujahideen Shura Council in Iraq" [in Arabic]. Muslim Portal, January 15, 2005 (http://bit.ly/1kYCFg9).

"A Statement by Abu Muhammad Al-Maqdisi" [in Arabic]. Tawheed and Jihad Website, September 7, 2014 (http://www.tawhed.ws/r?i=07091401).

"A Statement Issued by the Association of Muslim Scholars in Iraq," [in Arabic]. July 1, 2014, website of the Association of Muslim Scholars in Iraq (http://www.iraq.amsi.com/Portal/news.php?action=view&id=75741&a1bfc 65ffeb113d564f8878229f9aa54).

"A Statement Issued by the International Union for Muslim Scholars" [in Arabic]. July 22, 2014, website of the International Union for Muslim Scholars (http://iumsonline.org/ar/Default.asp?ContentID=8198&menuID =7).

"A Year Since the Establishment of the Freedom and Justice Party" [in Arabic]. *Al-Masry Al-Youm* newspaper, Egypt, June 6, 2012 (http://www.almasry alyoum.com/news/details/184089).

"Abu Muhammad Al-Maqdisi: A Jihadi Ideologue who Never Performed Jihad" [in Arabic]. Al-Araby Al-Jadeed website, June 17, 2014 (http://www. alaraby.co.uk/politics/09d87ce9-982b-4950-9d9c-736f28b4a690).

"Abu Mus'ab Al-Zarqawi" [in Arabic]. Aljazeera.net, June 9, 2006 (http://bit.ly/ 1pDLJFM).

"After Getting Only the Ministry of Environment: Al-Noor Party Withdraws from Qandeel's Government" [in Arabic]. *Al-Ahram* newspaper, Egypt, August 2, 2012 (http://digital.ahram.org.eg/articles.aspx?Serial=981853 &eid=7266).

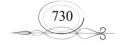

"Al-Fajr Media Center" [in Arabic]. Assakina website, April 6, 2012 (http://www.assakina.com/center/parties/14220.html).

"Al-Qa'eda and Technology: From the War of Faxes to Facebook" [in Arabic]. Religion and Politics Center for Studies, February 10, 2011 (http://www.rpcst.com/downloads.php?action=show&id=28).

"Al-Qa'eda in Iraq" [in Arabic]. Islamist Movements Portal, May 15, 2014 (http://www.islamist-movements.com/2602).

"Al-Qa'eda's Battalions in the Maghrib Defect and Join ISIL" [in Arabic]. *Al-Ittihad* (UAE), September 15, 2014 (http://www.alittihad.ae/details.php?id=80560&y=2014).

"Al-Qa'eda's Third Generation and Electronic Jihad," [in Arabic] (http://bit.ly/1vAYGpw).

"Al-Qa'ida Appoints Algerian Abu Luqman as a New Leader of 'Ansar Al-Sharia' Movement" [in Arabic]. *Al-Ittihad* newspaper, UAE, January 14, 2014 (http://www.alittihad.ae/details.php?id=3880&y=2014).

"Al-Qaida and the Internationalization of Suicide Terrorism" [in Arabic]. Aljazeera.net, September 21, 2005 (http://www.aljazeera.net/NR/exeres/1D636886-D4FD-4736-AB8C-F41D2343FCB8.htm).

"Al-Tahawi: Democracy is Un-Islamic" [in Arabic]. Ammon News Website, June 1, 2013 (http://www.ammonnews.net/article.aspx?articleno=141318).

"Al-Zawahiri Announces the Cancellation of ISIL and Al-Baghdadi Rejects the Decision" [in Arabic]. Alarabiya.net, November 9, 2013 (http://bit.ly/1uNr8C9).

"Al-Zawahiri Cancels the Islamic State in Iraq and the Levant" [in Arabic]. Aljazeera.net, November 8, 2013 (http://bit.ly/1nKG8JG).

"Al-Zawahiri Denounces ISIL and Stresses that 'Al-Nusra is our Branch in Syria'." [in Arabic]. *Al-Watan Al-Arabi* website, January 20, 2014 (http://bit.ly/1qHVIJX).

"Al-Zawahiri Dissolves 'ISIL' and Gives 'Al-Nusra' Jurisdiction in Syria …. and Al-Baghdadi Rejects" [in Arabic]. *Al-Sharq Al-Awsat* (London), November 9, 2013 (http://classic.aawsat.com/details.asp?section=4&article=749530&issueno=12765).

"Anwar Al-Sadat ... the Reasons and Repercussions of his Assassination, Part 2" [in Arabic]. Aljazeera.net website, October 24, 2005 (http://bit.ly/1qUp Ezp).

"Apostasy and Freedom of Belief: A New Islamic Perspective" [in Arabic]. Religion and Politics Center for Studies, August 9, 2011 (http://www.rpcst. com/news.php?action=show&id=3910).

"Arab Countries and Turkey Support US Plan to 'Protect the World' from the Violence of ISIL" [in Arabic]. *Al-Hayat* (London), September 12, 2014 (http://goo.gl/582ZyH).

"Badie to his 'Clan': Be Prepared to Carry the Banner of the 'Mastership of the World' and Raise it in 'Al-Aqsa'" [in Arabic]. *Al-Watan* (Egypt), May 14, 2013 (http://www.elwatannews.com/news/details/181456).

"Biographies of Religious Scholars: The Sheikh of Islam Muhammad ibn Abdulwahhab" [in Arabic]. Al-Tawheed website (http://bit.ly/1iY07bC).

"Biographies of Religious Scholars: The Sheikh of Islam Muhammad ibn Abdulwahhab" op. cit. (http://bit.ly/1iY07bC).

"Book Review by Jalal Al-Deen Ezz Al-Deen Ali of *Islamists Shifts* (From the Flames of September to the Spring of Revolutions)" [in Arabic]. Aljazeera.net, November 20, 2012 (http://bit.ly/1qY0Ai6).

"Caid Essebsi is President of Tunisia, and Al-Marzooqi Congratulates him" [in Arabic]. Alarabiya.net, December 21, 2014 (http://goo.gl/AVa8GD).

"Charter of the Legitimate League of Scholars and Preachers in Sudan" [in Arabic]. The Legitimate League website, May 28, 2011 (http://rabetasud. org/index.php/welcome/fullarticle/1).

"CIA: ISIL has about 30,000 Fighters" [in Arabic]. BBC Arabic, September 12, 2014.

"Collection of scholars' opinions about Muhammad Suroor and Suroorism" [in Arabic]; (http://www.anti-ikhwan.com/?p=166).

"Comprehensive Encyclopedia" [in Arabic]; (http://islamport.com/d/1/mtn/1/ 89/3501.html).

"Controversy Regarding the Remarks by the General Guide of the Muslim Brotherhood group that the Group is Close to Establishing a Global Islamic Caliphate" [in Arabic]. *Al-Sharq Al-Awsat* newspaper, London, January 1, 2012 (http://classic.aawsat.com/details.asp?section=4&issueno=12087& article =656946&feature=#.U_w_8_mSzYA).

"Dabiq: Media Arm of the 'Caliphate State'," [in Arabic]. *Al-Sharq Al-Awsat* (London), July 21, 2014 (http://classic.aawsat.com/details.asp?section=37& article=780177&issueno=13019).

"Debate: Belonging to a religious party is not one of the pillars of Islam, Imam Muhammad Mutwalli Al-Sha'rawi rejects the linking between belonging to Islam and joining a Brotherhood organization or party" [in Arabic]. *Al-Arab* newspaper, London, October 23, 2013 (http://alarab.co.uk/?id=6604).

"Defections and Divisions in the Ranks of Al-Qa'eda because of Conflicting Interests" [in Arabic]. *Al-Nahar Al-Jadeed* (Algeria), April 18, 2014 (http:// bit.ly/1p02Imc).

"Defections within Al-Qa'eda and Al-Zawahiri Loses Control" [in Arabic]. Assakina website, February 4, 2014 (http://www.assakina.com/news/news2/ 37512.html#ixzz3Exb6rQt0).

"Disintegration Threats: The Internal Situations of the Middle East according to the 'Fragile States Index'," [in Arabic]. Regional Centre for Strategic Studies in Cairo, website of the Arab Orient Center for Cultural and Strategic Studies, August 3, 2014 (https://gallery.mailchimp.com/7e569236ec7284d 7724bc0525/files/c05d5385-f374-41af-8cf9-a0e244b1904a.pdf).

"Dr. Sufi Abu Taleb: the Project to Incorporate Sharia in the Laws has been Ready since 1983!" [in Arabic]. On Islam website, May 22, 2007 (http:// www.onislam.net/arabic/fiqh-a-tazkia/fiqh-papers/8081/95402-2007-05-22 %2013-51-30.html).

"Economists: Qandeel's Government is Confused, 'its Decisions are Ill-considered' and it is Operating without a Clear Vision or Goal" [in Arabic]. *Al-Youm Al-Sabie* electronic newspaper, Egypt, November 4, 2012 (http:// bit.ly/1qYmVuj).

"Egypt Presidential Elections and the Theory of Political Poisoning" [in Arabic]. The Contemporary Studies Center, June 4, 2012 (http://derasat.ara-star. com/full.php?ID=569).

"Egypt: A Harsh Blow to the Brotherhood that May Escalate Violence" [in Arabic]. Sky News Arabia, August 20, 2013 (http://bit.ly/1q6f6gK).

"Egypt's Brotherhood are Shifting their Policy and Pressing Hamas to Make Compromises with Fatah" [in Arabic]. *Al-Sharq Al-Awsat* newspaper, London, March 25, 2012 (http://bit.ly/1teLkej).

"Egypt's Parliament between Consensus and Alliances" [in Arabic]. Aljazeera.net, January 23, 2012 (http://bit.ly/1qQqm5X).

"Erbakan and Çiller say coalition government functioning in harmony." Hurriyet Daily News, March 25, 1997 (http://www.hurriyetdailynews.com/default. aspx?pageid=438&n=erbakan-and-ciller-say-coalition-government-functio ning-in-harmony-1997-03-25).

"Expert on Terrorism: Number of Al-Qa'ida Members Reduced to Half, but Funding Unchanged" [in Arabic]. *Al-Sharq Al-Awsat* (London), October 13, 2002 (http://classic.aawsat.com/details.asp?section=4&issueno=8720& article=129763&feature=).

"Explanation of the Forty Nawawi Hadeeths." Website of Sheikh Muhammad bin Salih Al-Uthaymeen, May 4, 2005 (http://www.ibnothaimeen.com/ all/books/article_17764.shtml).

"Fahmi Jad'an Calls for Liberating Islam of Misconceptions" [in Arabic]. *Al-Mirsad*, August 18, 2014 (http://goo.gl/8TF19A).

"*Fatwas* of Dar Al-Iftaa Al-Massriyya, *fatwa* issued by the former Grand Imam of al-Azhar, Jad Al-Haq Ali Jad Al-Haq concerning the 1979 Peace Treaty" [in Arabic]. Al-Maktaba Al-Shamila (http://shamela.ws/browse.php/book-432/page-2571).

"Final Results: Nidaa Tounes Wins the Tunisian Elections" [in Arabic]. Ahdath Info portal, October 30, 2014 (http://www.ssrcaw.org/ar/news.asp?nid= 1844388).

"First Christian Governor of Jakarta in 50 years" [in Arabic]. Aljazeera.net, November 20, 2014 (http://goo.gl/5D8WVj).

"First Saudi List of Terrorist Organizations Includes the Brotherhood, Al-Nusra and ISIL" [in Arabic]. BBC, March 7, 2014 (http://www.bbc.co.uk/arabic/ middleeast/2014/03/140307_saudi_terror_organizations).

"First Statement by 'Caliph' Al-Baghdadi to the Muslim Nation" [in Arabic]. *Elaph*, July 1, 2014 (http://www.elaph.com/Web/News/2014/7/919276. html).

"Flashback from 13 Years Ago: Prince Nayef Speaking about the Muslim Brotherhood" [in Arabic]. Assakina website, March 2014 (http://www. assakina.com/news/news2/40123.html).

"General Labor Union Proposes a New Initiative to Resolve the Political Crisis in Tunisia" [in Arabic]. *Al-Arab* newspaper, London, September 19, 2013 (http://www.alarab.co.uk/?id=4172).

"Governor of Luxor a 'Jihadist' who was Arrested after Sadat's Assassination" [in Arabic]. Arabic CNN, July 18, 2013 (http://goo.gl/VZr7Ph).

"Growing Fears of Transforming Egypt into a Religious State" [in Arabic]. November 28, 2012, Deutsche Welle website (http://bit.ly/1pdZcp5).

"Gulf Umma Parties Gather in Kuwait" [in Arabic]. *Al-Watan* newspaper, Kuwait, March 30, 2013 (http://alwatan.kuwait.tt/articledetails.aspx?Id=26 4204).

"Haikal: Part of Mursi's 'Decisive' Tone in the 'Summit' is Directed to the Brotherhood ... and the 'Group' is Experiencing a 'Shock'," [in Arabic]. *Al-Watan* newspaper, Egypt, March 28, 2013 (http://www.elwatannews.com/ news/details/155186).

"Haikal: The Brotherhood is Innocent of Sadat's Assassination and Nasser is the only President who did not Taste the Joy of Ceremonies" [in Arabic]. *Al-Watan* newspaper, Egypt, March 28, 2013 (http://www.elwatannews.com/ news/details/155259).

"Hamas Wins the Palestinian Legislative Elections" [in Arabic]. Al-Quds Center for Political Studies, January 1, 2006 (http://www.alqudscenter.org/arabic/ pages.php?local_type=123&local_details=2&id1=86&menu_id=-1).

"Hamas: Inception and Relationship with the Muslim Brotherhood" [in Arabic]. *Al-Sharq Al-Awsat* newspaper, London, June 9, 2001 (http://classic.aawsat. com/details.asp?section=28&article=42016&issueno=8229#.U_NNDP2oWic).

"History of Islamic Civilization." Rulers of Egypt Encyclopedia [in Arabic]; (http://www.islamichistory.net/forum/showthread.php?p=48001).

"How Christianity Rose to Dominate Europe." Worldology, September 8, 2010 (http://www.worldology.com/Christianity/rise_christianity.htm).

"Ibn Taymiyya: Works and Reformist Approach" [in Arabic]; (a group of authors). Papers presented at the symposium held at Mutah University, Karak, Jordan, March 28–29, 2001 (Amman: Dar Ward for Publishing and Distribution).

"Illusion of the Religious State: between Caliphate, Hakimiyya and the Guardianship of the Jurist" [in Arabic]. *Al-Arab* newspaper, London, January 8, 2014 (http://alarab.co.uk/m/?id=12317).

"ILO: Unemployment in Arab Countries Twice the Global Rate" [in Arabic]. Elaph electronic newspaper, February 27, 2014 (http://www.elaph.com/Web/Economics/2014/2/881222.html).

"Imam Ahmad ibn Hanbal" [in Arabic]. Islam Story website (http://bit.ly/1njd5T6).

"In a Voice Statement Recorded before he was Killed, bin Ladin Praises the Revolutions of Egypt and Tunisia" [in Arabic]. Alarabiya.net, May 19, 2011 (http://www.alarabiya.net/articles/2011/05/19/149662.html).

"In the Dictionary of the Islamic State, even the Eyes of Veiled Women are *Awra* [a part of the body that should be covered]" [in Arabic]. Middle East Online, July 31, 2014 (http://www.middle-east-online.com/?id=181431!).

"In the Words of its President, the Social Reform Society is in Line with the Thought of the Muslim Brotherhood" [in Arabic]. Kuwait Sound electronic newspaper, December 1, 2013 (http://bit.ly/1pdNL0B).

"Inflation and Political Conflict: Threats to the Sudanese Economy" [in Arabic]. Aljazeera.net, September 4, 2014 (http://goo.gl/PzWFhE).

"Interview ... Shaikh Abdul Fattah Moro: Ennahdha's Government has More Cons than Pros" [in Arabic]. Islam Online portal, February 17, 2013 (http://bit.ly/1qjtHGl).

"Interview with Shaikh Muhammad Suroor Zine Al-Abideen (talking about democracy)." Today Interview Program, Aljazeera.net, June 9, 2013 (http://bit.ly/1u0Ts4L).

"Interview with the Writer and Academic Dr. Ahmad Faraj." *Al-Hayat* newspaper, London, April 16, 2014 (http://alhayat.com/Articles/1614402).

"Is it Al-Maliki's Policies and Miscalculations or it is the Islamic State in Iraq and the Levant?" [in Arabic]. Situation Evaluation Paper, Arab Center for Research and Policy Studies, June 15, 2014 (http://bit.ly/1Dkpo78).

"ISIL Accuses Al-Qa'eda of 'Deviation from the Path of Jihad'," [in Arabic]. *Al-Wasat* (Bahrain), April 19, 2014 (http://www.alwasatnews.com/4242/news/read/877400/1.html).

"ISIL Announces the Establishment of an Islamic Caliphate and Takes the Oath of Allegiance to Al-Baghdadi" [in Arabic]. *Al-Hayat* (London), June 29, 2014 (http://bit.ly/1wwb1e7).

"ISIL Announces the Establishment of an Islamic Caliphate and Takes the Oath of Allegiance to Al-Baghdadi as Caliph of Muslims" [in Arabic]. France 24, June 30, 2014 (http://f24.my/1y8wA0Y).

"ISIL Assassinates Emir of 'Al-Nusra' in Idlib" [in Arabic]. *Al-Hayat* (London), April 17, 2014 (http://bit.ly/1szR6HW).

"ISIL Criticizes Al-Zawahiri, Denies being a Branch of Al-Qa'ida, and States its Position regarding Al-Sisi and Mursi in Egypt" [in Arabic]. CNN Arabia, December 23, 2014 (http://arabic.cnn.com/middleeast/2014/05/12/isis-zawahiri-egypt-army-sisi-morsi).

"ISIL has Fighters from 81 Nationalities around the World" [in Arabic]. *Al-Sharq Al-Awsat* (London), August 31, 2014 (http://www.aawsat.com/home/article/172201).

"ISIL: Al-Qa'eda in Iraq has become History" [in Arabic]. *Al-Quds Al-Arabi* (London), February 23, 2014 (http://www.alquds.co.uk/?p=136497).

"ISIL: History and Organization" [in Arabic]. Noon Post, May 7, 2014 (http://www.noonpost.net/taxonomy/term/3508/all).

"ISIL's Black Fatwas" [in Arabic]. *Addustor* newspaper, Egypt, October 26, 2014 (http://goo.gl/9pblbi).

"ISIL's Proclamation of an Islamic Caliphate and Reactions to it" [in Arabic]. Al-Sharq Al-Arabi Center for Cultural and Strategic Studies, July 2, 2014 (http://bit.ly/1pfcihc).

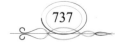

"Islamic Battles between Offensive and Defensive Jihads" [in Arabic]. Islamweb.net, the Da'wa and Religious Guidance Department of the Ministry of Awqaf (Religious Endowments) and Islamic Affairs, Qatar, April 5, 2012 (http://fatwa.islamweb.net/fatwa/index.php?page=showfatwa &Option=fatwaId&Id=177109).

"Islamic Hijab Allowed in Public Institution in Turkey" [in Arabic]. Voice of Russia Radio, October 8, 2013 (http://arabic.ruvr.ru/2013_10_08/1225 68913/).

"Islamic Parties and Organizations Reject the Announcement by ISIL of the Caliphate State" [in Arabic]. Al-Arab Al-Yawm (Jordan), July 3, 2014 (http://alarabalyawm.net/?p=332891).

"Issuing a Fatwa without having the Required Knowledge is a Crime that Deserves Tazeer [a discretionary punishment]," [in Arabic] Assakina website, January 28, 2012 (http://www.assakina.com/news/news1/12446. html).

"Jami Salafism: Loyalty to Rulers, Aversion of Politics, and Attacking the Muslim Brotherhood" [in Arabic]. Islamic Movements Portal, December 19, 2014 (http://www.islamist-movements.com/13327).

"Jihadi Salafism in Tunisia: Manpower and Sources of Finance" [in Arabic]. Al-Maghrib newspaper, Tunisia, February 19, 2014 (http://www.lemaghreb.tn/ 5722).

"Jordan Jihadis Divided: Some Support ISIL and Some Loyal to Al-Qa'eda" [in Arabic]. Al-Arab (London), July 24, 2014, p. 4 (http://www.alarabonline. org/?id=28746).

"Leading Women Ask the "Islamists" for a "Clear Explanation" of the "Supreme Imamate"," [in Arabic]. Al-Masri Al-Yawm newspaper, December 27, 2011 (http://www.almasryalyoum.com/news/details/137825).

"Lion of Jordan: Story of a King" [in Arabic] (part 14). Al-Sharq Al-Awsat newspaper, London, November 4, 2007 (http://classic.aawsat.com/details. asp?issueno=10568&article=444116#.VBaUbjqoWic).

"Main Macroeconomic Indicators Issued by the Central Bank of Egypt." Central Bank of Egypt website (http://cbe.org.eg/CBE_Bulletin/2014/Bulletin_ 2014_5_May/08_Indicator(Real_Sector)1.pdf).

"Major Terrorist Operations in Saudi Arabia" [in Arabic]. Assakina website, February 9, 2013 (http://www.assakina.com/center/parties/21860.html).

"Milestones on the Road to One Nation" [in Arabic]. Saaid Al-Fawaed website, no date (http://www.saaid.net/aldawah/r/010.htm).

"Militancy and Violence are Extension of Qutbism in Muslim Brotherhood's Behavior" [in Arabic]. *Al-Arab* newspaper, London, April 11, 2014 (http://www.alarabonline.org/pdf/2014/04/11-04/p13.pdf).

"Minister of Awqaf: 'The Brotherhood Embraced Dissimulation just like the Shiites and We are Purging them from the Ministry'," [in Arabic]. *Al-Masry Al-Youm* newspaper, Egypt, March 7, 2014 (http://www.almasryalyoum.com/news/details/406187#).

"Minister of Culture: Sadat Reconciled with the Muslim Brotherhood and Sought State Islamization" [in Arabic]. Al-Youm Al-Sabie electronic newspaper, July 14, 2014 (http://bit.ly/1uGXgoZ).

"Murderers of Al-Sadat: Executed by Shooting" [in Arabic]. *Al-Rai* (Kuwait), September 6, 2009 (http://www.alraimedia.com/Articles.aspx?id=144567).

"Mursi: Signs of Calming down between Hamas and Israel" [in Arabic]. Sky News Arabia, November 18, 2012 (http://goo.gl/RuslB5).

"Mustafa Farhat interviewing Rashid Al-Ghannooshi." Islam Online portal, April 7, 2012 (http://islamonline.net/selected/1665).

"New Islamic currents in post-revolution Egypt" [in Arabic]. Assakina website, September 7, 2012 (http://www.assakina.com/center/files/17922.html).

"New York Trial: The Prosecution Closes by Presenting Documents to Prove the Alliance between Al-Qa'eda, Al-Jihad and The Islamic Group" [in Arabic]. *Al-Sharq Al-Awsat* (London), April 6, 2001 (http://classic.aawsat.com/details.asp?section=4&article=33862&issueno=8165).

"Numan bin Uthman to *Al-Sharq Al-Awsat*: 'Sada Al-Malahim' is the Media Arm of 'Al-Qa'eda in Yemen'," [in Arabic]. *Al-Sharq Al-Awsat* (London), November 4, 2010 (http://classic.aawsat.com/details.asp?section=4&article=593832&issueno=11664).

"Numan bin Uthman, Comrade in Arms of bin Ladin on the 9th Anniversary of the Attacks: Your Alleged Path to Heaven is Full of Blood and Innocent

Victims" [in Arabic]. *Al-Sharq Al-Awsat* (London), September 10, 2010 (http://classic.aawsat.com/details.asp?section=4&issueno=11609&article=58 6097#.VFdGAzqoVaR).

"Obama before the Security Council: Number of Foreign Fighters on their Way to Conflict Zones in the Middle East is above 15,000 from 80 Countries," CNN Arabia, September 24, 2014 (http://arabic.cnn.com/world/2014/09/24/ obama-security-council-foreign-fighters).

"Obama: The Killing of Usama bin Ladin 'A Good Day for America'," [in Arabic]. BBC Arabic, May 3, 2011 (http://www.bbc.co.uk/arabic/world news/2011/05/110503_bin_laden_safer_world.shtml).

"Observers Talk about a Conspiracy to Remove the Sheikh of Al-Azhar after his Successful Tours in Saudi Arabia and the UAE while Mursi Failed to Build Bridges with the Gulf" [in Arabic]. *Al-Quds Al-Arabi* (London), April 30, 2013 (http://www.alquds.co.uk/?p=39267).

"Opinion Poll: Dispute between Erdogan and the Religious Cleric 'Gulen' Damaged the Reputation of Both" [in Arabic]. *Al-Shurooq* newspaper, Egypt, January 30, 2014 (http://www.shorouknews.com/news/view.aspx? cdate=30012014&id=871cf977-a832-4654-98f5-09783a1ed181).

"Opinions of Scholars about Salman and Safar" [in Arabic]. Al-Salafy network, July 6, 2012 (http://alsalafy.com/vb/showthread.php?t=335).

"Palestinian Liberation Organization" [in Arabic]. Al-Jazeera.net, October 3, 2004 (http://www.aljazeera.net/specialfiles/pages/74244504-9c64-41ff-88 87-b2d2dc94858e).

"Parliamentary Performance of the Brotherhood Deputies in the Balance" [in Arabic]. Swiss Info Portal, October 20, 2005 (www.swissinfo.ch/ara/detail/ content.html?cid=4777302).

"Principal Shari'a Society for Cooperation between Quran and Sunnah Scholars" (http://kfip.org/ar/principal-*Sharia*-society-for-cooperation-between-Quran-and-Sunnah-scholars/)

"Prohibition of Veils Expands in France ... Most Recently in Universities" [in Arabic]. Alarabiya.net, August 7, 2013 (http://goo.gl/9hTIz9).

"Project for Revival of Islamic Heritage" [in Arabic]. Islam Today website, February 11, 2012 (http://islamtoday.net/nawafeth/artshow-53-163032. htm).

"Pure Islam is Based on Centrism and Moderation" [in Arabic]. *Al-Riyadh* newspaper, July 25, 2008 (http://www.alriyadh.com/362159).

"Reality of Salafism" [in Arabic]. Islam Web (http://audio.islamweb.net/audio/ index.php?page=FullContent&audioid=4842&full=1).

"Results of the First Round of the Presidential Elections" [in Arabic]. *Al-Youm Al-Sabie*, May 28, 2012 (http://www.youm7.com/News.asp?newsID= 690592#.U48z5P1kpUY).

"Riyadh Wants to Make Sure of the Percentage of Saudis who Support ISIL" [in Arabic]. Erem News Agency, July 23, 2014 (http://www.eremnews.com/ ?id=52353).

"Russia's National Security Council Estimates ISIL's Fighters at 50,000" [in Arabic]. Russia Voice Radio, September 26, 2014.

"Salafi Scholars to 'Al-Anba': Muhammad Suroor's thought is a Dangerous Revolutionary *Takfiri* (excommunicating) one and is a Product of the Muslim Brotherhood's Qutbi Approach" [in Arabic]. *Al-Anab* newspaper, Kuwait, March 13, 2011 (http://www.alanba.com.kw/ar/kuwait-news/178645/13-03-2011).

"Secrets and Mysteries of the Muslim Brotherhood's Wealth: Investments Amounting to 180 Billion Pounds in 72 Countries" [in Arabic]. *Al-Ahram Al-Arabi* magazine, Cairo, November 20, 2013.

"Sectarian Sedition in Egypt: Political Fires Disguised in the Gown of Religion" [in Arabic]. Alarabiya.net, January 3, 2011 (http://www.alarabiya.net/ articles/2011/01/03/132018.html).

"Section Nine: The Cause of Difference" [in Arabic]. *Al-Dorar Al-Sunniyya*, no date (http://www.dorar.net/enc/firq/670).

"Statement: Umma Parties in the Gulf and Arabian Peninsula Reject Domestic and Foreign Policies Followed by GCC Governments which Pose a Threat to the Future of the Gulf" (http://bit.ly/1tZW3bD).

"Stating the Rights of Guardians on the Umma" [in Arabic]. Website of Shaikh Abdulaziz bin Abdullah bin Baz, September 13, 1996 (http://www.binbaz. org.sa/mat/8647).

"Statistical and Political Examination of the Results of the Second Palestinian Legislative Elections" [in Arabic]. Middle East Studies Center in the Hashemite Kingdom of Jordan, January 25, 2006 (http://www.mesc.com.jo/OurVision/vision_mesc/vote/vote1.pdf).

"Study: 7 Stages Planned by Al-Qa'eda's Strategic Ideologues to build their State in 2016" [in Arabic]. Assakina website, October 5, 2009 (http://www.assakina.com/center/files/4487.html).

"Suicide Bombing Kills MP Khalid Al-Fahdawi and Injures Chief of Sunni Endowment Court Ahmad Abdulghafoor Al-Samarra'i" [in Arabic]. Mawtani, August 31, 2011 (http://mawtani.al-shorfa.com/ar/articles/iii/features/iraqtoday/2011/08/31/feature-01).

"Suroorism in the Region: The Muslim Brotherhood Salafi version" [in Arabic]. Middle East Online, August 15, 2013 (http://www.middle-east-online.com/?id=160465).

"Suroorism: A Current that Excommunicates Shiites, considers South Sudan as 'Crusaders' and accuses Al-Turabi of Blasphemy" [in Arabic]. Al-Arabiya website, December 10, 2010 (http://www.alarabiya.net/articles/2010/12/10/129058.html).

"Suroorism" [in Arabic]. Arab Forum website, May 28, 2008 (http://arabcom.mam9.com/t80-topic).

"Suroorism" [in Arabic]. Yemen Sound website, February 26, 2007 (http://www.yemen-sound.com/vb/showthread.php?t=19646).

"Tablighi Jamaat" [in Arabic]. Said Al-Fawaid website. (http://www.saaid.net/feraq/mthahb/9.htm).

"Tablighi Jamaat" [in Arabic]. Umm Al-Qura University, Kingdom of Saudi Arabia (https://uqu.edu.sa/page/ar/199450).

"The Assassination of Hassan Al-Banna" [in Arabic]. Aljazeera.net (http://www.aljazeera.net/programs/pages/1af85e43-e9b5-4143-a93a-3eb022f4cd3e).

"The Beginning of Jihadi Groups in Egypt and the World" [in Arabic]. Assakina website, November 29, 2011 (http://www.assakina.com/news/news2/11005.html).

"The Brotherhood after Meeting Suleiman: Reform Proposals are Inadequate" [in Arabic]. BBC, February 6, 2011 (http://www.bbc.co.uk/arabic/middleeast/2011/02/110206_suleiman_meeting_opposition.shtml).

"The Charter of the Islamic Resistance Movement (Hamas)" [in Arabic]. Aljazeera.net website, 16 July 2005 (http://www.aljazeera.net/specialfiles/pages/0b4f24e4-7c14-4f50-a831-ea2b6e73217d).

"The Danger Organizations: 'Al-Qaradawi Union,' 'Cair,' the 'Islamic Organizations' and the 'American Society,' [in Arabic]. *Al-Watan* newspaper, Egypt, August 22, 2014 (http://www.elwatannews.com/news/ details/543704).

"The Emergence and Development of the term Political Islam" [in Arabic]. Babelmed electronic magazine (http://arabic.babelmed.net/societe/36-generale-culture/552-2012-04-27-19-54-55.html).

"The Empowerment Document and the Brotherhood's Intentions" [in Arabic]. *Al-Majalla* magazine, London, April 12, 2010 (http://www.majalla.com/arb/2010/04/article5542290).

"The Establishment of Hamas" [in Arabic]. alhoria.net website, December 14, 2012 (http://www.alhoria.net/article.php?id=12904).

"The Falsehood of Moderate Islam" [in Arabic]. A statement issued by Hizbut-Tahrir, November 25, 2002 (http://arabic.hizbuttahrir.org/index.php/culture/politics/195-moderate-islam).

"The Final Results of the October 23 Elections" [in Arabic]. Attounissia electronic newspaper, November 15, 2011 (http://bit.ly/XuBZ7u).

"The Freedom and Justice Party Program" [in Arabic]; (http://www.fj-p.com/Party_Program.aspx).

"The Future of the Struggle in Afghanistan (Episode 1): Dr. Fadl, Founder of 'Al-Jihad,' Writes the Full Story of the Birth of 'Al-Qa'eda' in Afghanistan" [in Arabic]. *Al-Sharq Al-Awsat* (London), January 25, 2010 (http://www.aawsat.com/home/declassified/744).

"The History of Coups d'état in Sudan: 13 Attempts since Independence with 4 Successes; Al-Numairi's and Al-Basheer's Regimes are the Most Lasting" [in Arabic]. *Al-Sharq Al-Awsat* (London), September 9, 2014 (http://classic.aawsat.com/details.asp?section=4&article=254457&issueno=9417).

743

"The ILO: Unemployment Rate in Arab Countries Double the Global Average" [in Arabic]. Elaph electronic newspaper, February 27, 2014 (http://www. elaph.com/Web/Economics/2014/2/881222.html).

"The IMF Loan Changes the Positions of Political Forces in Egypt" [in Arabic]. *Al-Sharq Al-Awsat* (London), August 29, 2012 (http://classic.aawsat.com/ details.asp?section=6&issueno=12328&article=692882#.VJ-JHULbE).

"The Islamic Group at a Dangerous Junction" [in Arabic]. Al-Quds Center for Political Studies, July 25, 2002 (http://bit.ly/1BMMnGj).

"The Islamic Group in Egypt" [in Arabic]. Aljazeera.net, March 16, 2011 (http://goo.gl/FGJfj2).

"The Kharijites" [in Arabic]. Ahl Al-Quran website, January 1, 2012 (http:// goo.gl/eU6eBZ).

"The Law of the Muslim Brotherhood Society (1930)" [in Arabic]. Wikisource (http://bit.ly/1vdRfo6).

"The Leader of Suroorism 'Sheikh Zine Al-Abideen' leaves Britain and moves to Jordan" [in Arabic]. Al-Arabiya website, October 27, 2004 (http://www. alarabiya.net/articles/2004/10/27/7492.html).

"The Muslim Brotherhood in Kuwait: A Journey of Understandings and Clashes with the Authorities" [in Arabic]. Islamic Movements portal, June 15, 2014 (http://www.islamist-movements.com/2800).

"The Muslim Brotherhood Group in Morocco: The Justice and Development Party" [in Arabic]. Islamic Movements portal, May 28, 2014 (http://www. islamist-movements.com/2674).

"The Muslim Brotherhood in Pakistan: 60 Years of Conflict between the Group and the Generals" [in Arabic]. Islamic Movements portal, August 16, 2014 (http://www.islamist-movements.com/3225).

"The Muslim Brotherhood in Sudan" *Al-Turabi's Ambitions: The Journey of the Rise and Fall* [in Arabic]. Islamic Movements portal, June 2, 2014 (http://www.islamist-movements.com/2701).

"The Ordeal of Imam Ahmad Ibn Hanbal" [in Arabic]. The General Presidency for Scholarly Research and Ifta, Kingdom of Saudi Arabia, no date

(http://www.alifta.net/Fatawa/fatawaDetails.aspx?bookID=2&View=Page&
PageNo=1&PageID=3591&languagename=).

"The Origin of Suroorism: Suroorism and Tawheed" [in Arabic]. Jihadi Media
Platform, January 6, 2014 (http://alplatformmedia.com/vb/showthread.
php?t=34811).

"The Parties Affairs Committee Approves the Establishment of the Strong Egypt
Party" [in Arabic]. *Al-Masry Al-Youm* (Egypt), November 12, 2012
(http://www.almasryalyoum.com/news/details/240914#).

"The Relationship between the Islamic Group and the Salafi Approach" [in
Arabic]. The Arab Observatory for Extremism and Terrorism, April 25,
2013 (http://arabobservatory.com/?p=6948).

"The Requirements of the (Supreme Imamate)" [in Arabic]. Islamweb.net, the
Da'wa and Religious Guidance Department of the Ministry of Awqaf
(Religious Endowments) and Islamic Affairs, Qatar, June 19, 2001
(http://library.islamweb.org/fatwa/index.php?page=showfatwa&Option=fat
waId&Id=8696).

"The Salafi Abu Qatada Al-Felistini Describes ISIL as Kharijites and Dogs of the
Inhabitants of Hellfire," [in Arabic]. Watan News, April 29, 2014
(http://www.elwtanews.net/alarab-news/37239.html).

"The Sheikh of Islam ibn Taymiyya" [in Arabic]. Islam Story website
(http://bit.ly/1cPxVFf).

"The Story of Abdullah Azzam and bin Ladin in Afghanistan" [in Arabic]. Donia
Al-Watan electronic newspaper (Palestine), 28 July 2005 (http://www.
alwatanvoice.com/arabic/news/2005/07/28/25812.html).

"The Story of the Founder of Suroorism: From Syria to the Najd" [in Arabic].
Middle East Online, November 8, 2013 (http://www.middle-east-online.
com/?id=165277).

"The Story of the Muslim Brotherhood's Emergence in Yemen (2-3)" [in
Arabic], April 29, 2007, Mareb Press (http://marebpress.net/articles.php?
print=1647).

"The Supreme Administrative Court Approves the Establishment of Al-Wasat
Party" [in Arabic]. *Al-Ahram* (Egypt), February 19, 2011 (http://gate.
ahram.org.eg/News/41458.aspx).

"The Suroori School, a 'Hybrid' Version of the Muslim Brotherhood and Salafism" [in Arabic]. *Al-Arab* newspaper, London, August 19, 2013, issue 9294 (http://www.alarab.co.uk/?id=1702).

"The Text of the Government's Statement Designating the Muslim Brotherhood as a Terrorist Group" [in Arabic]. *Al-Masri Al-Yawm* newspaper, December 25, 2013 (http://www.almasryalyoum.com/news/details/363925).

"The Thirty-Year War: Europe's Tragedy" [in Arabic]. *Al-Bayan* (UAE); (http://www.albayan.ae/paths/books/1288543294499-2010-11-13-1.303983).

"The True Position of Egyptian Salafism toward the January 25 Revolution" [in Arabic]. Arab Center for Human Studies (http://www.arab-center.org/index.php?option=com_content&view=article&id=167:25jan-revolution&catid=41:analysis-articles&Itemid=79).

"The Truth about the Salafi Call" [in Arabic]. Religion and Life program, Aljazeera.net, March 25, 2001 (http://www.aljazeera.net/programs/pages/409e086e-2203-478e-a9af-ae34f57c5d1b).

"The Unified Global Organization of the Muslim Brotherhood" [in Arabic]. *Al-Watan* newspaper, Egypt, September 2, 2013 (http://elwatannews.com/news/details/296054).

"The World's Neglected Food Basket" [in Arabic]. *Al-Sharq Al-Awsat* newspaper, London, April 11, 2008 (http://classic.aawsat.com/details.asp?issueno=10626&article=466415).

"Tolerance of Islam in Treating non-Muslims" [in Arabic]. Assakina website, February 11, 2011. (http://www.assakina.com/politics/6565.html).

"Turkey Enforced Erdogan's Threats by Banning 'Twitter'" [in Arabic]. *Al-Ittihad* newspaper, UAE, March 22, 2014 (http://www.alittihad.ae/details.php?id=25435&y=2014).

"UAE's Umma Party announces incorporation" [in Arabic]. National Kuwait Network, August 2, 2012 (http://www.nationalkuwait.com/forum/index.php?threads/239884).

"US Constitution" [in Arabic]. Human Rights Library, University of Minnesota, 1996 (http://www1.umn.edu/humanrts/arab/us-con.html).

"US PEW Center: 39% of Egyptians are optimistic about the Future" [in Arabic]. *Al-Shurooq* (Egypt), May 24, 2014 (http://www.shorouknews.com/mobile/ news/view.aspx?cdate=24052014&id=27d3b556-0b6c-4213-b4e0-77597f43 258d).

"Usama bin Ladin as Peter Bergen Knows him" [in Arabic]. Islamist Movements Portal, January 12, 2014 (http://www.islamist-movements.com/2187).

"USD 25 Billion Smuggled from the Arab World Every Year" [in Arabic]. Sky News Arabia, October 29, 2013 (http://www.skynewsarabia.com/web/ article/462271/).

"Wahhabism is not a New School but a Call to Unite Ahl Al-Sunna Wal Jama'a" [in Arabic]. discussion, Al-Alukah website, August 6, 2011 (http://www. alukah.net/web/triqi/0/33757/).

"Warnings from Increasing Number of Foreign Fighters in Syria" [in Arabic]. Aljazeera.net, May 29, 2014 (http://bit.ly/1qZAlDg).

"Washington and Sanaa Confirm Anwar Al-Awlaqi was Killed" [in Arabic]. BBC Arabic, September 30, 2011 (http://www.bbc.co.uk/arabic/middleeast/ 2011/09/110930_yemen_alawlaqi.shtml).

"We are Publishing the Reasons why the Supreme Committee Excluded Noor, Suleiman and Al-Shatir from the Presidential Race" [in Arabic]. *Al-Youm Al-Sabi'* (Egypt), April 15, 2012 (http://goo.gl/ypNQbM).

"Western Innovation" [in Arabic]. *Al-Ahram* (Egypt), November 2, 2004 (http://www.ahram.org.eg/Archive/2004/11/2/FACE7.HTM).

"What is ISIL? Journey since Defection from Al-Qa'eda until Announcing the Caliphate State" [in Arabic]. *Al-Hayat* (London), June 11, 2014, p. 9 (http://bit.ly/1p1YFmb).

"Who is ISIL and what are its Goals?" [in Arabic]. Al-Alam website, January 7, 2014 (http://www.alalam.ir/news/1552479).

"Who is ISIL? and What are its Goals? ISIL: A Terrorist Organization Fighting Everybody" [in Arabic]. *Al-Nahar* (Iraq), no date (http://bit.ly/1p9JOeG).

"Who is Muhammad bin Suroor bin Nayef Zine Al-Abideen and the Suroori Group?" [in Arabic]. Al-Rabanyon Religious Network, November 25, 2011 (http://www.alrbanyon.com/vb/showthread.php?t=8115).

A'la Boona, Yousuf. "A Look into the Thought of Sayyid Qutb [in Arabic]. *Al-Wa'i Al-Arab* journal, September 24, 2011 (http://elw3yalarabi.org/modules. php?name=News&file=article&sid=10645).

Abah, Al-Sayyid Walad. "Political Islam and the Concept of Umma: the National Trap" [in Arabic]. *Al-Ittihad* newspaper, February 17, 2014, p. 30.

Abah, Al-Sayyid Walad. "The Islamists: Politicizing Religion or Religionizing Politics?" [in Arabic]. *Al-Ittihad* (UAE), February 27, 2012 (http://www. alittihad.ae/wajhatdetails.php?id=64388).

Abdallah, Ahmad. *The Student Movement and National Politics in Egypt, 1923–1973* (London: Saqi Books, 1985).

Abdel Malek, Anwar. *Egypt: Military Society* (New York, NY: Vintage Books, 1986).

Abdelhaleem, Tariq "Suroorism in the Balance" [in Arabic]; (http://www.tariq abdelhaleem.net/new/Artical-72524).

Abdel-Malek, Anouar. *Egypt: A New Society Built by the Militarists* [in Arabic]; (Berirut: Dar Al-Talee'a, 1964).

Abdel-Malek, Anouar. *Egypt: Military Society; the Army Regime, the Left, and Social Change Under Nasser* (New York, NY: Vintage Books, 1986).

Abdo, Hani Khamis Ahmad. "Religion and Political Revolutions: Egypt as an Example" [in Arabic]. *Strategic Visions*, Issue 3, the Emirates Center for Strategic Studies and Research, June 2013.

Abdu, Imam Muhammad. *Islam between Science and Civility* [in Arabic]; (Damascus, Dar Al-Mada for Culture and Publishing, 2002).

Abdul Fattah, Saif Al-Deen. *State's Nationalization of Religion: A Look into the Records of Egyptian Citizenship; The Unholy March* [in Arabic]; (Cairo: Al-Shurroq International Bookshop, 2005).

Abdul Haleem, Mahmoud. *The Muslim Brotherhood: Events that Made History (an inside look)*, Part 1, 1928–1948 [in Arabic]; (Alexandria: Dar Al-Da'wah for Printing, Publishing and Distribution, 1979).

Abdul Majeed, Jad Al-Rab Ameen. Speech at a Ramadan evening, Emirates Writers Union, Abu Dhabi, 13 July 2014 (http://www.awqaf.gov.ae/News Item.aspx?SectionID=7&RefID=2343).

Abdul Majid, Nash'at Hamid. "The Afghan Arabs ... An Attempt for Definition" [in Arabic]. Iman1.net., October 7, 2001 (http://www.imam1.net/archive/showthread.php?t=68208&s=80c0d87bdc281941fe96de92b5b46301).

Abdul Malik, Ahmad. "Inquisition Courts Republics" [in Arabic] Al-Ittihad newspaper, UAE, August 30, 2012 (http://www.alittihad.ae/wajhatdetails.php?id=67764).

Abdul Nasser, Jamal. "The Muslim is More Sanctified than the Kaaba" [in Arabic]. Al-Ahram, July 27, 2013 (http://www.ahram.org.eg/NewsQ/2231 38.aspx).

Abdul Rahman, As'ad. The Nasserism: Bureaucratic Revolution or Revolution Bureaucracy? [in Arabic]; (Kuwait: Kuwait University Publications, 1977).

Abdulaal, Ali. "The Disagreement between the Muslim Brotherhood and the Salafis in Egypt" [in Arabic]. Democracy (http://bit.ly/1iZmRDQ).

Abdulaziz, Jumna Ameen. Leaves from the History of the Muslim Brotherhood [in Arabic], Part 3 (Cairo: Islamic House for Distribution and Publishing, 2003).

Abdulfattah, Basheer. "Beyond Political Islam in Turkey" [in Arabic]. Aljazeera. net, April 9, 2014 (http://goo.gl/dEGMBw).

Abduljawad, Jamal, et al. "Citizens' Attitudes Concerning the Most Important Political and Social Issues in Egypt" [in Arabic]. Arab Barometer Survey (Cairo: Al-Ahram Center for Political and Strategic Studies, June 2011); (http://www.arabbarometer.org/sites/default/files/countyreportyegyptII.pdf.

Abdullah, Hassan. "Hollow Political Islam Slogans Thwarted the Implementation of Sharia 3-2" [in Arabic]. Al-Ittihad newspaper, UAE (http://www.alittihad.ae/investigations_details.php?id=33).

Abdulmajeed, Waheed. "The Religious State between Islam and Christianity" [in Arabic]. Al-Ahram, November 23, 2010 (http://digital.ahram.org.eg/articles.aspx?Serial=339605&eid=891).

Abdulmajeed, Waheed. *The Muslim Brotherhood between History and the Future: How the Group was and How it Will Be?* [in Arabic]; (Cairo: Al-Ahram Center for Translation, Publishing and Distribution, 2010).

Abdulrahman, Waleed. "Al-Azhar in the Gown of the Revolution" [in Arabic]. *Al-Sharq Al-Awsat* (London), November 11, 2011 (http://classic.aawsat. com/details.asp?section=45&article=649395&issueno=12036#.U-MrbP2o Wic).

Abdulwahhab, Muhammad Helmi. *The Religious and the Sacrilegious: Religion and Politics in the Thought of Islamic Movements* [in Arabic]; (Cairo: Dar Al-Ain Publishing, 2009).

Aboul-Enein, Youssef H. "Al-Ikhwan Al-Muslimeen: The Muslim Brotherhood." *Military Review* (July–August 2003).

Abu Dah, Ibraheem. "Democracy and the Caliphate (2)" [in Arabic]. *Al-Ahram*, April 9, 2013 (http://digital.ahram.org.eg/articles.aspx?Serial=1247943& eid=1252).

Abu Faris, Muhammad Abdulqadir. *The Political System in Islam* [in Arabic]; (Amman: Dar Al-Furqan for Publishing and Distribution, 2013).

Abu Ramman, Muhammad. "The Muslim Brotherhood in Jordan's 2007 Parliamentary Elections: A Temporary Political Setback or an Erosion of Popularity?" [in Arabic]. Judran portal, December 23, 2007 (www.judran. net/?p=48).

Abu Rumman, Muhammad, and Hasan Abu Haniya. *The Islamic Solution in Jordan: The Islamists, the State and the Bets of Democracy and Security* [in Arabic]; (Amman: Friedrich Ebert Institution, Strategic Studies Center, University of Jordan, 2012).

Abu Rumman, Muhammad. "Revisions of Egyptian 'Al-Jihad Group' against the Revisions of 'Jihadis' in Jordan" [in Arabic]. Intellectual Revisions website (http://bit.ly/1gVTwr4).

Abu Rumman, Muhammad. "The Salafis and the Arab Spring: the Question of Religion and Democracy in Arab Politics" [in Arabic]. *Al-Mustaqbal Al-Arabi* no. 411, May 2013 (Beirut: Center for Arab Unity Studies, 2013).

Abu Shousha, Ahmad. "Nasser and the Brotherhood from Reconciliation to Rivalry: The Brotherhood's Support for Sidqi's Authoritarian Government

Accelerated the Conflict; The Mansheya Incident Put an End to the Group" [in Arabic]. *Sada Al-Balad* newspaper, Egypt, September 29, 2013 (http://www.el-balad.com/631747).

Abu Zahra, Imam Muhammad. *History of Islamic Schools in Politics and Faith and History of Jurisprudential Schools* [in Arabic], vol. 1 (Cairo: Dar Al-Fikr Al-Arabi, 1987).

Abu Zaid, Hajer (trans.). "Al-Qa'eda's Position Regarding the Arab Spring" [in Arabic]. Baghdad Center for Studies, Consulting and Media, December 2012 (http://bit.ly/1kzfPuE).

Abu Zaid, Muhammad. "The Islamic Group in Egypt from Years of Anger to Initiative to Stop Violence" [in Arabic]. *Al-Sharq Al-Awsat* newspaper, London, February 13, 2005 (http://classic.aawsat.com/details.asp?article=28 2643&issueno=9574).

Abu Zaid, Nasr Hamid. "Fear of Secularism: Separation of Religion and State" [in Arabic]. Al-Hiwar Al-Mutamaddin website, May 5, 2010 (http://www. ahewar.org/debat/show.art.asp?aid=215277).

Adwan, Bissan. "Hamas and the Culture of Elections" [in Arabic]. Modern Discussion website, April 12, 2006 (http://www.ahewar.org/debat/show. art.asp?aid=82523).

Agwani, M.S. "Religion and Politics in Egypt." *International Studies*, vol. 13, no. 3, July–September, 1974.

Ahmad, Abdulati Muhammad. *Political Thought of the Imam Muhammad Abdu* [in Arabic]; (Cairo: General Egyptian Book Organization, 2012).

Ahmad, Akbar S. *Religion and Politics in Muslim Society* (London: Cambridge University Press, 1983).

Ahmad, Diana. "The Muslim Brotherhood in Syria: A Suspicious Emergence and a Black History" [in Arabic]. Modern Discussion website, Issue 4002, February 13, 2013 (http://www.ahewar.org/debat/show.art.asp?aid=345458).

Ahmad, Noori. "Why Jamal Abdul Nasser executed Sayyid Qutb?" [in Arabic]. *Al-Mustashar* newspaper, Iraq, October 3, 2013 (http://almustashar-iq.net/ index.php/permalink/33278.html).

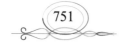

Ahmad, Refaat Sayyid. "Abdul Nasser and the Brotherhood: The Story of Blood and Fire" (1/5) [in Arabic]. Arab and Muslim Assembly to Support the Choice of Resistance, May 7, 2013 (http://www.khayaralmoukawama.com/ DETAILS.ASP?id=2970&param=NEWS).

Ajami, Fouad. *The Arab Predicament: Arab Political Thought and Practice Since 1967* (Cambridge: Cambridge University Press, 1981).

Aknur, Muege. "The Muslim Brotherhood in Politics in Egypt: From Moderation to Authoritarianism?" [in Turkish] *Uluslararasi Hukuk ve Politika*, vol. 9, no. 33, 2013.

Al-Aamri, Muhammad bin Musa. "Egypt's Al-Noor Party: an Opportunity or a Predicament?" [in Arabic]. Yemen's Scholars Forum (http://bit.ly/1gL ZB9j).

Al-Abideen, Muhammad Suroor Zine. 'Murajaat' talk show, Al-Hiwar TV Channel (http://www.youtube.com/watch?v=N5RSpkknVG4).

Al-Abideen, Muhammad Suroor Zine. "Refuting the Fabrications of Falsifiers" [in Arabic]. Website of Shaikh Muhammad Suroor Zine Al-Abideen, June 24, 2012 (http://www.surour.net/index.php?group=view&rid=852).

Al-Abideen, Muhammad Suroor Zine. *Studies in the Life of the Prophet* [in Arabic]; (Birmingham: Dar Al-Arqam Publishing and Distribution, 2nd Edition, 1988).

Al-Ahdal, Abdulla. "Jihad for Allah: Wasting Jihad Efforts by Acts of Sabotage" [in Arabic]. Ahl Al-Hadeeth Forum, August 5, 2014 (http://www. ahlalhdeeth.com/vb/showthread.php?p=2105371).

Al-Aineen, Muhammad Abu. "Expectations of the Future of Political Islam after the June 30 Revolution" [in Arabic]. *Al-Ahram*, September 13, 2013 (http://www.ahram.org.eg/NewsQ/231537.aspx).

Al-Ajlan, Fahd bin Salih. "Salafism: A Doctrine or a Group?" [in Arabic]. Al-Minhaj Preaching Blog (Islamic Electronic Magazine), no date (http:// bit.ly/1qF33Z3).

Al-Alawi, Saeed bin Saeed. "Strategy for a Second Arab Renaissance" [in Arabic]. *Al-Sharq Al-Awsat* (London), December 20, 2013 (http://bit.ly/1oFKLcw).

Al-Ameen, Hazim. "Jihadi Salafism in Jordan on its Way to ISIL after Spending Years with Al-Nusra" [in Arabic]. *Al-Hayat* (London), July 4, 2014 (http://bit.ly/1qUWbsL).

Al-Anani, Khaleel. "Mubarak and the Brotherhood: A Thirty-Year Experience [in Arabic]. Al-Jazeera Center for Studies, October 13, 2011 (http://studies. aljazeera.net/files/2011/08/201187113648385131.htm).

Al-Arab, Talal Abdul Kareem. "I am not the First to be Deceived by the Mirage" [in Arabic]. *Al-Qabas* (Kuwait), March 20, 2014 (http://www.alqabas. com.kw/node/849325).

Al-Arees, Ibraheem. "Islam and the Principle of Government according to Ali Abdul Raziq: A Battle over the Caliphate" [in Arabic]. *Al-Hayat* newspaper, London, September 27, 2014 (http://bit.ly/ZuoUML).

Al-Ashmawi, Muhammad Saeed. *Islam and Politics* [in Arabic]; (Beirut: Alintishar Alarabi, 1ˢᵗ edition, 2004).

Al-Attar, Imam Hasan. "Biographies." Egyptian Dar Al-Ifta website (http://dar-alifta.org/ViewScientist.aspx?ID=34&LangID=1).

Al-Awadi, Zaki Ali (ed.). *The Reform Movement in the Modern Age* [in Arabic]; (various authors), Minutes of the forum held at the Royal Cultural Center in Amman during the period 8–10 Sha'ban 1423 AH, corresponding to October 15–17, 2002 (Amman: Dar Al-Razi for Printing and Publishing, 2004).

Al-Awami, Maqboola Mas'ood. *Effect of Religious Factor on Emergence of Civilizations* [in Arabic]; (Cairo: Modern Dar Qiba, 2008).

Al-Awni, Haitham. "The Illusion of the Caliphate State" [in Arabic]. *Al-Arab* newspaper website, London, January 6, 2014 (http://alarab.co.uk/pdf/2014/01/06-01/p13.pdf).

Al-Badri, Muhammad Abdulsattar. "From History: Failure of the Crusades and the Beginning of European Reformation" [in Arabic]. *Al-Sharq Al-Awsat* (London), April 29, 2014 (http://www.aawsat.com/home/article/87181).

Al-Baghdadi, Ahmad. *Renewal of Religious Thought: A Call for Reasoning* (Beirut: Dar Al-Intishar Al-Arabi, 2008).

THE MIRAGE

Al-Bakeeri, Nabeel. "Suroorism: A Map of its Spread and Presence" [in Arabic]. On Islam website, March 4, 2010 (http://bit.ly/1qXZR0b).

Al-Banna, Hasan. *Five Tracts of Hasan Al-Banna* [trans. Charles Wendell] (Berkeley, CA: University of California Press, 1978).

Al-Banna, Hassan. "The Collected Epistles of Hassan Al-Banna" [in Arabic]; (the fifth general meeting), Daawa (http://www.daawa-info.net/books1. php?id=5126&bn=195&page=6).

Al-Banna, Hassan. *Memoirs of the Call and the Preacher* [in Arabic]; (Kuwait: Afaq Book Store, 2012).

Al-Banna, Hassan. *The Collected Epistles of the Martyred Imam Hassan Al-Banna* [in Arabic]; (Alexandria: Islamic House for Distribution and Publishing, 1992).

Al-Baz, Muhammad. "Treason Valley: Final Episode" [in Arabic]. *Al-Youm Al-Sabie* newspaper, Egypt, December 28, 2013 (http://www.youm7.com/ News.asp?NewsID=1421279).

Al-Booti, Muhammad Saeed Ramadhan. *Salafism: A Blessed Stage, not an Islamic School* [in Arabic]; (Beirut: Dar Al-Fikr Al-Mu'asir, 1998).

Al-Bulaihid, Khalid bin Saud. Said Al-Fawaid website (http://www.saaid.net/ Doat/binbulihed/11.htm).

Al-Dakheel, Khalid. "Separation of Religion and State in the Islamic History" [in Arabic]. *Al Hayat* newspaper, London, February 22, 2014 (http://alhayat. com/Opinion/Khaled-El-Dakheel/729863/).

Al-Dakheel, Khalid. "Separation of Religion from the State: Same Question Put Differently" [in Arabic]. Alarabiya.net, February 16, 2014 (http://goo.gl/ 86NMhD).

Al-Deen, Bilal Safi. *Decision Makers in the Islamic Government System: A Comparative Study* [in Arabic]; (Damascus: Dar Al-Nawadir, 2008).

Al-Deen, Hassan Yousuf Shihab. "The Phenomenon of Mirage between Science and the Facts of the Quran" [in Arabic]. Paper presented at the Tenth World Conference on Scientific Miracles in the Qur'an and Sunna, Turkey (March 11–13, 2011); (http://goo.gl/mSIsHR).

Al-Deen, Muhammad Al-Saeed Jamal. *Afghanistan between Domination Tendencies and the Will of Struggle* [in Arabic]; (Abu Dhabi: Zayed Center for Coordination and Follow-Up, March 2003).

Al-Deeni, Yousuf. "Suroor Left Buraidah and his Ideas Remained" [in Arabic]. in *Suroorism* (Dubai: Al-Mesbar, 2007).

Al-Demerdash, Muhammad. "Hassan Al-Turabi the Wizard of Sudan, Part 2" [in Arabic]. *Al-Masaeya* newspaper, Egypt (http://almsaeya.com/index. php/2014-02-11-17-19-41/item/5502-2).

Al-Dessouki, Mustapha. "Egypt from one Revolution to Another" [in Arabic]. *Al-Majalla* magazine, London, September 28, 2012 (http://www.majalla. com/arb/2012/09/article55238815).

Al-Dhahabi, Abu Abdullah. "Biography of Imam Muhammad ibn Abdulwahhab" [in Arabic]. Saaid Al-Fawaed website (http://www.saaid.net/monawein/ t/4.htm).

Al-Falahi, Abdulla Muhammad Ali. "From Misconceptions to Misbeliefs: the Phenomenon of Ideological Extremism and its Practice among some Contemporary (Islamic) Groups" [in Arabic]. *Al-Jamhooriyya* newspaper, Yemen, February 7, 2010 (http://www.algomhoriah.net/atach.php?id=277 55).

Al-Fateesi, Muhammad Saeed. "The Islamists and the Revolutions of the Arab Spring" [in Arabic]; (n.d.); (http://www.factjo.com/pages/print2.aspx?id= 2196).

Al-Fawaid, Saaid. "The Muslim Brotherhood" (http://www.saaid.net/feraq/ mthahb/10.htm).

Al-Filistini, Abu Qatada. "A New Viewpoint on Discrediting and Accrediting: Muhammad Suroor" [in Arabic]. Ana Al-Muslim network for Islamic dialogue (http://www.muslm.org/vb/showthread.php?353829).

Al-Ghaith, Fuad Abu. "The Group 'S' and the Disagreement that Brings One out of *Ahl Al-Sunnah Wal Jama'a*" [in Arabic]. March 26, 2012 (http://bit.ly/ 1pdGDAY).

Al-Ghamidi, Ahmad. "Salafism: A Group or a Doctrine? (1)" [in Arabic]. *Al-Yaum*, April 5, 2014 (http://www.alyaum.com/article/3130981).

Al-Ghannooshi, Rashid. *Approaches in Secularism and Civil Society* [in Arabic]; (Tunisia: Al-Mujtahid Publishing and Distribution House, 2011).

Al-Ghareeb, Hussein. "Principles of Islamic Jurisprudence: Origins, Importance and Evolution" [in Arabic]. Muslimonline website, August 13, 2009 (http://www.moslimonline.com/?page=artical&id=946).

Al-Hakeem, Grand Ayatollah Sayyid Muhammad Saeed Al-Tabatabai. "The Importance of Mind in the Quran and Sunna" [in Arabic]. Dar Sayyida Ruqayya for the Holy Quran website, September 5, 2012 (http://www. ruqayah.net/subject.php?id=1566).

Al-Hammadi, Sameer. "Wahhabism and Jihadi Salafism: Questions about the Relationship" [in Arabic]. Modern Discussion website, Issue 4461, May 23, 2014 (http://www.ahewar.org/debat/show.art.asp?aid=416173).

Al-Hammoori, Ghassan. "Challenges Facing Muslims in Western Societies" [in Arabic]. *Al-Waie Magazine*, issues 282–283, July/August 2010 (http://www. al-waie.org/issues/282-283/article.php?id=934_0_72_0_M).

Al-Haroob, Khalid. *Hamas: Thought and Political Practice* [in Arabic]; (Beirut: Palestinian Studies Institution, 1997).

Al-Hassan, Ihsan Muhammad. *Religious Anthropology: Analytical Study of the Interactive Relationship between Religious Establishment and Society* [in Arabic]; (Amman: Dar Wa'il for publishing, 1st edition, 2005).

Al-Henaki, Ahmad. "The Muslim Brotherhood between Abdul Nasser and Al-Sadat" [in Arabic]. *Al-Majalla* magazine, London, April 29, 2014 (http://www. majalla.com/arb/2014/04/article55250938).

Al-Hilali, Muhammad. "Moderate Political Islam: From Mosque to Government, or the Paradoxes of Conservative Social Islam" [in Arabic]. Al-Hiwar Al-Mutamaddin website, November 30, 2013 (http://www.ahewar.org/debat/ show.art.asp?aid=285435).

Al-Hubaishi, Ahmad. "Homeland in the Mirror of Deviant Thought?" [in Arabic]. *September* newspaper, Yemen, June 23, 2011 (http://26sep.net/ articles.php?lng=arabic&id=4824).

Al-Hubaishi, Ahmad. "Why do the Muslim Brothers Hate Jamal Abdul Nasser?" February 21, 2008 (http://www.metransparent.com/spip.php?page=article& id_article=3389&var_lang=ar&lang=ar).

Al-Hussein, Yasir Mahgoub. "The Future of the Political System in Sudan" [in Arabic]. Al-Sharq Portal, May 31, 2014 (http://www.al-sharq.com/news/details/242469#.U-MYGf2oWic).

Al-Huthaifi, Abu Ammar Ali. "Reservations concerning the Al-Ihsan Association" [in Arabic]; (http://wahyain.com/forums/showthread. php?t=3355).

Ali Hassan, Ammar. *Salafism: Discourse and Practice* [in Arabic]; Emirates Lectures Series no. 162 (Abu Dhabi: The Emirates Center for Strategic Studies and Research, 2013).

Ali, Abdul Raheem. *The Muslim Brotherhood: A Look into the Secret Files* [in Arabic]; (Cairo: the General Egyptian Book Organization, 2011).

Ali, Ali Muhammad. "Islamic Movement's Experience in Sudan: the Gap between Rhetoric and Practice" [in Arabic]. Digital Ahram portal, April 1, 2013 (http://digital.ahram.org.eg/articles.aspx?Serial=1383545&eid=592).

Ali, Maha. "Lords of War" [in Arabic]. *Al-Ahram* (Egypt), January 1, 2014 (http://digital.ahram.org.eg/Policy.aspx?Serial=1546067).

Ali, Muhammad Fadhel. "When Sadat Cried I was Wrong Laminating Releasing the Muslim Brotherhood Members from Prison" [in Arabic]. Sudanile Electronic Newspaper, August 17, 2013 (http://www.sudanile.com/index. php/2008-05-19-17-39-36/120-2009-02-03-19-32-31/57320-2013-08-17-11-52-13).

Al-Jabi, Nasser. *Report on Arab Barometer Survey (2011)* [in Arabic]. July 2011 (http://www.arabbarometer.org/sites/default/files/countyreportyAlgeriaII.pdf).

Al-Jabiri, Muhammad Abid. "Islamic Concepts: Dar Al-Islam and Dar Al-Harb" [in Arabic]. *Al-Ittihad* newspaper, UAE, August 18, 2009 (http://www. alittihad.ae/wajhatdetails.php?id=47406).

Al-Janabi, Ahmad. "Al-Manshiyya Incident," Aljazeera.net, 7 January 2013 (http://goo.gl/v9lCuF).

Al-Jehani, Salah Al-Sadiq. "The Muslim Brotherhood's Stance on Implementing Sharia" [in Arabic]. Modern Discussion website, July 03, 2014 (http://www. ahewar.org/debat/show.art.asp?aid=422203).

Al-Jehni, Muhammad bin Abdurrahman Abu Yousuf. "The Meaning, Evidence and Rules of Godliness and the Refutation of Denying it" [in Arabic]; (http://bit.ly/1pdemKP).

Al-Jiddawi, Mustafa. *Shiite Theory on Islamic Governance and Comparison with Western Principles of Democracy* [in Arabic]. Ph.D. Dissertation (Alexandria, no publisher, 1988).

Al-Khalidi, Salah Abdul Fattah. *American War through the Lens of Sayyid Qutb* [in Arabic]; (Amman: Dar Al-Uloom for Publishing and Distribution, 2003).

Al-Kharbawi, Tharwat. "Sayyid Qutb from America to Jahiliyya 1–2" [in Arabic]. *Al-Dostor* newspaper, Egypt, February 16, 2014 (http://www.dostor.org/ 81191).

Al-Khattab, Fares. "The Muslim Brotherhood in Egypt: A Journey of an Obscured Organization Exposed by Light" [in Arabic]. *Al-Ittihad* newspaper, UAE, June 8, 2014 (http://www.alittihad.ae/details.php?id=50721&y= 2014&article=full).

Al-Khattabi, Izz Al-Deen. *Modernity Questions and Bets in Society, Politics and Education* [in Arabic]; (Beirut: Arab Scientific Publishers, and Dubai: Muhammad bin Rashid Al Maktoum Foundation, 2009).

Al-Khayoun, Rashid. "Suroorism and Ahbash: The *Hakimiyya* Project and the Excommunication Weapon" [in Arabic]. *Al-Sharq Al-Awsat* newspaper, London, Issue 10305, February 10, 2007 (http://bit.ly/1pE0Crr).

Al-Khleif, Abdulhadi bin Abdullateef Al-Salih. *Efforts of Salafi Scholars in Najd in Responding to their Opponents (1200–1350 AH)*; [in Arabic]; (http://bit.ly/ 1ogcKha).

Al-Kinani, Ahmad Saad. "Salafis of Najd and Al-Ouda … A Red Line or Hidden Alliances?" [in Arabic]. Middle East Online, August 9, 2012 (http://www. middle-east-online.com/?id=136769).

Al-Kiswani, Haytham. "Tablighi Jamaat from India to the World" in *Tablighi Jamaat*, by a group of researchers [in Arabic]; (Abu Dhabi: Al-Misbar Center for Studies and Research, Book 35, November 2009).

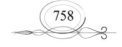

Al-Kuhl, Saeed. "Morocco's Justice and Development Party: Its Positions and Convictions Contradict its Slogans" [in Arabic]. Modern Discussion website, April 28, 2012 (http://www.ahewar.org/debat/show.art.asp?aid= 36301).

Al-Lami, Alaa. "Al-Barqawi, Al-Zarqawi and the Beginnings of Suicidal Salafism" [in Arabic]. *Al-Akhbar* (Lebanon); (http://bit.ly/1eAnV3C).

Al-Louz, Abdulhakeem Abu. "Inflexibility of the New Salafi Ideology" [in Arabic]. *Idafat Magazine*, Arab Sociological Association, issues 3–4, Summer and Autumn, 2008.

Al-Ma'aita, Atallah Najeeb. *Islamic Denominations and the Position of Sunni Muslims Towards them* [in Arabic]; (Amman: Dar Al-Farooq for Publishing and Distribution).

Al-Madeeni, Tawfeeq. *Amal and Hizbullah in Local and Regional Confrontations* [in Arabic]; (Damascus, Dar Al-Ahali for Printing, Publishing and Distribution, 1999).

Al-Madkhali, Rabi bin Hadi. "Islamic Sharia is Lenient and God Encourages Muslims to do What He has Allowed Them" [in Arabic]. Sahab Salafi Network, February 13, 2011, (http://www.sahab.net/home/?p=94).

Al-Mahdi, Al-Sadiq. "Fires of Extremism in the Islamic World" [in Arabic]. *Sudaress*, electronic newspaper, July 10, 2014 (http://www.sudaress.com/hurriyat/158115).

Al-Mahdi, Basma. "An American Researcher: The Opposition should Worry more about the 'Islamization' than 'Brotherhoodization' of the State" [in Arabic]. *Al-Masri Al-Yawm* newspaper, May 15, 2013 (http://www.almasry alyoum.com/news/details/316548).

Al-Mahmood, Muhammad Ibn Ali. "Europe and the Ages of Darkness ... The Struggle of Enlightened Mind" [in Arabic]. *Al-Riyadh* newspaper, Saudi Arabia, no. 14332, September 20, 2007 (http://www.alriyadh.com/280951).

Al-Mahmoud, Muhammad Ibn Ali. "We and Colonialism ... Reading through Ideology" [in Arabic]. *Al Riyadh* newspaper, May 27, 2010 (http://www.alriyadh.com/529448).

Al-Makki, Basim. "Power Struggle after the Death of the Prophet: Al-Saqifa Meeting as an Example" [in Arabic]. Mominoun Without Borders, November 29, 2013 (http://bit.ly/1q3rUUU).

Al-Marakishi, Muhammad Salih. *Ideology and Modernism in the Thought of Salafi Pioneers* [in Arabic]; (Tunis: Dar Al-Ma'arif for Printing and Publishing, 1995).

Al-Maseeri, Abdul Wahhab. *Partial Secularism and Total Secularism* [in Arabic]; (Cairo: Dar Al-Shurooq, 3rd edition, 2008).

Al-Masri, Muhammad. *Arab Barometer Survey II, Tunisia* [in Arabic]. September 2012 (http://www.arabbarometer.org/sites/default/files/Tunisia%20Country %20Report%20ABII.pdf).

Al-Masri, Muhammad. *Arab Barometer Survey: The Hashemite Kingdom of Jordan* [in Arabic]. August 2011, Strategic Studies Center, University of Jordan (http://www.arabbarometer.org/sites/default/files/countyreportjordan2_0.pdf).

Al-Mawla, Saud. *Islamic Groups and Violence: Encyclopedia of Jihad and Jihadis* [in Arabic]; (Dubai: Al-Misbar Center for Studies and Research, 2012).

Al-Mdaires, Falah Abdullah. *The Muslim Brotherhood Group in Kuwait* [in Arabic]; (Kuwait: Qurtas Publishing House, 1999).

Al-Mdaires, Salah Abdullah. "The Establishment Phase of the 'Muslim Brotherhood' and its Emergence in Kuwait" [in Arabic]. *Al-Qabas* newspaper, Kuwait, June 3, 2006 (http://www.alqabas.com.kw/node/167 864).

Al-Menbar National Islamic Society. "Introduction" [in Arabic]; (http://www. almenber.bh/about.php).

Al-Mesbar Studies and Research Centre. *The Muslim Brotherhood and the Salafis in the Gulf*, 2010.

Al-Mesbar Studies and Research Centre. *The Muslim Brotherhood: The Establishment* (various authors), 1st edition (Dubai: Al-Mesbar Studies and Research Centre, 2007).

Al-Meshouah, Mohammed bin Abdullah. "Preventing God's Mercy" [in Arabic]. *Okaz* newspaper, November 12, 2013 (http://www.okaz.com.sa/new/issues/ 20131112/Con20131112654043.htm).

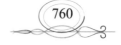

Al-Mezmaah Studies and Research Centre, "Before Issuing the Verdict" [in Arabic]. Part 4 (http://almezmaah.com/ar/news-print-1389.html).

Al-Minbar website. Sermon on the merit of mosque construction [in Arabic]; (http://www.alminbar.net/alkhutab/khutbaa.asp?mediaURL=9198).

Al-Monein, Abd [sic], Said Aly and Manfred W. Wenner. "Modern Islamic Reform Movements: The Muslim Brotherhood in Contemporary Egypt," *The Middle East Journal*, vol. 36, no. 3, September 1982.

Al-Mughrabi, Tariq. "Muhammad Abdulkareem, Abdul Hai Yousuf and Suroorism: Al-Qa'ida Sleeper Cells in Sudan" [in Arabic]. Kul Al-Salafiyeen website, August 14, 2012 (http://kulalsalafiyeen.com/vb/ showthread.php?t=40499).

Al-Mushawah, Khalid. "Religious currents in Saudi Arabia: Suroorism (3)" [in Arabic]. Jasad Al-Thaqafa website, November 16, 2007 (http://aljsad.com/forum9/thread113550/).

Al-Mustafa, Hamza Mustafa. "Jabhat Al-Nusra Li Ahl Al-Sham: From Establishment to Division" [in Arabic]. *Siyasat Arabiyya*, no. 5, November 2013 (Doha: Arab Center for Research and Policy Studies).

Al-Muwakkali, Ahmad bin Hasan. "Media Ideology of Al-Qa'eda: Challenges to Intellectual Security on the Internet" [in Arabic]. Paper presented to the First National Conference for Intellectual Security: Concepts and Challenges, 22–25 Jamada Al-Oola 1430 AH (May 16–19, 2009),

Al-Na'eemi, Salim Salimeen. "The Summer of the Fall of Activist Political Islam" [in Arabic]. Opinion section, *Al-Itihad* newspaper, UAE, June 25, 2013 (http://www.alittihad.ae/wajhatdetails.php?id=73227).

Al-Nabulsi, Muhammad Ratib. "The Concept of Following rather than Innovating" [in Arabic]. Lesson 11-70: Following Rather than Innovating, January 13, 2009 (http://www.nabulsi.com/blue/ar/art.php?art=2410&id=150&sid=775&ssid=776&sssid=777).

Al-Namnam, Helmi. "Dr. Abdulaziz Kamel: Shura According to Hasan Al-Banna is not Binding on the Ruler" [in Arabic]. *Al-Ittihad* newspaper, UAE, February 17, 2007 (http://www.alittihad.ae/details.php?id=98315&y=2007&article=full).

Al-Namnam, Helmi. *Hassan Al-Banna as Nobody Knows Him* [in Arabic]; (Cairo: Madbooli Bookshop, 2011).

Al-Nazeef, Ahmad. "Map of Salafi Groups in Tunisia" [in Arabic]. Africa News Gate, January 3, 2014 (http://bit.ly/1nWZcFL).

Al-Nima, Ibraheem. "The Mirage in the Quran: A Scientific Miracle" [in Arabic]; (http://www.beatona.net/CMS/index.php?option=com_content&view=article&id=1341&lang=ar&Itemid=84).

Al-Nogaidan, Mansour. "Islamist Map in Saudi Arabia and the Story of Excommunication" [in Arabic]. *Al-Wasat* newspaper, Bahrain, February 28, 2003 (http://www.alwasatnews.com/175/news/read/198071/1.html).

Al-Obaidi, Aouni Jaddou. *The Muslim Brotherhood group in Jordan and Palestine 1945-1970: Historical Pages* (Amman: 1st edition, 1991).

Al-Ola, Abdulrahman Abu. *A Reading of the Results of Egyptian Elections* [in Arabic]. Aljazeera.net, January 22, 2012 (http://goo.gl/cc4IPA).

Al-Omar, Nasser bin Suleiman. "Attributing unto God (Allah) Something of which you have no Knowledge" [in Arabic]. Al-Moslim website, August 7, 2011 (http://www.almoslim.net/node/150949).

Al-Otaibi, Abdullah bin Bejad. "Saudi Arabia and the Muslim Brotherhood: A Glimpse of History" [in Arabic]. *Al-Sharq Al-Awsat* newspaper, London, Issue 12072, December 17, 2011.

Al-Qadimi, Nawwaf. "The Jihadi Current in Saudi Arabia and Experiences of Dialogue and Reconciliation" [in Arabic]. Al-Asr website, May 12, 2009 (http://alasr.ws/articles/view/10859).

Al-Rasheed, Abdullah. "How Surooris in the Gulf Think: Democracy and the Dreams of the Caliphate" [in Arabic]. *Al-Majalla* magazine, London, March 25, 2013 (http://www.majalla.com/arb/2013/03/article55243687).

Al-Rasheed, Abdullah. "The Master of Hakimiyya [divine sovereignty] City: Papers of Muhammad Qutb (2)" [in Arabic]. *Al-Sharq Al-Awsat* newspaper, London, May 19, 2014 (http://www.aawsat.com/home/article/99311).

Al-Rasheed, Abdullah. "The Muslim Brotherhood in the UAE ... The Complete Story" [in Arabic]. *Al-Sharq Al-Awsat* newspaper, London, February 1, 2013 (http://www.aawsat.com/details.asp?article=715512&issueno=12484&sectio n=4#.UzWrtvldWSo).

Al-Rasheed, Abdullah. "The Muslim Brotherhood in UAE: The Roots of the Thought and the Organization" [in Arabic]. *Al-Majalla* magazine, London, February 10, 2013 (http://www.majalla.com/arb/2013/02/article55242417).

Al-Rawwaf, Uthman. "The Puzzle of ISIL in Syria and Iraq" [in Arabic]. Elaph electronic newspaper, July 13, 2014 (http://www.elaph.com/Web/opinion/ 2014/7/922955.html?entry=opinion).

Al-Regeb, Salih Hussein. *Our Contemporary Reality and Intellectual Invasion* [in Arabic]; (Gaza: Islamic University, 7th ed., 2004); (http://www.drsregeb. com/index.php?action=vb-k&nid=22).

Al-Saba', Imad Mas'ad Muhammad. "The Future of the Relations between the Muslim Brotherhood and America" [in Arabic]. Al-Hiwar Al-Mutamaddin website, August 16, 2011 (http://www.ahewar.org/debat/show.art.asp? aid=271596).

Al-Saeed, Refaat. *Hassan Al-Banna the Founder of the Muslim Brotherhood, When .. How .. and Why?* [in Arabic]; (Beirut: Dar Al-Talia Publishers, 1988).

Al-Saeed, Rifaat. *The Islamists: Terrorism and Sectarian Sedition* [in Arabic]; (Damascus, Al-Ahali for Publishing and Distribution, 1994).

Al-Sahab Media Production. "Status of the Islamic Nation: USS Cole Attack" (https://archive.org/details/state-of-the-ommah).

Al-Saidawi, Riyadh. "On the Rise and Fall of Islamic Movements in the Arab World" [in Arabic]. Al-Hiwar Al-Mutamaddin website, June 29, 2007 (http://www. ahewar.org/debat/show.art.asp?aid=101224).

Al-Saif, Tawfeeq. "Transformations and Future of Political Islam in Saudi Arabia" [in Arabic]. Afaq Center for Research and Studies, November 30, 2013 (http://aafaqcenter.com/index.php/post/1970).

Al-Sarhan, Saud. *Arab Barometer Survey: The Kingdom of Saudi Arabia* [in Arabic]. February 2011 (http://www.arabbarometer.org/sites/default/files/county reportysaudi2.pdf).

Al-Saud, Salah Abu. *Ancient, Modern and Contemporary History of the Kingdom of Saudi Arabia* [in Arabic]; (Giza, Egypt: Al-Nafiza Bookshop, 2014).

Al-Sawi, Abdulhafiz. "The Story of the Egyptian Economy: From Muhammad Ali to Mubarak." Book review [in Arabic]. Aljazeera.net, January 4, 2013 (http://bit.ly/1qEjaea).

Al-Sayyid, Abdulbaqi. *Zahiri School of Thought: Birth, Development, Doctrine and Key Features* [in Arabic]. Ahl Al-Zahir website (http://www.zahereyah.com/vb/showthread.php?t=83).

Al-Sayyid, Ridwan. "Fears for Religion: from the West, the Elite or Society?" [in Arabic]. *Al-Sharq Al-Awsat* (London), October 19, 2012 (http://bit.ly/1sfA8jK).

Al-Sayyid, Ridwan. "Religious and National Imbalances and Interferences Aimed at Dividing" [in Arabic]. *Al-Sharq Al-Awsat* (London), October 4, 2013 (http://classic.aawsat.com/leader.asp?section=3&article=745530&issueno=1 2729#.VFYJVTqoUSs).

Al-Sayyid, Ridwan. *Political Islamic Movements and the Future* [in Arabic]. Emirates Lecture Series no. 2 [in Arabic]; (Abu Dhabi: The Emirates Center for Strategic Studies and Research, 1997).

Al-Sayyid, Ridwan. *Revival, Reform and Other Options: Protecting Religion amidst Transformational Crises* [in Arabic]. Emirates Lectures Series no. 170 (Abu Dhabi: Emirates Center for Strategic Studies and Research, 2013), pp. 13–22.

Al-Shareef, Ashraf. "Transformations of the Salafis in Egypt: Politics Takes Ideology Apart" [in Arabic]. Al-Qantara (http://ar.qantara.de/content/lslfywn-fy-msr-thwlt-lslfyyn-fy-msr-ltsyys-mfkk-lydywlwjy).

Al-Shaybani, Ridwan Ahmad Shamsan. *Fundamental Islamic Movements in the Arab World* [in Arabic]; (Cairo: Madbooli Bookshop, 2005).

Al-Shayookh, Muhammad. "Suroorism: An Affinity between Salafism and the Muslim Brotherhood" [in Arabic]. Middle East Online, February 27, 2013 (http://middle-east-online.com/?id=150137).

Al-Shehabi, Ghassan. "The Bahraini Muslim Brotherhood: The Particularity of Thought and the Future of Activism" [in Arabic]. Al-Jazeera Center for Studies, June 10, 2014 (http://studies.aljazeera.net/reports/2014/06/20146 1062637721417.htm).

Al-Sheikh, Salah bin Muhammad bin Abdulrahman Al. *The Jurisprudential Approach of Salafi Imams in the Najd* [in Arabic]; (Riyadh: Dar Al-Somaie for Publishing and Distribution, 2009).

Al-Sheikh, Salih bin Abdulaziz bin Muhammad Al. "Research on Sheikh Muhammad ibn Abdulwahhab and his Revivalist Movement" [in Arabic]. February 12, 1999 (http://www.saaid.net/muslm/13.htm).

Al-Shihabi, Saeed. "Two Competing Islamic Enterprises: A Political and a Jihadi" [in Arabic]. *Al-Quds Al-Arabi* newspaper, November 12, 2013 (http://www.alquds.co.uk/?p=102771).

Al-Shinqeeti, Abu Al-Munzir. "The Benefit of Understanding the Verse of Al-Maa'ida: A Response to a Retreating Cleric in Morocco" [in Arabic]. *Tawheed* Wal Jihad website (n.d.); (http://webcache.googleusercontent.com/search?q=cache:7mNfX2rE6BQJ:www.tawhed.ws/dl%3Fi%3D09051010+&cd=2&hl=ar&ct=clnk&gl=ae).

Al-Shuaibi, Riyadh. "Tunisian Salafism: Labor of Transformation" [in Arabic]. Al-Jazeera Studies Center, November 15, 2012 (http://studies.aljazeera.net/reports/2012/11/20121115111741423396.htm).

Al-Siraji, Kareem. *Religious Principles of the Salafi Trends* (Beirut: Dar Al-Salam, 1st edition, 2010).

Al-Sirjani, Raghib. "Ibn Al-Haitham ... the Legendary Scientist" [in Arabic]; (http://goo.gl/JNnd1).

Al-Soofi, Faisal. "The Salafi Thought and the Church Obscurantism in the Middle Ages" [in Arabic]. Al-motamar.net (http://www.almotamar.net/1775.htm).

Al-Soos, Adnan Abdulraheem. *Hizbut-Tahrir and Political Practice* [in Arabic]; (Amman, no publisher, 1st edition, 2007).

Al-Suroori, Muhammad Abdulfattah. "Islamic Architecture: Debates on Modernity; Dissertation Review" [in Arabic]. *Al-Hayat* (London), March 21, 2014 (http://bit.ly/1vf0pkm).

[Al-Suwaidi], Jamal Ali Sanad. "Islam and Socio-Political Change: A Comparative Study of Egyptian, Kuwaiti and Palestinian Attitudes." Unpublished dissertation manuscript, University of Wisconsin, 1990.

Al-Suwaidi, Jamal Sanad, and Ahmad Rashad El Safti (eds.). *Political Islamic Movements and Authority in the Arab World: The Rise and Fall* [in Arabic]; (Abu Dhabi: The Emirates Center for Strategic Studies and Research, 2014).

Al-Suwaidi, Jamal Sanad. *Prospects for the American Age: Sovereignty and Influence in the New World Order* [in Arabic]; (Abu Dhabi: The Emirates Center for Strategic Studies and Research, 2014).

Al-Ta'ir, Abdullah Ibn Musa. "Muslim Brotherhood and Demonization of Others" [in Arabic]. *Al-Riyadh* newspaper, July 23, 2013 (http://www.alriyadh.com/854218).

Al-Tareeqi, Abdullah bin Ibrahim bin Ali. "Contemporary Salafi Schools: Diversity and Relationship with the Other" [in Arabic]. Al-Alukah, May 21, 2011 (http://www.alukah.net/web/triqi/0/32046/).

Al-Taweel, Kameel. *Al-Qa'ida and its Sister Organizations: The Story of the Arab Mujahideen* [in Arabic]; (Beirut: Dar Al-Saqi, 2007).

Al-Taweel, Tawfeeq. *The Story of the Conflict between Religion and Philosophy* [in Arabic]; (Cairo: General Egyptian Book Organization, 2011).

Al-Thubetat, Qasem Jameel. *The Muslim Brotherhood Group in Jordan 1945-1997: A Case Study* [in Arabic]; (Amman: Kunouz Al-Ma'refa Publishers, 2008).

Al-Wa'ee, Tawfeeq. *The Muslim Brotherhood: The Largest Islamic Movement: Suspicions and Responses* [in Arabic]; (Cairo: Al-Manar Islamic Bookshop, 2001).

Al-Waeli, Khalid. "Appealing to the Dead: A More Serious Form of Idolatry" [in Arabic]. Saaid Al-Fawaed website (http://www.saaid.net/feraq/shia/a/52.htm).

Al-Waqeedi, Muhammad and Ahmeeda Al-Naifar. *Why Did the Arab Renaissance Fail?* [in Arabic]; (Beirut: Dar Al-Fikr Al-Muaasir, 2002).

Al-Waseefi, Ali Al-Sayyid. *The Muslim Brotherhood between Religious Innovation and Political Bankruptcy* [in Arabic]; (Cairo: Dar Sabeel Al-Mumineen for Publishing and Distribution, 2012).

Al-Waseet Dictionary (Cairo: Al-Shurooq International Bookshop, 4th Edition, 2008),).

Alyan, Ibraheem Khaleel. "Religious State and Secular State." Working paper presented at the Third Baitul-Maqdis Conference 2012 (http://www. qou.edu/arabic/researchProgram/researchersPages/ibrahimElaian/r4_ibrahi mElaian.pdf).

Al-Yousuf, Abdullah Ahmad. "The Legitimacy of Disagreement: A Methodological basic Study of the Other Opinion in Islamic Thought [in Arabic]. 2nd edition, 2004 (http://alyousif.org/?ext=1&act=media&code= books&f=79).

Al-Zu'bi, Muhammad Falah. "Do the 'Muslim Brothers' Betray their Approach and the Founder of their Group?" [in Arabic]. *Fact International* (Jordan), June 16, 2012 (http://www.factjo.com/pages/print2.aspx?id=3858).

Ameenu, Amr. "A Disclosure: the Position of Each Arab State towards the War on Gaza" [in Arabic]. Al-Taqreer website, August 4, 2014 (http://bit.ly/ 1tN11Mc).

Amer, Yasir Ba. "Conservatives and Reformists in Muslim Saudi Arabia" [in Arabic]. Book review, Aafaq Center for Research and Studies, January 8, 2012 (http://aafaqcenter.com/index.php/post/969).

Anagreh, Muhammad. "Sharif Hussein bin Ali ... the Rebel King" [in Arabic]. *Addustour* newspaper, 13 June 2012 (http://bit.ly/1y10Af2).

Anderson, Charles W., Fred von der Mehden and Crawford Young. *Issues of Political Development* (Englewood Cliffs, NJ: Prentice Hall, Inc., 1967).

Anwar, Ahmad. "Theory and Methodology of Sociology" [in Arabic]; (faculty.ksu. edu.sa/75863/Publications/1.doc).

Arheelah, Abbas. "Reformation Movements in the Muslim World" [in Arabic]. *Al-Manhal*, issue 528, year 21, Sha'ban 1416 AH, December 1995.

Arif, Nasr Muhammad. "The Fatalist Circle: The End of Modernist Islamism of the Muslim Brotherhood" [in Arabic]. *Al-Siyassa Al-Dawliyya* journal, no. 194, October 2013.

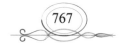

Arrahmah Islamic Network (http://www.arrahmah.com/arabic/tnzym-qadt-al-jhad-al-qyadt-al-amt-byan-bshan-alaqt-jmat-qadt-al-jhad-bjmat-ad-dwlt-al-islamyt.html).

Assyaukanie, Luthfi. *Islam and the Secular State in Indonesia* (Singapore: Institute of Southeast Asian Studies, 2009).

Atallah, Samir. "Sadat's Last Surprise" [in Arabic]. *Al-Sharq Al-Awsat* newspaper, London, September 20, 2010 (http://classic.aawsat.com/leader.asp?section=3&article=587449&issueno=11619).

Atawi, Muammar. "The Islamists of Turkey: from Sufism to Authority" [in Arabic]. *Al-Akhbar* newspaper website, January 22, 2010 (http://www.al-akhbar.com/node/59621).

Ateen, Hadi Ahmad Hassan. *The Muslim Brotherhood Invades the Gulf* [in Arabic]; (Cairo: Dar El-Hekma Printing, Publishing and Distribution) 2013.

Atwan, Abdulbari. *Beyond bin Ladin: The Next Generation of Al-Qa'eda* [in Arabic]. Saeed Al-Azm (trans.); (Beirut: Dar Al-Saqi, 2013).

Awadh, Shihata. "Enmity to the Muslim Brotherhood is an Obstacle in the Face of Egypt's Regional Role" [in Arabic]. Al-Jazeera.net, October 22, 2014 (http://studies.aljazeera.net/reports/2014/10/2014102184431755105.htm).

Awadhalla, Usama. "The Salafi Surooris: Who are they, Who is their God, Who is their Sheikh, Who are their Leaders and Institutions in Sudan? [in Arabic]. Al-Rakoba electronic newspaper, Sudan, April 12, 2013 (http://www.alrakoba.net/articles-action-show-id-42587.htm).

Ayesh, Muhammad Essam. "Jordanian Political Map after the Elections and Constitutional Amendments" [in Arabic]. Al-Arabiya Institute for Studies, May 8, 2013 (http://bit.ly/1qXPvxB).

Ayoob, Mohammad (ed.). *The Politics of Islamic Reassertion* (London: Croom Helm Ltd., 1981).

Ayoob, Mohammed. "The Future of Political Islam: The Importance of External Variables." *International Affairs*, vol. 81, no. 5, October 2005, accessed February 25, 2014.

Azb, Ahmad. "On this Day the Execution of the Muslim Brotherhood Member Sayyid Qutb" [in Arabic]. Al-Bawwaba News website (http://www. albawabhnews.com/759960).

Azbawi, Yusri Ahmad. "The Future of the New Political Parties after the January Revolution" [in Arabic]. Digital Ahram portal, August 1, 2011 (http://digital.ahram.org.eg/articles.aspx?Serial=672651&eid=8011).

Azeemi, Suhaila Allawa. *Revival Methodology according to Abu Al-A'la Al-Mawdoodi* [in Arabic]; (Damascus: Annahdah Publishing House 2008).

Badr, Badr Muhammad. "Religious Politics and Secular States" [in Arabic]. A review of a book with the same title by Scott W. Hibbard, Aljazeera.net, January 22, 2014 (http://www.aljazeera.net/home/print/92804797-74a7-4675-b919-6682990f8cbe/2c0e676c-4cc8-454d-9ebb-3b1f4d9eec4).

Baldhiafi, Munther. "Ennahdha Exiting the Government in Tunisia! Factors and Possible Scenarios" [in Arabic]. Al-Arabiya.net, January 13, 2014 (http://bit.ly/1pgospX).

Barhomeh, Muhammad. "85% of Al-Qa'eda's Victims are Muslims" [in Arabic]. *Al-Ghad* (Jordan), January 17, 2010 (http://bit.ly/1uAmF5A).

Barhomeh, Musa. "Interview: Fahmi Jad'an 'Political Islam' is an Ideological Innovation and a Deviation from the Purpose of Religion" [in Arabic]. Mominoun Without Borders, June 16, 2013 (http://goo.gl/2SeQXo).

Barnett, Michael, and Jack Levy. "Domestic Sources of Alliances and Alignments: The Case of Egypt, 1962–1973." *International Organization*, vol. 45, no. 3, Summer 1991.

Basheer, Hisham. *Theoretical Study on the Nature and Methods of Public Opinion Surveys* [in Arabic]; (Egypt: The Center for the Study of Developing Countries, no date).

Battar, Abdulqader. "When Excommunication becomes a Crime According to Islamic Sharia" [in Arabic]; (http://bit.ly/V0uxiJ).

Bellah, Robert. "Civil Religion in America." *Journal of the American Academy of Arts and Sciences*, vol. 96, no. 1 (Winter 1967).

Beshara, Joseph. "Inheritance, the Muslim Brotherhood and the Crisis of Political Parties in Egypt," Elaph electronic newspaper, June 3, 2006 (http://www. elaph.com/Web/AsdaElaph/2006/6/153224.htm?sectionarchive=AsdaElaph).

Bill, James A. "Resurgent Islam in the Persian Gulf." *Foreign Affairs*, vol. 63, no. 1, 1984.

Bill, James A., and Carl Leiden. *Politics in the Middle East* (Boston, MA: Little, Brown and Company, 1984).

Bin Ali, Yaseen. "Wahhabi Dissent against the Ottoman Caliphate" (Historical Reading and Sharia Discussion); [in Arabic], 2014 (https://da3msyria2.files. wordpress.com/2014/07/khourouj-wahabia.pdf).

bin Basheer, Hasheem. "Invaluable Statements by Imam ibn Taymiyya regarding the Kharijites" [in Arabic]. Majlis Alukah (http://majles.alukah.net/ t26910/).

bin Ghalib, Hisham. "Saudi Salafism in the Field of Authority" [in Arabic]. Al-Jazeera Studies Center, April 11, 2013 (http://studies.aljazeera.net/reports/ 2013/04/20134794152127903.htm).

bin Hijazi, Muhammad bin Hassan. "Disassociating the Salafi Call from the Qutbi Suroori Thought" [in Arabic]. Sudaress (Sudan Press), June 25, 2010 (http://www.sudaress.com/alsahafa/9001).

bin Hizam, Fares. "Islamist–Islamist Race: Dammam Elections Ignite the Suroorism and the Brotherhood" [in Arabic]. Al-Arabiya website, February 28, 2005 (http://www.alarabiya.net/articles/2005/02/28/10767.html).

bin Mees, Abdul Salam. "The Influence of Averroes on Western Political Thought" [in Arabic]. *Arab History* journal, no. 15, summer, 2000 (http://www.attarikh-alarabi.ma/Html/adad15partie13.htm).

Black, Cyril E. (ed.). *Comparative Modernization: A Reader* (New York, NY: The Free Press, 1976).

Black, Cyril E. *The Dynamics of Modernization* (New York, NY: The Free Press, 1966).

Bottomore, Tom. "Conservative Man." *The New York Review of Books*, October 8, 1970.

Brown, Heather. "Islamist Anomalies: The FIS in 1991, Muslim Brotherhood in 2005 and Hamas in 2006." Paper presented at the Annual Meeting of the Northeastern Political Science Association (Omni Parker House, Boston, MA, November 11, 2010).

Burhani, Manooba. *The Pragmatic Thought of Muhammad Rasheed Rida* [in Arabic]; (Beirut: Dar Ibn Hazm, 2010).

Bury, J. *A History of Freedom of Thought* [in Arabic]. Muhammad Abdulaziz Ishaq (trans.); (Cairo: National Translation Center, 2010).

Caiden, Naomi and Aaron Wildavsky. *Planning and Budgeting in Poor Countries* (New York, NY: John Wiley, 1974).

Calvert, John. *Sayyid Qutb and the Origins of Radical Islamism* (New York, NY: Columbia University Press, 2010).

Carmines, E.G., and R.A. Zeller, *Reliability and Validity Assessment* (Newbury Park, CA: Sage Publications, 1991).

Caromba, Laurence, and Hussein Solomon. "Understanding Egypt's Muslim Brotherhood." *African Security Review*, vol. 17, no. 3, July 2010.

Carroll, Terrance G. "Islam and Political Community in the Arab World." *International Journal of Middle East Studies*, vol. 18, no. 2 (1986).

Chilcote, Ronald. *Theories of Comparative Politics: The Search for a Paradigm* (Boulder, CO: Westview Press, 1981).

Corm, Georges. *The Religious Question in the 21st Century*, Khaleel Ahmad Khaleel (trans.); (Beirut: Dar Al-Farabi, 2007).

Dakeer, Ahmad. "The Reform Movement in the Modern Era: Abdurrahman Ahmad Al-Kawakibi as a Model" [in Arabic]. Al-Dhiaa for Contemporary Studies (http://aldhiaa.com/arabic/show_articles.php?articles_id=640&link_articles=alderasat_almoasereh/harakat_alaslah).

Dalacoura, Katerina. "The Uncertain Future of Political Islam," Global Brief, February 18, 2011 (http://globalbrief.ca/blog/2011/02/18/the-uncertain-future-of-political-islam/).

Dan, Salah Al-Deen Arga. *Political Backwardness in Contemporary Islamic Thought* [in Arabic]; (Beirut: Dar. Al-Nafa'is for Printing, Publishing and Distribution, 2002).

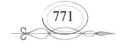

771

Davis, Kenneth. "America's True History of Religious Tolerance." *Smithsonian Magazine*, October 2010 (http://www.smithsonianmag.com/history/ americas-true-history-of-religious-tolerance-61312684/?no-ist), accessed April 14, 2014.

Deeb, Thaer. "From Hegel to Habermas: Religion and Secularism in Western Thought." Al-Hiwar Al-Mutamdden, 13 July 2006 (http://www.ahewar. org/debat/show.art.asp?aid=69855).

Dekmejian, Richard Hrair. "The Islamic Revival in the Middle East and North Africa." *Current History*, vol. 78, no. 456, April 1980.

Dekmejian, Richard Hrair. *Islam in Revolution: Fundamentalism in the Arab World* (New York, NY: Syracuse University Press, 1985).

Diamond, Larry, Juan Linz and Seymour Martin Lipset (eds.). *Politics in Developing Countries: Comparing Experiences with Democracy* (Boulder, CO: Lynne Riener Publishers, 1995).

Diyab, Muhammad Hafiz. *Sayyid Qutb: Discourse and Ideologies* [in Arabic]; (Cairo: Dar Ru'ya for Publishing and Distribution, 2010).

Durkheim, Emile. *The Elementary Forms of the Religious Life*. Joseph Ward Swain (trans.); (London: George Allen and Unwin, Ltd., 1915).

Eckstein, Harry, and David Apters (eds.). *Comparative Politics: A Reader* (New York, NY: The Free Press, 1965).

Eickelman, Dale, and James Piscatori. *Muslim Politics* (Princeton, NJ: Princeton University Press, 1996).

Eikmeier, Dale C. "Qutbism: An Ideology of Islamic Fascism." *Parameters*, Spring 2007 (http://strategicstudiesinstitute.army.mil/pubs/parameters/ articles/07spring/eikmeier.pdf), accessed February 27, 2014.

Eisa, Mahmood Shaikh. "Society: Can we Change it?" [in Arabic]. *Tishreen* newspaper, Syria, September 26, 2005 (http://tishreen.news.sy/tishreen/ public/print/50198).

Electronic Mus'haf Project. King Saud University [in Arabic]; (http://quran. ksu.edu.sa/tafseer/tabary/sura88-aya22.html).

El-Fahl, Mahir Yaseen. "The Sanctity of the Blood of Muslims" [in Arabic]. Said Al-Fawaid website (http://www.saaid.net/ahdath/77.htm).

El-Guindi Fadwa. "Religious Revival and Islamic Survival in Egypt." *International Insight*, vol. 2, no. 1, November–December, 1981.

El-Sherif, Ashraf. "The Egyptian Muslim Brotherhood's Failures." Carnegie Endowment for International Peace, July 1, 2014 (http://ceip.org/1ueqaNs).

Emirates Center for Strategic Studies and Research (ECSSR). *Islamic Movements and their Influence on Political Stability in the Arab World* [in Arabic]; (Abu Dhabi: ECSSR, 2002).

Encyclopedia of Islamic Jurisprudence (http://bit.ly/1qVeT0n).

Esposito, John (ed.). *Islam and Development: Religion and Socio-political Change* (New York, NY: Syracuse University Press, 1980).

Esposito, John L. (ed.). *Voices of Resurgent Islam* (New York, NY: Oxford University Press, 1983).

Fahmi, Ahmad. "Salafi Currents and Future Options," Majlis Al-Alukah, April 10, 2008 (http://majles.alukah.net/t14556).

Fakhida, Khalid. "Questions to the Muslim Brotherhood" [in Arabic]. *Al-Rai* newspaper, Jordan, March 24, 2012 (http://www.alrai.com/article/500913 .html).

Faqi, Abdulwahb. "The Revolving Door Game: Saudi Arabia and Smuggling Terrorism" [in Arabic]. Al-Hejaz.org, no date (http://www.alhejaz.org/ qadaya/038801.htm).

Faraj, Bassam Atiyya Ismael. *Ibn Taymiyya's Political Thought* [in Arabic]; (Amman: Dar Al-Yaqoot for Printing, Publishing and Distribution, 2001).

Farghali, Mahir. "The Salafis and Muslim Brotherhood: Disagreement of Ideology and Conflict of Politics" [in Arabic]. *Al-Hayat*, February 6, 2012.

Findley, Carter V. "The Turks in World History, Book Review" [in Arabic]. *Al-Bayan* newspaper, UAE, October 10, 2005 (http://www.albayan.ae/paths/ books/1128856924261-2005-10-10-1.983904).

Fouad, Muhammad. "15 Terrorist Incidents, the Most Infamous is the Luxor Massacre." *Al-Ahram* newspaper, Egypt, February 18, 2014 (http://digital. ahram.org.eg/articles.aspx?Serial=1540976&eid=749).

Fuad, Abdulfattah Ahmad. *Islamic Schools and their Origins of Faith* [in Arabic]; (Alexandria: Dar Al-Wafa for Printing and Publishing, vol. 1, 2003).

Fuller, Graham. "The Future of Political Islam." *Foreign Affairs*, vol. 81, no. 2, March–April, 2002.

Galston, William A. "Public Morality and Religion in the Liberal State." *PS*, vol. XIX, no. 4 (Fall 1986).

Gerges, Fawaz. *The Rise and Fall of Al-Qa'eda: Debunking the Terrorism Narrative* [in Arabic]. Muhammad Shiyya (trans.); (Beirut: Center for Arab Unity Studies, 2012).

Ghalioun, Burhan. *Critiquing Politics: State and Religion* [in Arabic]; (Beirut: Arab Institute for Research and Publishing, 2nd edition, 1993).

Gharaiba, Ibraheem. "Book Review: The Islam of the eras of Decadence" [in Arabic]. Aljazeera.net, February 12, 2008 (http://aljazeera.net/home/print/92804797-74a7-4675-b919-6682990f8cbe/37a440bd-c4f4-42aa-b715-1b3feb5f436a).

Gharaiba, Ibraheem. "Political Islam … Meteors Sparkled in the Sky of the Arab World and Burned out" [in Arabic]. *Al-Majalla* journal, December 31, 2013 (http://www.majalla.com/arb/2013/12/article55249377).

Gharaibeh, Ibrahim. *The Muslim Brotherhood Group in Jordan 1946–1996* (Amman: Al-Urdun Al-Jadid Research Center and Sindbad Publishing House, 1997).

Gibb, Hamilton A.R. "The Heritage of Islam in the Modern World (I)." *International Journal of Middle East Studies*, vol. 1, no. 1, January, 1970.

Gill, N. S. "Trojan Horse." About website (http://ancienthistory.about.com/od/troyilium/g/TrojanHorse.htm).

Gole, Nilufer. "Secularism and Islamism in Turkey: The Making of Elites and Counter-Elites." *Middle East Journal*, vol. 51, no. 1, Winter 1997.

Guirguis, Max. "Islamic Resurgence and Its Consequences in the Egyptian Experience." *Mediterranean Studies*, vol. 20, no. 2, 2012.

Habeeb, Rafiq. "Transformations of Contemporary Salafism between Reformation and Revival" [in Arabic]; (http://www.cha3biahli.net/kbirelhoma/index. php/2009-01-05-08-55-02/670-2009-07-13-12-02-34.html).

Habib, Kamal. "The New Islamic Alliance in Egypt" [in Arabic]. *Al-Youm Al-Sabie* newspaper, Egypt, June 24, 2013 (http://www1.youm7.com/News. asp?NewsID=1131000).

Haddad, Y., B. Haines and E. Findly. *The Islamic Impact* (New York, NY: Syracuse University Press, 1984).

Haidar, Khaleel Ali. "Religious Extremism ... and Fascism" [in Arabic]. *Al-Ittihad* newspaper, August 27 2006 (http://www.alittihad.ae/wajhatdetails.php?id= 22421).

Haikal, Muhammad Hassanein. *Autumn of Fury: The Beginning and End of the Reign of Anwar Al-Sadat* [in Arabic]; (Cairo: Al-Ahram Center for Translation and Publication, 1988).

Hamad, Muhammad Abu al-Qasim Haj. *Hakimiyya* [in Arabic]; (Beirut: Dar Al-Saqi, 1st edition, 2010).

Hamdan, Jamal. *Colonization and Liberation Strategy* (Cairo: Dar Al-Shurooq, 1983), pp. 64–76, 130–141.

Hamed, Muhiy. "Key issues in the Thought of Imam Hassan Al-Banna: The Brotherhood's Stance on Governments, Parties and Issues of Terrorism" [in Arabic]. *Al-Mujtama* magazine, Kuwait, issue 2069, March 5, 2014.

Hamid, Musa. "Sudan's Impossible Democracy" [in Arabic]. Ashorooq.net, January 29, 2013 (http://goo.gl/B9EVhU).

Hamid, Shadi. "The Brotherhood Will Be Back." *The New York Times*, May 23, 2014 (http://nyti.ms/1im2ijF).

Hamzawy, Amr. "Party for Justice and Development in Morocco: Participation and Its Discontents" [in Arabic] Carnegie Papers, Carnegie Endowment, July 2008 (http://carnegieendowment.org/files/cp93_hamzawy_pjd_ arabic.pdf).

Hanafi, Hassan. "The Relevance of the Islamic Alternative in Egypt." *Arab Studies Quarterly*, vol. 4, nos. 1–2 (Spring 1982).

Hanafi, Hassan. *The Concept of Centrism in Islam: Centrism in Theory and Practice* [in Arabic]; (Amman: Dar Jareer for Publishing and Distribution, Arabic Thought Forum, 1st Edition, 2005).

Hanna, Sami A. "Islam, Socialism, and National Trials." *The Muslim World*, vol. 58, 1968.

Harb, Usama Al-Ghazali. "Political Interest in the Behavior of the Muslim Brotherhood" [in Arabic]. Lecture presented at The Future of Arab–Islamic Culture Conference, The Emirates Center for Strategic Studies and Research, Abu Dhabi, UAE, 27–28; May 2013, *Al-Arab* (London), May 29, 2013 (http://www.alarab.co.uk/?p=40183).

Harfoosh, Muhammad. "Hezbollah: The Origins and Challenges" [in Arabic]. Al-Monitor (Lebanon), July 11, 2013 (http://www.al-monitor.com/pulse/ar/originals/2013/02/hezbollah-beginnings-challenges.html#).

Hasan, Ammar Ali. *Suicide of the Muslim Brotherhood: The Fade of Thought, Fall of Ethics and Collapse of the Organization* [in Arabic]; (Cairo: Dar Nahdat Misr for Publishing, 2013).

Hasan, Ammar Ali. *Suicide of the Muslim Brotherhood: The Fade of Thought, Fall of Ethics and Collapse of the Organization* [in Arabic]; (Cairo: Dar Nahdat Misr for Publishing, 2013).

Hasan, Usama. "Viewpoint: What do radical Islamists actually believe in?" *BBC News Magazine*, May 24, 2013 (http://www.bbc.com/news/magazine-22640614).

Hashim, Muhammad Younis. *Philosophical Schools: The Dialectic of Text, Mind and Interest* [in Arabic]; (Giza, Egypt: Dar Zohoor Al-Ma'rifa Wa Al-Baraka, 2013).

Hassanein, Sabri Abdulhafeez. "An Egyptian Scandal: Presidential Meeting on National Security Regarding the Renaissance Dam was Broadcast Live" [in Arabic]. *Elaph* newspaper, June 4, 2013 (http://www.elaph.com/Web/news/2013/6/816307.html).

Hatim, Lutfi. "The Evolution of National State and the Thought of Political Islam" [in Arabic]. Al-Hiwar Al-Mutamaddin website, October 7, 2012 (http://www.ahewar.org/debat/s.asp?aid=327279&t=4).

Hatti, Naseef. "The Transformational Course of the New Arab Order" [in Arabic]. Beirut, *Palestinian Studies*, Issue 93, Winter 2013.

Hayward, Emma. "Assessing Ennahda, Tunisia's Winning Islamist Party" [in Arabic]. the Washington Institute, November 18, 2011 (http://bit.ly/1tg3 Wf9).

Helmi, Majdi. "The Brotherhoodization of State: Plan and Execution" [in Arabic]. *Al-Wafd* newspaper, Egypt, September 6, 2012 (http://bit.ly/1y8 rt0M).

Heper, Metin. "The Strong State as a Problem for the Consolidation of Democracy." *Comparative Political Studies*, vol. 25, no. 2, July 1994.

Hijazi, Akram. "Introduction to Jihadi Salafism and its Jihadi Enterprise: Iraq" [in Arabic]. Jihadi Salafism Studies Series no. 4 (Amman: Arab Institute for Research and Strategic Studies, February 2008).

Hijazi, Akram. "Substantial Issues in the Thought of Jihadi Salafism" (From Tawheed to Leadership Making), [in Arabic]. Jihadi Salafism Studies Series no. 3 (Irbid: No Publisher, October 2007).

Hilal, Ali Al-Deen. *The Evolution of the Political System in Egypt 1803–1997* [in Arabic]; (Cairo: Center for Political Studies and Research, Cairo University, 1997).

Hilali, Saad Al-Deen. "Falsehood about Marriage of Minor Girls" [in Arabic]. *Al-Watan* newspaper, October 4, 2012 (http://www.elwatannews.com/news/details/57129).

Hirschkind, Charles. "What Is Political Islam?" *Middle East Report*, vol. 27, no. 205, Winter 1997 (http://www.merip.org/mer/mer205/what-political-islam).

Hoballah, Haidar. "Key Paper on Human Rights in Islam" [in Arabic]; (http://www.shahrodi.com/al-menhaj/Almen39/39000015.htm).

Hoballah, Haidar. "The Muslims' Tradition-based Interpretation of the Holy Quran: Concept, Roles, History, Works and Issues" [in Arabic] (http://bit.ly/1pxW3A4).

Hodgson, Marshall G.S. *The Venture of Islam: Conscience and History in a World Civilization*, three volumes (Chicago: University of Chicago Press, 1974).

Humaid, Salem. "The Story of the Brotherhood's Plot in the UAE, from the Infiltration of Thought to the Failure of the Scheme and Prosecuting the Accused Individuals" (Dubai: Al-Mezmaah Studies and Research Centre, Issue 4, 2013).

Hunter, Shireen T. (ed.). *The Politics of Islamic Revivalism: Diversity and Unity* (Bloomington, IN: Indiana University Press, 1988).

Hunter, Shireen T. "Islamic Fundamentalism: What it Really is and Why it Frightens the West." *SAIS Review*, vol. 6, no. 1, Winter 1986.

Huntington, Samuel P. and Joan Nelson. *No Easy Choice: Political Participation in Developing Countries* (Cambridge, MA: Harvard University Press, 1977).

Huntington, Samuel P. *Political Order in Changing Societies* (New Haven, CT: Yale University Press, 1968).

Hurvitz, Nimrod. *The Formation of Hanbalism: Piety into Power* [in Arabic]. Ghassan Alam Al-Deen (trans.); (Beirut: Arab Network for Research and Publication, 2011).

Hussain, Abdulghaffar. "The Muslim Brotherhood in UAE" [in Arabic]. *Al-Khaleej* newspaper, UAE, August 1, 2012 (http://www.alkhaleej.ae/studiesandopinions/page/f386335f-a354-4fc7-a6c2-dd476e573d3c).

Hussain, Freda (ed.). *Muslim Women* (London: Croom Helm Ltd., 1984).

Hussein, Hussein Al-Sayyid. "The Egyptian–Israeli Peace Treaty 1979 and its Impact of Egypt's Regional Role" [in Arabic]. *Historical Studies* journal, nos. 117–118, January–June 2012, pp. 447–497 (http://www.damascusuniversity.edu.sy/mag/history/images/stories/pdf/14.pdf).

Hussein, Imad Al-Deen. "Why did not Mursi Fight Israel?" [in Arabic]. Alarabiya.net, July 12, 2014 (http://goo.gl/Si67yK).

Ibraheem, Abdulwahid. "The Muslim Brotherhood's Ruling Experience in Sudan" [in Arabic]. Civic Egypt, January 28, 2013 (http://civicegypt.org/?p=34060).

Ibrahim, Saad Eddin. "Anatomy of Egypt's Militant Islamic Groups: Methodological Note and Preliminary Findings." *International Journal of Middle East Studies*, vol. 12, no. 4, December 1980.

Imad, Abdulghani. "God's (Allah) Sovereignty and the Guardianship of the Jurist: The Concept and Discourse" [in Arabic]. Tourathtripoli.org (http://tourath tripoli.org/phocadownload/dirasset_isslamieh/7akimiet%20alah%20w%20wi layat%20alfakieh.pdf).

Imad, Abdulghani. "Jihadi Salafism… or the Survivor Denomination" [in Arabic]. On Islam website, 10 March 2010 (http://bit.ly/O828n9).

Imad, Abdulghani. "Salafism and the Problem of the Other between Negotiation and Preference" [in Arabic]. Beirut, *Al-Mustaqbal Al-Arabi*, issue 224, February 2006.

Imad, Abdulghani. *God (Allah)'s Hakimiyya and Jurist's Authority: Examining the Discourse of Contemporary Islamic Movements* [in Arabic]; (Beirut: Dar Al-Talia Publishers, June 1997).

Iqbal, Muhammad. *Renewal of Religious Thought in Islam* [in Arabic] Muhammad Yousef Adas (trans.); (Cairo/Beirut: Egyptian and Lebanese Bookshop, 2011).

Ishra, Nermine. "Ibn Rushd Offers a Philosophical Present at the Anniversary of his Birth" [in Arabic]. *Al-Wafd*, April 14, 2014 (http://bit.ly/1wlJdGD).

Islamboli, Samer. *Divinity and Hakimiyya: A Scientific Study through the Quran* [in Arabic]; (Damascus: Dar Al-Awael Publishing, Distribution and Printing Services, 2000).

Ismael, Hamada Mahmood. *Hassan Al-Banna and the Muslim Brotherhood Group between Religion and Politics 1928–1949* [in Arabic]; (Cairo: Dar Al-Shurooq, 2010).

Ja'far, Hisham Ahmad. *Political Dimensions of the Hakimiyya Concept: An Epistemological Perspective* [in Arabic]; (Virginia: International Institute of Islamic Thought, 1995).

Jaafar, Hisham Ahmad Awadh. *Political Dimensions of the Hakimiyya Concept: Epistemological Perspective* [in Arabic]; (Herndon, VA: International Institute of Islamic Thought, Theses Series 14, 1995).

Jabir, Hassan, et al. *Renewal of Religious Thought* [in Arabic]; (Beirut: Institution of Contemporary Religious Thought, 2009).

Jabir, Hassan. "The Church in Confrontation with Reason and Science" [in Arabic]. Al-Najaf website (http://www.al-najaf.org/resalah/13/04_jaber. htm).

Jamal, Amaney, and Mark Tessler. "Attitudes in the Arab World." *Journal of Democracy*, vol. 19, no. 1, January 2008.

Jansen, G. H. "Militant Islam: The Historic Whirlwind." *New York Times Magazine*, January 6, 1980.

Jawad, Jamal Abdul. "Hizbullah's Political Document: What is New?" [in Arabic]. Digital Ahram, December 11, 2009 (http://digital.ahram.org.eg/articles.aspx?Serial=18068).

Jawda, Sulaiman. "It is not a State and it is not Islamic" [in Arabic]. *Al-Sharq Al-Awsat* newspaper, September 8, 2014 (http://www.aawsat.com/home/article/177041).

Jourchi, Salaheddine. "Tunisia's Salafism: A Critical Issue in a Fragile Transitional Period" [in Arabic]. Swiss Info Portal, September 3, 2012 (http://bit.ly/1sWMmgj).

Jumaih, Muhammad. "When Religion is a Means" [in Arabic]. Ma'reb Press, December 22, 2009 (http://marebpress.net/articles.php?lng=arabic&id=6224).

Kaheel, Abdul Azeez. "False Conflict between Text and Reason" [in Arabic]. Yaqzat Fikr website, December 16, 2012 (http://feker.net/ar/2012/12/16/12933/).

Kamal, Abdullah. "The Black Banners: Abdullah Azzam from Jihad to Assassination (1)" [in Arabic]. *Al-Sharq Al-Awsat* newspaper, London, May 1, 2002 (http://classic.aawsat.com/details.asp?issueno=8555&article=100961#.VGRdXzqoWRs).

Kamil, Ahmad Khamis. "The Dilemma of Empowerment: The Gap between Discourse and Practice in the Experience of the Islamic Movement in the Sudan" [in Arabic]. *Al-Siyassa Al-Dawliyya*, January 29, 2013 (http://goo.gl/3GfhY4).

Karawan, Ibrahim. "Sadat and the Egyptian-Israeli Peace Revisited." *International Journal of Middle East Studies*, vol. 26, no. 2, July 1994.

Kareem, Fakhri. "The Extremism Industry and its Most Inflammatory Elements (9), Incubators of Extremism and their Founding Beginnings: the Muslim Brotherhood" [in Arabic]. *Al-Mada* newspaper, Iraq, February 11, 2014 (http://goo.gl/ScQSTO).

Karlsson, Ingmar. "Islam and Europe: Confrontation or Coexistence?" Sameer Butani (trans.); (Cairo: Al-Shurooq International Bookshop, 1st edition, 2003).

Kassab, Muhammad. "Muslim Brotherhood … Three Decision of "Dissolution and Ban" in 85 Years" [in Arabic]. Al-Masri Al-Yawm website, September 2013 (http://www.almasryalyoum.com/news/details/321644).

Kassar, Ahmad Abdullah. "Centrism of Islam in Manners and Behavior" [in Arabic]; (http://www.iasj.net/iasj?func=fulltext&aId=78690).

Kenes, Bulent. "Moderation, modernization, and Malaysia." Today's Zaman, January 19, 2012 (http://www.todayszaman.com/columnists/bulent-kenes_269054-moderation-modernization-and-malaysia.html), accessed April 14, 2014.

Kepel, Gilles. *Jihad: The Expansion and Decline of Islamism* [in Arabic], Nabeel Saad (trans.); (Cairo: Dar Al-Aalam Al-Thalith, 1st edition, 2005).

Kepel, Gilles. *Jihad: The Trail of Political Islam* (London: I.B. Tauris, 2002).

Kepel, Gilles. *Muslim Extremism in Egypt: The Prophet and Pharaoh* (Berkeley/ Los Angeles, CA: University of California Press, 1984).

Khairallah, Dawood. "The Relationship between Religion and the State in the Arab Spring Era" [in Arabic]. *Al-Akhbar* (Lebanon), December 11, 2012 (http://www.al-akhbar.com/node/173416).

Khalaf, Khalaf. "Roots and Facts of the Hidden Conflict between Fatah and Hamas" [in Arabic]. Elaph electronic newspaper, December 17, 2007 (http://www.elaph.com/ElaphWeb/AkhbarKhasa/2007/12/288608.htm).

Khaleel, Majdi. "Citizenship Rights of the Copts between the Ruling Regime's Conduct and the Thought of the Islamists" [in Arabic]. Elaph electronic newspaper, May 6, 2007 (http://www.elaph.com/ElaphWeb/ElaphWriter/2007/5/231612.htm).

Khaleel, Salah. "Legislative Elections in Morocco: Division and Challenges" [in Arabic]. Digital Ahram portal, January 1, 2012 (http://digital.ahram.org.eg/articles.aspx?Serial=813871&eid=5239).

Khalil, Sabri Muhammad. "Al-Qa'eda: Birth, Intellectual Origins and Various Stances Towards it" [in Arabic]. Sudanile, November 16, 2011 (http://bit.ly/1lBflng).

Khalil, Sabri Muhammad. "Jihadi Salafism: Intellectual Origins and Various Stances Towards it" [in Arabic]. Sudanile, July 30, 2012 (http://www.sudanile.com/index.php/2008-05-19-17-39-36/252-2009-09-06-09-34-16/43048-2012-07-30-08-07-56).

Khalil, Sabri Muhammad. "The Concept of Hakimiyya in Political Islamic Thought" [in Arabic], September 15, 2010 (http://www.sudanile.com/index.php/2008-05-19-17-39-36/252-2009-09-06-09-34-16/18652-2010-09-15-15-34-33).

Khalil, Sabri Muhammad. "The Muslim Brotherhood: A Methodological Examination of its Intellectual Origins" [in Arabic]. Sudanile portal, June 5, 2012 (http://bit.ly/1pDHTwc).

Khan, M.A. Muqtedar. "The Political Philosophy of Islamic Resurgence." Cultural Dynamics, vol. 13, no. 2, 2001.

Khashoggi, Jamal. "Prince Turki Al-Faisal: Changes in the Personality of bin Ladin Started in 1990 when he Imagined he could form an Army to Fight Saddam in Kuwait" [in Arabic]. Al-Sharq Al-Awsat (London), November 7, 2001 (http://classic.aawsat.com/details.asp?section=4&article=65264&issueno=8380#.VBb5YzqoWic).

Khawaja, Saif Al-Deen. "The Role of Egypt … in the Coup of Hashim Al-Ata" [in Arabic]. Al-Rakooba website, September 23, 2014 (http://www.alrakoba.net/articles-action-show-id-53725.htm).

Khouri, Fred. The Arab-Israeli Dilemma, 3rd ed. (Syracuse: NY: Syracuse University Press, 1985).

Knudsen, A.J. "Political Islam in the Middle East." CMI Reports, R2003:3, Chr. Michelsen Institute, Norway, 2003 (http://www.cmi.no/publications/file/1548-political-islam-in-the-middle-east.pdf), accessed February 25, 2014.

Konakata, Hasan. *Ibn Taymiyya's Political Theory* [in Arabic]; (Dammam: Dar Al-Akhella' for Publishing and Distribution, 1994).

Lacroix, Stephane. "Sheikhs and Politicians: Inside the New Egyptian Salafism" [in Arabic]. Brookings Doha Center, June 2012 (http://bit.ly/1s1WtPK).

Lapidus, Ira. "The Separation of State and Religion in the Development of Early Islamic Society." *International Journal of Middle Eastern Studies* vol. 6, no. 4, October 1975.

Large Encyclopedia of Schools, Sects and Religions: Shiites [in Arabic]; (Beirut: Middle East Cultural Center for Printing, Publishing, Translation and Distribution, 2008).

Levy, Marion. *Modernization and the Structure of Societies* (Princeton, NJ: Princeton University Press, 1966).

Lewis, Bernard. "The Return to Islam." *Commentary*, January, 1976.

Lewis, Bernard. *What Went Wrong? Western Impact and Middle Eastern Response* (London: Phoenix, 2002).

Lia, Brynjar, and Katja H.-W. Skjolberg. "Why Terrorism Occurs: A Survey of Theories and Hypotheses on the Causes of Terrorism." Norwegian Defense Research Establishment (FFI), 2000 (http://www.ffi.no/no/rapporter/00-02769.pdf).

Lincoln, Bruce (ed.). *Religion, Rebellion, Revolution: An Interdisciplinary and Cross-Cultural Collection of Essays* (London: The Macmillan Press Ltd., 1985).

Lisan Al-Arab dictionary (Beirut: Dar Sadir Publishers, 2003).

Mahmood, Khalid. "Why did the Islamists Win the Elections in Egypt, Tunisia, Libya and Morocco?" [in Arabic]. Islam Times (http://islamtimes.org/vdcjyxev8uqe8vz.3ffu.html).

Mahmood, Sudfa Muhammad. Historical Evolution of Religion in International Relations [in Arabic], May 2010 (http://www.academia.edu/4097083/_).

Mahran, Nesrine. "The Last Decade of the Ottoman State was the Most Turbulent between the Arabs and the Turks" [in Arabic] *Al Ahram* newspaper, February 20, 2012 (http://digital.ahram.org.eg/articles.aspx?Serial=809438 &eid=840).

Makansi, Othman Qadri. "Reticence and Secrecy are Methods of Education in the Quran (21)" [in Arabic]. website of Al-Sham League of Writers, September 4, 2010 (http://www.odabasham.net/show.php?sid=38662).

Maleki, Muhammad. "Morocco's Justice and Development Party: Reform in the Context of Stability" [in Arabic]. Al-Jazeera Center for Studies, March 20, 2012 (http://studies.aljazeera.net/reports/2012/03/201231913332423267. htm).

Mamdani, Mahmood. "Whither Political Islam?" *Foreign Affairs*, vol. 84, no. 1, January/February, 2005.

Mamouri, Ali. "Lebanese Cleric offers Moderate Vision in 'Shiite Charter'." Al-Monitor, January 12, 2014 (http://www.al-monitor.com/pulse/ originals /2014/01/moderate-shiite-voice-organized.html), accessed March 5, 2014.

Mamouri, Ali. "The Roots of Radicalism in Political Islam," Al-Monitor, October 18, 2013 (http://www.al-monitor.com/pulse/originals/ 2013/10/ radicalism-political-islam-roots-sunni-shiite-fundamentalist.html).

Mansoor, Riad. "Jordan: Security Forces Arrest a "Terrorist ISIL" Cell in Central Amman" [in Arabic]. *Al-Madeena* newspaper, Saudi Arabia, September 11, 2014 (http://www.al-madina.com/node/556495).

Mansour, Ashraf. "Modern Philosophy: Development and General Features" [in Arabic]. Al-Hiwar Al-Mutamaddin website, December 12, 2010 (http:// www.ahewar.org/debat/show.art.asp?aid=238064).

Manzoor, Ibn. *Lisan Al-Arab* vol. 9 (Beirut: Dar Sader, 1994).

Maqdisi, Sameer, et al. *Arab Culture and the Issues of Development and Modernization* [in Arabic]; (Amman: Dar Al-Farsi Publishing and Distribution, 2011).

Markas, Yoachim Rizq. "Lectures on the History of the Western Church" [in Arabic]. St. Takla Church (http://goo.gl/YtjZ3i).

Marks, Robert. *The Origins of the Modern World: Fate and Fortune in the Rise of the West* (New York, NY: Rowman & Littlefield Publishers, Inc., 2007).

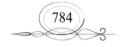

Massooh, Atiyya. "Secularism and the Arab Reality" [in Arabic]. Maaber (http://www.maaber.org/issue_december08/spotlights2.htm).

Masters, Jonathan, and Zachary Laub. "Hezbollah (a.k.a. Hizbollah, Hizbu'llah)," Council on Foreign Relations, Nabeel Zulf (trans.). *Al-Watan* newspaper, Kuwait, January 14, 2014 (http://alwatan.kuwait.tt/articledetails.aspx?Id=331527).

McCarthy, Bill. "Separation of Church and State, not Separation of God from State." Myfathershouse.com (http://www.myfathershouse.com/pdf/Separation_of_Church_and_State-not-separation-of-God-from-state.pdf), accessed April 13, 2014.

Merki, Peter M., and Ninian Smart. *Religion and Politics in the Modern World* (New York, NY: New York University Press, 1983).

Milton-Edwards, Beverley. *Contemporary Politics in the Middle East* (Cambridge, UK: Polity Press, 2000).

Mitchel, Richard. *The Muslim Brotherhood* [in Arabic]. Abdulsalam Ridwan (trans.); (Cairo: Madbooli Bookshop, 2nd Edition, 1985).

Mitchell, Richard P. *The Society of the Muslim Brothers* (London: Oxford University Press, 1969).

Mitz, Adam. *The Islamic Civilization in the Fourth Century AH or the Renaissance* [in Arabic]. Muhammad Abdulhadi Abu Zaid (trans.); (Beirut: Dar Al-Kitab Al-Arabi, vol. 1, no date).

Mohamad, Mahathir. "Islam is not an Obstacle to Modernization; the Problem Lies in Some Scholars Who Misinterpret Religion" [in Arabic]. *Al-Sharq Al-Awsat* (London), February 22, 2002 (http://classic.aawsat.com/details.asp?article=89611&issueno=8487#.VKJ_eULbE).

Mol, Hans (ed.). *Identity and Religion: International, Cross-cultural Approaches* (Beverly Hills, CA: Sage Publications Inc., 1978).

Monier, Elizabth Iskander, and Annette Ranko. "The Fall of the Muslim Brotherhood: Implications for Egypt." *Middle East Policy*, vol. 20, no. 4, Winter 2013.

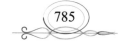

785

Muhammad, Ashraf Salih. "Our Glorious Civilization during the Middle Ages" *Alwaei Al-Islamic* magazine (Kuwait), no date, [in Arabic]; (http://alwaei. gov.kw/site/Pages/ChildDetails.aspx?pageId=168&Vol=581).

Muhammad, Jasim. "Al-Qa'eda's Generations Cloning" [in Arabic]. Al-Roaya News Network, July 28, 2014 (http://bit.ly/1oFLc2e).

Muhammad, Yahya. *History and Development of Jurisprudential Reasoning* [in Arabic]. Fahm Al-Din website, no date (http://www.fahmaldin.com/index. php?id=98).

Muntasir, Khalid. "We have Killed Ibn Rushd to Revive Ibn Taymiyyah" [in Arabic]. *Al-Watan* electronic portal, April 14, 2014 (http://www.elwatannews. com/news/details/461576).

Mursi, Muhammad. "The Muslim Brotherhood and Contemporary Islamic Parties" [in Arabic]. August 5, 2007, Ikhawanonline website (http://www. ikhwanonline.com/Article.aspx?ArtID=30200&SecID=390).

Musharbash, Yassin. "Al-Qa'eda in the Arabian Peninsula: Jihad over the Internet" [in Arabic]. Khadeejto Al-Hamid (trans.). *Al-Qa'eda in the Arabian Peninsula*, Al-Misbar Monthly Book, no. 10 (Dubai: Al-Misbar Center for Studies and Research, October 2007).

Muslat, Sa'ad Abdul Azeez. "The Political Project of the Justice and Development Party in Turkey [in Arabic]. *Regional Studies* journal, no. 12, 2008 (http://www.iasj.net/iasj?func=fulltext&aId=6499).

Muslim, Saheeh. *Book of Remembrance of Allah, Chapter on the Merit of an Assembly for the Recitation of the* Quran [in Arabic]; (http://www.alminbar.net/alkhutab/ khutbaa.asp?mediaURL=1811#_ftn3).

Mustafa, Assad Ahmad. *The Formation of the Muslim Brotherhood* [in Arabic]; (Dubai: Al-Mesbar Studies and Research Centre, vol. 12, December 2007).

Mustafa, Hala. *State and Islamic Opposition Movements between Appeasement and Confrontation in the Reigns of Sadat and Mubarak: The Political Regime and the Islamic Opposition in Egypt* [in Arabic]; (Cairo: Al Mahrousa Center for Publishing, Press Services and Information, 1996).

Mustafa, Rania. "From the 'Constant' of Popular Religiosity to the "Variable" of Political Islam" [in Arabic]. Al-Arab online, February 3, 2014. (http://www.alarabonline.org/?id=14392).

Myerscough, Rhea. "The Relationship between the State and Religion in the United States of America" [in Arabic]. Aljazeera.net, 27 December 2006 (http://www.aljazeera.net/specialfiles/pages/a02d95a9-ebda-4ac3-8dfe-c45c01302ba3).

Nab, Muhammad Abdullah. "Bickering between the Jamis and the Surooris in Saudi Arabia" [in Arabic]. Elaph electronic newspaper, May 20, 2005 (http://www.elaph.com/ElaphWeb/Politics/2005/5/63497.htm).

Nabulsi, Mohammed Rateb. "Interpretation of Quran, The Short Version, Surat Al-Ankabut (29)" Lesson 9-9, Verses 68-69 [in Arabic]. September 28, 1995 (http://www.nabulsi.com/blue/ar/print.php?art=5791).

Najeeb, Muhammad. "I was Egypt's President" [in Arabic]; (Cairo: Egypt, Modern Egyptian Office, 1984).

Naseera, Hani. *Al-Qa'eda and Jihadi Salafism: Intellectual Sources and Limits of Revisions* [in Arabic]. Strategic Booklets Series vol. 18, issue 188 (Cairo: Al-Ahram Center for Political and Strategic Studies, August 2008).

Nasser, Huda Abdul. "Biography of President Jamal Abdul Nasser." Website of President Jamal Abdul Nasser (http://nasser.bibalex.org/Common/pictures01-%20sira.htm).

Newman, Simon. "Religion in the Middle Ages." TheFinerTimes.com (http://www.thefinertimes.com/Middle-Ages/religion-in-the-middle-ages.html#sthash.If2pu26c.dpuf), accessed April 12, 2014.

Newport, Frank. "In US, 77% Identify as Christian." Gallup, December 24, 2012 (http://www.gallup.com/poll/159548/identify-christian.aspx), accessed April 14, 2014.

Nuwaihidh, Waleed. *The Political Contract: The Islamists, The State and the Issue of Democracy (1984–1996),* [in Arabic]; (Manama: Dar Al-Wasat for Publishing and Distribution, 2nd edition, 2009); (http://arabsfordemocracy.org/democracy/pages/view/pageId/1025).

Nuwwar, Ibraheem. "Egypt–Israel Relations: the Structure and Outcomes after One Year of Normalization" [in Arabic]. *Al-Ahram* newspaper, Egypt, July 1, 1981 (http://digital.ahram.org.eg/articles.aspx?Serial=215095&eid=13).

Nuwwar, Wa'il, and Feyzi Baban. "The Future of Political Islam: Two Lessons from Turkey and Egypt" [in Arabic] Al Monitor, January 29, 2014 (http://bit.ly/1vewCIs).

O'Connel, James. "The Concept of Modernization." *South Atlantic Quarterly* vol. LXIV (Autumn, 1965).

Official Website of the 2012 Egyptian Presidential Elections (http://presidential 2012.elections.eg/index.php/round2-results).

Omar, Khairy. "A Look into the Results of the Egyptian Parliamentary Elections" [in Arabic]. *Middle East Studies Journal*, Issue 5, Year 16, Spring 2012.

Othman, Ahmad. "Will the Islamic Caliphate Return in Cairo?" [in Arabic]. *Al-Sharq Al-Awsat* newspaper, London, January 2, 2012 (http://classic.aawsat.com/leader.asp?section=3&issueno=12088&article=657119).

Othman, Taj Al-Sir. "The Cover of Exploiting Religion in Politics is Exposed .. What Does it Mean that Islam is the Solution? A Solution for What?" [in Arabic]. *Al-Rakoba* newspaper, Sudan, April 9, 2012 (http://www.alrakoba.net/news-action-show-id-70531.htm).

Parsons, Talcott. "Some Sociological Aspects of the Fascist Movements." *Social Force*, vol. 21, no. 2 (December 1942).

Piscatori, James P. (ed.). *Islam in the Political Process* (London: Cambridge University Press, 1983).

Qaseer, Qassim. "Brotherhood and Saudi Arabia: Conflict and Convergence." Islamyun.net, October 5, 2013 (http://www.islamyun.net/index.php?option =com_k2&view=item&id=1711).

Qurbal, Noor Al-Deen. "Morocco's Justice and Development Party and Political Participation" [in Arabic]. *Hespress* newspaper portal, November 6, 2013 (http://www.hespress.com/writers/93243.html).

Qutb, Sayyid. *Ma'alim Fi Al-Tariq* (Signposts on the Road), [in Arabic]; (Beirut and Cairo: Dar Al-Shourouk, 1980).

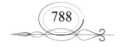

Rafiqi, Muhammad Abduwahhab. "Renewal and Revival in Salafi Thought" [in Arabic]. Aljazeera.net, March 13, 2014 (http://bit.ly/1BFlEvb).

Ramadan, Bassam. "Burhami: Interpretation of Sharia Principles in the Constitution 'Satisfactory'" [in Arabic]. *Al-Masri Al-Yawm*, December 4, 2013 (http://www.almasryalyoum.com/news/details/352377#).

Ramadan, Said. "Rakaiz Dawat Al-Islam." *Al-Musliman*, vol. 1, no. 6, n.d.

Reidel, Bruce. "Al Qaeda Strikes Back." *Foreign Affairs*, vol. 86, no. 3 (May–June 2007).

Richards, Alan, and John Waterbury. *A Political Economy of the Middle East*, 2nd ed. (Boulder, CO: Westview Press, 1996).

Rizq, Huda. "Struggles of Moderate Islam in Turkey" [in Arabic]. *Al-Akhbar* newspaper, Lebanon, January 21, 2014 (http://www.al-akhbar.com/node/199034).

Robertson, Roland. *The Sociological Interpretation of Religion* (New York, NY: Schocken Books, 1970).

Robinson, Bruce. "An Overview of the Reformation." BBC History, February 17, 2011 (http://www.bbc.co.uk/history/british/tudors/reformation_overview_01.shtml).

Rothchild, Donald, and Robert L. Curry, Jr. *Scarcity, Choice, and Public Policy in Middle Africa* (Berkeley, CA: University of California Press, 1978).

Roy, Olivier. *The Experience of Political Islam* [in Arabic]. Naseer Marwa (trans.); (Beirut: Dar Al-Saqi, 1st Edition, 1994).

Roy, Olivier. *The Failure of Political Islam* (London: I.B. Tauris, 1994).

Rubin, Elizabeth. "A Story of Reverting from Wahhabism: The Jihadi Who Kept Asking Why" [in Arabic]. Al-Hejaz.org (http://www.alhejaz.org/qadaya/031705.htm).

Rubin, Jared. "Printing and Protestants: Reforming the Economics of the Reformation." Munich Personal RePEc Archive (MPRA), June 2011 (http://mpra.ub.uni-muenchen.de/31267/1/MPRA_paper_31267.pdf), accessed April 12, 2014.

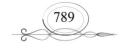

Rustow, Dankward A. *A World of Nations: Problems of Political Modernization* (Washington, DC: Brookings Institution, 1967).

Saad, Mahdi. "Mixing Religion and Politics is a Big Mistake" [in Arabic]. Al-Hiwar Al-Mutamdden, November 20, 2006 (http://www.ahewar.org/debat/show.art.asp?aid=81288).

Sachs, Susan. "Ayatullah Al-Sistani Rejects the Guardianship of the Jurist and Does not Pursue Political Ambitions" [in Arabic]. *Al-Sharq Al-Awsat* newspaper, London, January 19, 2004 (http://classic.aawsat.com/details.asp?article=213514&issueno=9183).

Saeed, Abdulmonem. *Religion and the State in Egypt: Thought, Politics and the Muslim Brotherhood* [in Arabic]; (Cairo: Nahdat Misr for Printing, Publishing and Distribution, 2008).

Saeed, Muhammad Al-Sayyid. "Resistance between Religious Sects" [in Arabic]. *Al-Ahram* newspaper. (http://www.ahram.org.eg/archive/2002/11/9/REPO 4.HTM).

Said Ramadan, "Rakaiz Dawat Al-Islam," *Al-Musliman*, vol. 1, no. 6, n.d., p. 37.

Saint-Prot, Charles. *The Future of Tradition between Revolution and Westernization* [in Arabic]. Wajeeh Jameel Al-Buaini (trans.), Refereed Works Series no. 113 (Riyadh: King Abdulaziz Public Library, 2010).

Salama, Sifat. "An Insight into the Contributions of Islamic Civilization in the Renaissance" [in Arabic]. *Al-Sharq Al-Awsat* newspaper, London, July 19, 2011 (http://goo.gl/ekcRej).

Salih, Hashim. "Christian Fundamentalism in the West: The Inquisition was the Culmination of Fanaticism and Violence" [in Arabic]. *Al-Sharq Al-Awsat* (London), October 4, 2000 (http://www.aawsat.com/details.asp?issueno= 8059&article=7390).

Salih, Hashim. "Europe Combines Religion and Modernity after Centuries of Separation" [in Arabic]. *Al-Sharq Al-Awsat* (London), March 7, 2004.

Salih, Usama. "Cautious Approach: Will the Rising Islamic Movements Restructure the Arab State?" [in Arabic]. *Al-Siyassan Al-Dawliyya*, no. 188, April 2012 (http://www.siyassa.org.eg/NewsQ/2369.aspx).

Salim, Hamdi Al-Saeed. "Secret Communications and Connections between Mubarak's Regime and the Muslim Brotherhood before the Revolution" [in

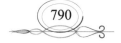

Arabic]. Middle East Panorama website, March 25, 2013 (http://bit.ly/1qT8Y0q).

Sarhan, Haytham. "Book Review of Awakening Time, by Stephane Lacroix" (http://goo.gl/wCDJOx).

Sha'ban, Ahmad. "Following the Teachings of Previous Religions" [in Arabic]. *Al-Ittihad* (UAE), July 23, 2014 (http://www.alittihad.ae/details.php?id=64586&y=2014&article=full).

Shahada, Usama. "Excommunication and Violence ... A Muslim Brotherhood Product!" [in Arabic]. Alalukah website, May 22, 2011 (http://majles.alukah.net/t82739/).

Shaheen, Abdul Hai. "Saudi Suroorism: A Phenomenon or an Intellectual Current?" [in Arabic]. Religion and Politics Center for Studies, September 21, 2010 (http://www.rpcst.com/articles.php?action=show&id=195).

Shalatah, Ahmad Zaghlool. *Contemporary Salafism in Egypt* [in Arabic]; (Cairo: Madbooli Bookshop, 2011).

Shammakh, Amer. *The Muslim Brotherhood and Violence: Reading in the Thought and the Reality of the Muslim Brotherhood* [in Arabic]; (Cairo: Al-Saad for Publication and Distribution, 2008).

Sharp, Jeremy M. "Egypt: 2005 Presidential and Parliamentary Elections." Congressional Research Service, Washington, DC, 2006.

Shehada, Marwan. *Transformations of the Salafi Discourse: Salafi Movements: A Case Study 1990–2007),* [in Arabic]; (Beirut: Arab Network for Research and Publishing, 2010).

Shenouda, Seti. "The Systematic Persecution, Kidnapping and Killing of Christians in Egypt" [in Arabic]. Al-hiwar Al-Mutamaddin website, June 17, 2014 (http://m.ahewar.org/s.asp?aid=419761&r=0&cid=0&u=&i=5396&q=).

Shihab, Mufeed. "Prospects for Cooperation between Research Centers in the Muslim World" [in Arabic]. The Supreme Council for Islamic Affairs, Egypt, July 1998 (http://www.elazhar.com/conf_au/10/46.asp).

Shuhaib, Abdul Qadir. "Legitimacy of Achievement" [in Arabic]. *Veto* newspaper, June 30, 2014 (http://www.vetogate.com/1093012).

791

Singh, Manoj. "The 2007-08 Financial Crisis in Review," Investopedia (http://www.investopedia.com/articles/economics/09/financial-crisis-review.asp).

Sirini, Ali. "Conclusions Regarding Political Reforms in Christian Europe in the Middle Ages" [in Arabic]. November 29, 2011 (http://www.ahl-alquran.com/arabic/show_article.php?main_id=8978).

Smith, Donald E. *Religion and Political Modernization* (New Haven, CT: Yale University Press, 1974).

Soroush, Abdul Kareem. *Tradition and Secularism: Structures and Pillars, Backgrounds and Facts.* Ahmad Al-Qabanji (trans.); (Beirut: Al-Jamal Publications, 2009).

Stowasser, Barbara F. (ed.). *The Islamic Impulse* (London: Croom Helm, 1987).

Ta'eema, Sabir. *Excess and Excessive Groups of Islamists in Light of Ancestors' Doctrine* [in Arabic]; (Cairo: Madbooli Bookshop, 2009).

Tabliyya, Al-Qutb Muhammad Al-Qutb. *Pioneers of Islamic Thought in Modern Age* [in Arabic]; (Cairo: Dar Al-Fikr Al-Arabi, 1st Edition, 2000).

Tahir, Bahaa. "Secular State and Religious State" [in Arabic]. *Al-Ahram* newspaper, September 11, 2011 (http://www.ahram.org.eg/archive/The-Writers/News/113764.aspx).

Tammam, Hussam. "The Brotherhood and Saudi: Is it the Time for Divorce?" [in Arabic]. *Al-Qahira* newspaper, Egypt, 2003.

Tammam, Hussam. "The Democratic Trend in the Brotherhood: Map of Proliferation and Obstacles" [in Arabic]. Modern Discussion website, Issue 1082, January 18, 2005 (http://www.ahewar.org/debat/show.art.asp?aid=30046).

Tammam, Hussam. "The Moroccan Experience in Distinguishing between Preaching and Politics" [in Arabic]. Islamism Scope portal, July 25, 2007 (http://www.islamismscope.net/index.php?option=com_content&view=article&id=140:2010-02-09-13-43-12&catid=37:articles&Itemid=67).

Tammam, Hussam. *The Transformation of the Muslim Brotherhood: Disintegration of Ideology and the End of the Organization* [in Arabic]; (Cairo: Madbouly Bookshop, 2006).

Taspinar, Omer. "Turkey: The New Model?" *Brookings Institution*, April 2012 (http://www.brookings.edu/research/papers/2012/04/24-turkey-new-model-taspinar), accessed March 8, 2014.

Tawfeeq Al-Saif, *Modernity as a Religious Need* [in Arabic]; (Beirut: Arab Scientific Publishers, 2006).

Taylor, Alan R. *The Islamic Question in Middle East Politics* (Boulder, CO: Westview Press, 1988).

Tessler, Mark, et al. *Determinants of Political Participation and Electoral Behavior in the Arab World: Findings and Insights from the Arab Barometer* (http://www.arabbarometer.org/sites/default/files/files/Determinants%20of%20Political.pdf).

Tessler, Mark. "Accounting for Variance in Popular Attitudes toward the Place of Islam in Political Life: Findings from the Arab Barometer Surveys in Algeria, Morocco and Other Arab Countries" (http://www.yale.edu/macmillan/africadissent/tessler.pdf).

Tessler, Mark. "Religion, Religiosity and the Place of Islam in Political Life: Insights from the Arab Barometer Surveys." *Middle East Law and Governance*, vol. 2, 2010 (http://www.researchgate.net/publication/233570622_Religion_Religiosity_and_the_Place_of_Islam_in_Political_Life_Insights_from_the_Arab_Barometer_Surveys).

Tessler, Mark. *The Civic Orientations of Arab Publics: Selected Findings from the Arab Barometer*, Emirates Lecture Series no. 115 (Abu Dhabi: The Emirates Center for Strategic Studies and Research, 2014).

Tessler, Mark. *The Civic Orientations of Arab Publics: Selected Findings from the Arab Barometer*, June 25, 2014 (http://www.arabbarometer.org/reports-presentation-abwave/arab-barometer-iii).

The Galileo Project (http://galileo.rice.edu/chr/inquisition.html).

The International Encyclopedia of Arabic Poetry (http://www.adab.com/modules.php?name=Sh3er&doWhat=shqas&qid=10650&r=&rc=5).

The Muslim Brotherhood: The Establishment, various authors (Dubai: Al-Mesbar Studies and Research Centre, January 2007), p. 131.

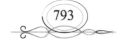

The Quran—Interpretation of Ibn Katheer [in Arabic]; (http://islamhudaa.com/e-Quran/images/katheer-p30.htm).

Trager, Eric. "Egypt's Muslim Brotherhood Pursues a Political Monopoly" [in Arabic]. The Washington Institute, April 4, 2012 (http://www.washington institute.org/ar/policy-analysis/view/egypts-muslim-brotherhood-pursues-a-political-monopoly).

Turner, Bryan S. *Weber and Islam: A Critical Study* (Boston, MA / London: Routledge and Kegan Paul, 1974).

United Nations (UN). "Human Development Report 2014, Sustaining Human Progress: Reducing Vulnerabilities and Building Resilience" [in Arabic]; (http://www.un.org/ar/esa/hdr/pdf/hdr14.pdf).

United Nations (UN). "The 2013 Human Development Report" [in Arabic]. The United Nations Development Programme in the Arab States, March 14, 2013 (http://bit.ly/1CGM7cj).

Uthman, Majid. "Results of a Public Opinion Survey on Egyptians' Assessment of the Muslim Brotherhood" [in Arabic]. The Egyptian Center for Public Opinion Research (Baseera); (http://www.baseera.com.eg/pdf_poll_file_ar/Towards-the-Muslim-Brotherhood-ar.pdf).

Uthman, Majid. "Results of a Public Opinion Survey on the Return of the Muslim Brotherhood to Political Life" [in Arabic]. The Egyptian Center for Public Opinion Research (Baseera) (http://www.baseera.com.eg/pdf_poll_file_ar/the%20return%20of%20the%20Muslim%20Brotherhood%20-ar.pdf).

Vatikiotis, P.J. *The Egyptian Army: Pattern for New Nations?* (Bloomington, IN: Indiana University Press, 1961).

Voll, John O. *Islam: Continuity and Changes in the Modern World* (Boulder, CO: Westview Press, 1982).

Wajeeh, Tamer. "Sayyid Qutb: Confrontation between the Group of Believers and the Jahiliyya of the Twentieth Century" [in Arabic]. *Al-Masry Al-Youm* newspaper, Egypt, May 8, 2012 (http://www.almasryalyoum.com/news/details/177399#).

Warburg, Gabriel R. *The Muslim Brotherhood in Sudan: From Reforms to Radicalism* [in Arabic]. Translated and summarized by Badr Al-Deen Hamid Al-Hashemi, February 19, 2014 (http://www.alrakoba.net/articles-action-show-id-55537.htm).

Wehbeh, Murad, and Mona Abu Sinnah (eds.). *Ibn Rushd and Enlightenment* (Cairo: Dar Al-Thaqafah Al-Jadeeda; Kuwait: Dar Qertas for Publishing and Distribution, 1997).

Welch, Alford T., and Pierre Cachia (eds.). *Islam: Past Influence and Present Challenge* (Edinburgh: Edinburgh University Press, 1979).

Wheatcroft, Andrew. *The Ottomans: Dissolving Images* [in Arabic]; (Abu Dhabi: The Emirates Center for Strategic Studies and Research, 2014).

Wickham, Carrie Rosefsky. *The Muslim Brotherhood: Evolution of an Islamist Movement* (Princeton, NJ: Princeton University Press, 2013).

Wiktorowicz, Quintan. "Anatomy of the Salafi Movement." *Studies in Conflict and Terrorism*, vol. 29, no. 3, 2006.

Wright, Robin (ed.). *The Iran Primer* (Washington, DC: United States Institute of Peace Press, 2009).

Wright, Robin. "'Quiet' Revolution: Islamic Movement's New Phase." *The Christian Science Monitor*, Friday, November 6, 1987.

Wright, Robin. "Religion and Politics: A Global Phenomenon." *The Christian Science Monitor*, November 4, 1987.

Wright, Robin. *Dreams and Shadows: the Future of the Middle East* (New York, NY: Penguin Books, 2008).

Wuthnow, Robert. "Two Traditions in the Study of Religion." *Journal for the Scientific Study of Religion* vol. 20 (March 1981).

Yaseen, Abduljawad. *Authority in Islam: A Critique of Political Theory* [in Arabic]; (Casablanca: Arab Cultural Center, 2009).

Yaseen, Al-Sayyid. "Egypt: the Problematic Relation between Religion and Politics" [in Arabic]. *Al-Nahar* (Lebanon), August 15, 2013 (http://news paper.annahar.com/article/58042).

Young, Crawford. *The Politics of Cultural Pluralism* (Madison, WI: University of Wisconsin Press, 1976).

Yousuf, Al-Sayyid. *The Muslim Brotherhood: Is it an Islamic Awakening?* Part 1 [in Arabic]; (Cairo: Al Mahrousa Center for Publishing, Press Services and Information, 1994).

Zaghlool, Ahmad. "The Islamists and Charity Work in Egypt" [in Arabic]. Non Post portal, December 27, 2013 (http://www.noonpost.net/content/1361).

Zaidan, Laila. "Palestine and the New Inquisition Colors" [in Arabic]. Palestine Website, December 2012 (http://palestine.assafir.com/Article.aspx?ArticleI D=2413).

Zayed, Ahmad. "The Islamists … Fear of Secularism" [in Arabic]. Middle East Online, January 6, 2014 (http://www.middle-east-online.com/?id=168890).

Zayed, Al-Sayed. "Suroorism: A Preaching Current or an Activist Organization?" [in Arabic]. On Islam net, December 31, 2008 (http://goo.gl/y0lkVF).

Zayed, Amani. "The Implementation of Sharia: The Brotherhood's Burned Card" [in Arabic]. *Al-Wafd* newspaper, Egypt, June 30 2013 (http://bit.ly/1qD DKvi).

Zooman, Ahmad. "Abu Bakr's Policy when Issuing Judgments" [in Arabic]. *Al-Ahram* (Egypt), 18 August 2013 (http://islam.ahram.org.eg/Category/24/ 40/NewsQ/2231.aspx).

Zraick, Karen. "Ground zero mosque opened to public Wednesday." *Christian Science Monitor*, September 22, 2011 (http://www.csmonitor.com/USA/ Latest-News-Wires/2011/0922/Ground-zero-mosque-opened-to-public-Wednesday).

Index

INDEX

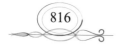